15

WITHDRAWN
FROM A.E.C.L

THE COCKROACH—VOLUME II

THE RENTOKIL LIBRARY

The Woodworm Problem
The Dry Rot Problem
Household Insect Pests
Pests of Stored Products
The Conservation of Building Timbers
The Insect Factor in Wood Decay
The Cockroach—Vol. I
Wood Preservation—A guide to the meaning of terms
Termites—A World Problem
Pest Control in Buildings—A guide to the meaning of terms

THE RENTOKIL LIBRARY

THE COCKROACH

VOLUME II

Insecticides and Cockroach Control

An account of the insecticides, formulations and equipment used for cockroach control, together with details of safety, resistance and test procedures.

P. B. CORNWELL

Director of Research
Rentokil Limited

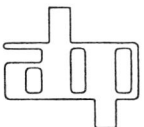

ASSOCIATED BUSINESS PROGRAMMES
LONDON

ASSOCIATED BUSINESS PROGRAMMES LTD

17 Buckingham Gate, London SW1

(Volume 1 published by Hutchinson & Co. (Publishers) Ltd, 1968)

First published 1976

The photographs used in this book are included only as illustrations of cockroach control problems. The author wishes to make it clear that no criticism of the premises or foodstuffs is intended.

© P. B. Cornwell 1976

Drawings © Rentokil Ltd., 1976, unless otherwise acknowledged
Assistance with illustrations from Hayward Art Group

Text set in 11 pt Photon Times, printed by photolithography and bound in Great Britain at The Pitman Press, Bath
ISBN 0 85227 102 6

CONTENTS

Acknowledgments   *page* 9

Preface   11

1. INTRODUCTION   13
The users of insecticides. Early attempts at cockroach control: gassing; baiting; trapping; sealing holes; biological control. Modern cockroach control: the insecticides most commonly used. The future outlook for insecticides.

2. THE COCKROACH AS A PEST   27
Pest Status. Infestations outdoors: in temperate climates; in the tropics; man-made habitats and sanitation; infestations in covered areas and entry into buildings. Infestation indoors: moisture; temperature, food; harbourage; lack of concern and the role of preventive pest control. Cockroaches and food poisoning. Pest cockroaches in different countries: U.S.A.; W. Germany; Finland; cockroaches in the U.K.

3. PRACTICAL COCKROACH CONTROL   67
The requirements. The action. The practical difficulties; restaurants; air transport; passenger shipping; hospitals; zoos. Reinfestation as a problem.

4. THE IMPORTANCE OF FORMULATION   74
The importance of contact: the treated surface. Components of formulations: technical material; premium grade; diluent; additives; dilution rate. Liquid formulations: oil spray; emulsion; wettable powder; suspension concentrate; lacquer. Solid formulations: dust; smoke; bait; attractants and feeding stimulants; response to pheromones; tests of performance. Insecticidal vapours.

5. THE EQUIPMENT TO USE   107
Selecting the right equipment. Equipment for inspection. Equipment for insecticide application: dust blowers; sprayers; motorised equipment; miscellaneous equipment; care of equipment; responsibility for maintenance. Equipment for self protection: dress; gloves; masks.

6. PRACTICAL SAFETY AND THE LAW   130
Poisoning and toxicity of insecticides: routes of entry into the body; ingestion, inhalation, dermal absorption. Measurement of toxicity; toxicity of organophosphorus and carbamate insecticides. Safety code: storage; self protection; the client and the public; the environment; the householder. Poisoning incidents: domestic animals; human poisoning; national poisons information centres; first aid. The environment and legislation: results of regulatory procedures. Approval schemes; international classification of pesticides. Crack and crevice treatment in food handling establishments. Training in health and safety.

7. REPELLENTS AND INSECTICIDE REPELLENCY   157
Repellents: Tabutrex; MGK R-11; MGK R-55; MGK R-874. Possible applications for repellents: bananas; movement of people and clothing; packaging materials; beer and soft drink industries. Avoidance and lethal action of U.V. light. Repellency of insecticides: the

cockroach and its need for harbourage; harbourage and the pest control operator; the insecticide and its effect on cockroaches. Tests of insecticide repellency: partial treatment of harbourages; recovery as part of the avoidance process; wall void tests; simple and complex environments; treatment of previously occupied harbourages; use of pyrethrins as a flushing agent.

8. THE EARLIEST INSECTICIDES (INORGANICS, FUMIGANTS AND OTHERS)   191
Borax and boric acid: physical properties; mammalian toxicity; use for cockroach control. Sodium fluoride and fluorosilicate: manufacture and properties; toxicity and symptoms of poisoning; activity against cockroaches; mode of entry; dusts containing sodium fluoride and pyrethrins. Desiccant dusts: chemical and physical properties; mammalian toxicity; action against cockroaches; use in cockroach control. Phosphorus: properties; application. Thallium sulphate. Hydrogen cyanide and other fumigants. Organic thiocyanates: chemical properties and toxicity.

9. THE NATURAL INSECTICIDE (PYRETHRUM)   218
Pyrethrum production and use: early history; effects of two World Wars; events between 1940 and 1960; awareness of the environment; influence of synthetic pyrethroids. Pyrethrins: pyrethrum flowers; pyrethrum dusts; pyrethrum extract; the pyrethrins. Effects of pyrethrins on cockroaches: early studies; susceptibility of species; developmental stages and sexes. Recovery from poisoning by pyrethrins: synergism; piperonyl butoxide; Tropital; MGK 264; sesame oil; safroxan; resistance to pyrethrins. Use in insect control: the contribution to cockroach control; indifferent performance; useful flushing action; effects on oothecae; toxicity to man and other animals; residues in food.

10. THE PYRETHRUM-LIKE INSECTICIDES (SYNTHETIC PYRETHROIDS)   254
History of development; properties of synthetic pyrethroids. Allethrin and bioallethrin: insecticidal properties; action against cockroaches; S-bioallethrin. Tetramethrin and biotetramethrin: insecticidal properties; action against cockroaches. Resmethrin and bioresmethrin: insecticidal properties; action against cockroaches; effect on oothecae. Other synthetic pyrethroids. Use of synthetic pyrethroids for cockroach control.

11. THE LONG-LIVED INSECTICIDES (ORGANOCHLORINES)   281
DDT: discovery; chemical and physical properties; early history of use and subsequent condemnation; wild life and the industrial user; insecticidal properties; performance against cockroaches; effects on species and sexes. Lindane: chemical and physical properties; insecticidal properties; effects on mammals. Chlordane: chemical and physical properties; performance against cockroaches; toxicity to man; chlordane in the environment. Dieldrin: chemical and physical properties; action on cockroaches; effects on mammals. Chlordecone: use in baits; toxicity to man.

12. THE SHORTER-LIVED INSECTICIDES (ORGANOPHOSPHORUS COMPOUNDS)   318
History of development; action and degradation. Diazinon: history of development and use; chemical and physical properties; effectiveness against cockroaches; toxicity to man and animals. Dichlorvos: chemical and physical properties; insecticidal properties; dichlorvos vapour; use of dichlorvos aerosols; spray applications; toxicity to man and animals; recommended uses. Malathion: chemical and physical properties; effectiveness against cockroaches; toxicity to man and animals. Chlorpyrifos: chemical and physical properties; effectiveness against cockroaches; toxicity to man and other animals. Fenitrothion: chemical and physical properties; effectiveness against cockroaches; toxicity to man and animals. Iodofenphos: chemical and physical properties; effectiveness against cockroaches; toxicity to man and animals. Trichlorphon: chemical and physical properties; effectiveness against cockroaches; toxicity to man and animals.

CONTENTS

13. THE NEWER INSECTICIDES (INSECTICIDAL CARBAMATES) 362

Origin of the carbamate insecticides; insecticidal properties. Carbaryl: chemical and physical properties; insecticidal properties; effectiveness against cockroaches; toxicity to man and animals. Bendiocarb: chemical and physical properties; insecticidal properties; toxicity to man and animals. Propoxur: chemical and physical properties; insecticidal properties; effectiveness against cockroaches; toxicity to man and animals. Other carbamate insecticides.

14. HOW INSECTICIDES KILL 383

Understanding insecticidal action—why it matters: the target for attack. The nervous system and nerve transmission; axonic transmission; synaptic transmission; interference by insecticides. Action of the pyrethrins: penetration of the cuticle; distribution in the insect; effect of temperature. Effects of pyrethrins on respiration; on heart beat; on haemolymph volume; effects in the gut. Action on the cockroach nervous system: on sensory nerve endings; physical damage; effects on nerve activity; on spontaneous nerve activity. Action of DDT: penetration, distribution and breakdown in the cockroach; effects of temperature on the susceptibility of cockroaches; effects on body reserves; on amino acids. Similarity of symptoms of DDT-poisoning and bodily stress; DDT-induced toxin. Interference with nerve function. Action of other chlorinated hydrocarbon insecticides. Action of organophosphorus and carbamate insecticides: acetylcholine and acetylcholinesterase in cockroaches; location of poisoning; response to diazinon; secondary effects of organophosphates. Action of carbamate insecticides.

15. RESISTANCE TO INSECTICIDES 422

Early history; resistance becomes a major problem; characteristics of resistance; resistance to the various insecticides; cross-resistance; detecting and measuring resistance. Resistance in cockroaches: the progress of resistance from 1951–1975; resistance among cockroaches in the U.K.; the ability to survive. The problem in retrospect and prospect; reproduction and the number of generations per year; frequency of exposure to insecticide; proportion of the population exposed and extent of inbreeding; inter-relationship of cockroaches with transport; ability to withstand temporary adverse conditions. Reactions of the pest control industry; an up-to-date perspective.

16. REARING AND COLLECTING COCKROACHES 460

Breeding and rearing cockroaches: conditions and equipment; diet; water; setting up cultures; cockroaches of known age; responsibility for cockroach culture; yield of insects; control of mites, psocids and nematodes in cultures; rearing of other cockroach species; handling of cockroaches; CO_2 anaesthesia; immobilisation and insecticide susceptibility. Collecting cockroaches: trap containers; suction methods.

17. TESTING INSECTICIDES 476

Test procedures; principles of testing. Tests of insecticide applied directly to cockroaches; immersion; direct spray methods; CSMA Cockroach Spray Method; CSMA Aerosol Test Method; topical application. Tests of insecticide picked up from treated surfaces; continuous exposure to a single dose; WHO resistance test; continuous exposure to a range of doses; varied exposure and/or multiple doses. Tests of insecticide repellency. Testing compounds for use as repellents.

Conversion Table 498
Bibliography and Author Index 499
Subject Index 537

ACKNOWLEDGMENTS

I wish to record my thanks to those who have helped me compile this volume. Particularly my indebtedness to Mr. Robin Edwards, our entomologist, for reading the text and making many useful comments. Also for his help with the tables and illustrations. Robin compiled the index and assisted with proof reading. He has again made a major contribution to getting this title of the Rentokil Library into print.

Shirley Edwards, my secretary, typed and retyped the manuscript through various drafts. I am grateful for her painstaking work, especially with the bibliography. She too has helped in no small measure with this production. I thank her for her considerable contribution.

Three other colleagues at Felcourt have given valuable assistance: Bob Smith, our photographer, designed and produced the jacket and has prepared many of the illustrations which appear in the text. He has also 'improved' those photographs taken by myself in difficult situations in various parts of the world. I am grateful to him for this. Also to Fay Church, our librarian, for obtaining most of the publications to which I have referred. Brian Ashworth has also helped with the content of various chapters.

Dr. Gordon Onions of Brunel University, kindly helped with the technical content of Volume I and has again advised on the information in this volume. I value the contribution he has made. I would also like to thank Denis Papworth, M.A.F.F. for supplying information on insecticide usage by Local Authorities in the U.K.

The others, to whom I offer my sincere thanks, are the many people in the United States with whom I have discussed the problems of cockroach control. Many are in industry and gave me the opportunity of seeing infestation problems. I would particularly wish to thank Norman Ehmann (Neil A. Maclean, San Francisco), Truly Nolan (Truly Nolan Exterminating Co., Tucson), Bill Spitz (Big State Exterminating Co., Houston), Bob Russell (Orkin Exterminating Co. Inc., Atlanta) and Noad Corley (Corley Pest Control, Dallas). For technical and scientific help may I also record my thanks to Dr. Phil Spear (National Pest Control Association of America), Dr. Clifford Roan (University of Arizona, Tucson), Prof. Walter Ebeling (University of Los Angeles), Dr. Charles Wright (North Carolina State University, Raleigh), Dr. James Grayson (Virginia Polytechnic Institute) and Dr. H. Schoof (National Communicable Disease Centre, Public Health Service, Savannah).

Many of my colleagues in Associated Companies of Rentokil overseas have helped provide background information on cockroaches in their respective territories. I would especially like to thank: Peter Meadows, Fred Westphal and many of their colleagues in Australia; Brian Phipps (New Zealand), Nigel Fisher-Jaine (Indonesia), Harry Khoo and Reg Perry (Singapore), Bob Blake (Malaysia), Ted Davies (Kenya), T. Faruki (Uganda), Les Cattermole (Mobasa) and J. van Someren (Tanzania). My special thanks to John Whitley and his colleagues in S. Africa, to Heine Jonker (Germany) and Chris Ries Høm and his staff in France, Holland, Denmark and Belgium. I am also grateful to Julian Macgregor for his help when manager of our Caribbean companies.

A number of companies have supplied illustrative material for this book. I record my thanks to Dow Chemical Co. Inc., Fisons Ltd., Neil A. Maclean Co. Inc., Sumitomo Ltd, Southern Mill Creek Products Co. Inc., Velsicol Inc., and Celamerck GmbH. Also to Dr. R. Winney, Director of the Pyrethrum Bureau, Nakuru, Kenya and to Dr. G. Haas, Director of Wuppertal Zoo, Germany.

In preparing both volumes about cockroaches it is my pleasure to acknowledge the stimulus of two close colleagues without whose encouragement neither of these titles would have been produced. They are Bob Westphal (formerly Joint Managing Director, Rentokil) and Dr. Norman Hickin (formerly Scientific Director, Rentokil). I thank the former for recommending the task and the latter for setting the example.

PREFACE

This book is the second volume about cockroaches, written for the pest control industry and for those in public health departments, food manufacturing, retailing and storage. Also for those in hospital, hotel and catering management—and all others who have the responsibility for hygiene and eradicating cockroaches from buildings.

There are many books on the chemistry and mode of action of insecticides written as reference texts for the research worker. They assume considerable knowledge of the reader and are intelligible only to those familiar with the structure of insecticides and insect biochemistry. They do not meet the needs of the many thousands of personnel engaged in *practical* pest control, who have the eradication of cockroaches as one of their major tasks.

This book is different. It acknowledges the fact that the pest control operator is not a graduate chemist and that his knowledge of insecticides comes from the use of proprietary products. By experience, he knows some of their merits, one formulation compared with another. The name of the insecticide in his spray or dust is known, not by its long chemical name, but by that given to it by the manufacturer, or by a Standards Organisation: this identification is sufficient since these names are used internationally and allow access to information through trade, advisory and technical press.

Most users of insecticides have an over-riding concern for good performance and safety in use and are not much concerned with how insecticides are made, or their detailed properties. This book is intended as a practical guide to the use of insecticides: hopefully it will help raise the standards of cockroach control achieved.

Experience proves that most engaged in industrial/domestic pest control have an interest in their job beyond simply applying pest control chemicals: they know something of the history of the insecticides used, their application outside cockroach control, but little of the way in which an insecticide kills. These subjects provide a broader interest in the job. Does the insecticide kill quickly or take time to have effect? How does it perform on different surfaces? Is it volatile or not, easily degraded by light or heat, or relatively long-lasting? Knowing the answers gives the pest control operator added confidence in his materials. Also, knowledge of unusual properties such as odour, or the discolouration of certain types of surfaces, might influence the choice of insecticide formulation used.

As a professional man, the pest control operator would wish, and indeed be expected, to know something of the toxicity of his materials: whether an insecticide accumulates in or is excreted by man; the risk to food, to children and domestic animals. This knowledge helps make him sympathetic towards government regulations which may, for example, allow an insecticide to be sprayed but not fogged, permitted in non-food areas but not in catering establishments.

The first volume on cockroaches written by the author was published in 1968. It reviewed the information then available about the more common pest species: their appearance and biology, aspects of behaviour and the reactions of these insects to man-made environments.

This second volume combines two things: (1) a personal assessment of cockroaches as pests, observed in different climates and different types of building, and the factors affecting their control, and (2) a review of information about the insecticides normally used to eradicate them. The properties of different formulations are considered, as well as the use and maintenance of equipment. There is also a chapter on resistance and how new insecticides are tested.

Many people have contributed to this book. It contains the views, ideas, facts and experience of people involved in the business of pest control. It is written with an understanding of the needs of that industry, and with experience of the rapid changes in recent years in legislation, influencing the insecticides permitted for use. There is perhaps an unconscious belief, that the next insecticide to become available for cockroach control will make the job much easier: hence the question often asked—'and what do you use for cockroach control?' There is often surprise and disillusionment with the answer: 'well-trained servicemen'.

In preparing each chapter an effort has been made to avoid unnecessary technical terms, so helping communication with the intended readership. However, to avoid the dangers of over-simplification some compromise has been necessary. To make the book a source of reference for technical personnel, a fairly full bibliography is included. Readers may thus find substantiation and enlargement for much of the information presented.

Few authors of books like this believe that their readers will start at the beginning and read to the end. Each reader will have particular areas of interest and it is hoped that the chapter headings will provide a guide. However, for those concerned solely with the practical task of eradicating and keeping buildings free of cockroaches, Chapters 2 and 3 provide essential reading.

1

INTRODUCTION

The users of insecticides—Early attempts at cockroach control: gassing: baiting: trapping: sealing holes; biological control—Modern cockroach control: the insecticides most commonly used—The future outlook for insecticides.

Pest control, as we know it today, is no more than 30 years old. We have within a generation accumulated an immense knowledge of insect pests and a detailed awareness of both the desirable and undesirable properties, of the insecticides technology has helped make available. Instead of burning sulphur, using hellebore, arsenic and nicotine, or applying turpentine as a cockroach repellent, we now make use of modern compounds, primarily developed for other purposes: each costing $5–10 million to discover and develop, 6–7 years to bring into use and 65 man-years to clear for marketing.[43,682]

Insecticides contribute to man's well-being by helping to supply sufficient food, protect housing and clothing, and as an aid to health. The use of insecticides for cockroach control has the principal benefits of eliminating a food contaminant, a carrier of disease organisms and the removal of an insect widely regarded with abhorrence. The insecticides now available are capable of eradicating these insects and maintaining buildings free of infestation.

In the United States, the German cockroach is the most important indoor pest[521,624,762] (Fig. 1). In Britain, the Oriental cockroach which is the most prevalent, occupies sixth place among pests dealt with by Local Authorities[216] (Fig. 2). No country is without cockroaches in industrial premises and homes.

The users of insecticides
Four groups of people are concerned with controlling cockroaches:

1. Householders who require ready-to-apply products, designed for domestic use and packed for ease of application (primarily aerosols and 'puffer packs').
2. Local health departments, serving primarily the domestic sector, requiring dependable ready-to-use products, and concentrates for dilution.
3. Hygiene staff in industry, for whom pest control is one of many responsibilities. Their expertise may encompass knowledge of pests associated with a particular food manufacturing process, or a group of products. Staff in food manufacturing, and the hotel and catering industries, depend in most cases on the professional services of pest control companies.
4. Servicing companies, with specialist knowledge of a wide range of industrial and domestic pests. The aim is to satisfy the demands from industry and the private sector, adopting new materials and techniques as they become

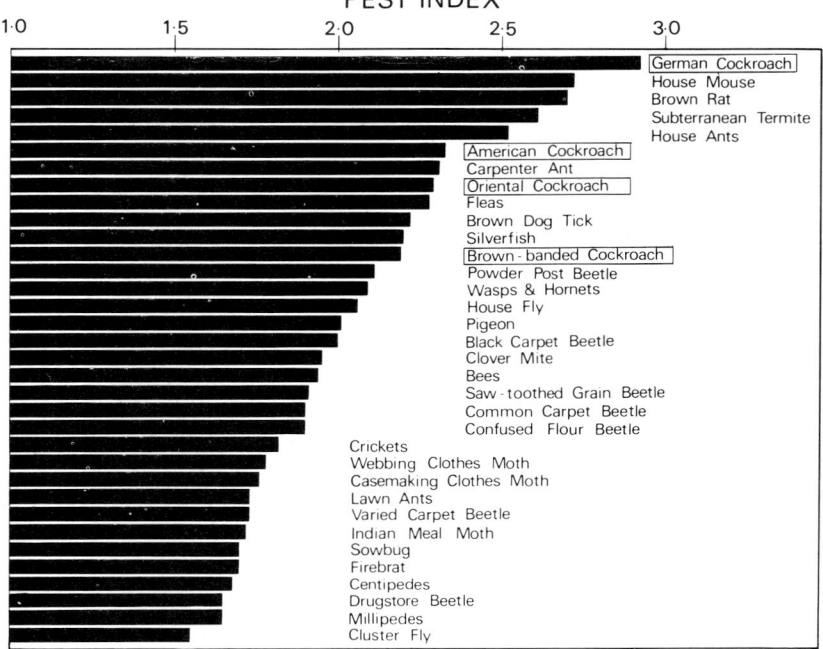

Fig. 1. Relative importance of pests, to 152 member companies of the National Pest Control Association in the U.S.A. (From NPCA[624]).

available. A few of these companies may purchase pesticides as active ingredients and formulate to their own requirements.

EARLY ATTEMPTS AT COCKROACH CONTROL

Two hundred years ago, Catesby[176] in his 'Natural History of Carolina' described cockroaches as 'very troublesome and destructive vermin, so numerous and voracious that it is impossible to keep victuals of any kind from being devoured by them without close covering'. At the beginning of this century, Morse[591] described them as 'travelling wherever man carried merchandise, and increasing vigilance and persecution are often not enough to exterminate them, once they have taken possession of favourable quarters'.

The extreme difficulty expressed by these two writers in eradicating established infestations of cockroaches stems from the relative inefficiency of the materials then available, and from the somewhat cumbersome procedures of gassing, baiting and trapping which had to be resorted to. In the absence of modern chemicals, Marlatt[528] refers to pyrethrum powder, or buhach, giving some relief, but not the perfect remedy: he recommends the 'burning of

INTRODUCTION

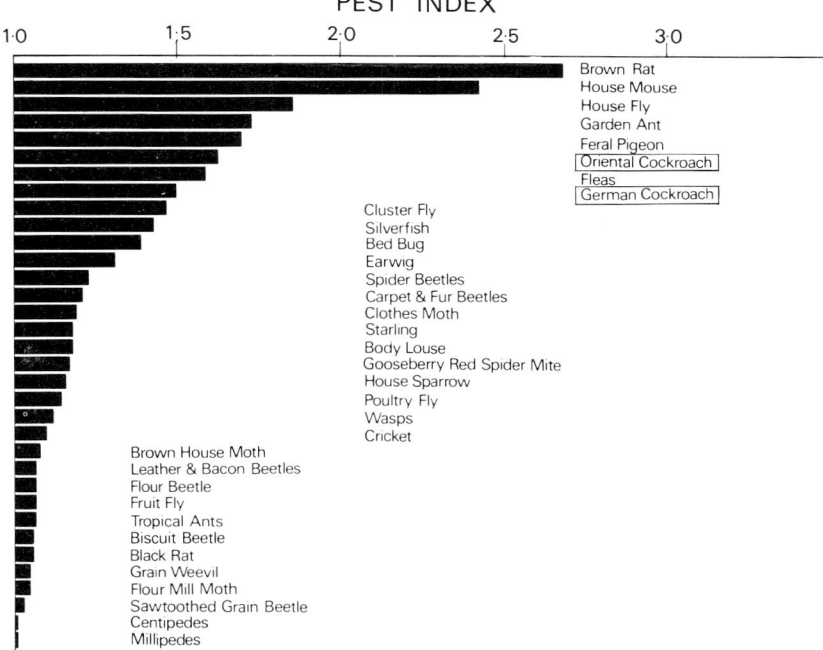

Fig. 2. Relative importance of pests to Local Authorities in the U.K. in 1968. (From Cornwell[216]).

pyrethrum' for 6–12 hours, and refers to the use of flowers of sulphur as a cockroach repellent.

Gassing

The use of hydrocyanic acid gas was widely recommended as an early control method but only by those experienced in such techniques. Another recommended method of fumigating small rooms, was to allow carbon bisulphide to evaporate from open dishes. A warning was given that the vapour dissipates rapidly unless the room is sealed up and it can also create an explosive hazard.

Fumigation with sulphur dioxide, generated by burning brimstone, was described as probably 'the easiest as well as the safest for the ordinary householder'. Because this may tarnish and corrode metal, bleach coloured fabrics and discolour wallpaper, it was not recommended for use on a damp day. 'At least 2 lb, preferably 4 lb, of sulphur per 1,000 cu ft should be burned: placed on an old iron shovel or tray, supported over a wide shallow vessel filled with water so that the risk of fire may be reduced, and set alight after being sprinkled with methylated spirit, or else by means of some glowing cinders'.

The only absolute Cockroach Exterminator is
BLATTIS,

The Union Cockroach Paste.

This is guaranteed to completely destroy them in all climates by the Sole Makers,

HOWARTHS, Crookesmoor, Sheffield, 10.

**Supplied by Order to the Royal Household,
- Royal Navy, Hospitals, Workhouses, -
Schools, Breweries, Shipping, etc. etc. . .**

BLATTIS the Union Cockroach Paste was first produced by Mr. E. Howarth, F.Z.S., then Curator of the Sheffield Museum, to clear the Workhouse of an overwhelming plague of Cockroaches in 1896. His remedy was quite efficacious, and there was such a wide demand for this remedy that arrangements were made for it to be supplied to the public generally.

The business then established has expanded until "BLATTIS THE UNION COCKROACH PASTE" is not only used in Great Britain but all over the world.

It is absolutely effective in all climes, and is guaranteed by the Sole Makers:—

HOWARTHS, 473, Crookesmoor Road, Sheffield, 10.

The following is an extract published at the time in the Chemist and Druggist. Similar comments appeared in the Press generally:—

"Much interest has been excited in the Sheffield district by a successful attack on Cockroaches. Mr. E. Howarth, of the Weston Park Museum, obtained permission from the Guardians to try a paste which the Cockroaches liked and which was certain death to such as ate it. He spread his paste about the kitchens and bakeries about two months ago, and at the end of six weeks, 'where' to use his own words 'the Cockroaches used to be found in thousands, there were not half a hundred to be found.' Where the floors used to be literally black with the insects, they were absolutely clear, and specimens even in favourite haunts were difficult to find. Since the experiments became known Mr. HOWARTH has been inundated with letters from people living near and far where his wonderful paste can be obtained."—*Chemist and Druggist*, August 29th, 1896.

BLATTIS The Union Cockroach Paste.

Safe.   Simple.   Sure.

Carry out the directions strictly, and all Cockroaches, Blackclocks and Blackbeetles will disappear. After eating the paste they retire to their holes; and there die, leaving no dead insects about, and they are so shrivelled up by the paste that no smell can arise. Absolute extermination is guaranteed. The real Blattis bears the name of E. Howarth across the label.

Must be kept in a cool place.

Free by Post

in Tins,

1/6, 2/6, 4/6.

Harmless to

Domestic

Animals.

Directions for Use.

Spread a thin layer of the paste with a knife on a few pieces of brown paper or cardboard (about 5 ins. by 3 ins.) and place them on the floor of the infested room at night. Burn the paper the next morning, and put down a FRESH supply each night for a week; afterwards, if necessary, put down a fresh supply every alternate night until all the Cockroaches will then have disappeared. Any subsequent invasion can be kept under by using the paste occasionally.

Sole Makers:
HOWARTHS, 473, Crookesmoor, Sheffield, 10.
Can also be obtained from Chemists generally.

Fig. 3. Advertising pamphlet for '*Blattis, The Union Cockroach Paste*' sold in the U.K. in the 19th century.

Requiring even greater care is the use of smoke from burning gunpowder, claimed to be very obnoxious and deadly to cockroaches, particularly 'the black English roach'. Marlatt[528] writes: 'on the authority of Mr. Thoe Pergande, gunpowder is commonly used in Germany to drive these roaches out of their haunts about fireplaces. The method consists of moulding cones of the moistened powder and placing them in the empty fireplace and lighting them. The smoke coming from the burning powder causes the roaches to come out of the crevices about the chimney and fire bricks in great numbers, and rapidly paralyzes or kills them, so that they may be afterwards swept up and destroyed'. This method again relies on the generation of sulphur dioxide.

Baiting

An ingenious baiting technique reported in early literature consists of 'mixing 1 part of plaster of paris with 3 or 4 parts of flour in a saucer and placing it where the roaches abound, with another nearby containing water, both supplied with several bridges to give easy access, and one or two thin boards floating on the water touching the margin. The insects readily eat the mixture, become thirsty and drink, when the plaster sets and clogs the intestines. The insects disappear in a few weeks, the bodies no doubt being eaten by the survivors'.

Early this century, and continuing up to a few years ago, phosphorus was sold as a sweetened flour paste to be spread on paper, or card, and placed where cockroaches ran. It appeared to be a very popular method of control in the United States. No doubt this was similar to the product 'Blattis—the Union Cockroach paste'—supplied by Order to the Royal Household, Royal Navy, Hospitals, Workhouses, etc.', advertised in Britain as 'the only absolute cockroach exterminator' (Fig. 3).

Trapping

Traps of one sort of another are often included in older recommendations: 'many of the traps on the market are good, success or failure largely depends upon the efficiency of the bait employed which should be changed from time to time. Beer and peeled banana have given very good results'. However, 'if a few cockroaches of the same kind are placed in the trap, they serve as decoys'.[389] Unwittingly this was perhaps an early observation of the benefits to be gained from the attraction of the cockroach aggregation pheromone (see p. 102.

When jam jars are used as traps with a stiff paper cone in the lid through which the black beetle is allowed to enter, emphasis is placed on 'runways laid from the floor to the rim of the jar to enable the insect to ascend.' One writer suggests that the sticks placed against the container should be bent over so they project into the interior of the vessel for a few inches.[528] The roaches then slip off: an effective method for Oriental cockroaches but not apparently for German. As an example of the results of a treatment using jam jar traps, 8,430 cockroaches were caught in one building in under three months, but Haber[389] warns that 'the satisfaction of seeing great numbers of pests cor-

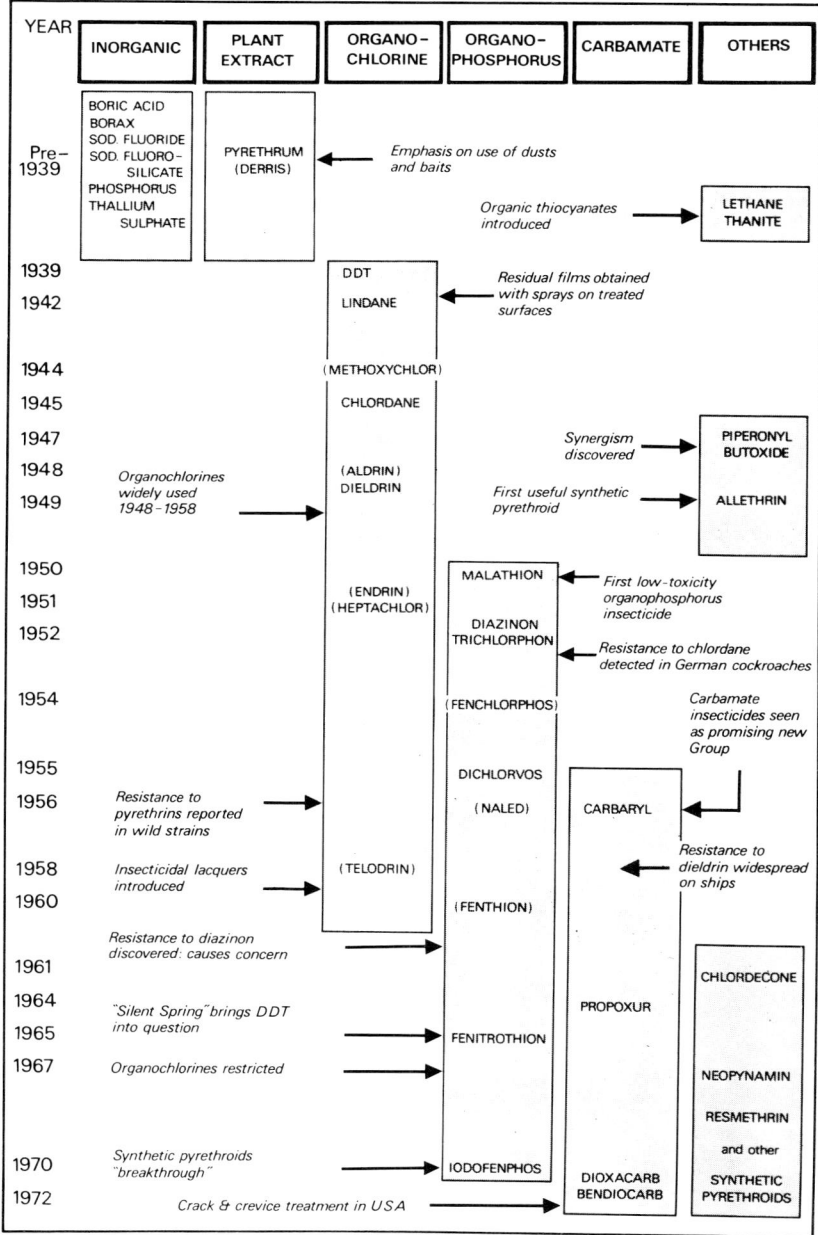

Fig. 4. History of development of insecticides showing when some of the more important ones were introduced. Those not commonly used for cockroach control are in parentheses.

nered may produce an unwarranted confidence in the efficiency of the method'. The same applies to the many cockroaches quickly killed by some currently used insecticides.

Another method recommended by the same writer is 'at night put old clothes dampened with dishwater in the sink or near their runways and places of seclusion. Darken the room and leave it. At half, or three-quarter hour intervals return with a liberal supply of scalding hot water and dash it upon the clothes, thus destroying many cockroaches which have secluded themselves in the folds of the cloth, or beneath it. The dead cockroaches should be collected and burned before the clothes are rearranged to trap more'. This clearly recognises the attraction which cockroaches have for sources of water.

Sealing holes
In an account of cockroach control written as little as 30 years ago,[494] the misleading impression is given that the age of the building is a great influence on whether or not cockroaches are likely to become a pest: 'houses that are particularly liable to invasion by cockroaches are generally old, or have many cracks and crevices, or have basement kitchens which, because of inadequate lighting, are not kept in good repair and scrupulously clean, or have been badly planned. It is not overstating the facts to say that the presence of cockroaches is an indication that repairs are needed. Cockroaches are not likely to establish themselves in a room, even in a basement, which has sound walls and floor, and furniture that stands clear of, or fits close to, the floor'. According to this authority the first essential step to be taken against cockroaches 'is to see that all places likely to provide harbourage are cemented up'. We now know that the most modern buildings can rapidly become infested with these insects—at least by German cockroaches.

Biological control
Apparently, if all else fails, success is likely to be achieved by biological control. Hedgehogs were, at one time, imported into houses to check cockroaches[747] and among other natural enemies of the roach are tree frogs: 'if these animals are enclosed in a room overnight, they will effectively clear it of roaches'.[528]

MODERN COCKROACH CONTROL

Methods of cockroach control practised today make use of chemicals of widely differing properties and include representatives of all the insecticide groups listed in Fig. 4. Products favoured during the mid-1960's was heavily biased towards the long-lived organochlorine compounds, although organophosphorus and carbamate insecticides were receiving increasing recognition. However, because of growing concern by governments about the undesirable, damaging side-effects of pesticides, the proportionate use of different insecticides changed dramatically, away from the long-lived chlorinated type towards the shorter-lived insecticides.

INTRODUCTION

Insecticides are now used in many different formulations: baits, dusts, sprays (of varying composition and properties), lacquers, fogs and smokes, and employing chemicals with vapour as well as contact action (see Chapter 4). Most are designed to be picked up by the insect in treated harbourages or when the insect walks over treated surfaces. Minute amounts of these insecticides kill insects. They have a high measure of safety to man.

The insecticides most commonly used

Many surveys have been made of the amounts of insecticides used against indoor pests. Pest control operators in the area of Tucson, U.S.A.* used four times more chlordane in the treatment of homes in 1966 than any other insecticide: chlordane usage was seven times greater than diazinon, and sixteen times greater than propoxur. But the *number of times* propoxur was used slightly exceeded chlordane—a reflection of the shorter life of the more frequently applied insecticide.

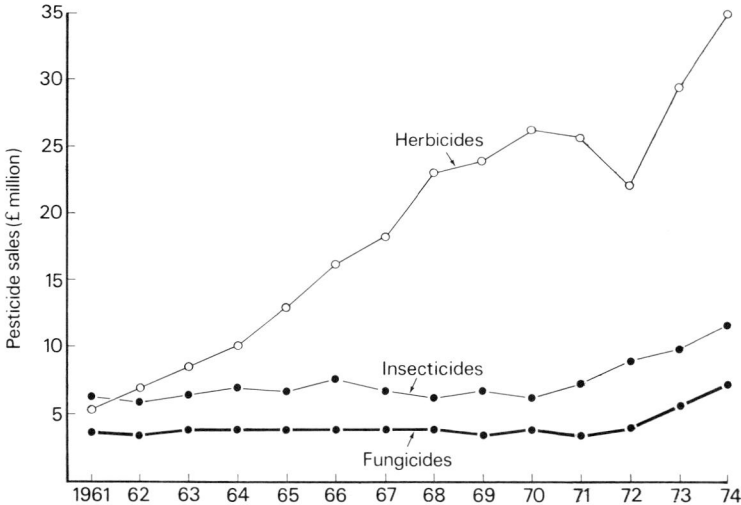

Fig. 5. Growth of manufacturers' sales of pest control chemicals in the U.K., corrected for changes in wholesale price index. (Source: *Business Monitor*, Dept. Ind., H.M.S.O.).

Also in 1966, commercial pest control companies replied to a questionnaire issued by the National Pest Control Association on the use of insecticides in 'general pest control'.[762] The results, more representative of the U.S.A., (Table 1), showed that diazinon was most frequently used for indoor work at that time. This reflects the widespread importance of the German cockroach and its resistance to organochlorine insecticides. The preferred formulation was a water emulsion spray.

* Information: courtesy C. Roan as part of the Arizona Community Studies Pesticides Project.

TABLE I

INSECTICIDES AND FORMULATIONS MOST OFTEN USED DURING 1966 AGAINST INDOOR PESTS BY 34 COMMERCIAL PEST CONTROL COMPANIES IN THE U.S.A.

(After Spear[762])

Insecticide and Formulation	Regularly (Score: 3)	Frequently (Score: 2)	Seldom (Score: 1)	Insecticide Index*
Diazinon (spray)	28	3	0	2·7
Chlordane (spray)	14	6	6	1·8
Dichlorvos (as additive)	11	9	5	1·6
Chlordecone ('Kepone' bait)	9	9	10	1·6
DDT dust	9	9	4	1·4
Synergised pyrethrins (spray)	8	7	6	1·3
Synergised pyrethrins (as additive)	9	7	4	1·3
Sodium fluoride dust	8	3	10	1·2
Dichlorvos (spray)	6	7	8	1·2
Propoxur (spray)	3	11	10	1·2

* Obtained by adding the scores for frequency of use and dividing by 34.

The history of use of insecticides for cockroach control in the U.S.A. has been reviewed by Burden.[141] But the problem most critical in that country in recent years (1972–73) has been the impasse about applying compounds with residual action in food handling areas. Such materials were not permitted during periods that food was being handled and prepared.[574] This caused a substantial, albeit temporary, increase in the use of pyrethrins. To some extent, the problem has now been resolved by regulations permitting 'residuals' in 'crack and crevice' applications (see Chapter 6).

In 1968, about half the Local Authorities in the U.K. replied to a questionnaire on the use of insecticides, specifically for cockroach control,[217] showing an overwhelming preference for DDT. This reflects, (1) the absence of resistance among Oriental cockroaches, the principal cockroach in British homes, (2) a lack of sophistication in the choice of insecticides and (3) the economy practised by local health departments. In this instance the preferred formulation was a dust, probably because of simplicity of application, effectiveness when applied to cockroach harbourages and the relatively low cost of dust formulations.

Insecticides used for general pest control in bakeries—ranging from small family bakers to large plant bakeries—were reported by 124 firms in the U.K.

in 1969.[575] Over 70 per cent used pyrethrins and 56 per cent used lindane: dieldrin and DDT were applied by less than 20 per cent. All but the small independent bakeries employed pest control contractors.

Two surveys of insecticides used by Local Authorities in Britain show the change in practice between 1968–69 and 1973–74.[599,657] Again, application concerned indoor pests, and not specifically the control of cockroaches (Table II). There was, (1) a change from DDT to lindane as the preferred insecticide (2) a greater interest in propoxur and fenitrothion and (3) more recent adoption of some carbamate insecticides. Additional data from the survey in 1973–74 indicates that about one third of Local Authorities use lindane to control cockroaches and two thirds apply pyrethrins alone, or in support of other residual insecticides.

TABLE II

ESTIMATED TOTAL QUANTITIES (kg TECHNICAL) OF INSECTICIDES USED BY LOCAL AUTHORITIES IN GREAT BRITAIN FOR PUBLIC HEALTH AND HYGIENE. COMPARISON OF THE TWO PERIODS, APRIL 1968–MARCH 1969 AND APRIL 1973–MARCH 1974
(From Muttrie, Papworth & Taylor[599])

Insecticide	1968–69		1973–74	
	Kg	No. of users	Kg	No. of users
DDT	3,852	1,102	1,609	438
Lindane	1,062	1,116	1,936	850
Pyrethrins	535	1,193	172	879
Malathion	464	294	160	177
Chlordane	375	144	368	204
HCN	196	368	14	19
Dieldrin	142	482	118	272
Diazinon	28	469	75	370
Dichlorvos	25	140	43	166
Propoxur	22	204	590	166
Fenitrothion	15	87	505	400
Rotenone	<0·5	8	1	20
Trichlorphon	<0·5	1	45	4
Additions				
Carbaryl	–	–	126	173
Dioxacarb	–	–	73	139
Bromophos	–	–	32	60
Bendiocarb	–	–	31	180
Iodofenphos	–	–	9	22
Chlordecone	–	–	8	90
Metaldehyde*	–	–	1	4
Sodium fluoride	–	–	<0·5	2

* Probably for slug and snail control.

Fig. 6. The cockroach is now recognised in most countries as an obnoxious intruder. It's presence in the home diminishes social status and often elicits fear. The horror with which some people react has been popularised in the science fiction film 'Bug': a tale of terror, of the frantic efforts to control a bizarre and deadly breed, unleashed from the bowels of the earth following an earthquake. (A Paramount Picture, distributed by Cinema International Corp.).

The future outlook for insecticides

The quite astonishing increase in agricultural productivity after World War II was helped substantially by the discovery of a range of synthetic organic pesticides, including materials which also contributed massively to improvements in public health. Some of these are now being relied upon for cockroach control.

In 1950, insecticides accounted for about two thirds of the £200 million world market in pesticides; fungicides and herbicides contributed the remaining one third. In the period 1960 to present day, the production of insecticides, as measured by sales in both the U.S.A. and U.K., has risen only slightly (compared with herbicides: Fig. 5). Pesticide production in Japan increased 2·5-fold in value between 1963 and 1969—again largely due to an increase in herbicides. The insecticide proportion of the world-wide pesticide market is now a relatively small fraction—below 30 per cent. The world use of insecticides is expected to double from £1 billion (in 1975) to £2 billion (in 1990),[9,20] with organophosphorus and carbamate insecticides being in most demand.

Fig. 7. German cockroaches attracted to a moist sandwich, to which they will impart a characteristic odour, will contaminate with excrement and possibly disease organisms. (Courtesy: Neil A. Maclean Co. Inc.).

Manufacture of many of the insecticides used today is dependent on the aromatic fraction of petroleum products. As a result, availability and price in future years will be dependent upon the world price of crude petroleum. Additionally, totally different criteria are now being applied to the introduction of new insecticides. Thus, in comparison with existing products there is a requirement for greater cost/effectiveness: whilst manufacturing facilities exist for the insecticides currently being used, new plant is becoming more costly to finance.

The already severe economic strain on manufacturers, of continual producing new chemicals, is still further intensified, if (1) the expected 'useful life' is limited through onset of resistance[849] and (2) the period of time required to obtain Government approval for use is further extended. In some countries, e.g. Japan, data showing completion of at least two years' toxicity tests must support applications for pesticide registration. Much higher standards of 'environmental acceptance' are being applied to new insecticides than was so with earlier materials.[682]

In the past, the insecticides used for cockroach control provided the manufacturer with a 'bonus' of sales: the amounts used were not large, but were *in addition to* the primary offtake for crop protection. With fewer new pesticides being submitted for registration in the U.S.A. (see p. 145)—the country in which 75 per cent of the world's pesticides are produced—the outlook for new insecticides for cockroach control appears bleak.

The controversy of the last decade makes it clear that one of our primary needs is for insecticides non-toxic to man and domestic animals, both when applied and when left as residues after application. As well as killing cockroaches and other indoor pests, the *ideal* insecticide should have properties which make it active only against insects and not against ourselves.

Thus new materials may justifiably come from the development of biochemically active agents specific to the pest: insect growth regulators which interfere with moulting,[9,10] sex attractants as lures, and aggregation pheromones, are examples. However, the commercial development of these would appear to be limited by the very thing we seek—specificity of action—since this must inevitably cause only very small amounts to be manufactured and used just for cockroach control. Would we expect industry to become involved in such far-sighted, but probably costly investments?

2

THE COCKROACH AS A PEST

Pest status—Infestations outdoors: in temperate climates; in the tropics; man-made habitats and sanitation; infestations in covered areas and entry into buildings—Infestations indoors: moisture; temperature; food; harbourage; lack of concern and the role of preventive pest control—Cockroaches and food poisoning—Pest cockroaches in different countries: U.S.A.; W. Germany; Finland; cockroaches in the U.K.

The natural habitat of cockroaches is outdoors. Contrary to what is often said—that cockroaches have adapted to our way of living—the fault is with us. *They* have not changed in any way: much that *we* have done by design, construction and heating of buildings, our food-handling practices and methods of disposing of waste, provide cockroaches with a favourable environment similar to their original habitat. We have encouraged them to come indoors.

The pest cockroaches live and reproduce in buildings, where we have come to regard them as objectionable, disease-carrying intruders. This is because of their usual association with food, with poor standards of hygiene, and their occupation of drains, toilets, sewers, and other locations in which infectious organisms exist.

The pest cockroaches which occur in buildings are:

Most common:	*Blattella germanica*	—German cockroach
	Blatta orientalis	—Common or Oriental cockroach
	Periplaneta americana	—American cockroach
Less common:	*Supella longipalpa*	—Brown-banded cockroach
	Periplaneta australasiae	—Australian cockroach
	Periplaneta fuliginosa	—Smokey-brown cockroach
	Periplaneta brunnea	—Brown cockroach
May be locally common:	*Leucophea maderae*	—Madeira cockroach
	Periplaneta japonica	—Japanese cockroach
Occasional intruders:	Cockroaches of about a dozen species accidentally introduced into buildings, but not necessarily establishing infestations (e.g. *Parcoblatta* spp. in U.S.A.).	

The appearance, biology and habits of cockroaches are described in Vol. 1 (Chapter 3). Here we shall re-examine briefly the pest status of cockroaches and the reasons for their control. We shall discuss the conditions

Fig. 8. Cockroach infestations outdoors: (top) in a refuse tip where *B. germanica* are encouraged by heating of organic debris (Sydney, Australia); (centre) alongside a railway siding by a godown where residues of cotton seed cake, maizemeal and bran accumulate through poor environmental hygiene and encourage *P. americana* (Dar-es-Salaam, Tanzania); (bottom) in a discharge area of warm factory effluent where it maintains *B. orientalis* (Netherlands).

outdoors which favour the association of cockroaches with buildings and the conditions which encourage insect entry. Also, the factors indoors which cause cockroaches to establish infestations. We shall then examine the incidence of the pest species in a number of countries, with particular reference to new survey data for the U.K.

PEST STATUS

Cockroaches do not eat large amounts, neither do they cause serious damage, as do insects normally living in stored foods. Nevertheless, there are six good reasons why pest cockroaches should be controlled.

1. The presence of cockroaches causes embarrassment, unnecessary distress and psychological harm to many people (Fig. 6). Entomophobia extends to many insects: fear of cockroaches is very common and comes, principally, from their speed and unpredictable direction of movement and the ease with which most can run over and cling to almost any surface.

2. Cockroaches, or parts of their bodies, in food sold to the public may result in considerable loss of business and goodwill. The revulsion which most people have on finding cockroaches in food comes from the mental association of these insects with filth. Most countries have laws regulating the wholesomeness of foods sold in cafes, restaurants, hotels and in retail trade. When contamination occurs, fines may be imposed following prosecution, but the resulting adverse publicity is the more damaging. Reputable companies have much to lose from an occasional lapse in hygiene. Nevertheless, the presence of insects in food is only one of many causes of complaint (Table III). Probably less than 10 per cent of foreign bodies in food get reported to Public Health Departments. There were 11,120 reported instances in the U.K. in 1974; prosecutions totalled 1,183, involving fines of £43,000. Most complaints by the public are resolved directly with retailers.

3. Food fouled and tainted by the characteristic odour of cockroaches is unfit for human consumption. Odours may remain even after cooking or processing. An allergen, which is also not destroyed by high cooking temperatures, can be detected in food partially consumed by cockroaches.[99] Two pest species of cockroaches excrete compounds related to active mutagens or carcinogens.[593]

4. Cockroaches can carry a number of disease organisms, notably *Salmonellae*, injurious to man and of importance in public health. However, the association of cockroaches with bacteria, viruses and a number of parasites is largely fortuitous (see Vol. I, Chapter 13). Because these insects live in situations where disease organisms are picked up on the outside of their bodies, or ingested, cockroaches have the opportunity of transferring them to foods and onto work surfaces, creating a potential health risk to man (see p. 56).

5. Cockroaches are omnivorous. Very little food is needed to sustain them. Thus, residues in kitchens—behind cupboards and under equipment—are sufficient to feed large numbers. Food left exposed overnight is readily con-

taminated (Fig. 7). But cockroaches also damage many articles other than foods, such as books, tapestries, leather goods and pictures. Some industries (e.g. cultivation of orchids) have special problems.

Fig. 9. Examples of poor sanitation, conducive to insect and rodent infestation: (top) caused by a street market (Kampala, Uganda); (left) behind slum housing (Djakarta, Indonesia); (right) alongside basement accommodation (Kuala Lumpur, Malaysia).

TABLE III

ANALYSIS OF 11,120 CONTAMINANTS OF DIFFERENT TYPES, REPORTED TO FOOD RETAILERS BY THE PUBLIC AND PUBLIC HEALTH DEPARTMENTS FOR DIFFERENT TYPES OF FOOD. FIGURES ARE PERCENTAGES OF CONTAMINANTS FOR EACH TYPE OF PRODUCT. (PERIOD INVOLVED: 1 YEAR. RETAIL VALUE £200 MILLION. U.K. 1975)

Contaminant	Cereal products: flour, bread, cakes, biscuits, savouries	Meats, pies, poultry and delicatessen	Groceries: canned & packet foods	Dairy products	Frozen foods	Sugar confectionery	Fresh fruit & vegetables	Average: all products
Insects: crawling and flying	7	12	10	13	7	10	68	10·1
Metal: all types	9	14	10	9	13	10	8	10·6
String, bristle, fibre, hair	19	14	6	14	17	6	1	15·4
Glass, plastic, rubber, wood	18	12	11	18	18	11	4	15·8
Dirt, oil and grease	30	11	19	15	18	19	4	21·9
Others: e.g. seeds, stones, moulds, paper, bones, cigarette ends	16	36	44	32	28	44	15	26·2
Total instances	5,720	2,200	1,030	890	620	500	160	

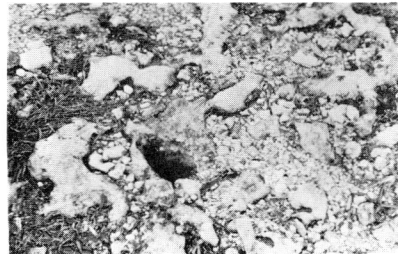

Fig. 10. Natural and man-made harbourage outdoors: (left) cavities in coral and limestone rock provide numerous harbourages for American cockroaches. Spraying of the complete ground area around buildings may be necessary where this problem occurs (Freeport, Bahamas); (right) electric meter point outside domestic property being treated with dust, also against *P. americana* (Houston, U.S.A.).

Fig. 11. Coconut palms, grown for shade or ornamental purposes around buildings provide harbourage for *P. americana*. Cockroaches breed in the leaf axils where rain water collects.

6. Public attitude towards cockroaches varies from abhorrence in developed countries, to acceptance in others. Relatively few people will tolerate cockroaches at their place of work and some may even assert that cockroaches have attacked them—an important consideration in the retention of employees.

In urban areas of the tropics where the density of people is highest, and where filth-borne diseases are common, cockroaches indoors are often accepted as part of normal living. Here the control of cockroaches may be practised in isolated locations, (the major hotels, restaurants and other public places), but elsewhere the association of cockroaches with man is intimate and unquestioned. It is in these countries that freedom from infestation is most difficult to achieve.

INFESTATIONS OUTDOORS

In temperate climates

Pest cockroaches cannot usually survive outdoors in cold winters. Back[68] refers to the inability of American and Oriental cockroaches to do so in the northern States of America.

Instances of cockroaches surviving the winter outdoors in Britain are also rare, but some have been reported. In Audenshaw, Lancs., for instance, a

Fig. 12. In warm climates, buildings are constantly re-invaded by cockroaches living outdoors. Sanitation in the areas immediately around homes, hotels and restaurants is important if the problem is to be reduced. Untended vegetation and accumulated trash provide ideal harbourage for cockroaches, encouraging infestation. 'Landscaping' helps reduce the numbers of insects which may enter from outside (Bahamas).

number of complaints were received from residents, of cockroaches both inside and outside their homes, adjacent to an open space, once a refuse tip.[376] Tipping ceased four years previously: no cockroaches, live or dead, could be found. The source of infestation was identified as a nearby road bridge, built in 1860, severely open-jointed and with perished pointing. The cockroaches had probably been there since closure of the tip, and had used the bridge for harbourage.

Fig. 13. Roadside culverts provide outdoor harbourage for American cockroaches: (left) moist dark conditions, at the entrance to each residential property (Houston, U.S.A.); (right) the same, outside city shops (Bridgetown, Barbados).

Beatson & Dripps[89] report three infestations of Oriental cockroaches breeding outdoors. One extended over about a quarter of a square mile, including two areas of modern housing in Essex, at the edge of a small pig farm and open common land. Occasional cockroaches were seen inside and outside these houses but the source was never established. The houses themselves did not apparently support infestations.

The second report was of cockroaches in soil and builders' rubble, about 100 yards from the nearest dwellings, in Kent. This was first reported in 1968 and the insects continued to occur there through the summer of 1970, 'gliding down from nearby trees'. The third infestation was on a disused chemical tip in Liverpool, of material 'unlikely to heat'; cockroaches were found over the entire area of 35 acres 'with groups of insects in various stages of development under stones and bricks'. There was no obvious food supply although a piggery was said to have been situated nearby, many years previously.

Fig. 14. Building construction affects the ease with which cockroaches may enter and infest homes: (top) the accumulation of timber around the walls of this home provides moist conditions for *P. americana*. Entry readily occurs between the timber cladding and the concrete base (inset, arrowed), especially when the cladding is in disrepair (Freeport, Bahamas); (bottom) residential properties built off the ground provide dark and moist crawl spaces (arrowed) favoured by *P. americana* and *B. orientalis*, especially where site sanitation is neglected (low class property, Houston, U.S.A.).

Fig. 15. Keeping properties free of cockroaches is difficult where facilities for refuse collection are not properly used: (top) a permanent garbage bin at the rear of a restaurant. Although the garbage is collected daily a residue of sludge builds up in the bottom, encouraged by continual exposure to rain. Cockroaches readily establish and breed in these bins throughout the year. A cover and periodic treatment with insecticides, would reduce the problem. In the example illustrated, site sanitation also needs to be improved; (bottom) an ill-maintained cesspool full of liquid effluent, not covered and providing favourable conditions for cockroaches. These will inevitably be heavily contaminated with pathogenic bacteria (Freeport, Bahamas).

The author has had recent personal experience of three cockroach infestations outside buildings under temperate conditions. In no case was it possible to establish whether the insects overwintered. The first of these, in London, was an infestation of *B. orientalis* which increased steadily in the uppermost bedrooms of an hotel. Isolated outbreaks in kitchens, wine cellars and passageways were eliminated quickly, but not those on the upper floors. These insects were eventually found associated with pigeons and their debris, on the flat roof and in roof ducts carrying hot water pipes and electrical conduits, which had become the main harbourage for the birds.

Fig. 16. Refuse should be incinerated or removed daily from food manufacturing sites. Collection areas should be capable of being hosed down.

The second example was at a small restaurant in Bromley, South London. Oriental cockroaches were periodically found in a kitchen built as a single storey extension to the rear of the property. Pyrethrins applied as a flushing tool, by a ULV generator (see p. 120), throughout the premises, failed to locate any harbourages indoors. However, a few minutes after the kitchen was 'aired off' by allowing the mist to escape *via* the kitchen door, cockroaches fell outside from the flat roof of the building, where they were harbouring under the bitumen felt.

The third outdoor infestation—of German cockroaches—was very extensive and occurred just below the exposed face of a refuse tip in Sydney, Australia. Probing of the debris, and pulling cartons and other refuse aside, revealed all stages of development. This source was the likely cause of cockroaches infesting nearby residential and industrial properties. It was encouraged by the obvious 'heating' within the mass of decaying refuse. Similar

Fig. 17. Entry of cockroaches into homes: (top) trees and shrubs, close to walls, or overhanging the roof, encourage the entry of cockroaches, principally *via* the roof void; foliage should be cut back wherever possible; (bottom) gaps left around ill-fitting air-conditioning units should be sealed (domestic property, Houston, U.S.A.).

infestations of cockroaches have been reported from locations in Europe, where hot liquid effluent from industrial processing provides local warmth for Oriental cockroaches outdoors (Fig. 8). In Japan nymphs of *Periplaneta japonica* have been reported hibernating outdoors in decaying wood heavily covered with snow, normally covered for about 70 days each year.[781]

Outdoor infestations in the tropics
In warm countries, cockroaches are common outdoors. They occur in natural and man-made habitats and are often encouraged by poor sanitation (Fig. 9). Crevices outdoors provide the necessary harbourage—between leaves, in the soil, under bark and in dead branches. Moist dark places are readily occupied: natural cavities in coral and limestone rock (Fig. 10 left), the crowns of coconut palms and the axils of fronds in which water collects (Fig. 11). Accumulations of trash adjacent to properties (Fig. 12) provide abundant protection for infestations of *Periplaneta* species with sources of organic matter as food.

The American cockroach is seldom found in kitchen cupboards or behind the refrigerator, as is the smaller German cockroach. *Periplaneta* spp. are common inhabitants of sewers, basements, and outdoor delivery areas, where vehicles unload.

Man-made habitats and sanitation
Harbourages often occupied by cockroaches close to properties include culverts, drains, gulleys and outdoor meter points (Figs. 10 right and 13). Ships in port often take on supplies of fresh water from tapping points within the quay, beneath metal plates. These chambers almost invariably contain cockroaches.

Accumulations of debris around domestic properties encourage cockroaches to use them for day-time harbourage; the insects then move indoors at night (Fig. 14 top). Facilities for refuse collection are often not used properly: waste is dumped in collection areas and left to provide food and breeding sites for rodents and insects. The number of refuse containers is often inadequate and they are not covered. Garbage cans should always have tight-fitting lids, particularly in basements. Outdoors, when the contents get wet a layer of organic matter accumulates inside: it is not removed when the bin is emptied and provides a continuing source of food for insect breeding (Fig. 15 top). Efficient disposal of refuse from food manufacturing industries is especially important if insect and rodent pests are not to be encouraged (Fig. 16). Daily removal, or incineration, is normally required.

Sewers and cesspools are favourite places where the larger pest cockroaches establish infestations. It is essential to maintain the free flow of effluent, to replace broken inspection plates and to ensure that they are tight-fitting. Cockroaches which migrate indoors from these locations at night are almost certain carriers of infection (Fig. 15 bottom and Fig. 126 bottom).

Methods of building construction and the materials used, often favour insect entry: dark moist crawl spaces beneath residential properties provide

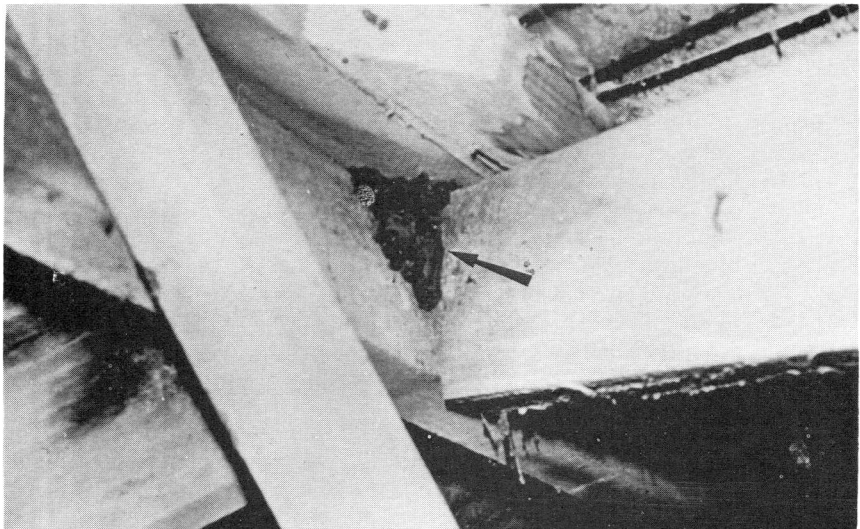

Fig. 18. Typical bat-roosting harbourage: (top) in the junction of roof timbers (arrowed); (bottom) droppings on the joists and ceiling below. Apart from producing an objectionable smell and staining ceilings, the droppings encourage cockroaches, especially *P. americana* (Georgetown, Guyana).

ideal resting places from which the cockroaches move indoors, through joints in the flooring (Fig. 14 bottom). Cladding, in disrepair, allows insects to get beneath and into the building through gaps in mortar jointing. It is common for owners of property to plant trees and shrubs close to the house: this allows *P. americana* easy access to the roof (Fig. 17 top). Roof spaces in temperate countries rarely contain cockroaches, as there is nothing to encourage them: temperatures are too low and there is rarely any food.

Fig. 19. Storm-water drains in markets are a particular health risk where cockroaches can readily contaminate food with disease organisms. The responsibility for treatment usually lies with the local health department (Bridgetown, Barbados).

However, in tropical countries, roof spaces with their low pitched roofs are often occupied by small fruit- and insect-eating bats, which foul the joists and ceiling boards with their droppings. These accumulations provide cockroaches with a ready source of food, and temperatures are favourable (Fig. 18).

A further example of the way cockroaches are encouraged to enter properties in the tropics is *via* air conditioning units. The air-intakes are rarely the exact size for the hole in the wall (often the lower part of a window) and are installed without a perfect seal (Fig. 17 bottom). This is a route by which cockroaches get into bedrooms, despite the screening of windows to prevent insect entry!

Fig. 20. The kitchen sink is a most favoured location for cockroaches: (top) in the home (U.K.) and (bottom) in a restaurant kitchen (Malaysia). All the requirements are provided: moisture, warmth, food residues and harbourage.

THE COCKROACH AS A PEST   43

Infestations in covered areas and entry into buildings
In warm climates cockroaches often enter covered areas such as markets, stadia, bars around hotel swimming pools, garages, covered patios and 'outbuildings'. Infestations here may provide sources of cockroaches within easy reach of other buildings. The food markets of tropical countries invariably have open storm water drains, providing good harbourage for cockroaches (Fig. 19). The insects may enter these areas voluntarily or be carried on commodities. Goods purchased from markets should be examined carefully before being taken into the home.

Most domestic properties in warm climates are proofed against flying insects (midges and mosquitoes), but for larger properties like restaurants and hotels, this can never be completely effective. Domestic garages provide 'over-

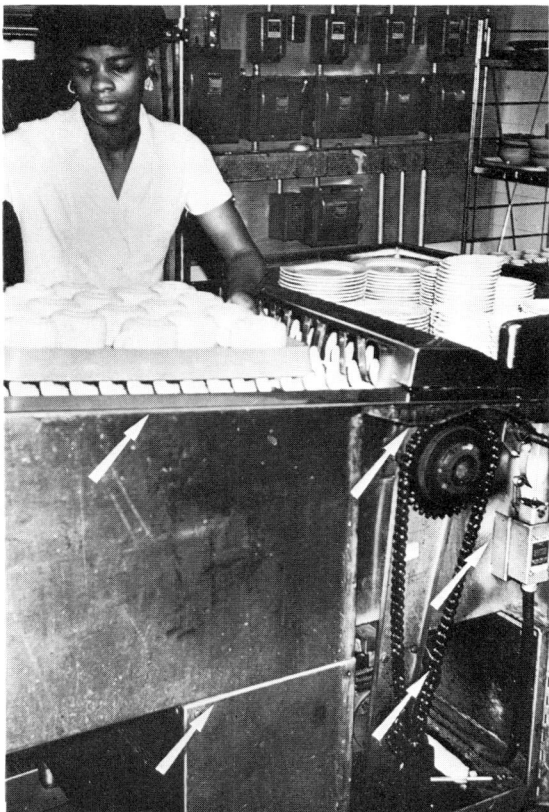

Fig. 21. Mechanical equipment for washing-up in cafeterias and industrial canteens provides numerous harbourages for German cockroaches, difficult to treat. Insecticides are also quickly lost. The warmth of electric motors encourages infestation. Arrows indicate typical harbourages (Atlanta, U.S.A.).

night' harbourage for cockroaches with easy entry into homes, especially garages which form an integral part of house construction where a service door may lead straight into the kitchen. Cockroaches may survive in garages on food put down for pets; there is also ample harbourage under garden equipment, tools, timber, children's toys and other clutter, making garages impossible to inspect and difficult to treat sensibly and safely (see baits, p. 103).

Fig. 22. Harbourage for German cockroaches within broken steam pipe insulation (arrowed at top of picture); also arrowed, condensation on cold pipes providing the insects with water (dairy: Atlanta, U.S.A.).

The proportion of premises in the tropics containing cockroaches is usually high. The possibility of these insects being carried into buildings already freed of cockroaches by treatment, is again high. Cockroaches can enter restaurants, and other food handling or processing establishments, every day, on incoming raw materials from suppliers. This stresses the importance of promoting good sanitation to make conditions in buildings as unfavourable as possible for the establishment of immigrant cockroaches (see p. 52).

Fig. 23. Modern kitchens with stainless steel surfaces give the appearance of cleanliness: (top) in large hospitals, German cockroaches are carried in the insulation of heated food carts (arrowed) used to transfer hot meals from kitchens to the wards (Tucson, U.S.A.); (bottom) the ducting and ventilation systems of modern ships help the spread of cockroaches from galleys to cabin accommodation. In both examples, harbourages occur between metal surfaces (Port of London, U.K.).

In temperate climates, the entry of cockroaches from outdoors is much less frequent, and then usually by introduction in goods.

INFESTATIONS INDOORS

The factors which encourage cockroaches to establish themselves in buildings are moisture, warmth, food and harbourage. Lack of concern about insect infestation may then allow cockroaches to breed and spread in an undisturbed environment.

Moisture requirements

Cockroaches may survive starvation for many weeks, but they have a far greater demand for water. Sinks and wash-up areas provide cockroaches with most of their needs. In infested houses, the kitchen is invariably the focus of infestation: the insects harbour beneath the draining board, in the poor jointing of wall tiles, within sink supports and inside the cupboard below. Sinks provide a constant source of water and food debris, and it is here that cutlery, china and glassware can be easily contaminated (Fig. 20). Secondary foci of infestation in the home occur in bathrooms and toilets where water is again readily available.

In large kitchens, which serve industrial canteens, cafeterias, restaurants and hospitals, washing-up is usually mechanised, but the equipment provides a multiplicity of harbourages, especially for German cockroaches (Fig. 21). The crevices in which they live are often inaccessible without removing stainless steel panels to treat inside, and insecticide applied is quickly lost (see Fig. 43). The moisture in shower and locker rooms and in the bars and service pantries of clubs, hotels and restaurants, also encourages infestation.

There are many food industries in which manufacturing processes involve heat and where sources of moisture are also available. This liquid—not always water—is sometimes a component of the manufactured product: cordials, soft drinks, milk products. More often it is effluent, pools of drainage water in gullies, washing water for equipment, and that resulting from 'hosing down' at night. Cockroaches favour the moist conditions often found in laundries and dairies. Condensation is sufficient to provide the water which cockroaches need (Fig. 22). Wooden surfaces hold water for long periods and crevices, when present, provide the locally high humidities which cockroaches prefer.

Temperature requirements

Cockroaches congregate near sources of heat, which speed growth and accelerate reproduction. Warmth is provided by central heating plant, radiators, ovens, tea urns, refrigerator motors, pumps and the variety of equipment which generates heat in industry. These sources provide the temperature range 20–29°C favourable to *B. orientalis* and the higher temperatures, 24–33°C preferred by *B. germanica* and *P. americana*.

Cockroaches in the tropics are not so dependent on artificial sources of warmth: breeding may continue unchecked throughout the year. Here

Fig. 24. Typical American drug store in which the contamination of retail products by cockroaches (top), is encouraged by the food service counter at the rear (bottom).

cockroaches occur in lunchrooms, washrooms, elevator shafts, or wherever there is available food or organic residues. Nevertheless, artificially heated areas do encourage 'hot spots' of infestation. Examples are around ovens, hot serving counters and heated cupboards in which meals are kept warm. The food carts (Fig. 23 top) used to distribute meals in hospitals[587] present special problems when cockroaches become established in the insulation material. The pest control operator's task is to discover where cockroaches are harbouring: it may be easier for him to locate sources of warmth and then to check whether cockroaches are infesting these areas.

Fig. 25. Harbourage of *B. germanica* provided by door hinges, illustrating the requirement of cockroaches for close contact with surfaces: (right) before and (left) after flushing with pyrethrins (hostel, Tucson, U.S.A.).

Food requirements

There is virtually no situation in which food is not available in some form, although we may not recognise it as such: the casein glue of book bindings, wallpaper paste,[798] fabrics,[302] floor sweepings usually of decaying organic matter—are sufficient to keep cockroaches alive. The more usual sources are residues behind kitchen equipment, in the crevices of work surfaces, the undersides of tables, in and behind cupboards, especially where standards of hygiene are low.

Fig. 26. Cockroaches congregate on rough surfaces and where temperatures are most favourable: (top) at the wall-ceiling junction around a pipe entry and between electrical cables (restaurant kitchen, Kuala Lumpur, Malaysia); (bottom) behind plastic skirting where floor washings have carried food debris beneath (fraternity house, Tucson, U.S.A.).

Moist foods are generally preferred, especially in a dry atmosphere: e.g. fresh fruits, vegetables, soups, beverages and moist organic debris. Problems arise in shops and other stores selling 'dry' merchandise, but which supplement their income by a counter service for beers, soft drinks and a limited range of meals. Normally these premises would be without the problem of cockroach infestation, but the catering facilities and eating area—as in the typical American drug store—encourage infestation which then spreads to retail counters (Fig. 24).

Three good reasons for cockroaches occurring in the auditoria of cinemas and theatres are the bar, the confectionery counter and the food debris left by the public.

Fig. 27. Brown-banded cockroaches are usually found in homes. Infestations are widely scattered throughout living rooms and bedrooms: the insects often occur in furniture and clothes cupboards. It is important that treatment does not mar decorations and furnishings; fine sprays are therefore used (Houston, U.S.A.).

Harbourage

Harbourage indoors is not difficult for cockroaches to find: the space between a door hinge and the timber is sufficient (Fig. 25). The domestic kitchen provides many crevices near warmth, food and water, where infestations become established. In the last 25 years, improvements in the design of kitchen equipment, and the greater attention to hygiene, have changed the appearance of kitchens, in homes, hotels, restaurants and in industry—but the cracks and crevices in which cockroaches hide during the day have not been eliminated. The galleys of modern ships are full of abutting stainless steel surfaces: units are firmly attached to bulkheads making it difficult to check for the presence of cockroaches (Fig. 23 bottom). Ventilation ducting and air extraction systems allow the insects access to other parts of the ship.

Fig. 28. Shop decor provides 'dead spaces' within counter display units, providing dark, undisturbed harbourage for insects and rodents. The motors of refrigeration units provide local sources of warmth, encouraging German cockroaches (U.K.).

Cockroaches tend to congregate on rough surfaces; often high up in rooms—at the junction of walls with the ceiling, where temperatures are highest. Points where pipe work passes through walls are commonly used (Fig. 26 top). The spaces between electric cables are often used for attaching egg cases. Harbourages may be superficial (Fig. 26 bottom) behind skirting boards, architraves, in jointing beneath tiles and under floor coverings—or deeper seated beneath suspended floors, in hollow walls, above false ceilings, in ducts and conduits.

The pest control operator who provides a service for cockroach control in warm climates may have to extend his treatment throughout the whole house, especially if Brown-banded cockroaches are present. The distribution of this insect in homes is much wider than *B. germanica*: detailed inspection and treatment may be necessary of the lounge and bedroom furniture, behind pictures, in telephones and television cabinets, behind light switches and in the wall cupboards of some apartments where ironing boards are a permanent fixture (Table VII and Fig 27).

Extensive panelling to enclose structures is part of modern decor, but behind this smooth facade are, of course, ample spaces suitable for cockroaches. The design of shops is intended to provide an appealing atmosphere in which customers will linger and buy, but this and the refrigerated display units in food stores are typical examples of man-made harbourages (Fig. 28). The crevices beneath gaskets which provide seals on smoke ovens for curing meats and other products provide ideal resting sites for *B. germanica* (Fig. 29).

Fig. 29. A smoke oven for meat products encourages cockroaches in broken insulation and under the moulded door seals (arrowed) (Dallas, U.S.A.).

Lack of concern and the role of preventive pest control

Our awareness of cockroaches as pests is greater now than ever before. Nevertheless, poor hygiene is responsible for many cockroach problems: there is massive ignorance of the benefits which can be obtained in reducing, or sometimes preventing, infestation from occurring, by methods of 'preventive pest control'. Sometimes both the poor hygiene and the presence of insects are ignored (Fig. 30). There are also occasions when fear or shame prevent the existence of an infestation from being disclosed. 'The "disgrace" is not in having cockroaches, but in allowing them to remain'.[68]

High standards of hygiene are predominantly important to our present mode of living, when many rely on the vigilance and quality of services provided by others. Preventive pest control involves action by those responsi-

Fig. 30. Grossly inadequate attention to hygiene in the food industry: (top) egg cases of American cockroaches swept into the corner of a warehouse (Antigua); (bottom) poor building structure encouraging the growth of moulds, and waste products not properly disposed of (Bridgetown, Barbados).

ble for hygiene, especially in food manufacture, warehousing, retailing and catering, (1) to deny entry of pests into buildings, then (2) to make conditions inside as unfavourable as possible for pest survival and reproduction.[140]

In 1937, Back[68] advocated that 'all cracks and pipes passing through floors or walls, as well as cracks leading to spaces behind baseboards and door frames, should be filled, particularly if cockroaches are known to be coming in from adjacent apartments or from outside'. In some properties—apartments and multistorey blocks of flats—it is possible to undertake 'chemical proofing' during construction by use of inorganic insecticides such as boric acid and silica aerogel.[266]

Because insects are more likely to be introduced into buildings inadvertently in goods (see p. 161), it is most important that scrupulous attention be paid to denying those insects the conditions in which to breed. Understanding the reasons why cockroaches may have established an infestation in a building, is the first step to preventing it occurring again. The action to be taken involves: (1) removing all food residues wherever possible, (2) eliminating 'dead spaces' where organic matter may accumulate, (3) thought being given to food storage, the inspection of raw materials, and waste disposal, and (4) stock rotation ('first in-first out') so that no packages remain long enough for infestation to develop.

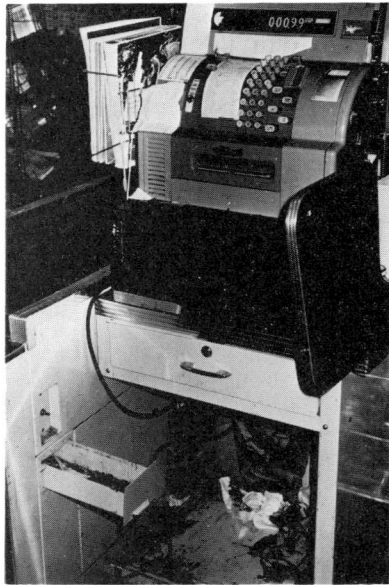

Fig. 31. The store room (left) and 'check out' (right) of a supermarket (Atlanta, U.S.A.). Pest infestation is inevitable, without proper stacking to allow for inspection, and the allocation of responsibility for storage to personnel aware of the importance of waste disposal. The poor hygiene and the motorised conveyor at the 'check out' are conducive to cockroaches infesting the cash desk.

When cockroaches do occur, they must be seen quickly. They are then more easily dealt with.

Look, for example, at the encouragement to cockroaches in the store room and around the cash desk in the supermarket shown in Fig. 31: not until large numbers of cockroaches occur will an infestation be noticed, especially as in these situations no one is likely to see the insects at night when they are most active. The problems of infestation by German, Oriental and American cockroaches in supermarkets were described in 1948 when this type of store first came into vogue.[228]

In applying preventive pest control, management should personally, (1) set and monitor the standards aimed at, (2) establish responsibility for the action to be taken, and (3) educate and motivate all staff to believe that high standards of cleanliness and good order are worthwhile (Fig. 32). Also, (4) co-ordinate preventive pest control with the activities (inspection and treatment) of a pest control contractor. 'Night inspections' (see Vol. I, Chapter 11) are the surest way of detecting infestations when they occur.

Fig. 32. Positive attempts at maintaining high standards of hygiene: (left) motivation of staff in kitchens of a cafeteria (Atlanta); (right) good storage, at least 30 cm off the floor, aids cleaning and inspection in the store of a large hospital. Education is needed, however, to prevent containers from being placed under the benching (Tucson, U.S.A.).

With a policy of this type it is possible that the use of insecticides can be eliminated, or perhaps that small amounts only need be used. In a test in New Jersey, U.S.A., homes with differing degrees of hygiene, showed no difference in the level of cockroach control achieved 10 days after treatment with sprays, dust and bait. Within a month, however, it was apparent that cockroach populations had increased noticeably in homes with bad sanitation, especially where no dust was used. In those with good sanitation, none of the treatments had lost their effectiveness two months after application.[384]

In an extension of this study[383] populations of cockroaches showed more pronounced fluctuations in numbers in homes with bad sanitation than where it was good. The adoption of 'community-oriented educational programmes' is suggested as a method of improving and maintaining adequate sanitary conditions both in and outdoors.

COCKROACHES AND FOOD POISONING

Contrary to general belief, food poisoning is seldom brought about by eating 'bad food'. Usually food which causes food poisoning, smells, tastes and looks normal. The presence of the harmful chemical, or bacteria, can only be shown by appropriate tests.

The most important bacteria involved are *Salmonellae, Clostridium welchii* and *Staphylococci*. The major sources are pigs, poultry and cattle: when animal feeding-stuffs are infected with *Salmonellae* these are excreted by the animal and may infect carcases during butchering. Meat and poultry thus introduce harmful bacteria into kitchens. The main source of the *Staphylococci* which cause food poisoning is the food handler.

The transmission of these organisms is of vital concern in kitchens which provide meals in schools, hospitals and restaurants. Foods vary in the extent to which they support and encourage bacterial growth. Favourable temperatures are between 10 and 60°C. Foods with a meat base, and fish and milk products, are highly susceptible. Meat products and poultry are implicated in about 80 per cent of all outbreaks of food poisoning reported in the United Kingdom (about 8,000 cases per year) where the source has been traced.[44]

Thorough cooking of food destroys active bacteria, but not all spores. Light cooking may not destroy toxins. A detailed study of the numbers and types of bacteria in a large number of industrial kitchens (to be published) shows a predominance of undesirable bacteria in areas of food storage and preparation, especially around sinks, on cutting surfaces and equipment. The numbers are somewhat less in cooking areas and are least in areas from which food is served.

The association of cockroaches with drains, gullies and waste traps, and with decaying food residues and other sources of putrefying matter brings them into intimate contact with thriving 'cultures' of harmful bacteria. The insects may also make contact with disease organisms on incoming, contaminated, raw materials. The fact that the association is casual—rather than the cockroaches acting as specific carriers (as do mosquitoes for malaria), makes them no less important in spreading infection to man.

The extent to which cockroaches do this and actually cause food poisoning, is unknown. It depends on whether susceptible foods are left exposed, (1) long enough to make contamination possible and (2) under conditions where bacteria can multiply readily.[816] The risk is clearly related to ambient temperature and the care in food-handling by catering staff. Figure 33 shows a typical hotel kitchen, the locations of cockroaches and approximate numbers found. The presence of cockroaches in such kitchens, in the evening, creates the additional risk—for management—that the insects may actually be noticed by clients.

In her survey of cockroaches in W. Germany, Döhring[236] describes vividly the presence of these pests in kitchens and other locations where they are cause for concern: 'cockroaches were found in industrial kitchens, in flour bins, bags of sugar and oats, in spice jars, among grated cheese on bread, in bread slicers, on meat balls and other cold meats, on buffets, in stored fats and oils, on spits and grills, in coffee machines and dishwashers, in hot plates, in kitchen cabinets and cutlery drawers, under the bars and serving hatches and underneath eating tables. Cockroaches were found around refuse bins next to larders: they were found running in large numbers over food, crockery and work tables. They were occasionally found on chopping blocks, in butchers' shops, which are known to be difficult to disinfect. Cockroaches were also found sitting on beer taps, in beer glasses, in and around soft drink

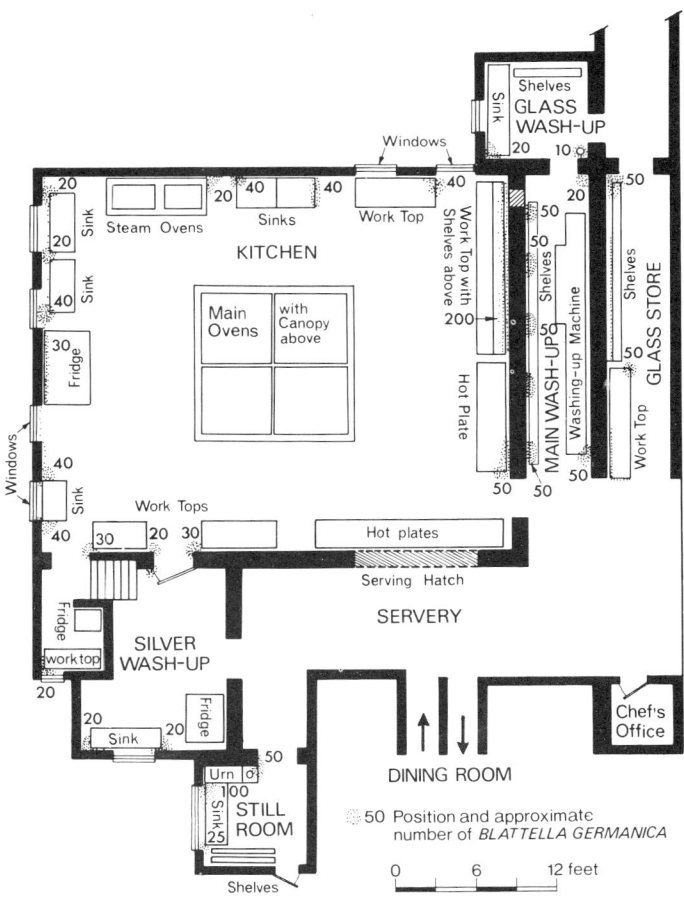

Fig. 33. Plan of an infestation of German cockroaches in a large hotel kitchen (London, U.K.).

machines. And, occasionally, the insects were reported in towel dispensers in toilets which certainly didn't supply hygienic towels'.

PEST COCKROACHES IN DIFFERENT COUNTRIES

The German cockroach has been described as the 'world's most successful commercial traveller': it has an international passport and uses all methods of transport. There is probably no country in which it does not occur.

The other pest cockroaches are not so generally spread: predominant species in one country may be almost absent in another. The best example is the American cockroach, which is common in Asia, parts of Africa and the U.S.A. and other warm climates, but is rare in most of northern Europe.

The history of introduction and spread of the Brown-banded cockroach in North America is detailed in Vol. I (Chapter 3). D. H. Murphy (personal communication: Univ. Singapore) says that originally this cockroach was unknown in S.E. Asia, except for a record from Christmas Island in 1915. The insect was certainly not conspicuous in Singapore in 1960 and the first specimen was brought for identification in 1965: by that time it had become locally common. Since 1967 this cockroach has appeared regularly and there are now probably few uninfested houses. The cockroach is an inhabitant of the upper floors of high rise flats, since it is a species characteristically inhabiting drier places than other pest cockroaches. At ground level, *P. americana* is the most conspicuous cockroach of public health importance, where it occurs as a 'sewer roach'. *P. australasiae* occurs only rarely in houses: it is essentially a garden pest in Singapore.

In the next few paragraphs, we will consider the cockroaches which occur as pests in the U.S.A., W. Germany, Finland and in the U.K. We will also look at the way 'what goes on' in buildings influences the species present.

U.S.A.

The German cockroach is the most common household insect in the United States.[521] In 1920, Morse[591] described it as an insect with a 'predilection for the society of man as a provider of the necessities and luxuries of life': although the smallest species (the Brown-banded cockroach was not regarded as a pest at that time), 'it makes up in numbers what it lacks in size'. He quotes Blatchley (from 'Orthoptera of Indiana') as saying that the German cockroach 'seldom if ever occurs in numbers in the country, but is one of the worst insect pests with which the inhabitants of the larger cities have to deal.' A survey of public housing projects in New Haven, Connecticut, revealed that 60 per cent of apartments were infested[34]: 90 per cent of kitchens and 50 per cent of bathrooms in low to moderate income apartments contained cockroaches.[587]

In the *city* of Boston, cockroaches are reported responsible for 68 per cent of pest infestations in commercial and industrial buildings, 70 per cent in flats, but only 12 per cent in private houses (where ants are more common). In the *suburbs* of Boston, cockroaches are less predominant: here, cockroaches comprise 55 per cent, 30 per cent and 2 per cent (ants 72 per cent) of pests in the three types of property.[39]

The distribution of the more important pest cockroaches in the United States varies with climate: *B. germanica* and *P. americana* are prevalent at all latitudes, but in the north, occur only indoors and in protected locations. Other species of *Periplaneta* are encountered most frequently in the south, where they occur outdoors, but are usually far less common than *P. americana*. The Oriental cockroach is a pest mainly in the north-central States.

Infestations of *B. germanica*, *B. orientalis*, *P. americana* and *S. longipalpa* in North Carolina, occur in the ratios 16 : 10 : 2 : 1, but the proportions vary in different properties.[863] In a military reservation in North Carolina, German cockroaches were responsible for 85 per cent of infestations, and *P. americana* for 14 per cent; *S. longipalpa*, *B. orientalis* and *P. fuliginosa* were seen only rarely. The Brown-banded cockroach is invariably associated with housing.[869]

Counts of German cockroaches (averages) in low-income homes, again in N. Carolina,[867] were as follows: kitchens (467), dining areas (241), the hall (47), living area (45), bedroom (37) and bathroom (21).

Populations of cockroaches in the U.S.A. tend to build up to a maximum during August and September (Fig. 34). There are many speculations as to

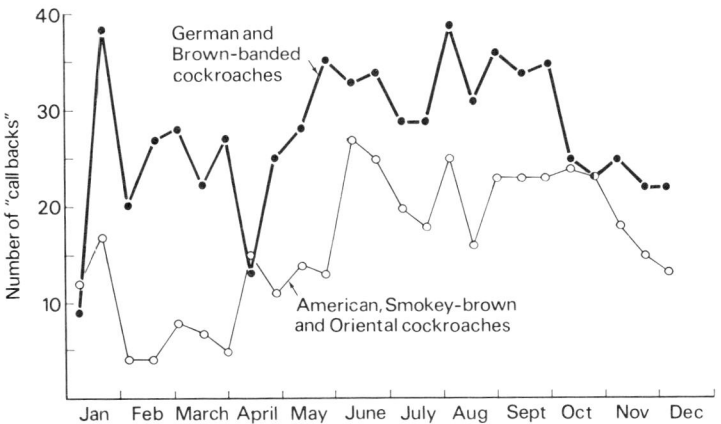

Fig. 34. Incidence of 'call backs' by clients for additional treatment for cockroach control (data supplied by a pest control company in the southern U.S.A. for 1966).

the cause, or combination of causes, but each year, almost without exception, such problems are reported to America's National Pest Control Association. (Phil Spear: personal communication). Warm humid conditions favour *B. germanica*, which probably responds by increased reproduction. Peaks also tend to occur for other species at the same time.[870]

W. Germany

In a survey by members of the West German pest control operators' association, 2,321 reports were made of cockroach infestations in buildings in 1970–71.[236] German cockroaches occurred twice as often as the Oriental cockroach. Towns tended to favour *B. germanica* (ratio German to Oriental 2·1 : 1) compared with rural areas (1·6 : 1). In large cities, the incidence of German cockroaches was 5 times greater than *B. orientalis*.[237]

The American cockroach was reported in 9 instances (0·4 per cent): in industrial kitchens, food factories, in the accommodation of foreign soldiers and in zoological gardens. There were six infestations of Brown-banded cockroaches: in a van recently arrived from India, in houses occupied by French soldiers, and in the accommodation of Korean nurses. These more unusual infestations illustrate the part played by people and transport in spreading cockroaches.

Cockroaches were found most often in industrial kitchens (35 per cent); in the small kitchens, washrooms and toilets of commercial buildings (11·4 per cent); in residential properties including the accommodation of foreign workers (9·1 per cent); in private homes (7·3 per cent); hospitals and clinics (7·0 per cent); bakers and confectioners and cafes (6·5 per cent), and in groceries, food manufacturing industries and warehouses (6·2 per cent). These seven groups account for 82 per cent of infestations.[236] Oriental cockroaches occurred most frequently in cellars and boiler rooms (45 per cent) and rarely above the first floor. German cockroaches occurred throughout infested premises, often making an appearance on the upper floors.

Finland

As an example of a country with a climate much cooler than others, brief information, published by the Department of Pest Infestation, is included for Finland.

About 3 per cent of all homes are infested with cockroaches (*cf.* 1 per cent bed bugs) and infestation is more prevalent in villages ('communes') than in small country towns and cities. German cockroaches occur almost exclusively in houses where Oriental and American cockroaches are rare. Infestations are noticeably greater in the eastern and central counties of Finland than in the west. However, levels of infestation in 1968 were said to be lower than ten years previously: 'control is neglected, or the measures taken are inadequate, in every fifth home infested.'[526]

Cockroaches in the U.K.

The last chapter of Vol. I gave an analysis of the incidence of pest cockroaches in buildings in the U.K. Data from 4,000 infested premises, surveyed and treated in 1964–66 showed that German cockroaches occurred in 21 per cent of infested premises and Oriental cockroaches in 89 per cent—a ratio of 1 : 4·1—with both species occurring together in 10 per cent.

Nevertheless, certain types of premises tended to favour *B. germanica* (*viz.* clubs, public halls, restaurants and cafes); others favoured *B. orientalis* (cinemas, theatres, houses and flats). Also densely populated areas (e.g. London and Glasgow) appeared to encourage German cockroaches irrespective of the type of property. The ratio of infestations, German to Oriental, increased from the south east of England to the west and north, where the Oriental cockroach is by far the most prevalent. The reader is referred to the results of the survey in the earlier volume.

During the 5 years, Oct. 1967–Sept. 1972, another survey was carried out in the U.K. in which the incidence of cockroaches was recorded in 13,500 infested buildings. The owners had requested a survey prior to treatment. Infestations of *B. germanica* (3,351) were again fewer than *B. orientalis* (11,552). The ratio of the two species fell from 1 : 4·2 in 1967–68, to 1 : 3·2 in 1971–72 (Table IV). This change in the ratio supports earlier findings (see Vol. I), which suggest that *B. germanica* is increasing in abundance relative to *B. orientalis* in the U.K.

TABLE IV

RELATIVE NUMBERS OF INFESTATIONS OF *B. GERMANICA* AND *B. ORIENTALIS* SURVEYED BETWEEN OCT. 1967 AND SEPT. 1972 (U.K.)
(Cornwell, unpublished)

Year	Infestations of		Ratio
	B. germanica	*B. orientalis*	
Oct. 1967–Sept. 1968	490	2,070	1 : 4·22
1968– 1969	640	2,262	1 : 3·53
1969– 1970	488	2,374	1 : 3·45
1970– 1971	750	2,370	1 : 3·16
1971– 1972	783	2,476	1 : 3·16
Total	3,351	11,552	1 : 3·45

Seasonal changes

The number of surveys in which German cockroaches were found remained unchanged throughout the year: this would indicate no period when this pest causes greater or less concern to occupants (Fig. 35). It is completely dependent for its survival and reproduction in the U.K. on an indoor environment: egg cases are carried by the female into the most favoured locations for hatching and growth. Slight fluctuations in the indoor environment of kitchens and similar places from month to month are therefore unlikely to have much effect on reproduction and the size of populations.

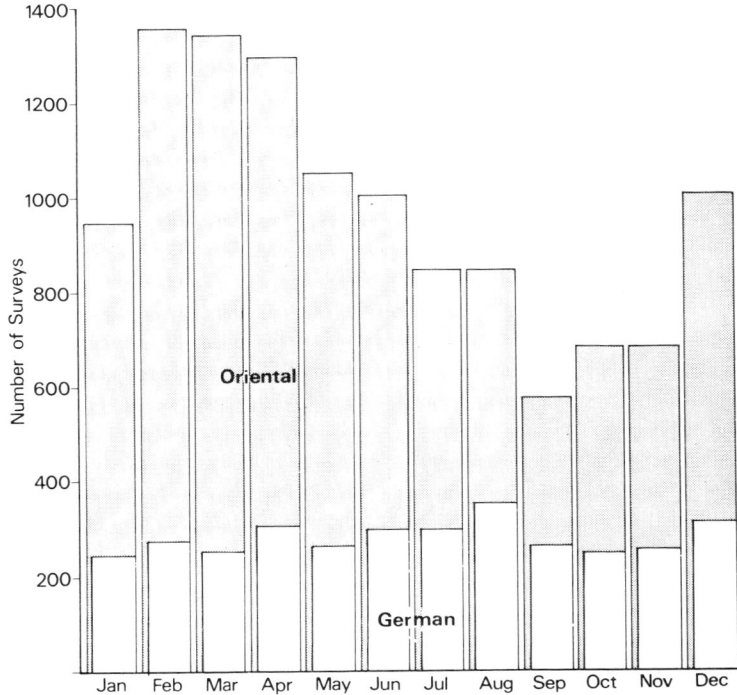

Fig. 35. Surveys of infestations of German and Oriental cockroaches in the U.K. 1967–72).

In contrast, the number of surveys involving Oriental cockroaches fluctuated from a maximum in February, to less than half that number in September. This pattern was repeated in each of the five years. *B. orientalis* prefers lower temperatures than *B. germanica* and its egg cases are deposited in locations where the return of a favourable temperature may be needed to encourage development and hatching (Fig. 36). More surveys in winter months suggest that this cockroach becomes more evident then: it may be encouraged to grow more rapidly by the higher indoor temperatures of December and January, causing more insects—as large nymphs and adults—to be seen in the following months.

Types of buildings infested
The buildings surveyed consisted of a mixture of industrial, food manufacturing, retailing, commercial and domestic properties. They were not in the same proportions as in the previous survey (Vol. I). For purposes of analysis properties were divided into convenient categories (Table V). Some were much more readily infested by German cockroaches, either because of a

favourable environment (e.g. animal locations), or because of movement with goods and people (e.g. buildings associated with transport or occupied by armed forces). Buildings with food readily available, especially industrial kitchens, favoured *B. germanica*. Cooler, less humid environments tended to favour *B. orientalis*.

TABLE V

NUMBERS AND RATIOS OF INFESTATIONS OF *B. GERMANICA*: *B. ORIENTALIS* IN DIFFERENT TYPES OF PROPERTY IN THE U.K., ARRANGED IN ORDER OF DECREASING INCIDENCE OF *B. GERMANICA*
(Cornwell; unpublished)

Type of premises	Infestations of:		Ratio*
	B. germanica	B. orientalis	
Pet shops and zoos	45	24	1 : 0.5
Transport: air, road, rail, shipping	51	36	1 : 0.7
Military establishments	119	96	1 : 0.8
Restaurants and cafes	857	1,261	1 : 1.5 (1.9)
Public houses	247	511	1 : 2.1 (2.8)
Clubs and Public halls	135	345	1 : 2.5 (1.7)
Offices	102	251	1 : 2.5 (4.2)
Breweries	27	79	1 : 3.0 (2.4)
Warehouses: food and non-food	46	145	1 : 3.2
Factories: chemical, engineering, foundries, paper and printing	147	487	1 : 3.3 (2.9)
Hospitals	231	859	1 : 3.7 (4.1)
Public baths	9	34	1 : 3.7
Factories; bakeries, milk, meat, fruit, vegetable, cereal, fish and other products	244	993	1 : 4.1 (8.1)
Shops (all types)	354	1,501	1 : 4.2 (4.5)
Hotels and boarding houses	309	1,395	1 : 4.5 (4.6)
Hostels and holiday camps	32	153	1 : 5.0 (5.6)
Cinemas and theatres	20	115	1 : 5.8 (12.3)
Laundries	52	316	1 : 6.0 (16.3)
Schools, colleges and convents	72	506	1 : 7.0 (7.3)
Houses, flats and convalescent homes	158	1,930	1 : 12.0 (17.0)
Textile factories	14	246	1 : 17.5 (7.8)
Farms	3	56	1 : 18.7
Miscellaneous	77	213	
Total	3,351	11,552	1 : 3.45

* Values in parentheses from previous survey (see Vol. I, Chapter 14).

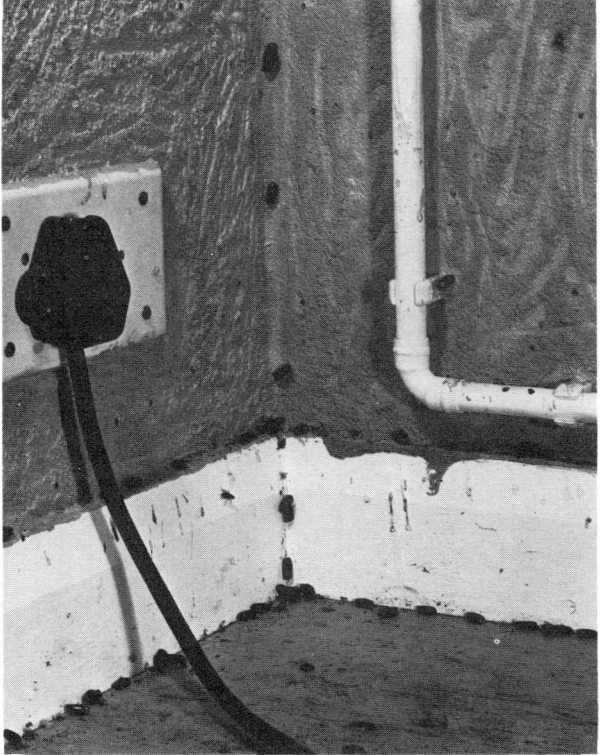

Fig. 36. Egg cases of the Oriental cockroach attached to surfaces. Note the 'vomit' marks (probably faecal contamination) on the skirting board (U.K.).

Geographical distribution of German and Oriental cockroaches
Infestations were recorded in all counties of the U.K.: no data was recorded for Eire. When ratios were calculated of the infestations of the two pest cockroaches (German: Oriental), for different parts of the country (as in Vol. I), London (1 : 1·1), and the south of Scotland—principally Glasgow and Edinburgh—(1 : 2·0) again had the lowest ratios. The ratio of *B. germanica* relative to *B. orientalis* was again low in the east (1 : 2·4) and the south east of England (1 : 2·5). Oriental cockroaches were much more predominant in the west (1 : 8·4), south west (1 : 8·9) and in the north (1 : 11·8). In these respects the relative abundance of the two species in different parts of the U.K. were much the same as reported previously. The north of Scotland, however, was an exception: here the ratio was much lower in the second survey, probably because of a different sample content.

TABLE VI

FREQUENCY (RATIO) OF ORIENTAL COCKROACH INFESTATIONS RELATIVE TO GERMAN, IN DIFFERENT TYPES OF PROPERTY, IN DIFFERENT GEOGRAPHICAL AREAS

(Cornwell, unpublished)

Geographical areas* (in order of increasing ratio)	All properties		Restaurants and cafes	Public Hses and Pub. halls	Hospitals	Food factories	Shops	Hotels	Houses and flats
	Old survey	New survey	(Properties in order of increasing ratio: left to right)						
London	2·8	1·1	0·5	0·6	1·7	1·9	1·8	1·2	3·0
S. Scotland	3·6	2·0	1·6	1·7	1·5	2·1	1·9	1·9	24·0
East	4·4	2·4	1·9	1·1	2·2	3·0	3·1	4·0	8·0
S. East	4·2	2·5	1·6	1·6	3·0	3·3	3·0	3·6	6·9
N. Scotland	20·0	3·8	4·3	1·5	4·6	4·1	8·3	3·3	20·0
Central	4·8	4·7	2·4	6·2	4·7	4·5	6·2	7·9	6·6
N. Ireland	4·7	5·7	3·3	2·4	7·0	4·8	—	7·5	10·4
West	7·8	8·4	5·0	5·1	4·8	8·7	7·2	10·3	22·9
S. West	7·3	8·9	10·1	6·2	14·0	12·8	11·4	12·6	17·4
North	11·0	11·8	4·4	8·1	8·2	8·3	12·5	11·6	47·0
Average for all areas			1·5	2·2	3·7	4·1	4·2	4·5	12·0

* The same geographical areas as in Chapter 14, Vol. I. —all infestations of *B. orientalis*.

Many more buildings were included in the new survey, so that the occurrence of the two cockroaches in different parts of the country could be examined in more detail. Restaurants and cafes, public houses and public halls, which tend to favour German cockroaches in London and the south of England, do likewise in the north and west, but not to the same degree. Those buildings in the south, which tend to contain a preponderance of infestations of Oriental cockroaches also have this cockroach strongly represented in other parts of the country, even more so than in the south (Table VI).

In this chapter we have examined the importance of cockroaches as pests: the conditions which encourage them, both outside and inside buildings: the relationship between cockroaches and locations favouring the spread of pathogenic bacteria. There are many reasons why every effort should be made to achieve the eradication of cockroaches from buildings, not least the aesthetic improvement of our environment. We no longer *have* to live with these insects.

The different pest cockroaches vary in occurrence in different countries: their presence is to some extent influenced by an ability to survive and breed outdoors. Conditions indoors, however, have a far greater effect on species distribution, especially in cooler latitudes. Thus the relative abundance of the pest cockroaches in different buildings varies with the functional use of the property and the environment which that function creates.

Much can be done, inside and outside buildings to discourage cockroaches by improvements in sanitation. High standards of housekeeping are of special relevance to food manufacturing and catering industries, for whom cockroaches are a special problem—by virtue of their easy introduction, establishment and spread.

3

PRACTICAL COCKROACH CONTROL

The requirements—The action—The practical difficulties; restaurants; air transport; passenger shipping; hospitals; zoos—Reinfestation as a problem.

The eradication of cockroaches is a practical task involving skill and experience. The chances of success are higher with an understanding of the insect in its environment, and the properties and limitations of the insecticides available for use.

There may be many readers of this book who would hope to find a clear-cut guide to how to do the job. There can be no such thing: many factors are involved, but the basic principles are summarised here: much that is said is discussed in greater detail in subsequent chapters, on the pages indicated. Some of the practical difficulties in various industries are then discussed.

THE REQUIREMENTS

1. Be able to identify the principal pest cockroaches. This is most important in tropical countries where many different species may enter buildings, but not all these insects will establish infestations[105,833] (see Vol. I, Chapter 3).
2. Know the biology and habits of the pest cockroaches: the places most favoured by the different species and where in infested buildings cockroaches are most likely to establish infestations (Table VII and see Vol. I, Chapters 8–12).
3. Understand the properties of different insecticides: the most appropriate use for each type of formulation and under what conditions each is likely to perform best (see p. 74).
4. Know the current status of resistance to insecticides by cockroaches, if appropriate to your territory (see p. 422).
5. Understand the potential health risks to yourself and others, associated with misuse of insecticides; ensure that use conforms with label instructions, e.g. 'crack and crevice treatment' in the U.S.A. (see p. 130).
6. Be suitably equipped to apply insecticides cleanly; application equipment should function efficiently; protective clothing should always be available and used where conditions warrant it (see p. 107).

THE ACTION

The following assumes that a contract service is being offered to a client for cockroach control. The steps necessary are:
1. Advise the client why he has an infestation of cockroaches: how the insects

TABLE VII

TYPICAL HARBOURAGE LOCATIONS OF THE PRINCIPAL PEST COCKROACHES

German	Oriental	American	Brown-banded
In crevices: in hot kitchens	*In crevices: in moist cooler places*	*On surfaces: in dark warm places*	*Scattered throughout very warm homes/offices*
Under table tops	Near bakery ovens	In outdoor service areas	High locations in rooms
Under kitchen equipment	In broken pipe insulation	In garages and outbuildings	Inside furniture
Beneath service counters	Behind heating plants	Food warehouses and packing plants	In clothes cupboards
Behind sinks	Within brickwork	Drainage manholes and grease traps	Behind curtain pelmets
In kitchen cupboards	In floor drains	Sewers	Behind pictures and picture mouldings
In motor compartments of fridges	In basements and service ducts	Roof spaces	In ceiling light fixtures
In electrical fuse boxes	Around waste disposal areas	Damp basements	In television and telephone units
Under broken plaster	In indoor coke-storage areas	Zoos and greenhouses (temperate countries)	Under sinks: in kitchen cabinets

PRACTICAL COCKROACH CONTROL 69

may have got into his premises; the conditions which encourage infestation. Don't make humour out of the problem: pests are not funny; neither is the act of killing. Do not demean the task of pest control. 'Professionalism' is becoming increasingly demanded.

2. Explain what you propose to do by way of treatment; that the materials you use have been approved for cockroach control; that treated areas should not be washed down; that pets should be kept out of treated areas for a day or so. Answer you clients' questions factually.

3. Ensure that you will be able to gain access to *all* parts of the building for inspection. Liaise on the most appropriate timing for subsequent visits (e.g. in respect of shift work, or restaurant working hours).

4. Inspect the building thoroughly for infestation; pay special attention to locations near warmth, water and food (see p. 46). Use a good torch and pyrethrins aerosol for flushing the insects from harbourages (see p. 247). The success of treatment depends on the detail of the inspection: be prepared to get dirty in searching for cockroach harbourages.

5. If treatment involves the dilution of concentrates ensure that quantities are measured accurately (see Table VIII). Make dilutions where spillage of concentrates can be easily removed. Wear protective clothing. Lock your vehicle while you are away.

6. Apply approved formulations with care, selecting each with regard to, (1) minimum environmental risk (see p. 130), (2) ability of the insecticide to withstand the treatment conditions (e.g wetness, type of surface to be treated, see p. 74), and (3) efficacy (e.g. distribution of the insecticide into harbourages and the problem of insecticide repellency (see p. 157).

7. Treat all harbourages thoroughly with the object of ensuring that no cockroaches are able to escape contact with insecticide. Do not treat exposed surfaces unnecessarily, with the hope that cockroaches will walk over them. Do not treat the air, in anticipation that the insecticide, as suspended droplets, will find its own way by drifting into harbourages (see p. 121).

8. Treat outdoors, where drains, gullies or other structures offer harbourage from which the larger pest species may obtain easy access to the property.

9. Advise the client where improvements in site sanitation would, (1) make inspection easier and more thorough (usually storage areas), (2) allow any further infestation to be seen quickly before large numbers of cockroaches might recur and (3) discourage the insects from becoming established (e.g. removal of food residues; regular cleaning of lockers in washrooms; exposure of harbourages, e.g. boxed-in pipe work) (see p. 52).

10. Discuss how reinfestation may occur; advise the client, if engaged in food manufacture, of the desirability of talking with suppliers of raw materials and packaging about infestation and control in their premises.

11. Do not make exaggerated claims about the duration of performance of the insecticides used (e.g. see p. 74). The objective is that your client should enjoy complete freedom from cockroach infestation. Achieve this quickly and maintain it by inspection of the premises at regular intervals. Re-treat only as necessary (see p. 73).

12. Should infestation in parts of the building not respond to treatment, carry out a 'night inspection' when cockroaches are most active. This will reveal sources of insects not located and harbourages not previously treated (see Vol. I, Chapter 11).

THE PRACTICAL DIFFICULTIES

Cockroach control cannot always be achieved as simply as the above section might suggest. Certain types of property and conditions present the pest control operator with special difficulties—not least an unco-operative client who expects his problems to be solved, being unappreciative of the contribution he himself should make.

When pest control operators in W. Germany were asked by questionnaire what makes cockroach control difficult, the reasons most often mentioned were, (1) reinfestation by insects in commodities and packaging materials, (2) the conditions of buildings providing inaccessible hiding places, making treatment difficult, (3) the movement of the insects from adjacent buildings and (4) insufficient hygiene in industrial kitchens. The cost of services was also reported frequently as a reason why infestations were not controlled.[237]

One or two examples of practical difficulties are now given which will not be unfamiliar to those experienced in cockroach control.

Restaurants

The control of cockroaches in restaurants is difficult to achieve because of, (1) limitations in the insecticides which may be allowed, (2) meals being served 24 hours a day, (3) wet conditions reducing the effectiveness of the formulations used, (4) cockroaches being introduced from outside.[35,36,37]

Cockroach control at London Heathrow Airport[104] where the problem has almost exclusively been caused by *B. germanica*, is complicated by the size and complexity of the site: 22 million passengers and over half a million sightseers per year in the terminal area, where more than 50,000 permanent staff work; these were the statistics for 1975. It has the catering amenities of a town, operating 24 hours a day. The daily intake of catering supplies, passenger baggage and animals with their food entail the continual risk of cockroach introductions. The building complex rises above a warren of underground service ducts.

Air transport

Insect control in aircraft creates special problems. Cockroaches cannot be altogether prevented from entering aircraft, and when they do get aboard all the conditions necessary to encourage infestation exist.

Airlines differ in their approval for use of different insecticides because of possible interference, over long periods, with the insulation of electrical cables, and the corrosion of metals, on the safety of the aircraft. Some infestations have to be dealt with by full scale fumigation using hydrogen cyanide or methyl bromide.[60,71] The latter may possibly interact with the upholstery and cause objectionable odour, although tests indicate that the risk is small. Under no circumstances should phosphine (e.g. 'Phostoxin') be used, due to its effect on metals. There is little difficulty in sealing an aircraft for gassing, but flight schedules often mean that treatment has to be done at short notice.

The repeated use of aerosols containing pyrethrins or synthetic pyrethroids[776] in the cabin of passenger aircraft to prevent spread of mosquito-borne diseases, may tend to keep cockroach populations suppressed. The use of dichlorvos in mechanical dispensers has been studied.[223,663,692,735] So have lindane vaporisers[12,687] and residual sprays.[671]

Passenger shipping
The control of cockroaches on passenger ships[117] is made difficult by (1) the rapid turn round of vessels in port, (2) the extensive ducting which interconnects all parts of a ship (Fig. 23 bottom), (3) high local temperatures, near engine rooms, reducing the life of some insecticides, (4) metal structures which often have to be drilled to get insecticide into cavities, (5) infrequent visits of ships to ports for inspection and re-treatment, (6) interaction of some formulations with newly applied paint (see p. 80) and (7) the likelihood of encountering resistant insects (see p. 452). These problems become exaggerated by the size of some modern liners: their passenger accommodation is equivalent to that of the larger multistorey hotels.

Hospitals
Difficulties in cockroach control often occur in hospitals and rest homes. In wards, special consideration has to be given because of people ill, or physically weakened where they are confined for 24 hours each day and often for long periods. Insecticides used must not produce an irritant vapour; whether or not to use cockroach baits in mental homes has to be considered very carefully.

Many of the buildings used as hospitals in the U.K. were not built for the purpose: structures are old and cause problems in maintaining required standards of hygiene. Infestations of German and Oriental cockroaches in central kitchens spread easily to ward kitchens, to the wards themselves and to nurses' homes.[791] The movement of insects is made easy by ducting systems which inter-connect the various buildings of a hospital complex.[87] The insects are also carried in food carts (Fig. 23): these do not present a problem when new, but as they deteriorate in use, openings occur which should be sealed immediately.[631] Otherwise heat sterilisation or fumigation may be needed to control the insects in the insulation.

With the re-organisation of the hospital service in the U.K., the spread of pests may have been encouraged. In the past, hospitals were relatively self-contained; now large laundries and stores provide services from a central point.[88] Infestation control in these 'depots' is essential if attempts to achieve cockroach control in the individual hospitals is to succeed. Difficulties in controlling cockroaches in hospitals in Germany have also been described.[567,790]

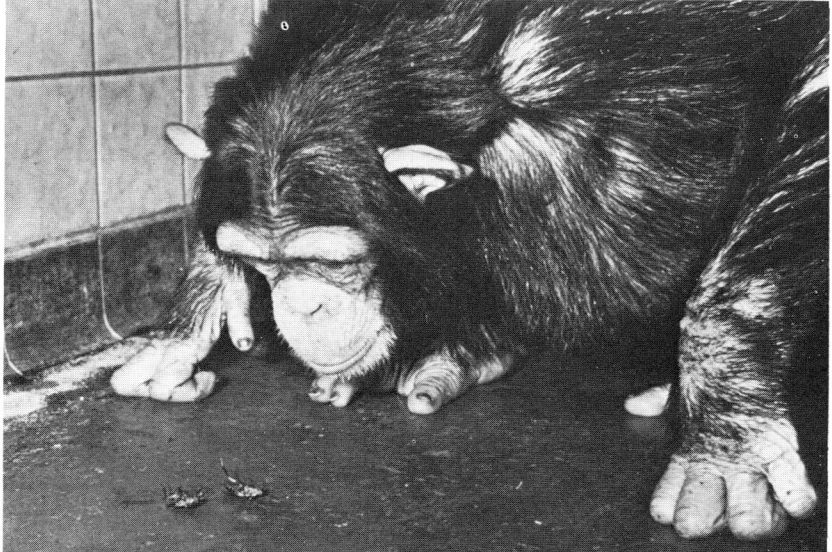

Fig. 37. The control of cockroaches in zoos requires the correct choice of insecticide and special care in application, to avoid endangering animals. Monkeys have been experimentally fed American cockroaches, treated with propoxur, without ill-effect. (Courtesy Dr. Haas, Zoological Garden, Wuppertal, Germany).

Zoos

Undoubtedly one of the most difficult locations in which to carry out cockroach control without risk to other animals is in zoos, aquaria and pet shops. The conditions for infestation—temperature, humidity, food residues, water and harbourage—are ideal for German and American cockroaches. It may be possible to move the more valuable animals into other quarters while treatment is being done.

Rachesky[689] has described the treatment of a zoo in the U.S.A. without harm to animals. In contrast, Brandes, Gangel & Kowalsky[120] describe an 'improper' treatment for cockroaches in an aquarium and terrarium in W. Germany. Animals started to die two days after treatment; within 3 days, 56 fish were dead. After about 5 months this figure had reached 313, representing 36 per cent of the fish stock. This example points to the great care needed in selecting the most suitable insecticide and formulation where animals are at risk. Experience has proved that such treatments can be carried out with complete safety. There is no evidence to suggest that secondary poisoning—the eating of poisoned cockroaches by the inmates—is likely to cause harm (Fig. 37).

REINFESTATION AS A PROBLEM

Reinfestation of buildings by cockroaches occurs much more readily in warm than in temperate countries. The ways in which this can occur are discussed in Chapters 2 and 7. It is difficult in the tropics to combat reinfestation with insecticides: spraying the surrounds of the property, the likely points of entry, and those indoor surfaces on which the insects might crawl is the best that can be done.

This underlines one of the important differences between cockroach control in warm and temperate climates: in the former, it may be necessary, (1) to apply insecticides as 'protective treatments' to counter cockroaches entering as casual intruders, (2) to apply these chemicals to exposed surfaces with which the occasional insect might come into contact, and (3) to repeat treatments more often (every month) because temperatures reduce the period over which insecticides remain active. In contrast, in most of Europe, for example, where infestation *via* goods is more likely, it is more sensible to rely on periodic inspection, once an infestation has been cleared than to apply chemicals unnecessarily.

This chapter outlines the basic principles of cockroach control. Success or failure on the part of a pest control contractor, depends in part on the materials he uses, but more so on his understanding of the problem, his thoroughness in carrying out inspection and treatment, and the degree of co-operation he receives from his client.

Examples are given of industrial and environmental problems which make cockroach control difficult. Rarely is it possible to achieve eradication in one treatment, although this should always be the aim. Some industries are more prone to reinfestation than others and the importance of frequent inspection for cockroaches is emphasised, since knowing the source of the infestation provides the key to effective treatment.

4

THE IMPORTANCE OF FORMULATION

The importance of contact: the treated surface—Components of formulations: technical material; premium grade; diluent; additives; dilution rate—Liquid formulations: oil spray; emulsion; wettable powder; suspension concentrate; lacquer—Solid formulations: dust; smoke; bait; attractants and feeding stimulants; response to pheromones; tests of performance—Insecticidal vapours.

Effective cockroach control requires the application of the proper amount and appropriate placement of insecticide, not only to eliminate the pest but to minimise environmental contamination. This is achieved with insecticides in various formulations.

It is the writer's view that too little attention has been paid to the development and evaluation of *formulations* for use in buildings, compared with testing of the insecticides themselves. It is not generally recognised that the difference in performance of a good and bad formulation of the same insecticide, can be greater than the difference between good and mediocre insecticides both well-formulated. A good formulation should enable the insect to contaminate itself with ease. It should also enable the user to apply it to harbourages without damaging surfaces.

In this chapter we look at the composition, properties and performance of formulations most often used for cockroach control. For convenience these will be divided into:

Liquid formulations:	oil sprays
	emulsions
	wettable powders
	suspension concentrates
	lacquers.
Solid formulations:	dusts
	smokes
	baits.
Insecticidal vapours:	gases
	volatile liquids and solids.

Manufacturers provide insecticides as ready-to-use products, safe to handle, and as concentrates suitable for further dilution as necessary. They contain components which enable the insecticide to be applied conveniently and to perform well according to instructions for use. Rarely is it possible for the pest control operator to obtain his insecticide as a technical material: exceptions might be some of the older compounds—sodium fluoride, borax or boric

THE IMPORTANCE OF FORMULATION

acid. Government departments which regulate the sale and use of pesticides, now have considerable influence on the maximum allowable concentrations of active ingredients in insecticidal products (see Chapter 6).

Subjects of concern to the insecticide manufacturer, such as chemical stability and aspects of the packaging of insecticides are outside the scope of this chapter. We must assume that these and related problems have been solved before a product is marketed.

THE IMPORTANCE OF CONTACT

Almost all the insecticides used for cockroach control rely for their action on *contact* with the insect. Whether or not an insecticide enters the insect by penetrating the cuticle, or by being picked up and then ingested, is secondary to the insecticide first getting onto the insect's body.

If one were to put together all the insecticide used to control cockroaches worldwide, in one day, it would add up to hundreds of thousands of litres of spray—mostly emulsion—and a few kilograms of dust. Of this total, only a fraction of 1 per cent actually does the job. Because cockroaches spend most of their time hidden and not within 'the line of fire' of spray droplets, relatively few insects are directly contaminated by insecticide at time of treatment. Accordingly, insecticides are more often used in those places where the insects are expected to be, knowing with confidence, that hours, days, or perhaps weeks later, some of the insecticide will, (1) continue to be available and (2) be picked up by the insects. A criticism of many pest control servicemen is that they frequently use formulations in ways that ensure that neither of these things happen.

Thus, cockroach control is much concerned with:

(1) Locating the places where cockroaches are and treating them so well that the insects cannot avoid insecticide. Success depends on the pest control operator's practical knowledge of cockroaches in infested premises, and the extent to which harbourages are found.

(2) Using formulations which will ensure that the toxicant remains on the surface of treated structures. Manufacturers' products, as supplied, are usually well-designed; it is *which one* the user chooses to apply and *where* he applies it which are vital.

(3) Contact of insecticide by the cockroach: the feet and undersides of insects are important areas of pick-up, but whether this happens again depends very much on the formulation used.

These three factors are the key to cockroach eradication. The serviceman who wishes to improve his ability to control cockroaches must start with an understanding of formulations: what they consist of and what happens to them when applied. The performance of an insecticide is not determined just by, (1) its chemistry, and (2) its ability to disrupt the insect's normal biochemistry, but more importantly by (3) its availability for removal from a treated surface.

The difference in susceptibility of the housefly and cockroach to some insecticides may depend, in part, on the anatomy of the insects' feet. The tarsi of houseflies (*Musca domestica*) are well-covered with chemoreceptors and have a cuticle only $12 \cdot 5-25\mu$ thick. In contrast, chemoreceptors have not been found on the tarsi of the German cockroach, and its cuticle is $60-90\mu$ thick.[417] To what extent the pad (arolium) between the claws, influences pick-up of insecticide is not known; as an adhesive organ which aids movement, its function in gripping surfaces should encourage contact. This structure is present in German cockroaches but absent in *B. orientalis*.

The treated surface
Formulation has a marked effect on insecticide performance. To appreciate this, it is helpful to consider what happens when a surface is treated. When a spray is applied at 1 litre/20m² (1 gal/1,000 ft²), only 5 mg of liquid is applied to each square centimetre. At a concentation of 1 per cent, the amount of active compound is only 50 μg/cm²—this equals about half a millionth of an ounce on this small area (Fig. 38). With a coarse spray (droplets as large as 1 mm across) about 5 droplets impinge on each square centimetre. As the size of the droplets gets smaller, to about one tenth of the above (100μ) the number of droplets increases greatly to 5,000. With 'mist-size' droplets (10μ) there will be as many as 5 million/cm².

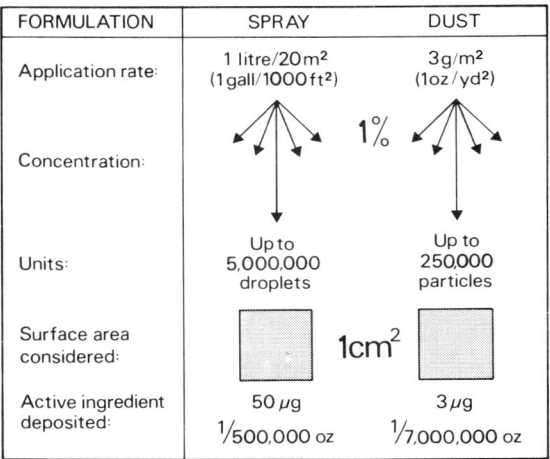

Fig. 38. Insecticide deposits obtained when surfaces are treated at usual application rates, assuming no 'run-off' or absorption of the spray.

Assuming good wettability of the surface, the droplets coalesce to form a continuous film. The thickness of the liquid film, assuming none is absorbed, or runs off, is about 50μ, which is perhaps only a fraction of the diameter of the original spray droplets.

If the treated surface is completely non-absorptive and the active compound is a solid dissolved in the spray, crystals of the toxicant are formed on the surface as the solvent evaporates. If, in contrast, the spray is absorbed *into* the surface more quickly than drying occurs by evaporation, then crystals of insecticide will be formed *below the surface*, in the matrix of the substrate, where they can have no future contact action. The same applies to active compounds which are liquids (like diazinon and malathion) miscible in the spray carrier, except in this instance there is no possibility of crystal formation.

A good insecticidal dust contains uniformly small particles, about 5μ across (one fifty-thousandth of an inch). When these are applied at 30 g/m² (about 1 oz/yd²), 25 million particles are spread over each square centimetre (or 250,000 active particles, if the insecticide content is 1 per cent). Their shape affects 'packing density' at the surface. If the particles fit like cubes, edge to edge, excluding air, their depth is 34μ, or about seven particles deep and each active particle is about 25μ apart. The distance between the tips of the claws on the foot of a German cockroach is ten times greater (250μ). The insect therefore cannot avoid making many points of contact with the active particles.

With a dust, there is of course no change of form of the insecticide on the surface, as happens with a spray, drying by evaporation. Particles cannot be lost by absorption into the substrate, and providing they remain discretely separate they are readily available to the insect. Accordingly, if there is a need to use a spray, there is a strong argument in favour of spraying solid particles as these would remain available for contact with the cockroach (see wettable powder and suspension concentrate).

The size of insecticidal particles, whether applied as sprays or dusts, affects their performance. Thus, with mosquitoes (of various species) walking on spray deposits, the kill by insecticides with low intrinsic toxicity (organochlorines) is highest with the better contact obtained from particle sizes in the range $0-20\mu$: sizes above 40μ are ineffective.[390,391]

In a study of the deposits of 42 insecticides applied as sprays to painted and unpainted metal, and to masonite and asphalt tiles, tests were made after various periods of ageing. There were marked differences in the number of weeks that treated surfaces killed 70 per cent or more of chlordane-resistant German cockroaches: 'not only is the response to a given compound different on the various surfaces, but the particular formulation employed also influences effectiveness on the insect'.[307]

COMPONENTS OF FORMULATIONS

Technical material
This is the active component of a formulation, in its undiluted form. In most cases technical materials do not contain 100 per cent of the specified insecticide; they also contain 1–5 per cent of other compounds, or isomers, which do not interfere with their action. To remove all the impurities would be too costly.

Premium grade

The objectionable odour of some technical materials may necessitate further refinement to eliminate contaminants. The best known example is malathion, which when first introduced was quite unsuitable for use indoors. This and many other organophosphorus insecticides have been 'cleaned-up' and marketed as 'premium grade' or 'deodorised' insecticides.

Diluent

The majority of commonly used insecticides are made available as *concentrates* (usual range 10–70 per cent active ingredient) and in a form suitable for dilution. The diluent of a dust is usually china clay or talc, appropriately chosen not to interact with or cause degradation of the active ingredient. The most commonly used diluent for sprays is water, but many are also diluted in a non-staining oil—kerosene (deobase), and other refined petroleum distillates from which the odorous fractions have been removed. The diluent can have a marked effect on the performance of an insecticide through its interaction with surfaces being treated. For instance, in kitchens, oil may cause insecticide to be taken up in grease, making the toxicant unavailable to kill cockroaches.

The diluent of a spray has many functions: (1) it reduces the concentration of the insecticide to a level acceptable for use; (2) it provides the mass to carry the insecticide from the spray nozzle to the surface being treated; (3) it provides the medium by which the insecticide is made to cover the surface being treated, and (4) it acts as a spreader for each droplet of insecticide when it reaches the target. The diluent also gives 'visibility' to the spray or dust being used; an indirect benefit important from the user's point of view.

Without a diluent, the uniform application of an insecticide would be difficult. An even spread can however be achieved by breaking up a liquid into tiny droplets and applying these more thinly. This is the principle of ULV application (see p. 118) in which air is used as the diluent and the concentration of toxicant in the formulation is higher.

Insecticides in solution can be applied as aerosols, mists or fogs; these are not differences in formulation, but in technique of application, as discussed in Chapter 5.

Additives

There are compounds, or mixtures of compounds, which when added to a formulation modify one or more of its physical/chemical properties. An additive may impart greater stability to an insecticide under cold or warm conditions of storage: it may increase the efficacy of the active ingredient. Strictly, additives include synergists, e.g. to enhance the action of pyrethrins (as discussed in Chapter 9).

The most common additives include co-solvents, to improve the solubility of insecticides in emulsions and oil sprays; emulsifiers, in emulsion concentrates, help indirectly in wetting surfaces to which diluted spray is applied; wetting agents in wettable powders help the wetting of the particles, making it easier to

THE IMPORTANCE OF FORMULATION

prepare ready to use sprays. Dusts include anti-caking agents, water-proofing agents and occasionally 'identifiable dyes', the latter to improve safety in use.

Pyrethrum formulations have been made with ultraviolet absorbers (screening agents) to extend their active life. This can also be achieved by incorporation of anti-oxidants.

Dilution rate

In most countries it is a Government requirement that the label states among other things: (1) the percentage of active compound in the concentrate, (2) the

TABLE VIII

DILUTION RATES FOR INSECTICIDAL CONCENTRATES

1. *If the label states percentage active ingredient in the concentrate, first calculate,*

$$\frac{\% \text{ insecticide required in ready-to-use spray}}{\% \text{ insecticide in concentrate}} \text{ Then,}$$

Multiply by:		To give the amount of concentrate required in:	To make this total amount of ready-to-use spray:
For Water spray	For Oil spray		
130	110	Ounces or fl. ounces	1 U.S. gallon
160	134	Ounces or fl. ounces	1 Imp. gallon
1,000	840	Grams or ml	1 litre

2. *If the label states the number of pounds active ingredient/U.S. gall, use the following Table to determine the number of parts of diluent (by vol.), to mix with 1 part of concentrate. For example: to make a 1% spray (wt./wt.), from a concentrate containing 8 pounds of active ingredient/gall, mix 1 part concentrate with 95 parts of water or 113 parts of oil.*

Per cent solution required	Pounds active ingredient per gallon of concentrate							
	2		4		6		8	
	Water	Oil	Water	Oil	Water	Oil	Water	Oil
0·5	47	56	95	113	143	170	191	227
1	23	27	47	56	71	84	95	113
2	11	13	23	27	35	42	47	56
3	7	8	15	18	23	27	31	37
4	5	6	11	13	17	20	23	27
5	$3\frac{3}{4}$	$4\frac{1}{2}$	9	10	13	16	18	22

percentage in the ready-to-use spray and (3) how much concentrate has to be diluted in the carrier to achieve the end-use concentration (i.e. the dilution rate).

If only the first and second are given, then the dilution rate can be easily calculated, using the data given in Table VIII.

LIQUID FORMULATIONS

Oil spray

An oil spray is the simplest of liquid formulations and consists of the active component in a suitable oil, acting as both solvent and diluent. The spray may contain 'co-solvents'—small amounts of more expensive ingredients, which help keep the insecticide (if a solid) in solution at low temperatures, especially if the product is being marketed as a concentrate. Most oil sprays have the advantage of being ready-to-use, with little risk of staining, but the spilling of oil sprays on floors of asphalt or vinyl tiles can soften and damage the surface.[27] Oil sprays are easy to apply and contain no solid particles to cause nozzle blockage. Uneven spraying is compensated by the creep of oils, carrying the insecticide in solution, over treated surfaces.

Oil sprays were at one time more in favour than today, their cost now being prohibitive. Other disadvantages are, (1) inflammability, (2) the greater bulk of fluid to transport (cf. dilution with water on site), (3) interaction with some materials of modern decor (adhesives, plastics), and (4) the major problem, of insecticide becoming lost in most surfaces unless completely non-absorbent. Oil-based sprays also lock-up insecticide in paint (Table IX). Their interaction with other surfaces is examined in detail in the section on emulsions. This aspect

TABLE IX

KILL (% AT 24 HOURS) OF GERMAN COCKROACHES EXPOSED TO OIL SPRAYS OF PROPOXUR (1%) APPLIED TO 'RUN-OFF' ON GLASS AND HARDBOARD, SOME COATED ONE WEEK PREVIOUSLY WITH GLOSS PAINT
(Cornwell, unpublished)

Exposure time (mins)	Glass		Hardboard	
	Unpainted	Painted	Unpainted	Painted
1	80	0	0	0
2	90	0	0	0
4	95	0	0	0
8	100	0	40	0
16	100	5	85	40
30	100	20	70	50

of treatment is probably the cause of more failures to eradicate cockroaches than any other aspect of insecticide use. Thus when fenitrothion (a liquid insecticide) is applied as an oil spray (2 per cent) to glass (non-porous) and to hardboard (porous) the difference in performance is dramatic (Table X).

TABLE X

EFFECT (KILL %) OF OIL SPRAYS APPLIED TO GLASS (NON-POROUS) AND TO HARDBOARD (POROUS) ON FEMALE *B. GERMANICA* CONFINED TO THE TREATED SURFACES AGED FOR DIFFERENT PERIODS. THE PROPOXUR FORMULATION CONTAINED A CO-SOLVENT WHICH QUICKLY VAPOURISED, CONVERTING THE INSECTICIDE QUICKLY TO CRYSTALS ON THE TREATED SURFACE BEFORE ABSORPTION IN SOLUTION COULD OCCUR

(Cornwell, unpublished)

Insecticide	Surface	Exposure (min)	Age of treated surface			
			1 day	3 weeks	6 weeks	12 weeks
Fentitrothion (2%)	Glass	4	100	95	100	80
		16	100	100	100	100
	Hardboard	4	0	0	0	0
		16	22	0	0	0
Propoxur (2%)	Glass	4	100	100	100	100
		16	100	100	100	100
	Hardboard	4	100	60	100	100
		16	100	100	100	100

The loss of an insecticide in an oil spray, by absorption into porous surfaces, can be partly offset by the choice of oil, or the use of an additive, modifying the behaviour of the insecticide. This is possible with solid but not liquid active ingredients.

For example, if propoxur (a solid insecticide) is retained in solution in an oil spray with methylene chloride, which evaporates from treated surfaces in seconds, the insecticide is almost instantaneously converted into crystals before the diluent starts to be absorbed. In this case the performance of the insecticide on glass and porous hardboard is the same, even after 4 month's ageing (Table X).

The speed with which oils penetrate absorbent surfaces has been demonstrated with larvae of the black carpet beetle (*Attagenus megatoma*), placed in contact 15 minutes after surfaces were sprayed. On glass and vinyl tile, mineral and vegetable oils were not very different in toxicity except that odourless kerosene killed none. All the others were almost 100 per cent lethal (Table XI). However, on absorbent surfaces, all the oils were harmless, or almost so, because absorption had removed the toxic material, out of reach of the larvae, within minutes of spraying.[752]

Emulsion

Most insecticides have to be dissolved in oil. An emulsion concentrate satisfies this need, yet provides the advantage of much lower cost of dilution and application in water. An emulsion concentrate contains emulsifiers—synthetic detergents—which act as a chemical bridge, allowing the user to mix and stabilise minute droplets of oil in water.

It is usual to add the concentrate to the water which is then agitated to ensure that the emulsion is uniformly distributed throughout the spray container. Not all insecticides can be made into emulsions since some (of the early carbamates for instance) are not sufficiently soluble in the oils normally used.

TABLE XI

KILL (% AFTER 24 HOURS) OF LARVAE OF *ATTAGENUS MEGATOMA* ON DIFFERENT SURFACES TREATED 15 MINUTES PREVIOUSLY WITH VARIOUS MINERAL AND VEGETABLE OILS. ABSORBENCY MARKEDLY AFFECTS KILL

(From Slominski, Gojmerac & Burkholder[752])

Oil	Glass	Vinyl tile	Asphalt tile	Plywood	Brick
Mosquito larvicide	100	80	0	0	15
Crop spray	100	100	100	0	0
Edible soyabean	93	98	65	0	0
Edible cottonseed	93	95	25	0	0
Paraffin	100	93	35	0	3
Odourless kerosene	0	0	0	0	0

Emulsion concentrates contain up to about 60 per cent of insecticide and are usually applied at 0·5–2 per cent. On dilution, the active component remains dissolved in, or miscible with the oil, which usually constitutes about 2 per cent of the ready-to-use spray. The water in the spray container does not contain insecticide; it simply provides the carrier for the oil. Not surprisingly therefore, a ready-to-use emulsion spray performs much like an oil spray. In the emulsion, the continuous phase of the oil is broken into droplets, each $1-10\mu$ in diameter, giving it a milk-white appearance. After spraying, when the emulsion is 'broken', the oil droplets coalesce on the treated surface. On some surfaces the much larger amount of water, compared with oil, may stop the oil droplets from spreading. The water and oil gradually disappear by absorption and evaporation.

The advantages of an emulsion spray are: (1) it allows an insecticide insoluble in water, to be applied in water, (2) it is cheaper than ready-to-use oil sprays, (3) there is less bulk (and weight) to be carried because water is available on site, (4) the amount of oil present is small, greatly reducing fire risk, (5) dermal absorption of the insecticide into man is similarly reduced and (6) the spray is less visible on treated surfaces than when a wettable powder is used (Fig. 39).

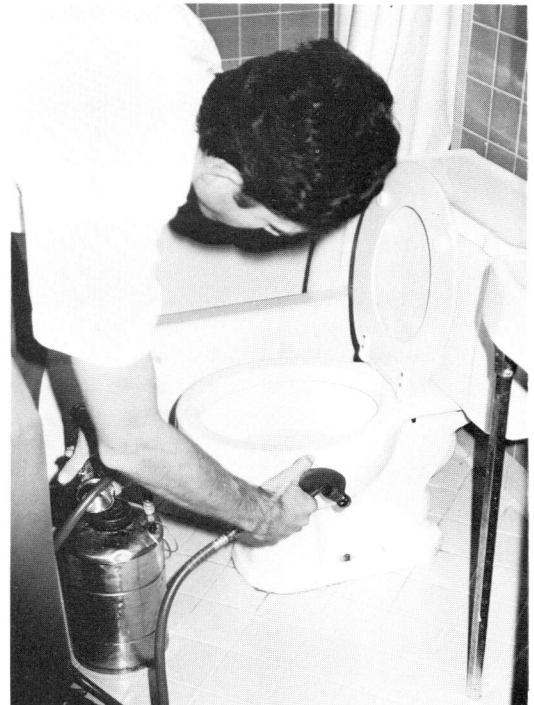

Fig. 39. Example of non-absorptive surfaces in the home on which emulsions perform well: vitreous enamel, ceramic tile and porcelain. In this instance, German cockroaches are harbouring beneath the toilet pedestal (Los Angeles, U.S.A.).

Emulsion sprays do, however, have a number of disadvantages: (1) water staining may occasionally occur on susceptible surfaces, although this is rarely serious, (2) the ready penetration of porous surfaces causes the treatment to have an exceedingly short residual life (in common with oil sprays), even when the emulsion contains an insecticide of long activity and (3) the convenience of using an emulsion encourages the pest control operator to use little else, when other formulations, e.g. wettable powder and dust, would in many locations be acceptable and infinitely more effective.

The subject of absorption of emulsion sprays into porous surfaces will now be examined in detail. It is first necessary to reiterate a number of points: (1) almost all the insecticides used for cockroach control kill by contact, (2) water and especially oil, poured onto a surface such as concrete are absorbed very quickly, (3) most of the surfaces which make up the harbourages of cockroaches (brick, plaster, woodwork) are similarly absorptive; (4) an oil, containing dissolved insecticide, is only capable of depositing insecticide on a surface if it dries quickly, before absorption, and (5) most of the cost of providing a professional service for cockroach control is not in the materials used, but in the labour, transport and overheads, of revisiting infested premises, when treatment fails.

When an emulsion concentrate is diluted in water, the properties of the insecticide are dependent upon the oil, for the oil droplets contain all the insecticide. Soon after the spray is applied, the oil passes into the treated surface: *cockroaches do not crawl through bricks, plaster and timber; they walk over the surfaces*. From the viewpoint of the cockroach, the insecticide has thus been locked away, a few millimetres deep, but unavailable, within the building structure. From the viewpoint of the serviceman he has virtually thrown insecticide away. The net result is poor cockroach control.

The exceedingly poor performance of emulsions of fenitrothion, propoxur and diazinon, in comparison with wettable powders is shown in Table CVI (p. 378). On painted hardboard, exposure of German cockroaches to propoxur emulsion had to be increased four times to give kill equal to that obtained with wettable powder (Table CV, p. 375). In this case the paint may have retarded immediate absorption and loss of the emulsion by penetration, otherwise the difference could have been greater. Chadwick[890] has shown the inadequacy of 1 per cent emulsions of fenitrothion and chlorpyrifos on many surfaces normally encountered in buildings.

A formulation which overcomes many of the disadvantages of both emulsion and wettable powder is the suspension concentrate (see p. 86).

Wettable powder
This formulation is often called a water dispersible powder, because the insecticide is dispersed as separate particles in the ready-to-use spray. Wettable powders consist of finely ground or 'micronised' insecticide, admixed with (1) a mineral diluent, to keep the particles separate and free-flowing during storage, and (2) wetting and dispersing agents to obtain the desired physical properties of the prepared spray. Wettable powders can be made of liquid active compounds (e.g. diazinon and fenitrothion) absorbed onto mineral fillers, or from solids. In either case, the end product usually contains from 30–50 per cent active ingredient (but may be as high as 76 per cent; see bendiocarb, p. 366).

A ready-to-use spray is made by adding the wettable powder to water. The wetting agents now used in manufacture have done away with the need to stir the powder into a cream before adding the bulk of the water. The powder can be dispersed quickly, and directly, with a few minutes agitation. Most have good suspensibility over many hours.

A wettable powder is the most effective spray for use on porous surfaces (e.g. on rough brickwork or rendered walls in hospital ducts, or in store rooms) where the presence of a white deposit is of no consequence (Fig. 40). Experience has proved that wettable powders can also be used without damage to decor in well-decorated locations, provided the spray is used carefully and directed into harbourages and not sprayed (with little ultimate effect) over large areas of wall.

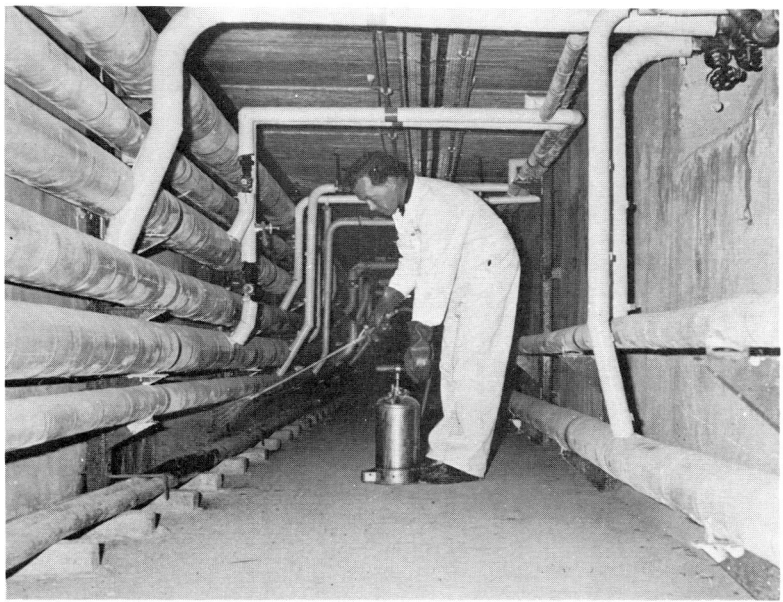

Fig. 40. Application of a wettable powder in a hospital duct where this formulation is the most appropriate; the white deposit left by the spray is of no consequence.

In many countries, cockroach control is offered as part of domestic contracts for the control of all insect pests in the home, with the unfortunate result that each application of spray has to act as a general purpose treatment for flying and crawling insects. Insecticide is therefore applied to a much wider area of exposed surface than would otherwise be needed to eradicate cockroaches alone. An emulsion or very finely divided oil spray is ideal for this purpose, in that the spray, on treated surfaces, is not readily seen; however, effectiveness against cockroaches is low.

The good performance of a wettable powder spray derives from the active particles remaining freely available to cockroaches, when the water has evaporated, or been absorbed into the fabric of a treated harbourage, and the surface dried. The particles are then easily transferred to the insects' legs, in much the same way that a cockroach picks up dust. A wettable powder is therefore considerably more effective and offers longer residual life on most surfaces, than an emulsion or oil spray. These same properties, without the

Fig. 41. Reinfestation of properties by cockroaches from outdoors is a serious problem in warm climates: (top) spraying of an amenity area around an apartment house (Los Angeles, U.S.A.); (bottom) treatment of climbing shrubs at a bungalow apartment (Tucson, U.S.A.). Wettable powders are least likely to damage plants; emulsions may do so and oil sprays should be avoided.

disadvantage of a visible deposit, are obtained with suspension concentrates. The wettable powder, is usually cheaper than other sprays.

No spray should ever be left in a sprayer overnight; this is especially important with wettable powders if nozzle blockage is to be avoided. Wettable powders are least damaging to plants and should be used in preference to emulsions and oil sprays whenever treatments are made outdoors (Fig. 41).

Suspension concentrate
Because most commercially desirable insecticides are insoluble in water, methods have been developed which allow their application in water, this being of particular relevance in the control of agricultural insects. Indoors the problem has been overcome by the use of emulsions and wettable powders, both having advantages and disadvantages as outlined on pp. 83 and 85).

A suspension concentrate* is a new type of formulation developed in the laboratories of Rentokil to offer the advantages of water based formulations without their disadvantages. It has been used with success by service staff to control cockroaches in the U.K. and other temperate and tropical countries, and for control of many other indoor pests. A number of insecticides can be applied in this way, provided they are solids and not soluble in water. The organophosphorus insecticide, iodofenphos, (p. 352) has been used extensively.

A suspension concentrate consists of an insecticide dissolved in an organic solvent, which is miscible with water. When the concentrate is diluted with water, the reduced capacity of the mixture to hold insecticide in solution causes crystals to form (Fig. 42). This reaction occurs on agitation of the spray container, helped by incorporation in the formulation of a substance (a 'nucleating agent') around which the crystals form, at millions of separate points in the spray liquid. The size of the crystals can be predetermined (say $3-5\mu$) to suit maximum pick-up and efficacy against the pest insect. The water when sprayed thus carries countless pre-formed crystals of optimised size and shape, and sufficiently small not to cause nozzle blockage or to be obviously visible. Each spray droplet, of say 1 mm^3, may contain upward of 200,000 separate crystals.

The characteristics of a suspension concentrate spray, in comparison with other formulations, are:
1. the suspension concentrate is diluted by adding the liquid concentrate to water (a cheap carrier), with the same convenience of mixing as an emulsion;
2. the spray consists of a suspension of 'tailor-made' insecticidal particles, each 100 per cent active, without the filler present in a wettable powder;
3. because the insecticide is applied as solid particles, there is no absorption of the active ingredient into treated surfaces, as with oil and emulsion sprays. The water evaporates or is absorbed and the crystals remain accessible to cockroaches;

---
* Patented in many countries and subject to patent application in others.

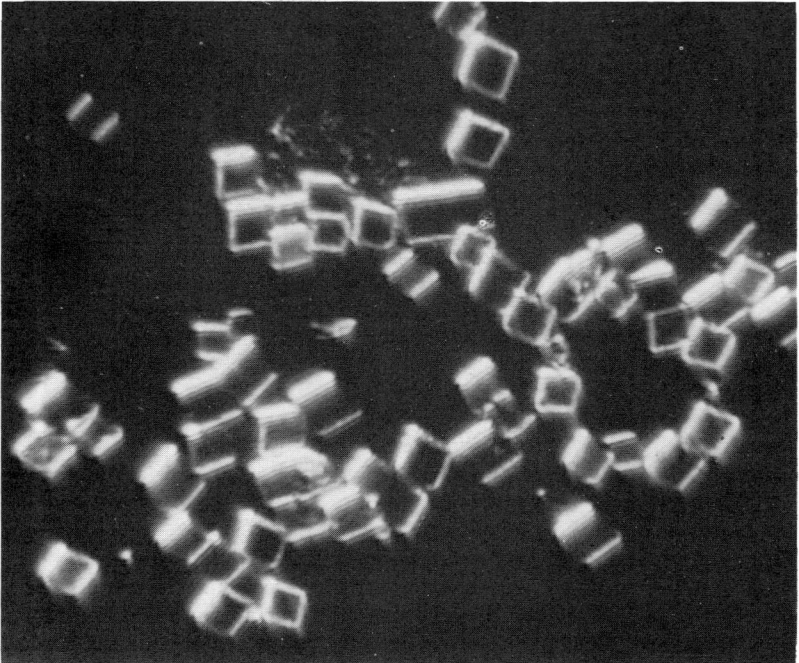

Fig. 42. Crystals of iodofenphos (× 1,000) on a surface sprayed with suspension concentrate: notice the uniformity of crystal size (3–5 μ).

4. the active particles are easily picked up from treated surfaces, as a wettable powder, but without the visible deposit of the dried film;
5. the suspension is easy to remix in the spray container, should it settle out on standing.

Much of the popularity of an emulsion derives from the lack of visible evidence of spraying in domestic properties. This is also obtained with a suspension concentrate, but can only be achieved if the sprayer is clean in the first instance; the solvent used in currently developed suspension concentrates strips out residues which may have dried in the spray tank. When these are sprayed they mar the surface being treated.

Lacquer
Insecticidal lacquers were developed in the U.K. in the mid-1950's with the co-operation of the National Research Development Council. They are resin formulations (a mixture of urea formaldehyde and oil-modified alkyd resins) into which an insecticide is incorporated at a relatively high concentration (4–10 per cent). Curing is encouraged by the inclusion of driers as used in conventional paints. Some lacquers require the addition at time of use of an acid 'accelerator' to speed drying.

The objective in the development of lacquers was to obtain a semi-permanent residual formulation capable of remaining on surfaces in a highly active state for many years.[116] A lacquer is a ready-to-use formulation designed for situations where sprays and dusts are quickly lost or rendered useless by frequent washings. (Figs. 43, 44 and 160). They have been used extensively in the U.K. for the control of crawling insects on ships, in hospitals, kitchens and in food manufacturing premises. The performance claimed for lacquers is influenced by the degree of hardness of the resin film and the concentration of insecticide.

Fig. 43. The application of a spray in this wash-up area achieves little, unless the cockroaches in the joints of the stainless steel are contaminated directly. Use of an insecticidal lacquer would be more appropriate (U.S.A.).

Lacquers offer a number of advantages for cockroach control:
1. the insecticide is produced on the treated surface in small amounts as a crystal 'bloom' (if the insecticide is a solid, e.g. propoxur), or as a minute amount of liquid (e.g. diazinon or malathion), imparting 'controlled release' and extending the life of the insecticide over many months. Thus, no difference could be detected in the performance against German cockroaches of dieldrin lacquer, applied to pieces of masonite and aged for 180 days, when some of the surfaces were wiped weekly with a dry cloth and others reused without wiping;[796]
2. the insecticide is available to the insect as 100 per cent active ingredient, without filler. The crystal size (about 10μ) is much smaller than is obtained with a dried film of an oil spray (usually greater than $1,000\mu$), influencing pick up and insecticidal activity;

3. only small amounts of insecticide become available on the surface of a lacquer film at any time; this affords a high measure of safety despite the high insecticidal content of the formulation. Nevertheless, flour in contact with newly applied lacquer containing dieldrin, may become sufficiently contaminated with insecticide to kill beetles (*Tribolium confusum*). Jute sacking gives better protection from contamination than kraft paper:[245, 248]

4. application is usually by brush, thus avoiding the contamination which can occur in the application of sprays and dusts. However, the solvent odours may be objectionable at the time of applying lacquer unless there is good ventilation.

Fig. 44. A brewery providing warmth and moist conditions for cockroaches, with harbourage in cracks in concrete and between tiles. Insecticidal lacquer or baits (above floor level) are appropriate (Berlin, W. Germany).

Lacquers can be applied to most surfaces, but where porous surfaces are treated, such as unpainted woodwork, plaster or brickwork, a sealer or second coat of lacquer should be applied after the first has dried. Recommendations for the use of lacquers have often included application by 'banding' on exposed surfaces, thereby providing an insecticidal barrier over which cockroaches have to pass. Lacquers should never be applied in this way. Firstly the resin base invariably discolours (tans) on ageing, so that application becomes obvious and unsightly. Secondly, as with other formulations, the control of cockroaches with lacquers cannot be obtained by expecting the insects to find the surface to which insecticide has been applied. Thus in the warm areas of kitchens, for example, lacquers should be used where cockroaches occur and where other formulations may be ineffective; around central heating systems, pipes, under sinks, kitchen equipment and tables, behind fixtures, at the backs of drawers and cupboards, in cracks and crevices around doors and skirting boards and where pipes go through walls.

In performance tests against *Tribolium confusum*, aged films of lacquer containing malathion at different concentrations were effective for at least one year.[246] Exposure for five hours to dieldrin lacquer kills 84 per cent of *T. castaneum*, six years after application; diazinon lacquer kills 57 per cent after 14 months, with a half hour exposure.[679]

Lacquers containing diazinon and propoxur are superior to those containing dieldrin and malathion, one week after application (Cornwell, unpublished). Formulations containing 6 per cent diazinon and 6 per cent chlorpyrifos are equally effective against *B. germanica* when tested after one week, but after four weeks some activity of the diazinon is lost, making it equivalent in performance to 3 per cent chlorpyrifos (Table XII).

In tests in Denmark[40] with various insecticides in lacquers applied at different rates, diazinon and dieldrin remained effective for about nine months and chlorpyrifos for five. A proprietary lacquer containing chlorpyrifos (Killmaster®) applied in low income housing in Arizona performed well for at least three months.[644]

TABLE XII

KILL (%) OF ADULT *B. GERMANICA* 48 HOURS AFTER SHORT EXPOSURES TO LACQUERS CONTAINING DIAZINON (6%) AND DIFFERENT CONCENTRATIONS OF CHLORPYRIFOS, AGED FOR 1 AND 4 WEEKS AT 25°C AND 65% RH
(Cornwell, unpublished)

Age of lacquered surface (w)	Exposure time (hr)	Insecticide				
		Diazinon 6%	Chlorpyrifos			
			2%	4%	6%	8%
1	0·5	100	60	85	100	100
	1	100	80	98	98	100
4	0·5	68	75	95	98	100
	1	93	80	98	100	100

When lacquers are applied to painted surfaces, some insecticidal activity is lost due to the solvent carrying the active compound into the paint film, thus making it unavailable to cockroaches. Transfer of insecticide into the paint also upsets the balance of active ingredient relative to other constitutents making the lacquer perform less efficiently (Table XIII). This is especially important on ships, where long life of an insecticide treatment is required because of infrequent visits to port, and painting is a continual occupation for maintenance crews when ships are at sea. Lacquers have been used to examine the susceptibility of cockroaches taken from infested ships; considerable resistance to dieldrin and a greater tolerance of diazinon and propoxur was evident among marine strains than insects reared in the laboratory (Table XIV).

TABLE XIII

KILL (% AT 24 HOURS) OF GERMAN COCKROACHES EXPOSED TO PROPOXUR AND DIAZINON LACQUERS ON GLASS. SOME PANELS WERE COATED WITH GLOSS PAINT ONE WEEK BEFORE APPLICATION OF LACQUER

(Cornwell, unpublished)

Exposure time (mins)	Propoxur		Diazinon	
	Unpainted	Painted	Unpainted	Painted
10	25	10	10	0
20	40	10	60	20
30	75	5	65	10
60	100	25	100	45
120	100	60	100	100
240	100	75	100	100

Most of the development work on lacquers, subsequent to their first introduction has been done at Rentokil. Attempts to produce a fenitrothion lacquer failed, because of very rapid darkening of the film after application. Lacquers are now little used in the U.K., experience having shown that long life can be obtained just as easily, and often more effectively, with the use of chlordecone baits.

Lacquers have never been popular in the U.S.A.: disappointing results were obtained by Smittle & Burden[759] from lacquers containing dieldrin, malathion and diazinon. More recently, the principle of the insecticidal lacquer has been developed further with the marketing of an adhesive-backed multi-layered plastic tape, impregnated with a toxicant (Hercon Roach Tape®). It consists of two layers of PVC with a pesticide reservoir layer sandwiched between. The upper one is porous to insecticide, the lower one is coated with pressure sensitive adhesive. The percentage of active ingredient in the total laminate for

®Herculite Protective Fabrics Corp.

cockroach control varies with the insecticide used; it ranges from 3 per cent (chlordane) to 10·5 per cent (carbaryl). The properties claimed for the product are exactly those of insecticidal lacquers, except that the use of a 2·5 cm wide tape provides the highest possible measure of safety in application.[50,51] The test data available suggest that relatively long exposures of cockroaches (24 hours) are required to kill.

TABLE XIV

KILL (%) OF LABORATORY 'SUSCEPTIBLE' AND 'DIELDRIN-RESISTANT' STRAINS OF B. GERMANICA EXPOSED TO INSECTICIDAL LACQUERS IN COMPARISON WITH COCKROACH STRAINS COLLECTED FROM SHIPS ('Rangitoto' and 'Matra')
(Cornwell, unpublished)

Strain	Exposure period (hr)	Insecticide		
		Propoxur	Diazinon	Dieldrin*
Laboratory susceptible	1	90	100	—
	4	100	100	78
Laboratory dieldrin-resistant	1	88	75	—
	4	100	100	3
Rangitoto	1	68	18	—
	4	88	100	8
Matra	1	10	15	—
	4	95	100	0

* Cockroaches exposed for 6 hours.

It is relatively easy to incorporate insecticides into conventional paints and achieve good cockroach control (Table XV). But the concentration of active compounds can be no less in paints than in conventional insecticidal lacquers, unless it is intended to treat considerably greater areas, thus possibly increasing the time that insects may be in contact. Lower concentrations might be effective for the control of flies and mosquitoes.

The concept of the 'controlled release' of insecticides to extend their length of life, and make them available to the pest without endangering the environment, has been considered for a number of crop sprays. Microencapsulation —coated droplets from which the pesticide diffuses—is a possible technique. Studies have been made with pyrethrins and other insecticides.[48]

TABLE XV

KILL (% AT 24 HOURS) OF GERMAN COCKROACHES EXPOSED TO INSECTICIDAL LACQUERS CONTAINING PROPOXUR (4%) AND DIAZINON (5·3%) AND TO VARIOUS PAINT BASES INCORPORATING THE SAME INSECTICIDES
(Cornwell, unpublished)

Formulation	Propoxur			Diazinon		
	Exposure time (mins)					
	30	60	240	30	60	240
Insecticidal lacquer	46	92	97	81	95	100
Paints:						
Gloss (enamel)	35	68	100	30	84	100
Lustre	55	55	97	43	94	100
Emulsion	100	100	100	—	—	—

Lacquers: one coat on glass
Gloss: one undercoat of lustre paint then one coat of gloss on glass
Lustre: two coats on glass
Emulsion: two coats on hardboard

SOLID FORMULATIONS

Dust
A dust is probably the most effective of all insecticidal formulations for killing crawling insects. Cockroaches live deep in cracks and crevices, in floor and wall cavities, which are often impossible to penetrate with a spray: their actual resting places may be some distance from where the serviceman can get his spray nozzle. Dust can be blown into these less-accessible harbourages to reach the insects directly. Apart from the easy dispersion of dusts, (1) they are more easily picked up by cockroaches than insecticides in dried spray films, (2) all the active particles remain available, none being lost into surfaces by absorption, (as with emulsion sprays, see p. 83), (3) dusts are usually the cheapest formulation of each insecticide. Dusts containing some insecticides may, however, be more repellent to cockroaches than sprays (Chapter 7). The excellent pick-up and kill obtained with a propoxur dust, in comparison with other propoxur formulations, is shown in Table CV (p. 375).

An insecticidal dust is a ready-to-use formulation in which a low concentration of the insecticide, usually 1–5 per cent, is uniformly mixed with a finely divided carrier, such as china clay or talc (aluminium and magnesium silicates). The powdered materials used as diluents are not pure, but mixtures of many minerals. The use of locally available diluents is of obvious economic interest to developing countries.[70] The choice is important because some active compounds are intolerant of acid or alkaline diluents.

Exceptions to the above occur among inorganic insecticides, such as sodium fluoride, which is used at 25–100 per cent, with or without pyrethrins, and boric acid used at 99 per cent, usually with 1 per cent free-flowing agent. 'Insorbicides' prepared by precipitating insecticides—trichlorphon, tetramethrin and others—onto kaolin talc and starch have been shown in laboratory tests to remain effective longer than conventional dusts against cockroaches.[122]

The diluent of an insecticidal dust helps spread the active ingredient uniformly over the surface of treated harbourages; fine dusts are more readily picked up by cockroaches and are therefore more effective than coarse dusts. Crystals of DDT (60μ and 400μ) had different toxicities to ants of different species, the size of particle having a much greater influence on the smaller insects.[515]

The increased toxicity of mixtures of insecticides with certain diluents has been attributed to a more rapid penetration of the toxicant after abrasion of the cuticle by the diluent. Increased desiccation may also be a contributory factor. Thus dusts of lindane plus the abrasive materials quartz and carborundum are much more toxic to *P. americana* than lindane alone, or when the insects are exposed to the diluent, prior to contact with lindane.[673] The diluent of a dust should be ground as finely as the active ingredient it carries. Too high a content of 'fines' however, may cause the dust to form a cloud during application. Gould[349] mentions the addition of a small amount of light oil to reduce dustiness of a pyrethrum/sodium fluoride mixture.

Dust can be distributed with small hand-operated equipment (Chapter 5) but it may be necessary to drill small holes to get it into hollow partitions and into 'dead spaces' beneath fixtures (Fig. 95). A light, uniform film is sufficient. Shelves and ledges above head height, should not be dusted, where there is a chance of the insecticide falling to contaminate surfaces below.

Insecticides used as dusts should be applied only in *dry* locations (Fig. 45): moisture causes the particles to clog. If dusts and sprays are used together, spray first and allow to dry, before applying the dust nearby: there is no merit in applying one on top of the other.

Dusts should never be mixed with water. It might help those not familiar with the terms 'dust' and 'powder' to differentiate by always using 'dust' to signify a *dry* formulation and 'powder' for admixture with *water*. Similarly confusion will be avoided by not doing a 'powder job' or using a 'powder blower' when a dust is being applied. Instances of people *dusting* with a 50 per cent wettable powder, believing it to be suitable for direct treatment are not uncommon.

Smoke

A smoke generator (or smoke bomb) consists of a mixture of an active ingredient (usually lindane) with a combustible material (an organic fuel) and an oxidant that makes it burn (sodium chlorate). On ignition the mixture

Fig. 45. In warm climates, provided conditions are dry, dusts can be used outdoors to protect against cockroach entry. A piston-type dust gun is being used (Houston, U.S.A.).

generates a cloud of water vapour, carbon dioxide, carbon monoxide and vapourised insecticide (Fig. 46). By this method, a much finer dispersion of a solid can be achieved, by allowing it to condense from a hot vapour, than by any mechanical means. Thus, initially, the particles of a condensing smoke are less than 0.1μ diameter, tending to aggregate as the concentration of smoke increases.[397]

A smoke generator may occasionally be of value in cockroach control: in a cellar, duct, sewer channel or other location impossible to reach by other methods. Stand the generator on a non-combustible surface before lighting. The smoke produced is dispersed over a relatively wide area (e.g. the whole of an attic) and cannot be directed especially to those places where the insects are harbouring.

There is a common misconception about the properties of an insecticidal smoke: that it is a fumigant. The insecticide is *particulate and not a gas*. As a result it is not able to diffuse in air into those crevices where insecticide may be most needed. The particles of a smoke fall out onto horizontal surfaces, with very little deposited on vertical or overhead surfaces. That which gets into cracks is carried by air circulation, the tiny particles having very little inertia or momentum of their own.

THE IMPORTANCE OF FORMULATION

Insects which crawl over surfaces covered with 'fall out' of the insecticide are readily killed because of the ease of pick-up of the finely divided deposit. Use of a smoke generator is probably the easiest, cheapest and most efficient way of dispersing a particulate formulation provided some account is taken of, (1) loss by ventilation, (2) failure of the smoke to penetrate insect harbourages and (3) the insecticide in the air has only transient properties against flying insects.

Fig. 46. Use of a smoke generator in a roof void to distribute particles of lindane (U.K.).

Bait

Baits containing stomach poisons provided one of the oldest methods of cockroach control, which together with trapping techniques and the use of early dust formulations, were once the only means of achieving relief from these insects (see p. 471).

Baits incorporate an insecticide in an attractive and palatable food. Their use lost favour when cockroach control was made easier by the development of sprays and other formulations. There has, however, been some renewed interest in recent years, with the emphasis on greater safety and the reduction in numbers of insecticides permitted for use.

There are a number of reasons why baits are not very popular with personnel engaged in cockroach control:

(1) early baits incorporated relatively inefficient materials which met with limited success; resort to their use today is considered retrograde;

(2) baits take much longer to kill than sprays and dusts; most people expect an instant remedy to their problem;

(3) residues on which cockroaches feed, compete with poisoned food laid as bait in the majority of locations where cockroaches occur. Nevertheless, many bait formulations do perform extremely well when other foods are freely available;

(4) every cockroach has to visit and feed on a bait for an infestation to be controlled—the chances of reaching every insect seems more probable with a dust or spray;

(5) placing baits out of reach of children and domestic animals can be more time-consuming than spraying.

Despite these disadvantages, baits do serve a useful function for the control of cockroaches in a number of locations:[619]

(1) in zoos (Fig. 47), animal laboratories[664] and pet shops, the use of sprays and

Fig. 47. A modern aviary for tropical birds in which central heating pipes and radiators below the cages encourage insect infestation. Food dropped by the birds and the public provide ample residues for cockroaches. Chlordecone baits may be used safely in this situation (W. Germany).

dusts can easily endanger animals. Baits, on the other hand, do not contaminate the air with insecticidal droplets, particles, or vapour;
(2) in the vicinity of electrical switch gear and in computer rooms, the methods of cockroach control must not interfere with relays and other electrical contacts;
(3) baits often provide longer residual activity against cockroaches than insecticides applied as sprays; they are therefore used to prevent re-infestation and are especially useful in shipping where inspection and treatment for cockroaches is necessarily infrequent. Here, as previously mentioned, baits have tended to replace insecticidal lacquers; also where resistance to dieldrin has occurred.[103, 814]

The insecticides incorporated into cockroach baits are boric acid, phosphorus, chlordecone, propoxur, trichlorphon and dichlorvos. Various mixtures of boric acid were used in the last century, but have now disappeared. Phosphorus is still used as a paste; it adheres well to crevices when pressed into place. Chlordecone is marketed as pellets and paste, incorporating groundnut oil as the attractant;[611] it is also used as a gel, satisfying the need of cockroaches for water.[670] Propoxur is marketed as 'crevice-sized' particles of bait, designed for light broadcast application and for direct application to cockroach harbourages. Trichlorphon is used as a sugar bait for the control of cockroaches and flies. Dichlorvos baits have not met with much success, although use of a 10 per cent formulation on Indian naval ships gave a noticeable cockroach reduction.[668] Lindane has also been tested experimentally.[672]

Attractants and feeding stimulants added to baits
A most important property of a bait is that it should be eaten in preference to other foods. The reactions of German cockroaches, before and after starvation, to diets containing non-nutritive substances have shown that consumption of dry matter is influenced by a number of factors.[900] The relative catches of German cockroaches in jar traps containing bread, beef, flour or nothing were 52, 33, 8 and 7 per cent, respectively (Ebeling & Reierson[258]). According to these workers, attractive foods used as baits must be placed in areas where cockroaches normally travel or congregate. If not, the insects do not find them. Thus, Miesch & Howell[569] found that baits were twice as effective when placed in thin lines, in locations favoured by cockroaches (such as under sinks and refrigerators) than when placed on cards or in bait cups.

One of the earliest studies to improve baits to control cockroaches examined the response of *B. orientalis* to essential oils.[204] The vapours were drawn through one arm of an olfactometer—a tube with a Y-junction—giving cockroaches the opportunity to show a preference. 'Positive' and 'negative' responses of the insects were recorded. 'Extremely strong attractant properties were noted for oils of banana, sweet orange, apple and pineapple, whereas responses to citronella and eucalyptus were completely negative'. A solid bait containing traces of the attractant oils, with gelatin (6g), beef broth (200 cc) and mercuric chloride (0·5g), killed cockroaches in 3 hours. Eisa[272] used the same toxicant to study the bait preferences of *P. americana*; pepsin in the bait is about six times more attractive than maltose although carbohydrates are generally regarded as the most attractive.[273]

Bare[75] attempted to find bait materials more effective than ordinary foods, toxicants that were non-repellent, and additives that would increase the attractiveness of baits. Powdered skim milk, butter, honey, confectioner's sugar and flours of malt barley, wheat and sorghum, proved no more attractive alone, or combined, than many other foods commonly available. Boric acid was non-repellent, but sodium fluoride was significantly so. Butyric acid, malt extract and stale beer had little to recommend them as attractants.

In another study of food-finding by cockroaches, 201 solid, semi-solid and liquid formulations of many kinds of food and pure chemicals were presented to German, Oriental and American cockroaches. Moist baits were more effective than dry: a semi-solid bait of 10 per cent dehydrated potato, 15 per cent sucrose and 75 per cent water was the most attractive to *B. germanica* and *B. orientalis*. American cockroaches were highly attracted to a semi-solid bait of persimmon, date, date sugar and sucrose, and to a water bait containing 20–30 per cent sucrose. The colour of baits had no effect.[568] The observation that cockroaches find their food by random searching, rather than as a response to odour does not offer much hope for the improvement of baits by the use of odorous attractants. However, more German cockroaches were caught by Sugawara and colleagues[916] in sticky traps of cardboard, baited with hexyl hexanoate and hexyl pentanoate than in unbaited traps.

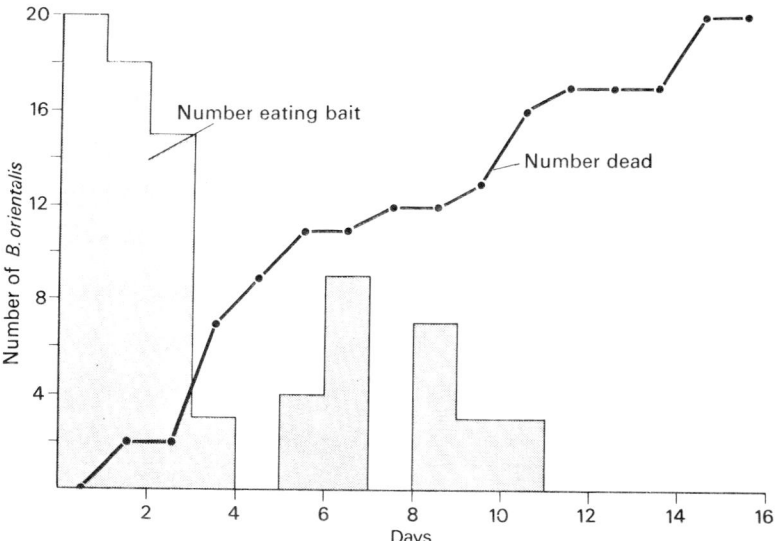

Fig. 48. Numbers of individually caged Oriental cockroaches eating chlordecone gel (0·25 per cent) each day; and cumulative kill (Cornwell, unpublished).

To examine the reaction of Oriental cockroaches to baits containing chlordecone, insects were caged individually with gel and alternative food. There was no evidence to suggest that poisoned cockroaches were in any way 'shy' of chlordecone, since all the cockroaches fed on the very first day, and most on the second and third. Feeding virtually ceased after four days when half the insects were dead (Fig. 48). There were then bouts of feeding by the survivors until almost all were dead or dying, in about ten days.

Aged gel baits, correctly formulated, lose little of their palatability to cockroaches even in the presence of alternative food and water. Thus gels containing 0·25 per cent chlordecone aged for 8 weeks, were eaten almost as well by German cockroaches as fresh gel. The amount eaten by Oriental cockroaches was slightly greater after ageing. The speed of kill, of both species, was unaffected (Fig. 49). (See also Chlordecone, p. 313.)

The factors which influence the acceptance of bait by cockroaches, and chemicals which elicit food-finding have been studied in Japan.[802,803] It is believed that for poison baits to be effective, 'insecticides with no repellency, as well as potent attractants and feeding stimulants—are essential'.[806]

A volatile fraction of rice bran, extracted with n-hexane, is both an attractant and a feeding stimulant. Sorbitol and mannitol, as well as several sugars, have a particularly marked stimulative effect on the feeding of *B. germanica*. Glycols, and some sugar alcohols also elicit a feeding response and a few glycerides are stimulative.[807]

Methyl myristate on filter papers is highly attractive to three pest cockroaches. Concentrations of 0·02 to 0·2 per cent more than double the amount of 20 per cent boric acid bait eaten. Addition of maltose and sucrose to baits of starch flour also increases intake (Table XVI). However, the incorporation of methyl myristate (0·1–0·5 per cent) in gel baits containing chlordecone (0·25 per cent) has the opposite effect, reducing the amount eaten and hence delaying kill (Table XVII).

TABLE XVI

AMOUNTS EATEN (mg) BY FEMALE *B. GERMANICA* OF STARCH FLOUR BAITS CONTAINING 20% BORIC ACID AND INCORPORATING DIFFERENT AMOUNTS OF METHYL MYRISTATE, MALTOSE AND SUCROSE IN CHOICE TESTS
(From Tsuji & Ono[806])

Methyl myristate (%)	0·0	0·02	0·2	2·0	4·0
Amount eaten	97	206	228	69	15
Maltose (%)		0	5	10	15
Amount eaten		5	8	16	64
Sucrose (%)		0	5	10	15
Amount eaten		−4*	10	11	55

* Negative value due to humidity changes, not corrected for.

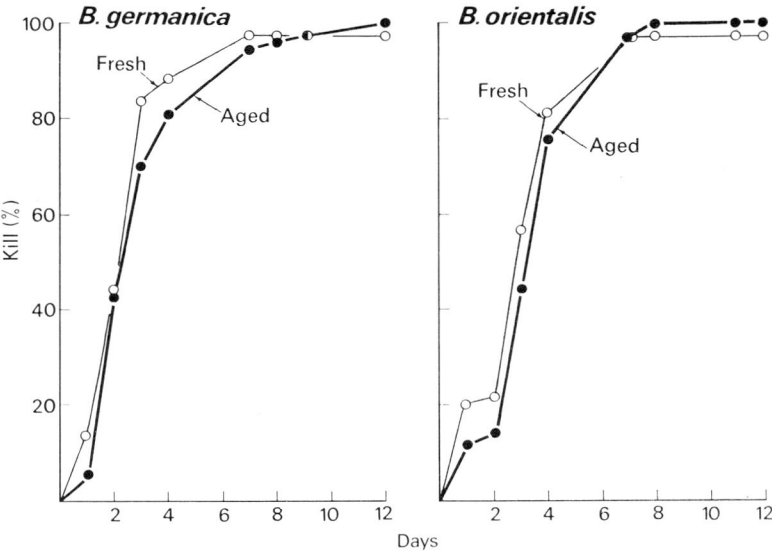

Fig. 49. Kill (per cent) of German and Oriental cockroaches fed gel containing chlordecone (0·25 per cent) and alternative food and water. Comparison between fresh and 8 week-old gel aged at 25°C and 65 per cent R. H. (Cornwell, unpublished).

Response to pheromones

Among substances attractive to insects, the most potent and specific are sex attractants. Gyplure—the sex attractant of female gypsy moths (*Porthetria dispar*)—has been isolated, prepared industrially and used in traps, with insecticide, for moth control in North America.[462] The attractants of other insects in some cases have been separated and identified. Male American cockroaches respond to the sex pheromone of females by moving about twice as rapidly: they respond to a source of pheromone to their left or right by turning towards it. The normal reaction of cockroaches to air currents is to turn away from them, but the reverse occurs if the air is carrying sex pheromone.[911] A purified extract from filter papers contaminated by female *B. germanica* is reported capable of attracting 99–100 per cent of males when used in traps.[828]

Other chemicals, such as the cockroach aggregation pheromone, might be used as attractants in insecticidal baits, to encourage strong preferential feeding where there is ample alternative food. Nymphs of *P. americana* stop and linger in the area when they encounter faecal pellets, their source of aggregation pheromone.[889] Very close contact is necessary to inhibit altogether, the movement of cockroaches.[911] Will male American cockroaches, starved for four weeks, still respond to the sex pheromone of the female as markedly when a food odour (banana extract) is also present? Responses to the pheromone in an olfactometer did not in fact diminish until 24 days of starvation, and even then remained dominant over the odour of food.[539]

TABLE XVII

KILL (%) OF ORIENTAL AND GERMAN COCKROACHES WITH ACCESS TO GEL BAITS CONTAINING CHLORDECONE (0·25%) AND INCREASING AMOUNTS OF METHYL MYRISTATE, WHICH REDUCED THE AMOUNT EATEN

(Cornwell, unpublished)

Cockroach	Methyl myristate (%)	Days					Amount eaten (g)
		2	4	7	9	11	
Oriental	0	20	91	100			13·8
	0·1	14	59	89	94	100	11·6
	0·2	12	47	87	99	100	12·6
	0·5	12	28	52	65	81	7·4
German	0	52	86	100			7·4
	0·1	43	81	97	100		6·2
	0·2	61	91	100			6·0
	0·5	52	94	100			5·4

Tests of performance

The recommended application of pelleted baits of chlordecone, to control German cockroaches, is that '2–3 tablespoonsful be used in each infested room, scattered or placed in a suitable container behind and under fixtures, not accessible to children or pets'.[512] Because some baits contain oil they are better placed in small trays, paper cups or bottle tops to prevent staining. This is also an advantage under wet conditions where disintegration of pellets may readily occur (Fig. 159).

The usual concentration of chlordecone in cockroach baits (e.g. Kepone®) is 0·125 per cent. Hawkes[403] has shown that 0·25 per cent gives much improved performance against German, Oriental and American cockroaches, without loss in palatability (Fig. 136). Also, a gel with a high water content, and incorporating glycerol to stabilise against water loss, is three times more readily taken by *B. orientalis*, four times by *B. germanica* and ten times by *P. americana*, than a paste containing half the chlordecone concentration.

In tests by Tabaru, Ono and Tsuji[782] all the insecticides incorporated into baits, at 0·1 and 1 per cent, showed some degree of repellency to cockroaches: propoxur was highly so, whereas trichlorphon had little repellency. Of cockroaches fed propoxur (0·5 per cent) and boric acid (20 per cent) in baits, at least 10 per cent of the insects survived. Baits containing propoxur (2 per cent) were noticeably more effective than those containing trichlorphon (1 per cent), especially against *B. germanica* (Table XVIII). In rooms and homes, none of the baits containing trichlorphon (1 per cent) tested against German cockroaches gave satisfactory control, although some reduction (75–90 per cent) was obtained of *Periplaneta* spp.[508]

Onset of poisoning symptoms and speed of kill are affected by the insecticide used. Thus 95 per cent of German cockroaches with free access to baits containing dichlorvos (2 per cent) die after one day, with propoxur (2 per cent) after 9 days, and with chlordecone (0·125 per cent) after 16 days. Baits of propoxur and chlordecone aged for six weeks were as effective as when fresh and continued to kill 90 per cent after 100 days. Dichlorvos bait killed only 68 per cent when aged for 6 weeks.[22]

The use of paraffin wax blocks containing trichlorphon (5 per cent) gave good control of German and Oriental cockroaches in living quarters and drains in a town in the Soviet Union.[685] American cockroaches in sewer access shafts in North Carolina did not feed on 'paraffin cakes' containing 2 per cent propoxur (in a commercially available bait formulation) with or without paranitrophenol as mould inhibitor: baits containing pellets of 0·125 per cent chlordecone, embedded in paraffin wax, were readily eaten by *P. americana* in sewers,[286] but were only partially effective.[871]

TABLE XVIII

KILL (%) AFTER 24 HOURS OF THREE PEST COCKROACHES FED BAITS CONTAINING PROPOXUR AND TRICHLORPHON, IN THE PRESENCE OF NON-POISONED FOOD

(From Quattrochi[688])

Cockroach	Propoxur		Trichlorphon
	2% in cereal (Baygon bait)	1% in sugar (Baygon fly bait)	1% in sugar (Dipterex bait)
B. germanica	90	75	5
B. orientalis	100	75	85
P. americana	100	95	60

When boric acid is force fed to adult German cockroaches, quite small amounts are lethal (LD_{50}: 150–200μg/insect). When boric acid (40 per cent) is fed in starch/flour 'tablets' the insects are not repelled by the taste, and feeding for one day on baits containing 20 per cent boric acid is sufficient to kill most in 4–6 weeks. When the cockroaches are continuously exposed to baits, 10–20 per cent boric acid kills in about 2 weeks, and 2·5–5 per cent takes 3–4 weeks (Fig. 50). The addition of 0·5 per cent lindane, or 0·5 per cent fenitrothion, to baits containing 20 per cent boric acid kills cockroaches more quickly, but there is some evidence of repellency.[806]

In practical treatments within buildings, changes in the populations of German cockroaches were monitored by trap counts before and after baits were used.[808] Those containing 20 per cent boric acid and 0·2 per cent methyl myristate caused a marked reduction within 2–3 weeks.

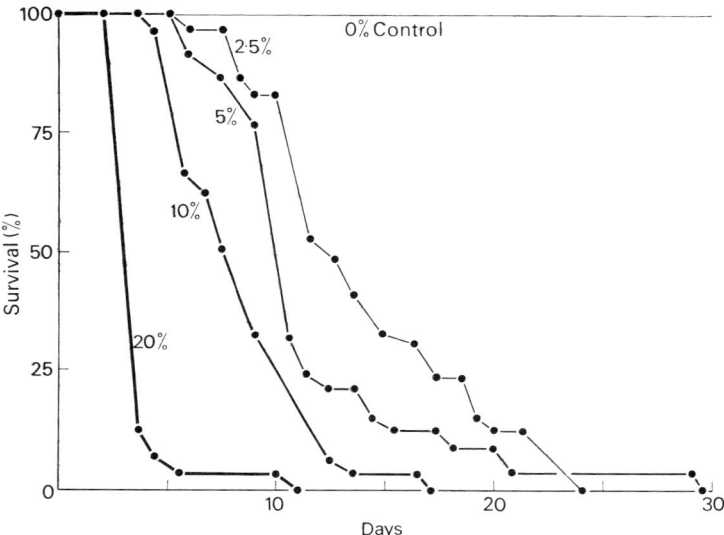

Fig. 50. Survival (per cent) of female *B. germanica* with continuous access to baits containing different concentrations of boric acid (after Tsuji & Ono[806]).

Freshly prepared gels containing 0·25 per cent iodofenphos fed in competition with alternative food killed adult Oriental cockroaches in two days compared with chlordecone in 7 days. Against German cockroaches, iodofenphos gel killed at the same rate as chlordecone taking about 2 weeks to provide 100 per cent mortality. The iodofenphos gel is still an experimental formulation (Cornwell, unpublished).

INSECTICIDAL VAPOURS

Fumigation is rarely used to control cockroaches (see Chapter 8), but incidental to the use of lindane, diazinon and dichlorvos as sprays and dusts, these insecticides may have some vapour action when applied to cockroach harbourages (see Table LXXXII), although the contribution to control is probably small.

The slow release of dichlorvos from resin strips (e.g. Vapona), cut into pieces and placed in kitchen units, is not effective in controlling German cockroaches (see p. 331). The use of dichlorvos in aerosols, applied in closed environments to control cockroaches, e.g. in buses, has proved effective where vapour concentration is high and can be held for sufficient time (p. 333). However, dichlorvos penetrates poorly into harbourages into which air cannot circulate, as shown by the inadequate control of cockroaches in simulated packages (p. 331).

In this chapter we have examined the properties and use of different formulations of insecticides for cockroach control: we have emphasised the advantages and disadvantages of each and attempted to explain their performance on treated surfaces.

A great deal has been written about the structural aspects of insect cuticle as they affect penetration of insecticides and the factors influencing toxic action.[327,616,729] Perhaps in the control of a crop pest, or in a spray programme against flies, when only tiny amounts of insecticide make direct contact with the pest, these factors are important. But in cockroach control, where the insects are sometimes so contaminated with spray as to be almost drowned in it, factors affecting penetration of the cuticle are not the ones which most affect kill. Rather, in warm climates where reinfestation readily occurs, the factors most important to cockroach control are those which affect maximum contact between insect and toxicant, some time after insecticides have been applied. Formulation has a marked effect on this principle.

To repeat the comparison with crop protection where large and costly amounts of pesticide are applied, the techniques used in applying crop sprays are of considerable economic importance. It is possible, in cockroach control, to optimise application—the sprayer pumped to the right pressure, the nozzle at the right distance from the harbourage or surface, with the nozzle moved at the right speed—but these considerations are far less critical than in agriculture. Most pest control operators devise their own way of working, which may, or may not, be the best.

However, what we use to control cockroaches appears too often to be influenced by 'convenience to the user' rather than 'effectiveness against the pest'. We seem more concerned with *all the other factors* which may dictate our choice: whether an oil based spray or the solvents of an emulsion, will damage a plastic or other type of floor covering; whether an oil based spray will create a fire risk; the deposit of a wettable powder which may be objectionable in well-decorated surroundings; the possible risk of short-circuits if a water spray is used near electrical installations.

We seem more concerned with the hotel manager's objections to the use of dusts, rather than the training of personnel to use this formulation expertly; dusts can provide first class results, and need not be unsightly if applied with care and good sense. Smokes, lacquers and baits all have a contribution to make to cockroach control, but so often treatments are carried out solely with the use of sprays—and emulsions at that!

Of course, all these things *are* important, but they are not the overriding factors! The decisions which have to be made when selecting formulations for cockroach control are, firstly, what is going to be the most effective, and secondly what are the possible risks if treatment is carried out in that way.

5

THE EQUIPMENT TO USE

Selecting the right equipment—Equipment for inspection—Equipment for insecticide application: dust blowers; sprayers; motorised equipment; miscellaneous equipment; care of equipment; responsibility for maintenance—Equipment for self protection: dress; gloves; masks.

The habits of cockroaches have considerable influence on how insecticides are best applied. Control requires knowing what these habits are and having appropriate equipment to apply approved insecticides safely and effectively. Although the control of cockroaches by the home owner has been simplified in recent years by (1) aerosol pressure packs which serve as spray applicators, and (2) plastic puffer packs to disperse dusts, he is often without the necessary knowledge and experience to do a thorough job.

Many liquid formulations are still sold for use in single stroke 'spray guns'. Additionally, in many countries there has been a boom in application equipment for garden products with the result that most households now have a small hand sprayer which serves for indoor use when required. These models are not, however, constructed for the professional user of insecticides, whose equipment has to withstand heavy and continuous use, on both industrial and domestic contracts.

Because of the range of insect problems normally tackled by servicemen, their equipment is varied. In tropical countries, for example, treatment for cockroaches often involves spraying around and under, as well as inside buildings; the amounts of insecticide applied may be large and powered equipment is therefore used. The control of cockroaches and crickets on refuse tips cannot be done effectively with the same equipment used to control insects in the domestic kitchen.

Nevertheless, on more than 90 per cent of occasions the equipment needed by servicemen to control cockroaches indoors is relatively simple: an efficient sprayer, holding 1–2 gallons, and a reliable piece of dusting equipment. Additionally he will need protective clothing and a good torch.

In this chapter, we examine the types of equipment most often used to control cockroaches. We shall not be concerned with detailed specifications, or the finer points of design; these can be obtained from equipment manufacturers.

Selecting the right equipment
The pest control operator undertakes what his client is unable, or unwilling, to do for himself. The operator aims to provide a reliable service, based on knowledge and experience of cockroaches and the safe and effective use of in-

secticides. The client has to be confident that the contractor will do the job 'professionally'. This will not occur if the serviceman arrives with dirty, ill-kept equipment, which drips insecticide from the spray nozzle and leaves ring marks from the bottom of the canister wherever it is put down. Neither will confidence be established if dust is applied in such a way that objectionable amounts get into the air and onto exposed surfaces.

The client is also unlikely to be impressed if the equipment used is of a type which can be bought from the local supermarket. As a result it is not uncommon for the equipment of service companies to be *far more* sophisticated than is necessary to do a relatively simple job. It often happens (regrettably) that a domestic contract is sold to 'Mrs. Smith' on the appearance—'the chromium plating'—of the equipment, rather than on the expertise of the user.

The problem is further complicated when the serviceman *does* adopt the attitude of a professional and uses protective clothing. The wearing of gloves and a simple dust, or fume mask is desirable when insecticides are handled every day. The serviceman, however, fears that the impression this may create could adversely affect the client's opinion of his work, believing that the materials used may create a toxic risk. As a result, the serviceman rarely dresses appropriately to do the job, whereas there is every justification that he should do so.

The professional pest control operator uses, principally, small transportable equipment and a number of criteria will influence his selection:
(1) reliability, (2) robustness, (3) appearance, (4) availability of spare parts, (5) suitability for a variety of tasks and (6) trade discounts from the supplier for quantity orders.

It is an advantage for a servicing company that has a number of employees to standardise on the same models, as parts from equipment 'beyond repair' can be used to maintain others. Very often, equipment is supplied through the same agents that market insecticides.

EQUIPMENT FOR INSPECTION

Location of cockroach harbourages is the first step in cockroach control and requires a good torch. Apart from personal preferences, there are a number of practical criteria which influence choice:

1. it should be possible to concentrate the light into a beam; a diffuse light over a large area serves little purpose;
2. the torch should not roll away when put down; nevertheless the large box-type torches can be inconvenient in some situations and cannot be carried in a pocket;
3. some food industries object to glass in processing areas; the 'lens' should be of plastic, or the torch rubber-cased to prevent breakage.

The second tool, essential for a thorough inspection, is a pyrethrins aerosol. The content of pyrethrins is of little consequence as very low concentrations stimulate cockroach movement when spray is directed into harbourages.

Short bursts along crevices, where there may be 'vomit marks' will confirm the truth (see p. 247). Aerosols containing dichlorvos are sometimes used for this purpose but are not so effective. Aerosol generators (e.g. Micro-gen®) have also been marketed as a tool to indicate whether cockroach infestations have been eradicated (see p. 118).

The third and a most important asset, to an inspection of large premises, is a map of the site—or at least an opportunity to examine one. This allows the surveyor to see the way buildings may be interconnected, perhaps by ducts. The experienced man will know the most favoured locations of cockroaches, and by studying the layout of a building complex, will be able to pin-point the 'high risk' areas. These may subsequently be confirmed to him, by the maintenance engineer, the hospital matron and by his own detailed inspection, as areas where infestations do exist. Nevertheless, all parts of buildings should be included in a survey. The use of a map:

1. allows the survey to be planned and ultimately saves time;
2. indicates the 'activities' in a building above and below 'high risk' areas;
3. shows which areas are interconnected by ducts and shafts;
4. can act as a 'check list' that all areas have been inspected.

No inspection of an industrial site can be carried out without getting dirty. Protective clothing is discussed on p. 125. Whether or not the knees of a surveyor's boiler suit are clean or dirty is a sure indication whether a survey has been carried out properly.

EQUIPMENT FOR INSECTICIDE APPLICATION

Dust blowers

There are four types of hand-operated dusting equipment. The *bulb duster* (Fig. 51), which holds 100–300g of dust and can be fitted with a small extension nozzle. Dust is ejected by simply compressing the bulb and then allowing air to be sucked back. The bulb duster has no moving parts and requires little maintenance except to ensure that the washer is correctly placed. Solvents should not be allowed to contact the rubber. The second type, the *bellows duster* (modelled on the original 'Getz Powder Blower') holds a little less insecticide and is again operated by compression. These two can be used to introduce small quantities of dust into cockroach harbourages without creating a dust cloud, or contaminating exposed surfaces. They are suitable for use in homes, for treating around refrigerators (Fig. 93), behind and under kitchen equipment, and in other areas where it is important to apply dusts cleanly.

The third is the *piston-type dust gun* (called a Dobbin duster in the U.K.) which holds about 500g of insecticide and is more suitable for applying dust in larger voids, in industrial rather than domestic properties (Fig. 52). It also has limited use outdoors (Fig. 45). The amount of dust applied is controlled by how vigorously the gun is pumped and whether the outlet nozzle is at the bottom or the top of the barrel. At the bottom (Fig. 53a) dust is ejected as a heavy deposit with little air; with the outlet uppermost (Fig. 53b), smaller amounts

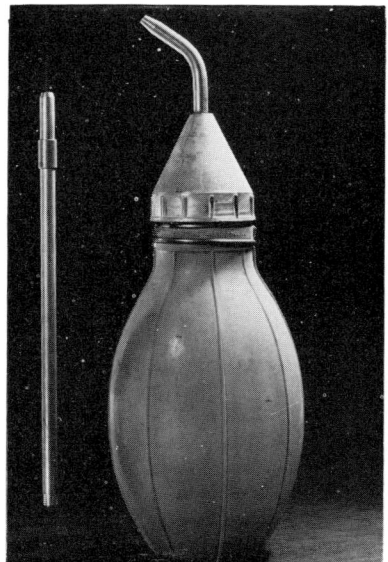 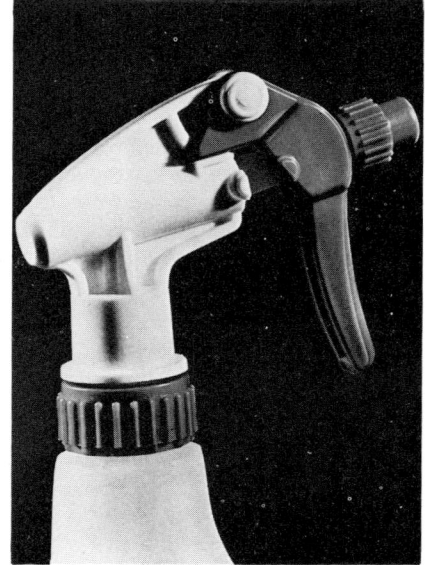

Fig. 51. Simple hand-operated equipment for cockroach control: (left) a bulb duster with extension tube (Rentokil photo); (right) nozzle of a suction sprayer which is fitted to a polythene bottle. (Courtesy: Tudor Accessories Ltd.).

are applied with the dust dispersed (as a cloud) in a jet of air. Provided the nozzle is well inside the harbourage, the latter type of dispersion is preferable for insect control, as it gives a thinner deposit which also coats vertical and overhead surfaces. Whichever equipment is used, it may be necessary to drill holes to get dust into closed cavities (Fig. 95). Also as the dust gun is the tool most likely to be used by service operators to apply rodenticidal contact dusts, it is preferable that separate dusters be used for these two purposes.

When cleaning this type of equipment it is sufficient to unscrew the cap of the barrel and tip out any unused dust; never wash a duster with water or solvent. Maintenance checks should consist of replacing the washers in the cap and plunger to ensure an air-tight and dust-tight seal.

The fourth type of hand-operated duster is the rotary type, of which there are a number of models holding up to 3 kg of dust (Fig. 54). This equipment is normally used outdoors for dusting refuse tips and other locations around properties, to control outdoor living cockroaches. The rotary duster is rested on the chest and held in place by shoulder straps. A crank handle rotates a geared worm-feed assembly through which the dust moves. The dust is not distributed as widely as with motorised dusters.

For large treatments, electrically- or petrol-driven dusting equipment is more appropriate (Figs. 55 & 56). Some powered units which are carried on the back ('knapsack') can be used for both dust and spray applications. They carry up to about 6 kg of dust. Additionally for treatments which involve large amounts of dust (perhaps the application of Dri-Die, or the extensive use of boric acid in roof voids and under properties), canisters which are pressurised from a separate compressed air source can be used to spread dusts at very high application rates.

Sprayers
The home garden market has resulted in a substantial increase in the number of manufacturers of spraying equipment. These provide a wider choice of design and materials of construction than hitherto. The single-stroke, hand-operated sprayer (or 'Flit' gun, as it is called in the U.K.) which gives an intermittent spray, is not of interest to the professional user. The portable, hand-operated, compressed air sprayer, with integral pump, is his major tool.

Nevertheless, the very simple, hand-operated sprayer, consisting of a compression mechanism which fits into a heavy gauge polythene bottle, is useful for careful work. This holds 0·5 or 1 litre of spray (Fig. 51). Experience in temperate countries proves that where cockroach infestations have been controlled, and the chances of re-infestation are small, little insecticide need be applied to maintain conditions free of cockroaches. For this situation reliance should be placed principally on detailed inspection, rather than protective spraying to maintain freedom from infestation. The simple sprayer described is useful where small amounts of spray are needed.

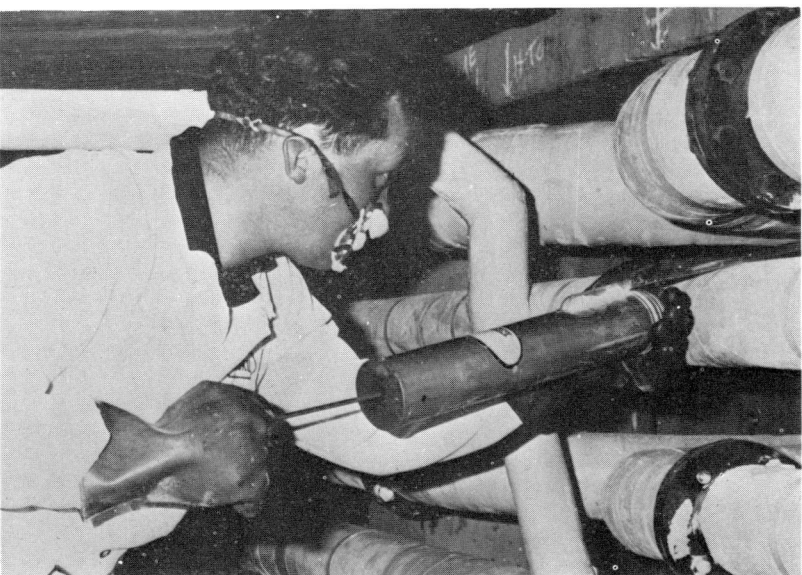

Fig. 52. Use of a piston-type dust gun ('Dobbin') to apply insecticide to crevices in insulation around steam pipes in a hospital duct. Note the use of gloves and a Martindale mouth and nose shield (U.K.).

112   THE COCKROACH

The sprayer normally used by the professional pest control operator consists of a canister of between 2 and 20 litres capacity (the 5 and 10 litre sizes are most often used) with a hand-operated plunger, or piston, which pressurises the air above the fluid level. The pressure forces the fluid *via* a hose to a lance assembly, terminating in a nozzle (Fig. 57).

In many models, the top of the plunger also acts as the carrying handle and the cap to the canister; thus the plunger assembly has to be removed to fill the

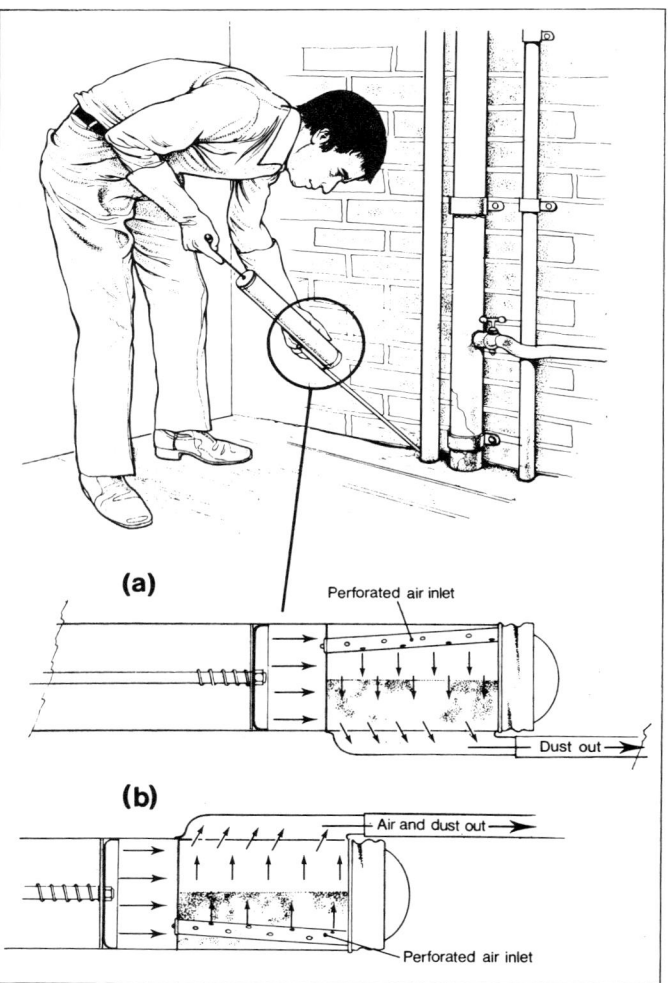

Fig. 53. Section through piston-type dust gun showing (a) delivery of a heavy deposit with little air and (b) delivery of the dust dispersed in air.

sprayer. The top of the canister is often flanged to provide a funnel for easy filling (Fig. 58). Construction is usually from galvanised (enamelled) or stainless steel, with a pressure gauge and relief valve as safety features. The lance assembly, usually of brass, contains filters, an on-off (trigger) mechanism and a nozzle to give the required spray pattern. Most nozzles allow a choice: for cockroach control a coarse wetting spray is usually required.

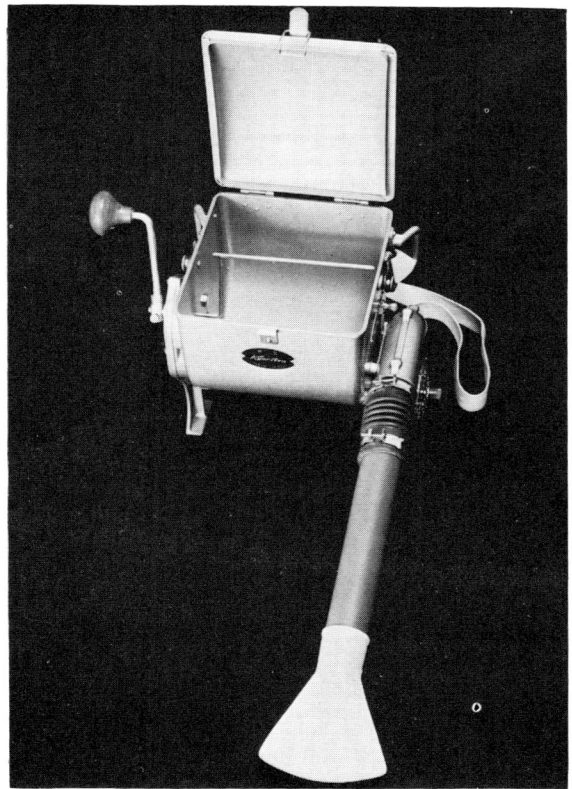

Fig. 54. The rotary 'Kyoritsu' duster which is equipped with shoulder straps, and rests on the chest. This equipment is most suitable for dust applications outdoors.

Ceramic jets are now commonly used; a 'flat fan' or 'pin stream' nozzle allows the insecticide to be directed easily into harbourages. An elliptical hole, 1·6 × 0·6 mm, is suitable for applying wettable powders; a smaller hole, 1·0 × 0·5 mm is appropriate for emulsions, oil sprays and suspension concentrates.

There are many variants to this basic design of sprayer: for example, the filler cap and piston may be separate; in some the flange of the filler cap fits inside the canister and is partly held in place by pressurisation (Fig. 59). In

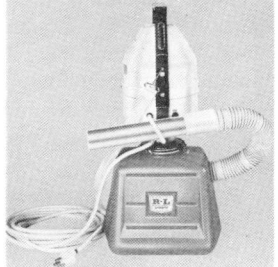

Fig. 55. Two electrically powered dust spreaders: (left) the 'Namco' insecticide blower, holding 2–3 kg of dust with a discharge volume of 3m³ of air/min. (Courtesy: Neil A. Maclean Co. Inc.); (right) the 'Atomite' with flexible discharge hose, holds 5 kg of dust and discharges at 40 kg of dust/hour over distances up to 15m. (Courtesy: Root-Lowell Corp.). Both are suitable for treatment of attics and crawl spaces.

others, the filler cap when opened, operates a release safety valve before the cap is fully removed. The hose of some is reinforced by a covering of nylon mesh. These are added safety features.

The outlet for the spray must, of course, come from the bottom of the canister, but sprayers are easier to handle and transport if the hose attachment is connected to a delivery tube at the top. Some sprayers have leak-proof

Fig. 56. Treatment outdoors with petrol-driven 'knapsack' equipment which can be used as a sprayer or duster. Knapsack refers to the method of carriage on the back.

swivel joints at this point, giving more freedom in use. There is also an attachment for the lance to the side of the canister making it easier to carry.

The most important feature of a sprayer, from the viewpoint of insect control, is what comes out of the nozzle. The higher the pressure in the canister, the smaller the size of droplet and the higher its velocity. High velocities cause

Fig. 57. Use of a hand-operated pressure sprayer. The canister is of stainless steel; the delivery hose is protected at point of attachment. The nozzle can be varied ('multee-jet') by rotating the tip to provide four different types of spray pattern (U.K.).

droplets to 'bounce' off surfaces; this makes the spray less effective and more likely to contaminate the operator.[712, 716] Nevertheless fine droplets become more widely dispersed in cockroach harbourages if forced into cracks and crevices at high pressures. If a spray is used intermittently with periods of more than a few minutes between, agitation may be needed to keep the spray content uniform.

Never fill a spray tank more than three-quarters full, or above the mark in-

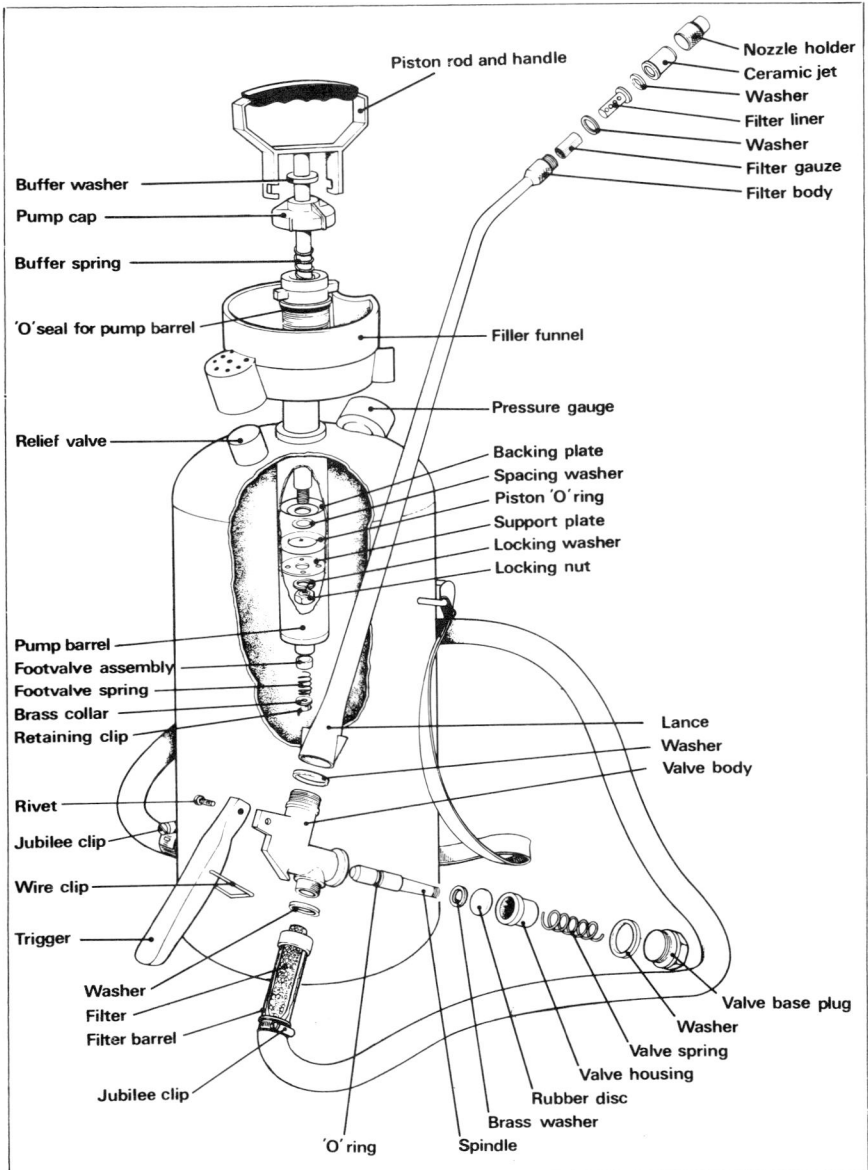

Fig. 58. Section through typical 1-gallon pressure sprayer showing component parts. Details vary with different manufacturers.

dicated. The sprayer may be pumped up more quickly when full, but this pressure is soon lost as the spray is applied. On most equipment, about 20–30 strokes of the pump gives about 30 kg (60 lbs) pressure but the normal pressure needed for routine crack and crevice treatment is no more than 3 kg/cm^2 (40 lb/in^2). This keeps spray drift to a minimum. The aim is to wet surfaces, just to the point of run-off.

Fig. 59. Top of hand-operated pressure sprayer showing safety filler cap separate from pump handle. The cap fits inside the canister and is held in place by compression. (Courtesy: Root-Lowell Corp.).

The application rates of sprays used in cockroach control vary with formulation and type of surface to which applied. Because, in practice, sprays are applied to crevices rather than to continuous surfaces the actual rates of application are difficult to measure. One litre of an oil or emulsion spray applied to point of run-off, covers about 70m^2 (= 1 gall/3,000 ft^2). Wettable powders are more often applied to rougher and more absorptive surfaces, and their application rate is usually less, about 1 litre/25m^2 (1 gall/1,000 ft^2).

Motorised equipment
Aerosol generators, mist blowers, foggers and ULV (ultra low volume) equipment (Figs. 60 & 61) are available to tempt those concerned with cockroach control that the output of spray, the number and size of droplets—particularly how small they are—and other advanced design features of the equipment, make the job easier, quicker, more effective and financially more rewarding.

Fig. 60. The Micro-gen® Chemical Dispersing Unit, model S1 W-5 which is powered by a 2·5 hp, 2-cycle engine and produces droplets in the range 1–15 μ. At recommended application rates the mist stays suspended in non-ventilated areas for 4–6 hours.

Ultra low volume spraying is a method of distributing insecticide over a *large* area, using a *small* amount of carrier. Specially developed nozzles break up the insecticide (by a cold process) into a mist of tiny droplets. Because of the small amount of liquid involved, higher than normal concentrations of insecticide are used, to ensure that treated areas receive adequate amounts.

The method was first employed for mosquito control outdoors, using concentrated insecticide sprayed from the air at no more than 6 litres/ha (½ gallon/acre). As the insecticide is undiluted, one or two droplets are sufficient to kill each insect. For agricultural use, the advantage is that in dry areas large quantities of water do not have to be carried to dilute the insecticide.[537]

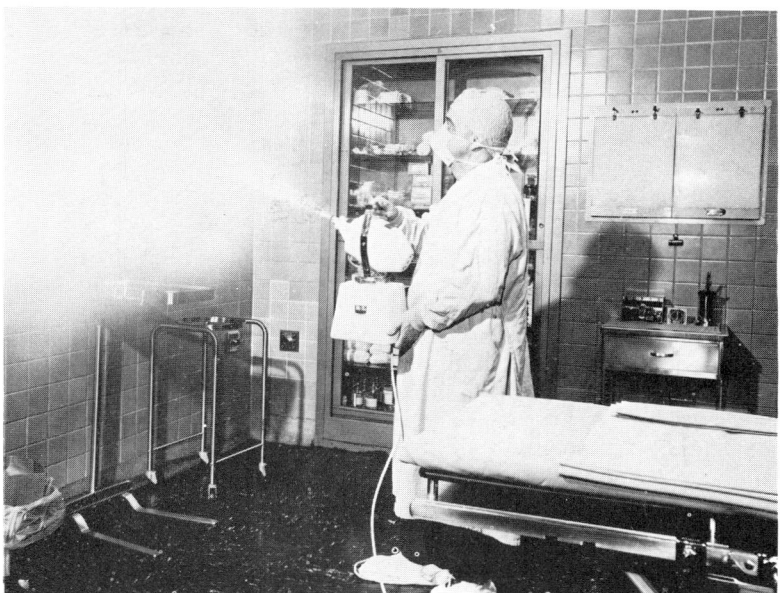

Fig. 61. Electrically powered sprayer/mist generator ('Atomist') suitable for application of insecticides, bactericides, deodorants and other products indoors and out. This equipment (like that in Fig. 60) can be used to apply high concentrations with minimum wetting of surfaces. Average particle size 17–20 μ; adjustable application rates (10–25 l/hr (1·5–5 gall/hr) over distances of 30 m. (Courtesy: Root-Lowell Corp.).

Now, with the aid of small, portable equipment, ULV has been brought indoors and advocated for cockroach control. This development has occurred principally in the United States: the equipment produces a mist, half-way between a conventional spray and a thermal fog. Technically the name ULV should only be applied to equipment giving droplets 1–30 microns in diameter. Conventional sprays deliver droplets in the range 50–100 microns and above.

Contrary to popular belief, the complexity of the equipment has little to do with practical cockroach control. A motorised sprayer, producing normal sized spray droplets does, of course, make the job of controlling cockroaches on the exposed face of a refuse tip much easier than doing it with a hand pump. Modern technology, in producing fine aerosols (droplets of 20μ and less) from pressurised packs and from powered equipment, achieves good control of flying insects: such equipment has a contribution to make in food manufacture, glasshouses and for the control of outdoor midges and mosquitoes.[693] But cockroaches do not fly—at least, not often—and rarely in situations where they are a pest! Much of the impetus in the development of mist blowers and similar equipment, has been to satisfy the demand for 'pest-free outdoor living' in yard, patio and garden where biting flies are a nuisance.

Mist blowers and ULV generators are claimed to project droplets 30m or more from the spray nozzle; wind outdoors carries these tiny droplets much further. Insecticides applied by ULV indoors are released at the rates of 0·5–1 ml/m^3 (fluid oz/1,000 ft^3). The function of the equipment is to break up a solution of insecticide into droplets of maximum efficiency, said to be about 10μ, (for mosquitoes) and to keep the particles airborne for as long as possible.[428] This increases the performance of an insecticide when used against flying insects, since the multiplicity of small droplets increases the number of points of contact.

Small droplets of insecticide impact well on the setae of exposed insects. (Fig. 62). Aerosol generators, ULV and fogging equipment can be used to treat surfaces, by directing the nozzle as if using a sprayer. Nevertheless a considerable amount of insecticide is lost in the air. However, by using a high concentration of insecticide in small droplets, active deposits can be achieved on surfaces without visible wetting. But unless the droplets are directed *into* cockroach harbourages, no greater amount of insecticide will actually make contact with the insects than by conventional spraying. Just because 1 ml of spray can, theoretically, be broken into 2 billion droplets, each only 10μ across, these small droplets are not going to find any more cockroaches to kill, unless given considerable acceleration to where the insects are. Such problems have been examined to optimise the penetration of finely atomised sprays in growing cotton: when generated by ground equipment, the sprays must be driven into the dense foliage by an air stream of optimised velocity and volume if they are to be efficient.

It is claimed that the tiny droplets produced by fogging and ULV equipment penetrate cracks and crevices and other hidden areas in which cockroaches live and are therefore effective in flushing the insects from their harbourages. This is considered useful in establishing locations where cockroaches are present. It is equally a property of hand-held aerosol packs when the insecticide is squirted directly into harbourages.

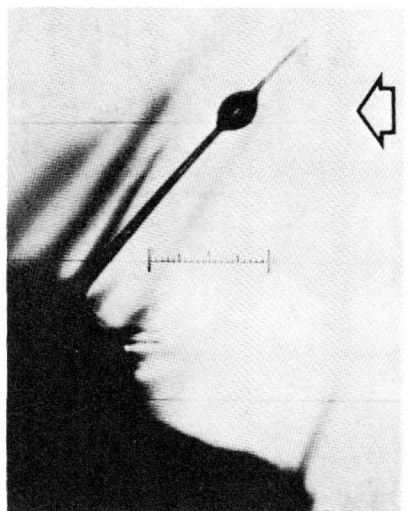 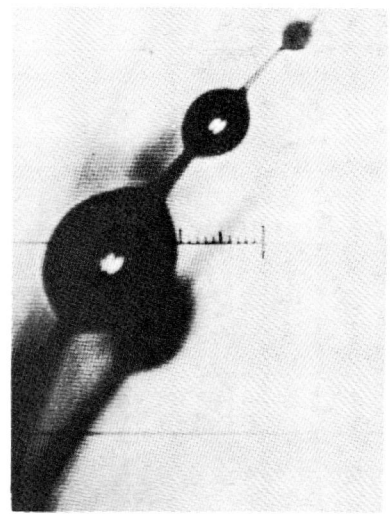

Fig. 62. Behaviour of insecticide droplets on setae of *B. germanica*: (left) impingement of 10 μ droplet; (right) additional droplets cause the first to enlarge and move towards the base of the seta and thus onto the surface of the cuticle. Scale indicates 50 μ. Arrow indicates direction of movement of aerosol. (Courtesy: Laser Holography Inc.).

Only by holding the valve of an aerosol pack close to a surface when treating it, can a reasonably good deposit of insecticide be obtained. Large pressure packs with extension nozzles are sold for this purpose (Whitmire Prescription Treatment®). The same can be achieved with hand-held pressure equipment (e.g. Hi-Fog®) which also produces a mist with droplets of small size (Fig. 63).

The use of aerosols, mists, fogs and ultra low volume sprays for cockroach control has several disadvantages:

1. most insecticide is put where it is *not* needed and very little where it is;
2. pyrethrins, some synthetic pyrethroids and dichlorvos, alone and in combination, are the only insecticides approved for use in these sprays in the U.S.A. or are likely to be approved in other countries. The pyrethrins and pyrethroids are expensive and not good cockroach killers;
3. works' personnel have to vacate treatment areas during a fog or ULV application. This applies whether the treatment is aimed at controlling the insects, or flushing them from their harbourages.

In an evaluation of the performance of the Micro-gen (S1 W-5) chemical dispersal unit (Fig. 60), for surveying for cockroach infestations, pyrethrins

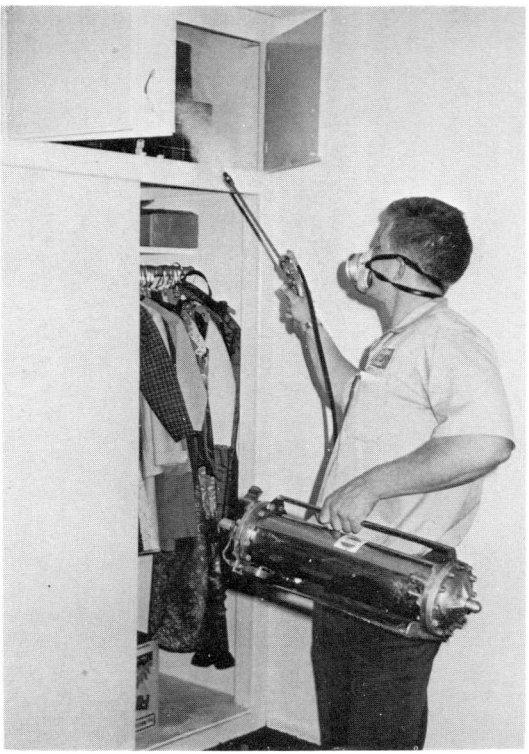

Fig. 63. High pressure aerosol generator (Hi-Fog) which can be carried in one hand and produces mist droplets of 10–15 μ. The cylinder is pressurised with nitrogen gas to 40 kg/cm^2 (600 lb/in^2) and the insecticide forced out of a nozzle at the end of a hose. In this illustration the equipment is being used to avoid excess wetting of surfaces in a clothes cupboard.

(1·3 per cent) had little effect on either German or Oriental cockroaches. Performance of the equipment was improved by using a higher content of synergised pyrethrins (6/60)—twice the recommended concentration—but German cockroaches in confined positions were little affected by the treatment. Good 'flushing' and knockdown of cockroaches was obtained when insects were in superficial harbourages (Table XIX)—where the insects were so obvious as not to need a flushing tool. The time taken to seal ventilation points, to prevent loss of fog, plus the observation period of flushing (30–45 mins) was estimated to be four times longer than was necessary with a hand-held aerosol to obtain the same results.

In other studies, ULV treatments were reported not effective in controlling cockroaches or other crawling insects, when used as the sole method of treatment.[95] 'ULV applications of synergised pyrethrins for German

Table XIX

KNOCKDOWN AND KILL (%) OF ORIENTAL COCKROACHES (NATURAL INFESTATION) AND OF GERMAN COCKROACHES (IN MESH-COVERED CONTAINERS) AFTER APPLICATION OF 60 ml OF PYRETHRINS/PIPERONYL BUTOXIDE (6/60) IN 2 MINS TO 130 m^3 BY MICRO-GEN (ULV) CHEMICAL DISPERSAL UNIT
(Cornwell, unpublished)

Time after treatment (mins)	B. orientalis (natural infestation)*		B. germanica (caged insects) Position			
	Flushing	Knockdown	1	2	3	4
1	25	0	40	0	0	0
5	97	0	100	20	0	0
10	98	3	100	20	30	10
17	98	9	100	40	30	20
30	99	50	100	50	30	10
40	99	86	100	50	30	10
50	99	87	100	30	10	10
60	99	88	100	30	30	10
Kill (24 hour)	—	20	70	10	0	0

* Harbouring in holes 10 cm deep in concrete ceiling.
1. Floor level.
2. Ceiling level.
3. Under boxes 10 cm clear of floor.
4. Within upturned box 1 m off floor.

cockroach control indicated that the concentrations needed to obtain effective control are prohibited by law. It was also found that the more complex the cockroach hiding areas, the less effective the treatments were in flushing and killing the insects.'[94] Treatments for the control of German cockroaches, in infested apartments in California, were considerably more effective when made with conventional dusting and spraying equipment (using boric acid and chlorpyrifos) than with 1·0–3·0 per cent pyrethrins applied by ULV microgeneration equipment (Table XX).

Miscellaneous equipment

The experienced pest control operator carries a number of tools and miscellaneous aids which help him in his job. These include a brush, pan and cleaning rags for removing dust and spray spillages; perhaps a brush and kettle for applying lacquer; a spatula, or knife, for applying baits and a tool kit. The latter should enable the serviceman to remove ventilator grills, open inspection plates and to drill holes in voids to insert dust. He may need to carry a ladder if treatments include attics and ceiling voids.

Care of equipment

Maintenance of sprayers is important if they are to function correctly. They are designed in the first instance to be time-saving and efficient pieces of equipment. Their good appearance should be maintained; worn or over-tightened washers and faulty shut-off valves lead to obvious drips on the client's property, which may soften floor tiles and mark polished floors. A slightly damaged hose may lead to a burst under pressure, and cause a health risk as well as extensive damage. These and other defects such as a broken carrying strap give a poor impression of a pest control operator's competence.

The rules for keeping equipment in good working order are:
1. do not abuse it;
2. clean it every day;
3. inspect it regularly, and
4. carry a stock of spare parts, especially washers.

The hole in a spray jet is carefully formed so that an even spray pattern is obtained and it is important not to damage it. If the spray is uneven, replace the jet. A blocked jet should never be cleared with a piece of wire or a pin; use an old toothbrush for the job.

The canister, the lance and jet, should always be washed out with clean water at the end of each day. Where possible, remove the pump and store the tank upside down; hang up the hose so that any remaining water can drain out.

For sprayers in regular use, follow this 10-point plan for weekly maintenance:[121]

1. inspect tank for pinholes or stripped threads;
2. clean tank with solvent, followed by detergent and hot water;
3. clean outside of tank. Repaint if necessary;
4. a drip of oil may be needed on the piston 'O' ring, but the leather cup washer (where fitted) must be oiled frequently (with oil no heavier than SAE No. 30);
5. inspect foot valve (or check valve). Replace parts if required;
6. check 'O' ring seal for pump barrel (or tank gasket, as it may be called);
7. wash hose thoroughly. This is best done after washing the tank. Refill with water and detergent, pump-up sprayer, and spray the detergent through the hose, shut-off valve and nozzle;
8. inspect hose for cuts and abrasions. Replace if necessary;
9. inspect shut-off valve and replace washer or worn parts if required;
10. remove and clean filters.

The responsibility for maintenance
Experience has shown that the best way to ensure that maintenance of equipment is carried out is to issue a sprayer to a serviceman and then make him responsible for its good working condition. The majority of men will take a pride in 'personal ownership' and ensure that their equipment never lets them down. This procedure is preferred to the 'equipment pool' from which men

TABLE XX

EFFICACY OF PYRETHRINS AND RESMETHRIN (SBP 1382) APPLIED BY A MICRO-GEN DISPERSAL UNIT (SI W-5), EITHER SEPARATELY, OR COMBINED WITH OTHER INSECTICIDES APPLIED IN CONVENTIONAL DUSTING AND SPRAYING EQUIPMENT. FOR EACH INSECTICIDE, APPLICATIONS WERE MADE IN 7 OR 8 APARTMENTS INFESTED WITH GERMAN COCKROACHES
(From Reierson[699])

Application equipment	Insecticide	No. of cockroaches trapped		Reduction (%) in one month
		Before treatment	After treatment	
Micro-gen	Pyrethrins (1%)	73	79	0
	Pyrethrins (3%)	208	153	26·4
		40	78	0
		426	520	0
	Resmethrin (3%)	78	72	7·6
Micro-gen and dust gun or sprayer	Pyrethrins (1%) then Boric acid dust	337	15	95·5
	Pyrethrins (3%) then Boric acid dust	196	4	97·9
	Pyrethrins (3%) then Chlorpyrifos spray (1%)	18	3	83·0
Dust gun or sprayer	Boric acid dust	679	4	99·4
		2,067	4	99·8
	Chlorpyrifos spray (1%)	13	3	77·0

draw a sprayer or dust gun each day; the 'pool' does not encourage pride and faults rarely get reported.

The less enthusiastic will put up with faults and inadequacies after a period of use. Herein lies the importance of regular monthly checks by a service manager: to give offenders the necessary training and to show them how to put matters right.

EQUIPMENT FOR SELF-PROTECTION

The principles of safe use of insecticides are discussed in Chapter 6. Here we consider briefly, the equipment which can protect the user against possible adverse effects. It should be stressed at the outset that the insecticides now permitted for application, by both the public and professional user, are most unlikely to cause harm, except where recommendations are ignored and gross spillage and contamination occur. Nevertheless, many servicemen appreciate the good sense of protecting themselves against the daily risks—however small—of applying insecticides, and do take notice of label recommendations about wearing gloves and mask wherever these are made.

Dress
Protection invariably means putting a barrier between the body and the chemical being used. The wearing of a dust coat or boiler suit is no hardship in temperate countries, but in the tropics, protective clothing can make the wearer unbearably hot. A study of the contamination of boiler suits worn by men spraying in roof voids shows that the areas in which most chemical is absorbed are around the cuffs, the lower legs and around the shoulders. These are the areas of the body most exposed when wearing an open-neck, sleeveless shirt, and shorts. Accordingly, even in warm climates, it is recommended that these areas be covered by normal dress, and that clothes are changed daily to prevent accumulation of pesticide on the skin. Some textiles are less absorptive than others and information on this should be sought when ordering. Protective clothing should be laundered regularly.

Where boiler suits can be worn with comfort these provide the best overall protection from chemicals. Also because the user's day clothes are being protected, there is less reluctance to 'get dirty'—an essential for good cockroach control on most industrial contracts. In some situations (basements and crawl spaces) a helmet (hard hat) should be worn (Fig. 68) and where in food manufacturing premises, or pharmaceutical works there are regulations about wearing head gear, to maintain appropriate hygiene standards, these should be observed. Many food producers insist on eliminating from processing areas, all articles which may fall and contaminate products. Thus metal fastenings (zips and press-stud closures which are detectable) are preferable to plastic buttons. The nylon hook and loop (Velcro) fastening may be specified.

Gloves
Liquids are more readily taken into the body than solids and the greatest risk occurs in handling concentrates. Without exception, gloves should be worn when diluting concentrates, making wettable powder sprays, and preferably, when applying all insecticidal liquids.

Much the same discomfort arises when wearing gloves in warm climates, as discussed above. This is why gloves of cotton and fabric are sometimes worn by service personnel, because they are cooler than neoprene or P.V.C. Fabrics which are absorptive offer no protection to the user; instead they increase the dermal risk, by holding insecticide close to the skin and by reducing the evaporation of volatile solvents. For the same reason it is not advisable to use lined gloves.

Another reason why gloves are sometimes not used is because they reduce movement of the fingers and make the handling of equipment more difficult. Undoubtedly this is so with the heavy gauge, P.V.C., gauntlet glove which provides the best possible protection, especially in preventing contamination *via* the cuff. At the other extreme the thin polyethylene (30μ thick) disposable glove (as worn by surgical staff) offers maximum dexterity, good sensitivity and adequate protection. They wear out quickly. Gloves sold for household use are flexible and provide easy hand movement, but most brands do not withstand hard wear.

Masks

All dust and spray applications put insecticide into the air, even though the amount may be small and invisible. The most rapid route of toxins into the body is *via* the lungs (Chapter 6), but inhalation can easily be prevented. To some extent the body already does this by trapping the larger particles and droplets in the nose and tracheal system, before they reach the lungs. It is therefore the smaller particles which are potentially the most damaging.

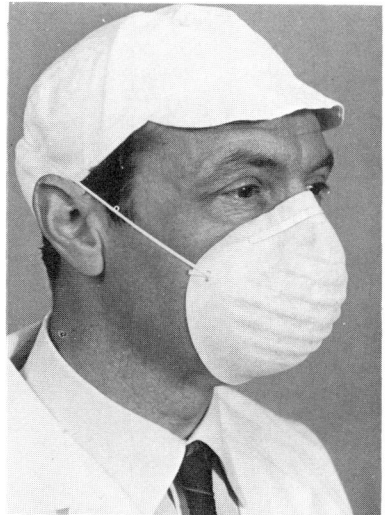 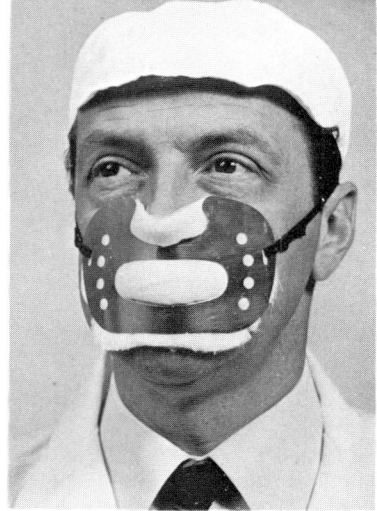

Fig. 64. Simple dust masks: (left) the preformed cup of non-woven fabric (3-M Company); (right) the Martindale mask of aluminium with a replaceable cotton pad.

The simplest form of dust mask consists of a light, moulded cup of non-woven fabric (made by 3-M Company) which fits over the nose and mouth and is held by a piece of soft metal which can be shaped to the bridge of the nose (Fig. 64 left). The Martindale dust mask is as comfortable to wear and consists of a soft, rolled aluminium former which can be moulded to the contour of the face to cover mouth and nostrils. It is fitted with replaceable cotton or polyurethane foam pads (Fig. 64 right).

Masks containing replaceable cartridges are also available to protect against dust particles and droplets. Many of those developed in the U.S. meet recommendations of the U.S. Department of Agriculture for protection against harmful dusts and sprays, and the requirements for protecting personnel in heavy engineering and other industrial locations. The Martindale, however, does not protect against extremely small toxic particles.

Light fume masks which protect against inhalation of droplets are designed to protect the user where long-term exposure to low and moderate concentrations of toxicants in the air may cause injury. They are not designed to protect against fumigants, for which specially designed gas respirators are required. Masks suitable for use against the spray droplets which may arise in cockroach control contain one or two filters (Fig. 65). General purpose safety goggles are also useful in ill-ventilated areas where dust or spray droplets may cause eye irritation.

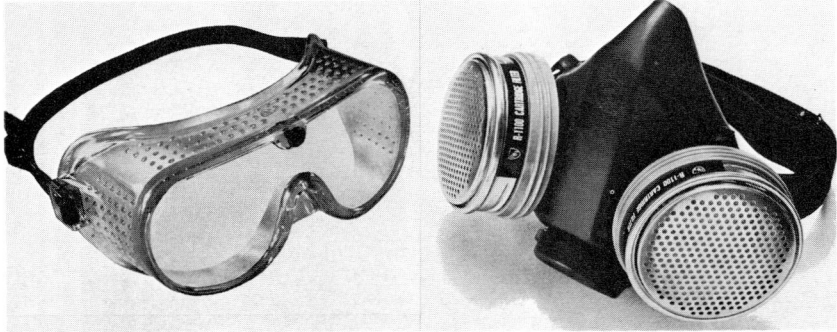

Fig. 65. Protective equipment: (left) goggles which allow spectacles to be worn; (right) light fume mask consisting of antidermatic rubber face piece covering the nose and mouth, fitted with cartridge filters to protect against fine dusts and convertible to protect against droplets by replacement with appropriate filters. (Courtesy: British American Optics).

Finally, it makes good sense for those employed in pest control to carry simple first aid kits, containing dressings, barrier and antiseptic creams to meet the normal hazards of a serviceman's job. There is no justification in service personnel having access to antidotes, e.g. atropine or protam chloride, to counter organophosphate poisoning. These should only be administered by a qualified medical practitioner.

In this chapter we have examined the equipment to apply and protect against insecticides. It is the way equipment is used—not the equipment itself—which controls insects; that needed for eliminating cockroaches is relatively simple.

The application of mists, fogs and aerosols by methods which put insecticide into the air is not appropriate for the control of insects such as cockroaches, which rarely fly, but which crawl on surfaces and live in crevices. Only where it may be difficult to treat otherwise, perhaps in sewers between manhole entrances, are such techniques applicable.

Service personnel cannot carry out their work with inadequate, or poorly maintained equipment. Inefficient equipment leads to frustation, a poor standard of workmanship and a poor impression among clients of a serviceman's competence. Regular maintenance extends the life of equipment and reduces breakdowns. Properly operating equipment reduces insecticide contamination and the possibility of damage to decorative surfaces.

Label instructions on packs of insecticides give guidance on safe application. Cockroach control requires the use of simple protective clothing and equipment to prevent insecticide getting onto and into the body. Safe use of insecticides is discussed in greater detail in the next chapter.

6

PRACTICAL SAFETY AND THE LAW

Poisoning and toxicity of insecticides: routes of entry into the body; ingestion, inhalation, dermal absorption. Measurement of toxicity; toxicity of organophosphorus and carbamate insecticides—Safety code: storage; self protection; the client and the public; the environment; the householder—Poisoning incidents: domestic animals; human poisoning; national poisons information centres; first aid—The environment and legislation: results of regulatory procedures. Approval schemes; international classification of pesticides. Crack and crevice treatment in food handling establishments—Training in health and safety.

Cockroaches and man have many physiological processes in common, with the result that they react to poisons in much the same way. The fortunate safeguard is that man is a much bigger animal, so that the amounts of insecticide required to kill are of a totally different order of magnitude. Additionally, some insecticides have a selective action in killing insects. Thus the dose, relative to body weight, to kill half a test group of rats (the animal most commonly used to estimate effects on man) is 70 times greater for malathion and 90 times greater for diazinon, when injected into the mammal, than when applied topically to some insects.[635]

Poisons cause some form of biochemical disruption: if we can prevent that occurring in man, pesticides can be used safely. Thus insecticides are safe in closed containers: it is only when they are used without care, that poisoning incidents occur. Of course, the least toxic insecticides generally present the smallest risks, but the safe use of all pesticides has much more to do with *how and where* a chemical is used than with how toxic it is.

Safe cockroach control is determined by five things:

1. the insecticide used, its formulation and toxicity;
2. where it is used, in relation to children, other animals and food;
3. how it is applied, minimising unnecessary contamination;
4. the precautions taken to prevent contact or entry into the body;
5. training of the user and his understanding of health risks.

Whether or not a particular insecticide may be used for cockroach control is decided in most countries by pesticide legislation. This regulates where and how insecticides may be applied and advises on appropriate protective clothing to be worn by the applicator. Such recommendations form part of pesticide labelling.

In this chapter we shall review briefly how poisoning of man occurs and the toxicities of different insecticides commonly used to control cockroaches. We shall examine the 'commonsense' precautions to avoid poisoning incidents and look at the functions of pesticide legislation and the way it regulates insec-

POISONING AND TOXICITY OF INSECTICIDES

Routes of entry into the body
To prevent injury from chemicals it is essential to have a clear understanding of how they enter the body. The three possible routes are:

1. through the mouth (oral): by ingestion;
2. through breathing (respiration): by inhalation;
3. through the skin: by dermal absorption.

Ingestion
Insecticide is taken into the mouth in *greatest amounts*, when drinking a liquid formulation or eating a dust, believing it to be food. Otherwise, accidental ingestion during use comes about by, (1) contaminating the hands and then bringing them in contact with the mouth during eating or smoking, (2) contaminating the face and lips and then transferring insecticide to the mouth by licking, and (3) inadvertently contaminating foods: the risk is greater with foods which are ready to eat than those processed or cooked after contamination.

Insecticide in the mouth is transferred to the stomach and then absorbed into the blood through the lining of the gut. This is not a rapid route of entry into the body; there is usually sufficient time, up to about 30 minutes, for remedial action to get rid of the toxicant by use of an emetic.

Inhalation
Fumigants (insecticides in the vapour phase) present the greatest risk of inhalation, but mists and fogs (tiny droplets) and dusts and smokes (finely divided particles) can also be taken into the body by breathing. This is especially so when insecticides are applied where there is poor ventilation.

The function of respiration is to supply oxygen to the blood through the wall of the lungs, for distribution throughout the body, and to remove carbon dioxide resulting from oxidation within the cells. The thickness of tissue between the air and the blood is only $0 \cdot 5\mu$: the exchange of gases occurs in numerous small sacs—the alveoli. The lungs fill about 80 per cent of the chest cavity; they have a capacity, in man, of about 5 litres and a respiratory surface area of 70–80m². Breathing for just a few seconds may thus bring insecticides into contact with a much greater area of absorptive surface, than by bathing in it!

The first reaction to inhaling a toxicant through the mouth or nose is often local irritation and inflammation of moist surfaces. This itself is a response of the body to an unwanted substance. Most dusts are filtered out in the nasal passages: 50 per cent of particles in the range $0 \cdot 25 – 6\mu$ are retained on moist surfaces in the respiratory tract before reaching the lungs. They are then swept back towards the mouth by a wave motion of the ciliated epithelium which lines the respiratory passages. The particles are finally cleared by coughing.

The risk of poisoning from inhalation depends on (1) the concentration of toxicant in the air, (2) its solubility in tissue fluid and the blood, (3) duration of exposure to the toxicant, (4) rate of breathing (related to degree of exercise) and (5) rate of blood circulation.

Toxic vapours, which are inhaled, become distributed throughout the whole body rapidly—within minutes—which leaves little opportunity for remedial action. Fortunately, very few of the insecticides used to control cockroaches present the risk of vapour inhalation.

Dermal absorption
The skin is a protective layer to the body and is much less reactive than the lining of the gut or of the lungs. Uptake of insecticide through the skin is therefore usually small but may extend over a number of hours. Some liquids can be absorbed, to a limited extent, through intact skin by entering the sebaceous and sweat glands. Certain solvents, chlorinated hydrocarbons, and fat soluble materials may be absorbed in this way. Absorption through lesions of the skin—cuts and abrasions—is much more rapid than through intact skin.

Brown[136] has reviewed the factors believed to affect dermal toxicity: it is not the *fact* of penetration but the *rate* of penetration which is responsible for producing undesirable effects. The following are considered important in modifying speed of movement through the skin:[137] (1) size and shape of penetrating molecule, (2) solubility characteristics of penetrant, (3) concentration of penetrant, (4) nature of vehicle (solvent or carrier), (5) temperature, (6) viscosity of the formulation, (7) ease of wetting the skin.

The greatest risks of dermal absorption arise from contaminating the skin when diluting liquid concentrates; or allowing protective clothing, contaminated by liquid insecticides, to remain in contact with the body for long periods. Dusts are less reactive on the body than liquid formulations, since to pass through the skin a toxic substance must be in solution. Systemic intoxication of the body by insecticides entering the eyes is possible, but rare. The epithelium of the eye is impervious to many substances provided it remains intact. The surface area for penetration is also very small.

There is no simple relationship between oral and dermal toxicity. Most chemicals are substantially more toxic when taken by mouth than when absorbed through the skin, although there are exceptions.

Measurement of toxicity
Toxicology is concerned with assessing the harmful effects of chemicals: the most powerful weapons of the toxicologist are experiments carried out with various animals. These provide him with the most reliable guide in judging the potential danger of a chemical to man, and hence give a measure of predictabili-

ty of its properties, but not with too great a precision. Toxicology lacks absolute exactitude in its application.[893]

The toxicity of an insecticide to man is usually measured by studies with rats. The chemical can be given in food, force fed, or may be brought in contact with the skin or inhaled. The measure of toxicity most indicative of potential risk, is the acute oral LD_{50} (50 per cent lethal dose). This is the amount of toxicant in mg per kilogram body weight of the test animal, which when given by mouth kills half the test group of laboratory rats (Table XXI).

Interest lies in the size of the single dose which causes *acute* poisoning. Most insecticides now used are degraded in the body and do not therefore accumulate (but see next section). The LD_{50} is measured with technical material: formulation and dilution reduce toxicity substantially. Considerable variations in the quoted figures occur due to differing methods of test and the different strains of rats used.

Measurement of *chronic* toxicity gives an indication of the likely long-term effects of a pesticide. This involves feeding animals (usually rats) on diets containing small amounts and observing changes in food intake, weight gain and general condition. At the end of the test (usually a minimum of 90 days) the animals may be post-mortemed to show any effects of the toxicant on body organs. Chronic toxicity is often recorded as ppm of toxicant in the diet which just produces measurable symptoms.

Those concerned with toxicology need to have information additional to the acute and chronic oral LD_{50}: namely, the sensitivity of, and the risk of poisoning *via*, the skin. There are special tests to examine eye sensitivity. Studies are often carried out on animals other than rats: e.g. on birds and fish to indicate risks to the environment—of special importance for insecticides used in agriculture.

An area of special study is the evaluation of pesticides as potential cancer-producing agents for which rats, mice, hamsters and many other animals are used.[901] Rapid test procedures, involving cultures of cells are being employed; but are not sufficiently well-developed to replace the typical 2-year feeding experiments with animals. There are some commonly used insecticides (e.g. DDT, benzene hexachloride, and chlordane) which are reported to produce tumours in the mouse but which have not been observed in rats. The most reliable information comes from case histories on exposures and symptoms in man recorded over many years. These examined retrospectively against a control group, not exposed to the toxicant, can give a direct measure of the carcinogenicity risk.

Questioning the validity of toxicity tests, Magee[516] believes it 'unlikely that any species of animal will be found which reacts to foreign chemicals in exactly the same way as Man. The decision on the safety of any chemical (pesticide, new drug, vaccine) to which Man is exposed must always depend on a very careful assessment of the balance of the possible benefits arising from use, against any possible risks'.

Toxicity of organophosphorus and carbamate insecticides

These have been selected for special comment because they are used most

TABLE XXI

ACUTE ORAL LD$_{50}$ (RAT) OF INSECTICIDES (TECHNICAL), AND CONCENTRATION OF USE OF THOSE MOST OFTEN APPLIED FOR COCKROACH CONTROL, INCLUDING SOME NOW LITTLE USED, AND NEW ONES WHICH SHOW PROMISE

(Averages from many sources including, Gaines;[320] Ben-Dyke, Sanderson & Noakes[93])

Type	Insecticide	Oral LD$_{50}$ (mg/kg)	Use concentration (per cent) by service personnel
Inorganics and miscellaneous	Phosphorus	1	1–2 (paste)
	Sodium fluoride	200	up to 50
	Thanite	1,000	2
	Silica aerogel	>3,000	100
	Boric acid	3,500	99
	Borax	5,000	100
Pyrethrins and synthetic pyrethroids	Allethrin	800	⎫
	Bioallethrin	860	⎬ 0·1–0·6
	Pyrethrins	1,500	⎭
	Resmethrin	1,700	
	Piperonyl butoxide	2,500	⎫ Synergists
	MGK 264	2,800	⎭
	Bioresmethrin	8,500	⎫ 0·1–0·6
	Tetramethrin	20,000	⎭
Organochlorine compounds	Dieldrin	60	0·5 (spray) 1 (dust)
	Lindane	125	0·5–1
	Chlordecone	125	0·125–0·25 (bait)
	DDT	250	5
	Chlordane	450	3
Organo-phosphorus compounds	Dichlorvos	70	0·5 (spray) 2 (bait)
	Chlorpyrifos	145	0·5
	Fenitrothion	325	2
	Diazinon	350	1 (spray) 2 (dust)
	Trichlorphon	500	1 (bait)
	Acephate	925	0·5–1
	Malathion	1,500	5
	Iodofenphos	2,100	1
	Chlorpyrifos methyl	2,000	(?)
Carbamate compounds	Bendiocarb	90	0·25–0·5
	Propoxur	100	1 (spray) 2 (bait)
	Dioxacarb	130	1–2
	Carbaryl	850	5

often for cockroach control. The expected results of exposure to most organophosphorus and carbamate insecticides—as measured by blood cholinesterase activity—is an initial depression of plasma cholinesterase, followed by a decrease in red blood cell cholinesterase. The rate and extent of decrease relate to the amount of insecticide absorbed. Symptoms of poisoning rarely appear until a 50 per cent depression has occurred in the normal activity. There is a large range (usually 25 per cent) in plasma and red blood cell cholinesterase determinations taken periodically from the same, normal, unexposed individual.[322] The normal range in cholinesterase activity for red blood cells is 0·39–1·02 pH/hr and for plasma 0·44–1·63 pH/hr. If the normal activity level of an individual is not known, only reductions in cholinesterase activity below 0·3 pH/hr need be regarded as significant. When an individual's level drops to less than 50 per cent of his usual value, he should be suspended from work and receive medical attention. Methods of measuring cholinesterase inhibition in human blood have been described.[234]

The depression of cholinesterase results in an increase in acetylcholine in the blood and brain: it rises 2–3 fold in the poisoning of cats and dogs. The symptoms of poisoning by organophosphorus and carbamate insecticides in man arise from parasympathetic stimulation, causing urination, defaecation, lachrymation, contraction of the pupil (myosis) and a slowing of the heart causing a drop in blood pressure. These insecticides also produce effects at neuromuscular junctions causing twitching of the muscles, leading to paralysis. In man, paralysis of the legs is associated with damage to the myelin sheath surrounding the nerves: this occurs about two weeks after poisoning but recovery is common. Demyelination of nerves does not occur with diazinon, dichlorvos and malathion.[637]

The risk from using organophosphorus insecticides is minimised by their rapid break-down in the body. But those concerned with repeated application—the day to day use of these insecticides for cockroach control—should be aware that if no precautions are taken, low levels of poisoning can have adverse effects over a long period. Use may *appear* to be without risk, since no ill-effects are experienced, and this 'confidence' leads to continued use without protective clothing, ultimately leading to a poisoning incident.

Atropine is the oldest successful antidote for treatment of poisoning by organophosphorus insecticides. It is a complex alkaloid derived from the plant, *Atropa belladonna*. Large quantities are needed in man, even in mild cases of poisoning (2 mg at half-hourly intervals) reaching 25–50 mg in a day. Pralidoxime chloride ('PAM') also reactivates cholinesterase and can be administered by tablet for mild poisoning cases.

SAFETY CODE

Everyone engaged in pest control has a responsibility to minimise risks from the use of insecticides. These risks may be to themselves, to their clients, to the public and to the environment. Risks are best reduced by *consciously creating the right condition for maximum safety*, plus the use of the least toxic materials at concentrations appropriate to greatest cost/efficiency.

Safety in the use of insecticides involves (1) safe storage and (2) careful application. Storage should be secure, tidy and with all containers properly labelled.

The safety code for pest control operators follows:

I. Storage

1. *Security*: keep all pesticides in a locked store, which is dry, cool, well-ventilated and protected from frost. Keys and duplicates should only be available to managers and service staff. Vehicles used for carrying pesticides must always be securely locked when unattended.
2. *Tidiness*: equip the store with shelving, and stillage for drums of liquid formulations. Keep stocks of concentrates at low levels to reduce the hazard from spillage. Replace tops on all containers. Dispose of redundant materials and useless equipment at regular intervals. Keep gloves, masks and other protective equipment in a separate cupboard.
3. *Labelling*: every can, canister, drum, bottle or bucket in which pesticides are kept, or from which they are dispensed, must carry an appropriate label. It is an offence in many countries to carry or dispense insecticides from unlabelled containers. Do not dispense into containers normally used for drinks or food.

II. Self protection

4. *Observe all precautions*: restrict application to the concentration and the pest for which the insecticide is approved. Do not mix different insecticides together, except in instances where this is recommended or permitted (e.g. the addition of pyrethrins for quick knockdown).
5. *Keep insecticides away from the mouth*: do not smoke, eat or drink whilst working. Wash hands and exposed skin before meals and after work.
6. *Wear protective clothing*: do not allow familiarity with insecticides to encourage careless application; wear a dust coat, overalls, or boiler suit as appropriate; wear gloves when dispensing and applying liquid formulations, otherwise use barrier cream on the hands; wear the appropriate mask to prevent inhalation of dust, spray droplets or insecticide vapour (see Chapter 5).
7. *Remove contamination*: wash off immediately any pesticide which contaminates the body, particularly the eyes. Change contaminated clothing.
8. *Improve the working environment*: ensure adequate ventilation when working in confined spaces; extinguish all naked flames, pilot lights, electric fires, and other heating appliances when using flammable liquids.
9. *First aid*: acquire a practical working knowledge of what to do in emergencies.

III. Protection of the client and the public

10. *Act responsibly*: do not give any pesticide to others for their own use.

11. *Note likely hazards to children and animals*: ensure that insecticide application does not present a risk to children; recommend to the client that he keeps domestic pets out of sprayed areas for 24 hours.

12. *Protect foods*: do not use insecticides in kitchens such that cooking utensils, work surfaces and foods become contaminated. Cover with a sheet (see Fig. 139 left), or confine application to pyrethrins or approved pyrethroids.

IV. Protection of the environment

13. *Observe proper disposal of toxic waste*: do not wash out sprayers so that residues may contaminate soil or water. If necessary, collect residues for approved methods of disposal. Burn, bury or crush pesticide containers if not returnable to supplier: this is to prevent re-use for other purposes.

14. *Make others aware of hazard*: for vehicles carrying pesticides, ensure that there is a list displaying contents and appropriate action in the event of a major accident.

15. *Know the answers*: in the rare event of serious spillage, ensure that you know what to do.

The householder

For those not routinely involved in pest control, the rules for safety in the home are simpler. These acknowledge that young children (usually under 5 years old), are most likely to suffer pesticide poisoning: and that most incidents, irrespective of age, are caused by thoughtless actions and can be prevented.

The householder's code follows.

1. Keep all pesticides, especially when NOT in use, out of reach of children.
2. DO NOT store pesticides under the sink, in the pantry or near food or medicines.
3. DO NOT transfer a pesticide into another container from the one in which it was purchased.
4. ALWAYS READ AND FOLLOW LABEL INSTRUCTIONS.
5. ALWAYS replace the lid (cap) firmly.
6. Do not save or re-use pesticide containers for any purpose: dispose of them safely.

POISONING INCIDENTS

In cases of suspected poisoning, the first question to be asked by a medical practitioner is: to what pesticide did the person have access and how much did he eat? If the answer is not available then there is no single observation by which poisoning from whatever cause can be recognised in man or domestic animals. Clinical signs can never be conclusive on their own. For example, a virus disease in a dog may produce exactly the same symptoms—convulsions—as DDT. Thus most of the information on which judgement, and thus medical treatment has to be made, is circumstantial.

You cannot ask an analyst to search for a poison in the body unless you have some evidence to suggest what he looks for.[189] Moreover, if there is evidence to show that very little pesticide may have been eaten, keeping a patient under observation, or just making him sick, may be more appropriate than treatment involving antidotes. With domestic animals too, it may be better merely to observe, than institute any unnecessary treatment.[769]

Domestic animals
Poisoning in domestic animals is much more common than is generally realised, but it is rarely possible for vets to diagnose poisoning with any certainty. There is a tendency to think that the *only* poisons to which cats and dogs get access are pesticides. Circumstantial evidence in the home is valuable in establishing the cause of an animal's malaise: enquiries should be made about the type of food eaten or any unusual substance, with which the pet may have had contact. Experience suggests that the poisoning of an animal usually arises from toxic substances in its housing, food, the medicines it is given or its immediate environment. Asking the owner the following type of questions may help establish the possible cause of poisoning.[190]

> Has any painting been carried out recently?
> Has any new domestic cleaner been used?
> Has there been any change in the diet?
> Could the animal have eaten a poisoned rodent,
>   or eaten the poison bait put down for rodents?
> Has the animal been given any proprietary medicine,
>   or any analgesic or tranquilizer intended for human use?
> Has any spraying been carried out in the garden?
> Has any bait been put down for slugs?

The answer to one of these questions may solve the problem more quickly than a scientific investigation of the animal. Cats are more likely than dogs to be poisoned by insecticides; cats have the habit of washing themselves thoroughly, when poisons on the coat or paws are rapidly transferred to the mouth.

Most poisoning incidents among animals occur through accident or negligence by the owners. The frequency with which pets are brought to vets in the U.K. (all ailments) is:

> dogs: 60 per cent
> cats: 35 per cent
> rabbits: 1·5 per cent
> budgerigars: 1·5 per cent
> hamsters, parrots and other pets: 0·5 per cent each.

The paper, 'Pesticides and domestic animals' by Stevenson and Carter[769] reviews the special problems facing veterinary surgeons who have to treat a pet with suspected pesticide poisoning. It provides sources of information from which he may obtain advice on treatment.

Human poisoning
Many materials which we eat, drink, or come into contact with, are poisonous: we can drown in water, be poisoned by alcohol or motor car exhaust fumes. It is the *dose* which determines whether the substance may be detrimental. Pesticides safety precautions aim to protect domestic animals, children and the user himself from contact with a dose liable to cause poisoning.

Two types of poisoning may occur:

1. *acute poisoning*, involving a large amount of toxicant at one time, as occurs in suicide attempts, or occasionally in accidents among production workers and those engaged in formulating;
2. *sub-acute or chronic poisoning*, as is more common among manufacturing personnel and users of pesticides, especially those engaged in day-to-day service application. It is rarely possible to isolate the real cause of a health disorder among pest control operators because of the large number of substances, other than active ingredients, which make up the formulations used.

For the consumer of contaminated food, the risk presented by a pesticide is also at two levels: the *one* occasion where a person accidentally eats contaminated produce; and the *repeated* consumption, over a longer term, of food containing only traces of active material.

Incidents involving humans (excluding the use of fumigants) arise most often from:

1. pesticides being put in containers normally used for soft drinks or foods, thereby being mistaken for edible materials;
2. children, through inquisitiveness, getting into cupboards, unlocked stores and vehicles where pesticides are kept;
3. preparations of service companies getting into the wrong hands.

National Poisons Information Centres
Centres established in a number of countries provide an information service on poisoning. In the United States 'Poisons Control Centres' were set up in local hospitals with the help of the U.S. Public Health Service, Dept. of Health, Education and Welfare, and are generally distributed in almost every part of that country. They contain staff members specially trained to treat cases of poisoning.

In the U.K., enquiries to Poisons Centres are permitted only from doctors and not the general public. Their function is to maintain an index of substances in common use (medical, industrial, agricultural and household) and the compositions of proprietary products. Details are also kept of toxicity and corrective measures to be taken in cases of poisoning.

In 1974, 19,133 emergency calls were made to the London National Poisons Information Centre: 9,979 concerned medicines and drugs, 5,738 involved household products and only 250 implicated pesticides. This total included 9 deaths due to unintentional self-poisoning.[354]

Among incidents of 'occupational disease'[28] in the State of California in 1968 there were 834 reports attributable to pesticides and other agricultural chemicals (excluding eye conditions). The rate for agricultural service workers (5·7 per 1,000) was higher than for structural pest control operators (4·3 per 1,000—cf. 3·2 per 1,000 in 1967). In 1969, poisoning among pest control personnel working in buildings numbered 8 cases only, compared with a continuing high level (5·9 per 1,000) among agricultural service workers.[31] No deaths occurred from the occupational use of pesticides.

The rate of deaths from pesticides in the U.S.A. is 0·65 per million people.[414,415] Where pesticides can be proven responsible for poisoning, about 99 per cent of cases recover.[413] These figures are approximate, because of many unrecorded incidents. Employers of pest control personnel are now required to maintain a log of occupational injuries and illnesses and must report within 48 hours any fatality or hospitalisation.[908]

First aid
The following is a simple guide to first aid for pest control personnel:

1. Do not panic.
2. Do not leave an unconscious victim.
3. Call doctor: advise him of the suspected poison: show him the container.
4. Loosen all tight clothing.
5. Keep victim warm.
6. Arrange transport to hospital.

I. *To counter pesticide taken by mouth*
(a) If oils, solvents or other petroleum products are the main ingredients; DO NOT INDUCE VOMITING.
(b) If victim is unconscious; GIVE NOTHING BY MOUTH.
(c) If unconscious and not breathing; loosen clothing at neck and begin artificial respiration AT ONCE.
(d) If unconscious but breathing; ensure that airway is not obstructed by any vomited material draining into the lungs. TURN AND KEEP VICTIM ON ONE SIDE.
(e) If conscious and breathing and
  (i) if oils and solvents have been ingested: give milk or tablespoon of vegetable oil;
  (ii) if other substances have been ingested: make victim vomit and dilute any remaining poison in the gut with 2–3 glasses of water or other bland fluid. (Keep vomit and send to hospital with patient.)

II. *To counter pesticide contaminating the skin*
(a) Remove victim from spillage.
(b) If unconscious: see I. b-d (above).
(c) Check for eye contamination: wash immediately and thoroughly with water under a running tap and cover with sterile pad.
(d) Otherwise, remove contaminated clothing and wash skin.

III. *To counter pesticide (vapour, dust or droplets) breathed in*
(a) Remove victim from further exposure to toxicant.
(b) If unconscious: see I. b-d (above).
(c) Keep patient rested: do not allow casualty to walk.
(d) Send any vomited material with patient to hospital and keep under medical supervision for 48 hours.

Experience suggests that routine tests for blood cholinesterase, on service staff using organophosphorus and carbamate insecticides to control insects indoors, are not necessary. Neither is there a need for them to carry antidotes: these should be administered only by physicians.

THE ENVIRONMENT AND LEGISLATION

An insignificantly small amount of insecticide is used to control cockroaches, compared with applications in agriculture, forestry and for killing animal parasites. Outdoor applications need very large quantities, and soil, air and water may become contaminated. The great increase in the use of agricultural chemicals has undoubtedly enabled us to grow more food, but it has also produced an emotional atmosphere of alarm among those concerned with the environment.

The current anxiety over pollution is centred on our use of synthetic chemicals (pesticides, food additives and new drugs). Examples of these anxieties arise from the recent banning of cyclamates (sugar substitutes), the extensive restrictions on certain insecticides (the organochlorines) and the tragedy of thalidomide (a sedative with teratogenic effects).

The prolonged litigation over the detrimental effects on the environment, by the use of DDT for insect control, was closed in the United States on June 14th, 1972 by a statement from the Environmental Protection Agency that general use of this insecticide would cease at December 31st, 1973. Applications then existing were for insect control in agriculture: for treating cotton, peanuts and soybeans. DDT has not been used in the U.S.A. to control public health pests for some time, and this suspension is now world wide.

The detailed discussion on DDT reflected undesirably on the properties of other insecticides: sweeping conclusions were being made about the broad pesticide groupings: strong pressures were exerted for a cessation in the use of all organochlorine insecticides. Decisions taken were irrational, without reference to the biological performance of individual insecticides. The effects of a pesticide on the environment cannot be predicted with certainty on the basis of its chemical affinity to other known pesticides or to its known action on just one or two animal species.[163] However, in 1959, O'Brien declared the objective: 'to make it possible eventually to outlaw the use of all insecticides that are hazardous to man or livestock'.[635]

The results of regulatory procedures
Procedures which have been developed to regulate the use of pesticides include (1) *monitoring* the levels of contamination in food and the environment,

and (2) *legislative schemes* to control the use of existing chemicals, and to approve the introduction of new ones. The same procedures which regulate the use of pesticides outdoors also control their use indoors. Thus, for those concerned with cockroach control, it may appear that over-elaborate procedures are brought to bear on a relatively small problem.

The approval of pesticides is confused by each country having its own regulatory scheme. Some, for example, may allow a dozen or more insecticides for cockroach control, but others only one or two. This implies different standards of assessment and a different technical judgement of what constitutes 'practical risk'. Some governments are concerned solely with approval for health and safety, but others have extended their role to testing the efficacy of pesticides. For the latter it is not unusual to have to submit samples for test in one country, although the insecticide may already have been approved for use in others.

Nevertheless, the measures taken in different countries have produced a number of desired results:

1. *A reduction in the levels of pesticide in home-produced food and international trade*

In 1965 the Ministry of Technology in the U.K. set up the Pesticide Residue Analysis Information Service to act as a communication and information service for those concerned about the possible ill-effects of pesticides. A study of organochlorine insecticides in foods (cereals, nuts, pulses and animal feeds) imported into Britain between July 1969–71 showed that BHC was present in all but 4 of the 248 samples, but only 10 per cent exceeded 0·5 mg/kg. DDT occurred in 39 per cent of samples.[427] In the U.S.A. there was strong evidence that essentially all storage of DDT in persons not occupationally exposed, resulted from the presence of the insecticide in the diet, especially, but not exclusively, in fats of animal orgin. Thus meatless meals in a cafeteria catering for meat abstainers contained only one quarter of the DDT in meals of ordinary restaurants. In vegetarians the amount of DDT in the body was 2·3 ppm compared with 4·9 in the general population.[416] Considerable scientific evidence now shows that the amounts of insecticide in food, resulting from recommended applications to crops, and during storage, is of minute proportions and is unlikely to have adverse effects on human health. Levels of organochlorine insecticides in the average British diet are now 'consistently low'[1].

2. *A reduction in the levels of pesticide in the environment with less harmful effects on wildlife*

Since restrictions were introduced in 1964, to limit the use of certain organochlorine insecticides, no widespread damage to wildlife has occurred in the U.K. The presence of organochlorine insecticides in rain water collected at 7 widely scattered sites in the U.K. suggested that contamination was a world wide phenomenon.[783] Some pesticides have an adverse effect on stream life at as low as 1 part/billion.[625] The effects of insecticides and photo-isomers on fresh water animals has been carefully studied.[323] Moore[584] has reviewed the experience in the development, control and safe use of pesticides in the U.K. in respect of wildlife.

3. *A better understanding of the potential risks of applying pesticides*

Valuable information has become available by improvements in analytical techniques (Fig. 66), and through financial support for studies into the behaviour of insecticides in the environment. Our ability to sample insecticides in food, soil, water and air,[571] and to measure minute amounts of pesticides has made striking advances since their presence was first questioned. However, our ability to detect and measure them should not be interpreted to mean that their presence necessarily makes them undesirable.

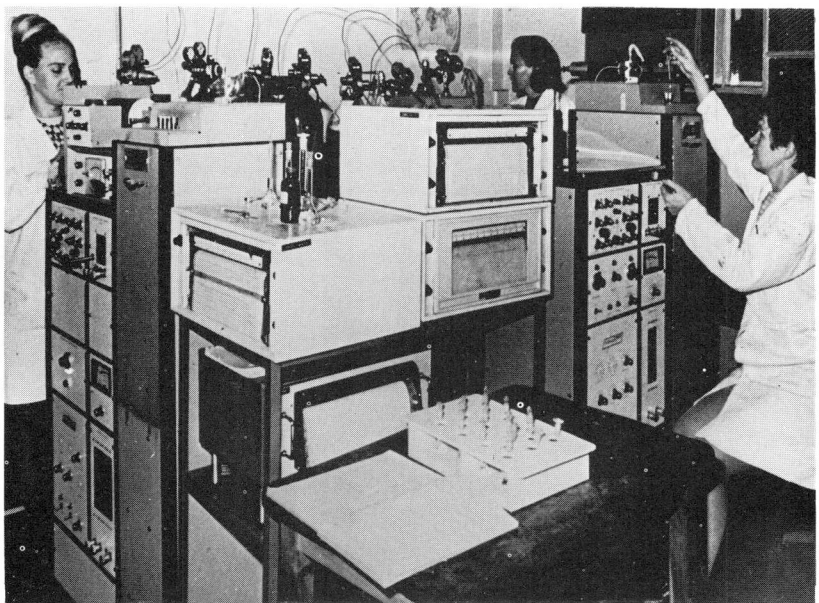

Fig. 66. Determination of pesticide residues by gas chromatography. (Courtesy: South African Bureau of Standards, Pretoria, S. Africa).

4. *Fewer incidents of poisoning among those involved in the routine application of pesticides*

Risks have been identified and there is now greater awareness of simple safety procedures (see p. 135).

5. *Fewer poisoning incidents among the general public by restrictions in the type of chemical to which they have access and improvements in labelling and packaging*

Considerable effort has been made by industry and government to make the domestic user of pesticides aware of 'directions for use' and 'precautionary measures'. The information on labels is carefully vetted and has a purpose.

Referring in 1960 to the safety record of the newer organophosphorus insecticides in the U.S. and other technically advanced countries, Hayes[412] states: 'in countries where labelling is poor or where illiteracy or irresponsibility tend to vitiate labelling, hundreds of cases of human poisoning have occurred'. Even where there is a high level of literacy it is regrettable that people still do not read labels.[822]

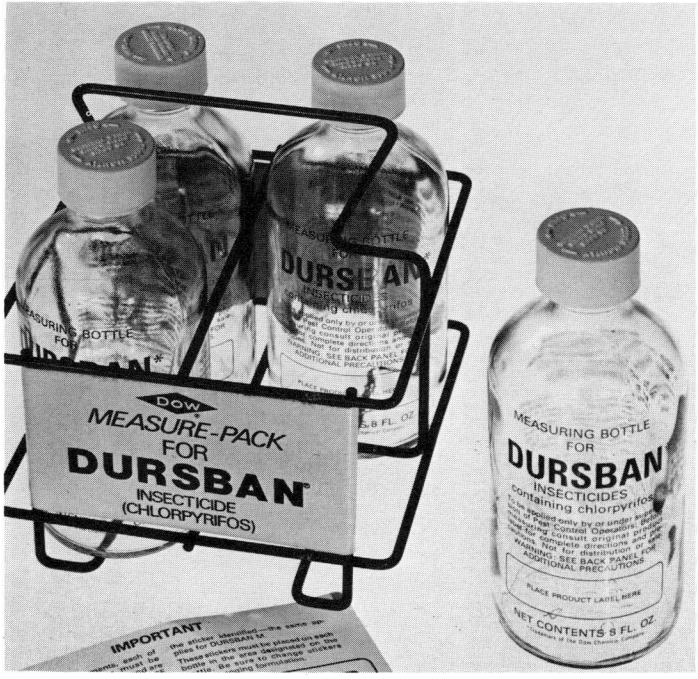

Fig. 67. 'Measure-pack' of Dursban* emulsion concentrate consisting of four calibrated bottles and a carrying rack to hold about a week's supply. Designed to help accurate dilution and reduce spillage and waste. (*Registered trade mark: photograph courtesy of Dow Chem. Co.).

Measurement of the required amount of emulsion concentrate for dilution in water is difficult when only small amounts of spray are prepared. Manufacturers of insecticide have contributed to improvements in safety by providing their products in calibrated containers (Fig. 67) and in sachet unit packs (see Fig. 153).

6. *The introduction of training and certification procedures for those involved in the day to day use of pesticides*

Training has become an important requirement for all those engaged in pest control. The larger servicing companies have developed and run their own programmes for many years. The smaller ones can benefit from membership of trade associations,[224] such as the N.P.C.A., which issues technical releases, training programmes and a certification manual. Some universities (e.g. Pennsylvania State University) run correspondence courses on 'Household pests and their control' and undertake courses for workers employed in pest control companies and municipal health departments. Specially prepared question and answer manuals for pesticide applicators[312] can do much to encourage 'do it yourself' tuition. Training tends to eliminate the 'less able' and probably the 'less well disciplined'.

In contrast to these advantages gained from regulating the use of pesticides, legislative schemes may also have had some undesirable effects:

1. *Reduced technical innovation and development*
Controls have tended to depress the number of new pesticides brought forward for approval. The amount of toxicological data and trials information now needed to support applications, constitutes a severe financial burden upon manufacturers and users. As a result, the long term development of potentially useful compounds is probably suffering.[52, 748]

2. *Reduced efficacy in use*
The determination by governments to make pesticides safe in use may in some circumstances have made them useless. This can occur through fear of exceeding the tolerances demanded in foods, resulting in under-dosing.

3. *The danger of 'environmental jitters'*
It is difficult to separate the effects of legislation, from the effects on public awareness, of excessive publicity about pesticides. In retrospect, there has probably been a great deal of harm done by unnecessary public alarm. 'Curbs on panic and pesticides',[32] 'How to ban chemicals without scaring people'[38] and 'Ecological whodunnits'[441] are examples of attempts to analyse environmental problems rationally and produce a steadying influence.

It is characteristic of man's thinking that he looks for a man-made cause for events which affect him. 'Scientists who encourage public fears on the basis of ill-digested evidence constitute a serious environmental problem': the recent call to ban fluorocarbon aerosol propellants may prove to be an example. 'People worry about the dangers we may bring upon ourselves if God is not in ultimate charge. The latest, new ethic is that we should not take a risk if harmful effects are predicted scientifically, unless we can *disprove* the theory in question'.[738] Precipitate and quite unwarranted action is therefore sometimes taken.*

---

* The notice of intent (July 29th, 1975) by the Environmental Protection Agency of the United States to suspend the manufacture of chlordane and heptachlor for most agricultural and household uses may illustrate this. Chlordane may continue to be manufactured, formulated and sold under current labels until such time as the suspension hearing ends and E.P.A. rules that current labels are suspended. The notice was made because of new evidence that these two insecticides cause 'significant numbers of cancers in test animals'. The compounds were thus cited as being an 'imminent human cancer hazard'.[53] The applications under attack include the use of dust and sprays of chlordane against cockroaches. On December 24th, registrations of chlordane for use by pest control operators (except against subterranean termites) were suspended, but allowed supplies in stock to be used up.[905]

Approval schemes

In the next few pages we shall examine the approval schemes of different countries to highlight the differences, especially between that of the U.K. and the U.S.A. In principle, approval schemes require the co-operation of notifiers (manufacturers and users) to submit data designed to provide evidence that a product will, (1) be effective against the pest(s) ultimately specified on the label and (2) not injure man, domestic animals or wildlife[809] when used as directed. Many schemes require the submission of a draft label, which incorporates the proposed claims for the product and precautionary measures. Bates[82] has reviewed the regulations in a number of countries.

The U.K. scheme

This is known as the Pesticides Safety Precautions Scheme and is unique in many ways.[653,654,655] It is concerned entirely with safety and not biological efficacy. Control is achieved through a voluntary procedure, agreed between Government departments and the major chemical and servicing companies, coupled with a minor amount of legislation for certain chemicals or their use.

The scheme (previously the Notification of Pesticides Scheme) came into effect 20 years ago. It puts the onus upon the notifier of a new chemical (or new use) to provide all the information required to satisfy government departments that the chemical will be safe when used in the way for which clearance is sought. Industrial representatives do not normally attend meetings of the approval committees, but may be invited to do so. The working group—the scientific sub-committee—is composed entirely of scientists chosen for their expert knowledge of some aspect of pesticides. The amicable relationship which exists between most companies and the secretariat has greatly eased the problem on the part of the notifier as to the nature of the information likely to be required for a particular chemical.

Recommendations for safe use are eventually agreed with the notifier, and made available to all those interested in the safe use of pesticides, in the U.K. and overseas. The advice which is to appear on the label is given in three sections concerning risks to operator, consumer and wildlife.

The great advantage of the U.K. scheme lies in its flexibility: especially the provision of a 'quick clearance' procedure for the least toxic substances, which enables the more formal committees to be by-passed. The methods used for assessing risks have proved satisfactory, in that incidents have not occurred from the correct use of cleared chemicals—in fact the scheme has provided an enviable record of safety. The integration of the U.K. scheme into those of the European Economic Community (Common Market) is currently being worked upon. It is to be hoped that the voluntary nature will be retained, especially as the scheme survived becoming a mandatory licencing procedure in 1968.[29,639]

Countries of the European Economic Community

These countries perhaps more than others, have recognised the need for international uniformity in classifying the risks to health from pesticide formulations. Accordingly, the committee of Ministers of the Council of Europe set out such proposals in a resolution in 1971. They recognised how dangers to health might arise, from accidental ingestion, skin or eye contact and by inhalation, in single and repeated incidents. Their efforts were directed towards:

1. Providing a toxicity classification based on the oral LD_{50} (rat) (Class I—greatest risk; Class IV—minimal risk).
2. The use of this classification to label products appropriately, with 'risk symbols' and standard safety phrases.
3. The use of this classification to recommend certain restrictions on sale and purchase of products.

The House of Lords (U.K.) Select Committee on the European Community has criticised the draft directives on pesticides and has suggested retention of the U.K.'s present voluntary system 'whose standards are higher and whose use has been largely successful'.[54] The new symbols indicating relative toxicity could be superimposed on present U.K. labels if believed desirable.

Pesticide regulations in Finland

Scandinavian countries have generally exercised more stringent measures than their European neighbours. Finland has had a Pesticide Act since 1952. The Act prescribes that before pesticides are marketed they must be tested by the Plant Protection Service, and given a 'sales licence'. Then, when more thorough testing is completed the pack may carry a triangular seal indicating that the product has been 'officially inspected and approved'. These two stages of approval are not unlike the stages of approval in the U.K.: 'limited clearance', 'provisional' and then 'full commercial clearance'.

The Finnish Plant Protection Service is responsible for carrying out biological, chemical and physical testing of pesticides and for supervising their production, importation and sale: also for monitoring the regulations concerning toxicity and for ensuring that use occurs only as indicated on the label. A Pesticide Statute provides for the setting of tolerances of pesticides in foods.

The main purpose of the Act is to safeguard users against ineffective products: for agricultural pesticides, approval may take 2–3 years, or longer for new compounds. Nearly 60 per cent of the preparations notified up to 1967 were insecticides and about 50 per cent of products were officially approved.[525]

Legislation in the U.S.A.

Policing is fundamental to the control of pesticides by legislation. It has to cover, among other things, the taking of samples for analysis, of products approved for use or sale, and checking that label instructions are observed. The purpose of the label has been described by Aubin,[63] and the usual information required (on pesticide labels) is given in Table XXII. Pesticide legislation thereby incurs the cost of monitoring for infringement and the need to impose penalties—which may mean revoking a licence to manufacture. On the other hand, compulsory safeguards allay the fears of the public and politicians, whether those fears are real or supposed.

In the United States, pesticides have been regulated, until recently, by registration under the Federal Insecticide, Fungicide and Rodenticide Act 1947 (F.I.F.R.A.), administered by the Pesticides Regulations Divison of the U.S. Department of Agriculture. Additionally, all States have introduced their own laws to regulate the introduction, shipment and use of pesticides. The purpose has been to assure, (1) efficacy against the pest designated on the label when the pesticide is used as directed; (2) that precautions for safe use

TABLE XXII

AN EXAMPLE OF LABEL INFORMATION. NOT ALL THESE PHRASES WOULD NECESSARILY APPEAR ON ONE PRODUCT

Information	Examples
Product name	— trade name, e.g. Baygon
Active ingredient content	— usually per cent by weight and by chemical name
Inert ingredients	— solvents (petroleum distillate per cent) or emulsifiers per cent
Type of formulation	— E = emulsifiable concentrate
	— S = solution; to be mixed with oil
Numbers after brand name	— Diazinon 4 = 4 lb active ingredient per gallon of formulation
Limitation on use	— by qualified pest control operators only
	— not for resale
Intended use	— for control of specified crawling insects: cockroaches, silverfish...
Cautionary phrase or symbol	— 'danger', 'warning', 'caution' or skull and crossbones relating to degree of toxicity
Dilution rate	— add 2 oz of concentrate to 1 gall of water...
Directions for use	— method of application: apply as residual spray to cracks and crevices where...
	— ensure adequate ventilation when...
Restrictions	— do not use as space spray
Warning	— protective clothing: wear gloves and light fume mask when...
	— do not contaminate food...
Disposal of container	— wash out thoroughly and bury...
Wildlife advice	— highly toxic to bees
Symptoms of poisoning	— headache, nausea, excessive sweating, blurred vision...
First aid advice	— if swallowed, induce vomitting by...
Guide to doctor	— this product contains an anticholinesterase...
	— atropine sulphate is antidotal (quantity)
Further advice from	— manufacturer's address and telephone number
	— local national poisons information centre

are adequately stated and (3) protection is given to people and animals who may consume produce on which pesticide has been used. Official tolerances are set by the Federal Food and Drug Administration: these state how much pesticide, if any, may be safely left on treated crops. A report prepared by the National Academy of Sciences, of the National Research Council of America, concluded in 1969 that adequate protection of man's food and health was being afforded by the system of controls then operating.[33]

Fig. 68. Cockroach control brings personnel in contact with health risks from chemicals (insecticides), physical risks (in cluttered industrial locations) and the risk of fire (if flammable solvents are used). The U.K. Health and Safety at Work Act (1975) makes safety the joint responsibility of employer and employee (U.K.).

On 2nd December 1970, the Pesticides Regulation Division became part of the Environmental Protection Agency, to which many of the pesticide activities of other Departments (Health, Education and Welfare) were also transferred.[47] Additionally new legislation was imposed to ensure that the label was read and obeyed. Under the old law, a pesticide needed to be registered so that a manufacturer could sell it: there was no law to control how it was used. Now it is illegal to use any registered pesticide in a manner inconsistent with labelling. EPA's duties are 'to establish and enforce standards, monitor and analyse the environment, conduct research and demonstrations to assist State and local government pollution control programmes'.[518]

This legislation (Public Law 92–516: the Federal Environmental Pesticide Control Act, 1972) gives the EPA new powers to regulate the use of pesticides: use involves acts of application, storage and disposal and some examples of misuse, leading to penalty warnings, have been detailed.[906] The EPA has assigned pesticides into different categories: 'general'—for use by the public, and 'restricted'—for use by trained personnel only.[420] The American pest control industry is in agreement with the principle that people should be trained, examined for their ability, and licensed to use restricted pesticides. Thus a new requirement for the industry is certification, by the State, of pesticide applicators. This must become effective by October 1976: results of early certification exams have shown that experience is a primary factor in acquiring adequate knowledge.[56]

The guidelines for obtaining data on a new pesticide submitted for registration to the EPA indicate a deeper probing into its chemical and biological properties than previously. The view has been taken that if the same were applied to pesticides already registered 'it could, conceivably result in the publishing of data not previously required for registration, perhaps casting doubts on the suitability of certain currently used products for continued use'.[41] In 1971, there were 35,000 registered pesticide products in the United States and up to 600 new applications for registration or renewals being made each week.

In 1975, there was an undercurrent of feeling within the American pest control industry, that the EPA had become more concerned with the activities of policing and enforcing pesticide control, 'than providing a sensible protection of the environment and nation's needs'.[55] Concern was being expressed at the way the Federal Insecticide, Fungicide and Rodenticide Act was being implemented. The NPCA expressed the view that the Federal Environmental Protection Agency had greatly exceeded many of the powers Congress intended it should have under the Federal Environmental Pesticide Control Act of 1972 (i.e. amended F.I.F.R.A.). This apparent antagonism now current in the U.S.A. between industry and government is mentioned simply to illustrate the inevitable difference between a scheme (as in the U.K.) in which equal partners—industry and Government— are committed to the success of pesticide regulation, and one of enforcement, which inevitably puts one party in the right and the other in the wrong.

International classification of pesticides
Attempts have been made to introduce a standard classification of pesticides: WHO have put forward tentative proposals based on *hazard* rather than *toxicity*. It recognises the greater risks that may arise when formulations are

used as liquids compared with dusts. The purpose is the same as in countries who have already adopted classification and registration procedures, *viz.* to advise the purchaser or user, through labelling, of the degree of risk by symbols and/or phases, and to advise safety procedures necessary in use. Also, from an international viewpoint, to be able to advise those concerned with the transport of chemicals, the likely hazards and precautions necessary.

International agreement on the technical meanings of toxicity ratings such as 'slightly', 'moderately', 'highly' and 'extremely hazardous' would certainly be valuable (Table XXIII).

TABLE XXIII

W.H.O. TENTATIVE CLASSIFICATION OF SOLID AND LIQUID FORMULATIONS OF PESTICIDES BY HAZARD
(From Papworth[656])

Class	$LD_{50}(rat)$ mg/kg			
	Oral		Dermal	
	Solids	Liquids	Solids	Liquids
Extremely hazardous	5 or less	20 or less	10 or less	40 or less
Highly hazardous	5–50	20–200	10–100	40–400
Moderately hazardous	50–500	200–2,000	100–1,000	400–4,000
Slightly hazardous	Over 500	Over 2,000	Over 1,000	Over 4,000

Crack and crevice treatment in food handling establishments

Insecticides are often applied for the control of cockroaches in kitchens and pantries. Food and cooking utensils should be removed before treatment, but this may not always be done. Accordingly, Wright and Jackson[868] treated cabinets, containing china saucers, with sprays of diazinon (1 per cent), chlordane (2 per cent) and propoxur (1 per cent) and measured insecticidal residues over the following four weeks. Significant residues were present in the 24 hours after spraying but then became much reduced. The maximum amount of insecticide likely to be ingested by man, from the upper surfaces of kitchen utensils within a few hours of treatment, is one thousandth of the acute oral LD_{50} dose to rats. Believing that such residues might cause harm, many countries have banned the use of residual insecticides in food areas.

In 1973 a code of practice for insect control in food handling establishments came into effect in the U.S.A., known as 'crack and crevice treatment'. This was introduced by the Environmental Protection Agency allowing the application of certain named insecticides as sprays, dusts or baits, but in such a way as to minimise the possibility of contaminating food.[238] It did not apply to private dwellings but to treatment in commercial buildings in which food is 'held, processed, prepared and/or served'. Previous to this, the EPA had made the ruling that *no residual insecticides* could be used in food processing areas. This was found to be too restrictive and limited industry's ability to provide effective services.

Crack and crevice treatment is not yet allowed in meat and poultry works, but some of the insecticides permitted for crack and crevice use may be applied there.

Insecticides permitted for treatment of cracks and crevices are:

borax	fenthion
boric acid	propoxur
carbaryl	malathion
chlordane*	MGK-264 (synergist)
chlorpyrifos	piperonyl butoxide (synergist)
dichlorvos	pyrethrins
trichlorphon	fenchlorphos (=ronnel)
diazinon	silica aerogel
bendiocarb (as from 3rd October 1975)	

Applications to the EPA are invited for the approval of additional residual insecticides, data being required to indicate that the insecticide does not increase the amount detectable in foods, above an acceptable level (tolerance).

Crack and crevice treatment means the careful and precise application of small amounts of insecticide into those harbourages in which pests hide, or through which they may enter a building. It is more precise than 'spot treatment' defined under American legislation as application to an area not exceeding 0.2 m^2. Examples of cracks and crevices are the expansion joints between different materials of construction and between equipment and floors. The treatment should be carried out to minimise as far as practical any contamination of exposed areas of floors or walls. It must not lead to contamination of food, containers or food-contacting surfaces. Incidental to ensuring safety in application, the confining of residuals to insect harbourages should reduce substantially the amount of insecticide used (cf. indiscriminate treatment of exposed surfaces) and greatly increase the cost/efficiency of cockroach control.

TRAINING IN HEALTH AND SAFETY

Training is a necessary requisite in any profession. Berns[98] has reviewed the history of the structural pest control industry in the United States (beginning in 1842) up to the present: 'the techniques employed by controllers of the day (the exterminating and fumigating industry) were as jealously guarded as they were crude. There seems to have been a pervading fear in the early firms that imparting too much knowledge to recent trainees was inherently a dangerous thing'. In contrast, the importance and current urgency of pest control certification in the U.S. has caused 'an overnight awareness of interest to sweep over the industry'. Rodgers[707] has described the policy and practice of training within Rentokil.

* Currently subject to investigation (see footnote to p. 145).

Fig. 69. Training and certification of pest control personnel is now a legal requirement for servicing companies in the U.S.A. Intensive training is provided by companies who supply products for pest control use. This is a school for supervisors held by Southern Mill Creek Products Company, Inc., Florida, U.S.A. (Courtesy: S.M.C.P.).

In the U.K., it is a requirement under the Health and Safety at Work Act, 1975 that pest control servicing companies advise and train their employees to recognise the risks to themselves in the application of pesticides: to make available all necessary safety equipment and for the pest control operator to recognise his responsibility in observing safety procedures.

The equivalent Act in the U.S.A. is the Federal Occupational Safety and Health Act, 1971 which is concerned with the issue and use of protective clothing and the safety of working conditions. Many of the regulations of this Act relate to pest control in their provision for safety equipment.[772] In the year ending 30th June 1975, OSHA recorded 26 violations of the Act by pest control operators.[907]

Training in pest control (Fig. 69) goes far beyond an appreciation of practical health and safety. Personnel engaged in applying insecticides must have a detailed understanding of:

1. the biology of the pests and their habits in situations where infestations occur;
2. the properties and performance of insecticide formulations used, and
3. the health risks and legal aspects of pest control chemicals.

But, most importantly, pest control operators should be trained in effective and safe application techniques. There is nothing difficult about applying pesticides safely, providing conditions likely to cause hazard are anticipated and there is a common-sense understanding of the following:

1. *the situations which present the greatest risks*: e.g. the extensive spillage and contamination of the body which may occur during dilution of concentrates. Make up sprays just before use, but if this is done on the client's premises, select an area where spillage can easily be removed;
2. *the ease with which the body can be protected from contamination*: gloves, masks and other protective equipment offer effective safeguards—but only if worn (Fig. 68). There is nothing effeminate about wishing to protect oneself from poisoning. Equally there is no place for bravado in the handling and use of pesticides;
3. *the responsibility to the public*: the object is not to take risks, but to keep food free of infestation and from pest control chemicals. If in doubt—don't;
4. *the proper use of equipment*: insecticide sprays must be applied at low pressures—to avoid spattering and 'bounce-back'—and just to the point of run off. A pin stream spray is needed to conform with the objectives of 'crack and crevice treatment' in the United States;
5. *the inquisitiveness of children*: their frequent involvement with pesticides has no malicious intent: most poisoning incidents occur among young children who are curious and meddlesome, and who cannot read. Remove all possible opportunity. It is the parents who ultimately suffer most;
6. *the need to maintain equipment in perfect working order*: most incidents with pesticides can be anticipated; very few are unforeseen. Well-maintained equipment allows controlled application: it puts insecticides only where they are wanted.

The reaction of service personnel to health and safety is often nonchalant, because:

1. they are not always trained to be systematic in their methods of working, and a minority are careless;
2. they see most systems as a form of disciplinary procedure (red tape) which create 'extra work';
3. they regard the observance of safety precautions as a requirement for others, but not themselves (lip service), especially when little is done to ensure observance;
4. few senior personnel have the ability or are prepared to spend the time necessary to meet the high standards required in operating safety precautions;
5. there may occasionally be a conflict of interests between the need to obtain immediately profitable business and the allocation of sufficient time to ensure that treatment is done efficiently with adequate attention to safety. There is no argument: application to ensure safety over-rides all other considerations.

The responsibility for training is often given to those 'longest in the business' and therefore to those believed most experienced—but often only experienced in the short cuts and methods of 10 and 20 years ago.

Legislation makes increasing demands on a new attitude to the use of pesticides: accidents are few when the individual knows and follows the proper procedures. The responsibility for training[311] must fall upon those aware of present-day needs and who welcome the requirements for certification in raising the status of the pest control industry and the professional ability of its members.

Safety is almost entirely a matter of discipline: its observance is largely a problem of supervision.

Training in health and safety is developing the intelligence and common sense to observe what is on the label.

Fig. 70. Pest cockroaches are often introduced into buildings with imported bananas. In the exporting countries, cockroaches infest the ground litter (top) and are carried with the harvested crop to the packing stations. The use of polythene sheeting to protect the bunches of bananas from leaf slashing probably encourages the transfer of cockroaches with the crop, to the packing sheds (below) (St. Lucia, West Indies).

7

REPELLENTS AND INSECTICIDE REPELLENCY

Repellents: Tabutrex; MGK R-11; MGK R-55; MGK R-874—Possible applications for repellents: bananas; movement of people and clothing; packaging materials; beer and soft drink industries. Avoidance and lethal action of U.V. light—Repellency of insecticides: the cockroach and its need for harbourage; harbourage and the pest control operator; the insecticide and its effect on cockroaches—Tests of insecticide repellency: partial treatment of harbourages; recovery as part of the avoidance process; wall void tests; simple and complex environments; treatment of previously occupied harbourages; use of pyrethrins as a flushing agent.

A pest problem, in a restricted area, may be reduced with chemicals which cause insects to positively dislike their food, host, or the environment in which they live. Insect control can thus, to some degree, be achieved without resorting to the use of insecticides. Repellents, which do *not* kill, are used mainly against disease-carrying insects which bite animals and man. Diethyl toluamide (DET) and dimethyl phthalate (DIMP) are well-known examples of the older type mosquito repellents, commonly incorporated into creams and lotions for personal protection.

There are a number of compounds which when applied to cardboard and other wrapping materials repel cockroaches for limited periods. These might be used, to advantage, to reduce the chances of cockroaches being carried into buildings and establishing infestations. The pyrethrins and some synthetic pyrethroids, as coatings to kraft paper, perform well for about 9 months in keeping stored food pests out of bags of wheat flour.[426]

Many of the insecticides commonly used to treat cockroach harbourages are repellent. The pyrethrins and to a lesser extent propoxur have a 'flushing action' and because they cause insects to move, they are helpful in locating harbourages during inspections for cockroach infestation. The repellency of other insecticides—although by no means so well marked—is a disadvantage. The objective, when eradicating cockroach infestations, is to obtain maximum pick-up of the toxicant by the insect. If the dust or spray repels cockroaches from their harbourages, the chances of successful contact with the insect are reduced.

In the first part of this chapter we shall look at some of the ways in which cockroaches are inadvertently carried in trade: at the way cartons and other wrapping materials become carriers of cockroaches and how this might be reduced by using repellent chemicals. Ultraviolet radiation has also been shown to have repellent effects. In the second part we shall examine the avoidance reaction of cockroaches to insecticides and how this reduces their performance.

Fig. 71. The use of shipping containers has speeded up the loading and unloading of vessels but cross-infestation of commodities can easily occur: (above) cockroaches are readily carried in the packing material for heavy engineering components (Hamburg, West Germany); (below) cockroaches on crates of rough wood delivered to a warehouse (Netherlands).

REPELLENTS

Methods of cockroach control which provide an alternative to the use of insecticides are of value where food may be contaminated. Though repellents may never completely stop the development of infestations, they may be helpful in preventing transport of cockroaches into uninfested areas. Some logical uses for repellents could be on cardboard cartons for food, soft drinks, or on beer crates; in juke boxes and other coin-operated machines.[343]

The early requirement of a good repellent was effectiveness against mosquitoes and other flies, but in 1952 Goodhue and Tissol[345] reported on ten of the best cockroach repellents chosen from over 200 compounds tested against *P. americana*. Burden & Eastin[146] suggest that a good repellent could be used either alone, or in conjunction with an insecticide as a residual treatment in business establishments or homes. However, if the repellent is intended to keep cockroaches away, combination with an insecticide would seem to the author to have little purpose. Examples of problems which might be overcome with the help of repellents are examined in detail on pages 161 to 168.

No country other than the United States has become much involved in the development of repellents, but renewed interest has recently been expressed there, probably because of restrictions in the use of insecticides near food. Much of the initial development of cockroach repellents was carried out in the U.S.A. by McLaughlin Gormley King Co. (MGK).

More recently, eleven of 31 compounds, related to cyanoacetic acid, have shown outstanding to excellent properties against four pest cockroaches. These repellents are easily synthesised from commercially available starting materials.[736] Among a further 30 compounds, chemically similar and tested to show the effect of structure on activity, there is no clear indication of what type of compound provides best results.[737] In a search among another group of compounds (heterocyclic amines), eleven are reported highly effective against the four cockroach species.[544] Diethylnonamide is claimed to be 100 per cent repellent.[545] In laboratory tests of alkane sulphonamides against *B. germanica*, one gave 97–100 per cent protection for two weeks and 82 per cent for a further week, equal to fencholic acid used as a standard.[546] Among chemicals examined in Canada, related to thujic acid (one of many compounds extractable from western red cedar, *Thuja plicata*), the diethylamide of the acid is 1·3 times as repellent as fencholic acid to *B. germanica*, and has the same repellency to *P. americana*.[896]

The following four cockroaches repellents (Tabutrex, R-11, R-55 and R-874), have been available for use by industry for about 20 years.

Tabutrex®
This is the trade mark of Glenn Chemical Co. for the cockroach repellent, dibutyl succinate, developed by Consolidated Research and Testing Laboratories, Chicago and introduced in 1955. It is formulated as an emulsion concentrate (20 per cent) and an oil spray (2 per cent). The oral LD_{50} (rat) is 8,000 mg/kg.

In trials of performance in an infested basement, treated surfaces remained 100 per cent repellent to *B. germanica* for three weeks. In laboratory tests, cockroaches were repelled from wooden beverage crates for 15 weeks.[13] A shorter performance of one week only, was reported by Burden & Eastin.[146]

MGK R-11

This insect repellent (hexahydrodibenzofurancarboxaldehyde = butadiene-furfural copolymer) was introduced by Phillips Petroleum Co. in 1949. It is a pale yellow liquid with a fruity odour, miscible with many organic solvents and compatible with most insecticides.

The repellent properties of R-11 against *B. germanica* were described in 1952. It is reported to improve the performance of sprays by acting as an agitator.[344] A typical formulation contains 0·075 per cent pyrethrins, 0·15 per cent piperonyl butoxide and 1 per cent R-11. For treating the inside of cartons, R-11 is applied as a 1 per cent emulsion incorporating 2 per cent of the synergist MGK 264. On beer cartons, R-11 gave better than 80 per cent repellency for 2 months, reducing to 60 per cent at 6 months.[520]

MGK R-11 is now used in pet sprays and in repellents for personal use. Of four materials evaluated for their odour, this repellent was the most pleasant.[680] The acute oral LD_{50} (rat) is 2,500 mg/kg; the dermal LD_{50} is more than 2,000 mg/kg.

MGK R-55

This repellent (tert-butylsulphenyl dimethyl dithiocarbamate) has been promoted by McLaughlin Gormley King Co. (and Phillips Petroleum Co.) as a rodent and insect repellent. It was the best of compounds examined by Burden & Eastin,[146] repelling *B. germanica* from treated cartons for 90 days (at 2 per cent) and for 63 days (at 1 per cent). DeLong[229] suggested it might be applied to basement and storage areas to give residual control. Experience by the author suggests, however, that this would create odour problems. It is more odorous and toxic than MGK R-11 and MGK R-874.

MGK R-874

The insect repellency of this compound (2-hydroxyethyl n-octyl sulphide) was discovered in 1955 by Phillips Petroleum Co. It is a light amber liquid with a mild mercaptan-like odour, slightly soluble in water but miscible with most organic solvents. It is used with MGK 264, a pyrethrins synergist (see p. 240). Formulations commercially available are: an emulsion concentrate, diluted with water and applied at 1–5 per cent by automatic spraying equipment, and an oil solution used at 1g active material/m². It is compatible with chlordane and many organophosphorus insecticides.

R-874 tested against German cockroaches by the 'slanting card test' (see p. 497 and Table XXIV) is marginally more effective than R-55 and lasts twice as long as R-11.[344] Toxicity is low: the acute oral LD_{50} (rat) is 8,530 mg/kg; dermal LD_{50} 13,590 mg/kg. Use of this repellent near food should not create a health risk.

TABLE XXIV

TYPICAL RESULTS FOR REPELLENTS, OBTAINED BY THE 'SLANTING CARD TEST'

(From Goodhue[343])

Interval (hours)	Number of cockroaches on cards treated with repellent (0·22 mg/cm^2)			
	R-11	R-55	R-874	Control
1	43	2	0	215
2	40	6	0	209
3	41	2	0	205
4	26	4	0	201
5	29	2	0	187
6	29	7	0	232
Total	208	23	0	1,249
% repellency	83	98	100	

POSSIBLE APPLICATIONS FOR REPELLENTS

There are many instances in international trade, of consignments infested with insects, passing between countries. The presence of insects is often quite fortuitous: for example, the infestation of cockroaches in a cargo of plywood, mentioned in the Chapter on *Movement* in Vol. I. The packaging of goods rather than the contents often acts as the 'carrier'.

Because of trade agreements between member countries of the European Economic Community (Common Market) the autobahns of West Germany have become the road links for trade between member countries. Some of the vehicles now using these routes are performing the function of the earlier 'box cars' of the United States railways—but in Europe, regularly carrying goods and possibly insects across national boundaries.

At a more local level there are many instances of goods highly attractive to cockroaches, passing from manufacturer to wholesaler, to supermarket and then into the home—again with the risk of carrying live cockroaches and their egg cases. The following are some examples of both the international and local problem.

Bananas

In temperate climates one of the routes by which pest cockroaches (e.g. *Periplaneta*) and some other cockroaches (e.g. *Panchlora viridis* and *Henschoutedenia* spp.) are introduced into port warehouses, and thence to hotels and restaurants, is in consignments of bananas. In banana plantations there is a thick ground litter of fallen leaves, moist beneath, and rich in insect life, including outdoor-living cockroaches (Fig. 70). These find harbourage in the 'hands' of bananas, between the individual fruits.

In some countries (e.g. St. Lucia) the fruit is enclosed in a large polythene bag while still ripening on the plant. This prevents leaves blown by the wind from damaging the fruit and reducing its quality. Any cockroaches which may be present between the bananas are hence carried within the bags to the packing station where the bags are removed.

Fig. 72. Cockroaches in holds, discharged with cargoes are always a threat to other commodities in dockside warehouses, especially where there are harbourages in the building structure. Here American cockroaches infested the flooring, built out on stanchions over the water (Paramaribo, Suriname).

The boxes in which bananas are packed provide harbourage and the commodity, a source of food. Treatment with a cockroach repellent could help discourage insects from accompanying the shipment. Quite apart from bananas, the treatment of shipping containers (Figs. 71 & 72) is suggested by Burden & Eastin[146] as an application for repellents which would be 'particularly helpful'.

Movement of people and clothing

There is an enormous gulf between the standards of living of peoples in various parts of the world; there are different attitudes towards pests in the home and the needs for pest control. Standards appear lowest in warm climates where insect multiplication is greatest: in tropical countries and in lower class properties, people co-exist with cockroaches. However, in the homes of the middle and upper classes, considerable effort is usually made to obtain freedom from cockroach infestation since a stigma is attached to having these insects in the home.

There are many families in the higher income levels that rely on the labour force of those from impoverished homes, to provide a 'daily help', as a nanny for the children, someone to do the laundry, and for carrying out other menial tasks. Unwittingly this labour force carries with it, on clothes and in personal effects, live cockroaches and egg cases into otherwise insect-free homes. People provide the means for reinfestation.

The problem is perhaps more severe for industry. As a further example from America, much of the work force in the southern states is coloured and there is a low standard of living among this and some sections of the white population. Efforts in these underprivileged homes to obtain freedom from cockroaches is by use of retail products: control is invariably inadequate and sanitation is often not a serious consideration.

Each day, hundreds of thousands of people from cockroach-infested homes go to work in different food industries—businesses highly susceptible to infestation. Whether or not this work force provides the continuing and serious threat of cockroaches ultimately finding their way into food processing areas, depends much on the standards of hygiene adopted by factory management. This applies throughout the works and especially in the staff cloakrooms (Fig. 73). Here sandwiches are eaten during lunch breaks and food residues and other accumulations—like soft drink cartons—occur in the bottom of lockers. For those companies which make a conscious effort to achieve freedom from cockroaches, the use of work's clothing, treated with cockroach repellent, may help minimise the risk of cockroaches reaching production areas.

The problem of cockroaches carried in clothing also occurs in laundries and dry cleaners. Incoming clothing, often tightly bundled, may easily bring cockroaches with it (Fig. 74). There, the environment of the steam laundry encourages the insects to become established, especially in the harbourage provided by broken insulation around steam pipes and in the cavities of modern presses. The motors of washing machines generate heat; floors are invariably wet, and drains and gulleys provide locations favoured by the larger pest cockroaches for daytime harbourage.

Clothes, when ready for return to customers premises, may carry cockroaches or egg cases in the folds of the material or in the polythene wraps, especially if finished items have been awaiting collection in infested laundries for some days. Laundries and dry cleaners should preferably be free of infestation—achieved by frequent use of insecticides—but this is not easy in warm climates. Enclosure of finished items in wraps treated with cockroach repellent would at least reduce the movement of cockroaches when articles are despatched or collected.

Packaging materials

A striking example of the ease with which cockroaches become introduced and distributed within buildings is provided by the infestations which occur in restaurants mounted high up on structures built primarily as communications towers (Fig. 75). The insects are most probably carried in foods or wrapping materials. Infestations known to develop on oil rigs at sea can only have arisen again through transfer of cockroaches by man.

Most shops keep stocks of paper bags, some now replaced by plastic. But in a room at the back of a supermarket, or other store, it is not unusual to find a cupboard or drawer of paper bags or cartons, perhaps forgotten, or for some other reason not used. If the building contains cockroaches it is here that their liking for paper and cardboard, as harbourage, is best demonstrated (Fig. 76). The greatest problem occurs with corrugated cardboard. A box of this material contains many thousands of tiny harbourages for cockroaches, quite apart from the folds and flaps of the box and the paper label on the top stuck down with casein glue (Fig. 77).

Whenever cardboard and other wrapping materials are brought into the production area of a factory there is a risk of introducing cockroaches (Fig. 78). Where have the cartons been previously? Are the premises of the supplier free of infestation? What else was being carried with the cartons in the vehicle at the time of delivery? This subject is of vital importance to those concerned with food packaging. Not only may cartons bring cockroaches into production areas, but foods packed directly into infested cartons may cause a purchaser to claim damages for food contamination (Figs. 79 & 80).

Fig. 73. Changing rooms in manufacturing premises are commonly used for lunch breaks (left), where cockroaches live on food residues and other debris in the bottom of lockers (slaughterhouse, Texas, U.S.A.). Unhygienic conditions in staff cloakrooms (above left) and inadequately maintained toilets (right) encourage rapid development of infestations (food factory, Barbados).

The beer and soft drink industries

The cockroach repellent, MGK-874 has been developed for commercial application to help solve 'the age-old problem of the spread of roaches through free rides in beverage cases'. It is applied by automatic equipment in beverage packing plants and is claimed to reduce drastically the number of insects returning to plants in empty crates. Additionally it protects the wholesaler, retailer and ultimate consumer by making the crates or cartons unattractive to cockroaches throughout the distribution chain.

Most soft drink plants already exercise a high degree of sanitation: it is essential to their reputation. The use of a repellent does not eliminate the cockroach problem at a bottling plant but it is claimed to make the 'rest of the sanitation problem easier to solve'.

Wooden beverage crates have in large measure given way to moulded plastic designs, with fewer crevices in which insects may hide: but the change is by no means universal. Returnable bottles have to a large extent also been replaced by throw-away cans. Apart from beverage crates providing harbourage, most soft drink containers invariably become contaminated with highly attractive syrup. More importantly, beers and soft drinks are dis-

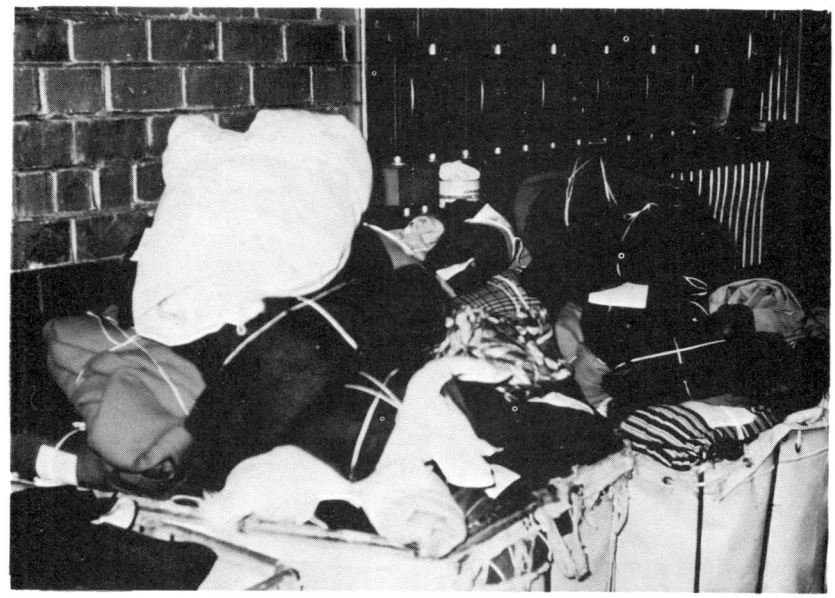

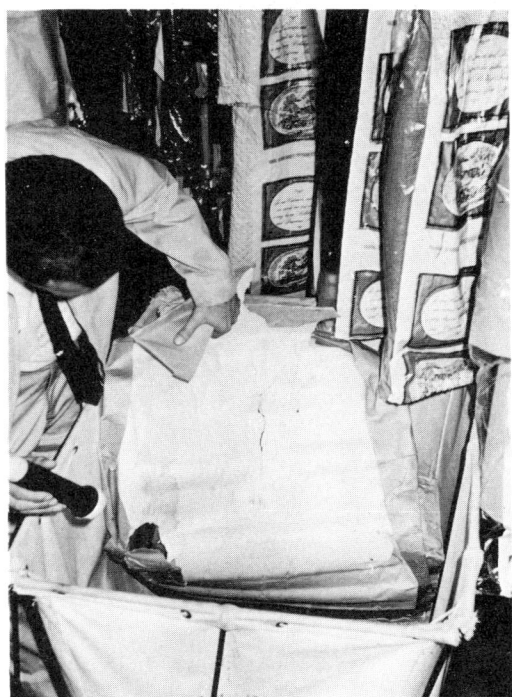

Fig. 74. Laundries and dry cleaners are especially prone to infestations of cockroaches and other insects: (top left) incoming bundles of clothes are very likely to introduce cockroaches from infested homes; (bottom left) steam presses and associated pipe work provide ideal harbourage, humidity and warmth; (right) cockroaches may become established in the trolleys used to convey laundry, or may be returned to customers with finished items under polythene wraps (Atlanta, U.S.A.).

tributed to a wide range of outlets—supermarkets, hotels, restaurants, public houses, cinemas and theatres, clubs and public halls—which are all prone to infestation.

It is unusual for crates to be returned to distributors immediately; often, bottles are transferred to vending machines and other automatic dispensers (Fig. 81). 'Empties' returned to these dispensers (there is often a rack for them at the side) are not rinsed and hence cockroaches find them attractive: more than 200 young nymphs in a single bottle has been known.[229] Cockroaches find harbourages in the machines—in the casings of the motors which circulate the coolant. Adjacent vending machines containing confectionery may also become infested.

Meanwhile the crates may collect debris or may be stacked one upon another to provide excellent dark harbourage, perhaps in the store room of an infested motel or night club. Alternatively, crates awaiting collection may be

stored against the outside wall of the local shop where outdoor cockroaches find them attractive (Fig. 82).

During return to the distributor, any cockroaches being carried may take up residence in the fabric of the vehicle. Or at the distributors, they enter the washing and sterilising plant and, left overnight, have an opportunity to find warm and wet areas in which to become established. The hollow stanchions of roller conveyors provide harbourage by day: the processing floors, unless scrupulously cleaned, provide food at night (Fig. 83).

Recommendations were made in 1960 to a large modern brewery in the U.S.A. to help solve its problem with cockroaches.[520] Included were the use of a repellent formulation on containers and insecticidal treatment of trucks and around loading platforms. The cost at that time was 0·6 cents per carton. The recommendations were put into action and results reported as successful: automatic equipment mounted over conveyor belts allows rapid treatment of thousands of beverage cases, with refilling of the spray reservoirs only once each day.

Fig. 75. Evidence of the way man assists in the transport of cockroaches is provided by infestations which develop in such structures as (left) restaurants on the top of telecommunication towers (Stuttgart, Germany) and (right) oil drilling platforms at sea (North Sea, east of Aberdeen, Scotland).

Avoidance and lethal action of U.V. light

A number of studies have been made of the effects on cockroaches (*P. americana*) of ultra-violet, germicidal light. Adult males are repelled and killed—emissions of 254 nm are the most lethal[202]—and fertility may be reduced. Young nymphs are more susceptible than older stages and the growth of survivors is suppressed.[841] Insects about to moult are the most sensitive.

The most detailed study of the avoidance by American cockroaches of U.V. light has been carried out by Gingrich.[334] He has also examined the effects on the hypodermis and the cuticle of newly-moulted American cockroaches.[335] Given the chance to escape into darkness, first and second stage nymphs avoid U.V. light (86 per cent of emission at 254 nm). This happens more quickly than their avoidance of white fluorescent light and of 'filtered' light (from which 99·9 per cent of U.V. below 345 nm is removed).

When cockroaches get older their avoidance of light is so rapid that differences between stages become undetectable. The avoidance of U.V. affects survival: the quicker the insects move away from the U.V. the longer they live. When the choice is between U.V. and white light of equal intensities (compared with U.V., dark or 'filtered' light), death occurs quickly because the insects fail to shun the U.V.: they have no preferred alternative (Table XXV).

TABLE XXV

TIME FOR 50% KILL (LT_{50}) OF NYMPHAL STAGES OF *P. AMERICANA* GIVEN A CHOICE OF REMAINING EXPOSED TO ULTRA VIOLET LIGHT OR MOVING INTO DARKNESS, 'FILTERED LIGHT' OR WHITE LIGHT
(From Gingrich[334])

Nymphal stage	LT_{50} (hours)		
	U.V. versus dark	U.V. versus 'filtered' light	U.V. versus white light
I	30	10	<24
II	50	29	25
III	53	20	18
IV	447	58	—
V	303	230	145
VI & VII	2,400	1,780	23
VIII & IX	—	1,660	53

U.V. light = 86% of emission at 254 nm.
'Filtered light' = 99·9% of U.V. below 345 nm removed.
White light = 15 W Cool-White® fluorescent of General Electric.

U.V. light in industry would presumably be used to protect some highly sensitive stage of manufacture (perhaps of pharmaceuticals) from contamination by cockroaches, where insecticides would be inappropriate. Depending on the wavelengths used, safety to personnel would need to be considered. Laboratory results show that repellency, at least of very young stages of cockroaches, occurs only after a period of 2 hours' exposure. It is not immediate and a dark area—as an alternative choice for the insects—seems necessary. Under these circumstances, results suggest that white light *versus* darkness would produce almost the same result.

Cohen et al[203] have examined the feasibility of using a crude aggregation pheromone to lure the insects to one place in conjunction with U.V. light—as an alternative to the use of insecticides.

There is no indication from any of the studies reported, of a likely interaction between the response to U.V. and the cockroaches' normal circadian rhythm (see Chapter 11, Vol. I).

REPELLENTS AND INSECTICIDE REPELLENCY 171

Fig. 76. Wrapping materials provide cockroaches with ideal harbourage: (below) paper bags, well-marked by cockroaches in the drawer of a food store (Antigua, West Indies); (top) the multiplicity of harbourages provided by corrugated cardboard.

REPELLENCY OF INSECTICIDES

The first part of this chapter is concerned with the properties and use of chemical *repellents* to keep cockroaches out of harbourages. Now we shall examine the properties of *insecticides* most often used to treat harbourages in the furnishings and fabric of buildings. It is here that we require intimate contact between insect and insecticide, and where repellency by the insecticide may cause it to be less effective.

The cockroach and its need for harbourage

Pest cockroaches become established in parts of buildings where chemical and physical conditions are most favourable. These include an optimal temperature [646] and humidity, proximity to food, absence of light, minimum air disturbance, close contact with surfaces[581] and the presence of other cockroaches.[805] An aggregation pheromone—a chemical produced by cockroaches from the rectal pads and released with faeces—tends to keep them together and in the absence of disturbance, cockroaches continue to use the same harbourages.[100, 108, 457, 458, 565, 714]

Cockroaches leave and return to their harbourages as part of an activity cycle (a built-in circadian rhythm, Chapter 11, Vol. I). They return to the same harbourage because environmental factors guide them there. When an infestation is eradicated and a new one for some reason is allowed to develop, months or even years later, there is every likelihood that the same harbourages will be reoccupied.

Fig. 77. The casein glue commonly used (left) to stick labels on to cartons provides cockroaches with highly attractive food. Conveyors often harbour cockroaches which infest finished products at despatch (right).

Additional factors to those already mentioned, which we do not yet know about, may affect the choice of harbourage, perhaps the roughness of the surface and the influence of other pest insects. Certainly, for cockroaches, the insecticides we use influence their behaviour. Some of the most detailed studies of the behaviour of cockroaches in typical infestations, (e.g. in cupboards containing clothes and household items) have been carried out by Ebeling and colleagues: a series of experiments were made to better understand how the chemicals used interact with the insect's affinity for its harbourage.

We now know that cockroaches can avoid deposits of insecticidal dusts and sprays. At least some cockroaches in a population are able to test and take an avoidance reaction, which becomes part of a learned behaviour.[259,265] This, plus the ability of cockroaches to fully recover from sub-lethal doses of some insecticides, allow the insects to survive better where there is a choice of treated and untreated harbourage. In field tests against German cockroaches in infested properties in Florida, dusts were more repellent than water-based sprays, and cockroaches, were observed avoiding dusted areas.[145]

Harbourage and the pest control operator
In various chapters of this book the author has stressed the importance of ensuring intimate contact between insect and insecticide if effective control of cockroaches—their eradication—is to be achieved. This applies whether the insecticide is a wet spray, residual film, dust, vapour or mist droplet. In doing his job, the pest control operator creates for cockroaches a range of situations, represented by the following extremes:

1. *Where an infestation already exists*: most cockroach harbourages are treated during the day, and if treatment is done thoroughly, the insects will be forcibly contaminated by insecticide projected into harbourages. The objective of the serviceman is to leave the premises with treatment complete, knowing that by his skill and thoroughness there cannot possibly be a live insect left by the time the insecticide takes its full effect. Egg cases remain, but any nymphs which may hatch will be dealt with in the same way on his next visit.

2. *Where an infestation has previously been controlled*: in this instance the serviceman is visiting the premises as part of a 'maintenance contract'—to inspect it for further infestation. Previously occupied harbourages and potential harbourages may be retreated: no cockroaches are likely to be seen at the time, but some may enter the building before his next visit and the insecticide is being used to counter these. Thus, the serviceman's objective is to make those harbourages most likely to be adopted by reinfesting cockroaches, completely untenable for them. But unlike the previous example, the cockroach when it arrives, has a choice.

In practice, of course, there are many conditions between these two extremes: where cracks and crevices (e.g. wall cavities and underfloor areas) have not been treated adequately and cockroaches survive because the serviceman has not taken the trouble to use a dust; where part of the premises

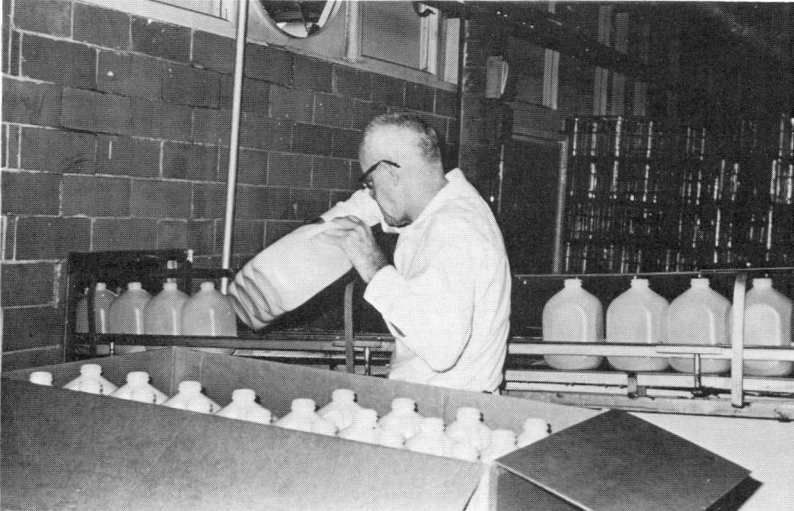

Fig. 78. Examples of poor practice in food manufacture which may result in the spread of cockroaches. Packaging materials should not be allowed into production areas. Infestation may be introduced. In a milk-processing plant: (top left) note the potential harbourages in steam pipe insulation; (bottom left) polybottles with open tops, unloaded direct from cardboard cartons onto conveyors for filling with milk; (top right) wooden crates containing milk bottles stacked adjacent to heat sterilisation plant providing an ideal local environment for infestation.

remains infested because the serviceman has failed to obtain a key to a store room and cockroaches wander from there into well-treated areas; where the serviceman ignores the treatment of harbourages altogether and hopes that an insecticidal mist will do the job for him, or that cockroaches will walk over exposed surfaces which he has sprayed.

The insecticide and its effect on cockroaches

We can now look at the likely effect of the serviceman's materials on the cockroach. The insecticide may:

1. *cause cockroaches to take an avoiding reaction*; they may be repelled by it, reducing the amount of contact and encouraging survivors to establish elsewhere. This can occur where the serviceman is not sufficiently objective in his efforts; he fails to understand the importance of treating all harbourages.
2. *be so very rapid in action that the insects have little time to take an avoiding reaction before being lethally contaminated*; however, if slow acting

insecticides of mediocre performance are used, the cockroach is given time to test the situation and make a choice.

3. *be so very toxic (or not broken down in the insect) that the smallest amount which contaminates the insects is effectively lethal, even if cockroaches leave treated harbourages quickly and do not return*; when insecticides are used which allow recovery from poisoning, the cockroaches are continuously able to make a second choice.

4. *have no repellent effect, permitting continued contact of cockroaches with treated harbourages*; under these circumstances the toxicity and speed of action of the insecticide are of less importance, as repeated contamination of the cockroaches occurs, leading to their eventual death.

This analysis pin-points the importance of repellency of insecticides in cockroach control. It may have little effect if *all* harbourages and potential harbourages are well-treated, and highly effective and quickly acting insecticides are regularly used. But repellency can affect the performance of a good insecticide as its activity is reduced. For example, where follow-up treatments are separated by long intervals, or insecticides with short residual life are used, the toxicant becomes gradually less effective and short excursions of cockroaches into treated harbourages becomes possible without penalty. As an insecticide loses its activity on a treated surface a point is eventually reached when attraction for harbourage overcomes the insects' avoidance reaction and is strong enough to enable some individuals to 'test' and survive. Females appear more adept in surviving a given deposit of insecticide, probably because they are inherently more tolerant than males, to most insecticides.

TESTS OF INSECTICIDE REPELLENCY

In a survey of the components making up commercially available formulations of insecticides for cockroach control in the United States—toxicants, synergists, solvents, flushing agents and emulsifiers—121 different materials were examined.[630] Tests on these showed that pyrethrins (considered a repellent for some years), MGK 264 (a pyrethrins synergist, see p. 240) and Triton X100 (an emulsifier) were noticeably repellent to both German and American cockroaches. The list of repellent materials also included a number of surfactants (wetting agents) and deodorants, but in no case were solvents implicated.[766] In laboratory studies for repellency, formulations containing 0.5 per cent acephate and chlorpyrifos did not function as repellents; but diazinon (0.5 per cent), propoxur (1 per cent), synergised pyrethrins (1 per cent), some synthetic pyrethroids and bendiocarb (1 per cent) were repellent for a week or more.[888] In an extensive test programme of many insecticides, avoidance of treated surfaces was observed more frequently with diazinon, than with any of the other materials.[895]

When German, American and Oriental cockroaches are given the chance of moving from light areas with food, into dark harbourages without, *B. germanica* accepts shelter most quickly. This is possibly a measure of its greater

REPELLENTS AND INSECTICIDE REPELLENCY 177

Fig. 79. Egg cases of American cockroaches in a supermarket: (top) attached to plastic wrappers of wafer biscuits, some of the wrappers having been eaten through and the biscuits themselves consumed by the insects; (bottom) attached to a cardboard box and to cans of vegetables (St. Lucia, West Indies).

agility. Observations over 5 days[261], however, show that German cockroaches are in fact least dependent on dark harbourages (79 per cent of insects), compared with *P. americana* (88 per cent) and *B. orientalis* (95 per cent).

Ebeling and co-workers have made extensive tests of the behaviour of *B. germanica* when given the choice of entering or avoiding areas normally attractive to cockroaches, such as dark voids, but which have been contaminated with sprays and dusts.

Their initial tests were made in a specially constructed kitchen, into which cockroaches were released.[263] Much of the work was subsequently done with choice boxes (Fig. 84): a partition with a single hole divides the box into two equal compartments. Insecticide is placed in one half which is kept dark (harbourage). The insects, with food and water, are introduced into the untreated half which is covered by clear plexiglass. Only after the cockroaches have become familiar with their new surroundings are they allowed to pass *via* the hole, into the section treated with insecticide.

Using this method, Ebeling has looked at the performance of various sprays and dusts. When the harbourage is untreated, cockroaches occupy it freely and most will be found there after two or three days (Fig. 85). When treated with borax and boric acid, about half the cockroaches occupy the harbourage, and presumed attractants (e.g. flour and sugar) fail to increase this.

Fig. 80. Goods in a warehouse, showing: faecal contamination of tins of tomato juice, and partial damage to paper labels by American and German cockroaches (St. Lucia, West Indies).

Ebeling suggests that probably no finely divided powder is completely non-repellent to *B. germanica*: when insecticides such as diazinon and propoxur are used, the initial numbers—those involved in exploratory behaviour—soon decrease.

It is this which Ebeling considers a 'learned modification of behaviour'. Learning occurs when there is an opportunity for repeated experience. Cockroaches which succeed in staying out of insecticidal deposits appear to have average susceptibility when later confined continuously to them. They are not much different in susceptibility from those that succumb, or from those that have not been through the 'learning selection process'. Under the unusual conditions of exceptionally high insecticide concentration, cockroaches succumb before learning to stay out (Fig. 86).

Experiments with choice boxes, treated with insecticides of different concentrations, show that the difference between 2·5 per cent and 1·25 per cent chlordane, or between 2 per cent and 1 per cent diazinon or propoxur, make the difference between complete kill (4–11 days later, depending on the insecticide) or incomplete kill in 30 days. These differences contrast with the very small changes in knockdown time (KD_{50}'s) when cockroaches are confined on deposits of these same concentrations in petri dishes.

Partial treatment of harbourages

When only parts of a harbourage (the corners of the dark compartment of a choice box, Fig. 84) are treated with dusts or sprays, compared with the whole, cockroaches appear able to avoid the insecticide and the incomplete treatment is accordingly less effective (Fig. 87). In most cases it is not possible for a serviceman to judge the size of the void he is treating or how much dust is required to give a uniform coating over all the surfaces. His main objective is to get the dust as widely distributed in the harbourage as possible, to ensure that any cockroaches present are contaminated. He is not likely to consider the merits of thin films of dust, which might cause less hesitation on the part of cockroaches to crawl over them, than heavy deposits which might be repellent.

In choice box tests the effects of 'light' (1 cc) and 'heavy' (8 cc) deposits (per 1174 cm²) of insecticidal dust were compared.[259] The amount used did not materially affect insecticidal efficacy; only with chlordane was the lighter deposit more effective. 'Heavy deposits may only be advantageous when placed in areas where cockroaches cannot leave their harbourage without crawling through them'.

The results with choice boxes are in accord with those of field experiments, particularly when application is not thorough and cockroaches are able to find untreated harbourages in which to breed. The inadequacy of propoxur in Ebeling's tests is most noticeable, and is confirmed by other tests where German cockroaches are allowed entry to treated and untreated cardboard boxes.[467] When cockroaches were given the choice of walking on treated and untreated paper towels, bendiocarb, diazinon and fenitrothion were more repellent than propoxur (Table XXVI).

Fig. 81. Refrigerated vending machines for soft drinks provide warmth and harbourage for cockroaches: (top) bottles returned to the rack (on the machine at far left) also provide residues of liquid food (hospital corridor, Tucson, U.S.A.); (below) the infestation then spreads to confectionery and other products (delicatessen, Melbourne, Australia).

TABLE XXVI

TIME FOR 50 PER CENT KNOCKDOWN (HOURS) OF GERMAN COCKROACHES (a) CONFINED ON PAPER TOWELS TREATED WITH VARIOUS INSECTICIDES (78 ml/m^2) OR (b) GIVEN THE CHOICE OF WALKING ON TREATED OR UNTREATED TOWELS. REPELLENCY FACTOR IS THE RATIO OF LT_{50}'s FOR THE TWO CONDITIONS
(From Jenkins, Taylor & Blow[467])

Insecticide	LT_{50} (hours)		Repellency factor
	(a) Confined	(b) With choice	
Bendiocarb 0·3% wettable powder	0·60	6·90	11·5
Diazinon 1% emulsion	1·04	5·90	5·7
Fenitrothion 1% emulsion	2·52	13·2	5·2
Fenitrothion 1% wettable powder	0·53	1·28	2·4
Propoxur 1% emulsion	0·60	1·50	2·5

Recovery as part of the avoidance process

Propoxur, understandably gives low kill in choice tests because cockroaches are able to recover quickly and completely from contact with sublethal amounts (see p. 377). On the other hand, because the avoidance of insecticides cannot be accomplished, as a learning process, without repeated contact, insecticides like chlordane and perhaps borax and boric acid are relatively more effective in choice situations because (a) slowness of action allows repeated 'testing' of the environment by the insect and (b) repeated contact combined with cumulative action can occur.

Ebeling cites non-recovery from short exposures to chlorinated insecticides as a reason for their good performance. When replacement insecticides, like diazinon were first used, reports were received of German cockroaches being much more widely distributed in buildings—suggesting a change in their behaviour associated with resistance (see p. 455). This may have been caused by the greater repellency of the new insecticides, encouraging cockroaches to make efforts to establish new harbourages.

Wall void tests

Tests of repellency have also been made using mock-up wall voids into which large numbers of German cockroaches can move: they can choose to enter the treated voids, or remain with food and water in 5-gallon cans, connected to the voids by short lengths of pipe. The relative performance of insecticides tested by this method have been confirmed by treatments of infested properties.

When groups of about 300 adult cockroaches were given the choice of entering wall voids treated with insecticidal dusts at normally used concentrations, the numbers alive, plus their progeny, at the end a 30 day test were: propoxur 791, sodium fluoride 452, silica aerogel 406, diazinon 205, boric acid 92 and control (untreated) 1017.

'Simple' and 'complex' environments

Every serviceman knows that some locations, in which cockroaches enjoy a multiplicity of harbourages, present him with a difficult problem. He may regard this as a challenge; to ensure that all infested harbourages are treated.

Fig. 82. Crates, some containing empty bottles, stacked outdoors, awaiting collection by the distributor. In warm climates, cockroaches living outdoors may use these as harbourage and be carried to the manufacturers plant (Melbourne, Australia).

Fig. 83. Cockroaches are often carried in bottle crates into factories, restaurants, hotels, supermarkets and the home. The crates provide ideal harbourage (top, St. Lucia, West Indies). On return to the bottling plant, empty crates require cleaning or insecticidal treatment before re-use (bottom, Dallas, U.S.A.).

184 THE COCKROACH

The domestic property, or the accommodation of a motel, are 'simple environments': the structure of the building and its fitments are of standard design and the serviceman by experience soon discovers those parts of the property where cockroaches are most likely to take up residence.

The 'complex environment' is typified by a large manufacturing site: perhaps a food factory covering many acres, with different manufacturing processes and intricate machines; false ceilings, underground ducting and gulleys; work going on in old buildings which by the nature of their construc-

Fig. 84. Methods of testing the repellency of insecticides involving the use (top) of 'choice boxes' consisting of two compartments: one containing food and water and the other (a dark harbourage) usually treated uniformly with insecticide. Cockroaches pass between them *via* the hole at the top of the partition. In some tests (bottom) the effect of partially treating the dark harbourage with dust (in corners only) is examined. (Courtesy: Ebeling, University of California).

tion contribute to the complexity of the problem. Here there is the need to achieve eradication without contaminating food products and this will limit the choice of insecticide. A further example might be a large industrial plant (Fig. 88); with many works canteens, cloakrooms and toilet areas; housing accommodation for immigrant labour, with low standards of hygiene, which make insect control difficult, without insecticide repellency contributing to it.

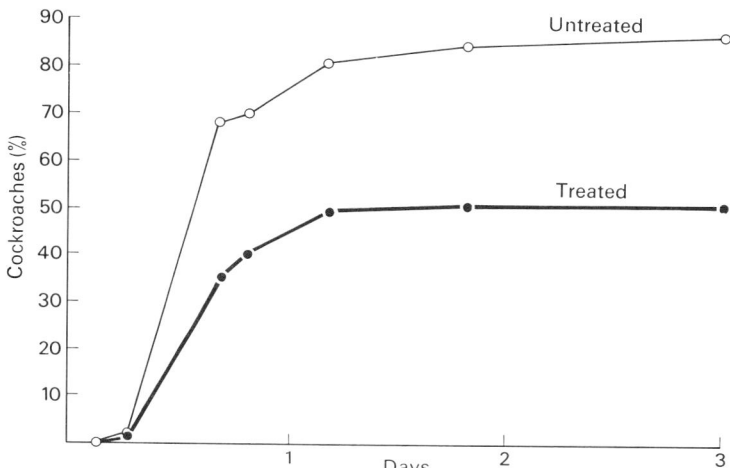

Fig. 85. Movement of German cockroaches from the light, to dark compartments of choice boxes during a 3-day period. The treated compartments (dark) received dust applications of various borax and boric acid formulations (Data averaged from Ebeling, Wagner & Reierson[265]).

If cockroaches can find abundant untreated harbourages they have less reason to crawl over treated areas. Thus, repellency of an insecticide becomes increasingly disadvantageous as the environment requiring treatment becomes more complex. Ebeling has demonstrated conclusively that a non-repellent insecticide does give better service in use; control is not so adversely affected by the insects' ability to discriminate.[260]

Treatment of previously occupied harbourages
So far we have looked at the evidence for insecticide repellency from experiments carried out in the University of California. Tests carried out in the laboratories of Rentokil have confirmed the relative non-repellency of boric acid compared with dusts containing organic insecticides. Combinations of boric acid with pyrethrins have also been examined.

The test procedure was not identical with that previously described. Populations of *B. germanica* were contained in 5 gallon pails, linked at the base by a 4 cm diameter tube, 15 cm long. Food, water and harbourage were placed in both pails. The harbourage consisted of four hardboard panels (30 × 15 cm) separated from each other by a 5 mm gap. An equal number of cockroaches was placed in each pail and allowed to acclimatise for 3 days. The harbourage of one pail was then shaken free of cockroaches and treated with dust at 3·5 mg/cm^2 and replaced.

This test was considered to best represent the practical environment where (1) harbourages at time of treatment are already contaminated by the odour, vomit, faecal material and aggregation pheromone of the insects, and (2) where the serviceman, by default, might treat only half of the already used harbourage in an infested premises. The tests were done under continuous artificial light and the following results obtained.

Fenitrothion and propoxur, both rapidly acting insecticides, are far less effective at killing cockroaches than boric acid. They thus allow reproduction to continue and these less effective insecticides also allow the nymphs produced to survive. The net effect on the total infestation is very low indeed (Table XXVII). Fenitrothion and malathion perform about the same; lindane is highly repellent and performs much less adequately (Fig. 145).

Boric acid, incorporating pyrethrins synergised with piperonyl butoxide (0·0625/0·625 per cent), kills much more quickly (in 4 days) than boric acid alone or with a lower concentration of pybuthrin (10–14 days), but after three weeks the incorporation of pybuthrin makes no contribution to improved kill (Table XXVIII).

TABLE XXVII

KILL (%) AND REPRODUCTIVE PERFORMANCE AFTER 3 WEEKS OF 500 ADULT GERMAN COCKROACHES IN REPELLENCY TESTS WITH DUSTS (3·5 mg/cm^2), WHEN THE INSECTS ARE GIVEN THE CHOICE OF OCCUPYING TREATED AND UNTREATED HARBOURAGES IN LINKED 5 GALLON PAILS

(Cornwell, unpublished)

Insecticide	Kill (%) of adults	Kill (%) of adults and nymphs produced**
Boric acid (99%)*	80	65
Fenitrothion (1%) + Boric acid (40%)	51	40
Fenitrothion (1%)	47	31
Propoxur (1%)	31	25
Boric acid (40%)	21	16
China clay only	15	7
Untreated control	8	2

* Plus 1% tricalcium phosphate: all other dusts formulated in china clay.
** 1800 nymphs were produced in the 'untreated control'.

Table XXVIII

KILL (%) AND REPRODUCTIVE PERFORMANCE AFTER 3 WEEKS OF 300 ADULT GERMAN COCKROACHES IN REPELLENCY TESTS WITH DUSTS OF BORIC ACID AND SYNERGISED PYRETHRINS (3·5 mg/cm^2), WHEN THE INSECTS ARE GIVEN THE CHOICE OF OCCUPYING TREATED AND UNTREATED HARBOURAGES IN LINKED 5 GALLON PAILS

(Cornwell, unpublished)

Treatment	Pyrethrins (%)/ pip. but. (%)	Kill (%) of adults	Kill (%) of adults and nymphs produced**
Boric acid (99%) only*	—	87	78
Boric acid +	0·0625/0·625	89	75
Boric acid +	0·0156/0·156	80	58
Boric acid +	0·004/0·04	88	75
Synergised pyrethrins only	0·0625/0·625	43	13
Untreated control	—	28	5

* Plus 1% tricalcium phosphate.   ** 4300 nymphs were produced in the 'untreated control'.

Use of pyrethrins as a flushing agent

The advantage most often cited for the inclusion of a flushing agent in dusts and sprays is that it helps those involved in cockroach control to find where the insects are during the day. A flushing agent should therefore contribute towards more complete treatment. The other advantage often claimed, is the possible loss of caution by cockroaches excited by pyrethrins, causing them to run over insecticides, thus picking up larger amounts than would otherwise be the case.[257]

In practical tests, the application into the harbourages of cockroaches of synergised pyrethrins as an aerosol, before dusting with boric acid, improved control when the insects were swept up and destroyed.[260] But when the aerosol was released indiscriminately into the room and the fallen insects disregarded, it 'added nothing to the long-term effectiveness of either a dust treatment with boric acid, or a residual liquid spray'.[698]

When synergised pyrethrins are applied *with* residual insecticides (as part of the formulation) they do not appear to improve control of German cockroaches, as shown by the numbers caught in traps before and after treatment (Table XXIX). The repellency of synergised pyrethrins may cause other insecticides with which they are mixed to become less effective when attempts are made to use mixtures as residual toxicants against German cockroaches.[760]

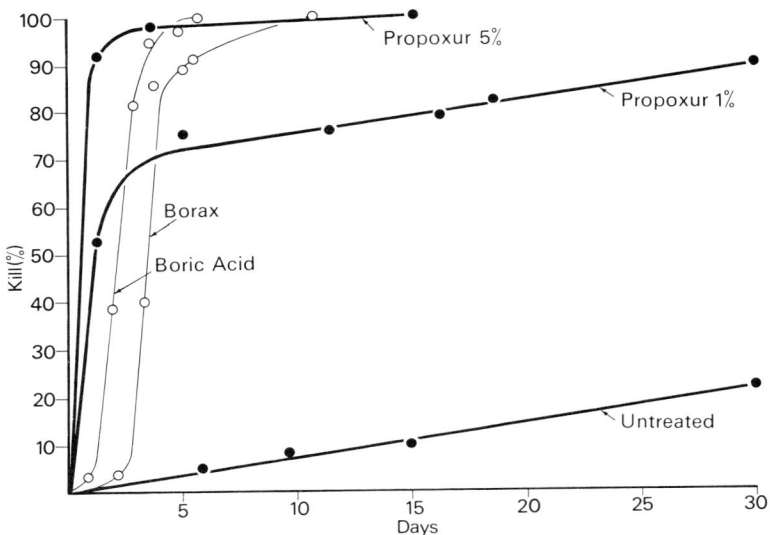

Fig. 86. Kill (per cent) of German cockroaches in light (untreated) and dark (treated) compartments of choice boxes. The entire inside surfaces of the dark compartments were treated with borax and boric acid and two concentrations of propoxur dust: 5 per cent is much higher than is normally used. (From Ebeling, Wagner & Reierson[265])

TABLE XXIX

CONTROL OF GERMAN COCKROACHES (%) BASED ON TRAP COUNTS BEFORE AND AFTER TREATMENT OF LOS ANGELES APARTMENTS, WITH AND WITHOUT SYNERGISED PYRETHRINS ADDED TO THE INSECTICIDE. RESULTS FOR EACH TREATMENT AVERAGED FOR 12–20 APARTMENTS

(From Ebeling & Reierson[257])

Insecticide	Interval after treatment (months)	Concentration (%) pyrethrins /pip. but.	Synergised pyrethrins Added	Not added
Boric acid (98%)	1	0·0625/0·625	98·6	97·4
	3		95·9	95·5
Boric acid (98·6%)	1	0·0625/0·325	95·5	97·0
	3		99·4	99·3
Propoxur (1%)	1	0·1/0·5	78·3	69·4
Malathion (2%)	1	0·5/2·5	81·9	91·7
Diazinon (1%)	1	0·1/0·5	98·4	96·1

In this chapter we have examined a number of applications of repellent compounds, which might help reduce cockroach movement in trade and transfer into buildings. The effective life of these chemicals on treated surfaces is no longer than many organophosphorus insecticides. Where the use of an insecticide is acceptable, there is surely more merit in treating to kill rather than to repel. Whether or not repellents become used more widely on packaging materials will depend on restrictions which may further curtail the use of insecticides.

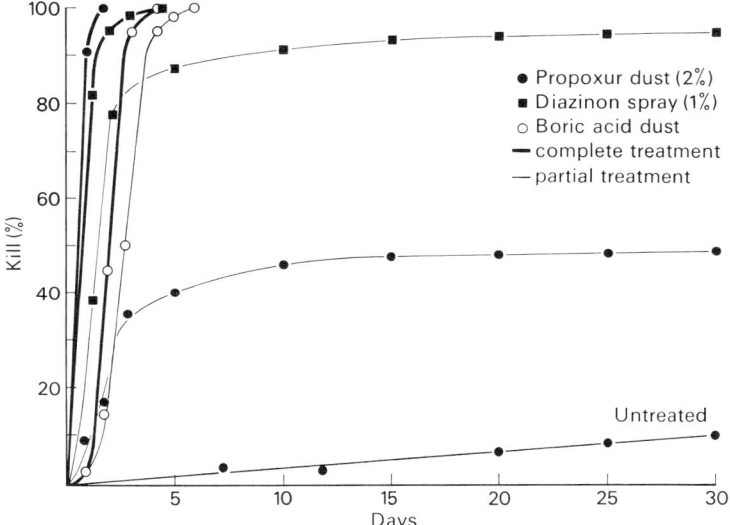

Fig. 87. Kill (per cent) of German cockroaches in light (untreated) and dark treated, compartments of choice boxes. Dusts and spray were applied to the entire inside surface of the dark compartment, or just in the corners (dusts) or on the floor only (spray). The comparison is therefore between 'complete' and 'partial' treatment of the harbourage. (From Ebeling, Wagner & Reierson[265]).

The repellency of insecticides used to treat cockroach harbourages is the more important issue since it affects our ability to obtain control. Clearly, how we use insecticides determines whether repellency is important in affecting our success. According to Ebeling, avoidance or acceptance of an insecticide deposit by cockroaches is never an 'all or none' phenomenon: differences occur in the number and duration of the trips that cockroaches make into insecticide treated areas. Insecticides which are sufficiently repellent to cockroaches to cause them to make only brief and tentative contacts with deposits have the inherent weakness that the cockroaches may learn to avoid them permanently and seek harbourage in untreated areas.

TABLE XXX

TIME FOR 50% KNOCKDOWN (MINS) OF GERMAN COCKROACHES EXPOSED CONTINUOUSLY AND FOR BRIEF PERIODS, TO DRIED RESIDUES OF INSECTICIDE SOLUTIONS (IN ACETONE) AND TO DUSTS. BRIEF EXPOSURES WERE 5 MINS FOR SOLUTIONS AND 1 SEC FOR DUSTS

(From Ebeling, Reierson & Wagner[259])

Insecticide	Application rate (mg a.i./ft²)	Exposure		Ratio of KD_{50}'s
		Continuous	Brief	
Solutions applied to glass (G) or masonite (M)				
Pybuthrin (1/10) (G) (Pyrenone)	0.04	24	>2,880	>120
Propoxur (M)	0.10	19	>2,880	>150
Diazinon (G)	0.15	22	>2,880	>130
Chlordecone (M)	0.30	180	1,440	8.0
Lindane (G)	0.60	51	780	15.3
Dusts (0.5 g/ft²) applied to paper				
Drione*	0.12	1	3	3.0
Propoxur	0.12	7	13	1.9
Diazinon	0.12	27	38	1.4
Chlordecone	0.60	134	240	1.8
Lindane	0.12	19	42	2.2
Silica aerogel (Dri-die 67)	2.20	58	176	3.0
Boric acid	12.00	384	780	2.0

* A formulation incorporating pybuthrin (1/10) but see p. 207 for detailed composition.

As a corollary: (1) insecticides which are repellent will perform poorly unless applied so thoroughly that no harbourage areas, favourable to cockroaches, remain untreated; (2) insecticides which are effective by being easily picked up from treated surfaces with the minimum period of contact will be the most successful; (3) hence with very short exposures, dusts are much more effective than dried films obtained from sprays (Table XXX); (4) judgements on the likely performance of new insecticides should be based on tests in which cockroaches are exposed to treated surfaces for extremely short periods and not continuously for many hours (see Chapter 17); (5) the ability to recover from poisoning predisposes the cockroach to any learning process associated with repellency; (6) the insecticides likely to be most efficient are those 'which it is practicable to apply in out-of-the way places in buildings; that enable cockroaches to carry away a lethal quantity and succumb to treatment, even if they never return to that deposit, or to other dust deposits in the building'. (7) The choice for the serviceman is boric acid, or a highly insecticidal, very quick acting dust, offering no chance of recovery.

8

THE EARLIEST INSECTICIDES
(INORGANICS, FUMIGANTS AND OTHERS)

Borax and boric acid: physical properties; mammalian toxicity; use for cockroach control—Sodium fluoride and fluorosilicate: manufacture and properties; toxicity and symptoms of poisoning; activity against cockroaches; mode of entry; dusts containing sodium fluoride and pyrethrins—Desiccant dusts: chemical and physical properties; mammalian toxicity; action against cockroaches; use in cockroach control—Phosphorus: properties; application—Thallium sulphate—Hydrogen cyanide and other fumigants—Organic thiocyanates: chemical properties and toxicity.

Early attempts at pest control were made with minerals and plant materials which were found by trial and error to have inherent biological activity—much in the same way that the taking of herbal mixtures and other mineral prescriptions preceded modern pharmaceuticals. At the beginning of this century the choice of materials available to kill insects was extremely limited. Emphasis was on the use of dusts. Pyrethrum was at that time available only as crushed, dried flowers. It is now difficult to contemplate a situation, before the advent of modern insecticides, when materials for cockroach control were largely 'refined' from minerals dug out of the ground!

Without any formulation technology, the inorganic insecticides were simple powders, often compounds of fluorine and boron, ground and mixed with fine clays and other minerals as diluents. Some (e.g. thallium sulphate, arsenic and phosphorus) were incorporated into foods to provide the earliest forms of baits. As a result, insect control was performed with chemicals, some highly toxic to man, many of which have now been rejected as unacceptable. However, in the years before World War II, boric acid, sodium fluoride and pyrethrum, used separately and in various mixtures, were very much relied upon for cockroach control.

This chapter is concerned with the use and performance of the early inorganic insecticides and the few organic compounds that preceded DDT. Many continued to be applied by pest control operators during the post-war years: sodium fluoride regained its popularity when chlordane failed to control German cockroaches in the U.S.A. Boric acid became used extensively in the U.K. on publication of the evidence that many of the synthetic organic insecticides were repellent to cockroaches (p. 172). The disiccant dusts, based on compounds containing silica, were a post-war development which found little application outside the United States.

BORAX AND BORIC ACID

Borax has been used for cockroach control since at least the middle of the last century. Slowly it lost favour to sodium fluoride which replaced it.[506] When sodium fluoride is dusted onto cockroaches (that are prevented from eating it) death occurs in 5–22 hours, compared with 2–10 days with borax.[741] Boric acid is more costly than borax and is intermediate in speed of action between it and sodium fluoride.[436]

Fig. 88. Examples of 'complex environments' for cockroach control: (above) the Opel motor vehicle works at Stuttgart; a miniature city involving one and a half square miles of plant, eating facilities and accommodation for the works' labour force. (Courtesy: Opel, W. Germany). (Below) International shipping; each vessel is like a multistorey building but with harbourages in inaccessible bulkheads which must be drilled to allow treatment with dusts (Hamburg, W. Germany).

Borax and boric acid also became less popular for cockroach control as the pyrethrins became more readily available; there was a preference for faster action. Later, when chlordane and other insecticides appeared in the U.S., with the opportunity to apply these as sprays, the use of borax and boric acid slipped into insignificance.

Renewed interest was however shown in boric acid in the mid-1960's with the emphasis then placed on the use of materials with low mammalian toxicity. Also as an insecticide with long residual activity (compared with the shorter-lived organophosphates), with no resistance by German cockroaches (cf. chlordane), and lack of repellency to cockroaches. These were all seen as reasons favouring the reintroduction of boric acid. It provided some quite remarkable results in an era of man-made insecticides, of considerably more complex chemical composition.

The excellent performance of boric acid has been vividly described by Walter[832] following his attempts in 1918 to control German cockroaches using traps in a cafeteria in the U.S.: 'When a new manager took charge of the cafeteria and saw the conditions he wrote to an agent of a roach poison company, who guaranteed to rid the place entirely in 30 days. The agent was employed, who used a white powder, scattering this every place that the cockroaches frequented. The agent would not tell what the powder contained, nor would he sell it, insisting on doing the work himself. The next morning, after the powder was scattered on the shelves, floor and in all corners, the floor was literally covered with dead and dying roaches and within a week's time scarcely any could be found, and a few days later, none at all. On analysis, the powder was found to be powdered boric acid'. The claim made in this quotation of many dead and dying cockroaches *after 24 hours* is perhaps an exaggeration: the action of boric acid against cockroaches is not that rapid.

Physical properties
Boric acid is a white crystalline solid, slightly soluble in water (maximum 6 per cent) and almost non-volatile. The last contributes to long stability. 'Free flowing' agents (e.g. tricalcium phosphate or fumed silicas) are usually incorporated at 1 per cent or less into dusts, to prevent 'caking' and the clogging of dusting equipment. These adjuvants are necessary to offset the effects of humidity on agglomeration of particles,[259] and compaction during transport.

Mammalian toxicity
In the days when the word 'toxicity' carried less emotional overtones and when sodium fluoride, phosphorus and arsenic were among the relatively few available insecticides, the claims made for boric acid being 'safe' and 'non-poisonous' to humans would have passed unchallenged. Not so today however!

The acute oral LD_{50} (rat) of boric acid is about 3,500 mg/kg. Because it is applied at concentrations approaching 100 per cent, toxicity to man is in fact greater than many organic insecticides now commonly used as dusts at only

1–2 per cent. About 15–20g of boric acid taken acutely is said to be fatal to man and about 5g to children.[820]

The acute oral LD_{50} (rat) of borax is 4,500–6,000 mg/kg. 'No effect' levels in dietary experiments with rats, fed sub-acutely, are 3,000 ppm for boric acid and 4,600 ppm for borax.

Compounds containing boron have been reported to accumulate in the brain, liver and fat body, indicating that the ingestion of repeated amounts should be avoided. The mechanism of toxicity of boron is not precisely known: there appears to be a decrease in oxygen uptake by brain tissues possibly resulting from the formation of complexes with brain cell sugars. Doses of 3g of boric acid and upward are rapidly excreted in the urine to the extent of 82–100 per cent.[848] Borax and boric acid are reported by Chittenden & Gies[187] to be eliminated quickly, 24–36 hours usually being sufficient for complete removal. Doses of 2g of boric acid administered in metabolism studies on humans were accounted for, to the extent of about 94 per cent, in the first week.[482]

Boric acid is not easily absorbed through the skin but repeated contact may cause eczema and localised oedema. Boric acid (= boracic acid) was first used on the skin as a mild antiseptic in 1875 when Lister introduced it for that purpose. All compounds containing boron are phytotoxic.

Fig. 89. The treatment of voids in apartment blocks with long-lasting insecticides such as boric acid and Dri-Die, during building construction and before occupation, has been tested. The incidence of cockroaches is much reduced: in warm climates, infestations of *B. germanica* would normally be expected within a year of occupation (Ventura, California. Courtesy: Ebeling).

Use for cockroach control

Powdered boric acid is more effective than borax in controlling German cockroaches[832] and there is no evidence to suggest that either substance acts better in a bait, than when liberally dusted into harbourages. Both are slow-acting stomach poisons: dust is ingested by cockroaches during grooming but penetration also occurs through the insect integument. That taken in by grooming distends the crop, but movement of the particles into the remainder of the alimentary tract is prevented by the proventriculus. Apparently movement only occurs of boric acid in solution.[891] Cockroaches with mouthparts sealed take longer to die than those unsealed, although penetration of the cuticle clearly occurs. The mortality of German cockroaches after short exposures to dust is shown in Table LXXXVII. Tricalcium phosphate, an adjuvant in boric acid dusts is not toxic below 5 per cent when fed to *P. americana* in diets.[385]

Varied uses have been made of borax and boric acid for cockroach control: as dusts without dilution, in places where other insecticides may be inappropriate; as diluents for pyrethrins, sometimes making up 50 per cent of the formulation, thereby reducing costs; as an extender or diluent for other insecticides, e.g. at a ratio of 3:1 with sodium fluoride; and in baits with sugar[882] flour and other cereal bases.[75,349,649] When boric acid is used as a diluent for pyrethrum and sodium fluoride, better results are reported than with mixtures using borax.[349]

A solution of boric acid (1·5 per cent) in 'vials' in infested premises is said to 'clean-up' the roach population.[79] This seems doubtful, although boric acid dissolved in warm washing water (5 per cent) for cleaning floors produces a thin film of boric acid crystals when dry, which may kill cockroaches by contact over a period of weeks.[259] The crystals are more difficult for the insects to pick up than when the insecticide is applied as a dust.

Boric acid has been used to treat wall voids and other cavities in buildings, to provide permanent control of cockroaches (see also Dri-Die, p. 205). The dust is introduced at various stages of construction or before apartment blocks are occupied, treating those locations which by experience invariably become infested.[587,786] This is possible with a long-lived insecticide and results are promising (Fig. 89).

Boric acid is the least repellent of insecticides tested as dusts against cockroaches (Table XXXI). In 'choice tests' boric acid performs better than carbamate and organophosphorus insecticides (Figs. 86, 87 & 145). Small amounts of other substances such as silica aerogels (e.g. Dri-Die® and Cab-o-sil®, see p. 205) which are highly repellent, can be added as anti-caking agents and increase speed of kill by sorptive action (Fig. 90). The greater repellency that results appears however to be compensated by the more toxic action of the mixture (Table XXXII). The results obtained for other toxicants mixed with boric acid depend on the relative insecticidal activity and repellency of the components.[259]

The amounts of borax and boric acid now used for cockroach control are not known, but they are probably very small. When boric acid dust was introduced for cockroach control in the U.K. and assessed for overall performance against a propoxur dust, service managers were not enthusiastic (Table XC). In a survey of dusts used in the United States in 1958, the advantages of cheapness and safety, relative to other materials then available, were not sufficient to outweigh the 'extreme slowness of action of boric acid'. German cockroaches confined in petri dishes are killed more rapidly by boric acid (KD_{50} 13·9 hr) than borax (17·6 hr) and not much affected by relative humidities between 2 per cent and 100 per cent.[259] Of German cockroaches, allowed to run through borax for 8 minutes, only 10 per cent of males and 7 per cent of females died in 4 days, but at 10 days, kills were 100 per cent and 95 per cent.[485] In dust settling tests, borax killed 61 per cent of *B. germanica* in 10 days compared with 94 per cent by boric acid.[350] Holt[436] described boric acid as 'useful' and borax as 'useless'.

TABLE XXXI

TIME FOR 50% KNOCKDOWN (MINS) OF AMERICAN COCKROACHES CONFINED ON DUSTS IN JARS, AND FOR 100% KNOCKDOWN IN CHOICE BOXES WITH THE DARK-HALF TREATED
(From Ebeling, Reierson & Wagner[261])

Insecticide	Concentration %	KD_{50} confined	KD_{100} in choice box	Repellency factor $\left(\dfrac{KD^{100}}{KD^{50}}\right)$
Boric acid	100	2,593	9,072	3·5
Sodium fluoride	100	200	6,192	31
Chlordane	2	130	5,328	41
Diazinon	1	46	3,312	72
Propoxur	1	10	2,880	288
Drione	1	3·3	3,883	1,177

When the four pest species of cockroach are confined on boric acid, adult males of the Brown-banded cockroach are the most readily affected (KD_{50}: 4·3 hr), compared with German (14·0), Oriental (15·1) and American (21·2 hr). In choice tests (see Chapter 7), Oriental and German cockroaches succumb more quickly (KD_{100}: 4·6 and 5·0 days, respectively) than Brown-banded and American cockroaches (6·2 and 7·4 days).[261] In mock-up wall voids (discussed in Chapter 7) boric acid dust was the most effective of all the insecticides tested against German cockroaches.

In low income houses in N. Carolina (one-storey dwellings) which were infested with *B. germanica*, boric acid proved as effective for 6 months, as various formulations of chlorpyrifos dust (1 per cent) and spray (0·5 per cent).[867] Treatment of domestic properties, with up to 2 kg of boric acid dust in each dwelling, and of commercial buildings with up to 23 kg, gave better control of *B. germanica* than organic insecticides sprayed at the usual dosages such as propoxur emulsion (Baygon), and diazinon, with or without

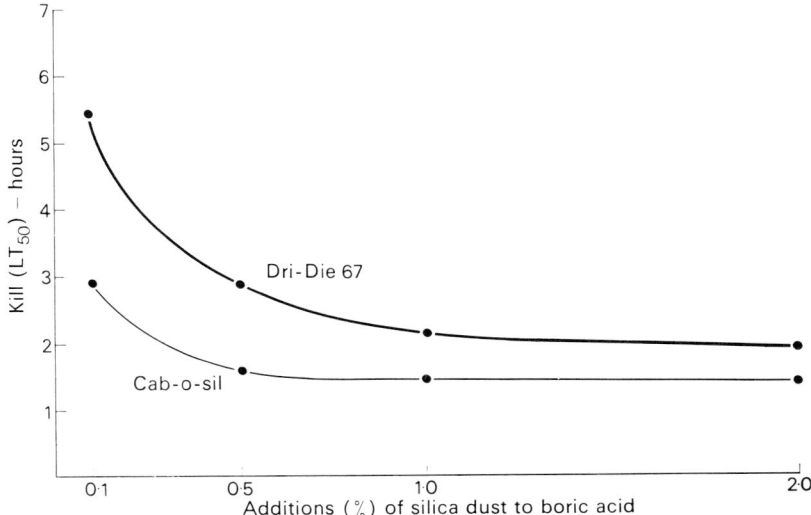

Fig. 90. Increase in the speed of kill of *B. germanica* confined on boric acid with additions of small amounts of silica dust. Boric acid alone killed 50 per cent in 12·4 hours; Dri-Die 67 and Cab-o-sil alone killed 50 per cent in 1·6 and 0·9 hours, respectively. (From Moore[586]).

dichlorvos (Table XXXIII). In comparison with inorganic insecticides, boric acid is more effective than Drione (silica aerogel plus pyrethrins) and sodium fluoride applied as dusts to control German and Brown-banded cockroaches. This is attributed to the lower repellency of boric acid in treated harbourages, with a longer residual than the organophosphates. Treatment with boric acid preceded by pyrethrins eliminated the cockroaches more quickly and prolonged the period of effective control.[260]

SODIUM FLUORIDE AND FLUOROSILICATE

Two compounds of fluorine have been used as dusts for cockroach control: (1) sodium fluoride, which is still used today in small amounts although almost completely superceded by modern, synthetic insecticides, and (2) sodium fluorosilicate, which played a temporary role in the early 1940's, when there was a need for alternative insecticides to counter the short supply of pyrethrum and sodium fluoride. Others have been used in agriculture.

The earliest reference to the insecticidal properties of fluorine occurs in a British Patent of 1896, entitled 'An improved composition or material for destroying insects'. It mentions effectiveness against cockroaches and advocates finely pulverised sodium fluoride and sodium silico-fluoride (sodium fluorosilicate).

Sodium fluoride was used in cockroach powders in the U.S.A. before 1900 but did not come into general use until 1915. There was apparently a severe outbreak of cotton worm and cotton boll weevil in 1923 which caused an acute shortage of arsenic; the need for a substitute stimulated a close examination of fluorine insecticides against field pests.[524] However, because sodium fluoride damages plants its use has been limited mainly to inclusion in poison baits and dusts for controlling household insects. It is also a component of some timber preservatives. In the years just before World War II the estimated annual consumption of sodium fluoride for the control of indoor pests was about 1500 tons.

Sodium fluorosilicate was the first of the fluorine compounds to be used against crop insects, as it is much safer on foliage. Nevertheless, fluorosilicate was not fool-proof for this purpose and became largely replaced by Cryolite (sodium aluminium fluoride).

Sodium fluorosilicate was once a popular mothproofing agent for textiles and found good use in baits for the control of crickets and grasshoppers. Lever[500] reports on its effective control of *P. americana* in homes in Suva, Fiji.

TABLE XXXII

KILL (%) OF ADULT MALE *B. GERMANICA*, GIVEN THE CHOICE OF ENTERING SIMULATED HARBOURAGES TREATED WITH BORIC ACID AND SILICA DUSTS, SEPARATELY AND COMBINED
(From Moore[586])

Dust	Days					
	1	2	3	4	7	10
Boric acid alone	3	18	70	98	100	100
Boric acid and						
Dri-Die 0·1%	0	12	70	95	100	100
Dri-Die 1·0%	0	2	13	42	88	98
Cab-o-sil 0·1%	0	15	72	97	100	100
Cab-o-sil 1·0%	0	7	17	28	72	80
Dri-Die and Cab-o-sil alone	0	0	0	0	0	0

Manufacture and properties

Rarely in this book has mention been made of insecticide manufacture, but here it is of interest. The ease and cheapness of manufacture of fluorine compounds were in part responsible for their becoming widely used for cockroach control. Sodium fluoride is made from fluorspar (calcium fluoride), reacted with sulphuric acid, and the resulting hydrofluoric acid is neutralised with sodium carbonate to give sodium fluoride. It is a colourless and odourless crystalline powder, with a specific gravity of 2·8. The vapour pressure is extremely low, imparting long residual life. It is soluble in water, 1 part in 25 at 15°C; aqueous solutions corrode glass.

Sodium fluorosilicate became available as a by-process of the fertiliser industry. Phosphate rock is composed largely of a double compound, of calcium phosphate and calcium fluoride. In the manufacture of superphosphate the fumes of silicon tetrafluoride were once allowed to escape, but this became prohibited because of injury to surrounding vegetation. This is an early example of action taken to prevent pollution of the environment by industry; some manufacturers recovered the fluorine gases to make the sodium salt.

Sodium fluoroscilicate is an odourless, granular, non-volatile powder, soluble 1 part in 150 parts of water at 17°C. It is insoluble in common organic solvents and has a specific gravity almost the same as sodium fluoride. Both are therefore rather heavy dusts.

Toxicity and symptoms of poisoning
Differences in the mammalian toxicity and the insecticidal effectiveness of

TABLE XXXIII

PERFORMANCE OF INSECTICIDES IN THE CONTROL OF GERMAN COCKROACHES, IN APARTMENTS OF DIFFERENT COMPLEXITIES, WITH RESPECT TO SANITATION AND THE NUMBER OF HARBOURAGES PRESENT
(From Ebeling & Reierson[255])

Insecticide*	No. of apartments	No. cockroaches trapped/apt. before treatment	Average survival (%) after treatment	
			1 month	3 months
Simple environments				
Boric acid dust	10	256	0.05	0.00
Propoxur spray (1%)	10	189	0.63	0.32
Diazinon (1%) and dichlorvos (0.2%) spray	10	46	0.94	0.22
Complex environments				
Boric acid dust**	12	24	0.3	0.0
Propoxur (1%) spray	12	17	68.0	131.0
Diazinon (1%) spray	12	7	11.2	21.0

* One lb of dust and 1 qt of spray per treatment.
** Plus 0.25 pint of Propoxur 1% emulsion in limited areas of kitchens and bathrooms.

fluorine compounds depend on the extent to which the toxic principle—the element fluorine—becomes available in solution. Both fluorine and fluorosilicates are protoplasmic poisons and toxic to virtually all forms of plant and animal life.

Sodium fluoride is regarded as a highly toxic poison. The acute oral toxicity (LD_{50}: rat) is about 200 mg/kg. The minimum acute lethal dose to dogs is between 50 and 100 mg/kg. The lethal dose for man is 75–150 mg/kg; deaths have occurred after ingestion of 2–4g. Chronic administration of 500 ppm of sodium fluoride in the diet of rats is toxic; 900 ppm is 100 per cent lethal in 10 days. Dusts of sodium fluoride are distinctly hazardous when handled in such a way as to make the substance air-borne.

Sodium fluoride 'ties up' calcium in the body by the formation of insoluble calcium fluoride. Recommended antidotes therefore include any form of calcium. Aluminium sulphate may be more effective through the formation of cryolite (Na_3AlF_6) which is relatively non-toxic to higher animals.[524]

Numerous fatalities have resulted from sodium fluoride being swallowed inadvertently:[744,745] in 1940, eleven men died from eating pancakes made with sodium fluoride mistaken for baking powder. Many instances of 'food poisoning' may, in fact have been mild cases of fluoride poisoning, traceable to wrong or careless use of dust in kitchens and restaurants.[14]

To avoid the hazard of mistaking sodium fluoride for food substances an early requirement in the U.S. was that commercial products must be coloured. This is now a requirement for insecticidal dusts in many countries; blues and greens are the usual pigments used.

When sodium fluorosilicate is swallowed, it would be expected to be more toxic than other inorganic fluorines, as 60 per cent of this molecule is made up of fluorine. The reverse, however, is true. The silicofluoride is safer than sodium fluoride because the former is less soluble: the acute oral LD_{50} (rat) is nearer 300 mg/kg. The oral LD_{50} (dog) is about 150 mg/kg. Dusts containing sodium fluorosilicate can cause intense nasal irritation if inhaled.

Activity against cockroaches
Sodium fluoride has been used in various formulations: as dust, poison baits, 3 per cent solutions, wet crayons and often blended with borax, pyrethrum and inert diluents. It has been claimed to act as a potent stomach poison in insects, destroying the epithelium of the mid-gut, and to act as a nerve toxicant. The formulation of sodium fluorosilicate most widely used for cockroach control is a dust mixed 1 part with 2 parts of inert diluent.

When DDT first became available for use in retail products in the U.S.A. the performance of sodium fluoride acted as the standard against which the new insecticide was compared. Using a test chamber in which dust settled onto German cockroaches which were allowed to run through it for 8 minutes, concentrations of sodium fluoride below 50 per cent were not fully effective against 2-day old adults:[351] males are more easily killed than females and the addition of pyrethrum marc (see p. 226) increases both the speed of poisoning and kill. A dust containing 10 per cent sodium fluoride performs marginally less well than 25 per cent sodium fluorosilicate (Table XXXIV). The better activity of the fluoride has also been shown by Marcovitch & Stanley.[524]

TABLE XXXIV

KILL (%) AND SURVIVAL TIME (HOURS) OF GERMAN COCKROACHES TREATED WITH DUSTS IN A SETTLING CHAMBER. PYROPHYLLITE WAS USED AS THE DILUENT
(From Gould[351])

Active ingredient (%)		Kill		Survival time	
		Males	Females	Males	Females
Sodium fluoride	0·5	22	6	67	—
	5	52	14	78	90
	10	86	32	64	74
	25	92	74	53	68
	50	100	90	34	61
Sodium fluoride	10	92	48	35	64
Sodium fluoride + pyrethrum marc	90	100	58	15	40
Sodium fluorosilicate	25	100	49	46	77

With older German cockroaches, 10 weeks after the final moult, 100 per cent kill in 48 hours can be obtained with a dust of 33 per cent sodium fluoride.[337] These tests were done in 1 gallon jars dusted to cover the bottom and walls and the excess shaken out: 33 per cent pyrethrum (probably 0·33 pyrethrins) was less effective. A dust containing 7 per cent DDT was needed to give complete kill in 48 hours. Sodium fluoride is less insecticidal against adult female *B. germanica* than 0·5 per cent lindane, 5 per cent chlordane and 10 per cent DDT when dusted directly onto the insects and when picked up by them in treated containers.[615]

Susceptibility of the developmental stages of *B. germanica* to deposits of sodium fluoride is reported by Dewey:[232] adult males take 3–4 times longer to die than second and third instar nymphs; adult females take about 15 times longer. Sixth and seventh stage nymphs are the most resistant and require about twice the deposit to kill them in the same time as adult females. About 2g of sodium fluoride per cm^2 is needed to kill all stages within 24 hours. Homes treated with dust, in comparison with others treated with sprays of chlordane, diazinon and malathion, contained many more German cockroaches 3–4 weeks later when sodium fluoride was used (Table LXXVII).

The susceptibility of male and female American cockroaches varies with the way sodium fluoride is administered, by mouth, injection or by contact (Table XXXV).

TABLE XXXV

THE SUSCEPTIBILITY OF AMERICAN AND GERMAN COCKROACHES TO SODIUM FLUORIDE APPLIED BY DIFFERENT METHODS

Species	Kill	Dosage Males	Dosage Females	How applied	Refs.
P. amer.	LD_{50}	250	500 μg/g	Contact	558
		300	1,000 μg/g	Oral	
		120	140 μg/g	Injection into blood	
	LD_{50}	>2,000	1,200 μg/g	Contact	421
		300–400	100–200 μg/g	Injection into stomach via mouth	
	LD_{100}	350	850 μg/g	Contact	558
		1,300	3,500 μg/g	Oral	
		150	170 μg/g	Injection into blood	
	MLD	156–780 μg/insect		Oral injection	780
	LD_{70} (10 days)	1,833 μg/insect		Insects entering dusted area at will	549
		1,763 μg/g			
B. germ.	LD_{50}	130 μg/cm²		Topical: dust applied to insect	615
		40 μg/cm²		Insects caged on dust	
	LD_{70} (4 days)	158 μg/insect		Insects entering dusted area at will	549
		1,375 μg/g			

Mode of entry

Many insecticides used as dusts for cockroach control cause death by being picked-up on the integument and ingested when the insect grooms itself. This was the view of Shafer[741] and Hockenyos[431] for the entry of sodium fluoride; they believed that sodium fluoride may penetrate certain areas of the cuticle of American and Oriental cockroaches but absorption is slight and ingestion is necessary to kill. This view has been perpetuated in a more recent revision of 'Scientific Guide to Pest Control Operations'[799]: 'it (sodium fluoride) acts as a stomach poison and to a lesser degree as a contact poison against insects'. A review of the evidence suggests that the reverse is more probably the case.

American cockroaches fed 'pills' of ground beef and oatmeal containing 1 per cent sodium fluoride survived; at 5 per cent they refused to eat and 90 per cent died in 4 weeks, mainly from starvation.[596] Griffiths & Tauber[378] claim that American cockroaches have to be starved before they will eat a paste containing sodium fluoride; it then requires 4–6 days to kill them (Fig. 91), compared with only 33 hours for males, and 52 hours for females, allowed to walk through a dust. Cockroaches with their mouthparts sealed die before those not sealed, suggesting that ingestion does not contribute to kill. The ability of sodium fluoride to penetrate the cuticle, particularly unsclerotised portions is well-documented.[431, 433, 434, 596, 741]

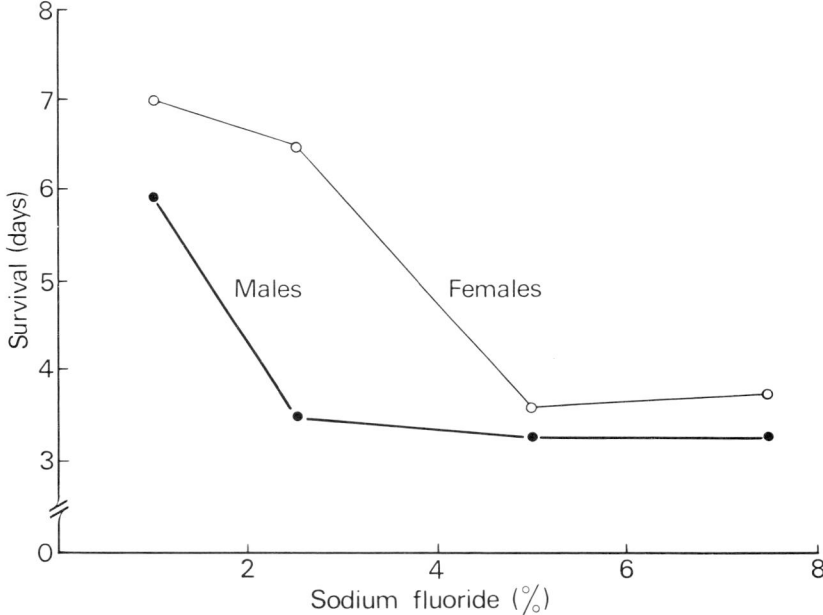

Fig. 91. Survival of adult *P. americana* fed starch paste containing sodium fluoride. (From Griffiths & Tauber[378]).

There would now seem a strong case for believing that the principal benefit of sodium fluoride as an insecticide is through its contact action, ingestion toxicity being only secondary. Additional support for this comes from the reaction of cockroaches poisoned by a dust combining sodium fluoride with pyrethrins; the latter causes paralysis so rapidly, that the cockroach is unable to clean itself and ingestion is thus much reduced (Marcovitch & Stanley[524]). These observers claim a synergistic action for the two materials: thus 100 mg of pyrethrum blown into a testing chamber kills 4 per cent of females in 24 hours; the same amount of sodium fluoride kills 12 per cent, whereas 50 mg of each, combined, kills 64 per cent in the same time. It must be assumed that the pyrethrum stimulates the insects to excessive movement during early stages of poisoning, causing them to become more readily coated with dust, than is so with sodium fluoride alone.

Examples of the susceptibility of American and German cockroaches to sodium fluoride, applied by different methods are given in Table XXXV.

Deposits of dust (3 mg/g) on adult American cockroaches kill in about 24 hours; heavier deposits do not increase speed of kill (Fig. 92). Symptoms of poisoning follow the sequence of irritability, torpor, sudden spasms, gradual decline in activity and death in 4–48 hours. When sodium fluoride is injected into the haemolymph in aqueous suspension, its toxicity to American cockroaches is about 1/60 for males, and 1/12 for females, of pyrethrins applied in the same way.[421]

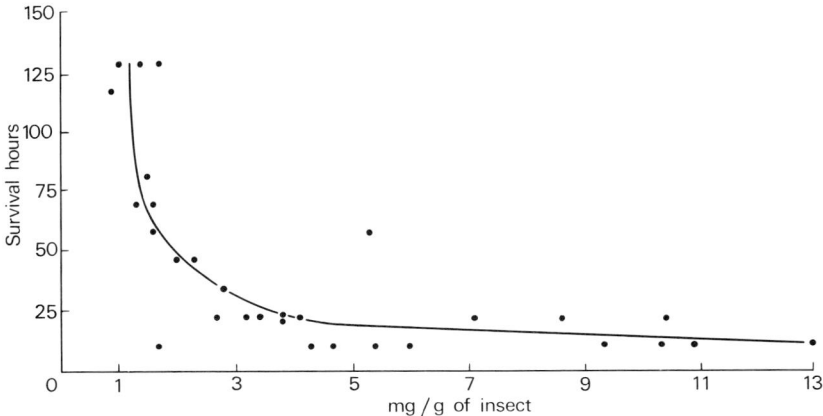

Fig. 92. Survival of adult *P. americana* exposed to contact with sodium fluoride powder for 15 seconds. (From Griffiths & Tauber[378]).

Dusts containing sodium fluoride and pyrethrins

Dusts of sodium fluoride for cockroach control (Fig. 93) are usually combined with pyrethrum to obtain quicker kill, the pyrethrum content varying from 25–50 per cent. The popularity of such mixtures, among servicing companies in the United States, was apparent in the years immediately following the discovery of resistance to chlordane by the German cockroach. At that time the older dust formulations regained some of their previous appeal because organophosphates such as diazinon, did not give the pest control operator the same residual as chlordane in the control of non-resistant *B. germanica*.[15]

A detailed study of the views of insecticide manufacturers and users at that time, highlighted the merits and disadvantages of sodium fluoride alone and in combination, relative to other dust formulations. The majority opinion in 1958 was that 75 per cent sodium fluoride with 25 per cent pyrethrum was the best all-round dust for cockroach control, with a 50/50 mixture as second choice. The actual pyrethrins content was probably 0·5 per cent or less. Sodium fluoride alone was considered not to knockdown cockroaches quickly enough: 'it lets the roach run away and die, out of sight, and this is not held to be good psychology for a bug killer. The housewife wants to see the roaches dead in their tracks'. It was for this reason that borax and boric acid were never popular in the United States. A summary of the relative merits of some of the older dusts used is given in Table XXXVI.

TABLE XXXVI

MERITS OF DIFFERENT DUSTS FOR COCKROACH CONTROL INCORPORATING INORGANIC MATERIALS AS ACTIVE INGREDIENTS AND DILUENTS
(Modified from Anon[15])

Insecticide	%	Material cost	Effectiveness	Speed of action	Deterioration
Sodium fluoride	100	Low	Excellent	Fair	No
Sodium fluoride + pyrethrum	75 25	Moderate	Excellent	Good	Moderate
Sodium fluoride + pyrethrum	50 50	High	Excellent	Fast	Yes
Pyrethrum (0·7% pyrethrins)	100	Very high	Good	Fast	Yes
Pyrethrum + borax	75 25	High	Good	Fast	Yes
Boric acid	100	Low	Excellent	Very slow	No
Borax + cocoa & sugar	50 50	Low	Poor	Very slow	No

DESICCANT DUSTS

Water is a most important requirement for cockroaches: it influences where they live and their behaviour to conserve body fluids. Silica dusts affect insects by causing water loss, by an abrasive or adsorptive action on the cuticle. Their desiccant action is superior to that of sorptive clays and diatomaceous earths. Silica dusts are available under a number of proprietary names, of which perhaps the best known is Cab-o-sil (Table XXXVII).

The use of dusts to kill insects by desiccation has been known for many years. Hockenyos[432] showed this with Oriental cockroaches in 1933. Diatomaceous earths, which have a high silica content, have been used to protect harvested grains against storage pests in warm climates. In a series of experiments, Tarshis[784] screened 90 compounds as dusts against cockroaches among which the silica aerogel (now designated Dri-Die 67®) proved most

®Dri-Die 67 —Trade mark of W. R. Grace & Co., Davison Chem. Div., Baltimore.

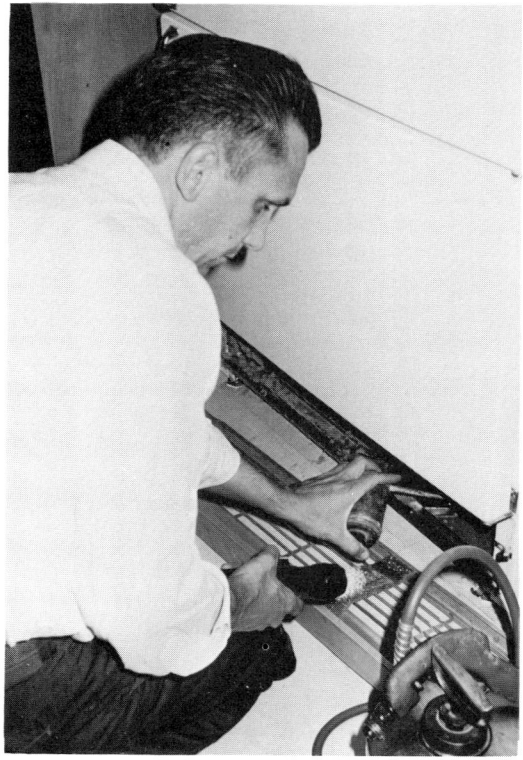

Fig. 93. Application of sodium fluoride dust admixed with pyrethrins by bellows-type duster to control German cockroaches infesting motor casings of a refrigerator. Note the absence of gloves and mask, which the operator should be wearing.

effective. Good performance was also obtained against 49 other insects of public health and veterinary importance.[787] Dri-Die has been developed for commercial application and is examined in some detail in the pages which follow.

Chemical and physical properties
Dri-Die 67 is a white, odourless, highly absorptive finely divided type of silica with an average particle size of 3μ and density of 72 mg/cm^3. The product consists of 95·3 per cent amorphous silica gel (i.e. 90 per cent non-crystalline silicon dioxide) and 4·7 per cent ammonium fluorosilicate, which prevents 'caking' when dry, and adds to insecticidal effectiveness. This additive had the original function of improving the properties of silica aerogel in paint manufacture.

Because the insecticidal activity of Dri-Die 67 depends on combined chemical and physical properties of the aerogel for absorbing cuticular wax, maintenance of the dust as discrete particles is essential for long life. During the first three months after application some insecticidal effectiveness is lost, to the extent that the deposit takes 2–3 times longer to kill German cockroaches. This is caused by a reduced pick up by the insects resulting from a loss in the electrostatic charge contributed by the ammonium fluorosilicate. Thereafter there is no deterioration and dusted voids remain completely repellent to cockroaches.[264]

TABLE XXXVII

KILL AT 48 HR (LD_{50} AND LD_{90} in mg/ft^2) OF ADULT MALE *B. GERMANICA* EXPOSED FOR 30 SECS TO PLYWOOD TREATED WITH VARIOUS SILICA DUSTS
(From Eastin & Burden[251])

Silica dust	LD_{50}	LD_{90}
Cab-o-sil	100	240
SG-67 (Dri-Die)	104	130
SG-68	109	150
Estersil-1	175	375
Santocel-C	205	455

Dri-Die in combination with synergised pyrethrins is marketed as a dust under the trade name Drione®. The chemical composition is:

Pyrethrins 1 per cent
Piperonyl butoxide 10 per cent
Silica aerogel 38 per cent
Ammonium fluorosilicate 2 per cent $\Big\} = 40$ per cent Dri-Die 67
Petroleum base oil 49 per cent

This formulation has less tendency than Dri-Die to 'float' in the air when applied by dusting equipment.

Mammalian toxicity
The acute oral LD_{50} (rat) of silica aerogel exceeds 3,000 mg/kg. Recommendations for use include the treatment of dogs and cats (30–60 g/animal) for the control of parasites. Because silica aerogel is amorphous, rather than crystalline, it is said not to cause silicosis in man. Nevertheless, the use of a mask is recommended to protect against nasal and throat irritation.

Action against cockroaches
Chemically inactive dusts, of fine particle size, kill insects by interacting with

Drione®—Trade mark of FMC Corporation.

the waterproofing surface of the cuticle, either by adsorption of the lipids or by abrasion. The size of dust particles affects adhesion to the insect.

In the American cockroach the outer layer of the cuticle is only 2 μ thick and the lipid or wax layer about 0·6 μ (see Chapter 4, Vol. I). The cockroach retains its body water through the properties of the film covering the cuticle.[84,691] As silica aerogels are capable of removing the soft covering wax of the cockroach, even when the insect is motionless, their action must be primarily adsorption of the soft cuticular wax onto the dust particles, rather than abrasion.[847]

In tests of the reaction of different cockroaches, males and females were allowed to crawl through silica aerogel for 1 minute and then shaken to remove all possible dust adhering loosely.[784] *Blattella germanica* is the most susceptible and *P. americana* the most tolerant (Table XXXVIII). About 0·5 mg on adult German cockroaches kills in about an hour;[785] *Leucophaea maderae* and *Blaberus* species are knocked down in 12 hours and are dead in 24 hours.[787] Relative humidities from 25–100 per cent scarcely affect speed of kill.

Silica dusts are more rapidly insecticidal than boric acid but strongly repellent.[586] When up to 1 per cent of silica dust is added to boric acid the mixture is more effective and only slightly more repellent than boric acid alone.

TABLE XXXVIII

TIME REQUIRED FOR 100% KILL (LT_{100}) AND WEIGHT LOSS (%) OF ADULT MALE AND FEMALE, GERMAN, BROWN-BANDED, ORIENTAL AND AMERICAN COCKROACHES TREATED WITH DRI-DIE 67
(From Tarshis[784])

Species	LT_{100} (mins)		Weight loss at death (%)		Weight loss when completely desiccated (%)	
	Males	Females	Males	Females	Males	Females
German	45	95	20	20	66	61
Brown-banded	160	190	35	25	64	66
Oriental	180	240	19	17	64	66
American	270	450	21	28	70	67

Use in cockroach control

Although only small amounts of silica aerogel are needed to kill cockroaches, large amounts are necessary to ensure control in wall cavities, ceiling voids and in underfloor areas, where cockroaches harbour (Fig. 94). Thus application of about 5g/m² is recommended. Like most other insecticides, Dri-Die has no effect on oothecae so that residual quantities of dust in infested areas are required. In common with the use of other dusts, the pest control operator

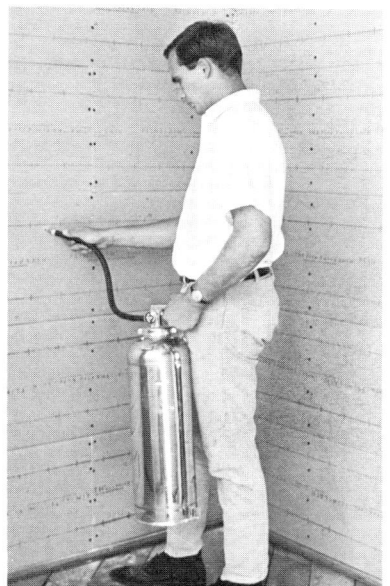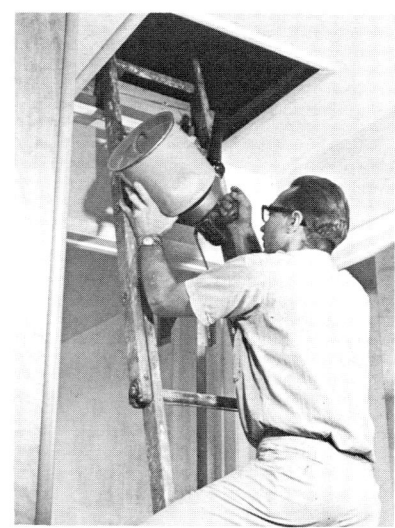

Fig. 94. Application of Dri-Die (left) into a mock-up wall void to test repellency and performance against German cockroaches, in comparison with other insecticidal dusts; (right) in a roof void using an electric dust-blower. (Courtesy: Ebeling, Reierson & Wagner; U.C.L.A.).

must often drill holes in the kick plates of wall units and other voids to get the dust into cavities occupied by cockroaches (Fig. 95).

Tarshis[787] describes results of an evaluation of Dri-Die and Drione for the control of cockroaches in a housing project, hospitals, schools and other public buildings in California, where attempts at pest control by tenants and professional personnel with conventional toxicants failed. The use of the faster acting Drione (incorporating pyrethrins) appeared necessary in the public areas, although Dri-Die was effective in concealed voids. The application of Dri-Die to attics, wall voids and other spaces during the construction of two to four-bedroom apartment units in California kept them free of cockroaches and other insects.[787]

Tests in Florida in single storey homes constructed of concrete blocks compared the performance of Dri-Die—up to 100g per home—with a 1 per cent diazinon dust.[251] Pre- and post-treatment counts of German cockroaches showed that the silica aerogels were less effective than diazinon (Fig. 96).

Good control of American cockroaches in sewers has been achieved by blowing Drione (135g) into every manhole along infested sewer lines.[264] This treatment was adopted by the Los Angeles Sanitation Division of the Department of County Engineers: 'apparently all active stages of the American cockroach are completely eliminated in one treatment, demonstrating the

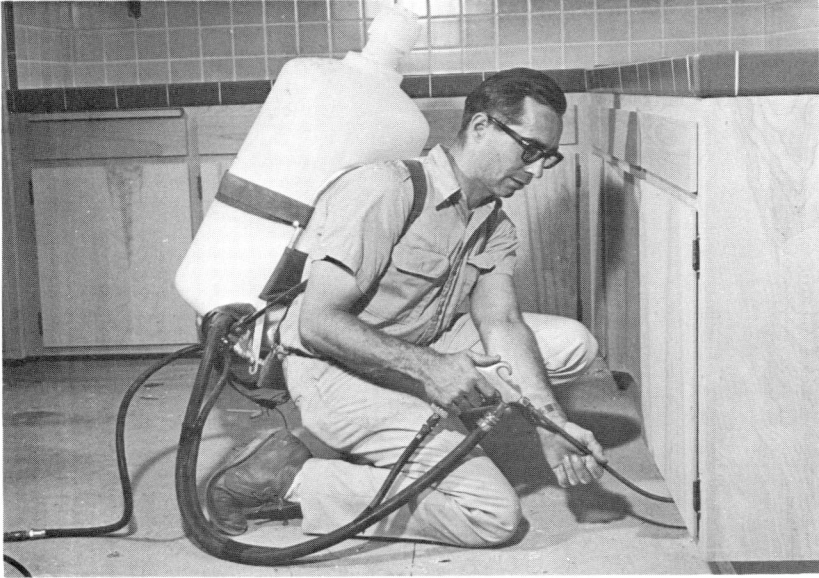

Fig. 95. Drilling a hole in a kick panel and applying insecticidal dust (Dri-Die) in the void under the cabinet with a compressed air blower. (Courtesy: Ebeling, Wagner & Reierson, U.C.L.A.).

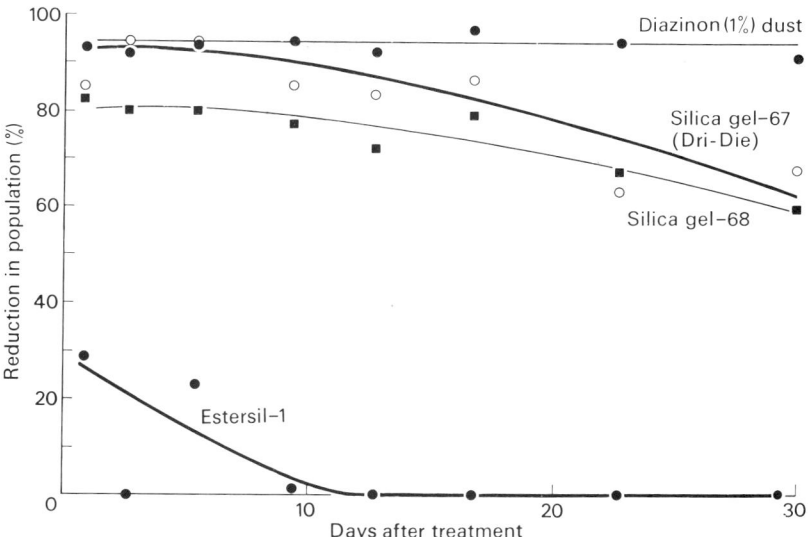

Fig. 96. Control of German cockroaches in Florida homes with diazinon and silica dusts (at average of 27°C and 79 per cent R. H.). (From Eastin & Burden[251]).

potential of a highly insecticidal (though repellent) formulation when the cockroaches have no way of escaping from it'.[261]

PHOSPHORUS

Yellow phosphorus has been used in baits for the control of cockroaches for at least 100 years. Proprietary formulations containing phosphorus at 1–2 per cent were among the earliest products sold for this purpose. Among the chronological events in the history of insecticides, Shepard[746] lists the use of phosphorus paste for cockroach control in Prussia in 1859. Products of this type are mentioned by Marlatt in 1896 in the United States[527] where they remained in use into the early 1960's. Risk to man and alternative safer chemicals, then resulted in phosphorus paste becoming largely replaced by baits of chlordecone (p. 313) and propoxur (p. 379).

Red phosphorus is not used in pest control but other inorganic compounds of phosphorus are of value in rodent control (zinc phosphide) and as an insecticidal fumigant (aluminium phosphide). Organic phosphates are, of course, widely used as insecticides (Chapter 12).

Properties
At normal temperatures, yellow phosphorus is inflammable, igniting spontaneously in air; but when baits are properly made, incorporating 98 per cent of non-flammable material there is no fire hazard. Phosphorus bait is highly

toxic: the fatal dose of phosphorus to man is about 50 mg, equivalent to 2·5–5g of formulated bait.

Phosphorus paste is most effective for the control of the larger pest cockroaches (*P. americana* and *B. orientalis*)[68] and for the smaller Brown-banded cockroach.[14] The American cockroach, for example, is 'attracted to and imbibes freely' from bait and is killed (oral LD_{50}) by a dose of 0·02mg phosphorus/g body weight. Poisoned American cockroaches receiving just a lethal dose, linger a month or more and become sluggish until they die. Insects which eat a large fatal dose die in 24 hours. Survival times for *P. americana* vary from 55 days at 0·01 mg/g to 10 days at 0·35 mg/g.

The German cockroach is not attracted, nor does it feed willingly: this species is also less susceptible (oral LD_{50}: 0·13 mg/g body weight).[186] These factors probably account for the relatively poor control of *B. germanica* with phosphorus paste.

Application

The bait is especially useful in damp, humid, tropical climates, or in other wet places where moisture may render dust useless. Bait is applied by spatula or the blade of a flexible knife (Fig. 97) onto basement walls, the ends of floor joists, or in other out-of-the-way places not accessible to children and domestic animals. In the treatment of homes, the bait is often used in garages and outbuildings, around the property, as a 'first line of defence' against outdoor living cockroaches (*Periplaneta* spp.) becoming established in the home. It can be spread on paper or cardboard (marked 'Poison'), or otherwise pushed into harbourages. The paste dries quickly on porous surfaces but on

 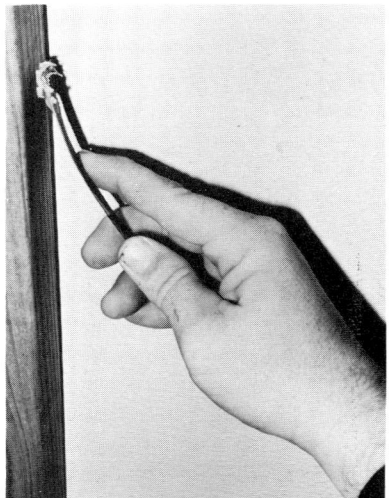

Fig. 97. Application of phosphorus paste with a spatula to crevices above head height in a domestic garage for the control of *P. americana*.

relatively non-porous surfaces, it remains soft and attractive for a number of weeks.

Life of the bait can be extended by rolling it inside cylinders of cardboard held with rubber bands: the more modern aluminium cooking foil is ideal for this purpose; it is not absorptive and is suitably maleable. Unless made inaccessible by insertion well into harbourages, or on the backs of kitchen drawer units, baits should be applied above head height; phosphorus should never be diluted with water, syrup or any other liquid which may cause it to drip. Also, because of its high toxicity, the bait should not be used where it may fall and contaminate food.

THALLIUM SULPHATE

This toxicant has been used in baits, usually at 1 per cent, for the control of rodents, ants and cockroaches. Thallium is one of the most toxic elements; the sulphate is particularly hazardous from the viewpoint of a high acute oral toxicity (LD_{50} rat: 16 mg/kg) and the accumulation of repeated doses in the body. The fatal dose for man is less than 500 mg. It is a tasteless, odourless and slow acting poison, readily absorbed through the skin.

In recent years there has been increasing restriction by Governments on the use of thallium sulphate for pest control; in the sale of products and later, of formulations used by servicing companies and health departments. The application of baits containing thallium sulphate for insect control can no longer be justified when far less toxic materials are available.

HYDROGEN CYANIDE AND OTHER FUMIGANTS

Before modern insecticides were available, the elimination of cockroaches from buildings was looked upon as difficult and sometimes accepted as impossible. Fumigations were carried out occasionally by health departments of local authorities, where infestations were extensive.

Hydrogen cyanide was used, but in common with other fumigants, it was recognised to have several limitations: the building structure was often not suitable and allowed gas to escape; treatment was expensive; it gave no protection against reinfestation; and because of the risk of cyanide to man, fumigation was often impracticable, especially of premises within congested or commercial areas. Buildings infested with bed bugs were also once fumigated; now however, treatment for both these pests is almost always carried out with residual insecticides.

Relatively long periods under gas are necessary for fumigants to be effective. Tests have been reported showing the effect of ethylene oxide[318] and carbon dioxide[80] on adults and eggs of *P. americana* (Table XXXIX) and on adult *B. germanica* (Table XL). Exposure of adult female *B. germanica* to carbon dioxide (94 per cent) for 3 hours at 32°C killed them in a few days, but nymphs hatched from oothecae deposited before the females died. Exposures

TABLE XXXIX

EXPOSURE PERIODS (HOURS) FOR 100% KILL OF ADULTS AND EGGS OF *P. AMERICANA* TREATED WITH AN AEROSOL FORMULATION CONTAINING 12% ETHYLENE OXIDE AT 27°C

(From Fulton et al[318])

Dosage (lb/1,000 ft^3)	Adults	Eggs
0·25	18	18
1	2	2
2	2	2
4	0·5	1

of 4·5 hours (at 31°C), or 7·5 hours (at 23°C) are needed to completely prevent hatching of German cockroach nymphs.[169] Where infestations are not amenable to treatment with sprays or dusts, as in electronic equipment, or in the wheeled food carts used in hospitals, infestations can be controlled by carbon dioxide (dry ice) fumigation.[795]

American cockroaches in pure carbon dioxide recover quickly if exposed for less than 2 hours; 2–2·5 hours causes paralysis which disappears in 5–7 days; exposures of 5 hours cause irreversible damage but not death; after 8 hours in CO_2 the insects cannot be revived.[112] American cockroaches kept for 2 hours in oxygen-free nitrogen recover without apparent damage, but when kept for longer, irreversible damage occurs and an 8-hour exposure causes death.

Phosphine in extremely small amounts produces irreversible injury to *P. americana* provided the insects are exposed for a long enough time. But

TABLE XL

KILL (% AT 24 HOURS), OF ADULT *B. GERMANICA* EXPOSED TO DIFFERENT PERIODS OF FUMIGATION WITH CARBON DIOXIDE

(From Barnhart[80])

Exposure (hours)	Males	Females
0 (Control)	0	0
1	0	0
2	0	10
3	10	20
4	50	50
5	90	90
6	100	100

phosphine is not absorbed by insects in significant quantities unless oxygen is also present: oxygen is necessary for toxicity.[112]

Cockroaches are readily killed by fumigation with methyl bromide.[818] If treatment with vapour is necessary the use of methyl bromide or dichlorvos (see p. 331) is usually the most appropriate.

ORGANIC THIOCYANATES

These insecticides have now almost disappeared from use. They served a useful function during World War II when the allocation of pyrethrum, for military purposes, made it virtually unavailable for civilian use. At that time the search for other insecticides of low toxicity directed attention to the organic thiocyanates. They were extensively tested for insecticidal activity, and soon found uses in household sprays in the United States for the control of flies and cockroaches. Use outside N. America has always been small.

Two thiocyanates received particular attention: Lethane 384® (a 50 per cent solution of 2-butoxy-2-thiocyanodiethyl ether) and Lethane A-70® (a 90 per cent solution of 2–2 dithiocyanoethyl ether). Both cause rapid knockdown of insects and have good contact toxicity, but their unpleasant odour and irritation of the skin and mucous membranes undoubtedly limited their development. A third product: Thanite® (isobornyl thiocyanoacetate) is chemically related, but has the advantage of being a synergist for pyrethrum and some insecticidal carbamates, although combination with the latter is not of practical significance (see p. 363). Thanite has been incorporated in aerosol products for the domestic market (as a knockdown agent, usually at 2 per cent), and was rated 20th in efficacy in 1948 among 91 organic compounds tested against nymphs of *B. germanica*.[133]

Chemical properties and toxicity

The active ingredient of Lethane 384 is an odorous yellow to brown, oily liquid. It is virtually insoluble in water, but can be dissolved in most organic solvents. In addition to being irritant, the lethanes are readily absorbed through unbroken skin. The eyes are said to be particularly vulnerable in providing a route of entry into the body.

The organic thiocyanates are toxicants of the central nervous system and cause asphixiation on inhalation of vapours. Their action is said to involve the release of hydrogen cyanide, with consequent cyanide intoxication, but sublethal doses are excreted.

The acute oral LD_{50} of Lethane 384 (50 per cent) to the rat is 90 mg/kg; dogs are about 10 times more susceptible. Symptoms of poisoning in man include restlessness, depression, cyanosis and dyspnoea followed by tonic convulsions. Death involves respiratory paralysis and occurs swiftly after taking a lethal dose. Thanite has a much lower toxicity to mammals: an acute oral LD_{50} (rat) of 1,000 mg/kg.

Lethane 384® and Lethane A-70® are trade names of Rohm & Haas Co.
Thanite® —trade name of Hercules Inc.

TABLE XLI

RELATIVE TOXICITY (KILL %) OF LETHANE AND PYRETHRINS TO
B. GERMANICA APPLIED AS SETTLING DUSTS IN A TOWER
(Anon[11])

Insecticide	Dosage rate (mg)		
	100	200	400
Lethane A-70 (10%)	38	51	76
Pyrethrins (1%)	40	50	69
Pyrethrins (1%) and sodium fluoride (60/40 mixture)	33	53	77

Effects on cockroaches

Studies with American cockroaches suggest that the organic thiocyanates are poisons of respiratory systems where they also have an HCN-like action. They cause a marked decline in heart beat and blood circulation.[212, 647] In *Blatta*, thiocyanates cause a decline in heart contraction rate and an increase in dilation.

Swift onset of paralysis in *Blatta* is not preceded by the initial excitation characteristic of pyrethrins. Nevertheless, selective degeneration of nerve tissue by Thanite has been recorded in *P. americana*, similar to the condition found with pyrethrum.[701]

The organic thiocyanates have to be used at higher concentrations than the more modern organic insecticides to provide the same insecticidal activity. When dusts are allowed to settle on cockroaches, 10 per cent Lethane A-70 is as active as 1 per cent pyrethrins, and equal to a 60/40 mixture of 1 per cent pyrethrins and sodium fluoride (Table XLI). Male American cockroaches are twice as susceptible as females to Lethane 384 applied topically, which is considerably more active than Thanite (Table XLII). This larger species is also killed slightly more rapidly by Lethane dust than is *B. germanica* (Fig. 98).

TABLE XLII

SUSCEPTIBILITY (mg/g) OF *P. AMERICANA* TO ORGANIC
THIOCYANATES APPLIED TOPICALLY
(From Menusan[558])

Insecticide	LD_{50}		LD_{100}	
	Male	Female	Male	Female
Lethane 384	0·66	1·26	1·36	2·30
Thanite	4·80	—	6·00	—

Use of the old insecticides today

In this chapter we have looked at the properties and performance of some of the older insecticides once relied upon for cockroach control. Some are highly toxic (sodium fluoride, phosphorus and thallium sulphate) and their use cannot be justified today; others are very slow-acting—the boron-containing compounds—but boric acid can still provide excellent cockroach control because of its relative safety and non-repellency. The silicia aerogels can keep ceiling voids, wall cavities and other dead spaces free of cockroaches; these compounds are extremely repellent but are effective in killing cockroaches which become contaminated.

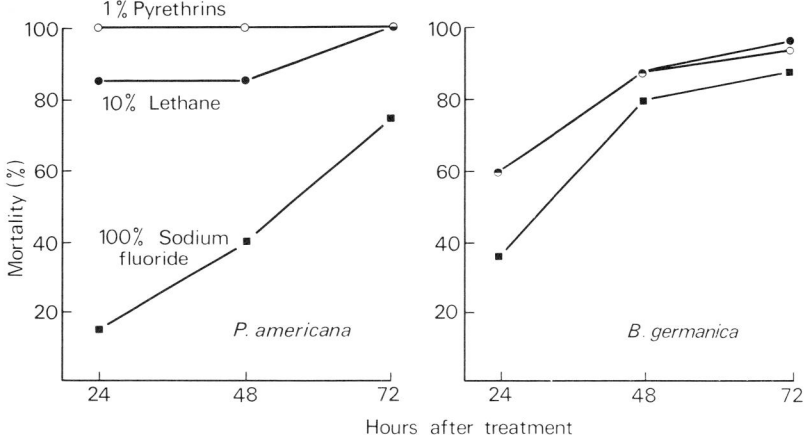

Fig. 98. Comparative kill of adult American and German cockroaches by insecticidal dusts containing pyrethrins, Lethane and sodium fluoride. (Anon.[11]).

Both boric acid and silica aerogels have sufficiently low toxicities to allow their use as 'protectants' against infestation in new building projects. This is a worthy objective with materials of almost permanent insecticidal activity. Their use can also be considered in food areas, and in cupboards and storage areas containing household effects without the latter having to be moved before treatment.

Fumigants no longer have a place in cockroach control unless dichlorvos is used (see Chapter 12): there are cheaper and less demanding ways of achieving cockroach eradication with the dusts and sprays currently available.

The organic thiocyanates have now been superceded by post-war insecticides—more efficient and more pleasant to use. Nevertheless, as we shall see from later chapters, the application of modern *organic* compounds has not been without problems, in a world many times more demanding in its attitudes towards health and safety, than when *inorganic* chemicals were virtually the only insecticides available.

9

THE NATURAL INSECTICIDE
(PYRETHRUM)

Pyrethrum production and use: early history; effects of two World Wars; events between 1940 and 1960; awareness of the environment; influence of synthetic pyrethroids—Pyrethrins: pyrethrum flowers; pyrethrum dusts; pyrethrum extract; the pyrethrins—Effects of pyrethrins on cockroaches: early studies; susceptibility of species; developmental stages and sexes—Recovery from poisoning by pyrethrins: synergism; piperonyl butoxide; Tropital; MGK 264; sesame oil; safroxan; resistance to pyrethrins—Use in insect control: the contribution to cockroach control; indifferent performance; useful flushing action; effects on oothecae; toxicity to man and other animals; residues in food.

Compared with 'man-made' insecticides, pyrethrum has one of the longest histories of safe use. In recent years, it has been promoted as 'the natural insecticide' to emphasise its plant origin. In the United States, there are probably more approved methods of using pyrethrins—extracted from pyrethrum—against household insects and pests of stored foodstuffs, than any other insecticide.[333]

The chemical and biological properties of the pyrethrins are well-established:[173] the insecticide has been used extensively for cockroach control, and although by no means the most efficient for this purpose, it is in some countries the only insecticide permitted in food handling areas. The synthetic pyrethroids—insecticides with similar properties to the pyrethrins, but man-made and with the promise of offering acceptable replacements for the natural product—are relatively new compounds for which effectiveness against cockroaches has only recently been documented.

In this chapter we shall look at the history of pyrethrum production and use; the properties which have lead to its universal adoption and the benefits of synergism. We shall look at the effects of pyrethrins on cockroaches and the effectiveness of the insecticide for cockroach control. The merits of some of the synthetic pyrethroids, in comparison with the natural product, are examined in the next chapter.

PYRETHRUM PRODUCTION AND USE

Pyrethrum is a common name for a group of plants belonging to the genus *Chrysanthemum*, some of which contain insecticidal substances. The commercially important plant is *Chrysanthemum cinerariaefolium*: it grows 45–60 cm high, resembles a field daisy (Fig. 99) and the flowers are picked and processed to yield 'pyrethrum extract'. This contains several constituents collectively referred to as 'pyrethrins'. That these flowers are capable of killing insects was no doubt discovered accidentally and the history of early use is uncertain.

THE NATURAL INSECTICIDE 219

A detailed account of the pyrethrum industry has been given by McLaughlin.[552] Now that chemical manufacturers face stringent requirements in bringing new pesticides onto the market, a review of the major events which have influenced the use of one of our oldest insecticides, is of interest.

Fig. 99. Flowers of pyrethrum (*C. cinerariaefolium*): one of the high yielding clones being cultivated to raise the pyrethrum content of the crop. (Courtesy: Pyrethrum Board, Kenya).

Early history
The original pyrethrum 'insect powder' was believed to have been derived from the plant *Chrysanthemum coccineum* (formerly known as *C. roseum*) from the Caucasus and northern Iran;[746] the nature of the powder was kept a secret there until the early nineteenth century.

Commercial use of pyrethrum is thought to have started in Persia as a mixture of the powdered, dried flowers of two plants, *Chrysanthemum coccineum* and *C. carneum*. The plant which was cultivated in Dalmatia (now Yugoslavia) in the mid 1800's, and which provided the first important source of pyrethrum, was the same as that grown commercially today. Shipment of dried flowers from Dalmatia to the United States began in about 1860. Pyrethrum was first grown experimentally in Japan in 1881.

In Europe, the dried flowers were probably used as an insecticide more than 100 years ago and provided the active constituent of 'Keatings Powder'—a domestic insecticide widely used in the U.K. in the early 1900's. Until 1920, pyrethrum was almost invariably used as a powder. The extraction of flowers with kerosene began in 1919, in the United States, allowing the development of pyrethrum sprays in various formulations.

Effects of two World Wars
Export of dried pyrethrum from Yugoslavia to the United States was interrupted by World War I when supplies were provided by Japan. The first pyrethrum seed from Yugoslavia, was planted in the highlands of Kenya in 1928, starting an industry which was eventually to provide the world's major pyrethrum source.[499] Commercial production in Kenya began in 1933 where it was soon discovered that the content of pyrethrin in African flowers and the yields per acre were higher than could be obtained elsewhere. Kenya now produces about 70 per cent of the world's pyrethrum, with Tanzania, Ecuador and Rwanda contributing important amounts (Fig. 100). The Kenya Pyrethrum Growers Association was also formed in 1933, and the Pyrethrum Board in 1935. The Board owns the processing factories and is organised on a co-operative basis with all profits returned to the growers.

The effort to establish production in Africa in those early years resulted in pyrethrum from Kenya replacing the Japanese product, the latter becoming unavailable because of World War II. Thereafter Japan never exported pyrethrum in any quantity, but as we shall see (p. 255), that country has since made a major contribution towards the technical development of synthetic pyrethroids.

A number of events then had a significant effect on the future use of pyrethrins. In 1934, work had begun in the U.K. to demonstrate the satisfactory control of stored food pests in warehouses by sprays of pyrethrins in heavy oils. On 29th July 1941 an application was made for a patent for an 'aerosol': a development which was quickly to become commonplace and which brought the insecticide firmly into use. During World War II pyrethrum was declared a strategic war material for malaria control, when it was much in demand by the armed forces.

Events between 1940 and 1960
The development of DDT and other chlorinated hydrocarbon insecticides (see Chapter 11) depressed pyrethrum production, especially as DDT appeared to have the property of long life, desirable at that time. Nevertheless, pyrethrum regained its position as a component of domestic aerosols in the late 1940's, coinciding with the first commercially viable synergist, piperonyl butoxide. This followed observations on synergism (see p. 235) made initially with sesame oil in 1940.

In the first years of World War II, pyrethrum powders were used extensively to prevent the spread of lice and typhus. Then and subsequently, synergism was to have a marked influence in reducing the cost of pyrethrins. This made them competitive with the newer synthetic insecticides which were becoming available at that time. DDT and others soon became popular as oil sprays among American householders and industrial users, for purposes not readily fulfilled by aerosols. As a result, sprays and aerosol formulations containing pyrethrins were combined with derris and DDT, to ensure that insects knocked down did not recover.

A review, projecting ahead, the requirements and likely supply of pyrethrum for 1944, said: 'The darkest spot in the insecticide picture is the pyrethrum outlook ... all new crop pyrethrum (1944 crop) will go to the production of aerosol insecticides and sprays for the armed forces in Britain and the United States and probably none will be available for any other purpose' ... 'for use against crawling insects such as roaches, ants, silverfish etc. under suitable conditions, mixtures of exhausted pyrethrum (flowers) with some 50 per cent of sodium fluoride, or sodium silicofluoride, and in some cases with added talc, or other inert dusts have been receiving attention'.[10] The total annual use of pyrethrum in the U.S. prior to 1942 was normally about 13 million pounds (nearly 6 thousand metric tons). The likely supply in 1944 was one tenth of this.

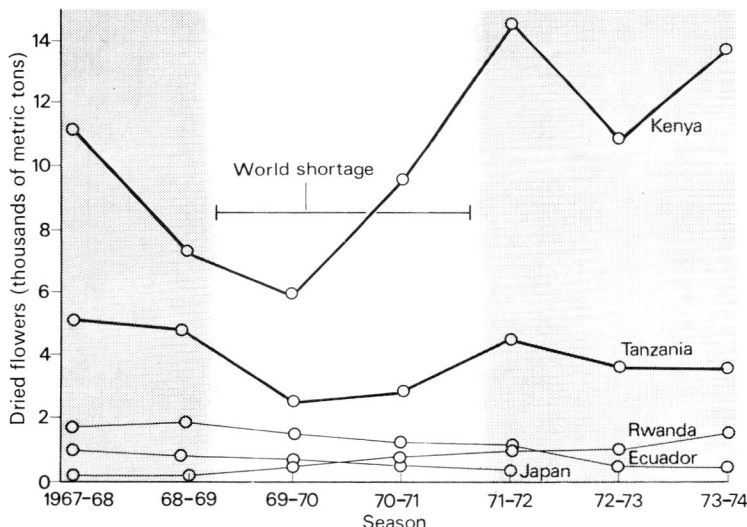

Fig. 100. Pyrethrum production in the major growing countries (1967–74).

In 1951, investigations began in Kenya into the production of a pyrethrum extract: a concentrated product which could make storage and shipment easier. The first of many extraction plants was completed in 1956 and these later replaced those of importing countries which had previously received consignments of the dried flowers. Not surprisingly, others saw the success being achieved by Kenya's pyrethrum industry and attempts were made in many countries to grow the crop during the 1950's, but without commercial success. The bulk of the world's production is near the equator at 6,000–8,000 ft (Fig. 101), where 40–60 inches of rain is spread throughout at

Fig. 101. Harvesting pyrethrum flowers. In Japan (top) the entire pyrethrum plant is uprooted when in flower and the heads removed by passing the plant through a 'comb'. In Kenya (bottom) where the plant is continuously flowering, the mature flower only is hand-picked; buds and immature flowers are left to grow. (Courtesy: Pyrethrum Board, Kenya).

least 7 months of the year. Flowering continues for up to 11 months but production can be badly affected by drought, frost and water-logging.

Because of Kenya's climate, production increased substantially during the post-war years, helped to some extent by extra demand created by early signs of resistance by flies and other insects to organochlorine and organophosphorus insecticides. Improvements were made in the refining of the pyrethrins; this eliminated complaints of staining with aerosols and the reported allergic reactions of some users to the cruder product (see p. 252). In 1960–61, the United States provided 47 per cent of the world market and nearly half of the insecticide was shipped as undiluted concentrate. At that time most pyrethrum was produced on farms larger than 50 acres. However, since Kenya's independence, over 90 per cent of production has come from small plot holders with less than 10 acres, some with pyrethrum plots as small as $\frac{1}{4}$ acre.

The post-war interest in fly control made increasing demands on the production of pyrethrum. Associated with this was the development of intermittent aerosol application equipment, such as the Syncro-Mist and Coopermatic, with electrically activated valves to deliver metered amounts of a mist into industrial and food manufacturing premises.[269,285] This, together with the growing demands of an international aerosol industry, caused the Kenya pyrethrum industry to over-produce in 1967–68, with 11,000 metric tons of dry flowers. Because of unsold stock, climatic factors and the promise of synthetic pyrethroids, years of shortage immediately followed (Fig. 100).

Awareness of the environment

In the last decade use of all insecticides has been influenced by the publication of 'Silent Spring'[170] and the concern for an environment free of pest control chemicals. But before that, in 1955, tolerances were being set for the amounts of insecticides permitted in food: toxicologists had become aware that small amounts of DDT and related insecticides could be detected in the environment, and action was being taken to minimise these and the possible risks which might follow.

The editor of *Pyrethrum Post* commented in October 1962 on the impact of 'Silent Spring' as follows: 'For a number of years there has been considerable disquiet amongst economic entomologists as to trends in the use, and particularly misuse, of insecticides. As is common in many spheres, the extremists on both sides are the most vocal and the man in the street is unlikely to get a balanced viewpoint from his daily newspaper whose function is to sell and not primarily to educate'... 'Whilst the insecticide industry will continue to search for safer insecticides, those of already proven safety, like pyrethrum, will of necessity, be in greater demand and beyond doubt, the highly organised pyrethrum industry will be able to raise flower production accordingly'.

Whilst Rachel Carson[170] mentioned pyrethrum as a 'less toxic chemical' than the 'synthetic ones' (referring to organochlorine and organophosphorus compounds), the general and immediate effect of her book was to reduce the use of all pesticides—including pyrethrins.

During the 1960's there was an interest in the United States in alternatives to chlorinated hydrocarbon insecticides for cockroach control because of widespread resistance by the German cockroach to chlordane. There was no new insecticide of outstanding merit at that time, and the alternatives which were adopted included the pyrethrins and organophosphorus compounds. Diazinon, and subsequently propoxur (Baygon® —a carbamate) provided the most practical replacements (see Chapter 15).

Influence of synthetic pyrethroids

After World War II considerable numbers of synthetically-produced insecticides—chlorinated compounds and organophosphates—became available to the pest control industry. None could match the pyrethrins, with their extremely rapid action at low concentrations and their very high margin of safety. These features, one had come to believe, were unique to pyrethrum.

This view has now been shattered. Quite rapidly there has become available a range of synthetic pyrethroids with properties closely matching those of the natural product. By 1968 it was apparent that the pyrethroids could challenge the position of pyrethrum: growers consequently replaced pyrethrum with other crops when attempts were made to reduce the pyrethrum price in 1968. This, combined with drought in the production areas, resulted in a desperate shortage of pyrethrum in 1970–71 with its effect continuing in trade through

Fig. 102. Field trials aim to increase pyrethrum yield, influenced by varietal differences, planting density, soil type and fertility, pests and diseases, and weed competition. (Courtesy: Pyrethrum Board, Kenya).

THE NATURAL INSECTICIDE 225

 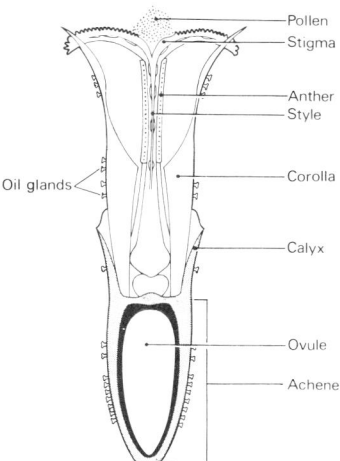

Fig. 103. A disc floret of the pyrethrum flower: diagrammatic section (right), showing notably the achene where the pyrethrins are located, and (left) electroscan photograph (mag. × 100) showing the pollen ready for insect transfer. (Courtesy: J. G. Brewer, Wageningen, Holland).

the following two years (Fig. 100). However, Kenya produced crops of flowers in 1972–74 which may meet the demands of the growing interest in ULV application indoors (see p. 120).

The world demand for dried flowers in the first half of the 1970's was about 23,000 tons/annum.[339] Part of this was met by special clonal stocks, developed for high pyrethrum content, by irrigated nurseries for vegetative propagation, and nurseries producing high quality seed (Fig. 102). Many fields now produce flowers with over 2 per cent pyrethrins content (crop average over 1·4 per cent in 1972/73) and yields well in excess of 900 kg/ha. Each pyrethrum flower head contributes 2–4 mg of pyrethrins to the total yield.

PYRETHRINS

Pyrethrum flowers
The flower head of pyrethrum is typical of the daisy family (the Compositae), made up of a collection of small florets: yellow disc florets in the centre (Fig. 103) and white-petalled ray florets around the edge. The time from first appearance of the bud to the fully open flower is about one month; the sequence in which the florets open encourages pollination mainly by Hymenopterous insects.[227]

More than 90 per cent of the pyrethrins in the flower head are contained in the achenes—the seed and seed coat.[184] Flowers are picked when they have the greatest pyrethrins content and the interval between picking is regulated to minimise the number of 'over blown' flowers, as these tend to reduce the plant's flowering capability and thus the yield of pyrethrins.

Pyrethrum dust

The flowers when picked contain about 80 per cent water. They are dried naturally in the sun, or artificially, to about 10 per cent and then sent for processing (Figure 104). As long as drying temperatures are kept below about 80°C this does not affect the content of pyrethrins.[338]

For many years pyrethrum was used as a dust: the dried flower heads were finely ground and diluted with a non-alkaline carrier. Dusts of pyrethrum flowers are not particularly efficient, because a large proportion of the pyrethrins remain within the unbroken cell walls of the plant material. Subsequently pyrethrum dust became combined with other active ingredients; borax, boric acid, and sodium fluoride, as 'extenders' to impart residual action.

Pyrethrum extract

Dusts are now made by adsorption of liquid pyrethrum (from pyrethrum extract) onto suitable carriers. This same extract, exported principally from Kenya (Fig. 105), provides the starting material for sprays, aerosols and other products manufactured all over the world.

Extracts are made with a light petroleum solvent, giving a dark viscous oleoresin. Since pyrethrins are unstable compounds, the liquid extracts are concentrated with minimum heating. They are then either standardised to contain 25 per cent pyrethrins, or further refined to provide a superior decolourised and dewaxed 'pale extract', principally for the aerosol industry (Fig. 106). The residue of the pyrethrum flowers—finely ground pyrethrum marc—is widely used for the manufacture of mosquito coils, as a filler for insecticide powders and livestock feed.[19]

The pyrethrins

Not surprisingly the extract from the pyrethrum flower provides a complex mixture of substances. The insecticidally active constituents—jointly called the 'pyrethrins'—are esters (acid-alcohol combinations). There are six components which together are responsible for knockdown and kill.

cinerin I	cinerin II
jasmolin I	jasmolin II
pyrethrin I	pyrethrin II
jointly pyrethrins I fraction	jointly pyrethrins II fraction

There is some evidence[801] to show that the Pyrethrins I are more responsible for the lethal action of the insecticide, and Pyrethrins II for the rapid action (knockdown).

Fig. 104. Pyrethrum Marketing Board's storage and extraction plant (top); sacks of dried pyrethrum flowers awaiting processing (bottom). (Courtesy: Pyrethrum Board, Kenya).

Forty years of analytical chemistry were required to discover the jasmolin esters, isolated only as recently as 1965 and 1966.[340,341] It is not known what accounts for the repellent properties of the extract.

The pyrethrins I and II are usually present in extracts in about equal amounts. They are clear, viscous, high boiling point gums: the remainder of the extract is mainly fatty acids. The pyrethrins are complicated molecules and as they are refined towards 100 per cent, their stability tends to drop; they are highly unstable in the presence of light (UV radiation), moisture and air. Minor changes in their chemical structure result in a complete loss of insecticidal activity.

Fig. 105. East African pyrethrum has been in commercial production for more than 40 years and extracts are exported world-wide. (Courtesy: Pyrethrum Board, Kenya).

All products containing pyrethrins should be stored away from light. The precise wavelengths, 290–300 nm, which are destructive to pyrethrins (and the synthetic pyrethroid, allethrin) were found by measuring the transmittance of borosilicate glass and soft window glass: the former transmits radiation beginning at 290 nm and soft glass only about 300 nm.[576] Pyrethrins were not destroyed when sunlight was filtered through soft glass but were through borosilicate. Provided products containing pyrethrins are formulated properly, no storage requirements are necessary, additional to those commonly adopted for other pesticides. The pyrethrins should not, however, be dispensed and stored in 'see through' containers.

Fig. 106. Refining extracts from dried pyrethrum flowers yields a pale oleoresin used in the manufacture of aerosols and other formulations. (Courtesy: Pyrethrum Board, Kenya).

EFFECTS OF PYRETHRINS ON COCKROACHES

Even with one of the oldest insecticides, we must admit an incomplete knowledge of the way in which the pyrethrins kill insects. How complex chemical substances produce fatal lesions in insects is by no means a simple matter, as evidenced by the pattern of symptoms which insects show in the process of knockdown and dying.

Much of the experimental work to find out how insecticides affect insects has been done by research biologists and chemists with little or no interest in the use of these materials for insect control. Their interest has been to explain how and why an insecticide kills. What they have discovered helps to explain the reaction of cockroaches to the pyrethrins and their performance in the control of infestations.

The activity of the pyrethrins results from the joint action of the six constituents and these vary in their toxicities to different insects. The net effect on a cockroach, comes from their combined rates of penetration and detoxification, as well as their intrinsic activities in the insect where poisoning occurs. This is of interest to the biochemist (Chapter 14), who wants to know which components are responsible for pyrethrin-like activity, but not to the pest control operator who has to accept that his formulation contains a mixture of active compounds over which he personally has no control.

Early studies

The first thorough study of the way insecticides kill, led to a misinterpretation of the action of pyrethrum: Shafer[740,741] believed it acted as a fumigant, through 'volatile bodies in the powder'. He failed to ensure that his tests were free of contamination by airborne particles of pyrethrum.[167] However, using honeybees, and carefully excluding particles of powder and droplets of pyrethrum extract, it was established that pyrethrins do have the low volatility which is now widely recognised.[336]

Much of the recent information on the susceptibility of cockroaches to pyrethrins comes from comparisons with synthetic pyrethroids (see Chapter 10); but among the earliest studies[764] were those of Staudinger & Ruzicka in 1924. These showed that pyrethrin I (at 0·01 per cent) was somewhat more active than pyrethrin II, killing cockroaches in 10–20 minutes compared with 20–40 minutes, respectively. The LC_{50} of a suspension of pyrethrin I in water to the German cockroach after 24 hours was 10 mg/1, compared with 12·5 mg/1 for pyrethrin II. In kerosene solution, applied topically to *P. americana*, the LC_{50} for pyrethrin I was 1 mg/1, compared with 1·5 mg/1 for pyrethrin II. The latter, however, caused more rapid knockdown of the American cockroach.[558]

The symptoms produced by insects which come into contact with pyrethrum are, after a latent period: (1) excitation, (2) convulsions, (3) paralysis and (4) death.[484] Excitation, convulsion and paralysis can be interpreted as an effect on the insects' nervous system. Early studies had suggested that duration of the latent period—between application and response—depended where the insecticide was placed: the closer to the large ganglia, the quicker the response (O'Kane et al.[540]).

Considering that the experiments of O'Kane were carried out over 40 years ago they were quite ingenious. Using an extract of 0·15 per cent pyrethrins, minute droplets of 0·05–0·1 mg were placed at various points on the surfaces of Oriental, German and American cockroaches. In fact this was probably the first instance of 'topical application'. The normal reaction of a cockroach when contaminated with insecticide is to clean its appendages with the mouthparts (Fig. 107). However, in these experiments cockroaches were provided with collars (Fig. 108) to stop the insects cleaning off the droplets placed on their appendages. This prevented the possibility of ingestion. The time between placing the droplet and the onset of convulsions was used as a measure of the permeability of the cuticle and of the distance from the point of application, to where in the central nervous system the insecticide was acting. With the exception of the tips of the antennae, convulsions occurred wherever droplets were placed on the cockroach. A droplet on the middle of the antennae produced symptoms, but if amputated below the point of application when first effects appeared, convulsions were prevented. Sclerotised areas were ap-

THE NATURAL INSECTICIDE 231

parently 'less sensitive' than membranous ones; symptoms of poisoning occurred in half the time when pyrethrins were applied to the neck and intersegmental areas. For areas of cuticle equally sclerotised, response was faster the nearer the application to the ganglia.

Most of the early experiments with pyrethrum and cockroaches were obviously done with formulations made from dried flowers: thus a dust said to contain 25 per cent pyrethrum, effectively contained only 0·25 per cent pyrethrins (assuming an active ingredient content in the flowers of 1 per cent). Experiments by Hockenyos[433] using such a formulation applied to the cuticle

Fig. 107. Typical cleaning responses of an American cockroach using the mouthparts as a 'comb' through which the antennae (top) and legs (bottom) are passed.

of Oriental cockroaches, produced no reaction in 1·5 minutes, but at 2 minutes there was sudden intense excitement during which antennal cleaning occurred: paralysis then followed, starting usually with the metathoracic legs, spreading to the others, with the insect helpless in 8 minutes. He maintained that the effects of poisoning were localised if application was restricted: that at least half of the surface of the insect had to be dusted to ensure total paralysis in 12 hours. With the knowledge that the pyrethrins are very rapidly distributed in insects, Hockenyos' observations are now questionable.

Fig. 108. Collar fitted to a cockroach to prevent it removing insecticide placed on different parts of the body. (From O'Kane et al.[640]).

In experiments with different concentrations of pyrethrum in talc, the time separating onset of paralysis and prostration of Oriental cockroaches, varies inversely with the concentration. This is as expected. However, in Hockenyos' experiments, dusts of 25 per cent pyrethrum were more efficient than 50 per cent, or any concentrations less than 25 per cent. Campbell[167] comments that if Hockenyos' observations were not due to chance, then they may indicate a difference in adherence of his mixtures to the insect cuticle.

Dust applied only to the appendages does not paralyse cockroaches,[433] but a minute drop of pyrthrum *extract* placed on almost any part of an appendage is effective.[640] This shows the clear difference in speed of action of these two formulations.[167] The work of O'Kane, Hockenyos and others also demonstrates that neither liquid nor dust need enter the tracheal system to paralyse; direct penetration of the cuticle is sufficient, as has been confirmed recently by more sophisticated methods[158] (see p. 387).

In feeding experiments, powdered pyrethrum is reported to be relatively ineffective, probably through degradation in the gut before the insecticide can exert an effect.[859] However, death can sometimes occur in feeding experiments,

TABLE XLIII
DOSAGE OF PYRETHRINS (μg/g) FOR MORTALITY OF *P. AMERICANA*
(From Menusan[558])

Method of application	50% Kill Males	50% Kill Females	100% Kill Males	100% Kill Females
Topical	4	9	6	12
Injection	3	8	6	11
Oral	14	29	20	40

possibly due to contact action through the cuticle of the mouthparts.[722] Differences in the amounts needed to kill *P. americana* when applied topically or injected into the body cavity are small (Table XLIII), but three times the amount is needed to kill by oral ingestion. About four times more pyrethrins applied topically to American cockroaches is required to kill at 35°C than at 15°C (Fig. 109).

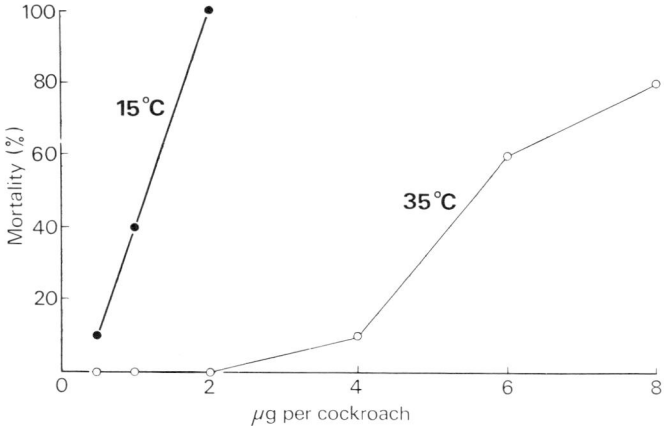

Fig. 109. The effect of temperature on the kill of *P. americana* when pyrethrins are applied topically. (From Blum & Kearns[109]).

Susceptibility of species, developmental stages and sexes

Large nymphs of the German cockroach have a susceptibility to pyrethrins between that of adult males and females: adult females are the most difficult to kill.[547] The relative susceptibility of adult females : males : second stage nymphs is 4·5 : 2·5 : 1, as determined by the concentrations of spray deposits needed to kill 50 per cent.[860] Dusts of pyrethrum applied topically to *B. germanica* cause males to succumb more quickly than females (Table XLIV). In contact tests (unpublished) in which pyrethrins (0·4 per cent) were incorporated in oil sprays containing also residual insecticides, 100 per cent knockdown of males and females took 1·5 and 2·2 minutes, respectively: bioallethrin took longer; males, 7·0 and females 9·3 minutes.

TABLE XLIV

EFFECTS OF PYRETHRUM DUSTS ON THE SEXES OF *B. GERMANICA*
(From Dewey[232])

Treatment	Kill (%)		Av. survival time (hrs)	
	24 hrs	96 hrs	Males	Females
0·9% pyrethrins at 0·8 mg/cm^2	14	100	7·8	49·3
25% pyrethrum + 75% pyrophyllite	81	86	3·5	26·6

In tests against all stages of the German cockroach the first instar is the most susceptible and the sixth instar is the most tolerant.[167] If speed of knockdown is used as the criterion of susceptibility, the younger nymphal stages of the German cockroach are more susceptible to most insecticides than the old, and adult males respond more quickly than females (Fig. 129).

When pyrethrins are sprayed directly onto the dorsum of adults and large nymphs, those of the American cockroach are more readily killed than those of the German cockroach: in these tests the nymphs of both species were slightly more difficult to kill than the adults (Table XLV).

TABLE XLV

PER CENT KILL OF *P. AMERICANA* AND *B. GERMANICA* BY PYRETHRINS APPLIED TO THE DORSUM
(From McGovran et al.[548])

Developmental stage	Species	Deposit (µg/ml)		
		280	560	960
Adults	American	56	100	—
	German	27	72	100
Large nymphs	American	52	77	—
	German	25	60	87

RECOVERY FROM POISONING BY PYRETHRINS

Cockroaches and other insects recover completely from sublethal doses of pyrethrins if poisoning does not pass beyond the initial stages of paralysis.[873] This should be seen as part of infestation control, if the value of pyrethrins in controlling cockroaches is not to be greatly over-estimated. The application of pyrethrins does result in many cockroaches lying on their backs, but given time most will get up and walk away none the worse for the experience!

In the process of killing insects, contact insecticides migrate from the surface of the body to a site of action, inside the insect. This may be reinforced by the insect also ingesting insecticide during the process of grooming. Inside the insect the pesticide may be lost in many different ways: by excretion, by being stored in body fat, or being broken down into non-toxic substances. Whether or not the insect dies, depends on a balance between insecticidal effect and the detoxifying effect (see Fig. 162, p. 388).

Some pest insects treated extensively with insecticides now have the ability to break them down—they have become resistant—with the result that whole populations are now able to survive. Resistance is an important practical demonstration of 'recovery from insecticide poisoning'; it is genetically transmitted from one generation to the next and brought about by the insecticide acting as a selecting agent (see Chapter 15).

Recovery is an outward expression of the insecticide being lost, detoxified or 'locked up' within the insect at a faster rate than the poisoning process: in the case of pyrethrins, however, if molecules of the insecticide do actually penetrate nerve cells, it is difficult to visualise how they leach out again so that recovery from paralysis can occur. In most cases inactivation of an insecticide involves a change of the molecule: studies of pyrethroids containing radioactively labelled carbon, and of the mode of action of synergists, suggest that the breakdown of pyrethrins occurs by oxidation of the insecticide. A synergist prevents this breakdown, thus enhancing the action of the insecticide which would otherwise be lost.

Synergism

A synergist is a chemical, non-toxic or negligibly so at the dosage used, which enhances the toxicity of a pesticide with which it is combined. The objective is to obtain a pesticidal activity greater than a simple additive effect, thus reducing the amount of toxicant needed with a consequent saving in costs.

Perhaps we should digress here for one moment to clarify the difference between synergism and potentiation. The end result, in both cases, is greater toxic action. If the combination of two compounds—one insecticidal on its own and the other not—results in the two being more toxic than the insecticidal component alone, then *synergism* is said to have occurred. If two compounds are each separately toxic, and the toxicity of the combination is greater than that expected from the sum of the toxicities of the separate components, *potentiation* has occurred.[425] In practice, synergism usually involves increased action against insects; potentiation refers to increased toxicity of pesticides to man, and is usually the concern of the pharmacologist.

The history of synergism goes back to 1938 when the first synergist for pyrethrum (N-isobutylundecyleneamide) was discovered having practical value. Later, in 1940, sesame oil was found to improve insecticidal action (attributable to the active components sesamin and sesamolin). Since then hundreds of similar compounds have been examined.

The synergist most widely used to enhance the action of pyrethrins is piperonyl butoxide, developed in the United States.[829] Without the advantage of synergism, the pyrethrins would probably have been priced out of the market when synthetic pyrethroids first appeared. According to Hewlett,[425] of 375 pyrethrin products being marketed in the U.S.A. in 1966, 94 per cent contained synergists and of these, 94 per cent contained piperonyl butoxide with or without the support of other synergising ingredients. The addition of piperonyl butoxide to pyrethrins does not make the insecticide on a treated surface any more persistent.[424]

Piperonyl butoxide
For the pyrethrins, piperonyl butoxide remains the most widely used synergist. Combinations are referred to as Pybuthrin[(R1)]. In the United States, Tropital[(R2)], MGK 264[(R3)] and other compounds are occasionally incorporated. Whilst a greater insecticidal effect may be obtained by applying synergist and insecticide separately, giving the synergist time to act, it is invariably uneconomic to do so. The synergist which may be the best for pyrethrum, or for each of the newer synthetic pyrethroids will depend on two things: first, the relative speeds of entry of insecticide and synergist into the insect; secondly, the speed of action of the synergist in negating the biochemical processes within the insect tending to inactivate the insecticide.

In experiments in which sesamex or piperonyl butoxide was applied directly to the exposed nerve cord of cockroaches, the time required for pyrethrum to block nerve conduction was considerably shortened, depending on the concentration of synergist. This suggests that the synergist may alter the rate of penetration of pyrethrins into the nerve,[153] or perhaps reduce the rate at which the penetrated pyrethrins are oxidised.

The various constituents in pyrethrum extract, which make up the pyrethrins, are synergised to varying degrees with piperonyl butoxide, and one would expect the same to occur with the synthetic pyrethroids (see p. 257). If a pyrethroid fails to respond to synergism (and most are less well synergised than natural pyrethrins) it can be assumed that the compound is less responsive to degradation. If piperonyl butoxide or other synergist fails to increase insecticidal action in a particular species (Fig. 110), the insect can be assumed to have little or no detoxifying mechanism. Piperonyl butoxide, itself, is only slowly metabolised. Current knowledge of the biochemical basis for the action of synergists has been the subject of recent reviews.[172,850,851]

(R1) Registered trade name of Cooper McDougall & Robertson.
(R2) and (R3) Registered trade names of McLaughlin, Gormley King Co.

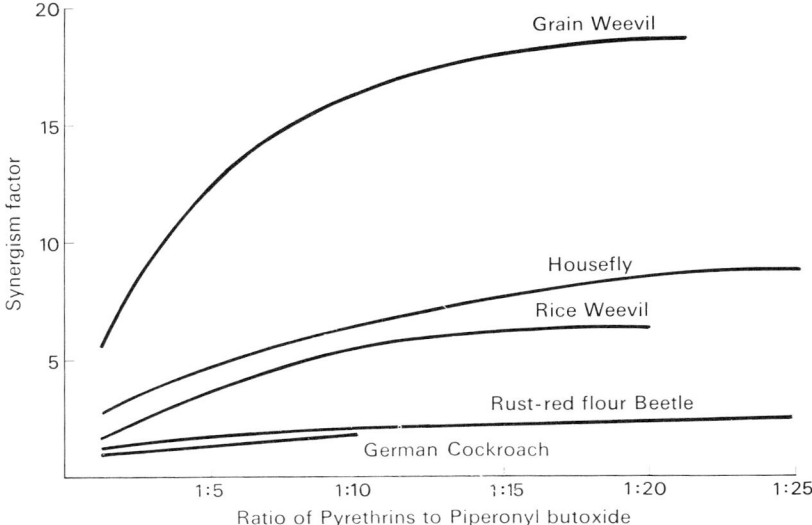

Fig. 110. Examples of the response of food storage pests to different mixtures of insecticide and synergist (after Brown et al.[135] and from Chadwick[179]). Note the difference in response of closely related species (e.g. weevils), and between these and other beetles. Also the small synergistic effect against German cockroaches compared, for example, with houseflies.

Action in houseflies

For those concerned with industrial/domestic pest control, the standard for assessment of the performance of piperonyl butoxide as a pyrethrins synergist is undoubtedly its action in houseflies. Piperonyl butoxide itself has virtually no activity against houseflies, but ratios between 1:5 and 1:10 of pyrethrins to piperonyl butoxide, substantially increase kill and to a lesser extent rate of knockdown. The degree of synergism in flies is lowest in the first few minutes after application, probably because it takes time for the synergist to reach, or bring about its desired reaction in the insect; then it increases rapidly for 2 hours.[725,726,727]

It is possible to use only one quarter, or less, of the amount of pyrethrins, when synergised, to achieve a given level of kill. The effectiveness of an insecticide synergist is usually expressed as the ratio of the LD_{50} of the insecticide alone, to the LD_{50} of the insecticide with the synergist. This ratio is the 'synergism factor'.

Action in cockroaches

The synergism factor of pyrethrins by piperonyl butoxide against houseflies is not less than 4. With stored food pests, factors up to 20 can be obtained. In contrast, there is very little benefit from synergising pyrethrins with piperonyl butoxide for the control of cockroaches. There is a slight acceleration in

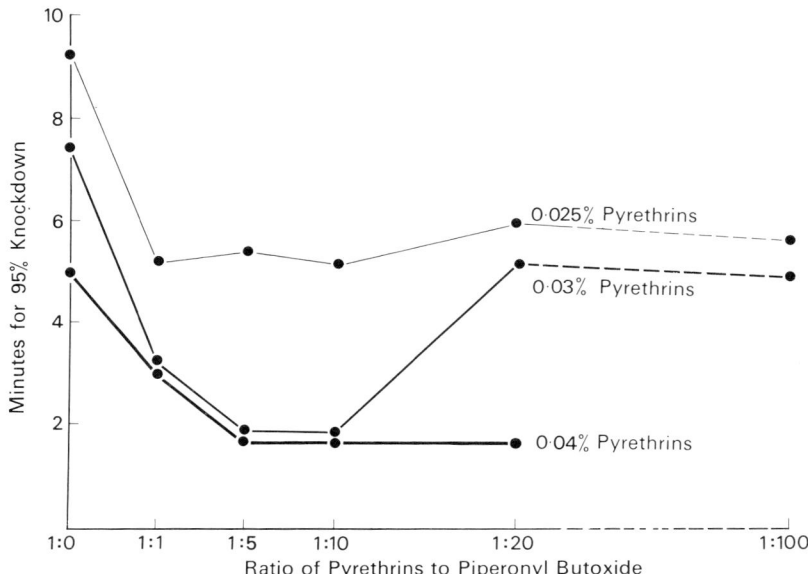

Fig. 111. The slight acceleration in knockdown of German cockroaches with synergism ratios of 1 : 1, 1 : 5 and 1 : 10; retardation at 1 : 20 and 1 : 100. (From Chadwick[179]).

knockdown of German cockroaches at ratios of 1 : 1, to 1 : 10, but this is lost at higher ratios (Fig. 111). Some improvement in 48 hour kill of *Periplaneta brunnea* is obtained with pyrethrins plus piperonyl butoxide applied topically.[177,178] There is also some improvement by direct spray methods, against nymphs of Oriental and American cockroaches (Table XLVI). Pyrethrum dust synergised 1 : 5 with piperonyl butoxide, applied directly to adult German cockroaches,[179] improves kill (synergism factor 2·3) but not so with spray (1·1) (see Tables LVI, LVII & Fig. 120). Even with sprays synergised 1 : 10, the synergism factor reaches only 1·6. However, as this minimal effect allows smaller quantities of pyrethrins to be used, a cost saving is clearly evident.

The toxicology of piperonyl butoxide has recently been reviewed.[134] The acute oral LD_{50} (rat) is not less than 2,500 mg/kg and this applies also to cats and dogs. Long-term animal feeding studies show no tumour formation, establishing no carcinogenic properties. Piperonyl butoxide has been used as a pyrethrum synergist for over 20 years without untoward effect. It is unlikely that the amounts ingested by man could ever be sufficient to prevent the rapid detoxification of pyrethrins which may enter the human body.

Tropital
Tropital is the registered trade name of a useful pyrethrins synergist, discovered in 1965 in the research laboratories of the Pyrethrum Board, Kenya.

(Chemically, it is an acetal of piperonaldehyde and gets its name from Heliotropin acetal). The compound is a pale yellow oil with a faint bland odour. Tropital is completely soluble in pyrethrum extracts and a wide range of organic solvents. The acute oral LD_{50} (rat) is above 4,000 mg/kg: it has a low irritancy and is easily destroyed by sunlight—sharing the degradative, non-residual properties of pyrethrins.[513]

TABLE XLVI

KILL (%) 48 HOURS AFTER APPLICATION OF PYRETHRINS, WITH AND WITHOUT SYNERGISTS, TO 3 PEST SPECIES OF COCKROACH (CSMA DIRECT SPRAY METHOD) IN COMPARISON WITH THE U.S. OFFICIAL TEST INSECTICIDE

(From Baker[72])

Insecticide and synergist (% wt)	Cockroach species and dose applied		
	German: 4th stage nymphs (0·6 ml)	Oriental: half grown nymphs (0·8 ml)	American: half grown nymphs (0·5 ml)
Pyrethrins/pip. but. (0·075%/0·375%)	70	34	46
O.T.I.*	47	34	44
Pyrethrins/pip. but./MGK 264 (0·075%/0·15%/0·25%)	83	70	42
O.T.I.*	54	34	34

* O.T.I. contains 0·125% pyrethrins.

The synergistic action of Tropital is reported to equal that of piperonyl butoxide in pyrethrin mixtures against flies, but is said to have greater potency against cockroaches. Tropital has similar effects with some synthetic pyrethroids (see p. 261).

In the American CSMA Cockroach Spray test, pyrethrins plus piperonyl butoxide (0·03 per cent/0·24 per cent) killed 16 per cent of German cockroaches in 24 hours and 21 per cent in 48 hours. When Tropital was used, the kill increased to 29 per cent and 32 per cent, respectively.[442] An aerosol formulation of pyrethrins plus Tropital (0·25 per cent/1·25 per cent),[496] gave the same kill of male German cockroaches as the Official Test Aerosol (0·4 per cent pyrethrins with 2 per cent DDT). In tests against stored food pests, pyrethrins supported by piperonyl butoxide, performed better as a contact insecticide, than when synergised by Tropital.[540]

MGK 264

This synergist is a viscous, faintly yellow liquid, miscible with a wide range of organic solvents, very stable and compatible with most pesticides. It was introduced commercially in the late 1940's. Chemically, it is a dicarboximide with an acute oral LD_{50} (rat) of 2,800 mg/kg. Claims are made that with a ratio 1:2:3·3 (pyrethrins: piperonyl butoxide: MGK 264) better performance is obtained in sprays and aerosols, and at lower cost, than a 1:5 ratio of pyrethrins to piperonyl butoxide. The evidence for this with cockroaches (Baker[72]) is given in Table XLVI.

Using a number of different insect species, Chadwick[178] challenged the claim for improved synergistic action made by Baker: at the same total synergist concentration (1:5 and not 1:5·3 as above), mixtures of MGK 264 with piperonyl butoxide are less effective than piperonyl butoxide alone. In most cases MGK 264 is less than half as effective as piperonyl butoxide against houseflies, cockroaches and other insects, when represented as the sole synergist in pyrethrin formulations (Table XLVII). The same conclusion is reached by Incho & Odeneal[455] comparing MGK 264 and piperonyl butoxide, as separate synergists for pyrethrins, against houseflies by topical application. MGK 264 is more active as a synergist for allethrin than for pyrethrins, but is less effective than safroxan with both these insecticides. Only when MGK 264 is used in space sprays and aerosols, at concentrations higher than piperonyl butoxide, does it compare favourably in synergistic action.

Sesame oil

This synergist was discovered by Eagleson[250] among 35 vegetable oils, tested by mixing with pyrethrins in kerosene solution: it gives an outstanding increase in toxicity to houseflies. Those flies which fail to die, are delayed in their recovery.

Considerable interest was shown in this synergist in the U.K. in the early war years when pyrethrum was in short supply and the manufacture of DDT not yet established.[659] The oil was cheap, presented no toxicological risk and

TABLE XLVII

KILL (% AT 48 HOURS) OF *PERIPLANETA BRUNNEA* (AV. FOR BOTH SEXES) BY PYRETHRINS WITH SYNERGISTS AT 1:5. TOPICAL APPLICATION OF 0·5 µl DROPLETS
(From Chadwick[177, 178])

Pyrethrins concentration (w/v%)	Pyrethrins +		Pyrethrins +	
	Piperonyl butoxide	MGK 264	Piperonyl butoxide	Safroxan
0·40	100	65	100	85
0·25	45	10	60	70
0·15	5	0	50	45

allowed a drop in pyrethrins content of sprays, from 0·1 per cent to 0·05 per cent, without loss in performance.

Sesamin, a crystalline solid, is the active principle in the oil which itself is non-toxic to insects.[393] Sesame oil also contains sesamolin which is a more effective synergist than sesamin. No great use has been made of either synergist in formulations for cockroach control.

Safroxan

Developed in Japan, this compound is an analogue of piperonyl butoxide. At room temperature it forms soft white crystals sparsely soluble in odourless kerosene. Like all synergists, safroxan varies greatly in its synergistic effect on different insects. It is much inferior to piperonyl butoxide against houseflies.

By 1961 about 60 per cent of the total production of pyrethrum was being used with synergists for fly control.[724] The poor performance of safroxan in this regard, hindered commercial development: the knockdown action of pyrethrins with safroxan in the first 15 minutes is not improved and safroxan is only one third as effective as piperonyl butoxide after 24 hours. Chadwick[177] rates the potency against houseflies, of pyrethrins synergised by safroxan and by piperonyl butoxide, as 1·0 and 0·6. However, in tests against *Periplaneta brunnea*,[177] piperonyl butoxide and safroxan are equally effective synergists for pyrethrins (Table XLVII).

Resistance to pyrethrins

Resistance to an insecticide demonstrates the ability of an insect to recover from, or tolerate, the concentration of toxicant in its environment. The methods by which insects have developed resistance to the pyrethrins is best understood in houseflies.[159] In some cases it appears to be an increased ability of the resistant strain to detoxify the insecticide; in others, decreased absorption or penetration of insecticide—the development of a cuticular barrier as a resistance mechanism. Resistance may also have arisen from reduced nerve sensitivity. (See Chapter 15.)

Resistance to pyrethrins can result from selection with pyrethrins, and from the presence within the insect of detoxifying enzymes developed through the use of other insecticides (e.g. DDT) (see cross-resistance, p. 446). Houseflies and grain weevils resistant to pyrethrins have shown even higher levels of resistance to some synthetic pyrethroids (e.g. allethrin). This cross-resistance can be developed in the laboratory.[300]

Resistance is often expressed as the ratio of the LD_{50} of the susceptible strain (or standard) to that of the resistant strain. German cockroaches taken from populations in the United States with previous exposure to DDT and cyclodiene compounds[477] have been found resistant to pyrethrins ($\times$ 13) and to synergised pyrethrins ($\times$ 8), but this creates no practical problem in their use for cockroach control. Other insects of economic importance for which there is reported resistance to pyrethrins[301] include bedbugs (*Cimex hemipterus*) in Kenya, houseflies in Sweden, cattle ticks (*Boophilus decoloratus*) in S. Africa and body lice (*Pediculus h. humanus*) in France.

USE IN INSECT CONTROL

The extensive use made of pyrethrins for the control of insect pests, both indoors and out, reflects this insecticide's many useful properties. Reference has already been made to some:

1. a wide spectrum of insecticidal action;
2. rapid knockdown;
3. enhancement of activity by relatively cheap synergists;
4. low toxicity to mammals;
5. no evidence of accumulation in the environment;
6. little evidence of resistance developed by insects under practical conditions.

The pyrethrins have been used primarily against flying insects: aerosols in pressure packs containing synergised pyrethrins are still a favoured method for controlling mosquitoes, houseflies and other flying insects in homes. Present international health regulations recommend products of this type for insect control in aircraft on international flights.

Formulations of pyrethrins, usually with synergists, have proved of immense value for the control of insects in food storage and processing: there are no adverse effects from the use of this insecticide in situations so close to man. Pyrethrins have long been the insecticide of choice where food may possibly be contaminated. In these applications relatively low concentrations are dispersed mechanically, or by thermal fogging, in light mineral oil or other suitable carrier. The object is to produce an aerosol (a suspension of insecticidal droplets uniformly dispersed in the air), on a larger scale than can normally be obtained with pressurised packs, to kill flying insects in warehouses and factories (Fig. 112).

Outdoor applications involve the use of fogs to obtain rapid knockdown of flies on refuse areas; the insecticide may kill the adults, but makes no contribution to killing the larvae likely to be developing within the refuse (Fig. 113).

The contribution to cockroach control

There appears to be a mistaken belief on the part of many pest control operators that, (1) cockroaches have the same high level of susceptibility to pyrethrins, as houseflies, (2) insects crawling on surfaces respond as well to tiny droplets of insecticide in the air as do flying insects, and (3) because pyrethrins can be put safely into the air, as an aerosol, mist or fog, this imparts some magic properties to it: making the insecticide behave almost as a gas—which it does not—penetrating the harbourages, however tiny or deep, of crawling insects, in the fabric of a building.

This misunderstanding about the properties of a mist is a major cause of bad cockroach control. Unfortunately misting is accepted by some as the modern and efficient way to control cockroaches: that fine droplets, mechanically or thermally produced, perform much more effectively than a spray or dust positively directed into infested harbourages. The latter is invariably more successful, but requires more time and more intelligent thinking.

The pyrethrins are well known for their lack of residual activity. This, of course, is one of the properties which allows all horizontal surfaces in an infested home to be coated with the 'fall out' of a pyrethrum aerosol, without risk to the occupants. But because of no residual effect, the misting process must be repeated regularly, further increasing the amount applied. Often the total exceeds that of an insecticide with residual properties and which more carefully placed, would provide infinitely better control.

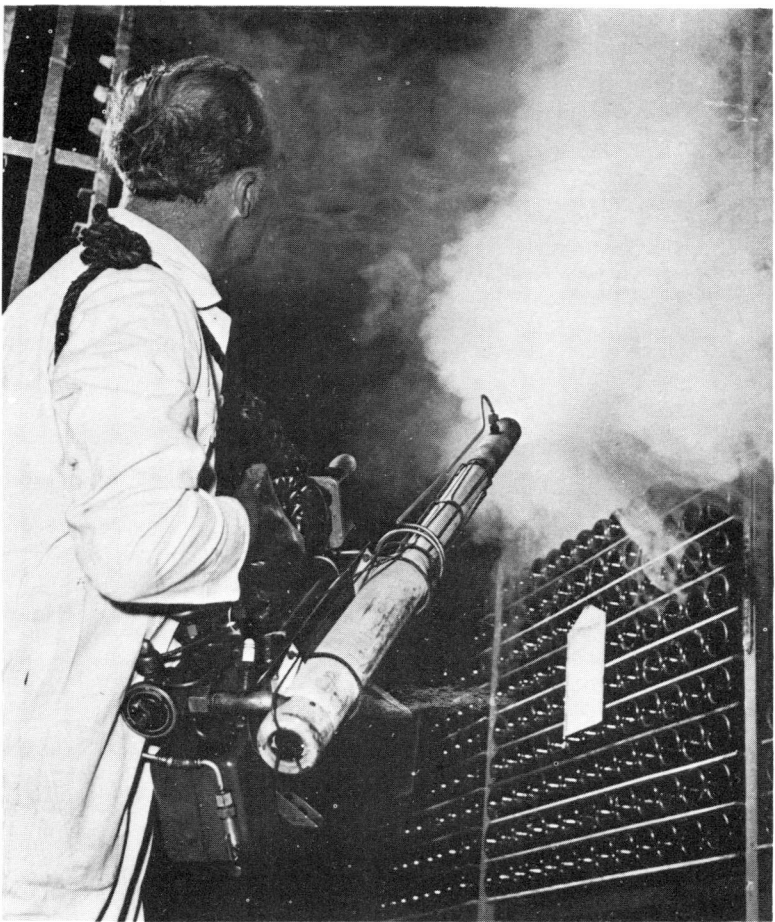

Fig. 112. Use of a Swingfog and synergised pyrethrins to control flying insects in bottle stores. (U.K.).

Fig. 113. Use of a thermally-produced fog of synergised pyrethrins to give quick knockdown and kill of adult flies on a refuse tip. Note that the wind carries the fog away from the operator up the tip face. Treatment offers no residual action and larval stages are unaffected. (U.K.).

To some extent this mis-use of pyrethrins for cockroach control has been perpetuated by word of mouth: misting or fogging in the home (Fig. 114) is mistakenly described by 'Mrs. Smith' as *fumigation* (that was the word the salesman used). Unable to control the cockroaches herself, by a dust or spray bought from the local shop, she has now seen the very complicated equipment being used by the visiting serviceman: (thinks) 'no wonder her efforts were unsuccessful'. Fumigation is what she now recommends to 'Mrs. Jones'; 'I had to leave the house for 3 hours while it was being *fumigated* and the numbers of cockroaches struggling on their backs when I returned was unbelievable!'

THE NATURAL INSECTICIDE 245

Much of the interest in the early 1970's, in the use of pyrethrins, undoubtedly came from an over-reaction by the pest control service industry to what they believed was a well-informed public—or at least an alerted one—on the subject of pesticides and the environment. It was a recognition by the industry that the housewife, through the successful efforts of many media, knew about the health risks which might arise in the application of insecticides in her home; skin contamination by possible contact with residues, or the inhalation of spray droplets. Referring to the way DDT was singled out for attack towards the end of the 1960's, the editor of *Pyrethrum Post* commented as follows:[30] 'The desire of the Press to have a good "news" story coupled with the tremendous impact of T.V. taken into people's homes, takes the problems of pesticide residues out of the arena of learned discussion and into the hands of those who wish to exploit sensationalism. We never anticipated using editorial space in *Pyrethrum Post* to defend DDT; in fact we are defending the age of reason'.

Not surprisingly then, the use of pyrethrins in the home became promoted under the banner of 'safe pest control': they are without untoward effects on children and domestic animals. Thus pyrethrins have been used to 'sell' safety.

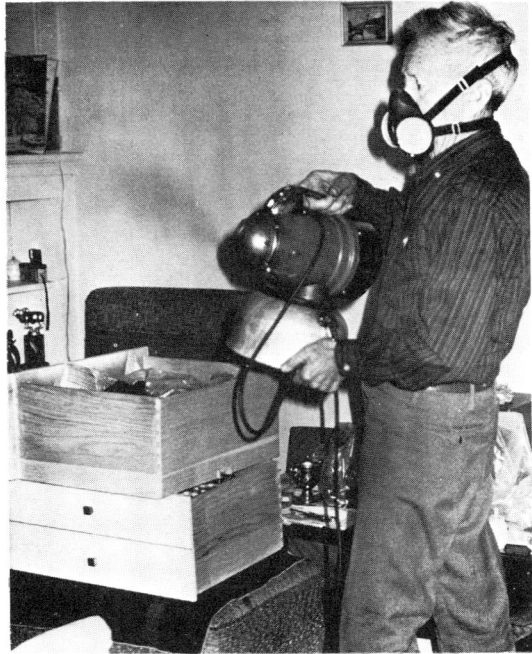

Fig. 114. Use of a mechanically-formed mist to control cockroaches in a home. Note that drawers have been taken out of wall units to increase distribution of the mist. Despite this, the insecticide is unlikely to reach all crevices occupied by cockroaches. A mask is being worn but the operator has no other protection. (Los Angeles, U.S.A.).

Indifferent performance

In contrast to flies, the record of performance of the pyrethrins for cockroach control is disappointing. Pyrethrins themselves are not highly insecticidal against the principal pest species, and residues of pyrethrins in harbourages do not remain active for long. For cockroach control, pyrethrins are sometimes incorporated as a minor part of a formulation, combined with an insecticide having residual action (p. 247). In trials with unsynergised pyrethrins (2·8 per cent), applied at 1g/50 m² in truck vans. German and American cockroaches survived. A formulation of 0·45 per cent pyrethrins synergised with sulfoxide, or Tropital, at 2·7 per cent and dispersed at 1 g/m³ killed *P. americana* but was ineffective against *B. germanica*.[142]

In tests to compare the performance of oil-based formulations of pyrethrins plus piperonyl butoxide (0·4 per cent/2 per cent), of malathion (5 per cent) and dichlorvos (3 per cent), applied as thermal fogs in homes at 6 ml/m³ all were *unsatisfactory* against natural infestations of German cockroaches (Table XLVIII).

Application of insecticides indoors by ultra low volume (U.L.V.) has been heralded as a promising new way to use synergised pyrethrins as a space treatment against cockroaches. The results obtained do not compare with the systematic treatment of cracks and crevices occupied by cockroaches using an insecticide with residual action (see Chapter 5). The elaborate equipment devised for application by U.L.V. in no way overcomes the inadequacies of mists for cockroach control. It may however make a favourable impression on

TABLE XLVIII

EVALUATION OF INSECTICIDAL FOGS AGAINST NATURAL INFESTATIONS OF *BLATTELLA GERMANICA*
(From Gillenwater & Burden[333])

Formulation	*Replicate number*	*Pretreatment count*	*Reduction in cockroaches (%) after indicated days*		
			1	*7*	*14*
Pyrethrins/piperonyl butoxide (0·4%/2%)	1	1,042	43	22	35
	2	699	0	0	0
	Average	870	22	11	18
Malathion (5%)	1	430	80	55	24
	2	229	16	36	31
	Average	330	48	45	28
Dichlorvos (3%)	1	100	76	85	74
	2	92	90	66	64
	Average	96	83	76	69

the housewife! It may help to 'sell' the service for cockroach control but in no way improves the performance of the insecticide used.

Useful flushing action
To obtain control of cockroach infestations, the pest control serviceman's primary objective should be to find out where the cockroaches are. He may already make use of the insect's greater activity at night, to show him where they may remain after previous treatment (see 'Night inspection', Vol. I). Additionally he may make use of the exceptional property of the pyrethrins, in flushing cockroaches from their harbourages. Used in this way the serviceman is exploiting the repellent—or irritating—action of the insecticides (Fig. 115). None of the synthetic pyrethroids has this property so strongly developed (see Table LVIII). One or two very short bursts of a pyrethrins aerosol, directed into cracks and crevices are fool-proof in showing whether or not cockroaches are present: experience suggests that German cockroaches may respond a little more readily than Oriental cockroaches.

The technique of flushing with an aerosol might, in some instances, cause cockroaches to go even deeper into floor or wall cavities. It is most unlikely that all the insects in a harbourage will behave in this way and the few that do emerge should indicate, unmistakably, the need for thorough treatment at that location. When the infested crevice has been located and the appropriate insecticide for treatment selected, the object is to make the whole of that harbourage—in depth—untenable to cockroaches. In this regard an insecticidal dust, rather than a spray, will more readily cover the internal surfaces and reach more of the insects themselves. It is in this type of situation that pyrethrins, as a mist or fog, clearly cannot perform adequately. The droplets, however small, have insufficient momentum to reach the concealed places.

A further, suggested use of pyrethrins and their flushing action, is to apply a residual insecticide first and follow immediately with pyrethrins to get the cockroaches out of their hiding places, and into contact with the residual. However, if residuals are being applied correctly in the first place—in harbourages and not over exposed surfaces—there should be no need to stimulate cockroach activity.

Many servicemen favour formulations for cockroach control in which a small amount of pyrethrins is mixed with an insecticide of good, long-lasting activity. This provides the flushing action previously referred to, and by stimulating movement encourages the insects to become readily contaminated with the more potent insecticide. There is some evidence that improved control can be obtained when aerosols containing pyrethrins are directed into harbourages before or after residual insecticides are applied. Mixed formulations, however, containing pyrethrins, are no more effective than a residual insecticide alone (Table XLIX). Frequently the incorporation of pyrethrins is designed to prove to the client how good the serviceman's materials are and how good he is at his job. Within seconds, the cockroaches are laying on their backs with their legs thrashing the air (Fig. 116). This demonstrates the mistaken belief that quick knockdown is desirable as a part

248 THE COCKROACH

of good cockroach control, and that all the cockroaches knocked down will, in fact, die (see Table LXIV).

There is some justification for arguing that flushing agents should never be used. Insecticides which cause cockroaches to move will inevitably make harbourages unsuitable for re-occupation; accordingly there is little purpose in following up flushing action with a residual insecticide or combining it in the

Fig. 115. Typical harbourage of German cockroaches in a domestic kitchen unit: (top) the work surface gently lifted to expose them; (bottom) the same with the work surface replaced and the harbourage 'flushed' with a pyrethrins aerosol. (Dallas, U.S.A.).

Table XLIX

CONTROL (%) 1 MONTH AFTER TREATMENT OF APARTMENTS INFESTED WITH GERMAN COCKROACHES, USING INSECTICIDES WITH AND WITHOUT SYNERGISED PYRETHRINS (PYBUTHRIN). ASSESSMENTS BASED ON TRAP CATCHES
(data from Ebeling & Reierson[257])

Insecticide content			Control achieved (%)	
Principal insecticide	Pyrethrins (%)	Piperonyl butoxide (%)	With pybuthrin	Without pybuthrin
Boric acid (98% dust)	0·0625	0·625	98·6	97·4
Boric acid (98% dust)	0·0625	0·325	95·5	97·0
Ronnel (2%) in oil	0·1	0·5	19·0	72·6
Propoxur (1%) emulsion	0·1	0·5	78·3	69·4
Malathion (2%) in oil	0·5	2·5	81·9	91·7
Diazinon (1%)	0·1	0·5	81·9	96·7

formulation. But because pyrethrins are so short lived it is doubtful if this argument applies. A further contention is that those cockroaches which disperse, and are not hit by pyrethrins, do not pick up a lethal dose while attempting to escape. They may seek new harbourages in untreated areas of the building, or move into another apartment, next door or even above or below.[257] Better perhaps to take the cockroaches by surprise, without first causing them to venture outside their harbourages into new situations which are often favourable for re-establishment. Here is perhaps an argument for quick-acting insecticides. The repellency of insecticides and their use in cockroach control is discussed in detail in Chapter 7.

Effects on oothecae

In warm locations, pyrethrins are exceedingly short-lived and nymphs emerging from oothecae might easily survive previous treatment.

Eggs within the ootheca of *B. germanica* are more resistant to sprays than the adult females. When a 2 per cent spray is applied as a settling mist (at 0·8 and 1·2 mg/cm^2) onto females carrying their first oothecae, pyrethrins cause most females to drop their egg cases (82–95 per cent): between 83 per cent and 96 per cent of the females die, but only 53–64 per cent of oothecae are prevented from hatching.[658,860] It must be assumed that dropping of the oothecae is caused by contraction of the abdominal muscles as part of the symptoms of poisoning.

Van den Heuvel & Shenker[824] put females of a dieldrin-resistant strain in glass vials previously treated with emulsions which had been allowed to dry. Both synergised pyrethrins and diazinon were tested. The German cockroaches were carrying egg cases 11–16 days old. At a favourable humidity (90 per cent), 7 out of 8 oothecae dropped by females treated with pyrethrins, hatched. When the capsules were removed from the treated surface within 24 hours, these oothecae each produced an average of 30 nymphs. If the egg case was left in contact, only 5 out of 10 hatched (average 13 nymphs). The results for diazinon under similar conditions were 10 out of 10 (av. 21 nymphs) and 3 out of 7 (av. 1 nymph), respectively. Hatching occurred when the egg cases were 28–30 days old, namely 2 weeks after insecticide treatment.

These experiments show conclusively that eggs of the German cockroach, enclosed in an egg case, may not be seriously affected by the death from poisoning by pyrethrins of the female carrying it. Moreover when the ootheca is prematurely dropped, hatching will take place under favourable conditions.

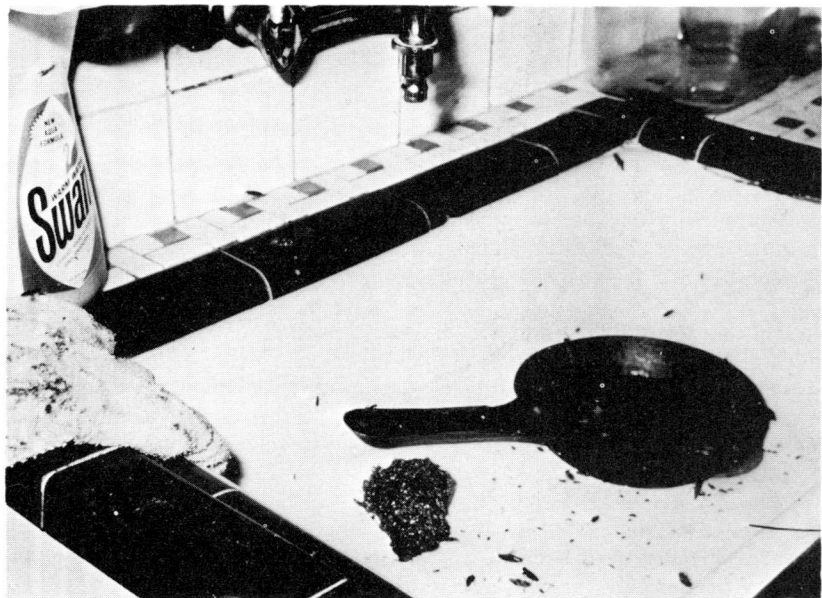

Fig. 116. A kitchen sink of a low-income family provides German cockroaches with water, warmth, harbourage and food. Pyrethrins have given spectacular knockdown, but recovery readily occurs. (Dallas, U.S.A.).

This occurs sufficiently long after separation from the adult for the activity of the insecticide originally applied to have been lost.

Toxicity to man and other animals

One of the earliest uses of pyrethrum was for the control of human internal parasites. In his excellent review of the 'Mammalian toxicology of pyrethrum', Griffin[377] lists several intestinal worms against which pyrethrins were recommended.

Pyrethrum has been used safely as an insecticide, world-wide for at least 50 years. Nonetheless, the considerable amount of work done on the toxicology of pyrethrum and the pyrethrins, 'is not complete enough to permit registration of the pyrethrins as a new insecticide if it were introduced to the market today'. Barthel[81] was presumably referring in this statement to registration in the United States, where the requirement for notification and approval of new pesticides is particularly stringent. Under normal conditions of use the pyrethrins do not harm mammals.

Not many years ago, pyrethrum was the sole insecticide of outstandingly low toxicity to man. It has now been overshadowed by the lower toxicity of some synthetic pyrethroids and newer organophosphorus compounds. In all these instances, it is the rapid breakdown of the chemical in man and other animals which underwrites safety in use.[281]

The average oral LD_{50} of pyrethrins for all higher animals is about 1500 mg/kg. The considerable variation in oral toxicities (from 200 mg/kg–2600 mg/kg) reported in the literature is most likely caused by differences in purity of the material tested. Unpurified oleoresin (oral LD_{50} (rat): 820 mg/kg) is twice as toxic as a purified extract of pyrethrins (oral LD_{50} (rat): 1870 mg/kg).

The mechanism of breakdown of pyrethrins in mammals has been studied using tritium-labelled pyrethrins fed to rats.[174] The symptoms of poisoning, arising from contact with large doses include excitation, tremors, incoordination and convulsions, suggesting action on the nervous system.[612] Because the insecticide is metabolised so readily, chronic accumulation in the body is a far smaller potential hazard than with more persistent insecticides.

When pyrethrins are given by mouth to rats, identifiable decomposition products appear in the excreta and 30 per cent of the dose is excreted as unidentifiable metabolites. Much of it, however, is not changed in the body and appears entirely in the faeces, indicating failure of absorption through the gut wall.

The pyrethrins are, nevertheless, intrinsically highly toxic, as can be shown when injected into animals intravenously (LD_{50} (rat) 10·5 mg/kg). However, animals which are injected and which survive a near lethal dose recover quickly and soon appear completely normal. The difference between the intravenous and oral values emphasises the ease with which pyrethrins are detoxified in the body. It is this rapid metabolism of the pyrethrins which explains why teratogenic effects have not been observed in mammals: unmetabolised pyrethrins do not reach the gonads or reproductive system sufficiently rapidly, although chick embryos show such effects following injection of eggs. The level of synergist (piperonyl butoxide) which might occur as residues in food, is never likely to reach a sufficient level to inhibit the detoxification of pyrethrins in man. There is no evidence that pyrethrins are carcinogenic or mutagenic in test animals.

Pyrethrins can be irritating to the eyes and mucous membranes of susceptible individuals. During use, the insecticide is likely to be more toxic to man by inhalation than by any other route.

Severe dermatitis was at one time reported among factory workers having occupational contact with pyrethrum, which cleared up on removal from exposure. Pyrethrum dermatitis is most common among those involved in e.g. picking, grinding or extracting of the pyrethrum flowers, although cases of allergy among users of unrefined pyrethrum extracts have also occurred. Attempts have been made to establish which agents in pyrethrum flowers cause skin reactions by testing extracts on previously sensitised guinea pigs.[703] There is evidence to suggest that the dermatitis is caused by impurities not present in the commercially available, refined pyrethrins.[702] The dermal toxicity of pyrethrins is negligible as they are poorly absorbed through intact skin.

The pyrethrins are toxic to fish and to the aquatic insects and crustaceans normally eaten by fish. Pyrethrins at 0·02 ppm in water are harmful to carp; 0·05–0·1 ppm is lethal to carp and disabling to trout. Birds are not usually affected. In outdoor treatment, at 0·1 and 0·2 kg pyrethrins/ha, residues on tree foliage and in water are greatly reduced or become undetectable in 1 to 5 days.[669] The ease with which the pyrethrins are degraded, accounts for their failure to give rise to persisting residues in the environment.

Residues in food

There are many situations where pyrethrins are used to control insects closely associated with food. Applications before harvest are degraded within 12–24 hours in the presence of air and sunlight, and residues are therefore non-existent on the crop when picked.

Against stored food pests, pyrethrins are applied to bulks of cereals, dried fruits and other commodities as a protectant. Applications are also made to processing plants to prevent infestations arising in food. In these situations, pyrethrins are not so liable to rapid breakdown.[583]

Pyrethrins are used for cockroach control in a great variety of situations. It is in industrial food processing areas and more especially in kitchens, shops and self-service counters, where meals are being prepared, or commodities sold directly for human consumption, that insecticides used for cockroach control may contaminate food. In many instances, pest control servicemen are required to work where food manufacturing plant is continuously operating, and where kitchens are in constant use throughout day and night.

In many countries the pest control serviceman may be required to use pyrethrins to control cockroaches in industrial food handling areas because other, long-lasting insecticides are not permitted. The latter could potentially contaminate food even though the practical risk may be extremely small:

much depends on the experience and skill of the man, his recognition of a risk situation and his ability to place insecticides only where they are really needed. Insecticides *can* be applied safely in these locations provided care is taken to reduce to a minimum, contamination in the air.

Legislative departments of some countries, have adopted the pyrethrins as the sole insecticide permitted in food areas. They have been slow to recognise that a number of the newer organophosphorus compounds (Chapter 12) are many times less toxic to man than pyrethrins and are speedily broken down in the body. These insecticides offer a residual activity in harbourages, lacking in the pyrethrins, but which in industries susceptible to cockroach problems, is so necessary for continuous freedom from infestation.

United States legislation has set tolerances for 'food processing areas and food storage areas: provided that the food is removed or covered prior to such use'. Those currently allowable are 1 ppm for pyrethrins and 10 ppm for piperonyl butoxide or MGK 264. No tolerances have been established for restaurant foods.

In this chapter we have examined the history of development, production, and use of the pyrethrins, but have not considered the other insecticides derived from plants. The pyrethrins are by far the most important, and for the others the interested reader should consult the book, 'Naturally occurring insecticides'.[463] More especially, we have looked at the properties of pyrethrins in relation to practical cockroach control, for which they have both advantages and disadvantages.

Advantages
1. Rapid action and quick knockdown—often thought to be desirable—are unsurpassed by other insecticides.
2. Flushing action is a most useful attribute.
3. Safety to man is well established, making the pyrethrins of considerable value where insect control may inadvertently contaminate food.
4. There are no undesirable residues and no evidence of adverse effects in the environment.

Disadvantages
1. Unfortunately, the pyrethrins do not kill cockroaches except at high and uneconomic concentrations.
2. Pyrethrins do not respond well to synergism, when used for cockroach control, whereas for other insects low concentrations are made more effective.
3. Cockroaches readily recover from knockdown doses of pyrethrins.
4. More importantly, rapid deterioration of the insecticide in treated harbourages gives no protection to premises against reinfestation.
5. Nymphs which hatch from egg cases, subsequent to treatment, are likely to survive.

A number of these limitations in the use of pyrethrins may be overcome by the synthetic pyrethroids, whose properties and use for cockroach control, are examined in the next chapter.

10

THE PYRETHRUM-LIKE INSECTICIDES
(SYNTHETIC PYRETHROIDS)

History of development; properties of synthetic pyrethroids—Allethrin and bioallethrin: insecticidal properties; action against cockroaches; S-bioalletnrin—Tetramethrin and biotetramethrin; insecticidal properties; action against cockroaches—Resmethrin and bioresmethrin: insecticidal properties; action against cockroaches; effect on oothecae—Other synthetic pyrethroids—Use of synthetic pyrethroids for cockroach control.

To avoid growing pyrethrum, picking its flowers and extracting the insecticide, compounds with many of the advantages and few of the disadvantages of the pyrethrins are now being synthesised. If one were to ask: where today are the most striking advances being made in the development of new, commercially useful insecticides, with properties which fit the requirements of the 1980's, the answer must surely be with the synthetic pyrethroids. We have discovered what it is that gives the natural product many of its remarkable properties: we are now able, artificially, to put together the chemistry of the pyrethrins. This provides a supply of pyrethrin-like compounds, free from political factors and climatic changes.

The first synthetic pyrethroid—allethrin—a slight modification of pyrethrin I was produced by Schechter and his colleagues in 1949 in the United States Department of Agriculture.[733] This was the beginning of 25 years' intensive effort to produce the variety of synthetic compounds now beginning to be used widely.

Increasingly in the future, the pest control operator will be offered formulations containing synthetic pyrethroids. These will be accompanied by advertising claims that a combination of numbered or coded compound X, with compound Y, will give him all the necessary properties for 'ultra rapid knockdown', 'high kill activity' against 'a broad range of insects' and with the last word in 'human and animal safety'.

Those companies well-established in the sale of pyrethrum-type formulations have already enlarged their market with newly registered formulations of synthetic pyrethroids. With the many that exist it is now possible to optimise performance against a particular pest—to tailor-make a product to fit the insect's susceptibility. Much of the interest in the promotion of the pyrethroids has been by formulators of aerosols, towards housefly and mosquito control. Historically, this has been the market for the natural product and is seen, too, as the area of use for these new compounds. Most of the insecticidal testing has therefore been carried out on flies, with performance against cockroaches and other crawling insects being secondary.

In this chapter we shall compare the performance of the major synthetic pyrethroids with the pyrethrins, confining our interest to those available to industry, and mentioning only briefly, related compounds which have not yet progressed beyond the laboratory. Our main aim will be to discover which of the pyrethroids score over the natural product for cockroach control, but incidental to this we shall see something of their performance against flies.

History of development
Use of the natural pyrethrins is limited by high cost and short life. In their favour are the outstanding merits of remarkably high activity at low concentrations against many flying insects, and in normal use, an absence of adverse effects on man.

Since allethrin was produced, attempts have been made in many countries, principally in the U.K., Japan, U.S.A. and France to improve upon it. Not long after its discovery, allethrin became available commercially, as a replacement for natural pyrethrins, mainly in aerosols. Along with later pyrethroids it was considered more seriously for this and other purposes during the shortage of pyrethrins in the early 1970's (see Fig. 100).

At the time allethrin was receiving recognition, a number of other compounds related to allethrin were being synthesised: the most promising were barthrin and dimethrin, but little commercial interest was shown in these, as allethrin was available and the new ones appeared to have few advantages.

The testing of new synthetic pyrethroids slackened in the 1950's and early 1960's, until the Japanese in 1965, announced tetramethrin. However, during this interval, Elliott and his co-workers at Rothamsted in the U.K.,[280] were beginning to reap the benefit of many years' study of the relationship of pyrethrum-like activity with chemical structure. This was to be seen later in a range of synthetic pyrethroids (NRDC compounds) with quite surprising properties.

In 1967 the commercial development of bioallethrin was announced: this too had been synthesised in 1949 and shown then, to be more effective than allethrin. When allethrin was first manufactured it was a mixture of the isomers of a basic molecule. It so happens that one of these (the (+)-*trans* isomer and now called bioallethrin) is the most active insecticidally. In 1970 it was claimed that bioallethrin could be manufactured, uncontaminated by the less active isomers.[73]

Since Schechter's early work in discovering allethrin an increasing number of pyrethroids has become available each with a slight permutation in chemical structure and molecular shape (in the words of the chemist; analogues and stereo and optical isomers), but with markedly different properties. All the early pyrethroids were synthesised esters of chrysanthemic acid; of mixed isomers, some of which have now been separated. A number of the more recent pyrethroids have been produced from different acids. Examples are pyrethric acid (NRDC 106), dimethyl and tetramethyl cyclopropane carboxylic acid (NRDC 143 = permethrin and NRDC 108, respectively), and ethanochrysanthemic acid (RU 11679). Unfortunately, the pyrethoids have become known by a variety of confusing chemical names,

TABLE 1.
NAMES, CODES AND SYNONYMS OF SYNTHETIC PYRETHROIDS

Standard, common or adopted name	Code name	Proprietary name	Chemical name
Allethrin	—	Pynamin® (Sumitomo)	(±)-3-allyl-2-methyl-4-oxocyclopent-2-enyl (±)-cis-trans-chrysanthemate
Bioallethrin	—	D-trans Conc® (MGK Ltd.)	(+)-trans isomer of allethrin
Tetramethrin (= phthalthrin)	SP 1103 FMC 9260 NIA 9260	Neo-Pynamin® (Sumitomo) Tetralate/Butamin (FMC Corp.)	3,4,5,6-tetrahydrophthalimidomethyl (±)-cis, trans-chrysanthemate
'Biotetramethrin'	—	(d-trans-Neopynamin)	(+)-trans isomer of tetramethrin
Resmethrin (= synthrin)	NRDC 104 SBP 1382 NIA 17370 FMC 17370	Chryson® (Sumitomo)	5-benzyl-3-furylmethyl (±)-cis, trans-chrysanthemate
Bioresmethrin	NRDC 107 SBP 1390	—	(+)-trans isomer of resmethrin

'Biotetramethrin' is an adopted name. The chemical nomenclature in the last column is adopted throughout this chapter, e.g.: (+)-trans ≡ d-trans.

code numbers, registered trade marks and as proprietary branded products. The information (Table L) on synonyms of the more important compounds should help resolve this confusion.

Properties of synthetic pyrethroids
Natural pyrethrins combine good knockdown with adequate kill of a wide range of insects and this is what the housewife is looking for in a household aerosol.[855] But if the reader has a primary interest in cockroach control his requirements will be different: we have already stressed (in Chapter 9) the relative inadequacy of the pyrethrins for the control of many crawling insects, and we shall be looking to see whether the pyrethroids can offer something better.

Tests with many of the synthetics have indicated their superiority over the pyrethrins in killing insects. Action is by no means so readily synergised by piperonyl butoxide and in some cases not at all (Table LI). Those pyrethroids that kill well are also not necessarily as good at causing rapid knockdown and paralysis. It is in killing cockroaches, once knocked down, that the pyrethrins are inefficient.

Some of the synthetic pyrethroids do have excellent knockdown properties. As well as combining certain of them 'for optimised fly control'—a process already well advanced[918]—we should also therefore consider whether something similar is justified for cockroach control.

TABLE LI

RELATIVE POTENCY TO HOUSEFLIES (*MUSCA DOMESTICA*) OF SYNTHETIC PYRETHROIDS COMPARED WITH NATURAL PYRETHRINS: SHOWING THE LOWER SYNERGISTIC ACTION IN BIOALLETHRIN AND ABSENCE IN BIORESMETHRIN
(From Davies[225])

Insecticide	Pyrethrins	Bioallethrin	Bioresmethrin
LD_{50} (%) alone	0·20	0·11	0·012
Relative potency (× factor)	1	1·8	17
LD_{50} (%) when mixed 1 : 5 with piperonyl butoxide	0·04	0·05	0·01
Relative potency	5	4	18
Increase in relative potency when synergised	5	2·2	1·1

The synthetic pyrethroids, as typified by allethrin, act in a manner similar to the pyrethrins in causing initial excitation of the nervous system followed by block (paralysis), and have been tested on the giant fibres of the cockroach nerve cord using micro-electrode techniques.[604,605] Allethrin is about 30 times less active than pyrethrin I in blocking conduction in the giant fibres of the American cockroach,[154] although the difference in toxicity between these insecticides is not quite so marked under practical conditions of cockroach control.

It is not possible to predict whether the pyrethroids may ultimately lose their value because of insect resistance. There is no reason why this should occur any more, or less, readily than with the chemically-related natural pyrethrins. Compared with organochlorines, the short persistence of both the pyrethrins and pyrethroids on treated surfaces is in their favour, in providing only a temporary selection pressure. Resistance could, however, be encouraged in the future by the wide scale adoption of the pyrethroids, at the expense of other insecticides with differing modes of action.

Safety in use of the pyrethroids would not appear to be a problem either. Most of the commercially available pyrethroids combine good activity against insects, with low toxicity to man (Table LII), but we should not take it for granted that because the chemist is putting together compounds modelled on the pyrethrins, we shall always have this happy combination. A good example of the reverse has recently been demonstrated[277] with a new insecticide related to the pyrethrins which is considerably more active than any other compound (LD_{50} about 0·0003 μg/housefly). The pure isomer (NRDC 161) is many times more active than bioresmethrin against flies (itself more potent than most insecticides), and about one and a half thousand times as active as pyrethrin I. This synthetic has a synergism factor of × 18 with sesamex. However, the LD_{50} to the rat (intravenous) is about 2 mg/kg and severe toxic effects are obtained orally, with some deaths at 25–63 mg/kg.[78]

TABLE LII

TOXICITIES (ACUTE ORAL LD_{50} RAT) OF SYNTHETIC PYRETHROIDS
(From Wickham & Chadwick[846] and other sources)

Insecticide	mg/kg
Natural pyrethrins	580 – 1,500
Allethrin	680 – 920
Bioallethrin	860
S-Bioallethrin	680 – 784
Resmethrin	1,400 – 2,000
Bioresmethrin	8,000 – 9,000
Tetramethrin	6,500 – >20,000
NRDC 106	>10,000
Permethrin	3,185
Cismethrin	100
RU 11679	63

ALLETHRIN AND BIOALLETHRIN

In its pure form allethrin is a pale yellow oil containing a mixture of isomers. One of these, bioallethrin,* is similarly an amber coloured, viscous liquid with a slightly aromatic odour.

When allethrin was first described[733] it had outstanding insect-killing and paralysing action, compared with the other insecticides available at that time.[328] The oral toxicity to man is similar to that of the pyrethrins (Table LII) and appropriate tests to demonstrate possible irritation of the skin have been negative.

Not surprisingly perhaps, caged canaries and budgerigars exposed to aerosols containing 50 times the normal amount of insecticide (bioallethrin with piperonyl butoxide, or with bioresmethrin), have suffered temporary eye and skin irritation but no other effects.[225]

Insecticidal properties

The effectiveness of allethrin (unsynergised), against houseflies, is about the same as pyrethrins (see Fig. 121), but allethrin performs less well against other household insects. Insects of medical and agricultural importance are also generally less susceptible to allethrin than to pyrethrins. Action of allethrin is enhanced by synergists, though it is less responsive than natural pyrethrins to piperonyl butoxide. In aerosols, the knockdown of flies by allethrin is slow, but bioallethrin is somewhat better. The usual concentration in kerosene formulations, as sprays and aerosols, and in impregnated dusts, is 0·1–0·6 per cent.

Both these pyrethroids are more persistent than natural pyrethrins on treated surfaces. In tests of photodecomposition, films on glass produced by evaporating acetone solutions, were illuminated for several hours by a 500 watt lamp held 70 cm above the plates. Allethrin persisted far longer than pyrethrins but not so long as tetramethrin and resmethrin (Table LIII).

TABLE LIII

RESIDUE (%) OF NATURAL PYRETHRINS AND VARIOUS SYNTHETIC PYRETHROIDS, AS FILMS ON GLASS, ILLUMINATED AT 25–30°C. (LAMP: XENOLIGHT UXL-500D, 500 WATT GIVING 7,000–7,800 LUX)
(From Fujimoto et al.[314])

Insecticide	Hours of exposure		
	4	8	24
Pyrethrins	—	40·0	19·0
Allethrin	94·1	85·8	59·5
Tetramethrin	95·6	95·0	87·0
Resmethrin	97·9	94·7	92·2

* The proposed common name, depallethrine, is being considered by the International Standards Organisation for this insecticide.[885]

Action against cockroaches

Allethrin interferes with the passage of nerve impulses in the cockroach nerve cord in the same way as pyrethrins. This is seen in the poisoned insect as stimulated activity, followed by paralysis and sometimes death—much as described for the pyrethrins (p. 230) and depends on the concentration of insecticide to which the cockroach has been exposed.

When allethrin and pyrethrins are compared, the latter are 2–4 times more toxic to *P. americana*, varying with the method of test,[106] and 5 times more toxic to German cockroaches.[582] Also, by topical application, pyrethrins are more toxic than allethrin to organochlorine-resistant and susceptible strains of *B. germanica*, and to susceptible strains of *P. americana* (Table LIV).

TABLE LIV

RELATIVE TOXICITY (LD_{50} : μg/INSECT) OF ALLETHRIN AND PYRETHRINS TO *B. GERMANICA* AND *P. AMERICANA* BY TOPICAL APPLICATION

(From Mitlin & Babers[579])

Cockroach	Allethrin	Pyrethrins
B. germanica: adults chlordane-susceptible	0.95	0.04
B. germanica: adults chlordane-resistant	1.12	0.03
P. americana: last instar nymphs	10.96	1.68

Bioallethrin is claimed to compare favourably with pyrethrins for fast knockdown and kill of flying insects, and for responding well to synergists. It too is not as good as pyrethrins against cockroaches, although Baker[73] says that it can be formulated with MGK 264 to make effective sprays against *B. germanica* (Table LV). On glass treated with 10 ml/m² of 0.5 per cent propoxur compared with the same, incorporating 0.03 per cent bioallethrin with 0.15 per cent Tropital (dried for 24 hours before test), German cockroaches are knocked down slightly quicker with synergised bioallethrin present. There is no difference after 20 minutes, or to the kill at 24 hours.[73]

Hayashi & Tanaka[411] have compared the performance of allethrin and bioallethrin, against *B. germanica*, on impregnated and dusted filter papers: bioallethrin was superior.

Lhoste and co-workers[504] have compared the effects of allethrin, bioallethrin and the pyrethrins on a number of insects. They show: (1) the superiority of bioallethrin over the mixed isomers to *B. germanica*, (2) the same superiority when tested alone or combined with piperonyl butoxide and

TABLE LV

EFFECT OF DIFFERENT SYNERGISTS: (A) TROPITAL, (B) PIPERONYL BUTOXIDE AND (C) MGK 264 ON THE KILL (%) OF *B. GERMANIC* BY BIOALLETHRIN AFTER 48 HOURS, COMPARED WITH OFFICIAL TEST INSECTICIDE (CSMA COCKROACH SPRAY METHOD)
(From Baker[73])

Bioallethrin (%) in petroleum distillate	Standard	Synergist (%)	Kill (%)
0·075		Tropital 0·375	34
0·100		0·500	53
0·125		0·625	65
	OTI		70
0·075		Piperonyl butoxide 0·375	32
0·100		0·500	41
0·125		0·625	62
	OTI		62
0·075		MGK 264 0·075	73
0·100		0·900	81
0·125		1·125	90
	OTI		70

(3) the obvious superiority of the pyrethrins over both pyrethroids (Fig. 117). Also (4), that allethrin is least effective in killing *Leucophaea maderae* and (5) given time, this cockroach has a strong ability to recover from knockdown and sublethal doses of pyrethrins and pyrethroids (Fig. 118). These studies also show (6), the considerably greater susceptibility of Oriental cockroaches compared with German, to all three insecticides, and no evidence of recovery from poisoning of *B. orientalis* over 5-day periods (Fig. 119). Applications of insecticide to plywood (1g/m^2) show no greater activity of pyrethroids, compared with pyrethrins, to cockroaches over 5 weeks.

The most extensive tests in the laboratory of synthetic pyrethroids against cockroaches, applied as dust and by direct spray, show that allethrin is among the least effective in killing *B. germanica*: natural pyrethrins are 3–5 times more toxic (Table LVI). Bioallethrin is a little better, but requires concentrations 1½ times those of the pyrethrins to give the same kill. Bioallethrin used as a direct spray is about as toxic to German cockroaches as lindane.[181]

TABLE LVI

CONCENTRATIONS FOR 50% KILL (LC_{50}:WT %) OF NATURAL PYRETHRINS AND SYNTHETIC PYRETHROIDS WITH AND WITHOUT PIPERONYL BUTOXIDE (1 : 5), APPLIED AS DUST AND SPRAY DIRECTLY TO ADULT MALE *B. GERMANICA*

(From Chadwick[179])

Insecticide	LC_{50} alone	LC_{50} with pip. but.	Synergism factor
DUST			
Bioresmethrin	0·016	0·014	1·1
Pyrethrins	0·045	0·020	2·3
Bioallethrin	0·053	0·036	1·5
Resmethrin	0·053	0·036	1·5
NRDC 106	0·084	0·057	1·5
Biotetramethrin	0·087	0·053	1·6
Allethrin	0·110	0·064	1·7
Tetramethrin	0·162	0·078	2·1
SPRAY			
Bioresmethrin	0·020	0·021	1·0
Pyrethrins	0·034	0·031	1·1
Resmethrin	0·038	0·029	1·3
Bioallethrin	0·045	0·062	0·7
NRDC 106	0·145	0·106	1·4
Biotetramethrin	0·148	0·103	1·4
Allethrin	0·178	0·101	1·8
Tetramethrin	0·287	0·152	1·9

For the same knockdown (50 per cent in 5 minutes or 95 per cent in 15 minutes), bioallethrin succeeds at about ⅓ the concentration of allethrin (both unsynergised) and at ⅔ the concentration of allethrin (when both are synergised). Bioallethrin is about four times less effective than natural pyrethrins in knocking down German cockroaches (Table LVII); the same applies when bioallethrin is substituted for pyrethrins at low concentrations in formulations combining residual insecticides, such as diazinon and fenitrothion (unpublished).

Synergism of the two pyrethroids at a ratio of 1 : 5, makes only a small difference to their activities, certainly of no practical significance. Surprisingly, bioallethrin with piperonyl butoxide at ratios up to 1 : 100 tend to *delay knockdown* rather than shorten it. Only when the ratio of bioallethrin to piperonyl butoxide reaches 1 : 100 is there any evidence of *improved kill* of German cockroaches; ratios below 1 : 10 tend to reduce kill (Fig. 120).

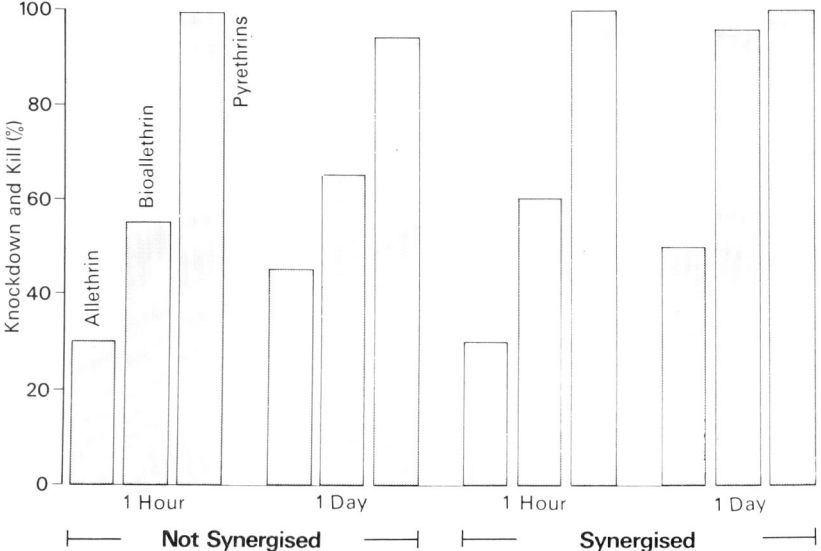

Fig. 117. Effects of allethrin, bioallethrin and pyrethrins (1 μg/insect) applied topically, alone and synergised (1 : 8, pip. but.) on German cockroaches. Results 1 hour and 1 day after treatment. (From Lhoste, Rauch & Lambert[504]).

TABLE LVII

CONCENTRATIONS FOR 50% KNOCKDOWN IN 5 MINS AND 95% KNOCKDOWN IN 15 MINS OF NATURAL PYRETHRINS AND SYNTHETIC PYRETHROIDS, WITH AND WITHOUT PIPERONYL BUTOXIDE (1 : 5) APPLIED AS A SPRAY DIRECTLY TO ADULT MALE B. GERMANICA
(From Chadwick[179])

Insecticide	KD_{50} (5 mins)		KD_{95} (15 mins)	
	alone	+pip. but.	alone	+pip. but.
Biotetramethrin	0·01	0·01	0·012	0·005
Pyrethrins	0·015	0·018	0·020	0·015
Tetramethrin	0·05	0·05	0·04	0·05
Bioallethrin	0·07	0·10	0·06	0·09
Bioresmethrin	—	—	0·07	0·08
NRDC 106	0·10	0·09	0·09	0·07
Allethrin	0·27	0·17	0·14	0·13
Resmethrin	—	—	0·15	0·07

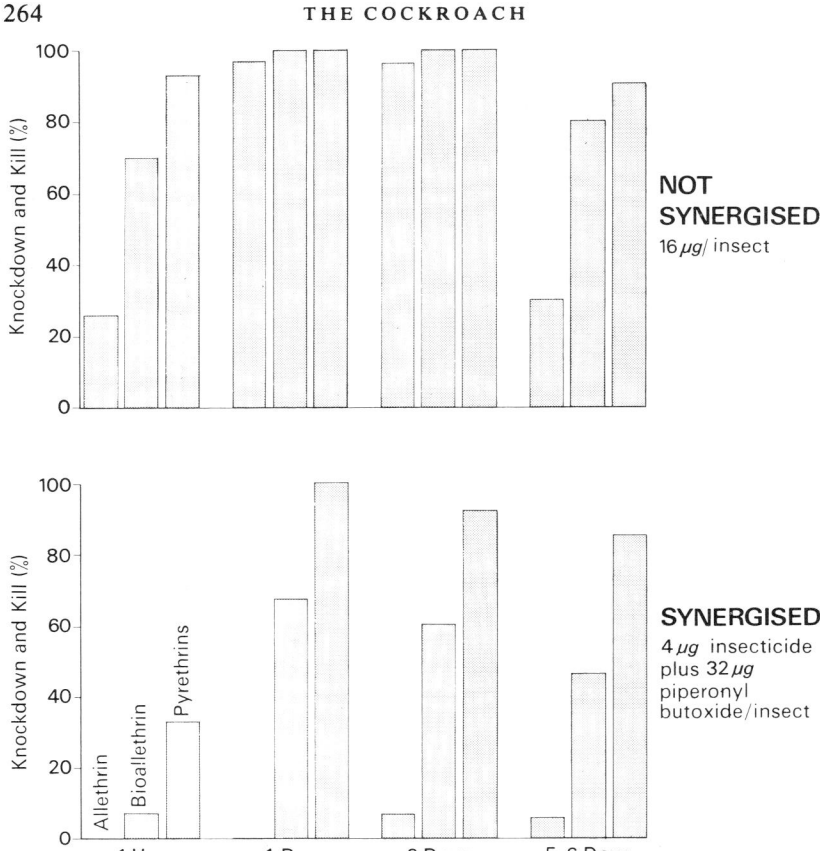

Fig. 118. The effects of allethrin, bioallethrin and pyrethrins, alone and synergised (1 : 8) on the knockdown and kill of *Leucophaea maderae*. Results 1, 24, 48 hrs and 5–6 days after topical application. Note with all three insecticides, the increase in symptoms of poisoning up to 24 hours and recovery thereafter. (From Lhoste, Rauch & Lambert[504]).

Flushing of insects from their harbourages is one of the most valuable properties of the pyrethrins. In a laboratory simulation of conditions where sprays might be used to flush German cockroaches from crevices, none of the pyrethroids tested as 0·3 per cent sprays, did as well as 0·3 per cent synergised pyrethrins (ratio 1 : 10). Bioallethrin was however, superior to cismethrin and bioresmethrin (see Table LVIII), and had similar flushing activity to biotetramethrin (see Fig. 123).

S-bioallethrin

This pyrethroid is bioallethrin—with a 'different chemical shape'—described as a 'third generation' pyrethroid. The first allethrin produced, was a mixture of eight isomers all varying in insecticidal performance but jointly con-

TABLE LVIII

PER CENT OF COCKROACHES FLUSHED OUT AND THE 50% FLUSHING OUT TIME (FO_{50}) OF ADULT MALE GERMAN COCKROACHES FROM A SPRAYED ARTIFICIAL HARBOURAGE. FORMULATIONS IN ODOURLESS KEROSENE
(From Chadwick & Evans[181])

Insecticide	(w/v) (%)	Minutes			FO_{50} (mins)
		5	10	15	
Pyrethrins/ pip. butoxide	0·3/ 3·0	71	77	79	2·2
Pyrethrins/ bioresmethrin/ pip. butoxide	0·05/ 0·25/ 0·25	65	75	75	2·9
Bioallethrin	0·3	54	62	65	3·9
Cismethrin	0·3	43	70	73	6·0
Bioallethrin/ bioresmethrin/ pip. butoxide	0·12/ 0·18/ 0·60	35	51	55	9·5
Bioresmethrin	0·3	28	48	58	10·5
Propoxur	0·5	24	38	41	>15
Odourless kerosene	—	15	22	27	—
Unsprayed control	—	4	11	16	—

tributing to the properties of the whole. Then came bioallethrin announced by Lhoste et al in 1967, and produced by Roussel-Uclaf in France, in which the acid part of the molecule was of a particular form:[501] it was substantially more active than the older allethrin and was introduced into the U.S. in 1969. S-bioallethrin[694] introduced in 1972 remains the same molecule as allethrin and bioallethrin, except that the alcohol side of its structure is now in a configuration which gives the compound still greater insecticidal activity.

Its appearance in pure form is the same as bioallethrin; toxicity to man is unchanged and like all pyrethroids it remains sensitive to U.V. light. Results for water-based sprays show an improved action, compared with bioallethrin—the same kill at half the concentration—against nymphs of the German and Oriental cockroach.[74]

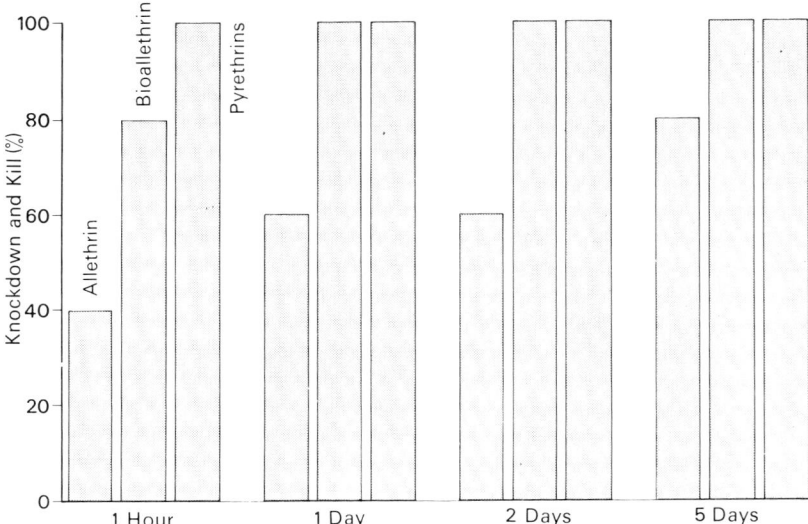

Fig. 119. The effects up to 5 days of allethrin, bioallethrin and pyrethrins (1 μg/insect) applied topically to Oriental cockroaches. Note their greater susceptibility than *B. germanica* (cf. Fig. 117) and absence of recovery (cf. Fig. 118). (From Lhoste, Rauch & Lambert[504]).

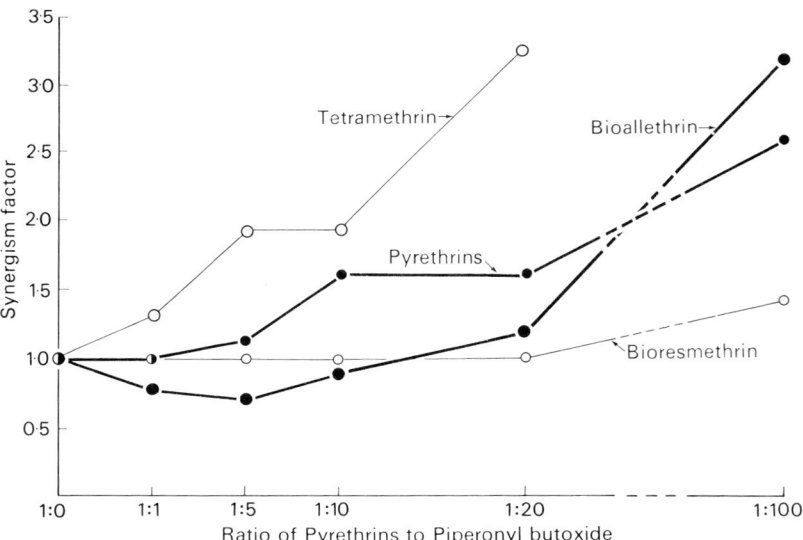

Fig. 120. Effect of piperonyl butoxide on the kill obtained with pyrethrins and three synthetic pyrethroids when applied to German cockroaches by direct spray. (From Chadwick[179]).

TETRAMETHRIN AND 'BIOTETRAMETHRIN'

Tetramethrin was introduced in 1965: in its pure form it is a light yellow powder, soluble in most organic solvents. It is available to the pest control operator as concentrates for oil sprays, and in forms suitable for water-based pressurised packs. Tetramethrin is used as space and residual sprays in combination with piperonyl butoxide and with other insecticides. In formulating dusts, care has to be taken to select the diluent because of high surface activity: antioxidants are used to stabilise the product.

A notable property of tetramethrin is its very high acute oral LD_{50} to the rat (Table LII), indicating extremely low toxicity to man. There is no potentiation of toxicity for formulations which combine tetramethrin with natural pyrethrins. Photodecomposition is slower than pyrethrins and comparable with other synthetic pyrethroids (Table LIII).

Like allethrin, tetramethrin has a chemical structure which exists in several forms (isomers). It is in fact a mixture of isomers: biotetramethrin is a coined name for the (+)-*trans* isomer of tetramethrin (as bioallethrin is the accepted name for the (+)-*trans* isomer of allethrin). Biotetramethrin has some good properties against cockroaches but is not yet available commercially.

Insecticidal properties

Again it is of interest to see first how tetramethrin rates against pyrethrins and other pyrethroids in controlling flying insects and then to look at performance against cockroaches.

Tetramethrin is good in producing early knockdown of flies: the times, for example, for 50 per cent knockdown of house flies by tetramethrin, pyrethrins and allethrin (0·1 per cent in oil without synergist), are 68, 85 and 138 seconds, respectively. There is very little difference between the three insecticides (Fig. 121) in their ability to *kill* houseflies.[139,290,291] Accordingly, efforts have been made to combine tetramethrin—for its good knockdown—with a pyrethroid, such as resmethrin which has good killing activity. These two pyrethroids together give an 'optimised fly control formulation' equal to the activity of synergised pyrethrins.[2,314] In topical application tests with both resistant and non-resistant flies this combination is thought to show synergism.[454]

The best combination of tetramethrin with the synergist, piperonyl butoxide, for improved action against flies, lies between 1 : 3 and 1 : 5. At these ratios the recommended amount of tetramethrin in household sprays is 0·1–0·15 per cent. For fogging solutions it is 0·25–0·4 per cent. Aerosol formulations contain 0·25–0·5 per cent. All three formulations are labelled for cockroach control, but this low synergism ratio is not the best for *B. germanica*.

Action against cockroaches

The early praise for tetramethrin against cockroaches has found little support. It was claimed that *aerosols* containing the high concentration of 2 per cent tetramethrin caused knockdown of female German cockroaches (chlordane-resistant) equal to 2 per cent pyrethrins, but was ineffective in killing these and large nymphs of *P. americana*.[290] However, in tests with *sprays*, tetramethrin caused greater knockdown than pyrethrins and was only slightly less effective in killing.[291] With an aerosol containing 0·2 per cent tetramethrin, 80 per cent of the German cockroaches knocked down on the first day had recovered by the second (Table LXIV).

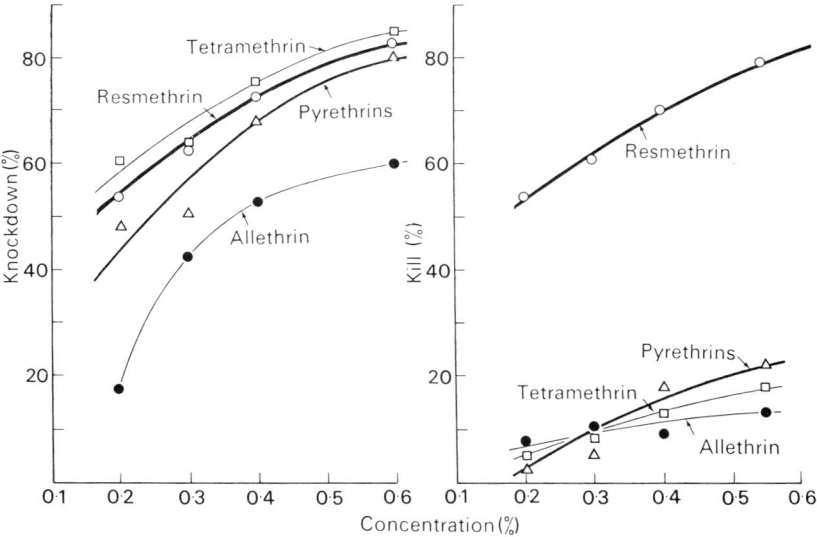

Fig. 121. Relative efficiency of tetramethrin, resmethrin, allethrin and the pyrethrins in knockdown of houseflies (at 15 mins) and kill (at 24 hours): CSMA Aerosol Test Method. (From Fujimoto, *et al*.[314]).

Tetramethrin was the poorest of all the pyrethroids in killing German cockroaches, as dust and spray,[179] whether or not synergised with piperonyl butoxide (1 : 5) (Table LVI). At this ratio, only half the concentration of tetramethrin was needed for 50 per cent kill, a small gain but nevertheless high for the pyrethroids as a whole. A ratio of 1 : 20 markedly improved the activity of tetramethrin towards German cockroaches compared with other pyrethroids (Fig. 120). A marked improvement of dust formulations can be obtained by combining tetramethrin with silica (Table LIX).

We now come to examine the performance of biotetramethrin—the (+)-*trans* isomer of tetramethrin—against cockroaches, and first the tests carried out in the United States.[296] Aerosols containing biotetramethrin or pyrethrins, applied (by the 'pen method' of Fales *et al*[294]) to large nymphs of *P. americana*, gave the same knockdown, but the pyrethroid was not half as good in killing them (Table LX). This contrasts with the greater knockdown

TABLE LIX

EFFECTIVENESS OF TETRAMETHRIN IN DUST FORMULATIONS AGAINST *B. GERMANICA*, BY PICK-UP FROM TREATED SURFACES
(Unpublished data: courtesy Sumitomo)

Composition (mg/m²)			Knockdown (%)				Kill (%)
Tetramethrin	Piperonyl butoxide	Silica*	25	50 minutes	100	300	24 hours
250	0	0	0	7	13	13	33
250	1,250	0	0	10	17	30	53
250	1,250	500	0	87	100	100	100

* Amorphous silica hydrate.

and kill of biotetramethrin, compared with pyrethrins, against flies. Biotetramethrin and pyrethrins were equally good in knocking down adult *B. germanica* when applied as sprays but pyrethrins gave slightly better kill at low concentrations. Against large nymphs of *B. germanica*, there was no difference between the pyrethroid and natural product, either in knockdown (at 3 mins.) or kill (at 24 hours).

The persistence of biotetramethrin has been tested on glass. German cockroaches resistant to chlordane were exposed to deposits of about 1 mg per 100 cm² in jars (the method of Keller, Clark, Lofgren & Wilson;[478] Bodenstein & Fales[110]). The pyrethroid remained insecticidal for up to 12 weeks and caused rapid knockdown for 8 weeks. In the same test, malathion performed well for only 1 week.

Assessing these results against those for the mixed isomers—tetramethrin—Fales and co-workers conclude that the single isomer—biotetramethrin—is more effective against flies, but less effective against cockroaches. This conclusion is not, however, supported by Chadwick:[179] he shows that biotetramethrin is about twice as active as tetramethrin in killing *B. germanica*,

TABLE LX

KNOCKDOWN AND KILL (%) OF LARGE NYMPHS OF *P. AMERICANA* BY AEROSOLS CONTAINING 2% BIOTETRAMETHRIN AND 2% PYRETHRINS
(From Fales et al.[296])

Insecticide	Dose (g/28m³)	Knockdown in mins			Kill in days		
		10	20	30	1	3	5
Biotetramethrin	47.5	35	65	100	0	20	40
Pyrethrins	45.8	24	75	95	0	25	100

and marginally better than allethrin (Table LVI). Biotetramethrin is less well synergised by piperonyl butoxide than tetramethrin, as is bioallethrin relative to allethrin.

It bears repeating that the deficiency of natural pyrethrins for cockroach control, when unsupported by an insecticide with residual properties, is the very high and totally uneconomic concentrations needed to achieve good kill. Tetramethrin and biotetramethrin are also poor in killing German cockroaches, although the knockdown achieved is excellent. Chadwick finds that biotetramethrin acts slightly more rapidly than pyrethrins, which in turn act more rapidly than tetramethrin (Table LVII). But because of poor kill, it would appear that neither of these synthetics provides an effective replacement for pyrethrins.

RESMETHRIN AND BIORESMETHRIN

These two synthetic pyrethroids are among a number of very active compounds developed by Elliott and co-workers in England. When announced[276] resmethrin had 'an insecticidal activity greater than any previous compound containing only carbon, hydrogen and oxygen'. It is an ester of chrysanthemic acid and is about 20 times more toxic to houseflies than natural pyrethrins. Like allethrin and tetramethrin, resmethrin is also a mixture of isomers: a white waxy solid in its pure form, containing about 70–80 per cent of the (+)-*trans* isomer, bioresmethrin, which is liquid and more active than resmethrin *per se*.

Resmethrin and bioresmethrin match other synthetic pyrethroids in decomposing on exposure to air and light, but much more slowly than the pyrethrins (Table LIII). Their toxicity to man lies between allethrin and the extremely safe tetramethrin (Table LII).

Insecticidal properties
There have been numerous results published on the performance of these compounds against flies.[125, 126, 292] In Peet Grady tests, oil formulations of 0·25 per cent resmethrin, 0·25 per cent synergised pyrethrins and the Official Test Insecticide, knocked down 88·3 per cent, 85·9 per cent and 73·4 per cent of flies in 15 minutes, respectively. Of the flies knocked down, 97·3 per cent were killed by 0·25 per cent resmethrin in water (78·0 per cent by synergised pyrethrins) and 96·0 per cent killed by 0·25 per cent resmethrin in oil (85·0 per cent by synergised pyrethrins). This effectiveness against houseflies is quite exceptional: both resmethrin and bioresmethrin are many times more insecticidal than unsynergised natural pyrethrins.[225, 641, 845] Rate of knockdown is slow, but somewhat quicker than with allethrin, and more importantly, flies knocked down do not recover.[846]

The German cockroach is also unable to recover (Table LXIV). Unfortunately the synergists commonly used with the pyrethrins, do nothing to increase the effectiveness of resmethrin and bioresmethrin (Tables LI, LVI & LVII, and Fig. 120). However, houseflies, selected for resistance to resmethrin,

THE PYRETHRUM-LIKE INSECTICIDES

are killed more readily than non-resistant flies by a combination of resmethrin and piperonyl butoxide.[913]

With such promising compounds for pest control, their effects on a large number of crawling insects have been examined. Brooks and co-workers[125] list 40 species against which resmethrin has been found effective. Tests with fabric pests (*Attagenus megatoma* and *Tineola bisselliella*), indicate that resmethrin can remain effective as a short-term protectant for woollens, for up to six months.[138] Registered uses for resmethrin in the U.S. include 0·05–0·15 per cent for space treatment against flying insects and 0·25–0·5 per cent for contact sprays against cockroaches and other crawling insects.

Action against cockroaches

The toxicity of resmethrin to German cockroaches (Fig. 122) lies between that of fenitrothion and propoxur, both of which have been used extensively for cockroach control because of their good residual properties. By dust and direct spray methods, resmethrin has much the same performance as natural pyrethrins in killing German cockroaches (Table LVI): synergism with piperonyl butoxide (1 : 5) does little to enhance action (an improvement in LC_{50} of × 1·3–1·5). Resmethrin is one of the poorest of the pyrethroids in knocking-down German cockroaches: about equal to allethrin (Table LVII).

These findings are not too different from those of Okuno *et al*[641]: resmethrin is inferior to pyrethrins and tetramethrin in knocking-down German cockroaches, but the first is about 1·5 times more toxic than pyrethrins.

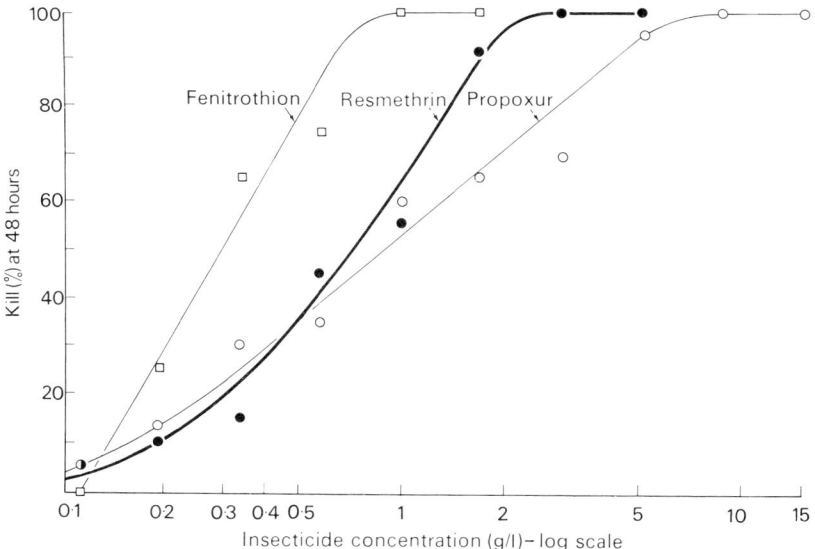

Fig. 122. Relative toxicity of resmethrin, fenitrothion and propoxur applied topically to adult German cockroaches. (Cornwell, unpublished).

Resmethrin is more effective on 'residual contact'. When adult male German cockroaches[125] were allowed to walk on and off unpainted, emulsion-sprayed, plywood panels, for 48 hours, 70 per cent died up to 10 weeks after treatment with $0 \cdot 3$ g/m^2 and up to 21–22 weeks at $0 \cdot 5$–$1 \cdot 0$ g/m^2. A kill of 70 per cent is not of course an acceptable level in practice. At least 70 per cent of adult female cockroaches exposed for 1 hour to surfaces treated with resmethrin wettable powder ($0 \cdot 2$ g/m^2), continued to die for up to 4 weeks on glass, up to 15 weeks on paper and 16 weeks on plywood. The equivalent periods for surfaces treated with pyrethrins were less than 1 week, 4 weeks and 10 weeks. These results suggest that in an average room, resmethrin might have longer residual activity than the pyrethrins,[126] as confirmed by photodecomposition tests (Table LIII).

In field trials, resmethrin (1·33 per cent) formulated directly in propellents (Freon 11 and 12) and applied as an aerosol at $3 \cdot 5$ g/m^3 to a large mess hall infested with *B. germanica*, caused small nymphs 'to fall out of crevices' in 15 minutes and adults in about 30 minutes: cockroaches knocked down did not recover.[379] From this trial, resmethrin was considered equal to, or better than, natural pyrethrins in flushing out German cockroaches: 'the insects do not seem to appear as quickly, nor are their movements quite so frenzied as those exposed to pyrethrins. However, after about 15–20 minutes more of the total population is exposed providing a more accurate estimate of the infestation level'. This same application rate in tests of aerosol formulations by Sullivan *et al*[777] was unsatisfactory in killing American and German cockroaches. In laboratory tests, the time for half of male German cockroaches to be flushed from simulated harbourages by kerosene sprays was 2·9 minutes for pyrethrins and 5·1 for resmethrin (see Fig. 123).

In infested houses the residual activity of resmethrin applied by spray (at 0·2–0·4 g a.i./m^2)—to all baseboards, architraves, and other likely cockroach harbourages—was sufficient to give control for 5–6 weeks. This formulation is claimed to have contained an undisclosed additive extending residual activity 5-fold.[165,166]

The merits of bioresmethrin may now be considered. It is already known to be more effective than the mixed isomers (resmethrin) in killing flies: '55 times as toxic to adult houseflies (*M. domestica*) as natural pyrethrins' demonstrates that bioresmethrin is a potent killer. We might therefore expect excellent performance in controlling cockroaches, which is an encouraging starting point.

Bioresmethrin has been examined in aerosols and sprays against *P. americana* and *B. germanica* (susceptible and chlordane-resistant) and against *S. longipalpa*.[297,298] By the 'pen method' of Fales *et al*.[294] an aerosol containing 2 per cent bioresmethrin does not give adequate knockdown or kill of large nymphs of the American cockroach (Table LXI). Pyrethrins perform better. However, against German cockroaches, a spray containing bioresmethrin (0·25–1·0 mg/l) gives results similar to the Official Test Insecticide containing 1 mg/l of pyrethrins (Table LXII). Bioresmethrin therefore appears to be somewhat more effective than pyrethrins against *B. germanica*, but no concentration of bioresmethrin (from 0·06 to 2 per cent) provides any knockdown in 30 seconds, whereas 1 per cent pyrethrins gives 84 per cent.

TABLE LXI

KNOCKDOWN AND KILL (%) OF LARGE NYMPHS OF *P. AMERICANA* EXPOSED FOR 30 MINS TO AEROSOLS CONTAINING 2% BIORESMETHRIN AND 2% PYRETHRINS
(From Fales et al[297])

Insecticide	Dose (g/28·3 m³)	Knockdown in mins			Kill in days		
		10	20	30	1	3	5
Bioresmethrin	40·1	0	2	30	2	22	52
Pyrethrins	44·5	5	32	45	0	35	100

Fales comments that in previous, similar tests[292] 0·25 mg/l of resmethrin had only half the performance of bioresmethrin.

In residue tests against German cockroaches resistant to chlordane, bioresmethrin is more effective than malathion (both at 1 mg/100 cm²), when first applied, and after 1 week, but the pyrethroid is less effective after 2 weeks. These results show bioresmethrin to have poorer performance than resmethrin previously tested by the same method.[292]

When cockroaches have a choice of harbouring in cartons, some treated with bioresmethrin (1 per cent in acetone at 1 ml/80 cm²) they are clearly repelled: only 2 per cent of German, 4 per cent of American and 2 per cent of Brown-banded cockroaches occupied the treated cartons. Wickham & Chadwick[846] claim specific differences in response of cockroaches to

TABLE LXII

KILL (%) OF ADULT MALE *B. GERMANICA* BY SPRAYS CONTAINING BIORESMETHRIN, APPLIED BY CSMA COCKROACH SPRAY METHOD, AND COMPARED WITH THE OFFICIAL TEST INSECTICIDE
(From Fales et al[297])

Bioresmethrin concentration (%)	Kill (%) in days	
	1	2
0·0625	30	62
0·125	62	68
0·25	92	98
0·50	95	98
1·00	100	100
2·00	100	100
OTI (Pyrethrins 1%)	98	100

bioresmethrin: 'it quite rapidly flushes out *P. americana* while *B. orientalis* shows little response.'

The results of Chadwick's experiments[179] with bioresmethrin against *B. germanica* tend to support the observations from the United States: with dusts and sprays applied to the insects directly, bioresmethrin is about twice as effective in killing cockroaches as pyrethrins and therefore also about twice as effective as resmethrin. Bioresmethrin is the most active of the pyrethroids tested, although the difference between it and pyrethrins is less marked than with houseflies. Bioresmethrin is inefficient at causing knockdown, and is unresponsive to piperonyl butoxide at 1 : 5. In fact Chadwick's experiments with synergism ratios up to 1 : 100 show little or no effect on bioresmethrin (Fig. 120). It is also the poorest of the pyrethroids tested for 'flushing action' against German cockroaches (Table LVIII and Fig. 123).

Effect on oothecae

Chadwick & Evans[181] have investigated the effect of bioresmethrin on the hatching of oothecae of *B. germanica* and undertaken trials with mists in in-

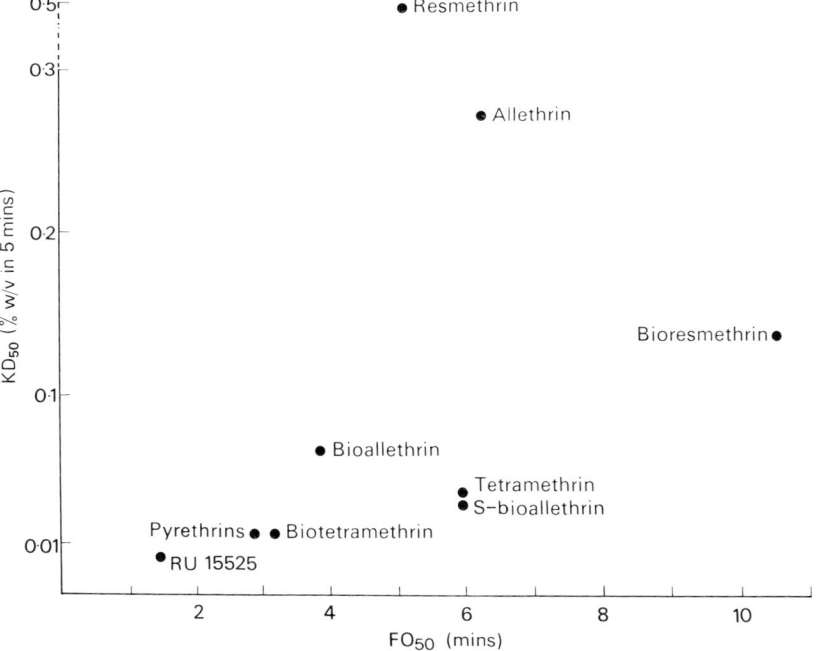

Fig. 123. Flushing and knockdown by synthetic pyrethroids in odourless kerosene of male *B. germanica*. FO_{50} is the time (mins) for 50 per cent to be flushed out by a 0·3 per cent (w/v) solution. KD_{50} is the concentration (w/v per cent) for 50 per cent to be knocked down in 5 minutes. (From Wickham & Chadwick[846]).

fested premises. The female German cockroach carries her egg case until the nymphs emerge and insecticides often cause it to be dropped prematurely. Little effect on hatching has been observed previously with pyrethrins[860] or with pyrethrins and diazinon.[824]

In tests with bioresmethrin, droplets (0·5μg in 1μl of odourless kerosene) were applied topically to females carrying an ootheca. The egg case is dropped within 24 hours and the adult dies: the ootheca invariably hatches, but 70 per cent of the nymphs die within 24 hours. This demonstrates the effect of contact of the insecticide with the parent only.

When the ootheca, near to hatching, is removed manually most nymphs will usually emerge. However, when the isolated ootheca is treated in the same way as the parent, very few nymphs hatch and 90 per cent of those that do, die very rapidly. Estimates suggest that bioresmethrin used as a fog would reduce the numbers of surviving nymphs, in the generation subsequent to treatment, to about one third.

In field tests with bioresmethrin (0·3 per cent), applied as mists (1 litre/ 100–200m³), good control was obtained of *B. germanica*, although this pyrethroid gave the slowest knockdown and stimulus to the insects to move from harbourages. Poor activation and knockdown was also obtained of *B. orientalis* even when the formulation incorporated synergised pyrethrins.[181] With fogs blown down sewers to control *P. americana* in Singapore[182] repeated applications of bioresmethrin were necessary to keep populations suppressed (Fig. 124).

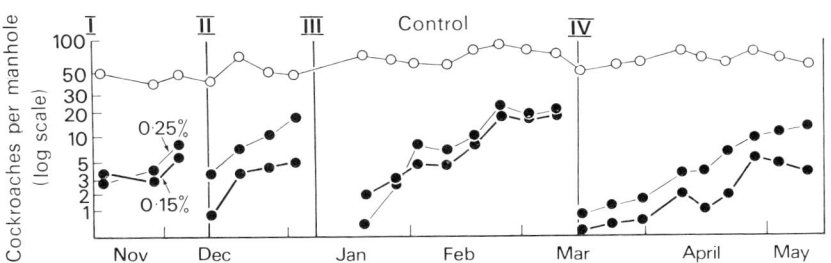

Fig. 124. Effect of thermal fogging with bioresmethrin on the numbers of *P. americana* in sewers in Singapore. I–IV are the dates when fog was applied. (From Wickham & Chadwick[846]).

OTHER SYNTHETIC PYRETHROIDS

There are a number of pyrethroids which have been examined experimentally but which have not yet reached commercial development. For instance NRDC 106 (= RU 12061) is related to bioresmethrin in that the former is a synthetic pyrethrate, whereas the latter is the corresponding chrysanthemate. The knockdown of male German cockroaches by NRDC 106 is poor—about equal to bioresmethrin: direct application of NRDC 106 as dust and spray is five to seven times less insecticidal than bioresmethrin (Table LVI). This NRDC compound has a very low toxicity to man (Table LII).

Another pyrethroid examined for performance against flies and cockroaches is NRDC 119 (= RU 12063 = the (+)-*cis, trans* isomer of resmethrin), called 'cismethrin'; its knockdown of flies is as rapid as unsynergised pyrethrins, and by topical application NRDC 119 is about 20 times more toxic than unsynergised pyrethrin I.[277]

In tests on German cockroaches by direct spray,[181] cismethrin at 0·25 per cent gives somewhat slower knockdown than bioallethrin, but is twice as rapid as bioresmethrin (Table LXIII). The flushing performance of cismethrin is not as good as bioallethrin, and is about 2–3 times slower than synergised pyrethrins (Table LVIII). Cismethrin gives equal kill at one quarter the concentration of synergised pyrethrins and bioresmethrin, when applied by direct spray: the LC_{50}'s (wt per cent) of these insecticides to German cockroaches are respectively, 0·0063, 0·031 and 0·020. Unfortunately, cismethrin has a relatively high mammalian toxicity.

Related to resmethrin and bioresmethrin, but containing a different acid component is the recent pyrethroid RU 15525. This flushes German cockroaches from harbourages just as quickly as pyrethrins and has the same knockdown performance—but in both cases at half the concentration of the natural product (Fig. 123).

TABLE LXIII

TIME (MINS) FOR 50% KNOCKDOWN (KD_{50}) OF MALE *B. GERMANICA* BY BIOALLETHRIN, CISMETHRIN AND BIORESMETHRIN APPLIED BY DIRECT SPRAY

(From Chadwick & Evans[181])

Concentration (wt/v %)	KD_{50} (mins)		
	Bioallethrin	Cismethrin	Bioresmethrin
0·30	0·1	—	2·9
0·20	1·6	2·1	4·2
0·10	2·4	3·7	5·9
0·05	—	5·6	—

Another promising pyrethroid of a new type, RU 11679 (made from ethanochrysanthemic acid),[502] has good stability to light, like bioresmethrin, but no knockdown properties.[845] Topical applications of RU 11679 to German cockroaches are four times more insecticidal than bioresmethrin.[503] RU 11679 is also marginally more toxic than bioresmethrin to houseflies, but is unfortunately one of the more toxic pyrethroids to man (Table LII).

Prothrin, another pyrethroid, of Japanese origin, with good insecticidal properties against flying insects, especially houseflies, has been dismissed by Fales et al[295] as, 'not effective in aerosols and sprays against crawling insects such as cockroaches'. This pyrethroid has an oral LD_{50} (rat) of about 10,000 mg/kg.[638] It was 'greatly less effective' than pyrethrins against *P. americana* ('pen method' of test) and against *B. germanica* as sprays (CSMA Cockroach Spray Method). Its residual activity against German cockroaches was no greater than a week.

The performance of prothrin, and the related proparthrin, as reported by Hayashi,[406] suggests that they are unlikely to be so effective against German cockroaches (see Table LXIV) as the synthetics discussed in more detail in this chapter. However, the synergism between proparthrin and tetramethrin, in doubling the toxicity of the former, and trebling that of the latter, to German cockroaches is of interest.[407]

TABLE LXIV

EFFECTIVENESS OF PYRETHRINS AND SYNTHETIC PYRETHROIDS AGAINST GERMAN COCKROACHES, BY TOPICAL APPLICATION (LC_{50} μg/INSECT) AND BY 0·2% AEROSOL. NOTE THE RECOVERY WHICH CAN OCCUR FROM PYRETHRINS AND TETRAMETHRIN
(From Hayashi[406])

Insecticide	LC_{50}*	Knockdown/mortality (%)**	
		at 24 hrs	at 48 hrs
Resmethrin	0·240	100	100
Pyrethrins	0·505	90	19·1
Tetramethrin	1·120	100	21·1
Allethrin	1·922	50	63·3
Proparthrin	2·162	27·8	42·2
Prothrin	3·584	15·6	18·9

* by topical application.
** by aerosol.

Finally, among synthetics with a good possibility of becoming commercially available in the next 2–3 years is NRDC 143, or permethrin. It has a low mammalian toxicity (Table LII) and quite remarkable residual life[278]: a deposit of 300 mg/m² on plywood gave 100 per cent kill of German cockroaches after 12 months exposure of the deposit outdoors. This stability to light is quite exceptional.[97] Wettable powders of permethrin can be made which are chemically stable.[846]

USE OF SYNTHETIC PYRETHROIDS FOR COCKROACH CONTROL

Synthetic pyrethroids have many of the properties needed for the future: as lethal to insects as the most potent of the chlorinated hydrocarbon insecticides and organophosphorus compounds (Fig. 125) and acting more rapidly (Fig. 129). Yet they are far less toxic to man, being degraded sufficiently rapidly to non-toxic by-products so as not to present a hazard in the indoor environment. Because of this short life, they are unlikely to give insects sufficient time to develop resistance; instances in field use are rare, but the increased use of pyrethroids which will undoubtedly occur, may increase the risk of resistance developing.[912] The greater resistance of pyrethroids to degradation on treated surfaces is a distinct advantage over the natural product.

The deficiencies of the pyrethrins for cockroach control are: (1) recovery from knockdown, (2) high concentrations needed for good kill, and therefore (3) high cost for fully effective formulations, and (4) short residual life.

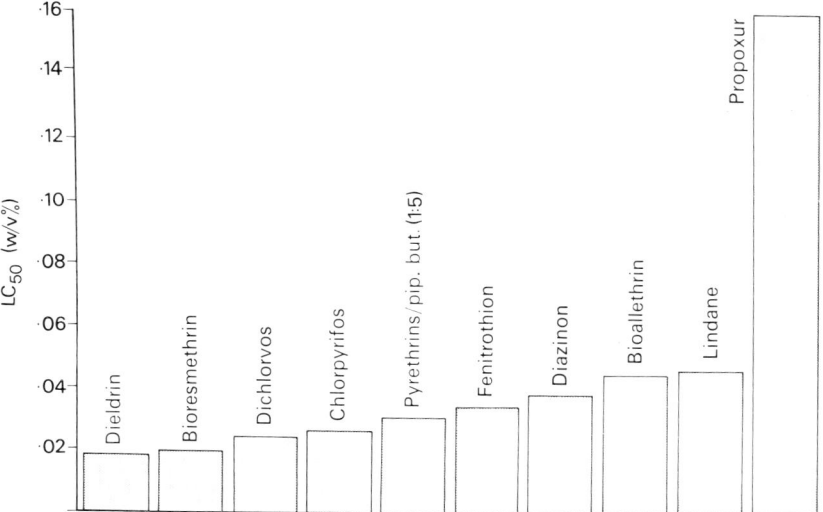

Fig. 125. Relative effectiveness of synthetic pyrethroids and other insecticides applied as direct sprays to male German cockroaches. (From Chadwick & Evans[181]).

Whether or not synthetic pyrethroids will replace established uses of the pyrethrins is questionable. They will undoubtedly succeed if there are any further short falls in production of natural pyrethrum. Suppliers are eager to introduce synthetics into the market, especially insecticides which have already received government registration, and formulators are unlikely to tolerate a repeat of the uncertainties surrounding the supply of pyrethrins as experienced in 1970–71. Assuming that clearances are given for indoor use against a range of pests other than houseflies, an increasing number of synthetic pyrethroids would seem likely to challenge the position of the pyrethrins. On the other hand, it is possible that the pyrethrins could retain, in large part, their currently favoured position, should the effort to lower costs by producing pyrethrins from high content plants, succeed.[514]

It is foreseeable that some pyrethroids, like permethrin, could also replace insecticides that have residual properties. Those known to have satisfactory performance against cockroaches provide good initial kill and sufficient activity to kill any immigrant cockroaches, or nymphs which may subsequently hatch: a requirement for good cockroach control is an insecticide which, in warm conditions, lasts longer than the development time of oothecae.

Some would add rapid action as a useful advantage in cockroach control, and others, a lack of repellency in treated harbourages. The pyrethrins offer flushing action—as a useful 'tool' in searching for cockroach infestations—and this property is better developed in the natural product than in the synthetics.

Despite their limitations, extensive use has been made of synergised pyrethrins, unsupported by other insecticides, to control cockroaches in food factories. In some countries only the pyrethrins are permitted. In others, however, pressure-packed cockroach sprays, often contain pyrethrins with a second insecticide to give residual action. Early pyrethroids, like allethrin, have not been widely used as substitutes, because their properties—knockdown and kill—are not equal to the pyrethrins. There are now, however, some synthetic pyrethroids with considerable merit against cockroaches; but among those which are so far available, commercially, it is still difficult to select any *one* which mirrors all the useful properties of the pyrethrins and gives good kill.

There is a temptation to separate the pyrethroids into two main groups.[503] (1) Those with reversible knockdown—substances which appear to reach the nervous system quickly and cause disturbances, spectacular rather than injurious, and cause marked excitement among poisoned insects. These symptoms are temporary and disappear without leaving after effects, although synergists tend to complement their action. (2) Pyrethroids which do not show any noticeable knockdown, but have powerful lethal properties and do not respond to synergism. It must be assumed that compounds of the second type take considerably longer to reach their site of action but do not need 'the protection of synergists' in retarding degradation. In relating structure of the pyrethroids to activity, those made from (+)-*trans* chrysanthemic acid are more active in knockdown and kill than those made with the (+)-*cis, trans* mixture of acids. The evidence with houseflies is that with the exception of sesamex (which is slightly superior in some cases, but too expensive to use and not sufficiently stable) there is no better synergist for the synthetic pyrethroids than piperonyl butoxide.[845]

If it were possible to put together insecticides, with all the properties commonly expected of a good formulation for cockroach control, but without help from the pyrethrins, we might choose the following: a combination of bioallethrin, or biotetramethrin, for good flushing action, tetramethrin—or better still biotetramethrin—for very rapid knockdown and bioresmethrin for the best kill. The latter would allow no recovery of German cockroaches and we would anticipate that these two or three insecticides, together, would also perform well against other pest cockroaches.

TABLE LXV

KNOCKDOWN (% AT 1 HOUR) AND KILL (% AT 48 HOURS) OF NYMPHS OF GERMAN AND AMERICAN COCKROACHES BY A MIXTURE OF TETRAMETHRIN (0·25%) AND RESMETHRIN (0·12%) BY THE CSMA COCKROACH AEROSOL TEST METHOD
(From Incho[457])

Species	Insecticide	Dose (g)	Knockdown	Kill
German	Pyrethroid mixture	1·17	100	74
	* Official Test Aerosol	1·01	96	62
American	Pyrethroid mixture	0·95	64	44
	* Official Test Aerosol	0·74	75	69

* OTA formulation: Pyrethrins   0·4%   Deobase   6·6%
                    DDT   2·0%   Propellents 85·0%
                    Velsicol AR-50 6·0%

This objective, set by Incho[457] resulted in a water-based formulation of tetramethrin (0·25 per cent) plus resmethrin (0·12 per cent) which gave somewhat better knockdown and kill of nymphs of German cockroaches, but inferior kill of *P. americana* (Table LXV). The comparison was made with 0·4 per cent pyrethrins. One would hope for better results against both pest cockroaches when using the (+)-*trans* isomers.

If pyrethrins were to form part of a composite formulation, they would undoubtedly produce better flushing action than bioallethrin or biotetramethrin, and contribute sufficient speed of knockdown. By sacrificing considerable safety to man, the more recent RU 11679 would be an excellent substitute for bioresmethrin to ensure that all cockroaches were killed.

We do not yet know sufficient about the properties of RU 15525 and of permethrin in practical cockroach control, but the speed of action of the first and the residual life of the second, suggest they may have a useful part to play.

11

THE LONG-LIVED INSECTICIDES

(ORGANOCHLORINES)

DDT: discovery; chemical and physical properties; early history of use and subsequent condemnation; wild life and the industrial user; insecticidal properties; performance against cockroaches; effects on species and sexes—Lindane: chemical and physical properties; insecticidal properties; effects on mammals—Chlordane: chemical and physical properties; performance against cockroaches; toxicity to man; chlordane in the environment—Dieldrin: chemical and physical properties; action on cockroaches; effects on mammals—Chlordecone: use in baits; toxicity to man.

The use of chlorinated hydrocarbon insecticides in the U.S.A. reached a peak of about 150 million pounds a year in 1959. Ten years later, it had dropped to only 71 million pounds, and has now fallen to insignificant quantities. The turning point, about 3 years before DDT was publicly criticised, was caused by greater use of other types of insecticide, mainly organophosphates: superimposed upon this has been the restricted use of the chlorinated insecticides, resulting from public alarm and the pressure of conservationists.[287]

In this chapter we shall look at the chlorinated insecticides used for cockroach control, and try to put in perspective the criticism which has arisen from use, mainly in agriculture.

Chlorinated hydrocarbon insecticides ('organochlorines') form a large group from which about half a dozen have been used extensively indoors. They are all synthetic insecticides; all contain chlorine in their composition and some remain biologically active for exceptionally long periods. Those of primary interest for cockroach control have been DDT, lindane, chlordane and dieldrin. DDT is probably the best known of all insecticides, both through extensive use and much adverse publicity. Chlordecone—a chlorinated ketone—is probably one of the least well-known insecticides.

The criticism of the organochlorine insecticides is their long persistence in small amounts in the environment; it is on this point that the furore about pesticides has centred in the last decade. Among problems attending the use of organochlorines is the 'early notion that they were completely inert biologically—except to insects'. Lack of knowledge of their mode of action, and the possibility that we may be doing ourselves harm, through not knowing the long-term effects, have added emotional overtones.[124]

Ironically the chlorinated hydrocarbon insecticides are more dangerous to humans as acute, rather than chronic poisons. Many become stored principally in body fat where they appear largely inactive. The body can store more than that which becomes a lethal dose if given at one time. There is no evidence that low levels of residues are harmful.[287]

The reader familiar with present-day attitudes towards the 'persistent' insecticides, such as DDT and dieldrin, may be surprised to find a chapter on chlorinated hydrocarbons in a book on cockroach control written in the mid-1970's. In some countries legislation prohibits the use of many pesticides which, in the past, have served the pest control industry well. There is considerable discrepancy, however, in the permitted and non-permitted uses of insecticides in different parts of the world (see p. 291).

Countries in Europe, particularly Scandinavia, have effectively banned all uses of chlorinated hydrocarbons for insect control where food is involved. Others have been very severe, and allow special applications only. Some have been more rational, and recognised that there are differences in the properties of insecticides of this group: they may all incorporate chlorine into an organic molecule, but that alone does not condemn them equally. They differ widely in insecticidal activity and in toxicity to man: examples are endrin which is highly toxic (LD_{50} (rat) 11 mg/kg) and methoxychlor (LD_{50} 6,000 mg/kg) which is relatively safe. Some are broken down rapidly in the body, but others are not.

Some 'enlightened' countries have not banned the use of all insecticides of the group. These countries have been able to separate 'practical risk' from 'theoretical risk'. The actual hazard presented by any pesticide is a function of three things: the biological properties of the compound, the location and method of use, and the knowledge and care with which it is applied. In the U.K., for example, a number of insecticides included in this chapter are still available to pest control servicing companies, and to government and local health departments for cockroach control. Readers in other countries will, however, find much of the information in this chapter of historical rather than practical interest.

DDT

DDT (*d*ichloro*d*iphenyl*t*richloroethane) is often described as the first synthetic organic insecticide. This is not strictly true since lethane (an organic thiocyanate) was used for the control of flying and crawling insects, some ten years before DDT, in household products in the United States. Lethane has the advantage of very rapid action, almost equal to the pyrethrins, but is irritant to the skin (see Chapter 8).

When pyrethrins were in short supply during World War II, and the use of organic thiocyanates made up the bulk of the deficit, the promise of the new insecticide, DDT, was received in the USA with considerable enthusiasm: 'if it is as effective as some reports indicate, it looms large as one of the most important post-war insecticide products and could offer very strong competition to pyrethrum, rotenone (derris) . . .'[10] DDT did in fact push lethane and other organic thiocyanates into the background, especially as DDT was effective at lower concentrations.

For the first time a residual deposit could be obtained on treated surfaces. This was seen as the major advantage that DDT had to offer. In the early

1940's, pyrethrins, derris, inorganic insecticides and the shorter-lived organic thiocyanates, were the only alternatives. By today's standards, of course, the residual activity of DDT is a serious disadvantage; also by today's standards—now that very effective organophosphorus compounds are available—DDT, by comparison, is one of the least effective insecticides for cockroach control.

Discovery

DDT was first synthesised in 1874 by allowing two chemicals—anhydrous chloral and chlorobenzene—to react in the presence of concentrated sulphuric acid.[881] Some 65 years were to pass before it was known that DDT killed insects. One wonders what effect DDT might have had on pest control, and on other living organisms, had its insecticidal properties been discovered in 1874 instead of much later, concurrent with the outbreak of World War II. Equally one wonders what the outcome of the War might have been without DDT.

The insecticidal properties of DDT were discovered by Paul Müller and a patent was assigned to Geigy, Basel in 1940. The most recent U.S. Patent is entitled: 'Devitalizing Composition of Matter' issued to Paul Müller in 1943: an appropriate title for a material, later to have untoward effects on many different types of living organism.

Military requirements for DDT brought about a new industrial interest in insecticides. A DDT dust for the control of human lice was first marketed in Switzerland under the trade name, 'Neocid'. DDT for agriculture first came into use under two trade names, 'Gesarol Dust Insecticide' (3 per cent) and 'Gesarol Spray Insecticide' (5 per cent). Experimental work by the U.S. Bureau of Entomology and Plant Quarantine, to appraise the usefulness of DDT as an insecticide, indicated that 'the loss of DDT by evaporation from spray deposits will occur too slowly to decrease its effectiveness appreciably'.[9] At that time, of course, it was not realised that the stability of DDT was to make it last far beyond most insecticidal requirements.

By 1955, 100 million pounds of technical DDT was being produced annually: extensive use then, and later, can be attributed to its long life after application and to its relatively low toxicity to man. By 1965 the total world production of DDT, as technical material, was about 3,500 million lb—practically 1 lb (450g) for every living person[321]—and spread evenly over the earth's land surface, would give a 'deposit' of about 20 mg/m^2.

Chemical and physical properties

A great deal has been written about DDT and related compounds, much of which forms the early history of the pesticide industry. Such has been the remarkable speed of development of new pesticides, and our change in attitudes towards pest control chemicals, that events of only 35 years ago have become archival material. The reader interested in the detailed chemistry of the compound is referred to the account of Metcalf.[560]

Chemically pure DDT is a practically colourless, odourless solid, which cannot be dissolved in water but is readily soluble in most organic solvents. The insecticide has a long life due to its low water solubility, relative insensitivity to light, low volatility (vapour pressure: $1 \cdot 5 \times 10^{-7}$ mm Hg at $20°$ C), and stability to heat. Pure DDT does not decompose below 195°C but the technical material, from which pest control formulations are made; decomposes at about 100°C due to impurities. Even so there are few situations where the insecticide would need to withstand this temperature. Under certain conditions, DDT may lose chlorine from its molecules to form DDE.

Dechlorination makes it almost non-toxic to insects, but DDE is still about 20–40 per cent as toxic as DDT to mammals. The major impurity of technical DDT is DDD (or TDE) which is only a quarter to one half as insecticidal as DDT, but 10 times less toxic to mammals (LD_{50} (rat) 3,400 mg/kg). However, DDD is superior to DDT for the control of certain insects, such as mosquito larvae (*Anopheles maculatus*).

A change in the positions of the chlorine atoms in the molecule of DDT provides isomers, with different insecticidal properties. Activity of the compound is also modified when the chlorine in DDT is replaced by other elements, such as fluorine, which produces a very active compound, or by bromine and iodine, producing compounds less toxic than DDT. None of these however, have challenged the position of DDT for insecticidal activity or economy in manufacture. One of the many compounds of similar structure to DDT, which has received successful commercial development, is methoxychlor.

Early history of use and subsequent condemnation
Because DDT has a wide spectrum of activity against insects of importance in agriculture and public health, great use was made of it in its early years. Its low toxicity to man (acute oral LD_{50} to rats is 250 mg/kg), enabled DDT to play a major role in the control of body lice, responsible for transmitting typhus, and for the control of mosquito vectors of malaria. Its contribution in reducing the incidence of malaria has been outstanding: each year, before the advent of DDT, 25 million people suffered attacks of the disease resulting in a toll of $2 \cdot 5$ million deaths annually. By 1962 the use of DDT, together with the antimalarial drug quinine, had resulted in the eradication of malaria over an area supporting 330 million people, with campaigns in progress in areas containing a further 740 million. In India alone, through the use of DDT, malaria cases dropped from 75 million a year in 1952 to one tenth of a million in 1964: the tonnage of DDT used[77] rose from 375 tons in 1952 to a peak of 21,000 tons in 1961.

Notwithstanding these massive achievements, DDT has fallen into disrepute. Its use between 1940 and 1970 has drawn attention to the disadvantage of introducing complex organic compounds of chlorine (and other elements) into the environment, in which there are no biochemical processes to break them down into less toxic constitutents. The effects of DDT in worldwide use have been responsible for the now modified views that long stability

Fig. 126. Locations which become readily infested by cockroaches, typical of many situations where the use of DDT and other persistent organochlorine insecticides could have no possible effects on wildlife, or cause residues in food. Treatment of hospital ducts (Netherlands; above). Infestations in drainage manholes (Mombasa; below).

and residual action are not, in themselves, desirable properties of an insecticide.

Wildlife and the industrial user
There is evidence that DDT and compounds of this type have caused deleterious effects on wildlife through selective accumulation (more aptly termed 'biological magnification') in plant and animal food chains.[446] Whilst this problem had been recognised for some time, it was brought forcibly to public attention by Rachel Carson[170] in her book 'Silent Spring'.

Many and varied effects of DDT on the environment have been reported. What then should be the views of a pest control serviceman carrying out cockroach control in hospital ducts (Fig. 126), in the basement of an hotel or in an industrial kitchen? He might rightly ask: what has my use of DDT, dieldrin or similar compounds got to do with birds laying thin-shelled eggs, the decline of numbers of the Golden Eagle (in Scotland), the absence of fish in some previously well-populated river, or the amount of dieldrin in home grown or imported lamb? The answer, of course, is absolutely nothing. Restrictions on his use of chlorinated hydrocarbon insecticides have been due to all-embracing regulations which have failed to distinguish 'end use' and 'the practical risk'.

The medical significance of accumulations of DDT in our environment, in our food and in human body tissues, has still not been fully explained. But many Governments have set up legislation and national monitoring systems by which a further increase of DDT and other organochlorine compounds in the environment is prevented. If there are effective alternatives to organochlorines for cockroach control then these should be used. Whilst there is no evidence that the low levels of DDT in our body fat does us any harm, it would be preferable, or less disturbing to the medical profession if it wasn't there—since none of us was born with it! Had we not become so adept at measuring incredibly small quantities of DDT in animal tissues we would not be aware that it was there.

Irrespective of residues, there is now evidence that DDT has almost reached the end of its useful life as an insecticide because of resistance: at least 98 species of insect are now resistant to it.[131] The use of alternatives has become essential if pest species are to be controlled.

Insecticidal properties
In the last 35 years almost every insect pest of economic importance must have been treated with DDT, perhaps not always in control operations, but at least in evaluation trials. Data on the performance of DDT against indoor pests is considerable, especially against flies and cockroaches.

From the symptoms shown by dying insects there is evidence that DDT has an effect on the nervous control of the insect's muscular system. Seven stages in the poisoning of the American cockroach have been defined:[793]

1. hypertension of legs, body raised, instability;

2. tremulous movement of head, body and appendages;
3. staggering and hyperactivity to touch and noise (indicating nervous impairment);
4. repeated falling onto back and inability to regain feet;
5. high frequency tremor of legs, together with slow extension and flexion (indicating muscle stimulation);
6. disappearance of tremors; isolated movements of integument, tarsi, palps, cerci and antennae (eventually leading to paralysis);
7. prolonged beating of heart for many days before ultimate death.

Performance against cockroaches
DDT is not very efficient in killing cockroaches, and compared with modern insecticides, is very slow in action. In the first field trials carried out during 1944–45, by servicing members of the National Pest Control Association of America,[226] a 10 per cent DDT powder gave excellent control of American and Oriental cockroaches, but most reports gave negative results for German and Brown-banded cockroaches. The conclusion from these trials was that 'everything considered, sodium fluoride, with or without pyrethrum is perhaps still superior to DDT, at least in the hands of the commercial operator'.

Until the American Armed Services made tests with DDT, they too were using and getting satisfactory control of American and German cockroaches with sodium fluoride with or without pyrethrum[233]—'the thoroughness and not the heaviness of application being the prerequisite for success'—a maxim still true for the insecticides used today. When DDT was applied as a 10 per cent dust, a 5 per cent kerosene solution, or 20 per cent emulsion, 'it was evident to an even more marked degree than with sodium fluoride, that complete coverage of all crevices was essential'. Both 5 per cent DDT in an oil spray and a 10 per cent dust were said to give excellent results wherever tried. Mixtures of sodium fluoride and 10 per cent DDT dust gave as good, but no better control than DDT alone, when properly applied.

In retrospect it is interesting to note the high concentrations used in these trials, probably because DDT is incredibly slow in killing insects, compared with the very rapid action of the pyrethrins. The rate of knockdown (KD_{95}) of male German cockroaches in the WHO test of resistance (54 mg/m^2) is: pyrethrins 2·1 min., lindane 0·4 hr, heptachlor 2·3 hr, chlordane 2·5 hr (but at double application rate), dieldrin 3·4 hr, and DDT greater than 24 hours.[180]

Many of the early laboratory and field evaluations of DDT against cockroaches are reviewed by West & Campbell[840] in their book 'DDT and other persistent insecticides'. Included are the reports of Ginsburg[337] that DDT dust is about 5 times as toxic as sodium fluoride to adult German cockroaches on deposits in glass jars. A bait containing 1 per cent DDT kills *P. americana* and *B. germanica* in 3 weeks[590] and a narrow band of 5 per cent DDT dust kills both species in cage tests in 48 hours.[319] Sprays of 2 per cent DDT in kerosene applied directly to German cockroaches are less effective than 0·4 per cent pyrethrins.[551]

In practical treatments of Army mess rooms in Florida, infested with German cockroaches, 5 per cent sprays and 10–25 per cent DDT dusts 'killed very large numbers of cockroaches'; sprays more quickly than dusts (Gahan & Knipling[319]). These workers, however, did not obtain complete eradication: 'but this was to be expected as in Florida the cockroaches breed out-of-doors'. They believed that DDT, applied as oil and emulsion sprays, did 'not produce a residue sufficiently toxic to provide protection in buildings from German cockroaches for more than a few days'. In contrast, Froelicher[313] reported extremely satisfactory control of cockroaches, from a properly applied dust of 5 per cent DDT, 'owing to its unusual residual property'.

Effects on species and sexes

In tests against different species, American cockroaches appear to be more readily killed by DDT than German cockroaches. Males of *B. germanica*, of both susceptible and resistant strains are killed by smaller amounts of DDT than females.[356] This is true also of American cockroaches treated with other insecticides: sodium fluoride and arsenicals.[419] The greater susceptibility of males to DDT is also reported by Munson & Gottlieb,[598] and by Cochran[192] using a number of organochlorine insecticides (Table LXVI). Cochran could not, however, detect differences between the sexes of last stage nymphs of *P. americana*.

TABLE LXVI

LD_{50} OF CHLORINATED HYDROCARBON INSECTICIDES APPLIED BY MICROINJECTION TO ADULT MALE AND FEMALE *P. AMERICANA*
(From Cochran[192])

Insecticide	LD_{50} (mg) males	females	Ratio of susceptibility males : females
Lindane	0.0008	0.0044	5.5
Dieldrin	0.001	0.005	5.0
DDT	0.0045	0.020	4.4
Methoxychlor	0.007	0.018	2.5
Chlordane	0.026	0.052	2.0

When DDT is injected into the haemolymph of *P. americana*, the LD_{50} (4 days) is 5 μg for adult males, 20 μg for adult females and 35 μg for male and female last stage nymphs.[193] Male and female nymphs, and adult females of the Oriental cockroach are all more tolerant of DDT than adult males.[700]

The oral toxicity of DDT to cockroaches is not very great. If DDT and other commonly used insecticides are given to American cockroaches by mouth with a micrometer-driven syringe (Fig. 127), DDT and chlordane are among the least toxic and dichlorvos the most toxic.[479] Exposure of adult German cockroaches to non-lethal amounts of DDT (0.1 per cent) in a ground Purina chow, does not affect reproductive ability as indicated by the number

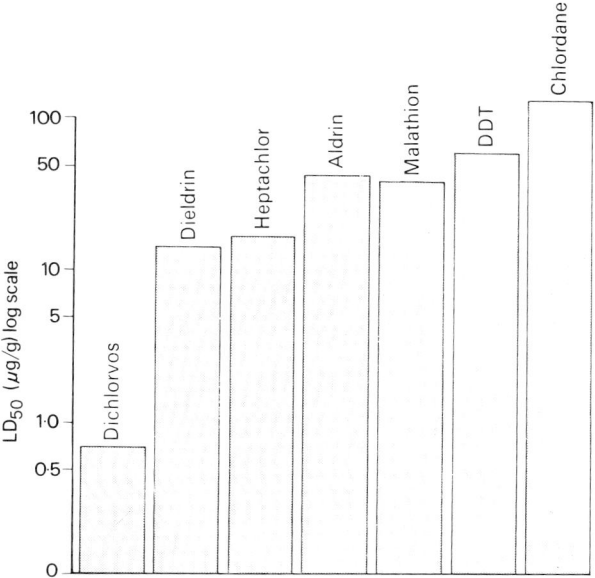

Fig. 127. The oral toxicity (LD_{50}) of DDT and other insecticides administered in 10 μl of refined kerosene to adult male *P. americana*. (From Keller & Liang[479]).

of ovarioles. It prolongs nymphal development by 20–44 days and smaller adults are produced, resembling 4th or 5th stage nymphs of untreated cockroaches.[381]

When successive doses of DDT are given to American cockroaches, to see whether they become habituated to the insecticide and thus survive larger total doses, they die whether the insecticide is injected in one dose or in up to six sub-doses (Table LXVII). Chang & Crowell,[185] who did the experiments, claim that their results are consistent in showing fewer survivors in groups receiving greater numbers of injections of DDT regardless of the severity of the initial treatment. Intervals between treatments of 1 and 4 weeks make no difference: more cockroaches are killed, the greater the number of injections, indicating increased sensitivity to DDT. These workers appear to ignore the fact that insects receiving the most doses also receive a greater total amount of insecticide.

With many insecticides, an increase in temperature usually increases the sensitivity of insects. A notable difference occurs with DDT, (see p. 400) and to a much lesser degree with lindane and pyrethrins. With these, the amount of insecticide required to kill German cockroaches, for example, becomes greater at higher temperatures (Table LXVIII). A dose of 10 μg per cockroach kills 80 per cent of *P. americana* at 15°C, but 50 μg causes only 20 per cent mortality at 35°C.[827]

TABLE LXVII

PERCENTAGE OF MALE NYMPHS OF *P. AMERICANA* KILLED BY SUCCESSIVE INJECTIONS OF INCREASING AMOUNTS OF DDT (20 INSECTS/TEST; INTERVAL BETWEEN TREATMENTS, 1–4 WEEKS)
(From Chang & Crowell[185])

No. of injections	Successive doses (μg/g of cockroach)						Total dose (μg/g)
	2	3·2	5	8	12·7	20	
6	0	10	25	40	50	95	50·9
5		0	5	20	45	90	48·9
4			0	10	40	90	45·7
3				10	35	90	40·7
2					15	85	32·7
1						60	20·0

TABLE LXVIII

EFFECT OF TEMPERATURE ON THE RESPONSE (LD_{50}) OF GERMAN COCKROACHES TO DIFFERENT INSECTICIDES
(From Guthrie[386])

Insecticide	$LD_{50}(\mu g)$ at the following temps. (°C)		
	14·5	22	32
DDT	2·1	12·9	40·8
Dieldrin	1·1	0·35	0·22
Lindane	0·07	0·10	0·18
Pyrethrins	0·32	0·80	1·45

LINDANE

'Persistent' is the word most often used to describe chlorinated hydrocarbon insecticides. With the knowledge that DDT and some related compounds remain biologically active for long periods, it is commonly believed that *all* organochlorines have exceptionally long life and accumulate in the environment.

This is not so. Lindane is an exception. That there are differences in the properties of the various chlorinated insecticides is worth re-emphasising. There can be no justification in prohibiting the use of lindane because it happens to be a synthetic, chlorinated hydrocarbon with some chemical affinities to DDT. On this basis, we should not permit the use of the very safe malathion because it is chemically related to the highly toxic parathion.

Of 112 countries reporting[107] on their uses of lindane, 33 (30 per cent) had no pesticide regulations of any type, 18 (16 per cent) had national restrictions on pesticides, but none relating to lindane, 59 (53 per cent) had some restrictions for lindane, varying considerably in severity, and 2 countries had banned lindane altogether. Many countries with restrictions on lindane do not allow its use for the control of stored food pests, or in areas where food is prepared, eaten or sold. This effectively prevents its use for cockroach control. The 'poison classification' given to lindane in different countries, also varies considerably: 'highly toxic' (Venezuala, Bolivia); 'medium toxicity' (Chile); 'poisonous substance' (Taiwan); 'innocuous pesticide' (Malaysia).

Lindane has played a major part in pest control during the last 30 years, in agriculture and public health. It has a useful and continuing contribution to make. We should clearly establish the behaviour of lindane, in relation to other organochlorines, in the environment, in their risk to man and as a danger in food. If we do this for the chlorinated insecticides of interest in cockroach control, we obtain the following three categories:

1. Persistent, bio-accumulative, slowly excreted insecticides with average to good contact action: DDT and dieldrin.
2. Less persistent, non bio-accumulative, readily excreted insecticides with good contact action: lindane and chlordane.
3. The same as 1, with good insecticidal action when eaten, but no contact action: chlordecone.

Lindane has been widely used to treat pest insects indoors, primarily because it can be relied upon to control the many different species that get into, or infest, buildings. It also remains sufficiently effective on treated surfaces, and in harbourages, to kill young stages which may emerge after treatment, or cause reinfestation.

Another reason for lindane's continuing popularity is that, although it is a chlorinated hydrocarbon, lindane has emerged from detailed examination of adverse side-effects with a relatively 'clean bill of health'—at least in the U.K. It has therefore come to replace previous uses of DDT where resistance to organochlorine insecticides is not restricting. As an example, production of technical BHC in Japan (the mixed isomers including lindane) reached 45,000 tons in 1968, having increased 3-fold in 8 years. The amount of DDT and other organochlorines used in Japan during that period was less than 5 per cent of that of BHC.[348]

Relatively little lindane has been used for indoor pest control in the United States where chlordane has served equally well as a general purpose insecticide. Both have given relatively good performance in cockroach control, but neither lindane nor chlordane rate among the most effective for this purpose; some of the more recent organophosphorus insecticides are considerably more efficient. A reason for the geographical preference could be the greater frequency of infestations of German cockroaches in the United States whilst the Oriental cockroach is the more prevalent pest in the U.K. and parts of Europe. Chlordane and lindane perform equally well against *B. germanica* but lindane is the more effective against *B. orientalis* (see Table LXIX). Origin and location of manufacture, affect cost and availability, making chlordane preferred in the United States and little used in Europe. Lindane is not now permitted for use in food handling, processing or serving establishments in the U.S.A.

Chemical and physical properties
Compared with other chlorinated hydrocarbon insecticides, the chemical structure of lindane is relatively simple. This, as we shall see, imparts biological properties in distinct contrast to DDT and dieldrin, making lindane more readily biodegradable.

TABLE LXIX

SUSCEPTIBILITY (LD_{50} μg/INSECT) OF GERMAN AND ORIENTAL COCKROACHES TO TOPICALLY APPLIED INSECTICIDES, ARRANGED IN ORDER OF DECREASING EFFECTIVENESS WHEN AVERAGED FOR BOTH SEXES
(Fenton, Williams & Bennett, unpublished)

B. germanica			B. orientalis		
Insecticide	Male	Female	Insecticide	Male	Female
Heptachlor	0·20	0·36	Dursban	0·40	1·03
Fenitrothion	0·26	0·36	Propoxur	0·26	2·17
Dieldrin	0·15	0·49	Heptachlor	0·97	1·64
Dursban	0·28	0·38	Aldrin	0·85	2·31
Aldrin	0·20	0·68	Dieldrin	1·02	2·23
Propoxur	0·23	0·68	Lindane	1·68	1·89
Chlordane	0·28	0·80	Diazinon	1·19	3·05
Diazinon	0·50	0·63	Fenitrothion	0·94	3·78
Lindane	0·74	1·10	Chlordane	2·16	5·19
Malathion	1·26	1·50	Malathion	2·06	7·31
Bromophos	1·83	3·07	Bromophos	3·73	10·70
Pyrethrins	2·16	4·15	Pyrethrins	6·35	12·30
Chlordecone	4·12	8·91	Carbaryl	1·81	32·10
DDT	10·40	45·11	DDT	9·00	50·40
Carbaryl	40·90	42·50	Chlordecone	33·10	50·30

Lindane originates from benzene hexachloride (BHC), a substance discovered by Faraday over 150 years ago. Its insecticidal properties were not recognised at that time. The performance of an insecticide is dependent not only upon the atoms present in its composition, but the way they are spatially arranged. This is the case with benzene hexachloride, which consists of a mixture of eight isomers and byproducts, of which gamma-BHC (now called lindane) has assumed overriding importance.

The prefix 'gamma' designates the structural isomer of BHC with significant insecticidal properties. Lindane makes up about 15 per cent of the commercially available BHC and is named after the Belgian chemist, van der Linden, who discovered it in 1912. Kurihara and colleagues[492] have measured the rate of disappearance of the isomers of BHC from the surface of the cuticle of American cockroaches and appearance and accumulation in the head of the insect. Penetration of the gamma isomer is the most rapid, but not sufficiently so to account for the striking difference in insecticidal activity.

The other isomers of BHC are 50–10,000 times less active than lindane, which tempted Metcalf in 1955 to say:[560] 'there are few insecticides which have as critical structural requirements for activity as lindane'. At that time, lindane may have appeared remarkable in this regard, but he would certainly not have commented so, had he known of the research to follow into the structure/activity relationships of the synthetic pyrethroids and organophosphates (Chapters 10 and 12).

The insecticidal properties of BHC were not revealed until 1933: those of lindane were announced independently in France and in England in 1942. Lindane therefore became one of the first organic insecticides to be developed after World War II—along with DDT.

BHC is still used for some outdoor applications, but because of its characteristic musty odour, it has been largely replaced by lindane. This is especially so indoors, where BHC is in most cases quite inappropriate. But for the discovery of lindane, as the active principle, there is no doubt that BHC would have found extremely limited use against cockroaches. Fortunately, the purification processes which follow extraction of the gamma isomer, make lindane practically odourless.

Lindane forms colourless crystals (Fig. 128) which are virtually insoluble in water, but which are nevertheless 10 times more soluble than DDT. Lin-

Fig. 128. Crystals of lindane. (Courtesy: Celamerck GmbH.)

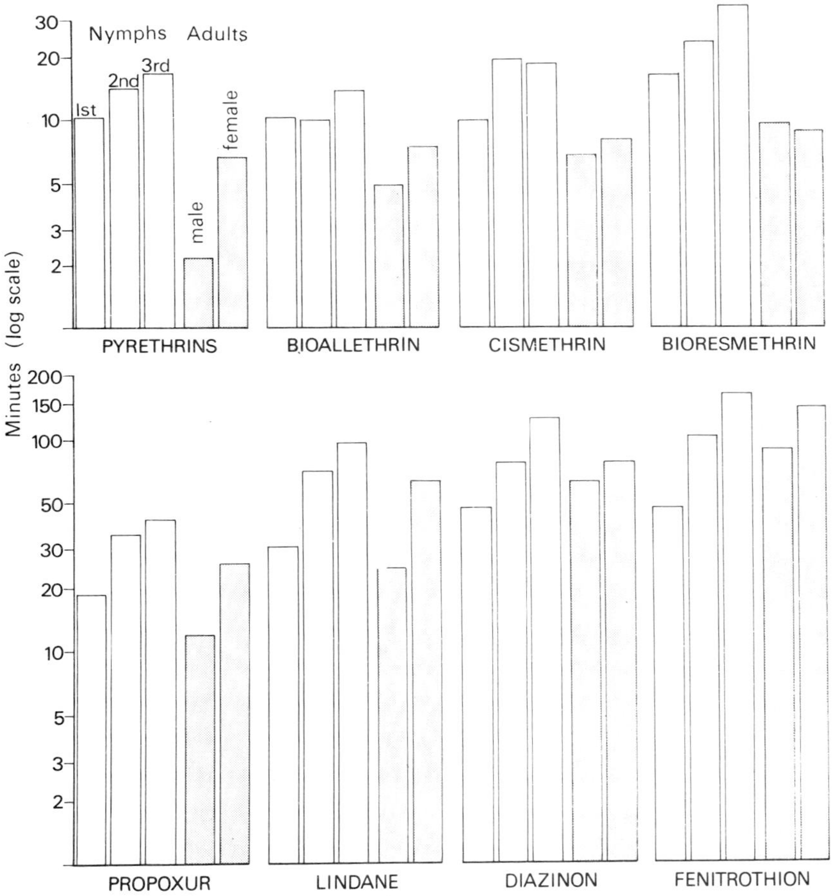

Fig. 129. Time for 95 per cent knockdown of 1st, 2nd and 3rd stage nymphs, and male and female adults of *B. germanica* exposed to different insecticides. (From Chadwick[180]).

dane is not broken down in the presence of light and heat, but like many insecticides, does become inactive in contact with alkali (e.g. lime-washed walls). The principal formulations are dusts and sprays (0·5–1·0 per cent) which involve the use of organic solvents at some stage in manufacture. Solutions in oil may be fogged and lindane is often a constituent of domestic aerosol packs, alone or in combination with pybuthrin or synthetic pyrethroids. Lindane smoke generators provide an easy way of distributing lindane particles.

One of the useful properties of lindane is its fumigant action—a function of the insecticide's vapour pressure ($9·4 \times 10^{-6}$ mm Hg at 20°C). High volatility partly accounts for the lower persistence of lindane compared with other organochlorine insecticides (e.g. dieldrin). In a laboratory experiment, deposits of lindane (32–43 mg/cm^2) on glass plates evaporated completely within 50–60 days.[800]

In enclosed spaces, such as poorly ventilated harbourages infested by cockroaches, the concentration of lindane in the air may rise to relatively high levels soon after treatment. But a large part of the evaporated lindane may be redeposited elsewhere, on untreated surfaces, so that the amount in the vapour phase becomes reduced.

Insecticidal properties
The first study[751] of the effects of lindane on cockroaches was made in 1945. A year later lindane was reported more toxic than sodium fluoride, pyrethrins and DDT to German cockroaches, but less toxic than pyrethrins and DDT to *P. americana*.[549] Poisoned insects show tremors, staggering movements, convulsions, knockdown (prostration) and death by paralysis, much the same as with DDT, but symptoms occur more rapidly.[723] They are all consistent with the action of lindane on the nervous system.

Although quicker in action than DDT, lindane is not very rapid compared with the pyrethrins and some of the pyrethroids (Fig. 129). However, lindane knocks down German cockroaches 10 times more quickly than dieldrin, and 2–3 times more quickly than diazinon and fenitrothion.[180] The insecticidal performance of lindane, as tested by topical application, is shown in Table LXIX.

Insects can be killed by ingesting lindane, and its vapour too, may contribute to its performance. The LD_{50} for lindane applied topically and injected into American cockroaches is 5 and 4 µg/g, respectively, showing that it penetrates the cuticle very readily.[241] The German cockroach is somewhat more susceptible: topical LD_{50} 3·8 µg/g.

The LD_{50} of lindane to German cockroaches exposed to dusts is variously reported[615] from 0·2 µg/cm^2 to 0·8 µg/cm^2. Half the cockroaches in contact

TABLE LXX

THE EFFECT OF LINDANE (BY DIPPING) ON MALE AND FEMALE GERMAN COCKROACHES OF A SUSCEPTIBLE AND CHLORDANE-RESISTANT STRAIN (CORPUS CHRISTI)
(From Grayson[358])

Strain	LD_{50} (mg/l)		LD_{90} (mg/l)	
	Male	Female	Male	Female
Susceptible	10·3	24·2	15·5	43·0
Chlordane-resistant	59·5	94·0	76·0	185·0

with a spray deposit[133] die at $2 \cdot 8$ $\mu g/cm^2$. When lindane is injected, 1 and $2 \cdot 5$ $\mu g/g$ kill 50 and 90 per cent of German cockroaches, but 23 and 75 $\mu g/g$, respectively, are required to kill a chlordane resistant, Corpus Christi strain.[164] In dipping experiments[358] males are considerably more susceptible than females of both susceptible and chlordane resistant strains (Table LXX).

In injection experiments with American cockroaches the LD_{50} (4 days) is $0 \cdot 8$ μ/g for adult males and $4 \cdot 4$ $\mu g/g$ for females.[192] Half of the males injected with lindane emulsified in arachis oil and introduced *via* the 5th and 6th abdominal sternites (Fig. 130), die in 1, 3 and 6 days, after treatment with 18, 8 and 5 μg per insect, respectively.[821]

Use of lindane for about 30 years has resulted in resistance being developed by many indoor pests, including *B. germanica* (see Chapter 15). This has come about by the insect being able to break down the insecticide more rapidly, or having a greater ability to inactivate the insecticide in the fat body. In some instances, resistance is only of local importance, but this is not so with *B. germanica*.[230] Instances of resistance to lindane in cockroaches, reported between 1955–65 are given in Table LXXI. In answer to a questionnaire, 6 per cent of pest control personnel in the Federal Republic of Germany mentioned resistance by cockroaches as a problem, in particular to lindane.[237] Resistance to chlordane confers cross-resistance to lindane.

TABLE LXXI

INSTANCES OF RESISTANCE TO LINDANE IN COCKROACHES REPORTED IN 1955–65
(From Demozay & Marechal[230])

Species	Year reported	Country
Blatta orientalis	1958	Germany
	1964	Czechoslovakia
Blattella germanica	1951	Texas
	1955	South East U.S.A.
	1956	North East U.S.A.
	1958	California, Panama, Cuba, Puerto Rico
	1959	Canada, Trinidad, Japan, Poland
	1961	Germany, England
	1963	Denmark, Hawaii, Australia, New Guinea
Periplaneta brunnea	1965	Florida

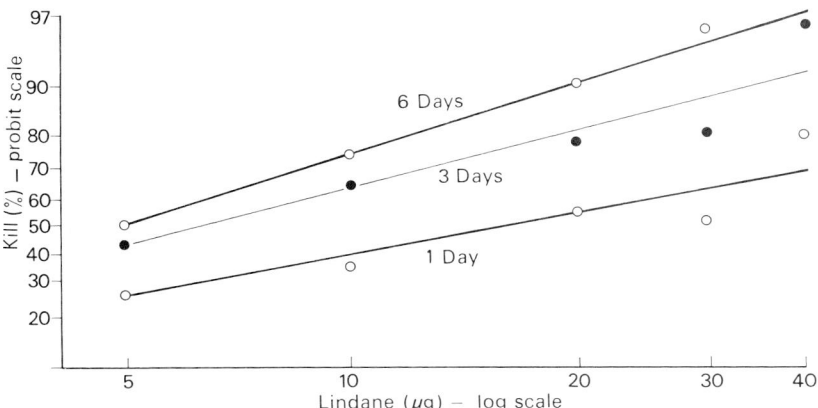

Fig. 130. Mortality of adult male *P. americana*, 1, 3 and 6 days after injection with lindane. (From Van Asperen[821]).

Effects on mammals

Lindane has similar toxicological properties to other chemically-related insecticides, except that lindane is excreted rapidly by vertebrates whether taken as single or repeated doses. The acute oral LD_{50} of technical BHC to mammals is about 1000 mg/kg, but the toxicity of the gamma isomer (lindane) to rats is greater (125 mg/kg). The symptoms of poisoning of lindane are hypersensitivity, tremors and convulsions.

A property common to all chlorinated hydrocarbon insecticides is their good solubility in lipids. For lindane, the body fat behaves as a simple organic solvent. Solubility of the insecticide in the body fat of rats is as good as that in benzene.[739] This is why after initial intake of lindane, it is stored preferentially in the fat deposits of the body. However, because of rapid degradation of lindane and the excretion of breakdown products in the urine, the insecticide does not accumulate in animal fatty tissue.

In rats, lindane activates those parts of the liver cells (the microsomes) responsible for enzyme production. Thus, there is some evidence that initial doses of lindane may accelerate the breakdown of subsequently absorbed doses. This self-induced metabolism of lindane counteracts the accumulation of residues. It is an important factor for maintaining the balance between uptake of lindane and excretion of its metabolites.

Long-term feeding studies show that accumulation of insecticide in warm-blooded animals occurs only in the first week of exposure. Subsequently, despite continual feeding, the residue level remains constant due to enzyme activation. When feeding is stopped, the substance in the body is reduced to half its level in one day and can virtually no longer be detected after 1 to 2 weeks.[497] During continuous ingestion, uptake by the body soon reaches a maximum: simultaneous breakdown then occurs, resulting in an equilibrium between intake and elimination.

Lindane is not therefore selectively accumulated by animals as are many other organochlorine insecticides (Table LXXII). It is of interest, however, that the beta isomer of BHC is eliminated much more slowly. This justifies the use of BHC as the pure gamma isomer only.

TABLE LXXII

CHLORINATED HYDROCARBON INSECTICIDES (ppm) IN THE FAT BODY OF HUMANS, REFLECTING THE COMBINED EFFECTS OF AMOUNT IN THE ENVIRONMENT AND ELIMINATION BY THE BODY
(From Wunscher & Acker[872])

Country	Year	No. of samples	Lindane	Dieldrin	DDT and conversion products
U.S.A.	1961–62	30	0.20	0.15	6.7
England	1961–62	131	—	0.21	2.2
U.S.A.	1962–63	282	0.56	0.11	11.1
France	1963	10	1.19	—	6.7
England & Wales	1963–64	64	0.42	0.26	3.3
U.S.A. (New Orleans)	1964	25	—	0.29	10.3
S.E. England	1964	100	0.015	0.21	4.2
U.S.A.	1965	64	—	0.31	7.7
U.S.A.	1966	42	—	0.22	10.7
N. Zealand	1966	52	—	0.27	5.8
Belgium	1966	20	0.09	—	3.3
Gt. Britain	1965–67	248	—	0.21	3.0
E. Germany	1966–67	100	—	—	13.1
W. Germany	1967	15	0.03	0.18	4.1

The toxicity of lindane to man, as measured by the acute oral LD_{50} to rats, makes the insecticide relatively safe for use by pest control operators. An average man (70 kg) would have to consume 875g, or about 1 litre of a 1 per cent spray, for 50 per cent chance of death. The dosage at which lindane has no effect in a two-year feeding study with rats is one hundredth of the acute oral LD_{50} (i.e. 1.25 mg/kg), indicating a large margin of safety in the use of dust and spray formulations. In other studies, some including administration by stomach tube, daily intakes up to 5 mg/kg were given without clinical symptoms. Lindane has a lower toxic action if administered in food (Table LXXIII) and at 5 mg/kg has no effect on fertility of mammals and the development of young is in no way impaired. The MAC (Maximum Allowable Concentration) value of lindane in the air is 0.5 mg/m^3.

TABLE LXXIII

ACUTE TOXICITY (LD_{50}) AND 'NO-EFFECT' LEVELS OF SOME CHLORINATED HYDROCARBON INSECTICIDES
(From Ulmann[819])

Insecticide	Oral LD_{50} (mg/kg)	No-effect level (ppm in food during chronic feeding by rats for 2 years)
Lindane	125	25–50
Chlordane	500	<2·5
DDT	250	1
Heptachlor	90	<1
Dieldrin	87	<1

Dermal absorption
Uptake of lindane through the skin can occur, especially with oil-based formulations. The least absorptive is crystalline lindane, as in a dust formulation. Lindane has, however, been used safely for many years in preparations for medical purposes, e.g. for the control of head lice, with good effect, without harm and no adverse skin reactions.

Poisoning incidents
From the statistical data available, lindane features among very minor causes of poisoning: lindane was responsible for only one of 25,000 cases of poisoning recorded[429] in San Francisco from 1958–67. Of 82 persons involved in accidental, acute, lindane poisonings, about one third (all children) had taken smoke generators (tablets or sticks) and 14 were cases of poisoning by wettable powder or emulsion concentrate. Eighteen of the 82 cases proved fatal.

There are records of acute and chronic lindane poisoning occurring in operators involved in mosquito control. Certain conditions have also developed in humans exposed to lindane vaporised in electrical devices, but these are now restricted in many countries. Occasional instances of allergy to lindane have also been reported.

Other animals
Birds are very similar to mammals in their sensitivity to lindane (LD_{50} sparrow 56 mg/kg; starling 100 mg/kg). Lindane concentrations critical for freshwater fish lie between 0·01 and 0·1 ppm (but see also p. 307).

CHLORDANE

Chlordane has been one of the most widely used insecticides for cockroach control, especially in the United States, in part attributable to location of manufacture (Fig. 131). Chlordane has not shared the same popularity in the U.K. (see p. 291).

Within less than 10 years from its introduction in 1945, extensive use of chlordane caused the development of a resistant strain of German cockroach in Texas (see Chapter 15). In spite of this, chlordane remained effective in most parts of the United States up to the mid-1960's. Only during the last 10 years has much of its use been replaced by organophosphates, especially

Fig. 131. Production headquarters of Velsicol Chem. Corp., where miles of pipeline form part of the production plant for manufacture of agricultural chemicals, including chlordane. (Courtesy: Velsicol, Memphis, Tennessee, U.S.A.).

diazinon. In recognition that the risk created in cockroach control is a function of *how* and *where* an insecticide is used, the United States allows the application of chlordane,* as one of 16 insecticides, for crack and crevice treatment in food areas (Fig. 132). The fogging of chlordane is not permitted.

Chlordane is said to have been discovered independently in the U.S.A. and Germany at about the same time. It became available very shortly after DDT and professional operators interested in cockroach control rapidly switched to this new and more rapidly acting insecticide.

Chlordane soon became adopted as a reliable, general purpose, household insecticide and gained a high reputation for its performance against ants. It has also been used extensively for the control of crop insects, termites and pests of soil and turf. Increasing use over a period of 30 years is attributed to a

* See footnotes on pp. 145 and 308.

wide spectrum of insecticidal activity and relatively low toxicity to man. There is now substantial evidence that chlordane does not bio-magnify in the environment[270] and that it has contributed virtually no residues to food.

Physical and chemical properties

Chlordane is a highly chlorinated insecticide. About 65 per cent of the technical product is chlorine. Its chemical structure set the pattern for a number of very active compounds (the cyclodienes) that were to follow.

Technical chlordane is a dark brown viscous liquid with a resinous cedar-like odour. The refined product is a pale yellow liquid, miscible with kerosene and other organic solvents and readily formulated as an oil spray (2 per cent). An emulsion concentrate (incorporating up to about 70 per cent) is probably the most widely used formulation for cockroach control. The percentages of active ingredient mentioned above are those commonly met with.

Chlordane is a mixture of chlorinated hydrocarbons: technical chlordane consists of at least two isomers; it probably contains others and impurities. One such impurity is heptachlor, originally present at about 6 per cent, but now reduced to 1 per cent by improvements in manufacture.

On treated surfaces, oil sprays tend to give a slow drying film because of the resinous nature of the insecticide. In common with related insecticides, chlordane breaks down readily on alkaline surfaces to produce non-toxic products. Its volatility is between that of DDT and lindane, but as a residual it is not as long-lasting as DDT.

Performance against cockroaches

The action of chlordane on insects is slow. It is more effective against cockroaches than DDT and compares with lindane in performance against *B. germanica* (Table LXXIV). The residual performance of chlordane on treated surfaces against American cockroaches does not extend to one week, under test conditions in which chlorpyrifos (= dursban—an organophosphate) and propoxur (= Baygon—a carbamate) are effective for 4 weeks (Table LXXV).

TABLE LXXIV

MORTALITY (%) OF *B. GERMANICA* EXPOSED FOR 5 DAYS TO RESIDUAL DEPOSITS OF DDT, LINDANE AND CHLORDANE
(From Kearns et al[474])

Deposit $\mu g/cm^2$	DDT	Lindane	Chlordane
1300	50	—	—
13	0	100	100
1·3	—	90	70
0·13	—	10	10

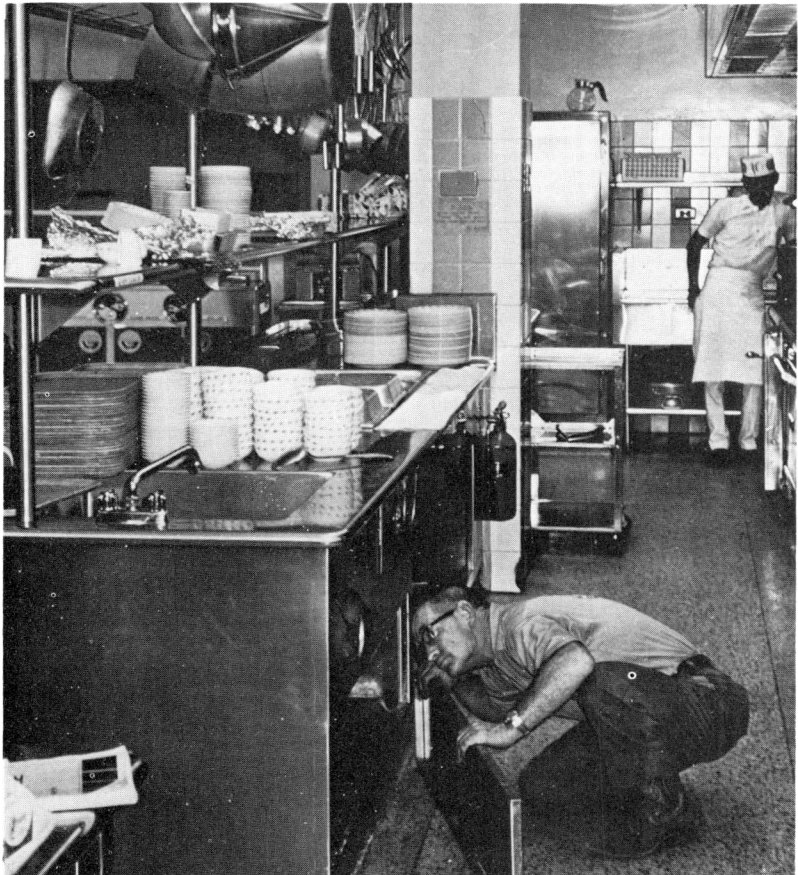

Fig. 132. Cockroach control is best achieved by applying insecticides to cracks and crevices where the insects hide. Treatment of harbourages also reduces the chance of food being contaminated with the insecticides used. This is the basis of crack and crevice treatment in the United States.

Modern counter units in shops display merchandise to maximum advantage. Made of metal, and with dark storage space beneath, they also offer excellent harbourage for cockroaches. The imitation grass beneath vegetables (top left) provides additional hiding places. (Atlanta, U.S.A.).

Poor jointing of brickwork against a rusting metal stanchion (bottom left) provides favourable harbourage for *P. americana* in a meat processing factory. (Dallas, U.S.A.). Crevices in the brickwork provide access to wall cavities, where large numbers of cockroaches congregate unseen.

The modern kitchen of a large hospital (above) gives the appearance of first class hygiene. Nevertheless, cockroach harbourages are provided beneath the metal flanges of the fixed stainless steel sink and other units, requiring frequent inspection if the appearance of good housekeeping is to be meaningful. (Tucson, U.S.A.).

TABLE LXXV

KILL (%) OF *P. AMERICANA* ON PLYWOOD TREATED WITH 1% SOLUTIONS OF INSECTICIDE IN ACETONE (100 mg a.i./m²) AGED FOR FOUR WEEKS AT 27°C AND 60% RH
(From Burden & Madden[150])

Insecticide	Weeks				
	0	1	2	3	4
Chlordane	80	0	0	—	—
Chlorpyrifos	100	100	100	100	80
Diazinon	100	100	0	0	—
Malathion	0	0	—	—	—
Propoxur	100	100	100	100	100
Fenchlorphos (Ronnel)	100	0	0	—	—

The symptoms of poisoning shown by cockroaches treated with chlordane are similar to those described for DDT. They become agitated with incoordinated movements before onset of paralysis and death. These symptoms indicate action on the insect's nervous system, confirmed by Lalonde & Brown.[495] But unlike other chlorinated insecticides (DDT, lindane and dieldrin), there is a delay before chlordane stimulates the production of electrical impulses in cockroach nerves. During the hyperactive stage of German cockroaches injected with chlordane (10 μg), oxygen consumption suddenly increases. Higher doses cause irregular pulsations of the heart of American cockroaches.[401]

Mention has already been made of the development of resistance to chlordane by German cockroaches. Residual sprays may select for resistance more rapidly and forcibly than insecticides inactivated quickly. In tests with chlordane against *B. germanica*, in conditions simulating natural infestations, the time required for 50 per cent kill (LT_{50}) was used to assess any change in the insect's susceptibility.[148] All strains developed measurable resistance to chlordane in 3 months (max. $\times$ 8) with further increases at 6 months (max. $\times$ 13).

Male cockroaches collected in infested homes in Orlando, Florida, and exposed to chlordane in jars showed an enormous range of susceptibility (Fig. 133), as measured by speed of kill.[509] Only six collections had LT_{50}'s less than the normal laboratory strain. On the other hand, on the arbitrary assumption that 'any group of cockroaches with an LT_{50} or LT_{90} three times as great as the normal is significantly resistant, 12 collections, or 43 per cent, were moderately to highly resistant'. On two occasions, both non-resistant and highly-resistant cockroaches were collected within the same housing block.

A comparison of the susceptibility to chlordane of different pest species of cockroach, as indicated by the time for 90 per cent kill of nymphs and adults, shows that the Brown-banded cockroach is killed most readily (4–5 hours).

German and Oriental cockroaches die more slowly (7–24 hours), and American and Madeira cockroaches take longest of all (up to 72 hours) (Table LXXVI). Adult males are in all cases more susceptible than females. Large nymphs are the most tolerant of stages in almost all species.

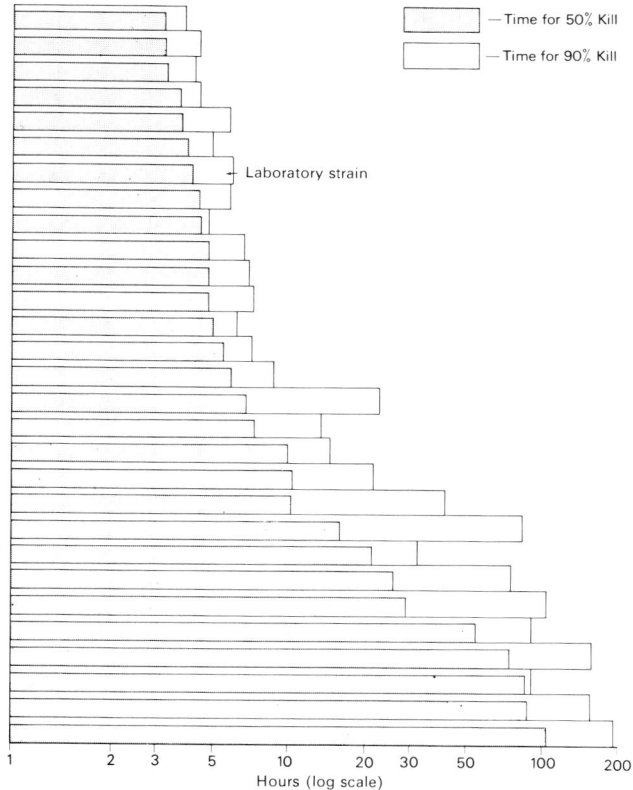

Fig. 133. Susceptibility to chlordane of German cockroaches collected from 28 different homes in Florida, ranked in order of increasing LT_{50}, compared with a laboratory strain. (From Lofgren, Burden & Clark[509]).

Among different insecticides applied as sprays and dusts against natural infestations of *B. germanica* in homes, chlordane (2 per cent) performed as well against non-resistant cockroaches (Table LXXVII) as diazinon (0·5 per cent) and malathion (2 per cent). Chlordane was noticeably less effective against resistant strains but still better than sodium fluoride. The thoroughness of treatment is stressed as being all-important.[509] Removable plywood panels, sprayed to run off with chlordane and other insecticides in kitchens, and taken to the laboratory at intervals for test, showed quite noticeable differences in residual performance against *B. germanica* (Table LXXVIII). In this instance chlordane was superior to diazinon and malathion.

TABLE LXXVI

RELATIVE SUSCEPTIBILITY (LT_{90}) OF COCKROACH SPECIES ARRANGED IN APPROXIMATE ORDER OF INCREASING TOLERANCE TO RESIDUES OF CHLORDANE (100 mg/m^2) BY THE JAR TEST METHOD
(Data from Fales & Bodenstein[289])

Species	Nymphs		Adults	
	Small	Large	Males	Females
Supella longipalpa	2–3	5–6	3–4	4–5
Diploptera punctata	2–3	7–24	4	6–7
Blattella vaga	4–5	6–7	4–5	7–24
Blattella germanica	4–5	7–24	4–5	7–24
Nauphoeta cinerea	6–7	24–48	7–24	24–48
Blatta orientalis	7–24	48–72	7–24	7–24
Periplaneta brunnea	7–24	72	7–24	7–24
Blaberus craniifer	4–5	48–72	7–24	24–48
Periplaneta australasiae	5	48–72	7–24	24–48
Blaberus giganteus	5–6	48–72	24–48	24–48
Periplaneta americana	5–6	72+	7–24	24–48
Eurycotis floridana	5–6	72+	7–24	48–72
Leucophaea maderae	7	72+	48–72	72

TABLE LXXVII

REDUCTION (%) IN NUMBERS OF GERMAN COCKROACHES IN HOMES GIVEN ONE TREATMENT WITH OIL SPRAYS AND DUST
(From Lofgren, Burden & Clark[509])

Insecticide	No. of houses treated	Days after treatment			
		1–6	8–16	19–27	29–41
Chlordane (2%)					
Non-resistant	3	90–97	99–100	100	95–100
Resistant	4	84–91	88–91	84–93	52–85
Diazinon (0·5%)	6	94–98	99	99	98–99
Malathion (2%)	8	97–99	98–99	98–99	97–99
Sodium fluoride dust	4	42–50	45–62	61	—

TABLE LXXVIII

HOURS (AV.) REQUIRED FOR 100% KILL OF GERMAN COCKROACHES EXPOSED ON PLYWOOD PANELS TREATED TO RUN-OFF WITH OIL SPRAYS, AND AGED IN HOMES
(From Lofgren, Burden & Clark[509])

Insecticide	Ageing period (weeks)			
	1	2	4	8
Chlordane (2%)	0.7	2.4	5.0	59
Diazinon (0.5%)	6.6	31	66	324
Malathion (2%)	10	20	75	—

Toxicity to man
The toxicity of chlordane to man is low relative to other organochlorine insecticides (acute oral LD_{50} rat: about 450 mg/kg—Table LXXIII, p. 299). It is thus one of the safer commonly used insecticides. Chlordane injected intravenously into rats is lost primarily *via* the faeces: 30 per cent is removed from the body in 60 hours, of which two thirds are breakdown products. Only 1 per cent is lost *via* the urine in the same period.[677] Both chlordane and lindane cause detoxifying enzymes to be produced by the liver microsomes, thus reducing the hazard from subsequently ingested doses.

Chlordane in the environment
Tolerances for chlordane in about 50 raw agricultural commodities were first set in 1955, by the Food and Drug Administration of the United States, at 0.3 ppm. A re-appraisal in 1965 produced facts to support the conclusion that there was no available evidence to indicate that chlordane contributed any real or potential hazard as residues in food (Table LXXIX) or as a contaminant in any other aspect of the environment.

In December 1967 chlordane was further reviewed by a Joint Meeting of the FAO and WHO Expert Committee on Pesticide residues. An ADI (acceptable daily intake, during an entire lifetime, which appears to be without risk, based on all known facts) was established for chlordane as 0.001 mg/kg of body weight per day. This compares with 0.0001 mg/kg for dieldrin.

From an environmental viewpoint the presence of heptachlor as a minor constituent of chlordane is the chief concern. Heptachlor has an acute oral LD_{50} (rat) of 100 mg/kg; it shares the high persistence of insecticides like DDT and dieldrin and undergoes oxidation to give residues of heptachlor epoxide which have occurred in foodstuffs.

The 24-hour LD_{50} of chlordane to fish (minnows) is 0.07 ppm and is not unlike other organochlorine compounds: dieldrin 0.02, DDT 0.03, lindane

TABLE LXXIX

RESIDUES OF CHLORINATED HYDROCARBON INSECTICIDES IN FOODS SAMPLED IN THE UNITED STATES IN 1964–65, WHEN THE PUBLIC WAS MOST VOCIFEROUS IN ITS CONCERN ABOUT PESTICIDES

(From Duggan et al[243])

Insecticide	Samples (%) in which insecticide could be detected	Maximum found (ppm)
DDT	39	0·86
DDE } breakdown products of DDT	38	0·92
DDD	22	0·29
Dieldrin	21	0·14
Lindane	17	0·21
Heptachlor epoxide	15	0·08
Heptachlor	1	0·01
Chlordane	0·5	0·03

0·06 ppm. A detailed account of the toxicological and pharmacological properties of chlordane* has been published as a monograph.[456]

DIELDRIN

This is another of the chlorinated hydrocarbon insecticides, first employed against insects in 1948 and used extensively for cockroach control, especially in the U.K. It is chemically related to chlordane and is formed as a decomposition product of aldrin (= aldrin epoxide). Unlike chlordane, however, dieldrin has pronounced residual action: it is most stable chemically, does not lose chlorine from its structure readily and has long persistence on treated surfaces. Because of these DDT-like properties, dieldrin is now banned by many countries and is no longer available for cockroach control. Many of its previous agricultural uses are also prohibited because of undesirable effects on wildlife. The use of dieldrin as a seed dressing on cereals, for example, has had serious effects on bird populations. It is also highly toxic to fish. It is however used widely in timber preservatives and for soil poisoning against termites.

Chemical and physical properties

In its pure form, dieldrin forms white crystals. Pest control formulations are

---

* At the time of going to press, chlordane is included in a suspension notice of the Environmental Protection Agency of the U.S.A. of July 29th, 1975. This threatens future use for cockroach control. (See also footnote on p. 145).

made from the technical product, a light tan flaky solid with a mild odour which is not sufficient to affect use. It is stable on alkaline surfaces and is not readily affected by light. It is less volatile than DDT ($1 \cdot 8 \times 10^{-7}$ mm Hg at 25°C) and its residual action exceeds that of aldrin of which it is only 1/30th as volatile. In countries where dieldrin was once used, many different formulations were available: oil sprays, emulsion concentrates (up to 20 per cent), wettable powder (usually 50 per cent) and dust, all with an end-use concentration of about 0·5 per cent. Dieldrin has also been used extensively as a lacquer with good performance against cockroaches and ants (Fig. 134). Dieldrin is not permitted for 'crack and crevice' treatments against cockroaches in the United States.

Action on cockroaches
Those who have used dieldrin for cockroach control, but are now using alternatives, will reflect on its striking performance against *B. germanica*. Males are more susceptible to dieldrin than to any of 14 other insecticides (Table LXIX). Female German cockroaches can tolerate 3 times as much insecticide as males, but dieldrin is still among the most toxic to this sex. Excellent insecticidal activity coupled with long life in treated harbourages made dieldrin one of the most effective insecticides available to the pest control operator. Oriental cockroaches are somewhat more tolerant than German.

Cockroaches poisoned with dieldrin behave similarly to those killed with other chlorinated insecticides. The process of poisoning superficially resembles that of DDT[409] but insects do not take quite so long to die (see p. 286). However, dieldrin applied to the cuticle, in just lethal amounts, may take up to 5 days to kill *P. americana* (Fig. 135): the topical LD_{50} (5 days) is $1 \cdot 3$ μg/g for adult females compared with $1 \cdot 1$ μg/g by injection. This indicates that dieldrin is efficiently absorbed and distributed to the site of action—the central nervous system.[330] Dieldrin applied topically (LD_{50} $1 \cdot 5$ μg/g) is six times more toxic than chlordane (LD_{50} 10 μg/g) to American cockroaches.[475]

The percentage of dieldrin (0·007 per cent) in a direct spray needed to kill 50 per cent of female German cockroaches in 72 hours is half that required in a bait (0·014 per cent) of ground dog chow.[447] The topical LD_{50} (48 hr) of dieldrin to German cockroaches reported by Fisk & Isert[306] is 0·5 μg/insect and is about the same for cockroaches resistant to DDT (0·62 μg/insect). However, 68 times as much dieldrin (LD_{50} 34 μg) is needed for cockroaches resistant to chlordane, indicating strong cross-resistance. When dieldrin is injected into German cockroaches half are killed by 6·6 μg/g and this must be increased to 68·4 μg/g for cockroaches resistant to chlordane (Corpus Christi strain)—a cross-resistance factor of ten times.[164]

Many attempts have been made to discover the mechanism for resistance to dieldrin and related compounds, but it is still unknown. O'Brien[637] attributes it to differences in the 'innate sensitivities of the nerves in susceptible and resistant insects'. There are now many economic pests, other than German cockroaches, which have developed resistance to dieldrin, and studies with houseflies have shown that dieldrin is not metabolised: in other words,

breakdown of the insecticide is not the reason why resistant insects survive. Aldrin-poisoned insects are able to convert the insecticide only to dieldrin, whether they are susceptible or resistant to the insecticide.

Experiments with strains of German cockroaches,[695] both resistant and susceptible to dieldrin, show that they are equally capable of absorbing dieldrin through the cuticle, and that the amounts that appear in the nerve cord are virtually identical: thus uptake, distribution and penetration to the part of the body where the insecticide acts, are not factors influencing survival of the resistant cockroach.

Effects on mammals
The acute oral toxicity of dieldrin for 12 different mammals falls between 20 and 70 mg/kg. The cat is among the most sensitive. The rat (female 51 mg/kg; male 64 mg/kg), monkey and therefore man (?) are intermediate in susceptibility. The dog is among the most tolerant. After an acute dose leading to death, symptoms of poisoning appear within an hour: they include hyper-

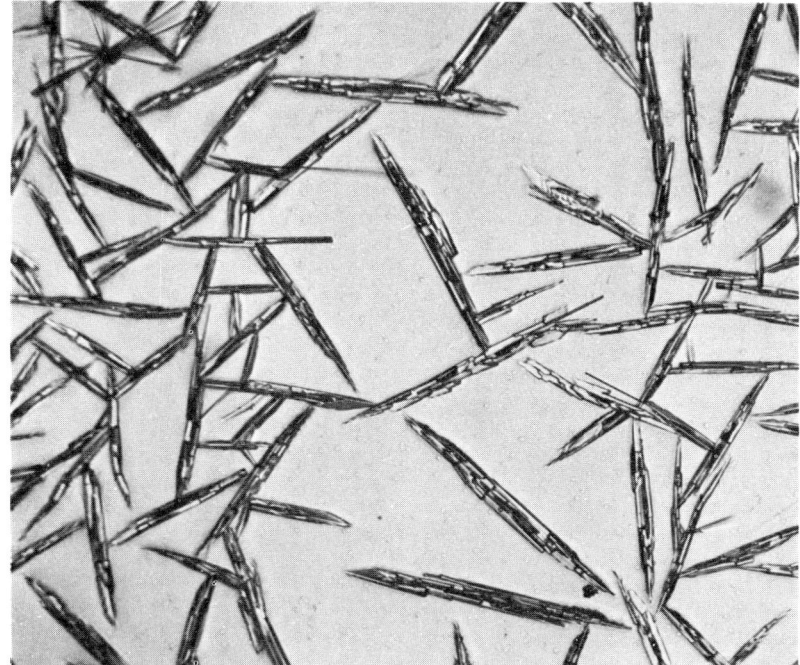

Fig. 134. Insecticidal lacquer is not washed away where other insecticides may be easily removed: (left) application of lacquer by brush to a metal stanchion of kitchen equipment (U.K.); (above) dieldrin crystals (× 180) on a dried lacquer film.

excitability, lack of co-ordination, exaggerated body movements and convulsions. Death occurs within 1 week. Dieldrin is readily absorbed through the skin.[899]

Diets containing 25 ppm of dieldrin fed to rats over two years cause no mortality,[797] but 2·5 ppm reduces pregnancies. The number of offspring per litter is unaffected by 25 ppm, but mortality is high among offspring suckled by mothers fed a diet containing 12·5 ppm.

In long-term feeding studies the first noticeable effect with all animals is an increase in enzyme activity of the liver, associated with an increase in its size. This reflects greater activity of the liver and not damage; it is a sign of exposure to insecticide rather than of injury or poisoning. Symptoms of intoxication by dieldrin are restricted to stimulatory effects on the central nervous system, but the mechanism by which the insecticide acts is still not fully understood. A review of recent literature is given by Jager.[464]

There were many cases of dieldrin poisoning during its early use, especially among workers taking part in control programmes of vector-borne diseases.

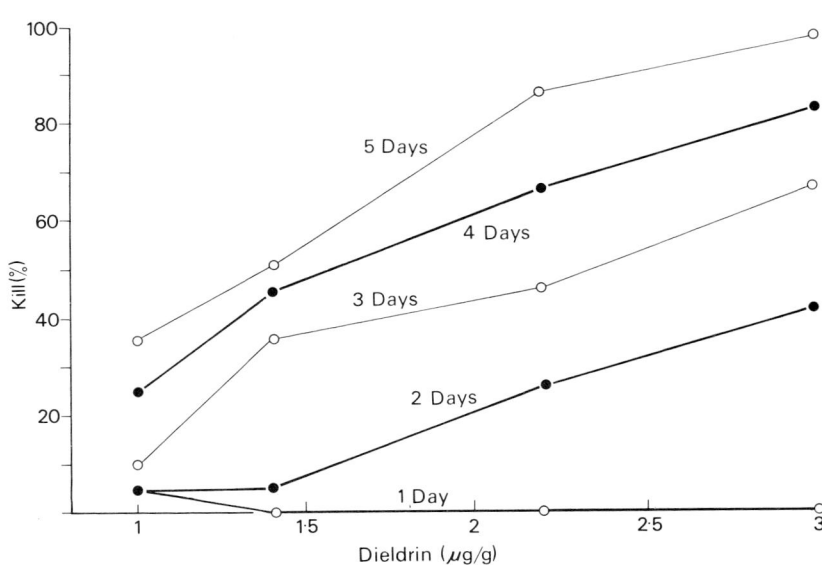

Fig. 135. Kill of female American cockroaches (at 1–5 days) after topical application of dieldrin. (From Gianotti et al.[330]).

These instances were the expected result of flagrant disregard of precautions suggested by W.H.O. Hayes reports on the symptoms which occurred[897] and documents cases from a number of countries.[898]

In men spraying dieldrin, 0·7 ppm in the blood does not bring about poisoning symptoms:[857] even after severe poisoning by dieldrin, complete recovery occurs, although this may take 4 weeks. The biological half life of dieldrin in rats, after prolonged feeding on the insecticide, is 15 days.[706]

Considering the public, and their exposure to dieldrin and other organochlorines, O'Brien[637] states that 'there is no evidence that persistent body burdens even at levels greatly in excess of that found in the general population have any adverse effect normally". Nevertheless, dieldrin has appeared as a contaminant in all the major reviews of insecticides in food, and more frequently than many other commonly used insecticides. Concentrations, however, have invariably been between 0·001 and 1 ppm but these intakes do not accumulate in the body indefinitely. In the United States, the levels in the body fat of the general public have averaged 0·15 ppm.[45]

In a study of 106 men, with an average of 7 years continuous exposure chiefly to dieldrin (and aldrin and endrin) and whose daily intake was 50–100 times greater than the average citizen (6–7 μg/man/day), twenty different clinical tests failed to show evidence of abnormality associated with exposure, or absence, through sickness, from manufacturing plant.[464] Nevertheless, in October 1974, the Environmental Protection Agency of the United States 'ordered an immediate interim ban on the production of dieldrin (and aldrin) which are claimed to be linked to cancer in mice and rats'.[862] The ban was not unexpected since it followed years of controversy over use of these two products. The evidence in connection with rats is not, at present, conclusive, and there is no direct evidence of a causal relationship with cancer in man. The action is seen as a further step, by 'environmental action groups' to prevent the use of long-lasting insecticides, following the banning of DDT.

CHLORDECONE

Chlordecone has been available for cockroach control for more than 10 years. Introduced in 1961 as Kepone® (cereal pellets incorporating chlordecone at 0·125 per cent), it provided an alternative to sprays and dusts against German cockroaches resistant to chlordane in the United States,[512] and to dieldrin in certain areas in the U.K.[814] It has also found application in the control of ants.[86]

Use in baits

Chlordecone is chemically unlike other chlorinated hydrocarbon insecticides. It is a chlorinated ketone, highly stable and the technical form is an off-white, odourless, crystalline solid. It does not dissolve in water but is soluble in many organic solvents. The stability of the insecticide allows it to withstand the hot situations in which cockroaches often occur and its stability in water allows the use of chlordecone in gels. The major use of chlordecone has been in baits, incorporated at 0·125–0·25 per cent, providing a long-lasting, but slow acting stomach poison. There is no indication that chlordecone affects the palatability of baits, which is exceptional for a synthetic insecticide (Table LXXX).

TABLE LXXX

PALATABILITY OF GELS WITH AND WITHOUT CHLORDECONE TO
P. AMERICANA
(From Hawkes[403])

Days of feeding	Gel eaten (mg) per surviving cockroach per day		
	No chlordecone	With chlordecone at	
		0·125 %	0·25 %
1	18·0	20·3	20·0
2	5·3	11·8	16·6
3	8·8	16·9	14·0
4–6	10·1	11·8	10·1
7–11	4·8	5·9	9·7
Mean	9·4	13·3	14·1

Kepone® —Registered trade mark of Allied Chemical Corp.

In feeding experiments, with alternative food available, German cockroaches are killed somewhat more readily than Oriental cockroaches with baits containing 0·125 per cent chlordecone, but there is little difference at 0·25 per cent. Males are more susceptible than females and death at the higher concentration occurs in 7–10 days (Fig. 136). Males of *P. americana* are also slightly more susceptible than females. All three species eat gel baits more readily than pastes (Table LXXXI).

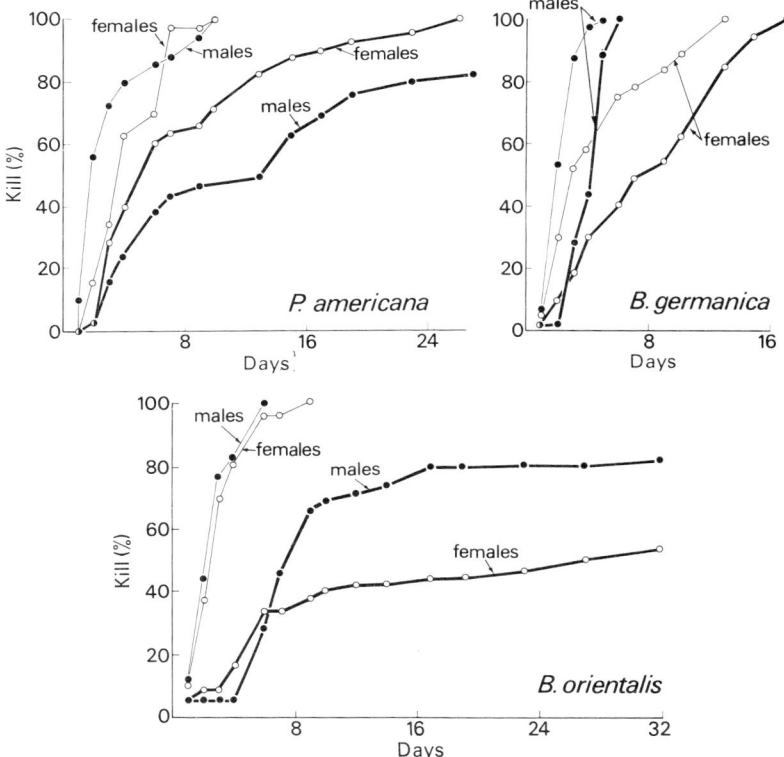

Fig. 136. Kill of *P. americana*, *B. germanica* and *B. orientalis* fed starch/groundnut oil paste, containing 0·125 per cent chlordecone (thick line) and gel containing 0·25 per cent chlordecone (thin line). (From Hawkes[403]).

The water in gels is believed to have an important effect on palatability, making gel baits readily acceptable as a source of moist food. The success obtained with chlordecone baits to control infestations of German cockroaches on ships, resistant to dieldrin, substantiate that there is no cross-resistance with this and other organochlorine insecticides.

Baits containing 0·125 per cent chlordecone embedded in paraffin blocks and placed in sewer manholes, were eaten by American cockroaches but not after mould became visible. Addition of p-nitrophenol reduced moulding but baits disintegrated in humid shafts with high ambient temperatures.[286,871]

TABLE LXXXI

PALATABILITY OF GEL (CONTAINING 0·25% CHLORDECONE) AND PASTE (0·125%) TO ORIENTAL, GERMAN AND AMERICAN COCKROACHES. TOTAL AMOUNTS EATEN (g)

(From Hawkes[403])

Species	Sex (and No. of insects)	Days of feeding	Gel	Paste	Ratio Gel : Paste
B. orientalis	Male (50)	0–6	3·8	1·1	
		7–32	—	0·8	3·4 : 1
	Female (50)	0–9	3·3	1·0	
		9–32	—	0·6	
B. germanica	Male (100)	0–6	3·2	0·7	
		6–7	—	0·1	3·6 : 1
	Female (100)	0–13	5·0	1·6	
		13–17	—	0·0	
P. americana	Male (50)	0–10	18·3	1·3	
		11–32	—	0·6	9·9 : 1
	Female (50)	0–9	18·5	2·4	
		9–27	—	0·4	

— indicates all cockroaches fed gel were dead.

Many personnel involved in pest control have discarded baits as being of little value in cockroach control because ingestion and action of the insecticide is slow. After laying 900 baits in a students hostel, seven storey's high and containing some 350 rooms, German cockroaches previously established there and resistant to dieldrin, started dying after three days. There was a marked reduction in infestation after a week, as shown by night inspection; after 7 weeks there was no living cockroach in the entire building confirmed by further examination at 10 weeks.[814] Action of chlordecone may be slow but results can often be very spectacular! Other examples of the use of baits are given in Chapter 4.

A wettable powder and emulsion of chlordecone are also available but these have not been used in sprays for cockroach control because of the poor contact action of the insecticide. Other uses of chlordecone have been against pests of turf and ornamental plants.

Toxicity to man

The acute oral LD_{50} (rat) is 125 mg/kg. Dogs can tolerate twice this amount. When fed in a diet to various birds, half die within 10 days on intakes of 100–200 mg/kg. A warm-blooded animal would have to eat bait, containing 0·125 per cent chlordecone, exceeding 10 per cent of its body weight to obtain a dose that would cause 50 per cent mortality. At doses given to cause poisoning of test animals, DDT-like tremors develop, reaching a peak of intensity during the second day, then gradually subsiding.

The safety in use of chlordecone in cockroach baits is quite striking: this comes from incorporation of the insecticide at exceedingly low concentrations and the placement of baits in locations, favoured by the insects and without access to children. A recommendation for pelleted baits is that they be scattered under fixtures: the number of pellets that a child might find is thereby reduced compared with pellets placed in bait containers. Gels and pastes should be squeezed into harbourages or applied to the backs of drawer units or on other surfaces in kitchens on which cockroaches collect.

Despite the exceedingly low risk presented by baits containing chlordecone, even in areas where food is being handled, some countries do not permit its use because of chemical similarity with the better known chlorinated hydrocarbons. Such restrictions reflect a lack of awareness of what can be achieved in practical cockroach control, especially by way of safe application of formulations, without risk of contaminating the air.

In this chapter, we have looked at the properties and performance of a number of insecticides, representative of the chlorinated hydrocarbons. These served the pest control industry well between 1945 and 1970. They were used effectively and safely in proven formulations by servicing companies. They also provided reliable constituents for household products, mainly for the control of crawling insects: cockroaches, ants, fleas, bedbugs and the immature stages of textile pests. The group includes some insecticides still in use against structural pests (termites and other wood-destroying insects) because adequate alternatives do not exist.

The adverse criticisms and consequent investigations of DDT in the environment have directed attention to the properties of other chlorinated hydrocarbon insecticides. Some of these have also come under attack. In some countries, however, lindane, chlordane and dieldrin continue to be available for cockroach control, for which they offer useful properties: a long life on treated surfaces underwrites their reliability for this purpose.

Insecticides of the chlorinated type are generally slow to kill cockroaches but there is little evidence that the insects recover once contact is made with a treated harbourage. To contribute to quick knockdown organochlorines are often combined with pyrethrins. The merits for cockroach control of using the two insecticides consecutively, or at the same time are discussed on p. 247.

Apart from Government restrictions, the use of organochlorines for cockroach control has declined rapidly in the last 10 years because of resistance, among German cockroaches. There is undisputed evidence of cross-resistance between insecticides of the group (see Chapter 15), with the result that resistance to one prevents effective use of others. There is no such cross-resistance, however, to chlordecone. This insecticide will, in the writer's opinion, make a major contribution to effective and safe cockroach control in the 1980's in countries where its use may still be permitted.*

For reasons quite unrelated to practical cockroach control (like the detrimental effects of insecticides on wildlife), the organochlorines have in most cases given way to the use of shorter-lived materials—organophosphorus and carbamate insecticides. These are chemically different from the chlorinated compounds and thus kill insects in a different way. They have provided valuable alternatives, acceptable on grounds of health and safety, for the control of cockroaches resistant to the organochlorines.

---

* This statement was written before the closure of manufacture in the U.S.A., in late 1975, due to inappropriate precautions in manufacturing and having nothing whatever to do with the safe use, or otherwise, of the insecticide.[884] (Comment added in press).

12

THE SHORTER-LIVED INSECTICIDES
(ORGANOPHOSPHORUS COMPOUNDS)

History of development; action and degradation—Diazinon: history of development and use; chemical and physical properties; effectiveness against cockroaches; toxicity to man and animals—Dichlorvos: chemical and physical properties; insecticidal properties; dichlorvos vapour; use of dichlorvos aerosols; spray applications; toxicity to man and animals; recommended uses—Malathion: chemical and physical properties; effectiveness against cockroaches; toxicity to man and animals—Chlorpyrifos: chemical and physical properties; effectiveness against cockroaches; toxicity to man and other animals—Fenitrothion: chemical and physical properties; effectiveness against cockroaches; toxicity to man and animals—Iodofenphos: chemical and physical properties; effectiveness against cockroaches; toxicity to man and animals—Trichlorphon: chemical and physical properties; effectiveness against cockroaches; toxicity to man and animals.

The aim in the development of new insecticides is to kill insects and leave man unharmed. In agricultural pest control it is also to kill the pest and leave other insects unharmed. To paraphrase O'Brien's[635] thoughts: in view of the apparent enormous differences between insects and man, at least the first of these problems ought to be capable of solution—but of course, it's not. Some of the most recent organophosphorus and carbamate insecticides do go part way to conferring toxicity, preferentially, upon the insect. The rest we have to obtain by using appropriate spraying equipment, protective clothing, and more recently, by self discipline. The last takes the form of legislative decisions, not to use certain insecticides in situations where they might cause harm.

The popularity of organophosphorus insecticides derives from their effectiveness against insects resistant to organochlorines. Also from the requirement that undesirable toxic residues shall not be allowed to pollute food or the environment: for our own sake, the insecticides used must break down readily if accidentally absorbed into the body.

Some of the organophosphorus insecticides used for cockroach control, considered in this chapter, have a very short residual life on treated surfaces. Others remain insecticidal for many weeks. If costs were equal, insecticides offering good initial kill of cockroaches and long residual life, would be preferentially used. These make the job of the pest control operator easier; service visits can be less frequent and 'guarantee periods' extended.

Among organophosphorus insecticides used for cockroach control there are some with acute toxicities to man greater than those of previously used organochlorine compounds. The preference now expressed for the shorter-lived organophosphates may have alleviated risks to wildlife outdoors. It may also have reduced by a fraction of a ppm, the amount of insecticide in food. But it may have put the user of pesticides at greater risk, especially in instances where gross accidental contamination or ingestion occurs.

Generalisations seldom apply to all members of a group of insecticides: in as much that all chlorinated hydrocarbons are not persistent and do not accumulate in the environment, neither are all organophosphorus insecticides highly toxic. In the control of cockroaches and other insects indoors, we should use those organophosphates with the best possible insecticidal life and lowest acute toxicity. In other words, make use of the materials in which the insecticide chemist has provided us with the maximum benefit of selective action against the cockroach.

History of development
There are many examples in pest control where the materials we use were initially researched for entirely different purposes. This is especially true of the organophosphorus insecticides. The organic chemistry of phosphorus began in 1820, to be followed in 1854 by the synthesis of the first insecticidal organophosphate. It was not known at the time, that 90 years were to follow before the potent insect-killing properties of this compound (tetraethyl pyrophosphate—TEPP) would be recognised.

The insecticidal action of the organophosphates was discovered in Germany during World War II and came about indirectly from the preparation of nerve gases as possible military weapons. The acute oral LD_{50} (rat) of TEPP for example is about 1 mg/kg. The earliest use of organophosphorus insecticides in agriculture[637] was in 1944, and among the early, highly toxic compounds used were some with effective systemic action in plants, e.g. schradan discovered in 1941 with an oral LD_{50} (rat) of 9–42 mg/kg, and systox, introduced later in 1951. Parathion,[219] with an acute oral LD_{50} (rat) of 4–13 mg/kg, appeared in 1947. The symptoms of poisoning caused by exposure of orchard spray men to parathion and TEPP have been described.[917]

Gradually, changes were made in the chemical (molecular) structure of these early organophosphates to provide useful, wide spectrum, contact insecticides with low mammalian toxicity. The first of these was malathion, developed in 1950, to be followed by dichlorvos (= DDVP, in 1951), diazinon (1952), fenitrothion (= sumithion, in 1959) and more recently, iodofenphos (1966).

By 1959, about 50,000 organophosphorus compounds had been made. Without the few which have been used, insect control from the mid 1950's onward would have proved most difficult. The carbamates, represented initially by carbaryl in 1957, had not been fully evaluated. By 1960, there was a large number of insect pests resistant to organochlorine insecticides and there was a need for chemicals with a different mode of action. This was especially true for German cockroaches resistant to dieldrin in ships and resistant to chlordane in the United States (see p. 428).

Action and degradation
The chemistry of organophosphorus insecticides is highly complex and no

attempt will be made here to divide them into subgroups on the basis of composition. Most are esters; combinations of alcohols with phosphoric acid. All can be hydrolysed and this affects their stability, insecticidal performance and mammalian toxicity.

The biological activity of the organophosphates is generally believed to derive from their interference with a vital enzyme (acetylcholinesterase) important to nerve function in insects and mammals. The insecticides owe their potency inside the body to conversion or activation, to compounds which are direct inhibitors of this enzyme. Thus malathion is converted to malaoxon which is the substance directly responsible. An insecticide acting itself, as a 'direct inhibitor', is dichlorvos which requires no activation in the body. 'Conversion of the insecticide by hydrolysis to activation and degradation products is of immense importance for toxicity; differences in the rates of these reactions can be all-important in determining whether death or survival will occur, after treatment with an organophosphate'.[637]

It is difficult to predict what might have happened in agriculture had the organophosphorus insecticides, and subsequently the carbamates, not become available. Would we have continued to use chlorinated insecticides and continued to inflict gross insecticide-poisoning on the environment in the 1960's? Or would public pressure have been sufficiently strong to cause a marked reduction in the use of these chemicals, to the detriment of insect control? Would there have been a stimulus to search for new compounds of totally novel mode of action? These questions we cannot answer. This stimulus never occurred because the type of insecticide needed was so readily satisfied by the organophosphates. These insecticides have made a major contribution to controlling insects of importance in agriculture and in public health.

The following are the organophosphates most often used for cockroach control. They differ markedly in speed of action and efficacy. They are arranged in order with the most preferred at the top, based on expressions of opinion to the author in different countries and as indicated in the published literature. To some extent the order of preference reflects industry's confidence in the older well-tested materials with newer materials tending to occur at the bottom.

Diazinon
Dichlorvos (DDVP)
Malathion
Chlorpyrifos (Dursban)
Fenitrothion (Sumithion)
Iodofenphos (Nuvanol)
Trichlorphon (Dipterex)

DIAZINON

Diazinon is the trade mark of Ciba-Geigy for an insecticide used worldwide to control cockroaches and other public health pests. It has many of the advantages of an all-purpose insecticide: (1) effectiveness against a wide range of crawling and flying insects, (2) versatility of use indoors and out, (3) availability in a range of formulations, of which the emulsion concentrate has proved most popular, (4) providing both contact and vapour action against insects, (5) not rapidly acting, but neither is it unduly slow, (6) cost effectiveness is good compared with other insecticides, (7) medium toxicity to man, with a good safety performance over 20 years of use.

However, for cockroach control, the primary disadvantage of diazinon is that good initial kill is not followed by good residual action in treated harbourages for more than a few days (Fig. 137).

History of development and use

Diazinon was synthesised in the laboratories of Geigy, Basle in 1951 and became available commercially in 1954. This was the year following first detection of resistance to chlordane in *B. germanica* in the U.S.A. Thus, diazinon was adopted as the best, readily available alternative and the pest control industry had shown considerable interest in it by 1956.

At that time diazinon was registered in America for use by pest control operatives for 'spot treatments', applied as a 0·5 per cent spray, and restricted to servicing companies. Its principal value was said to be for the treatment of infestations of German cockroaches not responding to chlorinated hydrocarbons. But pest controllers were advised that, 'for non-resistant roaches, the better-known cockroach materials, such as chlordane should be used. They have known effectiveness and are generally cheaper'.[618]

Subsequently, diazinon became widely used against ectoparasites of livestock (e.g. sheep blow fly in Australia) and against insect pests of forage crops, vegetables, garden ornamental plants and turf. Indoors, diazinon proved useful for insect control in processing plants and against stored food pests (notably *Tribolium castaneum, Sitophilus oryzae* and *Rhizopertha dominica*), and for the control of household insects and industrial pests.

A survey of insecticides used by the pest control industry in the U.S.A. in 1962 showed that diazinon (eight years after its introduction) was the insecticide most widely used by pest control operators.[622] At that time a 25 per cent emulsion concentrate was available.

Chemical and physical properties

Technical diazinon is a light amber to dark brown, slightly viscous liquid (about 95 per cent pure) and has a characteristic odour. It is miscible with many organic solvents but is sparingly soluble in water. The insecticide is hydrolysed by acids and alkalis. It is more volatile than malathion but not to the same extent as dichlorvos. The vapour pressure at 20°C is $1·4 \times 10^{-4}$ mm Hg; at that temperature, a cubic metre of air, fully saturated, contains 2·4 mg of diazinon. This imparts good control of adult flies but its vapour action contributes little to the control of cockroaches when the insecticide is used to treat harbourages (Table LXXXII). Diazinon vaporises 20 times faster at 40°C than 10°C, undoubtedly accounting for its short residual life in situations where German cockroaches often occur.

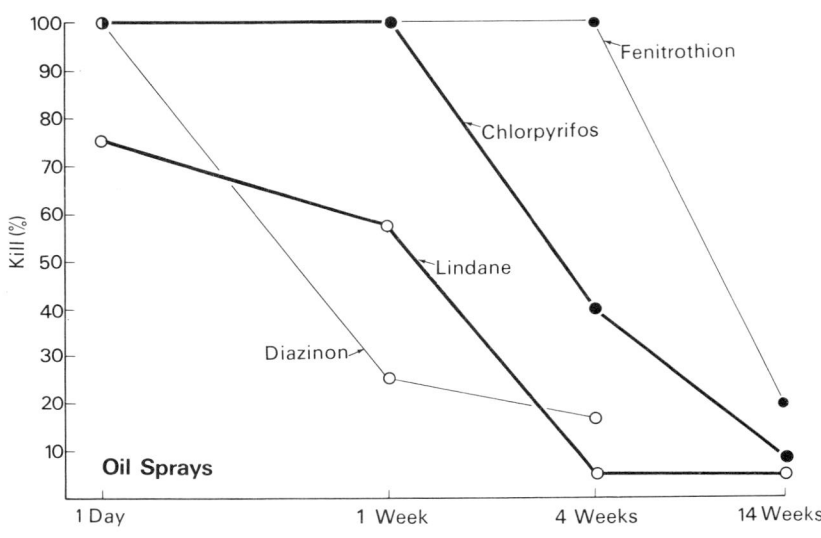
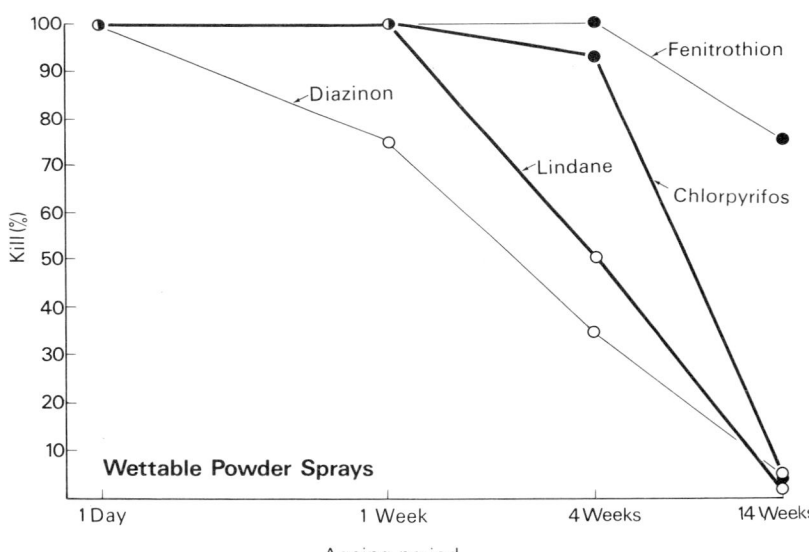

Fig. 137. Kill (per cent at 48 hours) of German cockroaches (both sexes) exposed for 12 minutes to various insecticides applied, as oil sprays on glass at 150 mg/m² and as wettable powders on hardboard at 500 mg/m². Treated surfaces were aged for various periods at 25°C and 65 per cent R.H. before test. (Cornwell, unpublished). (150 mg of active ingredient/m² is equivalent to a 1 per cent spray applied at 15 ml/m²; 500 mg/m² is equivalent to a 1 per cent spray applied at 50 ml/m².

TABLE LXXXII

KILL (% AT 48 HOURS) OF *B. GERMANICA* EXPOSED AT 25°C FOR SHORT PERIODS TO THE CONTACT AND VAPOUR ACTION OF 1% DIAZINON OIL SPRAY ON GLASS, AND FOR LONGER PERIODS OF VAPOUR ACTION ALONE, JUST ABOVE THE TREATED SURFACE
(Cornwell, unpublished)

Treatment	Exposure time (minutes)			
	2	4	8	16
Contact plus vapour action	80	95	100	100
	Exposure time (hours)			
	2	4	8	24
Vapour action alone	0	0	35	100

Diazinon is compatible with most other insecticides: there is no potentiation with malathion or other commonly used organophosphates. Pyrethrins are often combined with diazinon to impart flushing action and to give quicker knockdown of cockroaches.

The formulations most used by pest control operators are Diazinon 4E (47·5 per cent by wt of emulsion concentrate), Diazinon 4S (48·7 per cent by wt of diazinon in a concentrate miscible with odourless kerosene), Diazinon 2D (2 per cent ready to use dust for pest control operators only) and a 50 per cent wettable powder. Diazinon has also been formulated as a lacquer (see Chapter 4). Ready to use household sprays and pressure packs usually incorporate 0·5 per cent diazinon; spray treatments indoors by professional operators are best made with 1 per cent diazinon as 'spot' applications by coarse sprays direct into the insect's harbourages. Agricultural products incorporating diazinon are marketed under the trade name Basudin.

Effectiveness against cockroaches

The knockdown of cockroaches by diazinon on treated surfaces is slow. Only half of the German cockroaches exposed for short periods to spray deposits, giving good kill in 48 hours, are knocked down in 1–3 hours (Figs. 129 & 138). Residues on surfaces become ineffective within a month and at high temperatures (25°C and above) their effective life does not exceed one or two weeks (Table LXXV).

Diazinon (1 per cent) in acetone applied to plywood panels (2·5 ml/250 cm²) kills German cockroaches in about one third the time (LT_{50} : 1·4 hr) compared with American cockroaches (LT_{50} : 3·6 hr).[382]

Among various organophosphorus insecticides tested as sprays and dusts in homes against natural infestations of *B. germanica* in Florida, 0·5 per cent diazinon emulsion applied as spot treatments gave 95–99 per cent reduction during the following three months. Malathion as a 2 per cent spray gave 93–99 per cent. Diazinon dust (1 per cent) gave 'good to fair control' for 2 months but was unsatisfactory after 3 months. Control with malathion dust (4 per cent) was never satisfactory. The time for 50 per cent and 90 per cent knockdown of the cockroaches collected from these homes (29 strains) exposed continuously to deposits of diazinon at 0·1 g/m^2, ranged from 24–55 mins and 26–62 mins, respectively. These were about the same as for laboratory insects.[145]

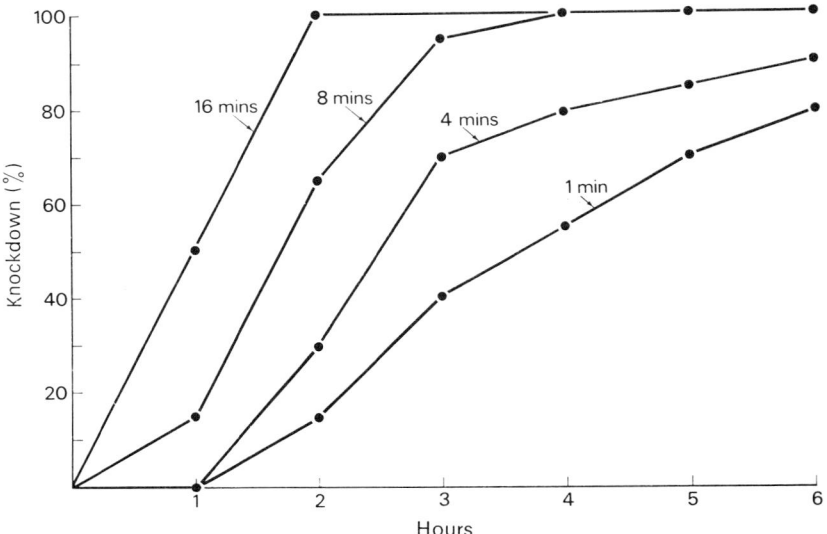

Fig. 138. Rate of knockdown of *B. germanica* exposed for short periods (1–16 mins) to 1 per cent diazinon applied as oil spray to run-off on glass. All treatments gave 95–100 per cent kill after 48 hours. (Cornwell, unpublished).

When organophosphorus insecticides and the carbamate, propoxur, were applied aboard ships of the U.S. navy, to control German cockroaches, diazinon (1 per cent) failed to give control on 4 out of 5 ships. Dursban failed at 0·25 per cent but performed excellently on 6 ships out of 7 when used at 0·5 per cent. Propoxur (1 per cent) gave excellent control on 3 ships but performed poorly on four. Malathion (2 per cent) was poor.[310]

In laboratory tests of oil formulations of diazinon, fenitrothion and propoxur, applied as 1 per cent sprays to a non-absorbent surface (glass), and aged for periods of up to 12 weeks, diazinon was least effective in killing German cockroaches (Table LXXXIII).

By topical application (Table LXIX) diazinon kills German cockroaches much more readily than Oriental; females of the latter are about 3 times more tolerant than males, but a sex difference in *B. germanica* is hardly evident. When the LD_{50} for both sexes is averaged, diazinon is as toxic to German cockroaches as chlordane, but less effective than propoxur, dursban, dieldrin and fenitrothion. For the Oriental cockroach, diazinon is twice as insecticidal as chlordane but again less effective than dieldrin, propoxur and dursban: it is also about as effective as fenitrothion but less so than lindane, notably against females.

TABLE LXXXIII

KILL (% AT 48 HOURS) OF *B. GERMANICA* EXPOSED FOR 12 MINS ON GLASS PLATES TREATED WITH 1% OIL SPRAYS OF DIAZINON, FENITROTHION AND PROPOXUR AND AGED UP TO 12 WEEKS
(Cornwell, unpublished)

Insecticide	Ageing period			
	1 day	3 weeks	6 weeks	12 weeks
Diazinon	100	12	0	0
Fenitrothion	100	82	56	5
Propoxur	100	100	100	100

There are a few reports of field resistance by German cockroaches to diazinon. Nevertheless, there is no evidence, after 20 year's use, that this insecticide will soon become ineffective (see Chapter 15). However, during the last 5 years there has been good reason to discourage the use of diazinon for cockroach control in favour of other organophosphorus compounds. In the 1960's diazinon became very popular for indoor insect control, with its relative freedom from odour (cf. malathion) and the claims then made for good residual life. It has in fact a relatively short life, especially when applied to porous and newly painted surfaces. It performed well, as an alternative to chlordane and dieldrin when, because of resistance, there was a need for an insecticide of good performance and acceptable safety. At that time there was virtually no alternative. But now much improved residual life can be obtained from other organophosphates, at little extra cost, and as an additional bonus, lower health risk to man.

Toxicity to man and animals
Diazinon is of intermediate toxicity to warm-blooded animals: ten times less toxic than parathion and about ten times more toxic than recent organophosphates, such as iodofenphos. Soon after commercial introduction, both technical and emulsifiable solutions of diazinon were found to deteriorate, producing a substance highly toxic to man. The acute oral LD_{50} (rat) for diazinon was at that time quoted as 80–150 mg/kg. Recent improvements in the manufacture and stabilisation of the insecticide have lowered the toxicity (to an oral LD_{50} (rat) of 300–400 mg/kg), but without change in activity to in-

sects. Nevertheless, opened concentrates should be used within 6 months.

The toxicity of diazinon to the housefly is about 40 times higher than to the American cockroach and 20 times higher than to the mouse. Accordingly, there is a good measure of selective action towards insects, brought about by different rates of hydrolysis of diazoxon, the actual toxicant, in both instances.[489] This difference in toxicity of diazinon is because the liver of mammals is considerably better than the fat body of cockroaches at degrading the insecticide.[316]

Chronic 2-year feeding of diazinon at 1000 ppm in the diet of rats causes no signs of toxicity or microscopic pathological symptoms. There is no tendency of the insecticide to accumulate when given by stomach tube at 20 mg/kg/day. Diazinon is readily broken down in the body: when administered to cows at 16 mg/kg, none is found in their milk.

The toxicity of diazinon through the skin is relatively low: the dermal LD_{50} (rat) for a 50 per cent emulsion concentrate is 2g/kg and in excess of this for a 50 per cent wettable powder. The aerosol (inhalation) LC_{50} of a 2 per cent diazinon aqueous solution to rats, exposed for 4 hours, is greater than 24 mg/1 of air. The LD_{50} for inhalation of a 50 per cent WP (as a dust aerosol) for rats exposed for 1 hour is greater than 120 mg/1 of air. Inhalation of spray droplets and vapour during the use of diazinon should obviously be avoided, but a mask is not necessary during application of 1 per cent sprays, unless an obvious mist is created, treatment is extensive or ventilation is poor. The conscientious operator will not take risks: with diazinon the chief risk is the spillage of concentrate which remains unnoticed on the skin.

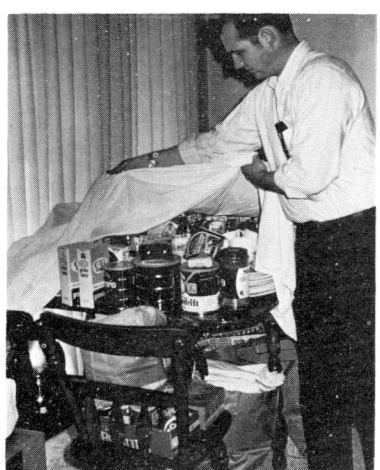
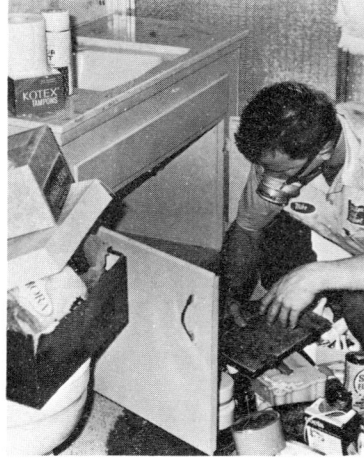

Fig. 139. Harbourages most frequently occupied by German cockroaches in domestic properties, are in store cupboards in the kitchen, and in bathroom cabinets beneath the wash basin. In both instances the contents should be removed or covered before treatment.

During the many years that diazinon has been used by pest control operators it has enjoyed an excellent record of safety and there have been few reported cases of illness. Analyses of blood samples of spray men have, nevertheless, shown reduced cholinesterase levels. Poisoning symptoms include headache, giddiness, blurred vision, nausea, cramps, diarrhoea and discomfort of the chest—all typical of body absorption of organophosphorus insecticides.

Where the use of diazinon may contaminate food, it is sensible to remove the food or cover it, and to cover all processing equipment (Fig. 139). In June 1974 interim labels[49] were granted by the Environmental Protection Agency of the U.S. for diazinon within food areas of food-handling establishments, allowing 'crack and crevice treatment'. Prior to that, diazinon was not labelled 'for use in commercial food preparation areas, or in edible product areas of food processing plants'.

The use of diazinon for cockroach control is unlikely to result in contamination of garden plants. However, the African violet—a popular indoor plant—is reported to be injured by diazinon sprays, but this may be caused by oil carriers or emulsifiers rather than by the insecticide itself. Bees are readily killed by diazinon and birds are highly susceptible. Fish are readily killed by small amounts, but diazinon is less toxic than DDT to them.

DICHLORVOS

This organophosphorus insecticide has been used extensively against industrial and domestic pests and is perhaps best known in 'slow-release' products (e.g. PVC resin strips) for fly control. It was first synthesised in the early 1950's and became popularly known as DDVP, by the trade names Nuvan® (Ciba-Geigy) and Vapona® (Shell). Compared with other commonly-used organophosphates, dichlorvos has some rather special properties. It combines high insecticidal potency at relatively low concentrations, especially against flying insects, with very rapid action and high volatility.

Chemical and physical properties

Dichlorvos is a colourless liquid which is miscible with most organic solvents. Because of its high vapour pressure ($1 \cdot 2 \times 10^{-2}$ mm Hg at 20°C) sprays and fogs applied in closed spaces, quickly result in dichlorvos filling the air space. When surfaces are sprayed, most of the active ingredient is taken up by the substrate and vaporises from it over several days. Thus in enclosed spaces a steady concentration of dichlorvos may remain present in the air.

Dichlorvos corrodes mild steel but not stainless steel or aluminium. The insecticide is broken down on alkaline surfaces, such as cement and concrete, markedly reducing duration of action. Should a formulation of dichlorvos be spilt, it can be removed by washing with strong caustic solution and rinsing with water.

The formulations of dichlorvos available for public health use include emul-

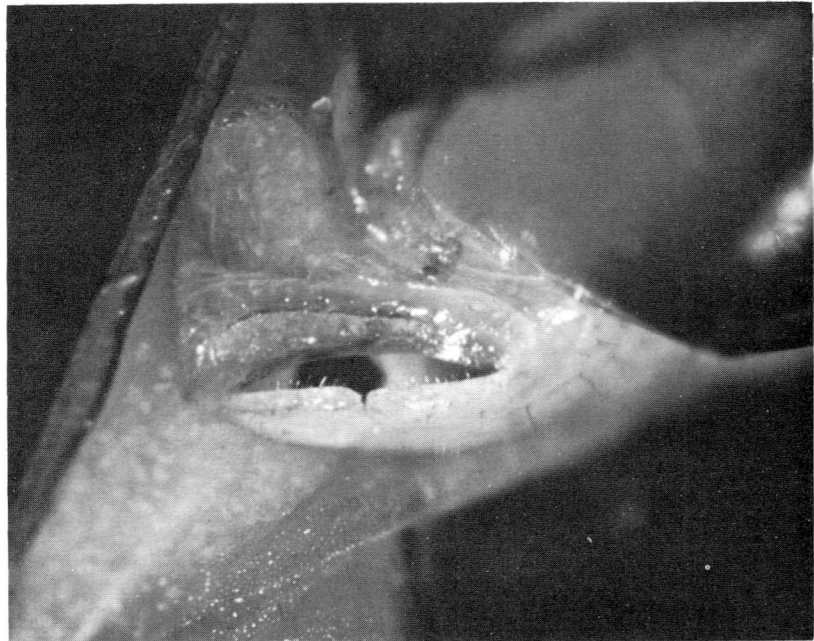

Fig.140. Parts of the cockroach respiratory system: (above) the first thoracic spiracle of the Oriental cockroach (× 100); (right) tracheae and tracheoles which carry oxygen and insecticidal vapour (e.g. dichlorvos) to the insect tissues. (Courtesy: Neil A. Maclean Co. Inc. & Stennett Heaton).

sion and oil concentrates for further dilution, usually to 0·5–1 per cent for spraying, and to 2 per cent for thermal fogging. Aerosols for domestic purposes usually contain 0·4–1 per cent, but there are 'non-stop' aerosols for professional use (for treating storage spaces) of 5–10 per cent. All containers for dichlorvos formulations should be tightly capped: first, to prevent build up of toxic concentrations of vapour in small ill-ventilated stores; secondly to prevent degradation of the product by the action of water vapour in humid environments.

In 'Vapona strip', dichlorvos is impregnated into PVC and slowly evaporates from the surface in small amounts over a 2–3 month period. Dichlorvos is often incorporated in formulations with residual activity, as a cheaper replacement for pyrethrins. It has their quick knockdown properties but the flushing action is not so good.

Wettable powders, dusts and granules do not last well in storage because the active ingredient is unstable. A Nuvan 'scatter bait' (0·5 per cent dichlorvos) is available, made from granulated sugar and impregnated carrier material, for use in dry places at 1 or 2 g/m². It is claimed to be effective against flies, cockroaches and ants over several weeks.

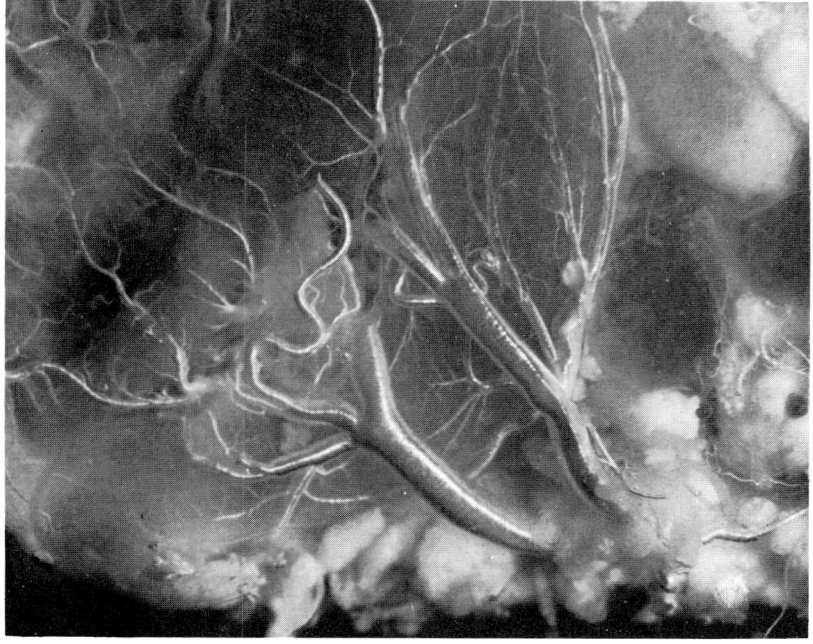

Insecticidal properties

Dichlorvos has contact, stomach and inhalation toxicity against a wide range of insects with outstanding action against the housefly (*Musca domestica*). The duration of insecticidal activity on surfaces normally encountered in buildings is relatively short. Contact action on treated wood is said to exceed 1 week.[626] Kill is not dependent solely upon contact: the insecticide has high volatility and activity in the vapour phase. Speed of knockdown of flies was not paralleled by any of 78 other insecticides tested as vapour toxicants.[451] Pyrethrins and some synthetic pyrethroids may be faster, but this derives from contact with insecticide droplets. Thus on plywood treated with dichlorvos (0·5 g/m^2), 50 per cent of flies are knocked down in 3 minutes compared with 13 minutes for diazinon and 121 for malathion.[268] Applications which aim to give extremely rapid control avoid the use of residual action but utilise the insecticide's vapour toxicity. In instances where prolonged action is required, dichlorvos has to be used in a 'controlled release' formulation.

Extremely small amounts of dichlorvos in air may be effective against many small *flying* insects and for some of these (filter and fruit flies, mosquitoes, cigarette beetles and tobacco moth) all that may be necessary to achieve control, e.g. in a warehouse, is to sprinkle dichlorvos in solution on the floor. However, for the control of crawling insects, especially those which live in cracks and crevices, the manufacturer's handbook says: 'it is very important to uncover the hiding places of these pests as much as possible before treatment. Control is best achieved by spot treatment of the usual resting places'. Despite the good vapour action of dichlorvos, do not rely on the insecticide 'seeking out' cockroaches in their harbourages.

Thus a 50 per cent emulsion released from a simple container onto free hanging absorbent surfaces (e.g. newspaper) failed to kill all cockroaches (98, 90 and 80 per cent in three separate tests): 'a continuous control operation is necessary followed by continuous treatment of foci of infestation'.[553]

It must be assumed that the reader of this book is interested in *effective* cockroach control and will not be offended by criticism of the inexperienced, who practice misting and fogging as a means to control—which are invariably imperfect. Thus despite the quite strikingly rapid action and volatility of dichlorvos, much the same condemnation can be made of its use when applied by these techniques, as had been made of the pyrethrins (see p. 244). The high volatility does not confer ready penetration of dichlorvos into cracks and crevices of a building fabric. That is not to say however, that the cockroach is unable to inhale and succumb to toxic vapours, should they be of sufficient concentration and maintained for long enough periods.

A study of different fumigants on the respiratory behaviour of the American cockroach—which normally ventilates the body 6–8 times per minute—suggests that ventilation and spiracular movements depend on the penetrating capacity of the toxicant. In addition to entry through the spiracles and tracheae (Fig. 140), which form the chief sites for exchange of gases,[101] penetration of the integument also appears to be important.

TABLE LXXXIV

AVERAGE MORTALITY (%) OF ADULT GERMAN COCKROACHES AFTER CONTINUOUS EXPOSURE FOR 48 HOURS TO RESIN STRIPS OF DICHLORVOS IN DIFFERENT SITUATIONS
(Data from Russell & Frishman[718])

Location	Area of strip cm^2/m^3	Males	Females
Ventilated rooms	8.6	20	20
	9.7	25	0
	19.4	45	10
	29.1	90	65
Air conditioned rooms	5.7		
(a) Open spaces		98	91
(b) Hidden areas		46	53

Dichlorvos vapour

We shall now look at some of the experiments to evaluate the performance of dichlorvos vapour against cockroaches. There is some evidence of successful use of dichlorvos strips to control cockroaches in sewer manholes in the U.S.A., in water meter boxes and dustbins. Much depends on the air-tightness of the harbourage and the concentration of insecticidal vapour developed.[254]

In tests in the laboratory with chlordane-susceptible and chlordane-resistant *B. germanica*, exposed to dichlorvos vapour from resin strips for 4 hours, the LD_{50} for females of the susceptible strain was 0·063 μg/l, and was four times higher for resistant insects (Fig. 141). More oothecae were dropped by treated females of both strains than untreated insects: 19 per cent were dropped at 0·1 μg/l, increasing to 95 per cent at 0·46 μg/l for the normal strain, but somewhat fewer (9 per cent and 63 per cent, respectively) for chlordane-resistant females.[718]

American and German cockroaches freely exposed to monitored concentrations of dichlorvos in sealed chambers of about 40 m³ are not all killed when exposed for less than 20 hours to concentrations below 1 μg/l. Levels above 7·4 μg/l for 2 hours are required for complete kill. Male American cockroaches are killed by relatively short exposures to low concentrations of vapour, but females are noticeably more tolerant. Moreover, the hatch of eggs from oothecae carried by females of *B. germanica* is not affected in vapour tests.[758]

In homes in Indiana, resin strip (240 cm² containing 20 per cent dichlorvos) was used per 30 m³ of room. Adult cockroaches were introduced in wire cages the day after the strips were installed. The insects were exposed on walls and hidden in such places as desk drawers. Tests were also made in air conditioned rooms. Only where rooms were unventilated was successful control achieved. One strip (of 160 cm²) per 6 m³ did not kill all cockroaches in well-ventilated rooms with a 2-day exposure (Table LXXXIV). Resin strips (one to 3–6 m³) reduced infestations of *B. germanica* to 5 per cent or less in three months in apartments in New Haven, Connecticut.[585]

Smittle & Burden[758] also exposed cockroaches to dichlorvos vapour when the insects were in Kraft paper bags with twisted tops, and in rolls of corrugated cardboard, with the ends covered to simulate cockroach harbourages. Much longer periods in dichlorvos vapour, or higher concentrations, were needed to kill the insects compared with cockroaches freely exposed (Table LXXXV). In most tests, mortality was reduced by more than half, by placing the insects in bags or boxes: this confirms that sufficient amounts of dichlorvos vapour are unlikely to penetrate the hiding places of cockroaches in buildings to provide adequate control. Far greater amounts are needed from slow release products than the established tolerance of dichlorvos in air to humans allows.

Seven weeks after treatment of enclosed kitchen cabinets (with dichlorvos ministrips at a rate of 7 cm²/m³), 75–90 per cent of German cockroaches were dead. The strips were attached to the tops of the back panels. Initially, these liberated 0·6–1·25 μg/l, the emission reducing with time. At the end of 12 weeks, about half the number of cockroaches were still living in the cabinets despite efforts to control them by other means in other parts of the kitchens. Treatment of the cabinets with dichlorvos, clearly did not keep cockroaches out.[866]

In similar tests in the U.K., in which strips were cut and passed through drilled holes into the dead spaces of buffet counters, inconclusive results were obtained: 'judged by the spasmodic yet continued appearance of one or two cockroaches (*B. germanica*) following application of a pyrethrins aerosol, complete control had not been effected, although one could never be certain if the cockroaches so disturbed were residents or wandering visitors. Whereas dichlorvos even at a high local concentration cannot be relied on to eliminate cockroach infestation, it has a valuable contribution to make as a population depressant'.[103]

Use of dichlorvos aerosols
In some countries, and the U.S.A. is an example, pest control operators have been known to add small amounts of dichlorvos to other insecticides for cockroach control. This is to impart better knockdown properties and flushing action to residual sprays. In this respect, dichlorvos is not as good as pyrethrins. However, dichlorvos has become a popular ingredient of aerosols from which the emission, as droplets, tends to give better performance against cockroaches than the vapour.

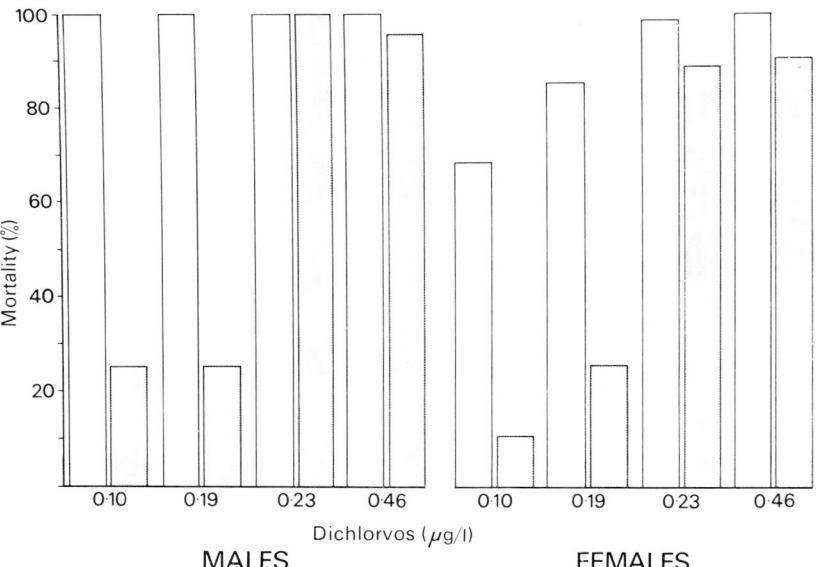

Fig. 141. Mortality (per cent) after 24 hours of susceptible (unshaded) and chlordane-resistant (shaded) *B. germanica* exposed to various concentrations of dichlorvos vapour for 4 hours. (From Russell & Frishman[718]).

TABLE LXXXV

MORTALITY (%) OF AMERICAN AND GERMAN COCKROACHES TO VAPOUR CONCENTRATIONS OF DICHLORVOS WHEN THE INSECTS ARE FREELY EXPOSED (UNCOVERED) AND WHEN CONTAINED IN PAPER BAGS AND CORRUGATED BOXES AT 27–29°C
(From Smittle & Burden[758])

Concentration	Species	Uncovered	In bags	In boxes
0·25 µg/l for 48 hr	P. americana	60	0	10
	B. germanica	98	90	2
1·04 µg/l for 24 hr	P. americana	100	60	10
	B. germanica	96	26	12

It is a common experience within the pest control industry to have a request to treat various forms of transport; ships, aircraft, vehicles and the accommodation of trains (Fig. 142). The requirement is usually: (1) that the insecticide shall not affect structural or electrical components (especially of aircraft[59]); (2) that the transport shall be available for treatment only on a specified date; and (3) that treatment shall not interfere with published schedules. Under these circumstances, the contact action of dichlorvos for control of crawling insects and vapour action against flying insects is useful. High volatility of the insecticide allows it to disperse rapidly when treatment is complete.

Specially developed aerosols containing 5 per cent dichlorvos were tested on buses commonly used in inter-city routes in the U.S.A. The volume of the vehicles is about 90 m^3 and they contain many places where German cockroaches can live: the seats, the lavatory, various small compartments by the driver's seat and the air-conditioning ducts. Food is often carried and eaten by many passengers and pieces dropped become available to cockroaches (Fig. 143).

Pest cockroaches were exposed in test containers in various parts of buses and one or two 100g aerosols released in the main aisle. Exposures of 45–60 minutes, while buses were being serviced between journeys, were sufficient to give good cockroach control.[293]

In another form of transport—U.S. Navy submarines—control of German cockroaches was investigated using an aerosol containing 6·5 per cent dichlorvos applied at 1·2 g/m^3. Treatment was supported with 2 per cent propoxur bait. First, all voids were opened and the ventilation system turned off. A 2·7 per cent pyrethrin aerosol was used just prior to releasing the dichlorvos to flush cockroaches from their harbourages. This made the insects more vulnerable to the dichlorvos which was directed into their harbourages. The submarines were kept closed for 2 hours before ventilating for 1 hour.

This treatment could best be described as fumigation. Not surprisingly it

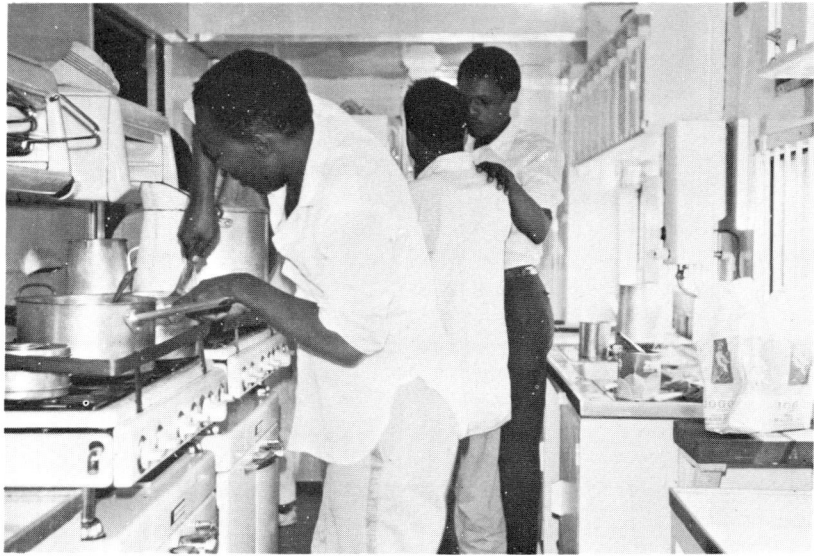

Fig. 142. Galley and dining car accommodation (East African Railways) where a tropical environment, high cooking temperatures, food residues, and harbourages behind panelling, encourage infestations of cockroaches. Regular treatment reduces the problem. (Nairobi, Kenya).

produced good results, with 97–100 per cent control after 24 hours. The propoxur bait was used to control nymphs hatching from the egg cases which survived the treatment with dichlorvos.[595]

Spray applications
Sprays of dichlorvos are normally applied at 0·5 per cent and are best used for the spot treatment of areas infested by cockroaches. Applied in this way, they have most value in reducing heavy infestations (providing a 'clean out'), which may subsequently need to be treated further with other, longer-lasting insecticidal formulations.

The LD_{50} of dichlorvos when applied topically to *P. americana* (laboratory strain) is 0·66 μg/g for males and 2·17 μg/g for females. About the same susceptibility and sex difference was found in a field strain collected in San Paulo.[557] Doses for 95 per cent kill are 2–3 times higher.

The oral toxicity to American cockroaches—important in respect of insecticide removed from the cuticle during grooming—is greater for dichlorvos than for seven other insecticides, including dieldrin and chlordane (Fig. 127).

Because of the short residual activity of dichlorvos on surfaces (Fig. 144) sub-lethal quantities are unlikely to cause selection for resistance among crawling insects. However, not unexpectedly, cross-resistance does occur among insects selected to other organophosphates. With flying insects there is the possibility of resistance developing among populations exposed for extended periods, to the non-lethal concentrations of slow-release dispensers.

Toxicity to man and animals
The acute oral toxicity of dichlorvos is relatively high: LD_{50} (rat) 60–80 mg/kg; dog 100–300 mg/kg. The acute dermal LD_{50} (rat) in arachis oil is 75–110 mg/kg: carriers which dissolve fats, such as xylene, aid penetration. Dichlorvos, at normally used concentrations, is not irritant to the skin; neither does the vapour affect the nasal membranes or eyes. Inhalation of 30 mg/l can be fatal to some rats in 5 hours. The accepted safe exposure to dichlorvos for humans, established by the American Conference of Government Industrial Hygienists (1960) is 1 μg/l of air for a maximum of 8 hours per day.[17] At dosage levels of 18–72 μg/l no symptoms of intoxication were noted in human volunteers who spent eight hours a day in this atmosphere, or in rats and monkeys confined continuously.[21]

Dichlorvos is potentiated by other organophosphorus insecticides, including diazinon and malathion. Symptoms of poisoning are typical of other organophosphates and include increased perspiration, miosis, lacrimation, salivation, headache, blurred vision, nausea, cramp, diarrhoea and dyspnoea. These usually occur within 2 hours of exposure and in severe cases may be followed by convulsions.

Dichlorvos is very unstable in mammalian tissues and is broken down by enzymes (esterases) to dichloracetaldehyde.[175] The process of degradation involves hydrolysis to non-toxic compounds which are excreted in the urine and faeces. The compound formed by interaction of dichlorvos with mammalian

Fig. 143. Transport is often implicated in the spread of infestation: (top) one of a fleet of vehicles used by a meat distributing company for its products, poorly maintained in the carrying section with corroded metal partitioning and flooring. The vehicles were treated regularly to reduce the risk of cockroaches establishing in the crevices (Dar-es-Salaam, Tanzania); (bottom) public transport is essential for communication in large cities. A characteristic of tropical countries is the large volume of personal effects carried by each passenger, with the possible unwitting transport of cockroaches and their establishment in the fabric of the vehicle (Kampala, Uganda). The quick 'airing-off' of dichlorvos makes it most suitable for the treament of vehicles.

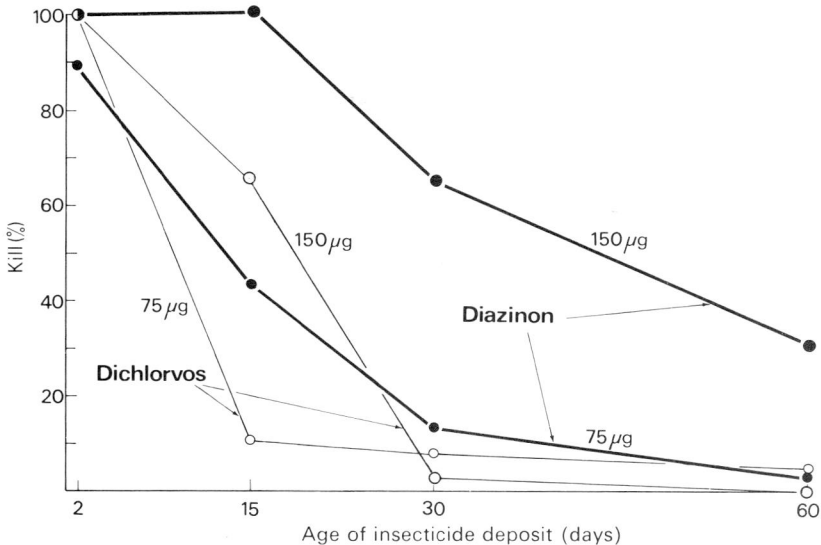

Fig. 144. Kill (per cent) of adult female *B. germanica* exposed for 24 hours to masonite panels treated with oil formulations of diazinon and dichlorvos at 150 μg and 75 μg/ft². (From Grayson & Townsend[372]).

acetylcholinesterase is unstable, but in insects the hydrolysis of this compound proceeds only slowly, imparting some selective action against susceptible insects.

The high volatility of dichlorvos, its short persistence and rapid degradation make this insecticide unlikely to be implicated as an environmental contaminant. It is sparingly soluble in water and toxicity to fish is lower than many other insecticides: the LC_{50} (24-hour) for trout is 500 μg/l compared with 8 μg/l for DDT and 100 μg/l for malathion. Other fish are more susceptible. Dichlorvos is not phytotoxic. Bees are highly susceptible.

Recommended uses

Considerable variation in permitted uses of insecticides in different countries makes it almost impossible to give meaningful and useful information on this subject. Notwithstanding geographical variations, legislation on approved uses of pesticides is subject to rapid change, such that recommendations for safe use now, may be different by the time this book is published.

Extensive use in the home of slow release products containing dichlorvos has brought this insecticide forcibly into the lime-light, with critical studies for adverse effects on man (including mutagenic and carcinogenic properties) being made.[62, 244] It has also been examined carefully as a possible contaminant of foodstuffs. Up to 1970, dichlorvos enjoyed liberal use by the pest control service industry in the U.S.A., but in that year, labelling changes restricted application near food. Resulting from this, resin strips were no longer permitted in kitchens and other areas where food is prepared or sold. Sprays of dichlorvos containing the active ingredient alone, or as an addition, also became unacceptable by the new labelling in commercial food preparation areas (of restaurants and hotels) and edible product areas of food processing plants. Eating areas of restaurants, food warehouses, and the dining rooms and kitchens of homes were excluded.

In tests for residues, in which unwrapped foods (milk, butter, cheese, meat, bread and water) were exposed to spray applications of 1–25 mg a.i./m^3, residues remained below 0·5 ppm with concentrations up to 4 mg/m^3 and below 1 ppm with 12 mg/m^3. This was so, when the ratio of surface area to bulk of the foods was not unduly exaggerated and spray was not directed onto them. Fatty products contain higher residues than fat-free or dry materials. Fat-containing products lose their insecticide content more slowly than others upon ventilation. The dissipation of dichlorvos in cereals of high moisture content is due to chemical breakdown. Cooking processes reduce residues by 80–100 per cent.[42]

MALATHION

This insecticide is another ester of phosphoric acid and was introduced by American Cyanamid in 1950. At that time, malathion was alone among commercially available insecticides (except for the pyrethrins) in having a low mammalian toxicity. It was therefore often quoted as an example, of what might otherwise have seemed to be the rule, that high toxicity is not intrinsic to organophosphorus insecticides. There are now, of course, many additional low toxicity organophosphates. The properties and uses of malathion in agriculture have been reviewed.[826]

The early malathion which became available to the pest control industry had a highly objectionable, mercaptan-like odour. This problem—caused by the presence of sulphur in its structure has now been largely solved by the manufacture of premium grade malathion.

Chemical, physical and insecticidal properties

Technical malathion is a light amber liquid, miscible with many organic solvents but not with odourless kerosene. It is not very volatile, is slightly soluble in water (145 ppm) and is stable to light. However, malathion residues on plants outdoors are rapidly lost: temperature, sunlight and rainfall all influence rate of breakdown. Certain plants and fruits are susceptible to damage. Degradation is rapid on alkaline surfaces but previous washing can extend the activity of deposits.[642] The insecticide is stable to weak acids but is degraded in contact with copper, iron, tin, lead and aluminium.

Malathion is available in all the commonly used formulations and has been combined with many of the early chlorinated insecticides, such as DDT, chlordane and methoxychlor. Considerable tonnages of the insecticide (as

TABLE LXXXVI

KILL (% AT 48 HOURS) OF GERMAN COCKROACHES EXPOSED FOR SHORT PERIODS TO MALATHION AND OTHER INSECTICIDES APPLIED AS WETTABLE POWDERS TO HARDBOARD AND AGED AT 25°C FOR 1 AND 4 WEEKS
(Cornwell, unpublished)

Insecticide	Application rate (mg/ft^2)	Ageing period (weeks)			
		1		4	
		Exposure period (mins)			
		0·5	2	4	16
Iodofenphos	90	100	100	100	100
	45	100	100	100	100
Fenitrothion	90	100	100	100	100
	45	100	100	30	45
Malathion	90	53	67	8	15
	45	0	10	12	22

(90 and 45 mg/ft² = sprays of 2 per cent and 1 per cent applied at 1 gal/1,000 ft²).

Cython®) have been used for the control of stored food pests, notably insects of cereals, to kill existing infestations and as a grain protectant. It has featured in the small package trade as a component of aerosol formulations (5–10 per cent) and often with pybuthrin for fly control. A concentrated aqueous emulsion of malathion with a fairly high content of sugar has been used as fly bait.

Provided sufficient co-solvent is used, malathion can be incorporated into deodorised kerosene, to give solutions (2 per cent) for thermal fogging indoors. Dusts (1–3 per cent) have been incorporated into many household products, but for this purpose premium grade is essential. Dusts have also been used to control poultry mite, and sprays to control parasites on pigs (lice), sheep, cats and dogs. All the formulations have had wide application in crop protection.

The relatively low mammalian toxicity of malathion has made it suitable for indoor use to control flies, mosquitoes, ants, silverfish, carpet beetles, moths attacking textiles, bedbugs and cockroaches. An emulsion (60 per cent) has been most popular, but to control many of these insects a 3 per cent ready to use spray is necessary. A knockdown agent is commonly incorporated in malathion sprays in the U.S.A.

Cython® is a trade mark of Cyanamid for premium grade deodorised malathion.

Effectiveness against cockroaches

The performance of malathion against cockroaches is not remarkable. Odour, and the need for concentrations of ready to use sprays higher than those of other products both detract from the wide-scale use of malathion as a preferred insecticide for cockroach control.

In tests of wettable powders applied to hardboard and aged for up to 4 weeks, malathion at 2 per cent, gives poor performance against adult German cockroaches even after 1 week, and at 1 per cent is almost without effect (Table LXXXVI). When adults are confined for very short periods to dusts, which are readily picked up from the rough surface of hardboard, malathion (at 1 per cent) immediately after application, performs better than boric acid (at 99 per cent) but not as well as fenitrothion (0·5 per cent) (Table LXXXVII).

TABLE LXXXVII

KILL (% AT 48 HOURS) OF GERMAN COCKROACHES EXPOSED FOR SHORT PERIODS TO DUSTS (30 g/m^2) OF MALATHION AND OTHER INSECTICIDES APPLIED EVENLY TO THE ROUGH SURFACE OF HARDBOARD

(Cornwell, unpublished)

Insecticide	Concentration (%)	Exposure period (mins)	
		1	4
Fenitrothion	1	100	100
	0·5	100	100
Malathion	1	95	93
	0·5	75	98
Boric acid	99	47	65

Adult German cockroaches given the chance of remaining in untreated harbourages with food and water, but also of straying into identical harbourages treated with various insecticidal dusts were killed equally by 2 per cent malathion and 1 per cent fenitrothion. Both were more effective than 1 per cent lindane and in the first week, more effective than 99 per cent boric acid. The boric acid was, however, the least repellent and gave better kill than all three synthetic insecticides from 1 to 6 weeks (Fig. 145).

The topical LD$_{50}$ of malathion to German and American cockroaches is 120 and 8·4 μg/g, respectively. *P. americana* reared on a protein-rich diet[57] are more tolerant of malathion (9 mg/kg) compared with insects reared on carbohydrate (7 mg/kg). Malathion penetrates insect cuticle very rapidly. Radioactive malathion applied topically in acetone accumulates in the cuticle of the American cockroach and appears to saturate it before passing into the body of the insect. Abrasion of the cuticle, by gently pressing cockroaches onto filter paper dusted with talc,[530] increases the permeability of the cockroach cuticle by a further 50 per cent.

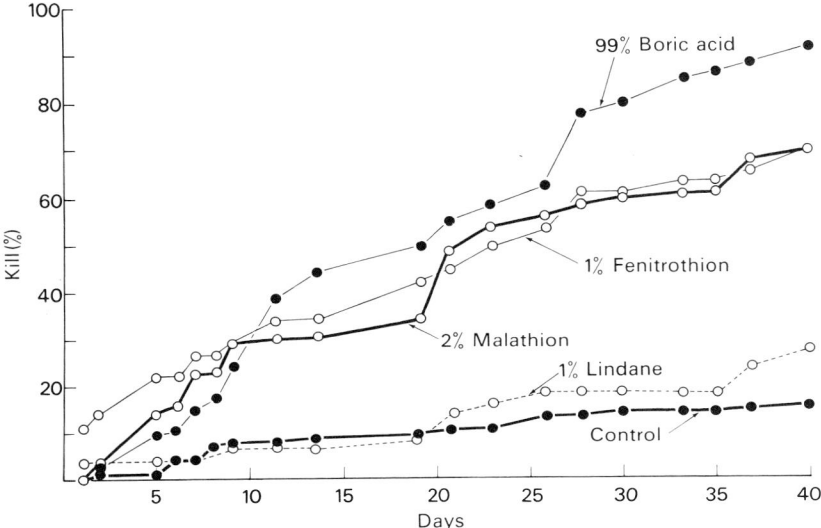

Fig. 145. Kill (per cent) of adult German cockroaches allowed access to treated and untreated harbourages in choice tests. Treated harbourages were dusted with formulated insecticide at 30 g/m². Food and water were provided in the untreated harbourages. (Cornwell, unpublished).

During the course of poisoning by malathion there is a reduction in blood volume in the cockroach. Evidence suggests that most of the water loss occurs *via* the spiracles and intersegmental membranes. When German cockroaches are poisoned by a dose which is lethal in 7 hours, reduction in blood volume is gradual up to 4 hours and then rises sharply when knockdown begins (Fig. 146). There is no evidence that fluid is redistributed between blood and the gut. A loss in wet weight of 70 per cent of the poisoned cockroach appears to be due directly to increased transpiration of the paralysed insect. Artificial blockage of the abdominal spiracles cuts water loss by 25 per cent compared with insects having open spiracles.[522]

Resistance to malathion has been reported among German cockroaches in the United States (Chapter 15), but appears to be of little practical significance at present in the use of malathion and other organophosphates for cockroach control. As with other insects, the inheritance pattern of malathion resistance appears to be the transfer from parent to offspring of a simple dominant character, probably for increased enzyme activity (carboxyesterase), making the resistant insect more capable of detoxifying malathion.[196]

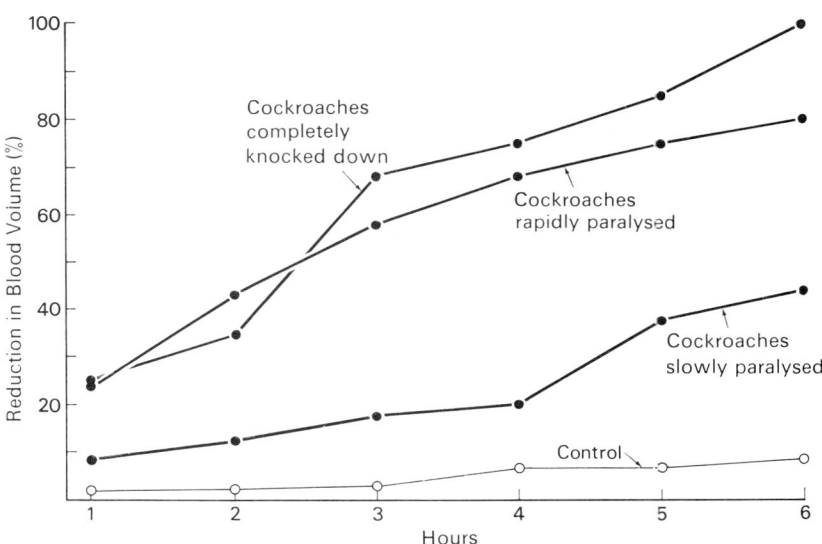

Fig. 146. Reduction in blood volume of male German cockroaches: (a) slowly paralysed by malathion-poisoning with knockdown occurring at about 5 hours; (b) rapidly paralysed with knockdown occurring at about 2 hours, and (c) of cockroaches completely knocked down. (Data from Mansingh[522]).

Toxicity to man and animals

In common with other organophosphorus insecticides, the pharmacological action of malathion is the inhibition of acetylcholinesterase, and a significant depression of this enzyme may exist long after gross evidence of toxicity has disappeared. In volunteer tests, 5 men took 16 mg of malathion daily for 47 days without effect on activity of plasma- or red blood cell cholinesterase. A daily dose of 24 mg for 56 days depressed the activity of plasma cholinesterase, the maximum depression (25 per cent of normal) occurring three weeks after administration ceased. The acceptable daily 'intake' of malathion by man is estimated to be below 0·02 mg/kg.

The acute oral LD_{50} (rat) for malathion most often quoted is 1,500 mg/kg, but as insecticide of higher purity is produced the value increases: 5,000 mg/kg has been obtained for male rats for 99 per cent technical malathion. The insecticide is not readily absorbed through the skin.

In feeding tests for short periods (33 days) diets containing up to 5,000 ppm of 95 per cent technical malathion produced no gross signs of toxicity in rats referable to inhibition of acetylcholinesterase: food intake and weight gain by the test animals was the same as controls (Table LXXXVIII). Over longer periods (2-year chronic tests involving repeated-feeding), few untoward symptoms of toxicity occurred at high concentrations: 5,000 ppm did not affect food intake, growth or survival, but red blood cell cholinesterase was markedly depleted.[418] The level of malathion which causes no significant toxicological effect in the diet of the rat is 100 ppm (= 5 mg/kg body weight per day). Malathion is rapidly absorbed from the intestinal tract where it is oxidised to the active form of the compound (malaoxon) and hydrolysed to less active metabolites. The allowable residue tolerance in foods (permitted under the Miller Pesticide Chemicals Amendment: U.S. Public Law 518) is 8 ppm.

TABLE LXXXVIII

EFFECT OF 33 DAILY DOSES OF MALATHION (95% TECHNICAL) FED TO MALE ALBINO RATS
(From Golz & Shaffer[342])

Conc. in diet (ppm)	0	100	1,000	5,000
Average dose (mg/kg/day)	—	10	90	470
Average food intake (g/rat/day)	14·7	16·5	16·0	15·4
Average weight gain (g/rat)	127	154	147	124
Cholinesterase activity as average per cent of control at end of test				
Plasma	—	94	94	78
Red blood cell	—	93	68	22

CHLORPYRIFOS

Chlorpyrifos is a relatively new organophosphorus insecticide, better known as Dursban®, introduced by Dow Chemical Co. in 1966. Much interest is now being expressed in its use for cockroach control in the United States, where somewhat better performance has been obtained than with other commonly-used organophosphates.[842] Dursban and Dowco 214 (chlorpyrifos-methyl) are closely related insecticides with very similar properties.[761]

Chemical and physical properties
Technical chlorpyrifos is a white crystalline solid with a mild sulphide odour which does not cause a problem in ready to use formulations. Its volatility is low ($1·87 \times 10^{-5}$ mm Hg at 25°C) but some vapour action is claimed.

Chlorpyrifos is soluble in most organic solvents but it does not dissolve in water (2 ppm only). It is unstable on alkaline surfaces and corrodes copper and brass. Chlorpyrifos can be mixed without difficulty with knockdown agents such as pyrethrins[394] and dichlorvos, to increase speed of action. Effectiveness is claimed against a wide range of flying and crawling insects. Formulations available include emulsion concentrates.

Effectiveness against cockroaches

In the WHO test for resistance the LT_{50} for chlorpyrifos is about the same as for diazinon.[180] Chlorpyrifos kills a little more slowly than diazinon (Table CXI), but has longer residual activity. In the laboratory, chlorpyrifos at 0·25 per cent is more effective against German cockroaches than diazinon,[761] although a higher concentration (0·5 per cent) is more likely to be required to control infestations.

At the Virginia Polytechnic Institute, chlorpyrifos in oil proved effective for 30 days in tests with German cockroaches resistant to diazinon and to malathion. In infested buildings, chlorpyrifos performs as well as propoxur, although the former has no flushing action and dead cockroaches are often not seen for four or more days.[627]

In tests by the U.S. Dept. of Agriculture, the LT_{50} of a laboratory strain of *B. germanica* exposed to chlorpyrifos on glass (5 mg/930 cm^2) was 57 minutes, whereas for propoxur, at a lower rate (1 mg/930 cm^2) it was only 19 minutes.[143] By topical application, the LD_{95} (24 hour) of chlorpyrifos is 9·3 µg/g to nymphs of *P. americana* and 3·3 µg/g to adult *B. germanica*.

By the CSMA cockroach spray method, oil formulations of chlorpyrifos perform slightly better than other commonly-used insecticides (Table LXXXIX). The kill of American cockroaches on treated surfaces is about as good with chlorpyrifos (in acetone) as propoxur after four weeks, and better than other organophosphates (Table LXXV). Chlorpyrifos dust applied at 11 mg of active ingredient/m^2, killed the three species of cockroach tested: half of adult male German cockroaches were knocked down in 120 minutes at 27°C, compared with 125 minutes for nymphs of *S. longipalpa* and 210 minutes for nymphs of *P. americana*.[481] Dusts containing 0·25 per cent chlorpyrifos were more effective against Brown-banded cockroaches than the other species.

TABLE LXXXIX

RELATIVE TOXICITY OF CHLORPYRIFOS AND OTHER INSECTICIDES APPLIED TO *B. GERMANICA*, AS SHOWN BY THE CSMA COCKROACH SPRAY METHOD
(Data from Kenaga, Whitney, Hardy & Doty[481])

Insecticide	(% wt/vol) LD_{50}	LD_{90}
Chlorpyrifos	0·032	0·05
Diazinon	0·028	0·10
Chlordane	0·06	0·14
Malathion	0·28	1·55

An extensive study by Japanese workers shows chlorpyrifos to be one of the most toxic of insecticides to German, American and Smokey-brown cockroaches (*P. fuliginosa*), with Dowco-214 the most effective against adult males of *B. germanica* (Fig. 147). German cockroaches exposed for short periods on treated plywood readily succumbed to Dowco-214; on treated glass, however, Dowco-214 was least satisfactory[483] (Fig. 148).

A comparison of the performance of chlorpyrifos with fenitrothion as wettable powders and oil sprays (Fig. 137), indicates the shorter persistence of chlorpyrifos.

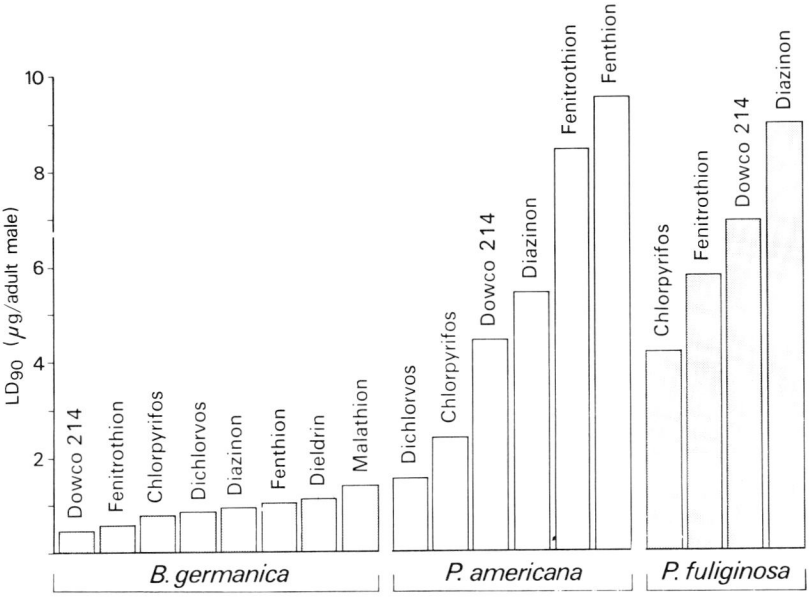

Fig. 147. The activity (LD_{90}) of chlorpyrifos and Dowco-214 in comparison with other insecticides, against three pest cockroaches by topical application at 25°C and 60 per cent R.H. (From Kitagaki, Nakayama, Sugiyama & Sakamoto[483]).

The real value of an insecticide is best demonstrated under field conditions, although its actual performance, in terms of percentage control, is more difficult to measure. Chlorpyrifos as 0·5 per cent and 0·25 per cent emulsions produced good results against German cockroaches in 18 Florida homes: the higher concentration reduced infestation by 97–99 per cent over 12 weeks; the lower gave 91–99 per cent reduction. From experience in the use of other insecticides under these conditions, chlorpyrifos (at 0·5 per cent) was said to perform better than diazinon (0·5 per cent), malathion (2 per cent) or propoxur (1 per cent).[144]

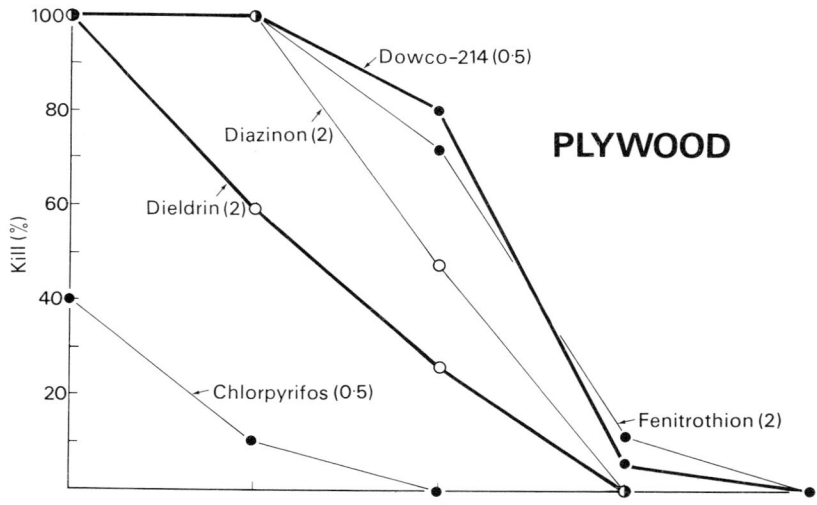
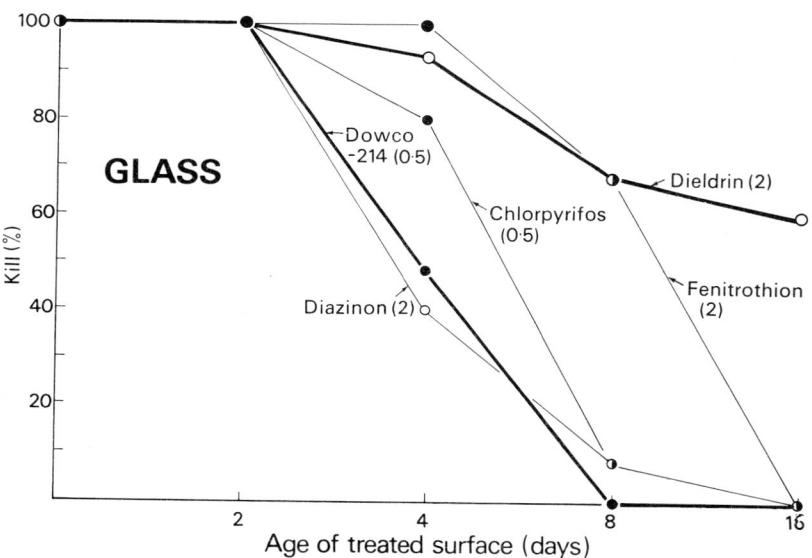

Fig. 148. Residual effectiveness of chlorpyrifos and Dowco-214 applied at 0·5 mg/100 cm² compared with other commonly used insecticides at 2 mg/100 cm² against adult male *B. germanica*. Insecticides applied to plywood (top) and to glass (bottom). (From Kitagaki, Nakayama, Sugiyama & Sakamoto[483]).

Toxicity to man and other animals

The acute oral LD_{50} (rat) of chlorpyrifos is 145 mg/kg, but it is more toxic to poultry (chicks; 32 mg/kg). The dermal toxicity is low and inhalation risks to man are believed to be no greater than when using diazinon.

The acute oral LD_{50} (rat) of Dowco-214 (chlorpyrifos-methyl) lies between 1,000 and 3,000 mg/kg for female rats. The toxicological data for the rat and other animals indicate that this insecticide presents a much lower risk to mammals than chlorpyrifos.

FENITROTHION

This insecticide is a relatively new, low toxicity organophosphate, discovered in 1959 by Sumitomo, Japan (Fig. 149). In some countries it may be better known by the trade name Sumithion®. Its chemical structure closely resembles that of parathion—a well known, highly toxic insecticide—one of the first organophosphates to be used commercially. Parathion is extremely limited in its application, but fenitrothion is currently one of the most promising insecticides for the control of a wide range of insects, on livestock, agricultural crops, in grain storage and of public health importance. It has excellent properties for the control of pest cockroaches.

Chemical and physical properties

Fenitrothion is a relatively non-volatile liquid (vapour pressure 6×10^{-6} mm Hg at 20°C). It is miscible with most organic solvents but not readily with odourless kerosene, and is practically insoluble in water. It has a slight odour. Contact of fenitrothion formulations with alkaline surfaces causes them to turn brown. Contact with iron causes gelation of liquid formulations. The insecticide is stable to light and compatible with most other commonly used pesticides. Emulsion concentrates and wettable powders (up to 50 per cent) and ready to use oil and dust formulations (1–3 per cent) are commercially available. Lacquers incorporating fenitrothion discolour rapidly and have not been marketed.

Effectiveness against cockroaches

Between 1969 and 1972 Rentokil service staff used fenitrothion, almost exclusively, to control cockroaches in temperate and tropical countries. The formulations were principally wettable powder and dust at 2 per cent. The success achieved confirmed much of the earlier laboratory data, demonstrating high initial activity, reasonably rapid kill and good insecticidal persistence on treated surfaces. An assessment by service staff of trial quantities of fenitrothion in various formulations, indicated good performance and use acceptance by operators and clients compared with previously used propoxur formulations (Table XC).

Fenitrothion applied topically to German cockroaches is equi-toxic with dursban and twice as insecticidal as diazinon (Table LXIX). Male German cockroaches succumb to the same amounts of fenitrothion and propoxur, but

TABLE XC

ASSESSMENT BY RENTOKIL SERVICE MANAGERS (U.K.) OF FENITROTHION FORMULATIONS, IN TRIALS USE, COMPARED WITH PREVIOUSLY USED PROPOXUR FORMULATIONS. A BORIC ACID DUST WAS ALSO ASSESSED AGAINST A PROPOXUR DUST
(Cornwell, unpublished)

Assessment	Fenitrothion formulations	No. of reports of comparison with propoxur		
		Better than	As good as	Worse than
Effectiveness against cockroaches	Oil spray	3	11	4
	Emulsion spray	2	11	5
	Wettable powder	2	11	6
	Boric acid dust	2	6	8
Ease of use by operators	Oil spray	4	14	0
	Emulsion spray	7	12	0
	Wettable powder	3	14	2
	Boric acid dust	0	5	12
Acceptance by clients	Oil spray	5	13	0
	Emulsion spray	4	15	0
	Wettable powder	3	15	0
	Boric acid dust	1	12	2
Total score	Fenitrothion formulations	33	114	17
	Boric acid dust	3	23	22

females are killed by half the amount of fenitrothion. It is about as toxic as diazinon to Oriental cockroaches whilst dursban and propoxur are superior against this species. Fenitrothion applied topically[315] is fifteen times more toxic to *B. germanica* (0·32 μg/adult) than to *P. fuliginosa* (4·7 μg/adult).

Whether or not these differences in insecticidal toxicity, measured in the laboratory, apply also to commercially formulated products, depends on the experience and skill in developing them for the pest control market. Availability of the insecticide to the insect by easy pick-up from treated surfaces, is absolutely essential for good insecticidal action. Thus in tests involving a comparison of wettable powders of fenitrothion and dursban to Oriental cockroaches, fenitrothion showed far better initial kill and performance up to four weeks

TABLE XCI

KILL (%) OF ORIENTAL COCKROACHES EXPOSED FOR 4 AND 12 MINUTES TO VARIOUS INSECTICIDES APPLIED AS WETTABLE POWDERS ON HARDBOARD. TREATED SURFACES WERE AGED FOR 1 AND 4 WEEKS AT 25°C AND 65% RH BEFORE TEST
(Cornwell, unpublished)

Insecticide applied at 90 mg/ft^2	Age of deposit (weeks)			
	1		4	
	Exposure period (mins)			
	4	12	4	12
Fenitrothion	100	100	100	93
Dursban	60	73	5	13
Lindane	35	45	5	8

(Table XCI), undoubtedly because of poorer pick-up of dursban. However good an insecticide is, poor residual toxicity will be obtained if the cockroach is unable to contaminate itself with insecticide from treated surfaces.

Wettable powders aged for 6 weeks before test against German cockroaches also showed the superiority of fenitrothion over propoxur and diazinon when 1 per cent sprays were used. At 2 per cent all three insecticides performed well (Table XCII).

TABLE XCII

KILL (% AT 48 HOURS) OF GERMAN COCKROACHES EXPOSED FOR SHORT PERIODS TO HARDBOARD SPRAYED WITH WETTABLE POWDERS (AT 1 gal/1,000 ft^2) AGED FOR 1 AND 6 WEEKS AT 25°C
(Cornwell, unpublished)

Concentration of spray	Insecticide	Exposure period (mins)			
		4		8	
		Ageing period (weeks)			
		1	6	1	6
2%	Fenitrothion	100	100	100	100
	Propoxur	100	100	100	100
	Diazinon	100	75	100	95
1%	Fenitrothion	100	60	100	20
	Propoxur	75	0	85	0
	Diazinon	5	0	0	0

Fig. 149. Manufacture (above) and shipment (right) of fenitrothion from Sumitomo's plant in Japan. (Courtesy: Sumitomo.)

In longer term tests, oil sprays on glass and wettable powders on hardboard demonstrate the superiority of fenitrothion, compared with dursban and diazinon, against *B. germanica,* when treated surfaces are aged for up to 14 weeks (Fig. 137). If adult German cockroaches are given the choice of entering harbourages, only half of which are treated with dusts, 1 per cent fenitrothion performs about as well as 2 per cent malathion (Fig. 145).

Strains of German cockroach taken from infested ships succumbed equally to fenitrothion and to propoxur when tested in the laboratory. They are not killed so readily by diazinon (Table XCIII).

Toxicity to man and animals
The acute oral LD_{50} (rat) of fenitrothion is about the same as diazinon (250–400 mg/kg). The acute dermal toxicity is reported greater than 3,000 mg/kg. Like other organophosphorus insecticides, fenitrothion does not ac-

cumulate in the body. Mice given fenitrothion by mouth at the rate of 80 mg/kg daily, survive for 4 weeks without symptoms, or effects on growth. Rats fed up to 160 ppm of fenitrothion in the diet for 16 weeks show normal weight gains, but a drop in plasma and blood cell cholinesterase (Table XCIV). The mammalian and insecticidal toxicity of fenitrothion derives from its inhibitory action on cholinesterase, not directly, but by 'oxo-sumithion' formed by enzymic oxidation of fenitrothion in the body.

TABLE XCIII

SUSCEPTIBILITY (LD_{50} μg/insect) OF MARINE STRAINS OF *B. GERMANICA* TO TOPICALLY APPLIED FENITROTHION, PROPOXUR AND DIAZINON
(Cornwell, unpublished)

Strain	Fenitrothion	Propoxur	Diazinon
Matra	0·62	0·60	1·10
Makrana	0·50	0·75	0·56
Neptune	0·46	0·58	0·70
Rangitoto	0·46	0·46	0·74
Nottingham	0·40	0·36	0·64
Benvraki	0·40	0·37	0·84
Average	0·47	0·52	0·76

TABLE XCIV

EFFECTS OF VARIOUS CONCENTRATIONS OF FENITROTHION IN THE DIET OF RATS FED FOR 16 WEEKS
(From Anon[20])

Treatment	Initial wt (g)	Final wt (g)	Increase (g)	Cholinesterase units	
				Plasma	Blood cell
Control	139·7	417·7	283·6	0·26	0·11
40 ppm	137·3	435·1	294·6	0·28	0·10
80 ppm	137·1	425·3	288·2	0·22	0·06
160 ppm	138·1	404·4	266·3	0·16	0·06

IODOFENPHOS

Iodofenphos is one of the newest insecticides to become available for the control of public health pests and is available under the Ciba-Geigy trade name Nuvanol N®. Its insecticidal properties were first described in 1969. It has excellent performance against some pest cockroaches, but not all. Iodofenphos offers promise for the protection of stored foodstuffs, as a residual insecticide for fly control and for the control of agricultural pests. A major advantage of iodofenphos compared with other insecticides is its wide spectrum of activity combined with low toxicity to man. It was for these reasons that Rentokil adopted formulations of iodofenphos for use in its pest control services in the U.K. in 1973.

Chemical and physical properties

Iodofenphos is closely related to the insecticide bromophos; the bromide atom being replaced by iodine. The technical product in pure form is crystalline and colourless, but the commercial product tends towards tan to purple, and the odour also varies with level of purity. Iodofenphos is relatively stable in weakly acid media but is unstable on alkaline surfaces. The insecticide is almost non-volatile (8×10^{-7} mm Hg at 20°C) and reaches only 0·0194 mg/m^3 in saturated air at 20°C. This extremely low volatility of iodofenphos (not unlike that of organochlorine insecticides) gives it a long residual life on treated surfaces, which is of great advantage when used against crawling insects.

Iodofenphos is insoluble in water (2 ppm), marginally soluble in odourless kerosene (2 per cent) but has better solubility in other common organic solvents.

In tests for possible taint, wheat was contaminated with iodofenphos at up to 48 ppm and the flour made into wholemeal bread. No off-odours were detected in the milled wheat, prepared doughs or in the hot or cold bread.

Organoleptic tests on the bread were also negative. The baking process reduced the iodofenphos content by two thirds.

The formulations of iodofenphos commercially available include an emulsion concentrate (20 per cent), wettable powder (50 per cent) and dust (5 per cent). This last concentration far exceeds that required in a ready to use dust for insect control indoors. A novel formulation—a 'suspension concentrate' of iodofenphos has been developed by Rentokil for service use (see Chapter 4), but this is not commercially available.

Both stomach and contact action is claimed for the insecticide against insects and mites. The recommended application rates (0·5–2 per cent) vary with the pest, somewhat higher concentrations (2–4 per cent) being used to control flies.

Effectiveness against cockroaches

Much laboratory work has been done to compare the insecticidal activity of iodofenphos with other compounds, especially with the relatively long-lived fenitrothion, and using a wide range of insects. For example, iodofenphos and fenitrothion are superior to lindane, malathion and bromophos in killing Rust-red and Saw-toothed grain beetles. Iodofenphos is notably more persistent than malathion on surfaces treated with wettable powders, when tested against Grain weevils.

There is very little published information on the efficacy of iodofenphos against cockroaches, but much test work has been done at Rentokil. Males of both Oriental and German cockroaches are more susceptible than females. Short exposures of adult cockroaches on hardboard treated with wettable powders show iodofenphos to have a far better residual life (up to 3 months) than fenitrothion (Table XCV). This may be because of better pick-up of iodofenphos from the treated surface.

TABLE XCV

KILL (% AT 48 HOURS) OF ADULT GERMAN COCKROACHES EXPOSED FOR 6 AND 24 MINS TO SPRAY DEPOSITS (1%) OF FENITROTHION AND IODOFENPHOS WETTABLE POWDERS ON HARDBOARD, AND AGED FOR 1 AND 3 MONTHS

(Cornwell, unpublished)

Age of deposit (45 mg/ft^2)	Sex	Fenitrothion		Iodofenphos	
		6	24	6	24
1 month	Male	23	38	100	100
	Female	45	60	100	100
3 months	Male	15	15	100	100
	Female	3	13	95	100

TABLE XCVI

KILL (% AT 48 HOURS) OF ADULT ORIENTAL COCKROACHES EXPOSED TO 4-HOUR-OLD DEPOSITS OF FENITROTHION AND IODOFENPHOS WETTABLE POWDERS AND IODOFENPHOS SUSPENSION CONCENTRATE FOR 0·5 AND 2 MINS ON TREATED HARDBOARD*

(Cornwell, unpublished)

Insecticide	Males		Females	
	0·5	2	0·5	2
Fenitrothion wettable powder (2%)	100	100	90	100
Iodofenphos wettable powder (1%)	80	90	45	20
Iodofenphos suspension concentrate (1%)	100	100	95	95

* 2% and 1% sprays applied at 1 gal/1,000 ft^2 = 90 and 45 mg a.i./ft^2

With extremely short exposures of up to 2 minutes, fenitrothion wettable powder applied at 2 per cent is more effective than iodofenphos wettable powder at 1 per cent, but about equal to iodofenphos (1 per cent) as a suspension concentrate (Table XCVI). The superiority of the suspension concentrate is noticeable against Oriental and German cockroaches (Table XCVII).

TABLE XCVII

KILL (% AT 48 HOURS) OF ADULT ORIENTAL AND GERMAN COCKROACHES EXPOSED TO 2-DAY-OLD DEPOSITS OF IODOFENPHOS WETTABLE POWDER AND IODOFENPHOS SUSPENSION CONCENTRATE ON HARDBOARD FOR LESS THAN 1 MINUTE (APPLICATION RATE 45 mg/ft^2 = A 1% SPRAY APPLIED AT 1 gal/1,000 ft^2)

(Cornwell, unpublished)

Formulation	Oriental		German	
	Males	Females	Males	Females
Wettable powder	48	8	98	94
Suspension concentrate	98	35	99	100

The speed of knockdown of cockroaches by iodofenphos is not as rapid as by fenitrothion (Fig. 150). There is however adequate experimental and field evidence to show that iodofenphos, as a 1 per cent spray of a suspension concentrate, is equal in effectiveness and persistence to fenitrothion wettable powder applied at 2 per cent (Fig. 151). This applies to infestations of German and Oriental cockroaches, but female American cockroaches are unfortunately considerably more tolerant of iodofenphos (Table XCVIII). No evaluations have been reported against other species of *Periplaneta*.

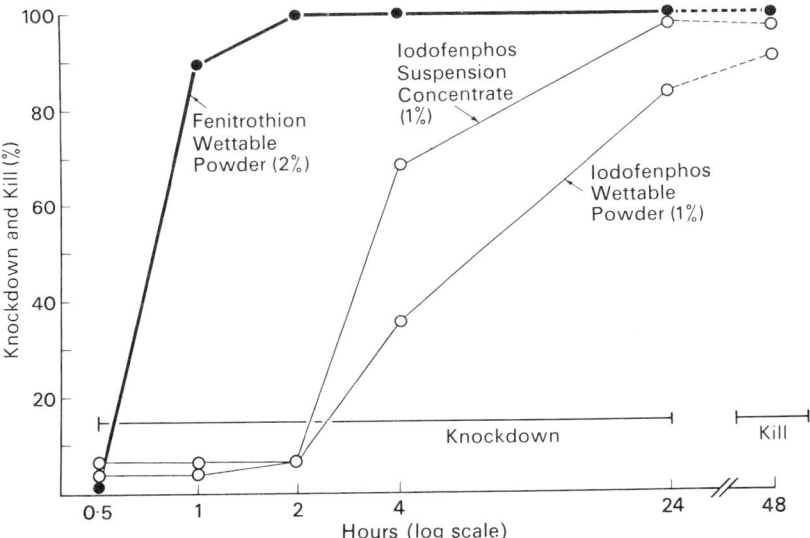

Fig. 150. Rate of knockdown and kill (per cent) of adult German cockroaches exposed for less than 30 seconds to 1-day old spray deposits of fenitrothion W.P. and iodofenphos W.P. and suspension concentrate. (Cornwell, unpublished).

An iodofenphos gel, developed for the control of Oriental and German cockroaches is as palatable to both species as chlordecone baits, when these contain 0·25 per cent of insecticide and are fed in competition with alternative food and water. Gels aged for 2 months remain as effective as fresh baits. This formulation of iodofenphos has not been marketed.

Toxicity to man and animals
Iodofenphos is of low toxicity to mammals: the oral LD_{50} (rat) is 2,100 mg/kg; it is 3,000 mg/kg to the mouse and dog. Dermal toxicities are lower and the insecticide is without irritant effect when 300 mg/kg is placed on the skin daily for three weeks. In feeding studies, 0·45 mg/kg daily in the diet for 90 days has no effect on the cholinesterase level of male rats and ten times this amount fails to produce clinical symptoms in females.

TABLE XCVIII

KILL (% AT 48 HOURS) OF ADULT *P. AMERICANA* EXPOSED FOR 1 AND 3 MINUTES TO 2-DAY-OLD SPRAY DEPOSITS OF FENITROTHION (2%) AND IODOFENPHOS (1%) ON HARDBOARD
(Cornwell, unpublished)

Insecticide formulation (a.i. applic. rate)	Exposure period (mins)			
	Males		Females	
	1	3	1	3
Fenitrothion wettable powder (90 mg/ft²)	100	100	100	100
Iodofenphos wettable powder (45 mg/ft²)	100	100	5	35
Iodofenphos suspension concentrate (45 mg/ft²)	95	90	0	0

Inhalation by rats of 242 mg/m³ of technical iodofenphos, 19 times for 6 hours daily, slightly reduced cholinesterase activity and produced mild clinical symptoms. Toxicity to fish varies with species: the tolerance limit in water to Goldfish exposed for 96 hours is about 1 ppm. Bees are highly susceptible (LD_{100} in 26 hours is 0·1 μg/bee).

TRICHLORPHON

The last organophosphorus insecticide to be mentioned here, has been used as a bait and spray. It is available commercially under the trade name Dipterex® from Bayer. It is not as effective against cockroaches as the more commonly used organophosphorus insecticides, but is useful where staining may be a problem, or lack of solvent odour is required. This is because trichlorphon, unlike most organophosphorus insecticides has an unusually high solubility in water (15 per cent).

Chemical and physical properties
Trichlorphon is a white to pale yellow crystalline solid with a faint, pleasant odour. The insecticide decomposes in water; solutions should therefore be freshly made up daily. It has no useful vapour action. Breakdown is rapid on alkaline surfaces, even on concrete.

Effectiveness against cockroaches
Trichlorphon is most effective as a stomach poison and is therefore best used as a bait for cockroach control. A mixture recommended for pest species of

Periplaneta includes:

>100 g of 80 per cent soluble Dipterex powder
>3 kg of cornmeal
>1 kg of powdered sugar

The concentration of insecticide in this bait is about 2 per cent.[628]

Admixture of trichlorphon with ammonium carbonate in baits increases their toxicity to cockroaches substantially. Against females, the LD_{50}'s of the insecticide with and (in brackets) without an equal part of ammonium carbonate were 16 mg/g (63) for a susceptible strain of *B. germanica*, 23 mg/g (82) for a resistant strain, and 2·2 mg/g (11) for *B. orientalis*.[61,754]

In laboratory and field tests, powdered sugar proved the most attractive to German cockroaches and dextrin with cornstarch, or cornmeal, was most attractive to *P. americana* (Table XCIX). In comparison with chlordecone, trichlorphon baits killed all *P. americana* in 15 days and *B. germanica* in 30 days. Chlordecone under the same conditions, was only 74 per cent and 92 per cent effective, respectively. Trichlorphon, however, has a much shorter life in baits.

In rooms and homes baits alone, containing trichlorphon, did not give satisfactory kill of German cockroaches. In homes, 1 per cent baits were effective in reducing *Periplaneta* spp. and 95 per cent kill of these was obtained in dairy barns.[508] Better control is likely to be achieved if baits are distributed widely rather than being placed as bait stations.

Sprays of trichlorphon do not last more than a week and have poor knockdown action.

Toxicity to man and animals

Trichlorphon has a low mammalian toxicity: acute LD_{50} (rat) of 500 mg/kg and extremely low dermal hazard. Cockroach baits are unlikely to present a risk to domestic animals: dogs fed 1,000 ppm of insecticide in the diet for 4 months showed no symptoms. Trichlorphon is potentiated by malathion and should therefore not be mixed with this insecticide. Acutely poisoned animals recover rapidly and completely.

In this chapter we have examined the properties and performance of a number of commonly used organophosphorus insecticides. In addition to the seven examined here, there are others (Ronnel® = fenchlorphos, Baytex® = fenthion and Dibrom® = naled), which have been used to a small extent to control cockroaches in the U.S.A. Had these been as efficient as the more commonly used organophosphates, they would no doubt have become more widely adopted.

One organophosphorus insecticide, not discussed in detail, but which appears to have good futured potential for cockroach control is acephate (Orthene®).[699,921] This is a product of Chevron Chem. Co., and its insecticidal properties were first described by Grayson[366] in 1972. The potential of this insecticide lies in its 65 per cent solubility in water at room temperature, combined with good contact activity against German cockroaches—unlike trichlorphon. Good water solubility can make an important contribution to minimising the cost of ready to use sprays, if emulsifiers and solvents can be dispensed with. Toxicity to mammals is also low: acute oral LD_{50} (rat), 850–1,000 mg/kg.

Trials against infestations of *B. germanica* on ships of the U.S. Navy have indicated good control by acephate alone (0·5–0·75 per cent) and when combined with dichlorvos (0·25 per cent) for periods of 5 weeks.[271] Control was better than by propoxur oil spray (1 per cent).

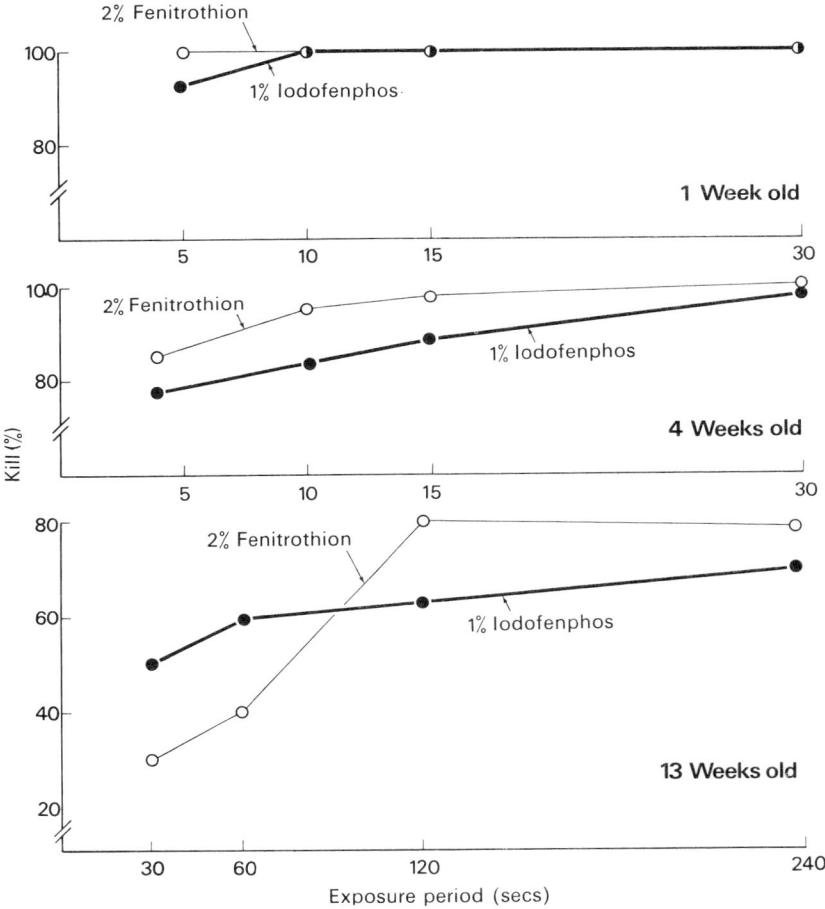

Fig. 151. The equal effectiveness and persistence of a 2 per cent spray of fenitrothion wettable powder (1 g/m²) and 1 per cent spray of iodofenphos suspension concentrate (0·5 g/m²) on hardboard to adult German cockroaches. (Cornwell, unpublished).

TABLE XCIX

ATTRACTIVENESS TO COCKROACHES OF BAITS CONTAINING 2%
TRICHLORPHON IN LABORATORY TESTS
(From Lofgren & Burden[508])

Food and percentage	Knockdown and kill (%) after:		
	2	4 (hours)	24
American cockroaches			
Powdered sugar (25) cornmeal (75)	13	27	100
Vanilla syrup	10	20	100
Dextrin (50) cornmeal (50)	0	70	100
Dextrin (50) cornstarch (50)	0	60	100
Pepsi-Cola syrup	0	40	100
Dextrin (50) peanut oil (50)	0	30	90
Dextrin	0	27	93
Coca-Cola syrup	0	25	95
German cockroaches			
Powdered sugar (25) cornmeal (75)	23	56	100
Cherry syrup	20	40	80
Sucrose water solution	10	10	90
Powdered sugar	5	80	100

An additional organophosphorus insecticide, with which there is still insufficient experience to judge its potential for cockroach control, is pirimiphos-methyl (Actellic ®). It is rapidly degraded on crops outdoors, but on inert surfaces—bricks, plaster and woodwork—several months of persistence is claimed.[886]

It is unfortunate that tests on insecticides are rarely carried out on more than two or three at a time, and then not under conditions which fully resemble those in buildings. An overall judgement of the merits of the seven examined in detail has therefore to be made from a number of separate comparisons and field assessments. If this is done, incorporating also propoxur—a widely used carbamate insecticide (see Chapter 13)—for the four criteria considered most important to their use—the following orders would be obtained:

® trade mark of ICI.

Safety (oral toxicity)

Iodofenphos (least toxic)
Malathion
Trichlorphon
Fenitrothion
Diazinon
Chlorpyrifos
Propoxur
Dichlorvos (most toxic)

Speed of action (at normally used concentrations)

Dichlorvos (fastest)
Propoxur
Diazinon
Chlorpyrifos
Fenitrothion
Malathion
Iodofenphos
Trichlorphon (slowest)

Initial contact toxicity to German cockroaches

Iodofenphos (highest)
Fenitrothion
Chlorpyrifos
Propoxur
Dichlorvos
Diazinon
Malathion
Trichlorphon (lowest)

Residual effectiveness to German cockroaches

Iodofenphos (longest)
Fenitrothion
Chlorpyrifos
Propoxur
Malathion
Diazinon
Trichlorphon
Dichlorvos (shortest)

If the insecticides in each column are now rated 1–8 (from top to bottom) and the score for each insecticide is totalled, the following overall merit rating is obtained:

Iodofenphos	10	easily the best
Fenitrothion	13	
Chlorpyrifos	16	just above average
Propoxur	17	
Diazinon	20	
Malathion	20	just below average
Dichlorvos	22	
Trichlorphon	26	clearly least satisfactory

Insufficient information is available to place chlorpyrifos-methyl (Dowco-214) in these ratings, but on present evidence it would be expected to appear near the top.[921]

Of the vast number of organophosphorus insecticides which are available to industry for cockroach control it is noticeable how few have been used. It must be concluded: (1) that those actually in use against cockroaches are performing well and are cost/efficient compared with newer alternatives, and (2) that in recent years legislative measures in some countries may have retarded the promotion of new insecticides for this purpose. It is perhaps for these reasons that so few carbamates—members of the most recent group of insecticides—are used. Those which have been employed in cockroach control are discussed in the next chapter.

13

THE NEWER INSECTICIDES

(INSECTICIDAL CARBAMATES)

Origin of the carbamate insecticides; insecticidal properties—Carbaryl: chemical and physical properties; insecticidal properties; effectiveness against cockroaches; toxicity to man and animals—Bendiocarb: chemical and physical properties; insecticidal properties; toxicity to man and animals—Propoxur: chemical and physical properties; insecticidal properties; effectiveness against cockroaches; toxicity to man and animals—Other carbamate insecticides.

'New insecticides are not necessarily better materials. The pest control operator must evaluate very carefully the choice of his chemicals. He needs to be informed and to investigate all potentially useful materials. He should not abandon successful ones for something only equally good, or just because it is new'. This was the advice given by the National Pest Control Association of America to its members when propoxur (Baygon[R1])—a new carbamate insecticide—first became available.[621]

Some insecticides have good kill with little or no knockdown, while others offer good knockdown with poor kill. it is rare among insecticides to find rapid action coupled with good residual activity on treated surfaces. Nevertheless, in the case of propoxur, these properties do occur together, making this a most valuable insecticide for cockroach control.

Few if any, cockroaches knocked down by organophosphorus insecticides ever recover, but with carbamate insecticides recovery is common. Some of the cockroaches knocked down by propoxur may get up and walk away apparently fully recovered. Hence the warning, coupled with the above advice, that 'carbamates will require considerable testing and evaluation before their value in pest control can be determined'.

In addition to propoxur, two other carbamates will be examined in this chapter: one is relatively old, namely, carbaryl (or Sevin[R2]), introduced commercially twenty years ago; the second, bendiocarb (Ficam[R3]), introduced much more recently. Others like mexacarbate (Zectran[R4]) and the new dioxacarb (Famid[R5]) will be mentioned briefly.

A very readable history of the early introduction of carbamates has been given by Metcalf.[562] The highlights of the story start with the occult practises of witchcraft followed, centuries later, by the manufacture and use of carbaryl 'in multi-million pound quantities'.

Trade marks of (R1) Bayer; (R2) Union Carbide; (R3) Fisons; (R4) Dow and (R5) Ciba-Geigy.

The thousands of experimental carbamates which have been produced are all man-made compounds chemically related to the alkaloid physostigmine. This is a naturally occurring substance, in the Calabar, or 'ordeal' bean, of French West Africa—the seed of *Physostigma venosum*—used by native witch doctors to determine guilt or innocence. If an accused was not fatally poisoned after being forced to eat one of these, his innocence was proved. Whether it was fast eating which caused vomiting, or slow eating which resulted in breakdown of the poison in the body, is not clear.

The drug was introduced into England in 1840, and the alkaloid identified in 1864. Its structure was described in 1923, and use was soon made of its pharmaceutical properties.

Attempts were then made to synthesise a number of compounds related to physostigmine, one of which (prostigmine) was subsequently used widely in medicine.[765] The compounds produced were not insecticidal: the breakthrough came in 1954 when Kolbezen, Metcalf and Fukuto in the U.S. produced some simple analogues, capable of dissolving fats.[486] These were able to penetrate insect nerves and were highly insecticidal. Simultaneously, Gysin[387] in Switzerland embarked on the synthesis of carbamates with a slightly different chemical structure. These gave rise to compounds now known as isolan, pyrolan and dimetilan.

Insecticidal properties

The carbamate insecticides are esters of carbamic acid. The first of real value was carbaryl, which is now used for the control of agricultural and orchard pests, ectoparasites, and insects of concern in public health. Most carbamates have a rather narrow spectrum of activity; carbaryl is an exception. In common with organophosphates, the carbamates also inhibit the enzyme acetylcholinesterase, which is vital to nerve function in insects. The carbamates, however, are not irreversible inhibitors of this enzyme, but compete with it, sometimes unsuccessfully, with the result that insects may survive poisoning.

The different carbamates vary in the rate at which they are broken down in the insect's body, making some more insecticidal than others and influencing the ease of selection for resistance. The age of an insect, of the housefly for example, influences its response, but neither acetylcholinesterase activity, nor its sensitivity to the insecticide, are sufficiently different to explain why 5-day old flies are less susceptible than younger or older flies.[375]

Detoxication of carbamates can be prevented by the use of pyrethrin-type synergists; piperonyl butoxide, sesamex, sulfoxide and others. Generally the more insecticidal the carbamate, the less well it responds to synergism. The degree of synergism varies considerably between species and the sexes. As an example, admixture of carbaryl, propoxur and mexacarbate, each as one part, with five parts of piperonyl butoxide gives synergism ratios for *Musca domestica* of more than 40 for the first and about 4 for the other two.[317] The activity of carbaryl and others to the German cockroach is also enhanced by piperonyl butoxide, sesoxane and sulfoxide.[588] Synergism also occurs between carbamates: admixture of carbaryl and pyrolan makes them more toxic to *B. germanica*.[325]

The carbamates as a group contain a number of compounds with quite varied action: some are weed killers, others are fungicides; some are active molluscicides, others are good acaricides. All the insecticidal carbamates, especially mexacarbate, are toxic to bees.[326]

There is no doubt that the wide spectrum of activity of carbaryl against insects, together with its low mammalian toxicity acted as a big stimulus to research and development into carbamates during the late 1950's and early 1960's. Propoxur, one of the best insecticides for cockroach control, was a result of this work.

CARBARYL

Carbaryl was the first insecticide of its type to show that carbamate insecticides are potentially safe, stable and relatively inexpensive. Carbaryl did for the carbamates what malathion was beginning to do for the organophosphates; each demonstrating the potential of its respective chemical group especially in terms of low health risk. Carbaryl was introduced in 1956 by the Union Carbide Corp. It will be better known to many as Sevin®.

Chemical and physical properties
In its pure form, carbaryl is a white crystalline solid, relatively insoluble in water (0·1 per cent) and not very soluble in organic solvents. It has a mild inoffensive odour and the vapour pressure is less than 5×10^{-3} mm Hg at 25°C. The insecticide is stable to light and heat and is non-corrosive.

Formulations commonly available are wettable powders (50–85 per cent), and dusts (5–10 per cent). Poor solubility in organic liquids has limited its use as an emulsion.

Insecticidal properties
Radioactively labelled carbaryl applied topically to houseflies penetrates the cuticle in about 4 hours, but is rapidly metabolised and excreted. Toxicity to the fly is about 2 μg/female. The German cockroach absorbs carbaryl more slowly, but breaks it down rapidly, which again results in carbaryl being relatively inactive: 20 μg/male cockroach (see Fig. 183). The synergist sesamex prevents breakdown of carbaryl in the fly and increases its toxicity 50-fold. Carbaryl and sesamex together reduce the LD_{50} of the insecticide to the cockroach from 20 μg to 0·4 μg (again a synergism factor of $\times 50$). 'But unlike many other combinations, this one has the *disadvantage* that the toxicant is cheap, while the added material is relatively expensive. Hence its practical use is limited'.[275]

The same improvement in response can be obtained with the synergist piperonyl butoxide: 5 and 10μg of carbaryl alone, applied to male German cockroaches, kills none and 5 per cent respectively. When combined with 50 and 100μg of piperonyl butoxide, mortality increases to 90 per cent and 100 per cent.[588] Quite marked synergism to the German cockroach can also be obtained by admixture of carbaryl with the related carbamates, dimetilan and isolan.[346]

Effectiveness against cockroaches

Carbaryl is about as inefficient a cockroach killer as DDT: about 100 times less toxic to German cockroaches than the best organophosphates. The data in Table LXIX show males and females of *B. germanica* equally susceptible to carbaryl: a 2- to 3-fold difference is obtained by Nagasawa & Shiba.[600]

Carbaryl cannot seriously be recommended for cockroach control when there are so many insecticides, both organophosphates and carbamates, which are more effective: some are also as safe as carbaryl to man and animals. Among five insecticides applied topically to a laboratory strain of German cockroaches, carbaryl clearly performed least well (Fig. 152). Because the insecticide is relatively ineffective, sprays and dusts usually contain high concentrations of carbaryl—about 5 per cent.

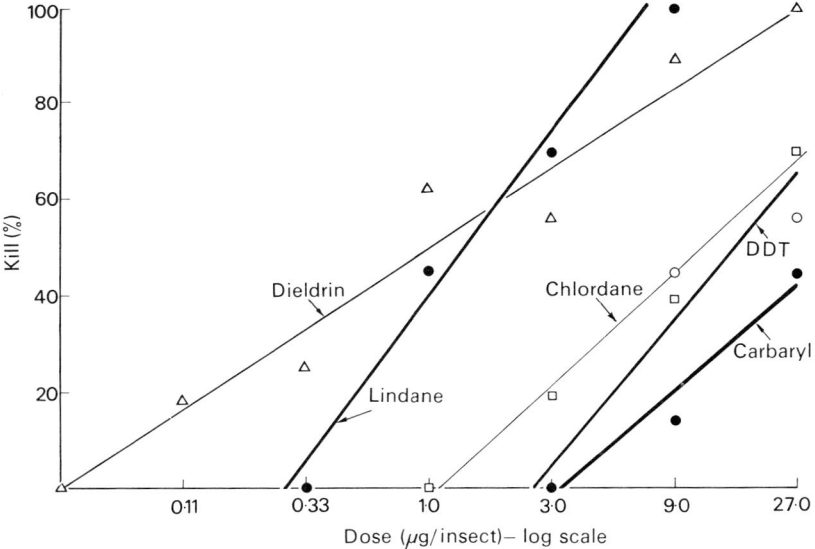

Fig. 152. Kill (per cent at 72 hours) of adult *B. germanica* treated topically with carbaryl and some chlorinated hydrocarbon insecticides. (Cornwell, unpublished).

Carbaryl as a wettable powder performed well against female German cockroaches, whether susceptible or resistant to chlordane, when these were confined on treated masonite panels, aged for two months. An emulsion performed poorly.[370] Carbaryl (2 per cent) was not as good as diazinon (0·5 per cent), but carbaryl (2·5 per cent) was better than chlordane (2 per cent) against a normal and resistant strain of *B. germanica* (Table C). There is no evidence of cross-resistance to chlordane[194] or to propoxur,[541] but cross-resistance does exist between carbaryl and DDT (see Chapter 15).

TABLE C

KILL (%) OF GERMAN COCKROACHES OF NORMAL AND RESISTANT STRAINS, EXPOSED FOR LONG PERIODS TO SURFACES TREATED WITH CARBARYL AND OTHER INSECTICIDES AGED FOR UP TO 30 DAYS
(From Grayson & Perkins[371])

Strain and Insecticide	Ageing period (days)			
	2	7	15	30
	24-hour exposure			
Normal strain				
Diazinon (0·5%)*	100	100	91	96
Carbaryl (2%)†	100	86	55	53
	72-hour exposure			
Normal strain				
Chlordane (2%)*	93	79	70	70
Carbaryl (2·5%)†	98	99	97	91
Chlordane-R				
Chlordane (2%)*	8	1	8	7
Carbaryl (2·5%)†	100	98	98	100

* Oil sprays; † Suspensions in water.

Toxicity to man and animals
Carbaryl is relatively non-toxic to mammals and offers a high measure of safety when applied in the home: the acute oral LD_{50} (rat) is 850 mg/kg; the acute dermal LD_{50} (rat) is more than 4,000 mg/kg. Rats fed two years on a diet containing 200 ppm suffered no ill effects. The insecticide is rapidly broken down in the gut of mammals to a degradation product (1-naphthol), which is then detoxified in combination with water and eliminated in the urine. Carbaryl fed to dairy cows (450 ppm) did not appear in their milk, either as insecticide or breakdown product. Domestic animals and poultry are not easily poisoned with carbaryl: hence its use for the control of ticks, fleas and poultry mite. A review of the toxicology of carbaryl is given by Back.[69]

BENDIOCARB

Bendiocarb was first synthesised in 1966. Early tests indicated likely application in agricultural pest control. It was subsequently introduced by Fisons in

1971 as an experimental carbamate for evaluation against insects of importance to public health. The insecticide was marketed for this purpose in 1972 under the trade name Ficam 80 W—a wettable powder containing 76 per cent active ingredient—which is unusually high for this type of formulation.

Bendiocarb is thus one of the most recent insecticides to become available for cockroach control. Currently, use is limited to applications by experienced pest control operators; it is not available to the general consumer market. During 1974 a trials programme was carried out in accordance with the requirements of the Environmental Protection Agency in the U.S.A. to check on the safety of bendiocarb in food establishments. It proved safe for use by trained personnel as a spot treatment. No residues occurred in food as a result.[771]

Chemical and physical properties
Technical bendiocarb is a white crystalline solid, slightly soluble in water (40 ppm at 25°C) and not readily soluble in organic solvents (0·1 per cent in odourless kerosene). It is odourless and is almost non-volatile (vapour pressure: 5×10^{-6} mm Hg at 25°C). A cubic metre of air saturated with bendiocarb contains 66 μg of insecticide at 25°C. There is no toxic vapour produced at normal working temperatures. Bendiocarb is broken down in water (neutral) to half its activity in 20 days at 25°C: hydrolysis is faster in alkali but slower in acid. There is no evidence of rapid atmospheric degradation or decomposition by sunlight.

Sprays of the wettable powder are claimed not to damage surfaces encountered in domestic and industrial situations where water alone is without effect. On drying, the spray leaves a fine white deposit, less so than most wettable powders because of the smaller amount of inert ingredient (filler).

Ficam 80 W is packed in sachets (Fig. 153) containing the measured amounts needed when mixed with water to give prescribed concentrations (0·25 and 0·5 per cent sprays). The prepared spray passes filters of 100 mesh/in and is said not to corrode spraying equipment. If flushing action is required to help locate cockroach harbourages during treatment, pyrethrins or pyrethroids diluted in water can be added to the previously dispersed wettable powder.

Insecticidal properties
Bendiocarb is reported to control a wide range of pests of importance in public health, by contact action and as a stomach poison; it is said to kill quickly and to have long-lasting residual activity. The insects for which control is claimed include cockroaches (tested as NC 6897),[365] mosquitoes,[76] ants,[856] silverfish, bedbugs, fleas, carpet beetles and other nuisance insects.[498] Insecticidal activity on treated surfaces is said 'to persist for weeks or months depending on the application rate and conditions in infested premises'.

The toxicity of bendiocarb to male German cockroaches (LC_{50} 0·015 per cent w/v) is ten times greater than propoxur (0·15 per cent) by direct spray application[771] and about the same as dieldrin (0·019 per cent). However, in

Fig. 153. Sachet pack of bendiocarb wettable powder (Ficam 80 W) premeasured to ensure accurate rate of admixture with water. (Courtesy: Fisons).

tests with these insecticides applied topically,[903] the LD_{50} of bendiocarb to male German cockroaches is reported as 1·6 μg/insect, only half as toxic as propoxur (0·9 μg/insect). On treated glass (0·2 g/m²) bendiocarb takes twice as long (55 mins) to kill males (LT_{50} propoxur: 23 mins) and five times as long (120 mins) to kill females (LT_{50} propoxur: 25 mins).

Cockroaches in contact with deposits of bendiocarb are knocked down in about half the time taken by fenitrothion, with little difference between the sexes (Table CI). Recommended application rates of 0·5 per cent and 0·25 per cent are proposed for initial and maintenance treatments, respectively. At these still low application rates German cockroaches require 30 times the length of exposure to bendiocarb wettable powder, to achieve the same kill as with iodofenphos, when treated surfaces are aged for four weeks (Table CII).

In tests to compare the performance of Ficam 80 W with iodofenphos and fenitrothion applied at the same rate, bendiocarb killed German cockroaches almost as well as the organophosphates 1 week after application. Bendiocarb was not as good as iodofenphos, but better than fenitrothion, at 4 weeks (Fig. 154). In comparison with propoxur, and a number of organophosphate insecticides as emulsions, applied to hardboard and to ceramic and vinyl tiles. Ficam performed well,[770] but so might the other insecticides if they too had been applied as wettable powders instead of emulsions.

TABLE CI

TIMES FOR 100% KNOCKDOWN (IN MINUTES) OF THREE PEST COCKROACHES, EXPOSED TO 250 mg/m² OF BENDIOCARB AND FENITROTHION ON GLASS

(From Story[770])

Species	Bendiocarb		Fenitrothion	
	Males	Females	Males	Females
B. germanica	47	52	65	110
P. americana	41	44	130	180
P. japonica	34	37	70	100

The performance of bendiocarb has been examined for the control of resistant German cockroaches. When these insects are exposed for long periods (24 hours) to high deposits (1·6 g/m²), kill on treated surfaces is good up to 60 days. These are not of course the conditions normally experienced by cockroaches in infested premises. The lower kills which were obtained with bendiocarb and propoxur, of cockroaches resistant to diazinon (compared with susceptible insects), suggests some cross-tolerance (Table CIII).

Sprays of 0·25 per cent bendiocarb applied in field trials are reported to give control of German and American cockroaches in warm climates for up to 4 weeks, and longer with 0·5 per cent. In hot steamy kitchens in the U.K.,

TABLE CII

KILL (% AT 48 HOURS) OF ADULT *B. GERMANICA* EXPOSED FOR DIFFERENT PERIODS TO 4-WEEK-OLD DEPOSITS OF IODOFENPHOS AND BENDIOCARB WETTABLE POWDERS

(Cornwell, unpublished)

Spray conc. (at 1 gal/ 1,000 ft²)	Application rate (mg/ft²)	Iodofenphos		Bendiocarb	
		Minutes			
		0·1	0·5	3	12
0·25%	11	10	21	11	15
0·5%	22	15	25	13	26
1·0%	45	53	85	33	59

TABLE CIII

KILL (%) AFTER EXPOSURE FOR 24 HOURS OF FEMALE GERMAN COCKROACHES, OF SUSCEPTIBLE AND RESISTANT STRAINS, TO INSECTICIDAL DEPOSITS (150 mg/ft^2) AGED FOR UP TO 60 DAYS
(Data from Grayson[365])

Insecticide	Cockroach strain	Age of insecticide deposit (days)			
		2	15	30	60
Bendiocarb	Normal	100	97	100	100
	Malathion-R	100	100	100	100
	Diazinon-R	100	92	90	80
Propoxur	Normal	86	100	100	92
	Malathion-R	100	100	100	100
	Diazinon-R	100	83	83	34

Oriental cockroaches are controlled for longer periods (3–4 weeks) than German cockroaches (a few days). Persistence is shorter in areas of high humidity; these require more frequent treatment.[771]

In a large scale project in the U.K. (the 'Birkenhead experiment') Ficam 80 wettable powder was used to establish a pest-free zone in a depressed urban environment. The zone was a half mile square surrounded by a 'buffer zone' to stop reinfestation. In 13 months the number of reports of cockroaches by residents dropped from 75 to 12, but in only 2 instances was there physical evidence of pests. Use experience in the United States has not revealed significant differences in performance between Ficam, and any of the other insecticides—diazinon, dursban or propoxur—used for cockroach control.[902]

Toxicity to man and animals

Ficam 80 W is intended for use by trained pest control operators and government health officials. The acute oral LD_{50} (rat) is between 60 and 120 mg/kg. Bendiocarb is therefore of moderately high oral toxicity to mammals. In common with other carbamates the mode of action is by direct, but reversible inhibition of acetylcholinesterase. The dermal toxicity of the insecticide is relatively low ($LD_{50} > 800$ mg/kg); it is non-irritant at normally used concentrations.

Cats are more susceptible (oral LD_{50} 8 mg/kg) but show no symptoms when continuously exposed for 33 days in rooms treated with 100 mg/m^2. Fish (guppies) are highly susceptible (LC_{50} 0·5 ppm for 24 hours).

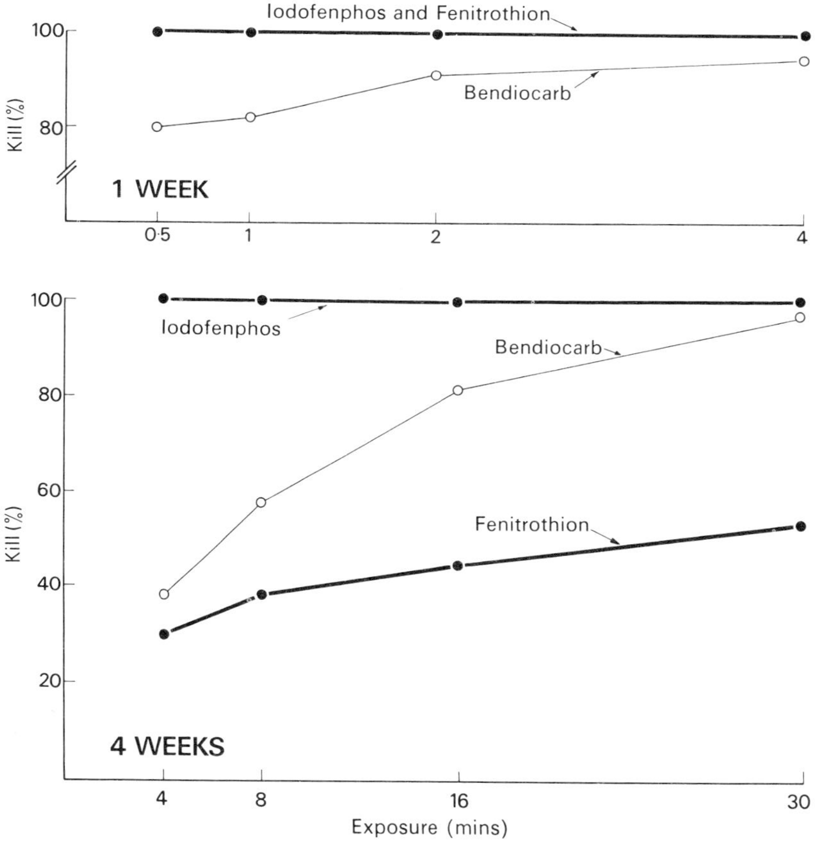

Fig. 154. Kill (per cent at 48 hours) of adult German cockroaches exposed for different periods to bendiocarb and two organophosphates applied as wettable powders (1 per cent spray) to hardboard at 0.5 g/m^2 and aged for 1 and 4 weeks at 25°C. (Cornwell, unpublished).

PROPOXUR

Propoxur is the most widely used carbamate insecticide for cockroach control and is better known by the Bayer trade names, Baygon® and Blattenex®. Before propoxur became established as the standard name, the insecticide was known in the U.K. as arprocarb. It was introduced as a coded compound (39007) in 1959 and became available commercially in the early 1960's. Formulations of propoxur were available in the U.K. for local authority use between 1966 and 1969, under Rentokil's trade mark, Insectrol®.

The early use of propoxur as an emulsion spray by the American pest control industry met with a number of teething problems; the solvents degraded certain types of hose and washers, and when used in sprayers for the first time acted as cleansing agents, loosening previous insecticidal deposits in the spray containers and causing blockage of nozzles. Blockage also occurred because of rapid evaporation of the solvents used. The water temperature for mixing sprays was also apparently critical; low temperatures caused crystallisation and high temperatures affected emulsification. Moreover, only two formulations were available; an emulsion concentrate, and later, a bait.

In the U.K. the Insectrol range of formulations included: a dust (1 per cent); a wettable powder (50 per cent) for use as a 1 per cent spray; an emulsion concentrate (20 per cent) recommended for application as a 2 per cent spray; a ready to use oil spray (1 per cent) and a self-drying lacquer (6 per cent). Rentokil also undertook initial test work on smoke generators containing propoxur. These (Undine®) were subsequently developed for the control of glasshouse pests.

Chemical and physical properties
Technical propoxur is a white crystalline solid with a faint odour and low volatility (vapour pressure, 3×10^{-6} mm Hg at 20°C). It is sparingly soluble in water (0·2 per cent at 20°C) and not readily soluble in commonly used solvents. It is degraded on alkaline surfaces, but otherwise, spray deposits have a residual life of many weeks. The crystals are needle shaped (Fig. 155)

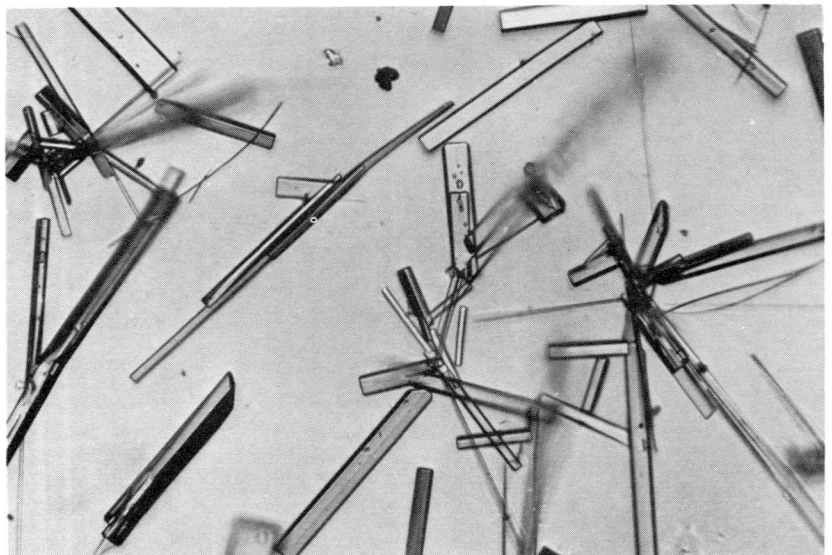

Fig. 155. Crystals of the insecticide propoxur ($\times$ 180).

® Undine is the trade mark of Pains-Wessex Ltd.

and easily picked up by crawling insects. Unlike some insecticidal carbamates, propoxur is not converted to other inhibitors of acetylcholinesterase by exposure to sunlight and ultraviolet radiation.[220] When applied in water (neutral), about 1·5 per cent of the active ingredient is decomposed per day at 20°C.

Insecticidal properties
Propoxur is undoubtedly one of the best insecticides developed for cockroach control, and but for the problems common to all carbamates of providing a range of formulations, propoxur may have gained even wider acceptance. In addition to controlling cockroaches, the insecticide has useful properties against mosquitoes, and crawling insects, including silverfish, crickets and ants.

Georghiou & Metcalf[326] have undertaken studies on the toxicity of a number of carbamates to 15 species of insects. When applied to the cuticle, German cockroaches require twice as much propoxur to kill them as houseflies. The action of all carbamates against *Musca domestica* is synergised by a factor of 4 times by piperonyl butoxide, at a ratio of insecticide to synergist of 1 : 5. However, synergists of the type studied by Fahmy & Gordon[288] and which improve the efficacy of carbamates against houseflies, fail to bring about as much synergism in cockroaches. According to El-Aziz, Metcalf & Fukuto,[274] piperonyl butoxide synergises propoxur against German cockroaches and reduces by half the amount of insecticide needed for 50 per cent kill. These results, however, could not be substantiated by tests in the U.K. (Table CIV).

TABLE CIV

KILL (% AT 48 HOURS) OF ADULT FEMALE *B. GERMANICA* TREATED BY TOPICAL APPLICATION WITH PROPOXUR ALONE AND WITH VARIOUS POTENTIAL SYNERGISTS AT DIFFERENT RATIOS
(Cornwell, unpublished)

Propoxur with potential synergists	Ratio of propoxur : synergist		
	1 : 1	1 : 3	1 : 9
	Amount applied/insect (μg)		
	0·33	1·0	3·0
Piperonyl butoxide	20	25	13
Lethane	28	18	38
Thanite	48	53	18
Bucarpolate	20	38	25
Dimethyl sulphoxide	33	43	38
N-isobutyl undecylanamide	23	13	35
Propoxur alone at 0·33 μg/insect		45	

Effectiveness against cockroaches

Blattenex emulsion was quickly evaluated by the pest control industry in the U.S.A. after its introduction: resistance by *B. germanica* to diazinon appeared as a potential threat to the industry's ability to provide cockroach control; there was evidence that propoxur could kill these insects. Blattenex provided industry with the alternative, and with an insecticide of better residual life than any available on the market at that time.

Experience soon showed that propoxur had a number of useful properties: a built-in flushing action which encouraged cockroaches to contaminate themselves on the wet surfaces of treated harbourages; rapid knockdown, about 2–3 times slower than the pyrethrins (Fig. 129), but considerably faster than organophosphorus and other carbamate insecticides (Table CXI): good persistence on treated surfaces (Table LXXV and Table LXXXIII), provided the insecticide was not absorbed into the materials being treated; and effectiveness against cockroaches resistant to organochlorine and organophosphate insecticides (see Chapter 15). Propoxur even proved effective in killing a carbaryl-resistant strain.[541] The effectiveness of propoxur against different species of cockroach on treated glass is shown in Fig. 156. In direct spray tests with an emulsion, German, Oriental, American and Madeira cockroaches were all knocked down within 12 minutes, by spray concentrations of 0·25 per cent and above.[92]

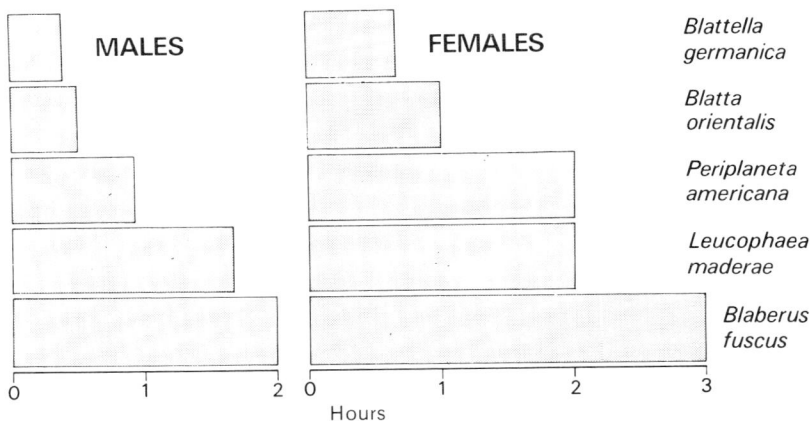

Fig. 156. The activity (LT_{100} hours) of propoxur on glass (10 mg/m²) to five species of cockroach. (From Behrenz & Böcker[92]).

The good residual life of propoxur on treated surfaces is now well established and many laboratory tests have compared its performance with other insecticides. First, however, it is of interest to compare the residual life of different propoxur formulations. As a dust it has exceptional properties. Those concerned with controlling cockroaches should need no further evidence to convince them of the merits of dust application, compared with other formulations, than that presented in Table CV. For a year, dust continued to kill German cockroaches on treated surfaces. This is because a dust in no way interacts with the surface on which it is applied, unless damp, and remains easily picked up by cockroaches. Moreover, dusts may be introduced into harbourages otherwise difficult to treat, or reach, with sprays (Fig. 157). Dusts may, however, cause cockroaches to be repelled from partially treated harbourages (see Fig. 87).

Sprays of wettable powder, oil and emulsion continue to kill cockroaches up to seven weeks, but lose most of their effectiveness in three months. However, the long residual life of propoxur tempted the National Pest Control Association of America to comment: 'its performance in this respect is more like that of the better chlorinated hydrocarbons than the organophosphates.

TABLE CV

KNOCKDOWN AND KILL (%) OF ADULT GERMAN COCKROACHES EXPOSED TO SURFACES TREATED WITH DIFFERENT FORMULATIONS OF PROPOXUR AND AGED FOR 15–52 WEEKS AT 18–24°C
(From Cornwell[214])

Formulation and treatment	Age of treated surface (weeks)	Exposure period (hours)	Knockdown (%) in minutes			Kill (%) at 24 hours
			20	40	60	
Dust: 30 mg a.i./ft² on hardboard	1	1	98	100	100	100
	7		98	100	100	100
	12		90	100	100	100
	22		92	100	100	100
	52		77	100	100	100
Wettable powder: 74 mg a.i./ft² on hardboard	1	1	75	100	100	100
	7		80	100	100	100
	13		0	8	20	30
	22		0	0	0	22
Emulsion: 84 mg a.i./ft² on painted hardboard	1	4	3	28	98	95
	7		0	3	17	100
	13		0	3	10	60
	22		0	0	2	77
Oil spray: 37 mg a.i./ft² on glass	1	0·5	0	100	100	100
	7		10	87	98	92
	15		0	50	75	40*

* Note the recovery from knockdown which may occur when inadequate insecticide is present or exposure is short.

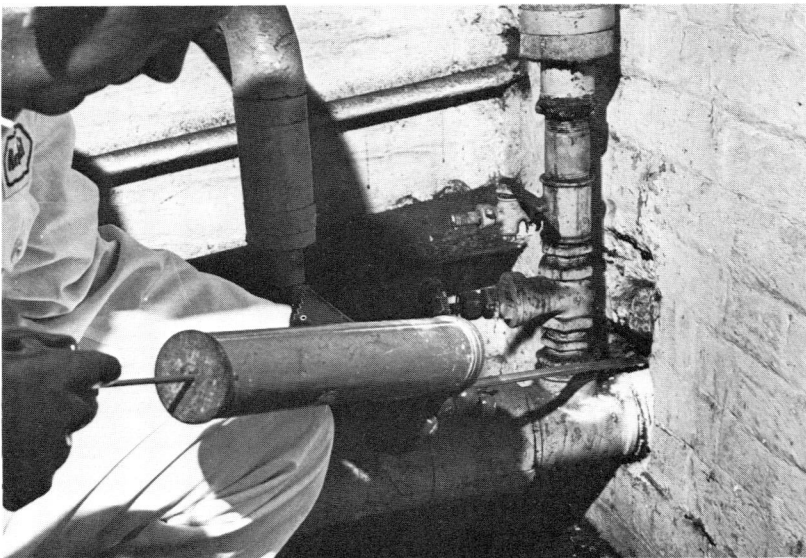

Fig. 157. Typical cockroach harbourages: (above) in electrical conduit impossible to treat effectively with insecticides other than a dust; (below) in brickwork around hot water pipes, where a dust gun is being used to ensure treatment of all surfaces of the harbourage.

Not only do the residues give long kill, but laboratory results show they provide knockdown as well'.[623] Not emphasised, however, is an important weakness of propoxur, that even during the period of exposure of cockroaches to treated surfaces, or shortly after, recovery from knockdown can occur if an inadequate amount of insecticide is picked up (Table CV and Fig. 158).

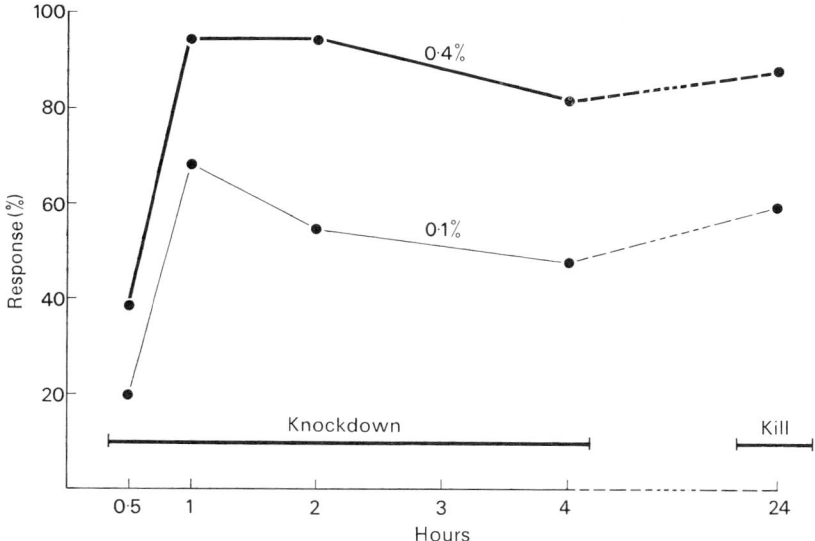

Fig. 158. Recovery from knockdown during 4 hours exposure of female *B. germanica* to surfaces treated with low concentrations of propoxur in oil sprays. Also kill at 24 hours. (Cornwell, unpublished).

In common with other insecticides applied as *emulsions*, the life of Blattenex on treated surfaces is extremely short. This is no criticism of the insecticide propoxur, but of the wrong choice of formulation for use on materials which soak up insecticide in solution. Insecticide within the substrate cannot possibly kill cockroaches walking over the surface (see Chapter 4). This is shown in Table CVI in which the performance of propoxur, fenitrothion and diazinon as wettable powders is clearly superior to emulsions. As 1 per cent sprays of wettable powder, the residual life of fenitrothion exceeds propoxur, and propoxur in turn is far better than diazinon. As 2 per cent sprays propoxur and fenitrothion perform equally well.

Topical application of fenitrothion, iodofenphos and dieldrin to German cockroaches provides LD_{50}'s less than propoxur; these are therefore more toxic (Table LXIX). When cockroaches of susceptible and resistant strains are exposed to surfaces treated with propoxur,[542] the sexes of *B. germanica* are killed in about equal numbers (average LD$_{50}$: males 0·018 and females 0·024 μl/cm^2). By topical application, a two-fold difference in susceptibility is obtained.[541] By tarsal contact, using mixed sexes of German cockroaches from Tunis stock, concentrations of 0·06, 0·12, 0·25 and 0·5 per cent killed half the insects in 22, 19, 18 and 15 minutes, respectively.[892] Propoxur is also highly active against Oriental cockroaches but unfortunately these have an 8-fold difference in the susceptibility of their sexes; males respond to much lower doses.

Treatment of natural infestations of *B. germanica* in homes in Florida, using 1 per cent emulsion sprays, reduced populations by 97–99 per cent in 6 weeks, but by only 90 per cent in 17 weeks.[151] Propoxur is more toxic to German cockroaches than chlordane but less active than chlorpyrifos. In comparative trials in Florida homes, propoxur applied as 1 per cent sprays per-

TABLE CVI

KILL (% AT 48 HOURS) OF ADULT FEMALE *B. GERMANICA* EXPOSED TO HARDBOARD TREATED WITH PROPOXUR AND TWO ORGANOPHOSPHORUS INSECTICIDES AS WETTABLE POWDERS AND EMULSIONS AND AGED AT 25°C BEFORE TEST
(Cornwell, unpublished)

Insecticide	Age of deposit (weeks)	Spray concentration %	Wettable powder			Emulsion
			Exposure time (mins)			
			6	24	90	90
Fenitrothion	1	1	100	100	100	0
	3		100	100	100	0
	6		40	43	100	—
	3	2	—	—	—	0
	6		100	100	100	—
Propoxur	1	1	80	90	100	—
	3		8	70	100	—
	6		0	83	100	—
	3	2	—	—	—	33
	6		100	100	100	—
Diazinon	1	1	3	10	60	15
	3		3	33	20	33
	6		0	10	18	—
	3	2	—	—	—	0
	6		80	73	73	—

formed less well against *B. germanica* than 0·5 per cent chlorpyrifos.[144] However, propoxur (1 per cent) gave excellent control of German cockroaches on three U.S. Naval ships, but performed poorly on four, on which chlorpyrifos (0·5 per cent) was again better.[310] Collections of German cockroaches taken from ships visiting the U.K., and tested with propoxur and fenitrothion applied topically, were equally susceptible to the two insecticides (Table XCIII).

To support spray treatments with propoxur (Baygon), the Chemagro Corporation recommend the use of, 'Baygon Bait Back up—a new concept in roach control. Baygon 2 per cent cockroach bait is designed for the pest control industry, in providing 'crevice-size' particles of insecticide, for use as an effective and long-lasting back up treatment between service calls: its killing power lasts so long as the bait remains dry enough to prevent deterioration by mould'.

Application is recommended at $1·2 \text{ g/m}^2$, loosely or in bait containers. The latter are obviously preferred where it is necessary to keep the bait dry (Fig. 159). Application to harbourages may be made by a dust gun having an enlarged nozzle. In some situations it might be more sensible to use a dust, but in food and animal locations where contamination may create a risk, placing bait in harbourages, thus making it more readily available to cockroaches, is likely to achieve better results.

Another way of extending the life of an insecticide is to incorporate it into a lacquer. This is described in detail in Chapter 4, but here in Fig. 160, the results

Fig. 159. Use of a bottle top to keep Baygon bait dry in wet surroundings (processing floor of soft drinks works, Dallas, Texas, U.S.A.).

380 THE COCKROACH

obtained with two self-drying lacquers—propoxur and diazinon—are compared. The use of a lacquer incorporating propoxur, together with other formulations of this insecticide to control German cockroaches at London's Heathrow Airport is described by Bills.[104] Observations on the performance of the lacquer, in the least favourable locations in the airport, indicated a minimum life of about eight months.

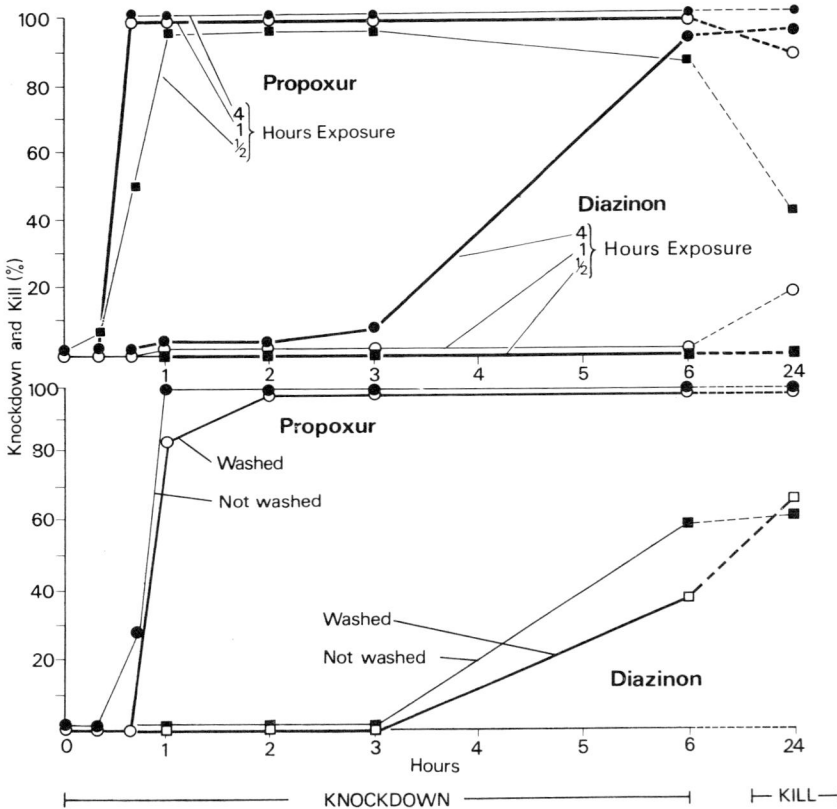

Fig. 160. Knockdown and kill of *B. germanica*: (top) exposed for periods of 0·5, 1 and 4 hours on surfaces treated with propoxur and diazinon lacquers; aged for 22 weeks; (bottom) exposed for 4 hours on lacquered surfaces aged for 16 weeks, and then washed weekly for 6 weeks with household detergents. (From Cornwell[214]).

Toxicity to man and animals

The acute oral LD_{50} (rat) of propoxur is about 100 mg/kg. The dermal toxicity is lower at 800–1,000 mg/kg. Skin function tests on the forearm of 8 human volunteers showed no symptoms.[92] Inhalation tests on a variety of test animals showed no effect of 2g of propoxur in ethanol sprayed into 2 m³, 20 times in 5 days. Samples of air taken in a submarine at intervals up to eight days after spraying a 1·1 per cent emulsion of propoxur gave levels not exceeding 0·009 μg of insecticide per litre of air.[904] The solvents used (methylene chloride and trichloroethylene) never exceeded 25 ppm, well below levels which have adverse effects on man.

Diets containing 250 ppm of propoxur had no ill effects in two-year animal feeding tests. Starlings are killed by acute oral doses (LD_{50}) of 15–30 mg/kg. Most Hymenoptera, especially honeybees, are highly susceptible to propoxur. A description of the safe use of Baygon emulsion and wettable powder, to control ants and cockroaches, in Wuppertal Zoo, Germany (Fig. 37), without harm to reptiles, birds and mammals is given by Haas.[388]

OTHER CARBAMATE INSECTICIDES

There are a number of relatively old carbamate insecticides which have been tested against cockroaches, but their high mammalian toxicities have restricted interest in them. Examples are mexacarbate (= Zectran: acute oral LD_{50} (rat) 15–60 mg/kg), and dimetilan (47–64 mg/kg), a stomach poison. Isolan and Pyrolan are no longer of commercial interest.

The topical LD_{50} of mexacarbate to American cockroach nymphs (5 weeks old) is half that of diazinon.[480] On surfaces treated with dusts (22 mg/m^2) the KD_{50} of these two insecticides is the same (30 mins), but the carbamate gives better kill at 48 hours (100 per cent for mexacarbate and 72 per cent for diazinon). The LD_{50} of Isolan to the German cockroach[346] is about 25 μg/g and that of Pyrolan about 400 μg/g.

A new carbamate insecticide, dioxacarb, marketed by Ciba-Geigy has been registered for cockroach control in some countries under the trade name Famid®. Like propoxur and bendiocarb, this carbamate has a low vapour pressure (3 × 10^{-7} mm Hg at 20°C) and promises long residual life in excess of three months, as a wettable powder, on treated surfaces. It has a low solubility in water (0·6 per cent) and in odourless kerosene (0·1 per cent). The recommended spray concentration of wettable powder to control crawling insects is 1–2 per cent. In tests of the susceptibility of dioxacarb to German cockroaches, the LD_{50}'s for nymphs and adult males and females were 10, 63 and 86 mg/g, respectively. This suggests an insecticidal effectiveness 4 to 8 times lower than propoxur.[773]

Dioxacarb knocks down German cockroaches (WHO test) in less than half an hour[180, 374] and is especially active against *P. americana*, offering both stomach and contact action. It has no flushing action; some problems of visible deposits on treated surfaces, difficult to remove, were reported in early trials with the wettable powder.

The acute oral toxicity to the rat (LD_{50}) is variously reported from 107 to 156 mg/kg. It is therefore moderately toxic to mammals—about the same as propoxur and bendiocarb—but dermal toxicity is low and no skin irritation is reported. Dioxacarb is claimed effective against a number of agricultural pests (as coded Compound 8353).[67] It is also effective against cockroaches resistant to organochlorine and organophosphorus insecticides (malathion and diazinon),[364] but this applies also to the other carbamates of similar mammalian toxicity.

In this chapter, three insecticides have been examined in detail but others only briefly. The limited solubility of the carbamates in normally-used solvents has adversely affected their development for industrial and domestic use. It was this which in the mid-1960's appeared to restrict interest in MCA-600 (a coded compound of Mobil), closely related to carbaryl.

The activity of propoxur against cockroaches is good. It is against this standard which new carbamate insecticides must favourably compare if they are to be adopted by the pest control industry. MCA-600 was inferior in insecticidal activity against both laboratory and field strains of *B. germanica*.[542]

Carbaryl is not likely to make any real contribution to cockroach control in the future: its insecticidal activity against the pest species is not sufficiently high. But propoxur has made a major contribution and seems likely to remain a successful insecticide for this purpose, with the new bendiocarb, and possibly dioxacarb, competing with propoxur in different geographical areas. These new carbamate insecticides may become more widely adopted, depending on their cost/efficiency compared with the well-tried and newer organophosphates of low mammalian toxicity.

14

HOW INSECTICIDES KILL

Understanding insecticidal action—why it matters: the target for attack. The nervous system and nerve transmission; axonic transmission; synaptic transmission; interference by insecticides—Action of the pyrethrins: penetration of the cuticle; distribution in the insect; effect of temperature. Effects of pyrethrins on respiration; on heart beat; on haemolymph volume; effects in the gut. Action on the cockroach nervous system: on sensory nerve endings; physical damage; effects on nerve activity; on spontaneous nerve activity—Action of DDT: penetration distribution and breakdown in the cockroach; effects of temperature on the susceptibility of cockroaches; effects on body reserves; on amino acids. Similarity of symptoms of DDT-poisoning and bodily stress; DDT-induced toxin. Interference with nerve function—Action of other chlorinated hydrocarbon insecticides—Action of organophosphorus and carbamate insecticides: acetylcholine and acetylcholinesterase in cockroaches; location of poisoning; response to diazinon; secondary effects of organophosphates. Action of carbamate insecticides.

An insecticide can kill insects by direct chemical poisoning or through the potency of a breakdown product formed within the insect's body. Insects may be *killed* because their tissues are unable to detoxify an insecticide, or because some poisonous metabolite accumulates. Insects may *survive* an insecticide because they can render it ineffective, as in resistant strains, by enzyme action on the poison.[589, 666]

This chapter describes the efforts made to unravel the action of insecticides, in which the cockroach, principally *P. americana*, has often been used. The very extensive literature dealing with the action of insecticides on other insects has been largely omitted.

Understanding insecticidal action—why it matters
For the pest control operator, it does not matter how his insecticide kills, as long as it is efficient and is in all other respects acceptable. Nevertheless, chemists in laboratories around the world have for years been trying to discover how insecticides work. The subject involves some understanding of the physiological processes in insects and the biochemistry of interaction between insecticides and insect tissues. The discussion which now follows is a technical one and is not easy to follow unless the reader is to some extent informed in these sciences.

Studies of the mode of action of insecticides tell us two things: they point to those aspects of the chemical structure of an insecticide responsible for its activity, and thus help us to develop new ones; secondly they may tell us something of how resistance in insects develops and might be overcome. A good example of this is the work in Australia to produce DDT-like compounds, not subject to detoxication by DDT-dehydrochlorinase—the enzyme which breaks down DDT in resistant flies. It is for these reasons that this subject is discussed in detail.

At a rough guess, probably between 1 and 2 million chemical compounds have been screened since World War II for pesticidal activity. A large proportion of these have been looked at as potential insecticides with the result that new compounds have continued to be promoted commercially. Their development has come about by (1) one Company copying the structure of another's compounds and making something like it: hence the enormous number of closely similar variants among the organophosphorus insecticides, or (2) making a compound similar to a naturally occurring toxin: hence the synthetic pyrethroids, with properties similar to the pyrethrins, and the large number of experimental carbamates with a basic structure related to physostigmine—the active principle of the Calabar bean (see p. 363). The success rate in developing a new pesticide for use, is about one new compound in 10,000 screened.

What we ought to be doing, perhaps, in our efforts to design insecticides for the future is to first beg the question: what are the vital processes of the insect which we might chemically interrupt? We should attempt to answer this by discovering those processes vital in the insect, but not so vital, or of low sensitivity in man.

The target for attack
All modern insecticides affect the 'control' mechanisms of the pest: they interfere with the nervous system. This is a highly sensitive system, which when damaged is apparently least tolerant of interruption and least capable of repair. We know this from the very rapid damage which occurs to brain cells in man when respiration or blood circulation fails.

There is now strong evidence that the action of organophosphorus and carbamate insecticides is on the enzyme acetylcholinesterase. But apart from this, the enzyme systems of insects are not much affected by the insecticides we use. It just so happens, the enzyme acetylcholinesterase plays an essential part in nerve function which, as we have said, appears to be a highly sensitive target.

From what we do know about the ways insecticides kill, it would seem that specificity—maximum activity against the insect with minimum detriment to man—comes from different rates of *uptake* and *breakdown* of the chemicals we use, rather than different *sensitivities* where they act. Nevertheless, the many studies made of the action of insecticides leave us in no doubt that insects themselves are resilient to most forms of chemical poisoning: they have defence mechanisms which can break down or get rid of poisons quite rapidly, so that insecticides, if not lethal, have only temporary effects.

In this chapter we shall look at the properties and action of insecticides inside cockroaches. We shall not be concerned with the differences in the fate of chemicals in insects and man, factors which might be responsible for selective action.

The nervous system and nerve transmission
To help understand how insecticides affect nerve function some knowledge of

the insect nervous system and the way it works is desirable. The nervous system of the cockroach is described in detail in Volume I (Chapter 7). It is sufficient here to summarise its structural components and the factors responsible for impulse transmission.

The central nervous system consists of a ventral nerve cord connected to the brain, the latter having a co-ordinating function. Ganglia around the oesophagus secrete hormones. The peripheral nervous system conveys stimuli (by afferent nerves) from receptors on the cuticle to the central nervous system. Motor (or efferent nerves) convey instructions to the muscles or other effector organs. These 'stimuli' and 'instructions' exist in the form of nerve impulses carried by the basic components of the nervous system, the nerve cells or neurones.

Short branched processes—the dendrites—convey impulses to the nerve cell. A long filamentous process—the axon—conveys information away, and to the next adjacent nerve cell. Bundles of these axons are grouped together to form the nerves, which take on a special grouping—as giant fibres—in the ventral nerve cord.

The transmission of nerve impulses is best considered in two parts: (1) movement along the nerve axon from one cell to the next, i.e. *axonic transmission* and (2) movement across the gap—the synapse—between the transmitting axon of one cell and the receiving dendrites of the next, i.e. *synaptic transmission*. The reason why this differentiation has been made is because some insecticides interfere with the first of these transmission processes and others influence the second.

Axonic transmission is best thought of as an electrical process although its actual basis involves physical chemistry. Synaptic transmission is essentially one involving enzyme biochemistry.

Axonic transmission
The inside of an unstimulated nerve axon is more negatively charged, electrically, than the outside. By using micro-electrodes it is possible to trace the sequence of electrical changes which occur inside the nerve, as an impulse goes by (Fig. 161a). Momentarily, the nerve becomes more positively charged ('the spike potential'): the membrane potential is reversed in sign during excitation. In the process of recovering quickly to its normal negative 'resting potential' there is a fraction of a second when polarity 'overshoots' the resting potential. The reversal in polarity constitutes an electrical wave—an impulse, or 'action potential'—along the axon.

Transmission of an impulse along a nerve axon involves rapid movement, and therefore a rapid change in the concentration of electrically charged ions of potassium and sodium inside, compared with outside the axon: these movements occur across the nerve membrane. We can therefore anticipate that any chemical capable of interfering with the porosity of the nerve membrane to these electrically charged ions, may be expected to disrupt normal nerve function.

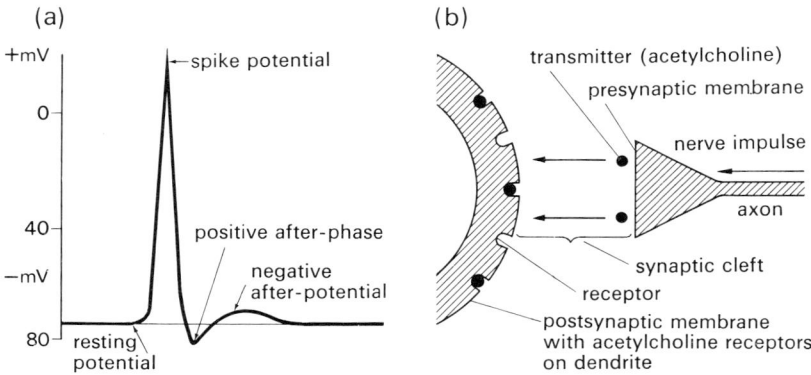

Fig. 161. Nerve impulse transmission: (a) action potential recorded inside the nerve membrane showing changes in electrical state with the passage of a nerve impulse (from Narahashi[606]); (b) diagram of a nerve synapse. (From Corbett[213]).

Synaptic transmission

This is the transfer of information from one neurone to the next. When an impulse reaches the end of an axon the change in electrical polarity dies out and is replaced by a chemical transmitter substance which crosses the gap and 'sparks off' another action potential in the next neurone. This substance is released from the end of the axon (Fig. 161b) and diffuses across the synapse—a gap of 10–20 nm (1 nm = one thousandth of a micron).[755]

There are two kinds of chemical transmitter substance, but the one which is important in insects is acetylcholine. A molecule of this substance is about 0·9 nm,[637] so that only small amounts are needed to stimulate a receptor on the other side of the synapse. When this happens, permeability to sodium ions changes, triggering an action potential.

It is obviously necessary that this chemical stimulator should be 'turned off', or nullified, ready for the next occasion—a fraction of a second later—when another impulse has to cross the synapse. Thus the transmitter substance acetylcholine is eliminated promptly by the enzyme acetylcholinesterase removing the acetyl group from the choline. In doing this, the enzyme returns the receptor to its resting position. Synapses occur in both the sensory and central nervous systems of insects and the zones of highest density are in the ganglia and brain.

In the normal insect the two substances—the transmitter and the enzyme which removes it—are in balance. Clearly any chemical which inhibits the production or action of the enzyme will seriously disrupt nerve function. The effect might be compared with a failure, simultaneously, of all the traffic lights in a large city. Communications would fail; chaos would soon result.

Acetylcholinesterase has the same function in man. The selective toxicities of organophosphorus and carbamate insecticides, which interact with acetylcholinesterase, are not therefore inherent in their sites of action. We do not know what transmitter substance is involved at the synapses between nerves and muscles—at the neuromuscular junctions of insects—or how it is eliminated.

Interference by insecticides
Much of this chapter is concerned with the experimental evidence which implicates insecticides as chemicals interfering with nerve function. We have no better interpretation of how insecticides work, and much of the finer detail is still missing. The pyrethrins, synthetic pyrethroids and DDT appear to disrupt axonic transmission by binding with the nerve axon. Other chlorinated hydrocarbons, such as lindane and dieldrin, appear to do likewise, but we do not know with any certainty how they work. The organophosphorus and carbamate insecticides inhibit acetylcholinesterase, but there is also evidence that they interfere with other non-specific enzyme systems (e.g. insect aliesterase).

In addition to action on the insect nervous system there have been many studies of the 'side effects' of insecticides. It is difficult to interpret the significance of these; whether they contribute to poisoning of the insect or occur as a result of it. The two books, 'Insecticides: action and metabolism' by O'Brien[637] and 'The Biochemical Mode of Action of Pesticides' by Corbett[213] provide useful reference texts for the reader who wishes to enquire into the subject in more detail than is given here.

ACTION OF THE PYRETHRINS

The important stages in the poisoning of a cockroach by a contact insecticide are (1) pick up, (2) penetration, (3) activation—of some chemicals only, (4) ability to withstand degradation and excretion, (5) distribution to the target and (6) attack of the target itself (Fig. 162). We shall start by assuming that the insect is already contaminated with pyrethrins which are beginning to penetrate.

The symptoms of poisoning by pyrethrins are first excitability, followed by prostration (knockdown), twitching movements, paralysis and death. These are what we see as outward expressions of the poisoning process.

Penetration of the cuticle by pyrethrins
When pyrethrins I, in almost lethal quantities (0·5 μg/insect), are applied to the cuticle of American cockroaches, about one quarter passes into the insect within an hour: this is the period when effects on nerve ganglia, measured by electrophysiological methods, are greatest. About half the amount applied penetrates in 6 hours, by which time the insect has long been prostrate. Concurrently, some of the insecticide is eliminated: the rate at which this occurs is so rapid that not more than one eighth of the applied dose can be found internally after 16 hours.[158] The amount of pyrethrin in the insect's body increases during the first hour or two, when symptoms of poisoning are severe and then—with a balance between penetration and loss—remains steady for at least 24 hours (Fig. 163).

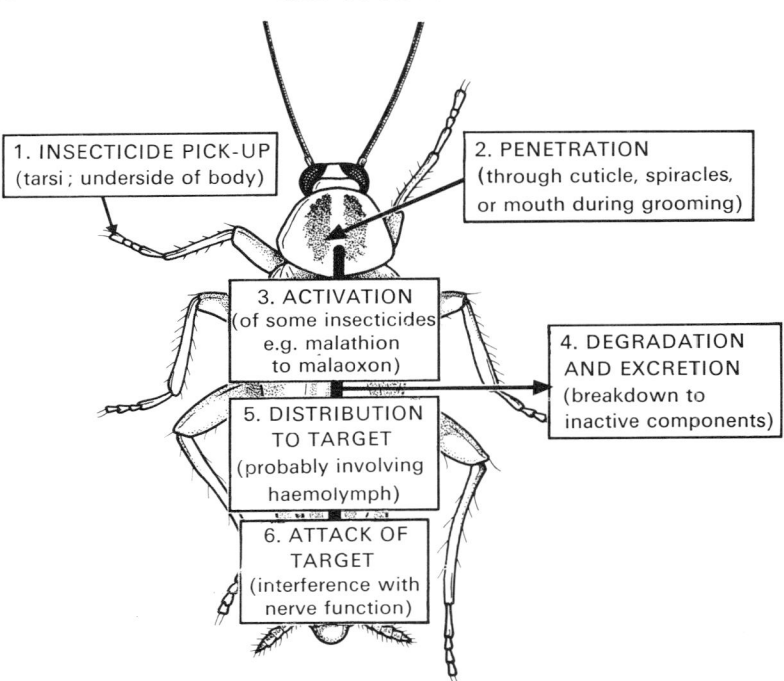

Fig. 162. Stages in the poisoning of a cockroach by a contact insecticide. (After O'Brien[635]).

To determine how rapidly pyrethrins penetrate into cockroaches, Hutzel[448] recorded the speed of onset of poisoning symptoms. Except for allowing the insects to make footprints in dust, the other methods he used put his cockroaches to severe indisposition. They had to run in a treadmill, exercise muscular traction on a rotating wheel, and in a 'leg jerk method' they recorded their responses *via* a human hair to a lever on a kymograph.

In summary, since cockroaches drag their abdomens when running, the amount of insecticide adhering to the body is increased. Liquid formulations of pyrethrum penetrate the insect and therefore cause symptoms more rapidly than dust (in 2 and 55 seconds, respectively). A threshold level occurs for stimulation by pyrethrins—0·006 per cent in a 1 μl droplet—and an increase in this dose does not affect the 'latent period' before onset of symptoms, but does shorten the interval before onset of paralysis. To prove that the nerve cord is implicated as part of the poisoning process, the cord may be cut beneath the third abdominal segment. Insecticides placed behind the cut produce no stimulation anterior to it, although the abdomen and cerci show typical twitching movements. Application next to the thorax and in front of the cut, results in the characteristic 'leg jerking' response.

Hutzel believed that the underside of the thorax was more sensitive to pyrethrum dust than the underside of the abdomen, where application often failed to bring about a response, irrespective of quantity. He concluded that a film existed on the surface of the cockroach cuticle, sufficient to moisten pyrethrum powder, so extracting the pyrethrins which then diffused to the sensory nerve endings. Also, because of the limited quantity of 'pyrethrum-extracting secretion' only that layer of dust actually making contact with the integument became effective. He considered the symptoms of poisoning to be reflex responses following stimulation of the sensory nerve endings. The drop in amplitude of 'leg jerks', following initial activation, were attributed to 'insect fatigue'. Onset of final paralysis was dependent on the speed with which pyrethrins spread to the thorax to inactivate the thoracic ganglia.[449]

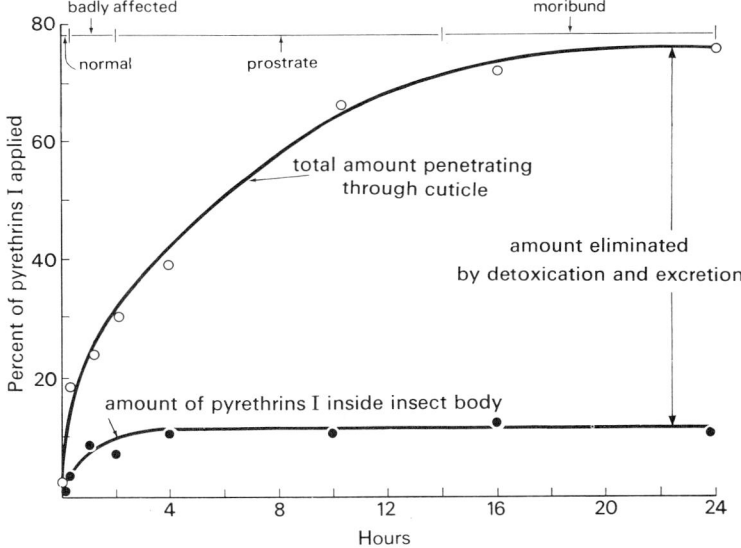

Fig. 163. Fate of pyrethrins I applied topically to *P. americana* at different stages of poisoning. (From Burt et al.[158]).

Distribution in the insect

The distribution of pyrethrins has been studied, in the body of adult American cockroaches, after administering it in different ways.[880] It was radioactively labelled. After spiracular perfusion of the mesothorax, the fore-gut contained the greatest amount of radioactivity, perhaps due to closeness of application. In males and females, two-thirds and three-quarters, respectively, of the radioactivity administered was retained in the remainder of the insect's body, indicating extensive distribution of the insecticide or its breakdown products.

Inside the cockroach, pyrethrins I becomes strongly associated with body solids: when equilibrium is established between penetration and loss, only one part in 30,000 of the insecticide is in solution. Thus at a dose that would normally kill 95 per cent of cockroaches, the concentration of pyrethrins in the haemolymph is very low indeed, and seems hardly adequate to account for the damage to the nervous system. Nevertheless, haemolymph from cockroaches poisoned by pyrethrins is able to cause symptoms typical of the insecticide, when applied to exposed nerves of normal cockroaches.

Haemolymph from the cut antennae and legs of treated cockroaches can be shown to be toxic by injecting it into other insects, such as Flesh flies (*Sarcophaga*). Blood taken several hours after complete paralysis of the cockroach has the same toxicity as that taken immediately after prostration. This indicates a fairly constant concentration of toxin—a balance of penetration and loss (Fig. 163).

There is no evidence that the insecticide produces effects on the insect's nervous system by spreading over the cuticle and then penetrating to the site of action through the tracheae.[158] In fact a deliberate attempt to achieve this by irrigating the respiratory system was somewhat less than successful.

From measurements of the insecticidal activity of pyrethrins and synthetic pyrethroids in Mustard beetles, the less toxic compounds penetrate the cuticle somewhat faster and thus become subject to more rapid detoxication.[279] Speedy penetration, and therefore availability of pyrethrins within the insect for immediate breakdown, could be a primary factor influencing (1) the relative susceptibility of species (e.g. house-flies compared with cockroaches), and (2) the relative insecticidal activity of the synthetic pyrethroids, one to another (see Chapter 10).

Effect of temperature

Cockroaches and some other insects are more rapidly affected by pyrethrins at low temperatures than high:[386] for instance, about six times more insecticide is needed to kill American cockroaches at 35°C than at 15°C.[109] This effect of temperature probably contributes to the poor performance of pyrethrins in hot, steamy kitchens.

Haemolymph from cockroaches poisoned by pyrethrins when the insects are held at 35°C, is completely non-toxic to flies, whereas haemolymph from treated cockroaches at 15°C contains toxin. If cockroaches are successively alternated between 35°C and 15°C, the blood is always toxic at the lower temperature but not at the higher. Use of radioactively labelled pyrethrins shows that penetration of the insecticide is more than twice as fast at 35°C than at 15°C. The rate of penetration through the cuticle therefore has nothing to do with the more severe poisoning at low temperatures.

Cockroaches prostrate at 15°C can be returned to normal by transferring them to 35°C and *vice versa*: this process can be repeated for several hours. Thus, *if* a toxin is produced at the higher temperature, it is ineffective (see also p. 392). When, however, a synergist (e.g. piperonyl butoxide) is used with the pyrethrins, both houseflies and American cockroaches are more susceptible at the higher temperature.[183] As the action of synergists is believed to increase the toxicity of pyrethrins by preventing their breakdown, it would seem that lack of poisoning symptoms with unsynergised pyrethrins at high temperatures is because very rapid detoxication is occurring (see also synergism of carbaomates p. 419). At high temperatures, the greater metabolic activity of the insect probably contributes to the more rapid breakdown of the pyrethrins, thus lowering insecticidal activity.[607] It could also be that the sensitivity of the nervous system varies with temperature as with DDT.[874]

Effects on respiration
Poisoning by pyrethrins and many other insecticides alters the oxygen intake and carbon dioxide production of insects. Hayashi[405] has investigated the effects of an emulsion of pyrethrins, with and without piperonyl butoxide, on the oxygen consumption of adult male American cockroaches. Unsynergised pyrethrins cause an increase in oxygen demand which reaches a maximum 50 minutes after application. Using synergised pyrethrins, the rate of oxygen consumption increases more rapidly after treatment and reaches a higher peak at 40 minutes (Fig. 164). With sublethal amounts, the normal level of respiration is reinstated within 90 minutes. Results obtained with allethrin are very similar.

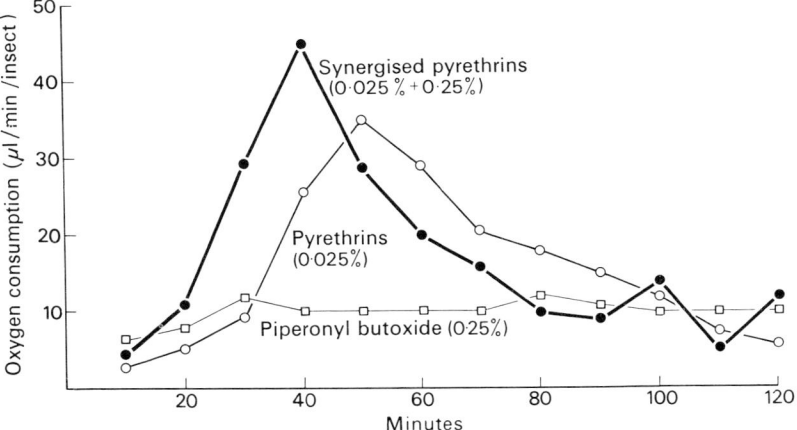

Fig. 164. The effects of pyrethrins and piperonyl butoxide, alone and together, on the oxygen consumption of *P. americana*. (From Hayashi[405]).

When radioactively labelled pyrethrins are applied to American cockroaches,[880] the initial excitation and convulsions of the insect are accompanied by abrupt increases in respiration rate and the production of $^{14}CO_2$. More pyrethrins are excreted (as radioactively labelled carbon dioxide and precipitated as barium carbonate: $Ba\ ^{14}CO_3$), after perfusion of the spiracles than by other methods of application. It is most likely that the effect of pyrethrins on the respiration of cockroaches comes indirectly from stimulation of the insect, and not as a direct cause of the insecticide.

Effect on heart beat

In poisoned *P. americana*, the heart continues to beat long after the appendages are paralysed, and in severe poisoning, circulation of the haemolymph ceases before the heart stops.[212] Pyrethrins at 0·5 ppm cause permanent alteration in frequency of heart beat of American cockroaches. At the lower 0·1 ppm, there is immediate depression in frequency of heart beat;[601] lower concentrations still (0·025 ppm), cause a temporary initial increase; very low concentrations (0·0025 ppm) increase the frequency which is maintained for some time. At all these concentrations the isolated heart of *P. americana* beats irregularly with an increased amplitude and occasional pauses in diastole.

Knowing that very low concentrations of pyrethrins stimulate the frequency of heart beat and high concentrations depress it, many experiments have been reported in which 'changes' in frequency are used to examine the fate of pyrethrins and other insecticides injected into the cockroach body. By injecting *P. americana* with pyrethrins (at 5 μg/g) and extracting haemolymph at intervals, it is possible to judge from effects on the beat of isolated hearts, what has happened since the insecticide entered the insect. By incubating pyrethrins with cockroach blood outside the insect's body it was hoped to learn whether substances additional to those in the haemolymph were involved in toxicity. Blood tested after 4 hours, irrespective of procedure, stimulated isolated hearts indicating a low concentration of pyrethrins and that detoxication was occurring in both instances.[774]

However, by extracting blood from cockroaches treated with pyrethrins maintained at two temperatures (35°C and 15°C), and using this on isolated hearts from untreated insects, a noticeable difference in effect on heart beat activity is found.[648] Some substance, having an important toxic effect, is apparently released by the action of pyrethrins at low temperature, which is not formed at the higher temperature.

Effects on haemolymph volume

Most insects poisoned by insecticides lose body fluids rapidly. Experiments have been carried out to determine whether American cockroaches killed by pyrethrins die because of loss of water, through increased respiration or increased diuresis.[155] The latter has been noted in other insects and may be a symptom of damage to the nervous system by the insecticide.

Cockroaches treated with just-lethal doses of pyrethrins I were weighed every half hour for 7 hours. One hour after treatment, the insects started to lose weight faster than untreated cockroaches. By this time the poisoned insects were already prostrate, suggesting that dehydration begins only when fatality is already assured. To further establish this, transfusions were carried out with the hope of alleviating poisoning symptoms. However, 20–50 μl of saline, or haemolymph from untreated cockroaches, injected four times within 7 hours failed to influence symptoms and none of the injected insects recovered.[155]

Effects of pyrethrins in the gut
The pyrethrins are used for their contact action and the ease with which they penetrate the insect cuticle is now unquestioned. There are many who believe that pyrethrins do not act as a stomach poison—that they are not toxic in the gut and are readily detoxified by the tissues.

If this is so, one would not expect pyrethrum to affect the enzymes of the gut (the non-specific alkaline and acid phosphatases) which are responsible for various digestive functions, such as the transport of digested food across the gut wall and the regeneration of the epithelial lining.[730]

Accordingly, starved American cockroaches were fed pyrethrum powder incorporated in glucose and gelatine, using a glass syringe and avoiding contact with other parts of the body. In subsequent autopsies, sections of the wall of the mid-gut and caeca were subjected to various staining procedures. Results showed that production of alkaline phosphatase drops sharply after ingestion of insecticide; after six hours the level is not only regained but is enhanced, but within 12 hours returns to normal. There is also a gradual loss in acid phosphatase activity from 3–24 hours.

These observations suggest serious disruption of the normal physiological processes of the mid-gut and caeca—where most of the digestion and absorption of food in cockroaches occur. Concurrently with the change in enzyme activity there is an accumulation of glycogen. This is the major carbohydrate reserve of insects, most of which is found in the fat body. The accumulation in the gut wall occurs first in the muscle layers of the mid-gut, progressing by 12 hours after feeding to the connective tissue and epithelial layer.[731] Additionally, there is a change in the phospholipid content of the gut wall: lipids which exist in many forms in the cockroach are important energy resources. Within 3 hours of ingesting pyrethrins, the phospholipids increase in the epithelial layer of the mid-gut, become sub-normal after 6 hours and then almost disappear.

Thus many physiological disorders occur in the tissues of the mid-gut, subsequent to ingestion of pyrethrins. However, because the changes occur so relatively slowly, compared with onset of excitation and paralysis, it seems that these disorders are more associated with the process of dying rather than symptoms of insecticide poisoning.

Action on the cockroach nervous system
There is now indisputable evidence that the toxic effects of pyrethrins are associated with direct action on the insect nervous system. Precisely what processes occur has not been fully resolved. For instance, because some flies may be knocked down by pyrethrins almost instantaneously, there is a temptation to believe that part of the action, and therefore the symptoms of knockdown, must result from interference with peripheral nerves. These sensory fibres, ending in receptors in the cuticle, are the first to be exposed to

pyrethrins when a flying or crawling insect encounters insecticide. The onset of knockdown is often so rapid that it appears unnecessary for deeper penetration of the insecticide into the insect.

Moreover, because pyrethrins are characterised by such manifestly different symptoms during the course of poisoning one would question whether these result from changes taking place at the same or different sites of the insect's nervous system.

In addition, it should be remembered that cockroaches and other insects are readily capable of recovering from knockdown. In some the dosage required to kill is often much higher than that to immobilise. Does the ability to recover from the poisoning indicate more than one site of action?

Action on sensory nerve endings
Some of the early studies of the effects of pyrethrins on the nervous system tend to favour action on the sensory nerve endings, as emphasised by Page & Blackith.[650] They say, in a review of previous work: 'Hartzell and his co-workers[398,399,400] have carried out an extensive histological examination of the nervous systems of insects poisoned by the pyrethrins, with and without various added synergists. Their studies[651] ... have shown that not only do the pyrethrins act primarily on the peripheral nervous system of the insects, but that the site of action is only a few thousandths of a millimetre from the external surface of the insects'.

When pyrethrins are injected into the abdomen, or into a spiracle of the cockroach, there is progressive weakening of the insect starting with the leg innervated by the ganglion nearest the point of injection. Symptoms then progress to the opposite leg and so on.[717] This observation suggests some limitation in speed of distribution of insecticide in the insect. Experiments with a number of insects in which more and more pyrethrins are applied to the cuticle, to speed up onset of paralysis, show that the minimum is 2·5 minutes. This is believed to be the time required for diffusion through the cuticle to the site of action. Three minutes is the time required to knockdown[651] 50 per cent of German cockroaches treated with 0·02 per cent pyrethrins (Fig. 165).

To establish conclusively whether the sensory nerve endings, or the central nervous system (the ganglia and nerve cord) is the primary site of attack by pyrethrins, Burt & Goodchild[155] applied pyrethrins I in acetone to houseflies. Application was made to the ventral side of the thorax (near to the CNS) and to the dorsum. Knockdown occurred much sooner with the pyrethrins applied to the underside of the thorax than above. Rate of knockdown was examined with pyrethrins applied topically and when injected. For 50 per cent knockdown in 2 minutes, 20,000 times more pyrethrins was required with topical application than by injection. Clearly injection allowed the insecticide to reach the site of action for knockdown much more quickly. This suggests involvement of the CNS rather than the sensory endings associated with the cuticle.

Using American cockroaches for such studies, the LD_{95} of pyrethrins I, applied topically, was compared with two synthetic pyrethroids: that for the pyrethrins (0·37 μg) was one quarter of that of bioallethrin (1·49 μg) and one third that of bioresmethrin (1·16 μg). When these compounds were applied directly to the exposed nerve cords of cockroaches, the toxicities of the individual compounds were greater: the pyrethrins were 100 times as active as bioallethrin and 10 times more active than bioresmethrin. Thus unlike the results with houseflies, it would seem that the relative ability of pyrethrins, compared with the pyrethroids, to kill cockroaches, depends on the poisoning process at the site of action and is much less influenced by processes such as penetration and detoxication.

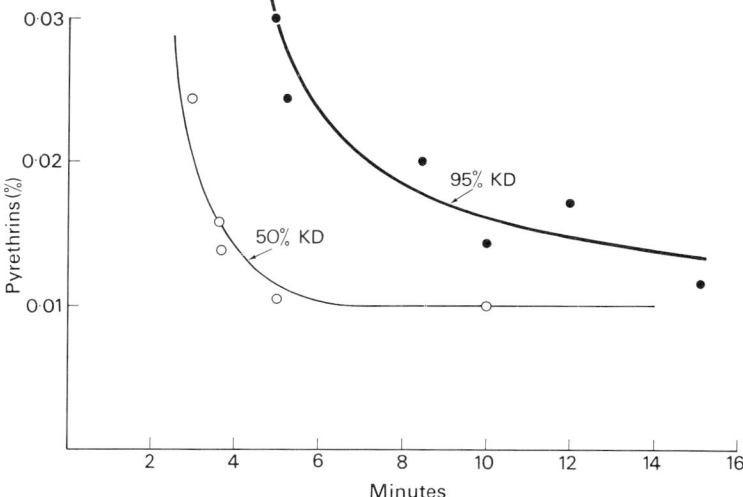

Fig. 165. Relation between pyrethrins concentration and times for 50 per cent and 95 per cent knockdown of *B. germanica* after spraying. (From Chadwick[179]).

Physical damage to the nervous system

If pyrethrins damage the central nervous system, what form does this take? To answer this, nymphs and adults of American cockroaches injected with insecticide, have been examined for possible damage associated with cessation of nerve action. In other experiments, pyrethrins have been applied to the cuticle; the insecticide has also been fed to the insects. Degenerated nerve tissue was found, proceeding from the region of application, but death of the insects had no fixed relationship to the degree of damage. All effects observed were subsequent to paralysis, without the insect's recovery, and were therefore post-mortem 'end-results' rather than 'cause'.[701]

The indications are that damage to nerve tissues from insecticidal poisoning develops slowly and it is questionable whether pyrethrum has any causal relationship to 'pyrethrum lesions' other than killing the nerves. In the opinion of Richards & Cutkomp,[701] studies of the pathology of damage to insect nerves might give 'some slight help in locating the action of insecticides, but that, at best, it is a crude and likely to be a misleading measure of physiological effect in insects.'.

Electron microscopy of normal American cockroaches and those exposed to pyrethrins applied topically to the pronotum, also shows no difference in the ultra-structure of the brain tissues or of the ganglia. If the primary site of action of pyrethrins is in the central nervous system, 'paralysis results from a chemical disturbance of neurones and is not detectable by the most recent methods of microscopy'.[168] This conclusion expressed in 1968 is in direct contrast to the views being expressed 20 years before when it was believed that the reaction of pyrethrins with insect nerves was one of physical interference: a reaction with the lipid surface of nerve axons.[839] The pyrethrins are readily soluble in lipids and this, it was believed, would facilitate entry of insecticide into the nerve cell membrane. Sufficient deposition there might interfere with and eventually block the conduction of impulses along axons to recipient dentrites of adjacent neurones.

Effects on nerve activity

We are left, it seems with poisoning by pyrethrins occurring through some chemical action on the cockroach nervous system. Much of the evidence now shows that at least two actions are involved. Following application of the insecticide, there is an initial 'excitatory action' in the central nervous system (as demonstrated by stimulated and convulsive movements of the insect) and a 'blocking action' (as seen by knockdown and paralysis). Both are supported by experimental evidence,[154,158] especially from neuropharmacological studies with allethrin.[612]

The simplest demonstration of the 'two actions' was made by Lowenstein in 1942 using Oriental cockroaches.[510] It is well known, that when the cerci of cockroaches are stimulated by a puff of air, there is a discharge of nerve activity in the last abdominal ganglion and a burst of electrical activity through the giant fibres of the nerve cord. This can be detected with fine electrodes and the activity recorded on an oscillograph or reproduced as a crackling 'noise' on a loudspeaker. Lowenstein used the time to suppress these discharges as a measure of the effect of pyrethrins applied to the exposed abdominal nerve cord. He discovered that under the influence of pyrethrum there is *first* a massive discharge of a number of types of impulses in the nerve cord (the initial excitatory phase), followed by a 'spontaneous, synchronised discharge of continuous trains of giant-fibre potentials'. *Second*, sensory stimulation becomes weak and eventually fails (blocking phase), with no further electrical activity in the nerve cord. The time taken from application of pyrethrins, to a disappearance of response in the giant fibres when the cerci are stimulated is closely correlated with insecticide concentration (Fig. 166).

For the Oriental cockroach 1·6 per cent pyrethrins applied to the cuticle of the insect produces the same toxic effect as 0·3 per cent applied directly to the insect's exposed central nerve cord.

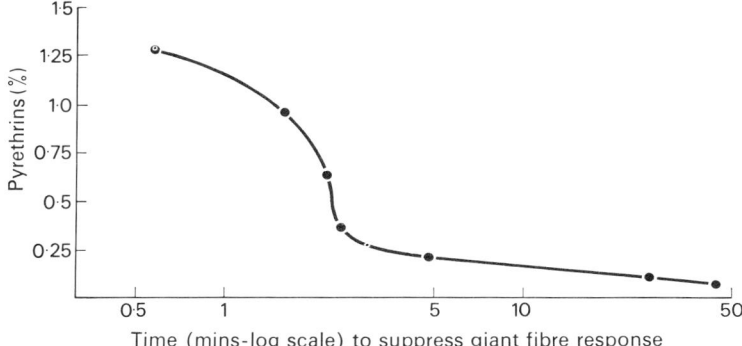

Fig. 166. Time/concentration curve for the suppression by pyrethrins of action potentials in the nerve cord of *B. orientalis*, arising from stimulation of the cerci. (From Lowenstein[510]).

Effects on spontaneous nerve activity

In the normal cockroach, electrical discharges occur in the nerve cord as a result of sensory stimulation, but there are also spontaneous (endogenous) nerve impulses arising in the last abdominal ganglion of the cockroach when all sensory connections with it are cut.[154] This spontaneous activity has been utilised to examine the course of poisoning by pyrethrins I.

Apparently, the processes which prove fatal to cockroaches occur within their ganglia, rather than in the axons of the giant fibres. This is based on three conclusions. First, the concentration of insecticide carried by the haemolymph, which actually penetrates the nervous system, is too little to affect conduction in the axons. Therefore impairment of nerve conduction in the giant fibres is not likely to contribute substantially to killing the insects. Such very small amounts of pyrethrins do, however, increase electrical activity in the last abdominal ganglion. Second, although cockroaches treated with 0.5 g of pyrethrins I are all prostrate 2 hours after treatment, and moribund after 16 hours, the giant fibres of these insects show few abnormalities until 4 hours after treatment. This argues that failure of nerve conduction (that is paralysis as a symptom of pyrethrin poisoning) is probably a secondary effect associated with general tissue degradation.

Third, and more importantly, changes which occur in the spontaneous activity of the last abdominal ganglion closely parallel the course of poisoning in cockroaches: 15 minutes after treatment, when abnormal symptoms begin to appear, spontaneous nerve activity increases; after 1 hour, when severe symptoms are evident, there are intense bursts of activity in the ganglion which continue until 4 hours when all insects are prostrate. The 'symptoms of poisoning' by pyrethrins therefore seem to be associated more closely with damage to neurones within ganglia than with impairment of conduction in axons outside them.[154]

Similar studies to establish the contribution of synergists in the poisoning of cockroaches by pyrethrins[155] provided no evidence that piperonyl butoxide modifies their action on the central nervous system, except for some depression of spontaneous activity. The addition of synergists to pyrethrum applied to the cockroach central nervous system shortens the time, compared with pyrethrum alone, to block conduction in the giant fibres,[153] but has little effect on the amplitude of action potentials in the giant fibres. The action of piperonyl butoxide and other synergists in enhancing the action of pyrethrins—by slowing detoxication—is thus confirmed to lie outside the nervous system.

It is now widely accepted that excitation in a nerve is caused by the movement of ions across the axon membrane. Normally the fluid surrounding the nerve cells is high in sodium ions and low in potassium; the reverse being true within the nerve cell. An action potential (nerve pulse) is caused by the influx of sodium and an efflux of potassium. Whilst there is no substantiating evidence, it seems likely that poisoning by pyrethrins is an expression of a block of the normal sodium and potassium currents associated with the formation of nerve impulses. This is not, however, considered to be the case with poisoning by allethrin, although interference with chemical permeability of the nerve sheath is probably involved.[604, 605]

THE ACTION OF DDT

Very few people engaged in pest control seem likely to apply DDT in the future and the way it brings about death of cockroaches is perhaps of little concern to today's insecticide user. However, because many readers will have used it in the past and seen the symptoms of poisoning of insects killed with it, some space for a review of the considerable work done to try to discover how DDT works is justified.

The symptoms of poisoning by DDT are described in detail in Chapter 11: first there is instability of the insect with tremulous movement of the head and appendages. It staggers and falls repeatedly on its back. Tremors give way to paralysis, but death may not occur until many hours or days later.

We are not much better informed about how DDT kills cockroaches than is the case with the pyrethrins, despite the fact that DDT has probably been the subject of more 'mode of action' studies than any other insecticide. Apart from the housefly, the cockroach has been used most often, and not surprisingly, there are many and varied accounts of the way DDT kills. Its ability to penetrate the cuticle and appear in the insect's fat body probably has much to do with the ease with which DDT can dissolve fats. As we shall see later, this may influence the ability of DDT to penetrate the lipid nerve sheath.

There is now little doubt that DDT acts *via* the nervous system of insects where it binds to the protein portion of the nerve membrane.[380] Here it interferes with the movement of ions, into and out of the nerve axon. But it is anomalous that non-toxic compounds related to DDT (*viz.* DDT analogues) do just the same, and that DDT binds to non-nervous tissue as well.[213] Studies with radioactive DDT and cockroach blood show that the insecticide binds to the blood proteins, indicating a possible route into the central nervous system.[919] Some of the lipoproteins which bind DDT in the haemolymph of American cockroaches have been isolated.[915] The interaction of DDT with the nerve membrane brings about abnormal discharges of electrical impulses in the cockroach nervous system. 'Trains' of nerve impulses in the ventral nerve cord of the poisoned insect coincide with body tremors and may frequently continue after the cockroach is prostrate.

Without actually explaining the insecticidal action of DDT, Martin[529] believed that ability (1) to penetrate, (2) to concentrate at, and (3) to be sufficiently stable to reach, the site of action were important attributes. Let us start by looking at how DDT gets into cockroaches and then at the effects it produces within.

Penetration, distribution and breakdown of DDT in the cockroach

One of the reasons why DDT performs poorly against *some* insects is because it is unable to penetrate the cuticle. For example, the amount, topically applied, to kill 50 per cent of American cockroaches is as little as 10 μg/g, but more than 9,000 μg/g is needed for the grasshopper, *Melanoplus femurrubrum*: 2 μg/g of DDT *injected* into this grasshopper is lethal.

If solutions of radioactive DDT are applied to the cuticle of American cockroaches, penetration can be readily measured. Half the DDT applied to the abdomen, beneath the wings, passes through the cuticle in 24 hours and 75 per cent in 48 hours. The insecticide becomes widely distributed within the insect, and by 3 days about 20 per cent of the absorbed DDT has been excreted. Most of the remaining insecticide or its breakdown products occur in the fore-gut, hind-gut plus malpighian tubules, and fat body. Less than 1 per cent of DDT applied to the cuticle, or injected, is lost by respiration as radioactive carbon dioxide.[705]

In similar studies with the Madeira cockroach sublethal doses of DDT (66 μg and 100 μg/cockroach) were applied ventrally to the thorax.[505] The amount makes no difference to the rate of penetration of the cuticle, or to excretion. About one third penetrates the insect in the first 24 hours (Fig. 167). This is less than that reported for *P. americana*, and may account for the greater tolerance of the Madeira cockroach to large doses. Only tiny amounts are excreted.

DDT injected in measured amounts into the haemolymph of American cockroaches *via* the thorax, becomes fully distributed in 3 hours. At doses which kill half the insects in 4 days (5 μg for males and 20 μg for females), most of the DDT is recoverable from the alimentary canal, principally the fore-gut, the thoracic muscles and fat body.[193]

The part of the body of both sexes which appears to be most important in the breakdown of DDT to DDE is the fat body. Cochran suggests that the greater tolerance of adult females and last stage nymphs of both sexes to DDT derives from their having considerably larger fat bodies than adult males; the insecticide is diverted to the fat body, rather than to more important sites of action.

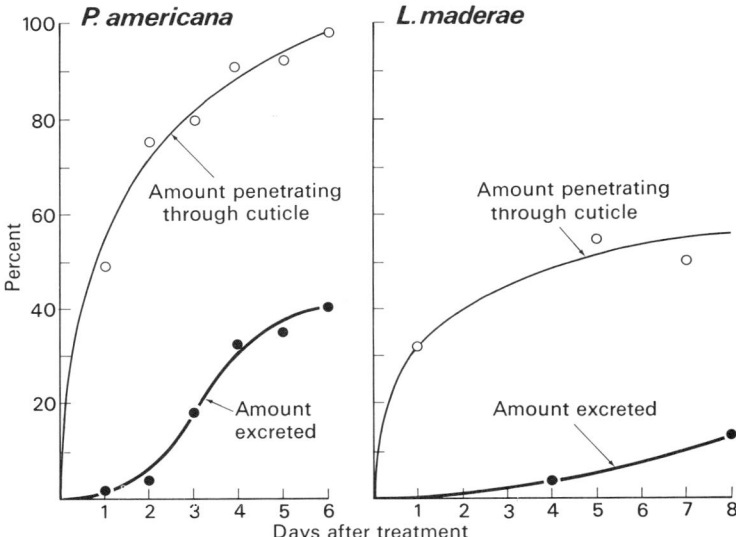

Fig. 167. Absorption of radioactive DDT and excretion of radioactivity in faeces following topical application of DDT: (left) to American cockroaches at 40 µg/insect (after Robbins & Dahm[705]); (right) to Madeira cockroaches at 66 µg/insect. (After Lindquist & Dahm[505]).

This was discounted by Munson & Gottlieb[598] three years earlier: they believe that the difference in susceptibility of the sexes of adult cockroaches is not accounted for by the small difference in lipid content. The change in lipid content with age of the cockroaches does however show a high correlation with the changing susceptibility of the insect to DDT.

Elimination of insecticide from DDT-susceptible insects is *via* the malpighian tubules rather than by detoxication. Degradation products of DDT do occur in such insects, but the process of breakdown is not sufficiently fast to prevent death. To study the effects of insecticides on the excretory efficiency of *P. americana*, dye was introduced into the haemolymph 24 hours before DDT (4–8 µg) was injected. Rate of clearance of dye from the blood of last stage nymphs shows that DDT has no effect; dieldrin (3–4·5 µg) retards excretion, and endrin (1·5 µg) almost completely inhibits it.[661]

Effects of temperature on cockroach susceptibility

We now come to some fascinating studies of DDT-poisoning. With most insecticides, the warmer the conditions the easier it is to kill insects. This is because the chemical processes of poisoning are speeded up, and the activity of cockroaches—and their contact with treated surfaces—is thus increased at high temperatures.[284] However, DDT and the pyrethrins (p. 390) both cause more pronounced symptoms of poisoning in cockroaches at low (15°C), rather than at high temperatures (35°C). One reason for this is, perhaps that the insect is less able to detoxify the insecticide when it is cool.[827] Symptoms of poisoning which are marked at low temperatures can be reduced by warming the cockroach, if the period previously at a low temperature has not been too long.

The greater toxicity of DDT to cockroaches at low temperatures can be readily demonstrated: the LD_{50} of DDT applied topically to *B. germanica* is 41 μg/insect at 32°C, only 13 μg at 22°C and 2 μg at 14·5°C—a difference in susceptibility of ×20 over this temperature range.[386] Methoxychlor, closely related to DDT, has the same properties. The response has been attributed to a difference in the ability of the cuticle, at different temperatures, to adsorb insecticide on to it.[299] Pradham[678] explains it as 'the balance at different temperatures of the opposing factors of DDT penetration, detoxication and elimination' from the insect.

The experiments of Vinson & Kearns[827] on DDT poisoning, justify description in some detail. For the American cockroach the 5-day LD_{50} for topically applied DDT at 15°C is 5–10 μg/insect. At 35°C it is 75–100 μg/insect, a difference in susceptibility for this species of 10 times.

Penetration is 2 to 2·5 times faster at the higher temperature: thus at 35°C, 85–95 per cent of the applied dose penetrates in 4 days, while only 35–50 per cent does so at 15°C. Cockroaches kept at the higher temperature, contain from 2 to 6·8 times as much *unchanged* DDT as insects similarly treated at 15°C. The proportion of absorbed DDT, to metabolised DDT, does not vary at the two temperatures; despite this, the large quantities of DDT which penetrate at the higher temperatures do not produce symptoms. They show up quickly, however, on transfer of the insects to a low temperature. This evidence establishes that factors other than penetration, detoxication and elimination of DDT, are necessary to explain the effect of temperature on the action of DDT. Pradham's suggestion made 3 years earlier was not proven.

Vinson & Kearns also investigated the effects of temperature when American cockroaches are injected with DDT. This eliminates cuticular penetration. The amount of DDT which must be injected to kill half the cockroaches in 5 days is 2–3 μg/insect at 15°C, and 25–30 μg/insect at 35°C; again a difference in susceptibility at the two temperatures of 10 times.

The breakdown of DDT in the body of the cockroach in the first 6 hours after injection is not very different at the two temperatures. But after 6 hours, metabolism at 15°C is practically negligible, but continues rapidly at 35°C. Poisoning symptoms in cockroaches do not appear in 1 hour at 35°C, whereas those at 15°C are knocked down within an hour and never recover. It seems then, that low temperatures drastically reduce the ability of the cockroach to detoxify high doses of DDT or, as suggested by Vinson & Kearns (*loc cit*), the insecticide is more effective at low temperatures in disrupting all bodily functions.

When this investigation is carried further and nymphs of the American cockroach are kept for two weeks at 34°C and 17°C before treating them with DDT, those held in the cool are *less readily affected by DDT* whether applied to the cuticle or injected. This is a reversal of the previous findings. In this experiment the temperature after treatment was 23°C, at which untreated cockroaches without food and water normally survive 4–5 weeks.

Munson[597] explains these results by suggesting that at 34°C the lipids in the cockroach are more fully saturated: DDT, being less soluble in them, is thus more readily available at the site of action to cause poisoning symptoms. He supports this argument by showing that temperature has a greater effect on poisoning symptoms when DDT is applied topically than when injected. Applied to the cuticle the insecticide is entering the haemocoel gradually and has less opportunity for preferential absorption by the fats.

A difference in the effects of DDT with temperature, and with method of application, is also reported by Eaton & Sternberg.[252,253] They confirm the results of Vinson & Kearns, that when the temperature is raised symptoms of poisoning in DDT-treated cockroaches are alleviated. Also that abnormal bursts of electrical impulses in the central nervous system are removed. In sensory nerves, however, changes in temperature do not affect the abnormal discharges caused by DDT. They continue throughout any temperature change.

What Eaton & Sternberg had discovered was that in the 'absence of high levels of sensory input' (as can be achieved by injecting DDT directly into the ganglia of the nerve cord, but not by application to the cuticle), the effects of DDT on the central nervous system increase with temperature, as in sensory nerves. Their explanation is that an excess of impulses stimulated by DDT in sensory nerves (those feeding information to the central nervous system) liberates 'excess transmitter substances' which accumulate at low temperature and ultimately block nerve transmission (indicating severe poisoning symptoms). These substances could be the 'DDT-induced toxin' described on p. 406.

It is now accepted that the change in toxicity of DDT with temperature has little to do with the effect of temperature on rates of penetration, detoxication and accumulation of the insecticide. The most likely explanation is that temperature causes an alteration in the sensitivity of the nerves with which the insecticide binds.[608] Greater amounts of radioactively labelled DDT are found in nerve tissue with increasing ambient temperature.[534]

Effects on body reserves

Cockroaches can live for many weeks without food. They survive on their body reserves, water being much more important to them. DDT-poisoning causes very noticeable hyperactivity, which may rapidly deplete the insects' reserves thus contributing to debility and eventual death. Dieldrin does not cause such hyperactivity and makes smaller demands on the insects' reserves.[188]

Normal and fatally poisoned American cockroaches lose 11–12 per cent of body weight when deprived of food and water for 18 hours. There is no weight loss if water can be taken. DDT-poisoning causes a 12 per cent loss in fats in 24 hours, but a DDT-poisoned cockroach does not lose more weight than can be accounted for by inability to feed and drink. The most marked reaction is a 90 per cent loss in body glycogen and glucose (Table CVII, 'Not anaesthetised' column).

TABLE CVII

GLYCOGEN AND GLUCOSE CONTENT (% WET WEIGHT) OF NORMAL AND DDT-POISONED ADULT MALE *P. AMERICANA*, WITH AND WITHOUT ANAESTHESIA, AND WITH AND WITHOUT GLUCOSE ADMINISTERED 12 HOURS AFTER TIME OF POISONING
(From Merrill, Savit & Tobias[559])

Time of capture	Treatment	Glycogen (%)		Glucose (%)	
		Not anaesthetised	Anaesthetised	Not anaesthetised	Anaesthetised
Winter	Normal	0·78	0·56	0·94	0·83
	DDT-poisoned	0·06	0·96	0·19	1·01
Spring	Normal	0·96	0·51	0·96	0·94
	DDT-poisoned	0·13	0·51	0·05	0·63

Time of capture	Treatment	glycogen (%) when glucose:		glucose (%) when glucose:	
		not given	given	not given	given
Summer	Normal	0·75	1·56	0·77	1·17
	DDT-poisoned	0·10	0·79	0·14	0·52

However, when cockroaches poisoned with DDT, are anaesthetised immediately symptoms appear, there is virtually no carbohydrate depletion (Table CVII, 'Anaesthetised' column) indicating that hyperactivity and not DDT is the cause. Insects recovering from anaesthesia show all the late symptoms of poisoning, and go on to die as if they had not been spared the early hyperactivity and fat loss. Administration of 10–30 mg of glucose to each insect, daily, for 3 days after poisoning has no influence on mortality, but does reduce body losses of glycogen and glucose (Table CVII).

When a cockroach is poisoned by DDT, the symptoms of incoordination are associated with increased respiration (Fig. 168). If DDT or methoxychlor is injected into German cockroaches at 100 μg/insect, consumption of oxygen increases 3–4 times above normal in half an hour, returning to normal after a few hours.[559]

Effects on amino acids

Only very small differences occur in most of the amino acids of the haemolymph of DDT-treated cockroaches at various stages of poisoning;

however the amount of proline is depleted in paralysed insects to one quarter of its normal content.[218] Relief of symptoms by transfer of poisoned cockroaches to warm conditions re-establishes the proline level, but this can again be reduced, with increased severity of poisoning, if the insects are returned to the cold.

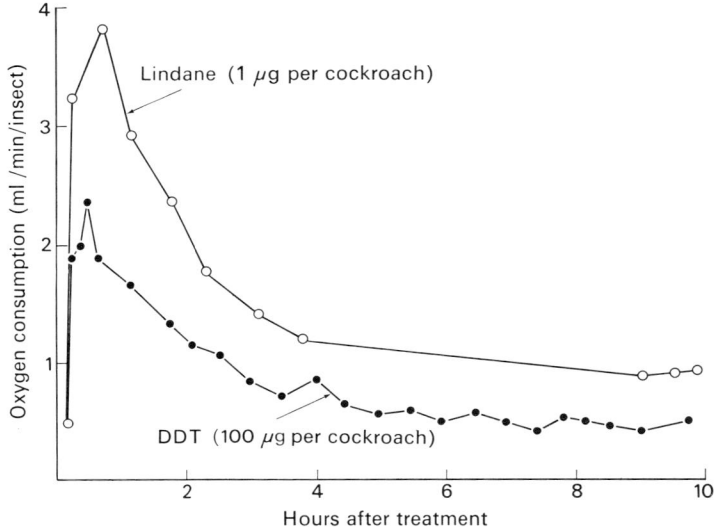

Fig. 168. Oxygen consumption of German cockroaches treated with 100 µg DDT and 1 µg lindane. (From Harvey & Brown[401]).

The changes in proline content of the haemolymph of cockroaches would appear therefore to be selectively correlated with symptoms of DDT poisoning, perhaps through a demand by the prostrate insect for oxidizable carbon. This suggestion gains support from the production of carbon-labelled carbon dioxide by American cockroaches, injected with radioactively-labelled proline.

Ray[696] has examined the amino acid content of the central nerve cords of normal and insecticide-treated American cockroaches. DDT and dieldrin were applied topically to the dorsal surface of the insects and the nerve cords dissected out. The principal amino acids in cockroach nerve cord are shown in Fig. 169. Both insecticides cause a loss of proline and rise in glutamine.

The marked drop in proline following insecticide poisoning certainly appears to be associated with prostration, the insect having previously experienced great muscular, nervous and respiratory activity, probably stimulating the oxidation of proline.

Similarity of symptoms of DDT-poisoning and bodily stress

In the next few pages we shall examine the results of experiments which help to explain the symptoms of poisoning by DDT. Prostration of DDT-poisoned

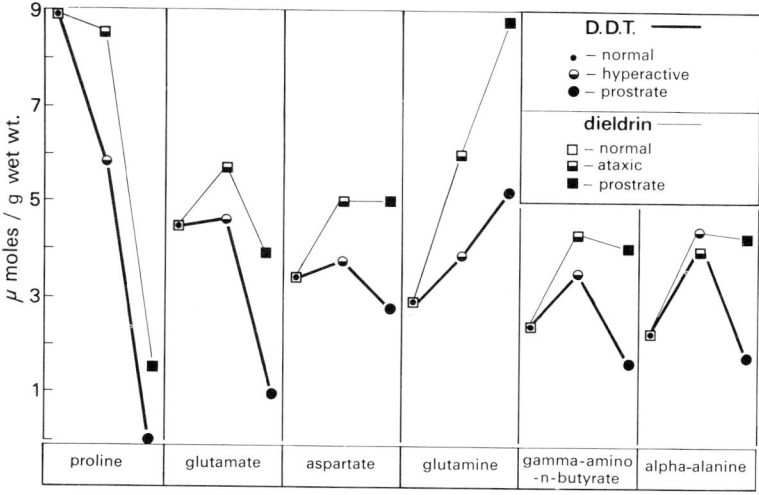

Fig. 169. Effect of topically applied DDT and dieldrin on the free amino acids of the nerve cord of *P. americana* at different stages of poisoning. (From Ray[696]).

cockroaches can be reproduced by inducing insects to struggle,[85] or more quickly by direct stimulation, using mechanical or electrical means (Vol. I, Chapter 7). Blood taken from American cockroaches, stressed by having their mouthparts sealed or by being dehydrated by silica aerogel, administered into the abdomens of honeybees produced in them a neuromuscular reaction. In some experiments fragments of leg muscle taken from normal and headless cockroaches, placed in contact with silica aerogel, were substituted for blood. The results suggest that the brain plays a part in producing substances associated with stress.[909]

Heslop & Ray[423] compared the effects of bodily stress and DDT-poisoning on the oxygen consumption and neuromuscular reactions of American cockroaches. When stress is imposed by immobilising cockroaches on their backs, or by applying 100 μg of DDT, there is in both cases, a surge of respiration preceding prostration and paralysis (Fig. 168). Cockroaches tied down but which do not become paralysed respire normally, like cockroaches free to move. Of two strains of *P. americana*, used in these tests, the one which was prostrated more readily by 20 μg of topically applied DDT was also the more readily paralysed by bodily stress.

According to Heslop & Ray, trains of nerve impulses in the ventral nerve cord of DDT-poisoned cockroaches always coincide with body tremors and frequently continue after prostration. Impulses were recorded in 30 of 45 cockroaches prostrated by DDT and in 8 of 13 paralysed by bodily stress. These studies suggest that because cockroaches subject to stress produce reactions so similar to DDT, insecticides of this type which first cause convulsions and then kill very slowly, may first produce symptoms of stress, obscuring the specific response to the poison.

DDT-induced toxin

DDT-poisoned cockroaches contain in their haemolymph a material which is not DDT but which on injection into normal cockroaches can be lethal. The action of this neurotoxin is independent of the DDT present in the blood. It does not excite the central nervous system of test insects if blood is removed from DDT-treated cockroaches held at 35°C, but will do so if removed from prostrate insects held at 15°C.[768] Haemolymph from DDT-poisoned cockroaches injected into the leg of another cockroach quickly causes high frequency discharges in the crural nerve; this active material accumulates in the haemolymph with the advancement of poisoning symptoms. Partially purified toxin, diluted 50-fold, greatly increases spontaneous activity in a cockroach isolated nerve cord. Higher concentrations block spontaneous activity.[767]

When blood is taken from American cockroaches treated with 125–150 μg of DDT and tested on excised nerve cords, the concentration of toxin in the blood increases as poisoning becomes more advanced.[742] Using electrical activity in the nerve cord as a measure of the toxin's effect, spontaneous nerve activity increases shortly after poisoning, reaches a maximum about half an hour after prostration, and then decreases. If blood from cockroaches, prostrate for some hours is diluted, this then produces an effect comparable to that of undiluted blood taken after only half an hour of prostration (Table CVIII).

TABLE CVIII

NUMBER OF NERVE IMPULSES/SECOND OF 50 MICROVOLTS AND LARGER, IN EXCISED NERVE CORDS OF MALE *P. AMERICANA* PERFUSED WITH UNDILUTED SUPERNATANTS OF HAEMOLYMPH FROM FEMALE *P. AMERICANA* IN VARIOUS STAGES OF DDT-POISONING. COUNTS TAKEN IN THE 1-MINUTE PERIODS INDICATED. ALSO THE EFFECT OF A 10 TIMES DILUTION IN PHYSIOLOGICAL SALINE OF SUPERNATANT TAKEN FROM COCKROACHES WHICH HAD BEEN PROSTRATE FOR 5 HOURS

(From Shankland & Kearns[742])

Stage of poisoning	Normal level	Minutes after perfusion						
		0–1	1–2	2–3	5–6	10–11	15–16	20–21
Hyperexcitable	0·2	9	6	15	13	8	9	12
Uncoordinated	0·4	2	6	1	3	14	21	9
Prostrate ½ hour	0	28	16	30	38	96	51	61
Prostrate 2 hours	1·0	6	16	17	9	13	1	17
Prostrate 5 hours	0·6	8	4	1	10	12	21	19
Prostrate 5 hours (diluted 10 times)	0·3	44	38	32	39	43	75	84

The DDT-induced toxin can also be produced in cockroaches by repeated mild electric shocks. Sternburg and colleagues suggest that because no such biologically active substance has been detected in the blood of untreated organisms, the toxin might result from excessive stimulation of the peripheral nerves: it may normally be involved in transmission of nerve impulses and the accumulation which occurs during DDT-poisoning may disrupt the entire nervous system.[767] Using chromatographic techniques, a substance produced in isolated nerve cords treated with organophosphorus compounds was found to be identical with that resulting in the intact insect following DDT-prostration.[404]

On the assumption that insects suffering bodily stress might produce the same, or a similar toxin, capable of giving DDT-like symptoms, a detailed examination of the haemolymph of *P. americana* has been made.[660] The insects examined were either normal, stressed by forced immobilisation, or poisoned with chlorinated hydrocarbon insecticides (especially DDT), or with organophosphates.

Physical stress and chlorinated hydrocarbons both cause the production of a compound with particular fluorescence characteristics, absent in normal cockroaches and not induced by organophosphorus-poisoning. This indicates that the American cockroach does respond in a similar biochemical fashion to the two situations. In contrast, Holzhacker & Giannotti[437] are unconvinced that the symptoms of DDT-poisoning—tremors and movements of legs—which may appear in different parts of the insect's body, are caused by a neurotoxin carried in the haemolymph. By severing the connectives of the ventral nerve cord of injected cockroaches they showed that symptoms of poisoning occur away from the site of injection, *only* when the central nerve cord is intact. They believe that the suboesophageal ganglion is a significant site of action of DDT in insects.

Interference with nerve function

The initial response of cockroaches to poisoning by DDT clearly indicates some impairment of the nervous system; body tremors, twitching of the legs, great excitability and eventual paralysis—all outwardly suggest an interference with nerve function.

The effects of DDT on conductance in nerves show this to be so. Application of DDT causes a repetitive discharge of impulses[609,610] and modifies the negative after-potential (see p. 386). In this respect, DDT, pyrethrins and the synthetic pyrethroids appear to affect nerve function in a similar way. The underlying cause is believed to be interference with the normal movements of ions of sodium and potassium through axon membranes. In normal insects sequential changes in permeability of the membrane to these ions is the very essence of nerve impulse conductance (see p. 385).

Almost from the day DDT was first used, attempts were made to discover how the insecticide interacted with insect nerves. Evidence showed that DDT caused spontaneous discharges in the nerve fibres, of motor nerves (those carrying impulses to muscles), thus producing the characteristic muscle twitches of poisoned insects.[877] Since these responses can be seen in amputated, DDT-treated legs of cockroaches, and decapitation or separation of body segments causes no reduction in DDT-tremors, it would seem that no specific target—nerve centre—is involved.[709] Tobias & Kollross[793] conclude that those parts of the insect's body necessary for the development of symptoms of DDT-poisoning 'are contained within the lateral half of a body segment, which contains the lateral half of a ganglion, leg nerves and peripheral structures'.

Roeder & Weiant have done much to pin-point the factors involved in DDT-poisoning. When silver electrodes are placed in contact with an exposed ventral nerve cord of an otherwise intact American cockroach, impulses in the nerve cord can be counted. If DDT is injected into the insect, the number of impulses per second jumps as much as 700 per cent. Cutting the nerve cord above or below the point of attachment of the electrodes shows that the impulses induced by DDT are in the 'ascending fibres', i.e. those arising from sensory sources and conducting impulses forward to the thoracic ganglia and the brain.

Confirmation that sensory structures and nerves are affected is seen in electrical discharges, when a leg, for example, is perfused with solutions containing as little as 0·01 ppm DDT. Roeder & Weiant believe that in the cockroach the tremors characteristic of DDT poisoning 'are due to an intense and patternless bombardment of the motor neurones by trains of impulses originating in sensory endings'. For the crural nerves, these sensory endings are believed to be the campaniform organs of the trochanter.[710] However, when small amounts of DDT are applied in acetone to the exposed suboesophageal and thoracic ganglia of the American cockroach, these cause strong electrical impulses, indicating that DDT acts on the central as well as the peripheral nerves of the insect.[894]

The speed of onset of electrical disturbances in nerves is correlated with DDT concentration—the greater the concentration the more rapid the symptoms (Fig. 170). When 1 ppm of DDT is injected into the American cockroach the interval before impulses arise is not modified by temperatures between 12°C and 32°C. This suggests that the period is occupied by a 'physical process'.[711] Washing of a leg preparation injected with 0·3 ppm of DDT, did not appear to remove the DDT, since stimulation of nerve impulses continued: discharges began with no greater delay than in an unwashed preparation (17 minutes). Since DDT cannot, apparently, be easily removed it seems that the insecticide becomes immediately bound at the surface of the sensory neurones. The time between application of the insecticide and the appearance of nerve impulses, is perhaps occupied by 'solution of the DDT in a lipid layer below the neurone surface'. In this respect symptoms of DDT poisoning are greater when the insecticide is injected into cockroaches in acetone than in an aqueous emulsion, the solubility of fat in acetone more readily fixing the insecticide in nerve tissue.[437]

Dresden[240] has established that DDT does not increase spontaneous nerve activity from the sense organs of the mesothoracic leg of the cockroach, or motor activity from the second thoracic ganglion. He also believes that it is unlikely that DDT induces spontaneous nerve activity in the nerve cord of *P. americana*. In his view, the specific cause of DDT symptoms is 'a facilitation of synaptic transmission' followed by 'synaptic block', the latter ultimately causing death of the insect. As described in the first part of this chapter, synapses are the points of chemical transfer of nerve information from one neurone to the next—the links in the nerve network. He could not establish that DDT had any specific action on the sense organs of the leg of *P. americana* or on the peripheral nerves. Eaton & Sternburg[252] also believe that synaptic transmission in the insect becomes impaired as DDT-poisoning progresses.

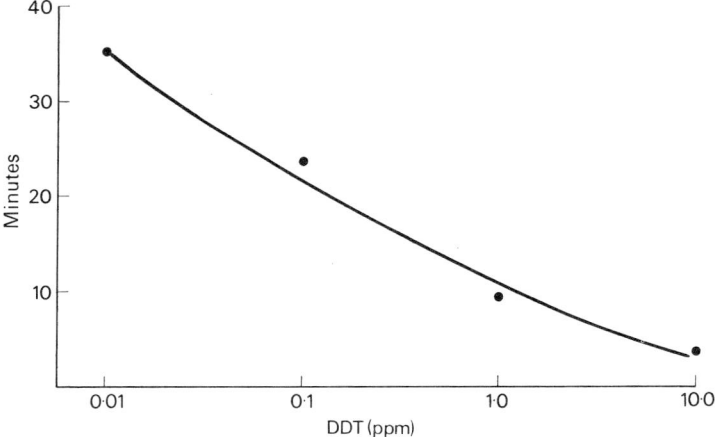

Fig. 170. Relationship between time from perfusion of the crural nerve of the metathoracic leg of *P. americana*, to the appearance of high frequency impulses induced by different concentrations of DDT in saline. (From Roeder & Weiant[709]).

The previous pages indicate the results and views of many workers on the action of DDT. Perhaps the nearest we shall get to an understanding of how DDT works is the discovery that the actual size and shape of a molecule of DDT make it particularly active on the membrane of a nerve axon. The way in which the molecule of DDT fits, physically, into the membrane structure of the nerve sheath, may cause it to act as a 'wedge' in the pores, influencing the movement of sodium ions.[435] In the normal insect, rapid and sequential changes in the permeability of the nerve membrane to sodium and potassium ions constitute 'the chemistry of nerve impulse transmission'. Interference with this porosity by physical blocking by DDT is a simple explanation of what may happen. Recent studies with ouabain (a heart stimulant) suggest that it may interact with DDT, synergistically; both compounds interfering in different ways with the membrane of nerve cells.[329]

ACTION OF OTHER CHLORINATED HYDROCARBON INSECTICIDES

Knowledge of the action and effects within the cockroach of insecticides related to DDT, is by no means so complete. The fate of lindane in insects has been studied most extensively in the housefly (*Musca domestica*). The site of action in cockroaches is believed to be, principally, the nerve ganglia. Unlike DDT, lindane does not stimulate the motor nerves of *P. americana*;[114] it does however, act through the ganglia in causing reflex tremors and twitching. It increases the frequency of spontaneous discharges in the cockroach nerve cord and prolongs 'synaptic after-discharge'.[608]

Experiments with lindane
One hour after injecting or spraying German cockroaches with lindane there is a five-fold increase in respiration rate.[401] This coincides with the period of muscular spasms and falls during the period of paralysis, as with DDT (Fig. 168). Lindane injected into American cockroaches at 100 μg/g does not affect the rate of heart beat but makes the pulse irregular.[647]

Again, like DDT, the toxicity of lindane is greater at low, compared with high temperatures, but with lindane this negative correlation is not so well marked: a temperature change from 12°C to 35°C causes a 20-fold difference in toxicity for DDT, but only 2·5-fold for lindane.[386]

In experiments involving radioactively labelled lindane, topically applied to American cockroaches (3 μg/g), the insects were subsequently frozen, sectioned and then autoradiographed. Lindane reached all parts of the central nervous system, crop and gizzard within 15 minutes, but most remained where it had been applied: 75 per cent had penetrated the cuticle in 6 hours and 90 per cent in 24 hours. Although lindane penetrates quickly, it accumulates only in the peripheral regions of the central nervous system.[491]

The acetylcholine level in the ventral nerve cord of American cockroaches made prostrate by lindane increases from 38 to 57 μg/g.[794] The level in the whole thorax of poisoned cockroaches increases by about three times.[831]

The increase in acetylcholine in the nerves of insects poisoned with dieldrin[208] is interpreted by O'Brien[637] as the consequence of unduly high nervous action induced by poisoning. On the basis of recent findings, dieldrin appears to act on the 'release side' of synaptic junctions causing excessive and spontaneous release of acetylcholine.[743] However, lindane and other chlorinated hydrocarbon insecticides do not have an effect on the enzyme acetylcholinesterase, whereas all organophosphates tested are inhibitory.[396]

Response to dieldrin
Dieldrin too, appears to interfere with nerve function in insects. It is efficiently absorbed into *P. americana* (topical LD_{50} 1·3 μg/g; LD_{50} by injection 1·1 μg/g) and efficiently transported to the site of action.[330,643] It is broken down in *P. americana* and *B. germanica*, to a number of metabolites, by both hydrolytic and oxidative systems.[613] A direct relationship with the CNS was observed by Yamasaki & Narahashi[875] who discovered that

nerves of *P. americana* poisoned with dieldrin show spontaneous bursts of action potential.

However, dieldrin takes at least 35 minutes to express its neurotoxicity in *B. germanica*, regardless of concentration.[835] Synaptic transmission across the metathoracic ganglion is greatly prolonged when American cockroaches are poisoned with dieldrin applied topically to the abdomen, but when applied directly to the exposed ganglion, the insecticide has virtually no effect on synaptic transmission. In the development of poisoning symptoms, dieldrin has a much smaller effect on sensory discharges than has DDT.[836]

The effect of dieldrin upon the ion-transport mechanism of the cockroach nervous system was determined by placing dissected abdominal nerve cords, taken from *P. americana*, into a saline solution containing radioactive ions, with and without dieldrin present. The same was done with heads of *B. germanica* cut in half. At the end of various incubation periods the amount of radioactive ions which could be effluxed was measured.[409]

TABLE CIX

EFFECT OF DIELDRIN INJECTED INTO GERMAN COCKROACHES ON THE RATE OF UPTAKE OF RADIOACTIVE IONS OF SODIUM AND POTASSIUM BY THE BRAIN (μ mole/g of tissue). AVERAGE FOR THREE STRAINS
(From Hayashi & Matsumura[409])

Ion	Hours after injection	*Injected with dieldrin in radioactive saline*	*Injected with radioactive saline only*
Sodium	0.5	13.1	3.4
	1	12.7	11.1
	2	11.0	11.0
Potassium ($\times$ 100)	0.5	3.5	1.2
	1	1.3	1.3
	2	1.2	1.3

Results were somewhat inconclusive: dieldrin applied simultaneously with the radioactive saline increased uptake of sodium ions, but when the insecticide was applied one hour before, uptake of sodium was reduced. In other experiments, dieldrin in saline incorporating radioactive sodium, potassium and other ions was injected into the abdomens of live German cockroaches. Uptake of sodium and potassium in the insect's head was much increased by the presence of dieldrin in the early stages of poisoning, but reached an equilibrium after one hour (Table CIX).

On balance, it seems that dieldrin-poisoning is likely to cause an accumulation of sodium ions inside the nerve, as with DDT. The binding of dieldrin to subcellular nerve components of cockroaches (fractions obtained by high speed centrifuging of homogenates of heads and nerve cord), suggests that the difference in response of susceptible and resistant strains of *B. germanica* to the insecticide is a function of the amounts bound to nerve cell membranes.[788] There is no difference in the anatomy (the ultra-structure) of the nervous system; differences are likely to be caused by less dieldrin being able to accumulate in the nervous system of the resistant cockroach.[789]

Other organochlorines
In their study of 17 organic insecticides applied to the surface of the leg of *P. americana*, Lalonde & Brown[495] measured the effect on sensory impulses to the central nervous system. Dieldrin produced a repetitive discharge after 2–4 hours and chlordane had a considerable latent period before stimulating action potentials. These insecticides were much slower in producing a reaction than DDT and lindane.

The haemolymph of *B. craniifer* is said to play an important part in transporting chlordane within the insect's body. The poisoning response in this cockroach is quicker following intracardiac injection than substernal injection.[614]

The biochemical mode of action of chlordecone is completely unknown, but because it is a chlorinated compound it is expected to be like that of DDT, lindane and other organochlorines. Certainly, ingestion of chlordecone is vital as a first step in the poisoning process: upon contact, the pest cockroaches are almost unaffected.

ACTION OF ORGANOPHOSPHORUS AND CARBAMATE INSECTICIDES

The symptoms of poisoning of organophosphorus and carbamate insecticides are hyperactivity, convulsions, paralysis and eventually death. Duration of hyperactivity is usually short so that not many insects show this at any time. Duration of the different symptoms varies considerably with different insecticides (Fig. 171).

All organophosphorus and carbamate insecticides act in insects on the enzyme acetylcholinesterase, which hydrolyses the synaptic transmitter, acetylcholine (see p. 386). The symptoms of poisoning are therefore associated with excessive activity at the synapse. Electron microscope studies, on nerve preparations from mammals, indicate that the acetylcholinesterase is manufactured, at least partly, within nerve cells and transported inside the axons to where it functions.[472] Whether or not acetylcholinesterase is formed just on the 'emitting' side of the synapse (from which the nerve impulse is coming) or on both the pre- and post-synaptic membranes in the insect is still uncertain.

The enzyme first appears in insect eggs shortly after the mid-point of embryonic development and increases progressively until hatching. The appearance of the enzyme coincides with the nervous system becoming fully developed but one cannot generalise in the same way for acetylcholine: in some insects it appears before the presence of acetylcholinesterase; in others it develops afterwards.[756]

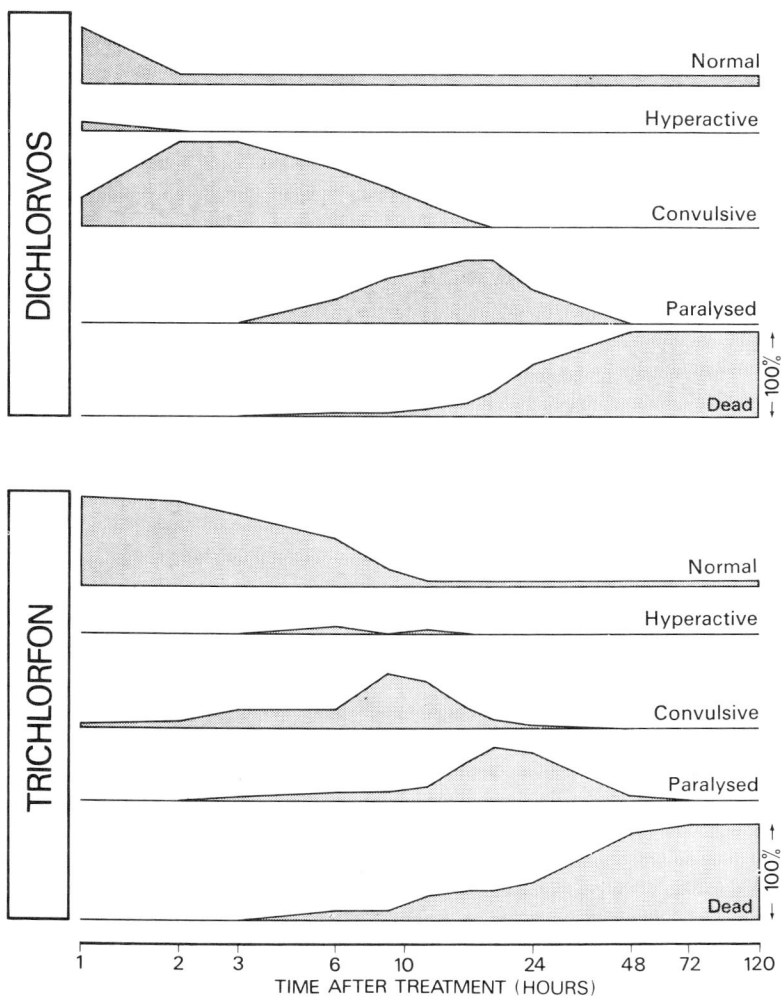

Fig. 171. Poisoning symptoms of American cockroaches treated with organophosphorus insecticides: dichlorvos (13·2 μg/g); trichlorphon (12·7 μg/g). (Data from Miyata & Saito[580]).

The naturally occurring carbamate, physostigmine, was for many years known to constrict the pupil of the eye and in 1930 was shown to inhibit acetylcholinesterase. It therefore provided a clue to the action of the insecticidal carbamates. The same applied to organophosphorus compounds being developed as warfare agents, and which were also shown to inhibit the enzyme.

How the inhibition occurs is still not fully understood: many of the insecticides have a chemical resemblance to acetylcholine on which the enzyme works, although this is not true, for example, of carbaryl.[7,854] A consequence of the inhibition of acetylcholinesterase must be the presence in poisoned insects of inhibited enzyme[636] and the accumulation of acetylcholine at nerve endings,[753] both of which have been demonstrated.

Selective toxicity towards insects of the commercially important organophosphates is partly explained by their being more stable in the body of insects than in mammals. A varying rate of breakdown may account for their effectiveness against different insects.[118] Depending on their structure, some of the organophosphorus insecticides, such as the phosphorothionates—malathion, diazinon and fenitrothion—are activated in the insect to other chemical forms which actually cause the poisoning.

The carbamates act on acetylcholinesterase in exactly the same way as organophosphates, except that the chemical reaction involving the carbamates is reversible. These insecticides also inhibit insect aliesterase[675]—a non-specific enzyme—but this is not thought to contribute much to insecticidal action. The action of many carbamates is enhanced by pyrethrin-type synergists, as first shown in flies,[588] but this is not of commercial interest (see Chapter 13). Synergists are believed to protect the carbamate from detoxication or influence its excretion by the insect.

We shall now turn our attention to the efforts made to measure acetylcholine and acetylcholinesterase in cockroaches and to discover the fate of organophosphates and carbamates in insects. It is unfortunate that most studies on cockroaches have been made with organophosphates of no practical use in buildings (e.g. parathion, schradan and TEPP). Some studies do, however, involve malation and diazinon.

Acetylcholine and acetylcholinesterase in cockroaches

The content of 'transmitter substance', acetylcholine, in nerve tissue varies greatly for different insect species and for insects of the same species. Thus Mikalonis & Brown[570] give 70 μg/g for isolated ventral nerve cord of *P. americana*, where Roeder[708] reports a value of only 37 μg/g.

Acetylcholine, and the inhibiting enzyme, acetylcholinesterase, both occur in the central and peripheral nervous systems of the American cockroach (Fig. 172). The highest concentration of acetylcholine is in the brain and nerve ganglia. The enzyme is strongly represented in the ventral nerve cord and the ganglia.

The acetylcholine content of the thoracic nerve cord of the cockroach is at its lowest at 15–20°C; there is a slight increase at 9°C and a more marked increase at 35°C (Fig. 173). (Temperatures outside this range are extremes for *P. americana*). The increase in transmitter substance at high temperature may arise from greater insect activity and therefore greater synthesis. At temperatures which cause the cockroach to be quiescent and almost immobilised by cold, little acetylcholine is required for nerve function and it may therefore accumulate.[205]

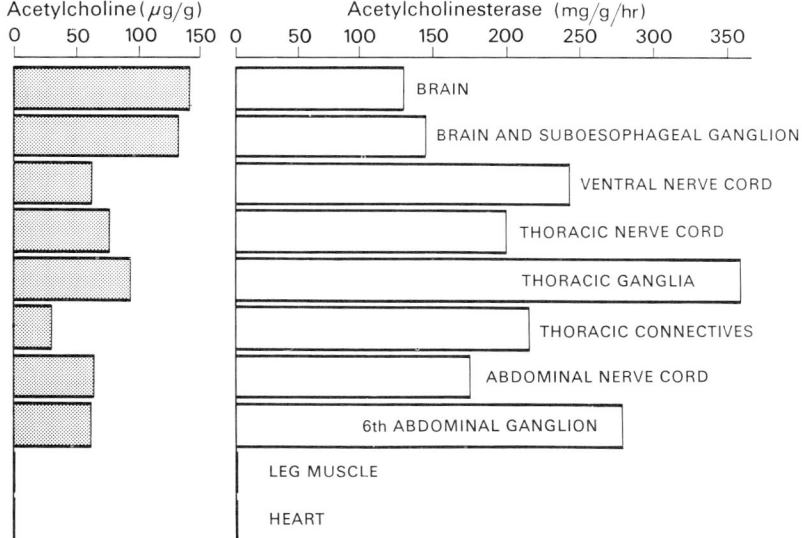

Fig. 172. Distribution of acetylcholine and acetylcholinesterase in tissues of *P. americana*. (From Colhoun[205, 206]).

Early attempts to prove that an accumulation of acetylcholine is toxic to insects failed, when no kill was achieved by injecting it into insects experimentally.[440] This cast serious doubts about the validity of the hypothesis for organophosphorus poisoning: the failure was later found to be caused by a protective sheath (the 'ionic barrier' of O'Brien[634]), preventing easy penetration of injected acetylcholine into the nervous system.[445, 810, 811] The sheath consists of a homogenous layer about 5 μ thick with an inner layer of epithelial cells, 1–3 μ thick. This same sheath is also presumably why acetylcholine does not readily escape from cockroach nerve tissue.[207]

Electrical stimulation of the nerve cord causes a substantial increase in acetylcholine (43 per cent). Stimulation of the cerci by puffs of air increases it far less (15 per cent), presumably because fewer nerve fibres are involved. These results were obtained using eserine to inhibit acetylcholinesterase allowing ready accumulation and measurement of the acetylcholine. The degree of stimulation, seen as electrical activity on an oscillograph suggests a direct correlation with the amounts of acetylcholine produced.[207]

Activation of organophosphorus insecticides

Paraoxon is the active compound formed in insects following application of parathion. Booth & Metcalf[113] used this to study movement of a typical phosphate in the body and accumulation in nerve tissue.

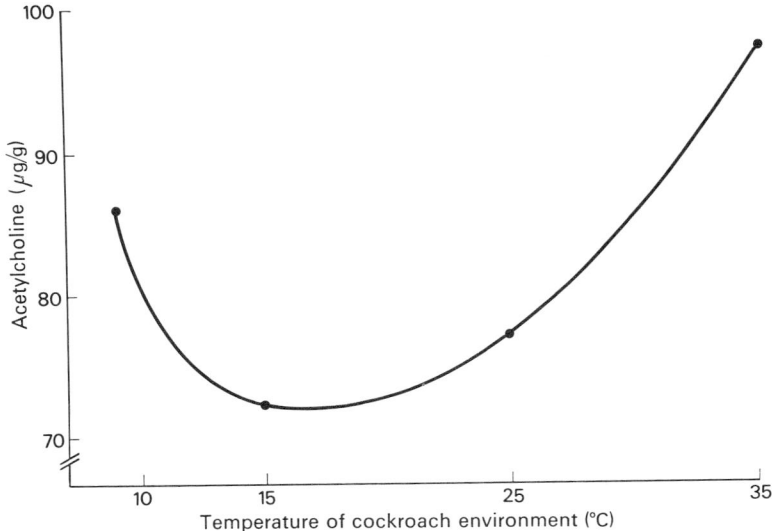

Fig. 173. The acetylcholine content of cockroach thoracic nerve cord at different temperatures. (Data from Colhoun[205]).

If applied to three different regions of the cuticle of the cockroach the pattern of inhibition of acetylcholinesterase in the brain remains the same. The position just influences the speed of onset of symptoms: fastest when applied to the head, slower on the thorax, and slowest when applied to the abdomen. Inhibition of acetylcholinesterase is greatest in the centre of the brain and less in the peripheral areas. A constant feature of all treatments is complete inhibition of activity in the mushroom bodies (the corpora pedunculata). These are among the most concentrated areas of synapses in the nervous system; many nerve tracts, sensory and motor, from all parts of the brain, from the ventral nerve cord and sense organs on the head, meet in these bodies. Fenitrothion applied topically to American cockroaches causes changes in the cellular components of the neurosecretory centres of the brain.[603]

The LD_{50} of malathion for the American cockroach and the housefly is about 10 μg/g. In these and other insects, malathion is a poor inhibitor of acetylcholinesterase. Again its action depends on conversion by the tissues to the more potent malaoxon which is not readily broken down, but accumulates sufficiently to be insecticidal. After poisoning with malathion (30 μg/g) the level of malaoxon in the cockroach reaches 0·4 μg/g.

Because the brain has a major control and coordinating function, damage here may be critical to the course of poisoning. For example, in locusts, *Schistocerca gregaria*, if activation of malathion to malaoxon occurs away from the sensitive head region, the insect is able to survive.[6] This also occurs where activation is slow or the circulatory system delays the arrival of malaoxon.

The German cockroach is not so readily killed by malathion as *P. americana*; the LD_{50} for *Blattella* is 120 μg/g. By using radioactive compounds it was hoped to show that this difference in susceptibility might be attributable to the fate of the insecticide in the insect body. However, both insects produced the same degradation products and at the LD_{50} both insects had degraded half the dose of malathion applied in 30 minutes. Surprisingly, both species activated malathion to malaoxon to exactly the same extent. 'The difference between the German and American cockroach must lie in penetration to the target, attack on the target or in the nature of the target'.[635] We must assume that in both species the ultimate cause of death is an accumulation of acetylcholine.

With some organophosphorus insecticides there is evidence that toxicity may be affected by availability. They become bound to many of the proteins in the haemolymph of the cockroach, to the extent that 80 per cent of the lethal dose (LD_{50}) is located there, possibly reducing considerably the amount available to cause toxic effects.[887]

Response to diazinon

The use of diazinon to control cockroaches results in the formation in the insect of diazoxon and it is this which brings about symptoms of poisoning. Thus, when the exposed last abdominal ganglion of *P. americana* is irrigated with diazinon, depression of acetylcholinesterase activity and the effects on nerve conduction closely resemble those of diazoxon.[157]

Diazoxon in the last abdominal ganglion is about 300 times more active than diazinon in inhibiting acetylcholinesterase. Its effect is to increase electrical activity in the nerve cord until conduction is blocked, even though some enzyme remains uninhibited.

The more diazoxon applied directly to the exposed metathoracic and terminal ganglia of the American cockroach the sooner blockage of nerve impulses occurs (Fig. 174). Activity of acetylcholinesterase is first inhibited in the outer zones of the ganglion; this may simply reflect delay in penetration. When diazoxon is applied to the outside of the cuticle, enzyme activity in the ganglia again decreases steadily, but the last abdominal ganglion always recovers normal function even in prostrate cockroaches. The condition of the poisoned cockroach corresponds much more closely to the functional status of the ganglia in the thorax which are three times more susceptible than the last abdominal ganglion.

The shortest time for severe symptoms of poisoning to occur in the metathoracic ganglion is about 45 minutes after application of an LD_{90} dose of diazoxon to the thoracic cuticle. The presence of large amounts of uninhibited acetylcholinesterase in prostrate insects (as with malathion—see above) suggests that functional effects of organophosphate poisoning come about by inhibition of the enzyme in restricted regions of the nervous system, rather than as a general level of inhibition.[156]

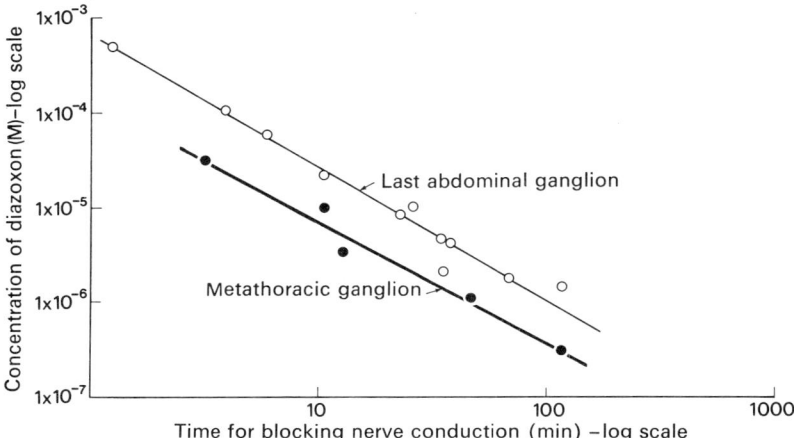

Fig. 174. Time taken by different concentrations of diazoxon applied to ganglia to block nerve conduction in giant fibre synapses of *P. americana*. (From Burt, Gregory & Molloy[156]).

Secondary effects of organophosphates

In addition to producing biochemical changes in the cockroach nervous system, organophosphates also have secondary effects: parathion causes the Madeira cockroach to accumulate large quantities of air and sometimes fluid in the fore-gut, during prostration and paralysis.[443] Acetylcholine and inhibitors of acetylcholinesterase have both stimulatory and toxic effects on peristaltic contractions of the cockroach intestine.[487] The fat body of the cockroach (*P. americana*) appears much involved in the enzymic activation of parathion, and presumably also other organophosphates.[602]

From time to time enzymes other than acetylcholinesterase are implicated in the physiology of poisoning by organophosphates. Some interfere with the synthesising enzyme choline acetylase. Low doses of fenitrothion applied repeatedly to *P. americana*, at one to two day intervals, cause an initial rise in the activity of phosphatases which may be involved in the metabolism of the insecticide.[914]

Action of carbamate insecticides

The chemical structure of this group of compounds has a marked effect on insecticidal activity. Variation is caused by the ability or otherwise of the chemical to penetrate the insect nerve cord and in the rate of detoxication.[171] Action of the insecticidal carbamates is again by interference with synaptic transmission. The carbamate competes with acetylcholine, by providing an additional substrate for reaction with acetylcholinesterase, allowing the 'transmitter substance' to accumulate.

Among three carbamate insecticides tested on bees at different temperatures, carbaryl was noticeably more toxic at low temperatures (LD_{50}

0·30, 1·12 and 1·14 μg/bee at 15·5, 26·5 and 32°C, respectively). Carbaryl, the least toxic, was also readily synergised by piperonyl butoxide, the mixture then having much the same toxicity at all temperatures (Table CX).

Further evidence of an interaction between carbamate detoxication, synergism and temperature occurs with *Musca domestica*.[283] Carbaryl is slightly more toxic to flies at 30°C than at 20°C. But in combination with synergists there is again little evidence of an interaction with temperature. Many noninsecticidal carbamates are active synergists for insecticidal carbamates. Some are as active as piperonyl butoxide in enhancing action against flies.[676]

TABLE CX

KILL (% AT 24 HOURS) OF HONEYBEES TREATED TOPICALLY (0·2 μg/insect). THE DATA ILLUSTRATES THE PRESENCE OF A DETOXICATION MECHANISM SENSITIVE TO BOTH SYNERGISM AND TEMPERATURE

(From Georghiou & Atkins[324])

Treatment	Temperature (°C)		
	15·5	26·5	32
Carbaryl alone	38	8	8
Carbaryl/pip. but. (ratio 1 : 5)	97	97	87

Carbaryl applied topically to German cockroaches at 5 and 10 μg/insect kills none and 5 per cent, respectively. At a ratio of 1 : 10 with piperonyl butoxide, carbaryl at the same rates of application kill 90 per cent and 100 per cent.[588] Carbaryl at the low rate of 0·5 μg/cockroach plus 10 times the amount of sesamex also kills 90 per cent of *B. germanica*.[275] In all instances the synergist prevents breakdown of carbaryl to its many metabolites. For German cockroaches, certain organothiocyanates are also carbaryl synergists.[282]

When radioactively labelled carbaryl is injected into *P. americana*, labelled carbon dioxide is released, in proportion to the amount of insecticide administered and broken down by the insect (decarbamoylation). Males are more susceptible than females; at doses which cause knockdown, females are more able to recover.[201]

The rate of heart beat of *P. americana* is accelerated by acetylcholine at extremely low dilutions (10^{-9}M). Carbamates applied to heart preparations similarly increase the rate of beating, substantially, causing erratic movements, often leading to complete arrest.[564]

In addition to the well-recognised action of the carbamates on acetylcholinesterase, they may also have an effect on the receptors of acetylcholine.[858] A detailed review of the relationship between chemical structure and the insecticidal activity of the carbamates has been made by Metcalf & Fukuto.[563]

SUMMARY: DIRECT AND INDIRECT ACTIONS OF INSECTICIDES

This chapter has described much of the work done in an attempt to determine how insecticides kill cockroaches. It spans about 25 years of study, and some of the experiments have been ingenious in their area of enquiry. They have involved some of the most modern techniques of electrical recording, chemical analysis and radiotracer chemistry. The experiments indicate that for each group of insecticides there are biochemical processes which (1) have a *direct* adverse effect on the well-being of the cockroach and (2) others which have an *indirect* effect, caused by a loss of that well-being.

Pyrethrins
For the pyrethrins, the direct effect of poisoning appears to be on the nervous system. Here the insecticide interferes with nerve transmission by causing electrical disturbances—a repetitive discharge in the nerves—followed by a block in nerve conduction. We see this as stimulation followed by paralysis. Repetitive discharges in nerves occur at high, but not at low temperatures, although death occurs more readily at low temperature. The negative after potential in the nerves of cockroaches is much increased in size (mv) and duration. The excitation in nerves lasts for a relatively long time, compared with DDT, unless the concentration of insecticide is so high as to block it. The processes which prove fatal to cockroaches probably occur in their ganglia rather than in the nerve axons.

All the other effects of pyrethrins are probably symptoms of the insect's debility—indirect effects: increased respiration, alteration in heart beat, depletion of haemolymph, interference with gut enzymes and physical degeneration of nerve tissue.

DDT and related compounds
The primary site of the action of DDT is again the insect nervous system: sensory nerves are very susceptible and their stimulation causes a spontaneous discharge of impulses, seen as body tremors. Electrical disturbances arise from an interaction—a 'binding'—of the insecticide with the nerve membrane, upsetting the normal movement of sodium and potassium ions into and out of the nerve axon. This seems to relate to the physical dimensions of the DDT molecule and the micro-structure of the nerve membrane. It causes electrical disturbances, seen with appropriate equipment as an increase in the duration of the action potential, associated with a longer negative after potential. Like pyrethrins, DDT causes a multiple response, a single stimulus of a nerve axon producing a repetitive discharge.

The symptoms of poisoning by DDT can be induced by subjecting cockroaches to stress, not involving the use of insecticide. The action of DDT is moderated by breakdown of the insecticide in the insect, storage in fat body, and by raising environmental temperature. The poisoning process reduces body reserves, lowers the proline content of the blood and increases respiration. It causes a toxin to be formed in the cockroach, which is not DDT, but which may be used to produce symptoms of DDT-poisoning in other insects. Other chlorinated hydrocarbon insecticides act in a similar manner but our knowledge of them is not so complete.

Organophosphorus and carbamate insecticides
These also cause malfunction of nerve impulse transmission by interfering with the chemical transmitter, acetylcholine, at the synapse. The insecticide brings about poisoning directly, or by conversion into a more toxic compound, inhibiting acetylcholinesterase. Carbamates compete with acetylcholine for the attention of acetylcholinesterase and their action is reversible. Essential to poisoning appears to be the inhibition of acetylcholine in the brain and the thoracic ganglia of insects.

Less important aspects of poisoning are interference in the production of the non-specific enzyme aliesterase, and with the synthesis of choline acetylase. The action of both the pyrethrins and some carbamate insecticides can be increased by combining them with synergists.

15

RESISTANCE TO INSECTICIDES

Early history; resistance becomes a major problem; characteristics of resistance; resistance to the various insecticides; cross-resistance; detecting and measuring resistance—Resistance in cockroaches: the progress of resistance from 1951–1975; resistance among cockroaches in the U.K.; the ability to survive. The problem in retrospect and prospect; reproduction and the number of generations per year; frequency of exposure to insecticide; proportion of the population exposed and extent of inbreeding; inter-relationship of cockroaches with transport; ability to withstand temporary adverse conditions—Reactions of the pest control industry; an up-to-date perspective.

Resistance in insects is one of the most significant factors affecting the development and application of insecticides. It is evidence of incomplete control, since the development of resistance needs survivors.

By WHO definition (1953, modified 1957), resistance to insecticides is 'the development of an ability in a strain of insects to tolerate doses of toxicants, which would prove *lethal* to the majority of individuals in a normal population of the same species . . .'

'Resistant' describes any pest population, normally susceptible to a pesticide, but which can no longer be controlled by the same concentration in the area concerned. In the case of cockroaches the area may be a single building or part of a building. The ability to survive is a developed attribute, consequent upon repeated use of insecticide, and is not by convention used to describe insects normally unaffected when an insecticide is first applied.

Resistance is often referred to as a phenomenon; that is, it contravenes all expectations. However, those aware of the innate variability of all biological material will not be surprised that one or two insects in a population can survive a toxicant which is lethal to most. This variability is essential to the evolutionary process of survival.

In this chapter we shall look at some of the factors responsible for the development of resistance and examine briefly the problem among insects as a whole. We shall then look at the subject in more detail as it affects the pest cockroaches and their control. Methods of testing insecticides and of measuring resistance in cockroaches are given in more detail in Chapter 17.

Early history

The first suggestion, based on field experience, that insects might possess an inheritable resistance to chemical insecticides is attributed to Melander.[554] In a paper entitled 'Can insects become resistant to sprays?' he wrote: 'There is a prevalent feeling in some districts that sulphur-lime is less efficient now, than formerly, in controlling San Jose scale, or orchard aphids or the brown mite.

There seems to be no question but that some years and in some places sulphur-lime is a rapidly acting insecticide ... that the San Jose scale should become acclimatised to a sulphur-lime environment is *not altogether a strange thing*'.

Early examples of resistance among agricultural pests include the strain of Codling moth (*Cydia pomonella*) in the Grand Valley of Colorado, which in 1928 needed as many as 10–12 sprays of lead arsenate to give the control afforded by two sprays in 1900. Peach twig borers (*Anarsia lineatella*) had developed resistance to lead arsenate in part of California in 1944; more of the larvae were then able to penetrate spray coatings of the insecticide than previously.[129]

The first documented case of resistance to synthetic insecticides was in 1947, in the housefly and in a species of mosquito in Italy. Initial use of DDT by the allied military government in Italy in 1944, was followed by extensive applications of residual sprays in the Spring of 1946 for the control of malaria mosquitoes.[577,578] In the next year, the first DDT-resistant houseflies and *Culex pipiens autogenicus* were observed.[592,721]

Up to 1951, two extensive reviews were made of insects then known to have developed resistance to insecticides.[64,65] There were many references at that time, to agricultural and veterinary pests, but no mention of resistance by cockroaches. A more detailed search shows that the first recorded indication of resistance was by *Blatta orientalis* to DDT: females collected from treated premises in Rome and Latina, Italy, in 1948 were more able to survive deposits of DDT (38 per cent), than females taken from untreated premises (only 8 per cent).[700]

In 1951, DDT-resistance was discovered in the body louse in Korea and in another species of mosquito (*Anopheles sachavori*) in Greece.[507] There, in addition to the failure of DDT to kill houseflies, resistance to DDT was noted among other domestic pests 'such as *Culex molestus*, fleas, bedbugs and cockroaches'.

The first record of resistance in a field population of German cockroaches[422] was in 1953—although in the 2 years previously, difficulties had been experienced in achieving control. Since then a great many papers have been published dealing with resistance in cockroaches, and many more have described experiments to investigate the biochemical and physiological aspects of the problem.

Resistance becomes a major problem

By 1955 insect resistance had become severe. It was established among many pests of economic importance—with DDT, dieldrin and lindane becoming less and less effective. That the same could occur also with organophosphorus insecticides was also apparent (Fig. 175).

In 1955 resistance to dieldrin was discovered in a third species of mosquito, in Nigeria, to be followed in 1959 by DDT-resistance diagnosed in the Oriental rat flea (*Xenopsylla cheopis*) in India, with the problem extending to dieldrin 3 years later. Resistance caused major setbacks in the control of vector species of flies, especially of mosquitoes—the targets of malaria eradication campaigns[734]—and in the control of the yellow fever mosquito in the Americas. Many people were beginning to think of insecticide resistance as essentially 'an American product' since of the 72 confirmed cases of resistance among insects and mites, recognised in 1958, no fewer than 50 occurred within the United States.[130]

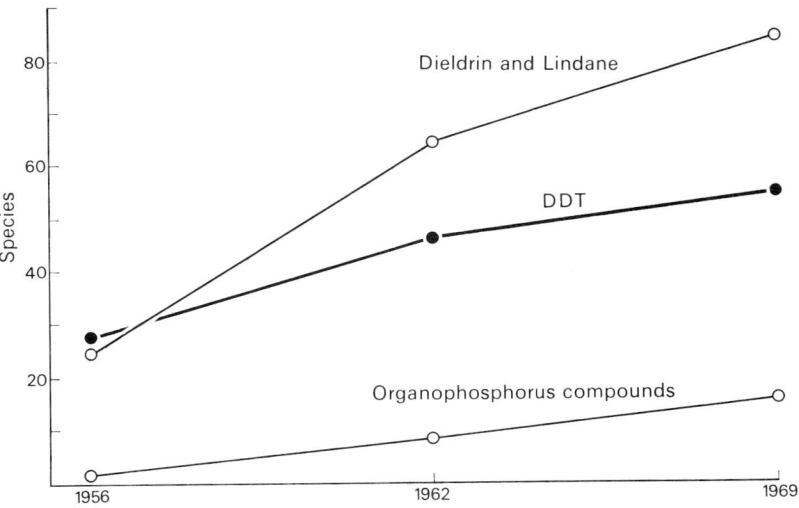

Fig. 175. Increase in the numbers of species resistant to insecticides, 1956–1969: some e.g. *B. germanica* have developed resistance to all three types of insecticide. (Brown & Pal[132]).

In the next five years there was a greater number of species capable of withstanding the commonly used insecticides. The major increase which then followed, between 1963 and 1969, was in the number showing resistance to more than one type of insecticide. Thus, by 1971 there were 104 resistant species, of which 18 showed resistance to organophosphates.

We have now come to recognise insecticide resistance as an international problem, the movement of people and goods by jet aircraft helping to spread resistant strains around the world exceedingly rapidly. These have become especially important in the control of insects transmitting disease. The reader interested in the detailed history should consult the monograph by Brown & Pal.[132] Resistance among insects of stored foodstuffs has occurred relatively slowly: 3 species in 1960, increasing to 16 in 1973, of which 11 species are beetles and 5 are moths.[247]

The characteristics of resistance
Among the early pronouncements of how resistance arises in nature are those of Painter (in 1930)[652] and Thorpe (in 1931),[792] both suggesting the presence of individuals within a wild population, which differ from the majority. Later

Dobzhansky (in 1941)[235] expressed the view that variability, with respect to insecticide resistance, is 'an example of the genetic variability typically existing in any population'. As an example of this Brown & Pal (*loc. cit.*) refer to the 31 different strains of pea aphid collected from various parts of the United States, which were found to fall into 5 biological races on the basis of size, reproductive rates and feeding damage. These provided a range of genetically differing insects of the same species (genotypes) from which the application of insecticides could select the most resistant ones.

In the same way, resistant insects have always been present to a greater or lesser extent, 'but have not manifested themselves because their numbers have been over-shadowed by the relatively enormous preponderance of what we call normal individuals. But now, the insecticidal suppression of the normal population has allowed the resistant individuals and their offspring to prosper, and claim our attention.'[704]

The most important feature of resistance, emphasised by Brown & Pal[132] is that an insect's ability to survive an insecticide is inherited. It is not possible for an insect to acquire resistance during its period of development from egg to adult. On the contrary, it is known that exposure to small amounts of insecticide during an insect's life span may make it more susceptible.

Insecticides do not induce mutations for resistance. There is, however, the possibility, though most unlikely, that a gene mutation for resistance can occur in the period during which chemical control is being applied.[129] In contrast, where the genetic make up exists, it is possible for resistant strains of insects to arise without any insecticide being applied. This can be shown artificially in the laboratory by selecting for characteristics, that by accident happen to be associated with resistance, e.g. for late development, or emergence. But for all practical purposes we accept that the factors making for resistance are present—are incipient in the population—before an insecticide is ever applied. Because it is an inherited character, resistance increases faster in insects that develop rapidly, and have many rather than few generations per year. This is why a major problem has arisen in such insects as houseflies and mosquitoes, which have life-cycles of only a few days. Equally it is a reason why resistance has not so far developed, for example, in wood-boring beetles which may take 2–5 years to develop from egg to adult.

Much has been learned about resistance by applying insecticide selection to insect populations in the laboratory. When this is done, as with cockroaches, it is unusual to see much change in susceptibility to the insecticide in the first few generations. Insects of later generations then require more insecticide to kill them and they take longer to die. Resistance can be expected to develop faster when the selection pressure is high, when most of the insects, say 80–95 per cent, are killed in each generation.

Experience suggests that insects in the laboratory do not respond to selection for resistance quite so rapidly as happens in the field. This is because the genetic 'make up' of insects in the laboratory is often not so varied. They may have been inbred previously for many generations. A common occurrence with resistant strains developed in the laboratory is that they nearly always revert: they become more susceptible when selection with the insecticide is removed, but this does not happen once the strain has become 'genetically pure' or homozygous for resistance.

In practice, suspicions of resistance arise immediately an insecticide fails. There are however a great many things that can lead us to this conclusion erroneously—faulty mixing of insecticide, wrong choice of formulation, or poor application—which have nothing to do with a change in susceptibility of an insect population. It is as well to check these before undertaking a quantitative test for resistance in the laboratory. Nevertheless only such a test will confirm that resistance really does exist (see p. 48).

Resistance to the various insecticides
Much of our knowledge of resistance in insects comes from observation and experiment, with the three different kinds of insecticide: (1) DDT, (2) dieldrin and related compounds including lindane, and (3) the organophosphates. Resistance to the most recent group of insecticides—the carbamates—has not caused major problems among insects of importance to public health.

Strangely, although the first two groups are both representative of organochlorine insecticides, resistance to DDT does not confer resistance also to the cyclodienes (dieldrin and chlordane). This was demonstrated as early as 1952. Selection to one type of insecticide may however cause 'cross-tolerance' to another, by increasing the vigour of the strain.

Experience over the last 30 years shows that resistance develops more rapidly, and reaches greater intensity to organochlorine compounds, than to organophosphorus insecticides and carbamates. There are three possible reasons for this. First, insects are so variable in their response to DDT and dieldrin (the response curve with increasing concentration is so flat), that a wide range of dose levels are experienced by insects in a field population and exert selection on the population. Secondly, greater quantities of organochlorines than other insecticides have been used in practical pest control, thereby exerting greater selection pressure. Thirdly, the chlorinated insecticides have much longer residual activity, exerting selection for a longer time than the shorter-lived organophosphates and carbamates. From this comes the inescapable conclusion, that our problem of insect resistance might not have been so severe had we exercised restraint and used insecticides only to kill and not to protect against insect infestation.

Cross-resistance
Many of the insecticides which have been used extensively are chemically related, thereby subjecting insects to similar physiological processes of toxication, as well as selecting for similar mechanisms of chemical degradation.

It is not surprising therefore that resistance to one insecticide confers cross-resistance to a related one. But, as we have seen, this is not true of DDT on the one hand, and of dieldrin and its related compounds on the other. Thus the resistance to chlordane which developed initially in the German cockroach in the United States[422] occurred without cockroaches first becoming resistant to DDT. Resistance to dieldrin does however confer resistance to all other cyclodienes, but the resistance which it confers to lindane is never so well marked.

Selection for resistance to chlorinated hydrocarbons does not confer resistance to organophosphates. Selection for the latter does however give rise to resistance to the former. With organophosphorus compounds, selection to one confers cross-resistance to others, but resistance is usually highest to the insecticide causing selection. There is one exception: malathion resistance is quite distinct in flies and *B. germanica*[369] and does not confer resistance to other organophosphates. This is because the mechanism in insects for detoxifying malathion is quite different from that for other organophosphates.[531]

Compared with earlier materials, the more recent carbamates have had relatively little chance to cause resistance on their own account. However, strains of housefly selected with one carbamate show some cross-resistance to all others, sometimes to organophosphorus insecticides, to lindane, dieldrin and usually strong cross-resistance to DDT. Likewise, there may be cross-resistance between organophosphates, as the selecting agents, and carbamates.

Strangely, strains of insects selected with pyrethrins *do* develop appreciable cross-resistance to chlorinated hydrocarbons; the common link is probably that both act on the insect nervous system although their susceptibility to detoxication is quite different. Such factors are explained in a review of cross-resistance mechanisms, and their relationship to the problem in cockroaches, prepared by Grayson & Cochran.[369]

Detecting and measuring resistance
Laboratory methods for measuring resistance are in all cases concerned with a mortality response, usually expressed as a percentage. The question is: can the strain of insects being tested survive more readily than 'the normal'? There are two ways of making this comparison. The first is to keep constant the time of exposure of the insects to the toxicant and vary the dosage; the mortality response is then related to the change in dose. The other is not to change the dosage, or concentration of insecticide, but to vary the time of exposure. The test method used can give quite striking differences in results.[210] In either case, log-probit paper is used to compare the changed mortality with concentrations or time. Values are derived for the *dose* for 50 per cent kill (LD_{50}) or the *time* for 50 per cent kill (LT_{50}). Sometimes an LC_{50} (lethal concentration, expressed as a percentage) is used.

The method of field-testing for resistance in cockroaches is to confine them in jars treated with a known deposit of insecticide (see p. 48). The insects are checked at intervals to give information on the LT_{50} or LT_{90}. When these values are compared with those of normal insects the ratio obtained—the 'resistance factor'—tends to be much higher than in tests in which the lethal dose (LD_{50}) is being measured.

Tests of this sort, raise the question of what is 'normal', since the degree of resistance is always comparative. In most cases, the ease of killing an in-bred laboratory strain, of a reputable research department, of University or Government, sets the standard (Table CXI).

TABLE CXI

KNOCKDOWN TIMES (LT_{50} HOURS) FOR 'NORMAL' STRAINS OF *B. GERMANICA* IN THE W.H.O. COCKROACH RESISTANCE TEST
(From W.H.O.[844] & Burden[143])

Insecticide	Adult males	Adult females	Mixed nymphs
Lindane[2]	0·5	0·8	0·9
Dieldrin[2]	2·4–2·9	6·6	7·4
Chlordane[1]	3·0–4·1	5·6–7·6	5·7–6·6
Diazinon[2]	0·5–0·7	—	—
Malathion[1]	1·0–1·2	1·9	1·7
Chlorpyrifos[2]	1·0	—	—
Propoxur[3]	0·3	—	—
Fenitrothion[2]	Males, females and nymphs combined 1·2		

Insecticides applied at: (1) 10 mg; (2) 5 mg and (3) 1 mg/ft².

How great a difference 'from the normal' there must be for the term resistance to be correctly applied, has not been precisely defined, but it is generally agreed that an increase of 5–10 times in the LC_{50} is strongly indicative of resistance. It should be understood, however, that when insects are first submitted to selection with an insecticide, it may increase the dose for 50 per cent kill, but not that for 90 per cent. This is because the insecticide may be killing a greater number of the more susceptible individuals, but not affecting the others.

RESISTANCE IN COCKROACHES

In most insects, development of resistance has been dependent, in large measure, on the extent of use of the various insecticides. Quite a few have been used for cockroach control: soon after DDT was discovered, it made an initial contribution to cockroach control, but was rapidly replaced by the more effective chlordane, at least in the U.S.A. Local authorities in Britain,[217] however, continued to favour DDT as late as 1968. DDT tended to displace the inorganic insecticides—sodium fluoride and phosphorus paste—and may have had a temporary influence on the demand for pyrethrins. Resistance to DDT has never been an important factor in the control of German cockroaches in the U.S.A., but several hundred-fold resistance to it has been seen in field-collected cockroaches in Europe.

The insecticides which have been used most extensively for cockroach control are chlordane in the United States and dieldrin in Britain (both organochlorines), and diazinon and malathion in the United States, and diazinon in Britain (both organophosphates). During 1954–55, the Orlando Laboratory of the U.S. Department of Agriculture tested 181 compounds in a search for the most effective and safe material for use against resistant German cockroaches. The most resistant field strain (from Phoenix, Arizona) succumbed as easily as laboratory cockroaches to six organophosphorus insecticides, among which diazinon gave the quickest kills.[478]

In the late 1960's, propoxur (a carbamate—Baygon®), became used extensively for cockroach control on both sides of the Atlantic. This was because resistance to diazinon had been detected in field strains, against which propoxur was effective. Propoxur was thus used by the pest control industry in America in anticipation that resistance to diazinon in the German cockroach was soon to create a problem. Subsequently, by 1969, chlorpyrifos (Dursban®—another organophosphorus insecticide) had also entered the pest control market in the U.S.A. Thus insecticides from all three groups have made a substantial contribution to cockroach control in recent years.

Outside Britain and the United States, chlordane, dieldrin and diazinon are also judged to have been the insecticides most widely used for cockroach control. In recent years, greater use has been made of pyrethrins, because of legislation affecting application of insecticides near food. But the switch from organochlorines to organophosphates occurred long before the industry became ultraconscious about the environment and contaminating food with insecticides. The main stimulus for the change from chlordane and dieldrin to diazinon, was the development of resistance, notably by the German cockroach.

In the next few pages we shall examine, in chronological order, the information on resistance in cockroaches as known mainly from the American literature. It concerns principally the German cockroach. Resistance has not occurred to any significant extent among populations of the Oriental cockroach, although there is some evidence of it in Europe. Similarly, resistance is not currently a problem in the control of *Periplaneta* species. Resistance in cockroaches in the U.K. will be considered separately.

A great deal of the laboratory information about resistance in *B. germanica* has come from the Virginia Polytechnic Institute in the U.S.A. In the period 1960–69, more than $125,000 was contributed by members of the National Pest Control Association of America to seek answers to many of the industry's most pressing problems.[629] A large part of this was spent on studies at V.P.I. into new insecticides for the control of resistant German cockroaches. There, much of the testing for resistance has been done and studies made into the genetic factors responsible for inheritance.

The progress of resistance from 1951–1975
The following notes are from the published literature describing, year by year,

how resistance in cockroaches developed, as seen by writers at the time.

1951 Unsubstantiated reports of German cockroaches, normally easy to kill with chlordane, indicate that they are proving difficult to control in Texas.[242]

Laboratory work begun in 1947 to breed and select German cockroaches resistant to DDT has now produced insects with 4 to 14-fold resistance to this insecticide. Little resistance is obtained with exposure to BHC (5 per cent gamma isomer).[356]

1952 For the past year German cockroaches have survived in buildings in Corpus Christi, Texas, treated with 2 per cent chlordane 'I have reached the conclusion that we have a breed of German roaches immune to the residual of chlordane.'[90]

A laboratory strain of *B. germanica* acquires 333-fold resistance to DDT. Much greater amounts of DDT are required to kill females of this strain than males (Table CXII). Both chromosomal and cytoplasmic factors appear to be involved in the inheritance of DDT-resistance, but little or no dominance for resistance is detected.[198,199]

TABLE CXII

RESISTANCE FACTORS AT THE LD_{50} OF CROSSES BETWEEN DDT-SUSCEPTIBLE AND DDT-RESISTANT STRAINS OF *B. GERMANICA* WHEN THE DDT-RESISTANT STRAIN IS IN THE 11th GENERATION OF SELECTION

(From Cochran, Grayson & Levitan[198])

Generation	Males	Females
Parent generation		
Non-resistant strain	0	0
Resistant strain	14·8	333·3
F.1 generation		
Non-R males × R females	2·7	5·4
Non-R females × R males	1·4	2·8
F.2 generation		
Non-R males × R females	3·7	6·1
Non-R females × R males	3·3	5·3

The resistance factor is the ratio of the LD_{50} of the susceptible strain to that of the resistant strain.

1953 Cockroaches taken from Corpus Christi, Texas, provide the first proven case of field resistance in *B. germanica*. Resistance to chlordane is more than 100-fold, with cross-resistance to lindane (10–12 fold) and to DDT (5–6 fold).[422,543] There are no reports of difficulty in controlling cockroaches with chlordane or lindane, elsewhere in the U.S.

German cockroaches selected for resistance to DDT and BHC have biological and morphological characteristics differing from the susceptible insect (Table CXIII). This is contrary to the majority of findings for resistant insects. In the 12th generation, 22 times and 198 times as much DDT is required to kill half the males and females, respectively. Also from 1·4 to 2·6 times as much BHC is required. Selection of the insects was as vigorous to both insecticides, yet the difference in response is most noticeable.[357] The lower biotic potential of insecticidally-selected strains is not considered the result of in-breeding.[368]

TABLE CXIII

REPRODUCTIVE AND WEIGHT DATA FOR A LABORATORY STRAIN OF *B. GERMANICA* SELECTED FOR RESISTANCE TO DDT AND TO BHC

(From Grayson[357])

Character	Measurement	Untreated	DDT-strain	BHC-strain
Size of empty egg case (mm) produced by 9th generation females	Length Width	8·0 3·7	7·3** 3·5**	7·8* 3·6*
Av. number of nymphs produced during 114-day period by 6th–10th generation females	Per female Per egg case	101 35	67** 28	89 32
Weight of adults (g) of 10th generation	Males Females	1·32 2·66	1·27** 2·37**	1·36 2·53

* Probability of 1 in 20 that the difference from the untreated strain is not due to chance.
** Probability of 1 in 100.

There is evidence from several sources that houseflies resistant to DDT can dehydrochlorinate the insecticide faster than susceptible ones. DDT applied topically to German cockroaches resistant to chlordane, is absorbed and broken down more rapidly than by a susceptible strain.[66]

A strain of *B. germanica* selected in the laboratory for resistance to DDT, and then bred for 9 generations without pressure, reverts to susceptibility. Reversion is not nearly so rapid in the chlordane-resistant field strain from Corpus Christi. Resistance to chlordane (100-fold) imparts high cross-resistance to dieldrin (70-fold) but not to DDT, diazinon or to allethrin synergised with MGK 264 (Table CXIV).

1954 Cross-resistance is confirmed in the Corpus Christi strain between chlordane (112-fold for males and 276-fold for females) and lindane (5·7–3·8 fold) but not to the organophosphate, TEPP. This strain also

Table CXIV

RESPONSE OF NORMAL, DDT- AND CHLORDANE-RESISTANT STRAINS OF B. GERMANICA (ADULT FEMALES) TO OTHER INSECTICIDES

(From Fisk & Isert[306])

Insecticide	LD_{50} (μg/female)			Resistance factor (ratio of LD_{50}'s)	
	Normal	DDT-resistant	Chlordane-resistant	DDT-resistant	Chlordane-resistant
DDT	13·5	25·0	19·0	1·9	1·4
Chlordane	2·3	4·1	250·0	1·8	108·6
Dieldrin	0·5	0·6	34·0	1·2	68·0
Diazinon	0·3	0·8	0·4	2·4	1·2
Synergised allethrin	0·8	1·3	1·0	1·7	1·3

differs in reproductive performance and weight from a laboratory chlordane-susceptible strain (Table CXV).

1955 Bedingfield[91] reports that 'Malrin' consisting of 1 part malathion and 2 parts perthane is wholly effective in controlling some cockroach in-

Table CXV

REPRODUCTIVE PERFORMANCE, SIZE OF EGG CASE AND WEIGHT OF ADULTS OF THE CHLORDANE-RESISTANT, CORPUS CHRISTI STRAIN AND A LABORATORY STRAIN OF B. GERMANICA

(From Grayson[358])

Character	Resistant	Non-resistant
Average number of nymphs produced:		
per female in 105-day period	122·6*	138·9
per egg case	34·7*	37·1
Empty egg case (mm)		
length	7·8*	8·1
width	3·5*	3·7
Average weight of adults (g)		
males	1·102**	1·205
females	2·015**	2·248

* significant at 5% probability; ** at 1% probability.

festations but entirely ineffective in others. Cross-resistance is shown between chlordane (32-fold) and heptachlor, dieldrin, lindane and aldrin when micro-injected into the Corpus Christi strain (Table CXVI). Resistance to heptachlor may have arisen through field use of chlordane containing heptachlor as an impurity.[164]

TABLE CXVI

SUSCEPTIBILITIES OF THE CORPUS CHRISTI STRAIN (CHLORDANE-RESISTANT) AND A NORMAL STRAIN OF *B. GERMANICA* TO VARIOUS INSECTICIDES AS SHOWN BY THE LD_{50} AND LD_{90}
(μg/g body wt.)
(From Butts & Davidson[164])

	Insecticide	Normal strain	Corpus Christi	Resistance factor
LD_{50}	Chlordane	81.3	1117.5	13.8
	Aldrin	26.5	127.6	4.8
	Heptachlor	9.1	174.2	19.2
	Dieldrin	6.6	68.4	10.4
	Lindane	1.0	23.1	22.7
LD_{90}	Chlordane	144.3	4648.8	32.2
	Aldrin	70.1	1113.6	15.9
	Heptachlor	19.9	1509.3	76.0
	Dieldrin	17.4	502.5	28.5
	Lindane	2.6	75.0	29.2

Varying degrees of chlordane resistance are demonstrated in 9 strains of *B. germanica* from infested premises in Texas (collected in 1954). The conclusion is reached that 75 per cent of infestations in Dallas have significant chlordane resistance.[493]

1956 Collections of German cockroaches from Jackson (Mississipi), San Antonio (Texas) and Phoenix (Arizona) are about 20 times more resistant to chlordane than 'the normal' on the basis of exposure time for 50 per cent knockdown. Resistance to lindane and dieldrin is also apparent (Table CXVII). The rearing in the laboratory of the Corpus Christi strain in the absence of selection by chlordane, causes resistance to drop to 14 times the normal in 2 years[164]; it is only 6 times normal after 3 years.[478]

Collections of cockroaches from Naval installations throughout the S.E. United States showed resistance to chlordane (10- to 25-fold) in at least 20 distinct strains. There was no evidence however of resistance among cockroaches aboard naval vessels.[242]

Twelve strains of *B. germanica* from premises in the United States prove resistant to chlordane, dieldrin and lindane. One (Fort Rucker strain)

TABLE CXVII

HOURS FOR 50% KNOCKDOWN OF GERMAN COCKROACHES CONTINUOUSLY EXPOSED TO INSECTICIDE DEPOSITS ON MASONITE PANELS

(From Keller et al[478])

Strain from:	Chlordane 100 mg/ft²	Dieldrin 50 mg/ft²	Lindane 50 mg/ft²
Jackson, Mississipi	81	24	1·6
San Antonio, Texas	61	31	2·6
Phoenix, Arizona	79	43	4·9
Laboratory	3·8	2·6	0·35

requires 31 times longer exposure to synergised pyrethrins than a laboratory strain to kill 90 per cent. (The others require 3–6 times longer.) Lethal concentrations for 50 per cent kill are shown in Fig. 176.

Both sexes of strains of *B. germanica* selected for resistance to DDT and to lindane, and of a naturally occurring strain resistant to chlordane, were

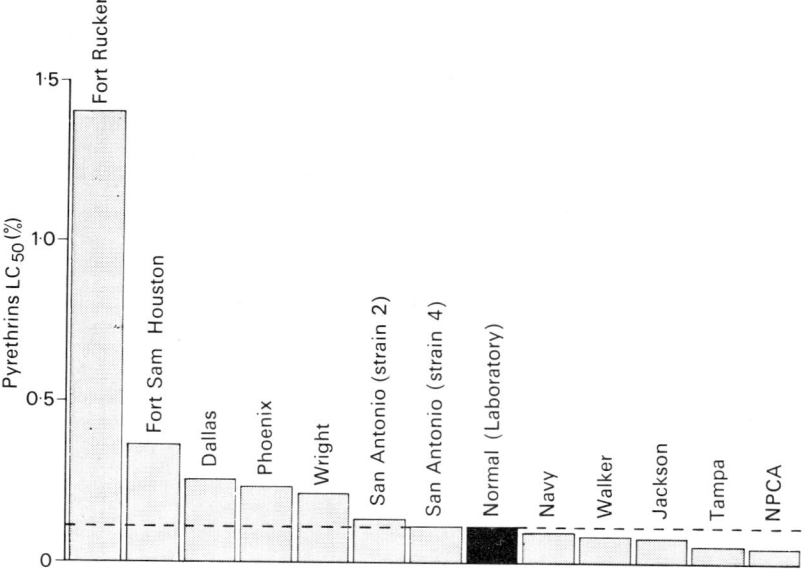

Fig. 176. Differences (LC$_{50}$ per cent) in the susceptibility of males of 12 field strains of *B. germanica* (all resistant to chlordane, dieldrin and lindane) and a laboratory strain, to pyrethrins applied as a contact spray. (From Keller et al.[478]).

consistently smaller than those of a normal strain, especially in the case of DDT.[517]

Routine treatments carried out with 2 per cent chlordane in Army kitchens and mess halls since 1950 in the Panama Canal Zone begin to fail. Chlordane resistance is now evident after 6 years' use.[883]

Diazinon, pyrethrins (as sprays) and sodium fluoride (as dust) are now being widely recommended for control of chlordane-resistant *B. germanica* in the U.S.A. Twelve out of 28 strains (43 per cent) of German cockroaches taken from infested homes (not receiving regular pest control service) in Orlando, Florida, were moderately or highly resistant to chlordane (Table CXVIII). At one location, both non-resistant and highly resistant cockroaches were collected from two dwellings within the same block.[509]

TABLE CXVIII

SUSCEPTIBILITY OF 28 STRAINS OF GERMAN COCKROACHES (MALES) COLLECTED IN VARIOUS FLORIDA HOMES AND EXPOSED CONTINUOUSLY TO CHLORDANE (10 mg/ft²) IN JARS. COMPARISON IS MADE WITH A LABORATORY STRAIN
(After Lofgren, Burden & Clark[509])

No. of strains		Range of LT_{50} (hours)	Range of LT_{90} (hours)
6 field strains		3·2–3·9	3·9–5·7
Laboratory strain		4·1	5·9
22 field strains	8	4·4–5·8	4·7–8·5
	5	6·6–10·0	13·0–40·0
	4	15·5–28·0	31·0–100·0
	5	52·0–126·0	88·0–190·0

See also Fig. 133.

1957 Little use has been made of DDT for cockroach control in the U.S. but the U.S. Armed Forces in Europe have used DDT throughout Germany and France since 1944. Unsatisfactory control of *B. germanica* is now reported in military establishments: insects from five locations are resistant to DDT and one to chlordane. Nymphs of Oriental cockroaches are resistant to DDT and in one instance to chlordane. The three strains of Brown-banded cockroach tested are not resistant. No species shows resistance to malathion (Fig. 177).

1958 Control failures with chlordane are now coming in from San Francisco and other areas of California: LT_{50} values for adult cockroaches are more than 25 times the normal.[566] Tests in Canada show 35-fold (St. Hubert strain) and 75-fold resistance (Goose Bay strain) by German cockroaches to dieldrin. Some infestations in adjacent buildings at the Goose Bay Air Force Station are normally susceptible to chlordane.[18]

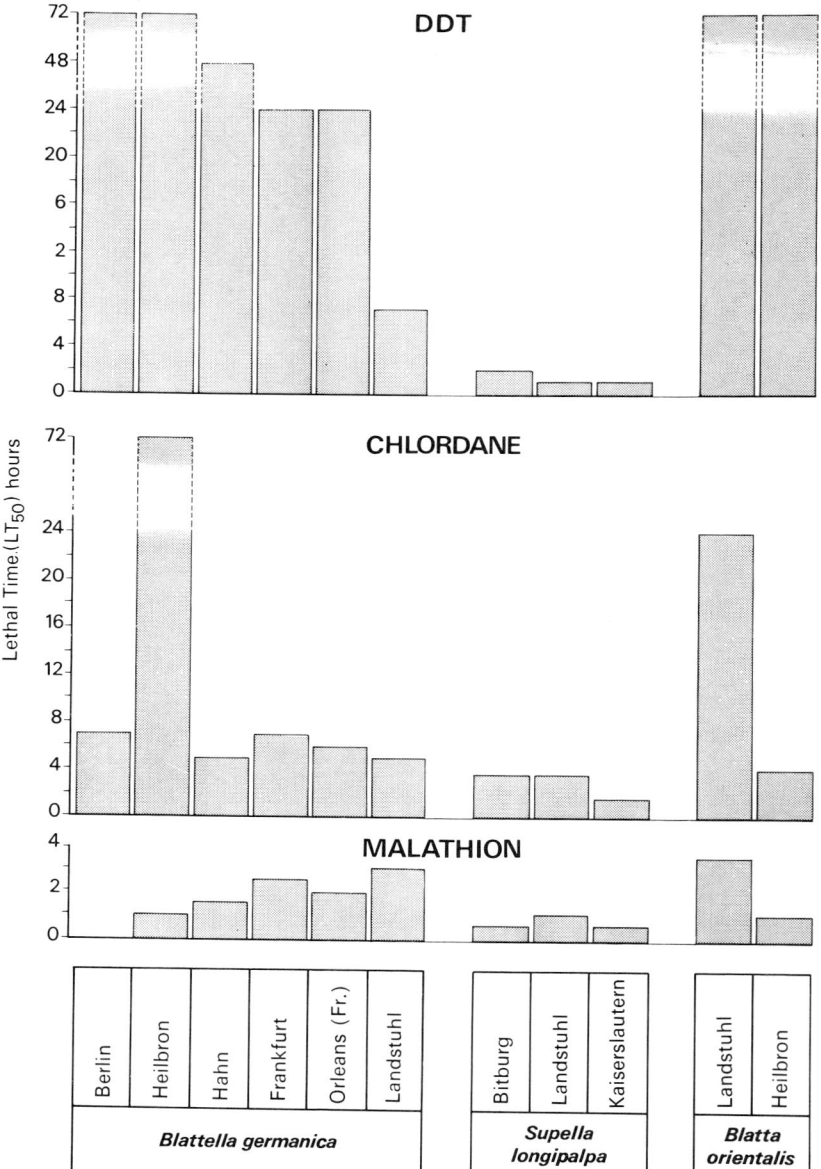

Fig. 177. LT$_{50}$'s for some European strains of cockroaches, taken from military installations, to DDT, chlordane and malathion. (Data from Webb[838]).

1959 German cockroaches from the Tunapuna area of Trinidad show strong resistance to dieldrin and DDT; organophosphates are effective.[645]

Resistance is now confirmed in *B. germanica* and in 71 other insects and mites. No fewer than 50 of these occur in the United States. Experience proves the conclusion: 'the speed of development of resistance to a particular insecticide (or at least its speed of recognition) is closely related to the extent of use of that insecticide.'[130]

Earlier generalisations by Metcalf[561] that cross-resistance occurs between closely similar insecticides but not between chemically dissimilar ones, is demonstrated in *B. germanica*. Cross-resistance is confirmed (Table CXIX) between DDT (497-fold) and methoxychlor (310-fold), and between chlordane (280-fold) and dieldrin (212-fold) but does not extend to organophosphates, allethrin or to lethane.[191]

TABLE CXIX

RESPONSE (LC_{50} μg/ml) OF DDT-RESISTANT, CHLORDANE-RESISTANT AND NON-RESISTANT STRAINS OF *BLATTELLA GERMANICA* (ADULT FEMALES) TO EIGHT INSECTICIDES APPLIED TOPICALLY

(From Clarke & Cochran[191])

Insecticide	Non-resistant	DDT-resistant	Chlordane-resistant	Resistance factor	
				DDT-resistant	Chlordane-resistant
DDT	0·032	15·900	0·026	497	0·8
Methoxychlor	0·035	10·800	0·037	310	1·1
Chlordane	0·010	0·034	2·800	3·4	280
Dieldrin	0·012	0·033	2·550	2·7	212
Prolan	0·082	0·125	0·100	1·5	1·2
Malathion	0·014	0·039	0·016	2·8	1·1
Allethrin	0·018	0·035	0·018	1·9	1·0
Lethane	0·074	0·175	0·078	2·3	1·1

There is no evidence of cross-resistance in *B. germanica* between chlordane and the carbamate insecticide carbaryl.[370] Resistance to malathion (4- to 11-fold) is obtained in German cockroaches after laboratory selection for five to ten generations.[147] Nine strains of *B. germanica* taken from U.S. Army Installations (Colorado, Illinois, Indiana, Kansas, Missouri and Nebraska) all had varying degrees of resistance to chlordane (Fig. 178). There was no pronounced resistance to malathion.[763]

1960 Loss of resistance to chlordane and lindane in laboratory-selected strains is slow when exposure to these insecticides is discontinued. In contrast, there is a rapid loss of resistance (within 3 or 4 generations) by DDT-

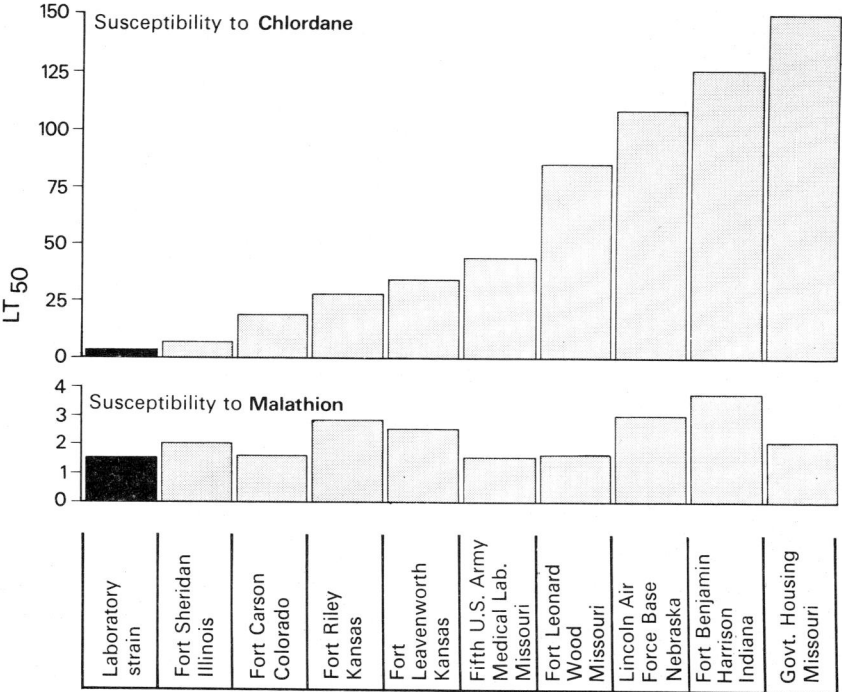

Fig. 178. Susceptibility (LT_{50} hours) of nine field strains of *B. germanica* to chlordane and malathion, in comparison with a normal laboratory strain. (Data from Stapp[763]).

selected strains.[359] Resistance to chlordane is rapidly restored (in two generations) when selection pressure is reapplied.

'The alternate or combined use of two insecticides (chlordane and malathion)[149] may retard slightly, but will certainly not prevent the development of resistance to each of these insecticides' (Fig. 179).

'Resistance to all chlorinated hydrocarbon insecticides is general in the Southern U.S. and is widespread in northern cities. Resistant populations are reported from Canadian cities'.[843] Proof of suspected resistance, beginning in Montreal, Toronto and Windsor (Ontario) in 1959, is confirmed by tests. Twenty-one collections were resistant to dieldrin (resistance factors up to 80-fold for males and 60-fold for females). One field strain had a 2-fold tolerance to pyrethrins and allethrin.[834]

A population of German cockroaches taken from the centre of Tokyo (Nihonbashi colony) shows a 10-fold resistance to dieldrin and lindane by residual contact and topical application. Susceptibility to diazinon is normal.[430]

'Many reports are now being received of infestations difficult to control with malathion and diazinon'. Resistance to malathion (43-fold) is ob-

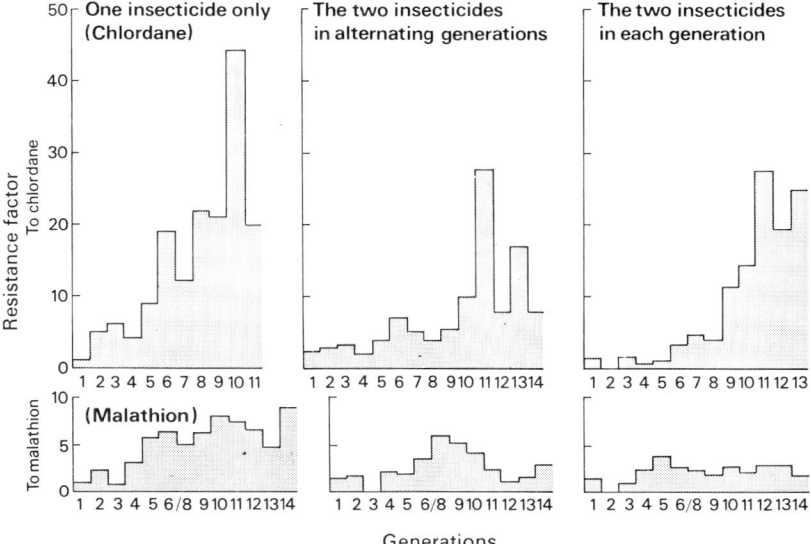

Fig. 179. Development of resistance in laboratory colonies of *B. germanica* by selection to chlordane and malathion, when applied separately, alternately and together. (Seventh generation omitted in tests with malathion). (Data from Burden, Lofgren & Smith[149]).

tained in a chlordane-resistant strain, after selection for seven generations to malathion at progressively increasing pressures. Selection to diazinon does not induce resistance.[359]

1961 Cross-resistance in *B. germanica* is demonstrated between DDT and the carbamate, carbaryl (75-fold) but not between chlordane and carbaryl.[194]

Diazinon has now been used to control cockroaches in the U.S. for about 5 years. Resistance to diazinon, (3- to 15-fold at the LC_{90}) is found among two strains of *B. germanica* collected from Kentucky (Fig. 180). Resistance to diazinon did not impart cross-resistance to malathion.[360] This was confirmed by getting control of the resistant field infestation with 3 per cent malathion, following the failure with diazinon.

Laboratory strains of *B. germanica* resistant to DDT and lindane have differences in egg incubation time, nymphal development (Fig. 181) and adult longevity compared with a susceptible strain. 'It is not clear whether these differences are correlated with resistance or are fortuitous.'[665]

1962 Resistance to chlordane is reported in Puerto Rico, the LT_{50} for *B. germanica* to chlordane and dieldrin exceeding 72 hours. Susceptibility to malathion is normal.[347] Control failures with dieldrin sprays, which have been effective since 1954, now occur in Hong Kong; malathion (2 per cent) is used instead.[713]

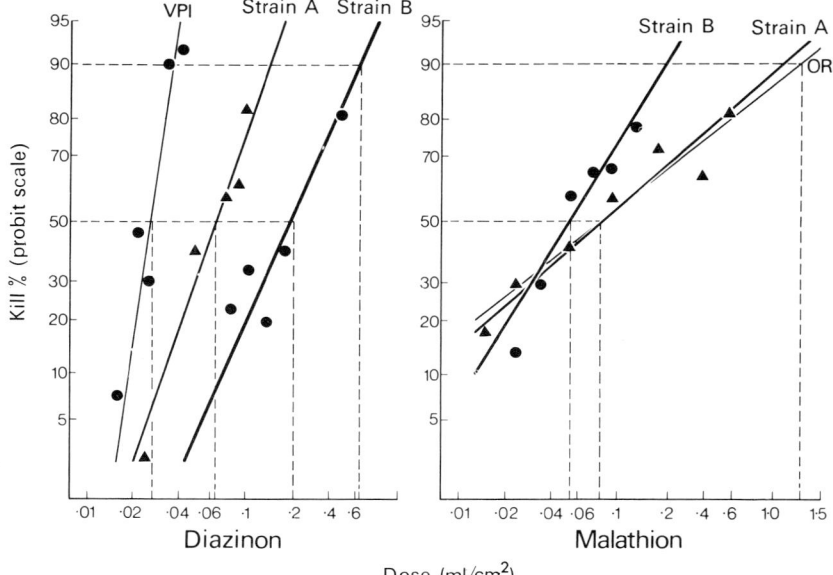

Fig. 180. Susceptibility to diazinon and malathion on treated filter paper, of two field strains (A and B) of *B. germanica*. Comparison is with Virginia Polytechnic Institute (VPI) and Orlando, U.S.A. (ORL) laboratory strains. (From Grayson[360]).

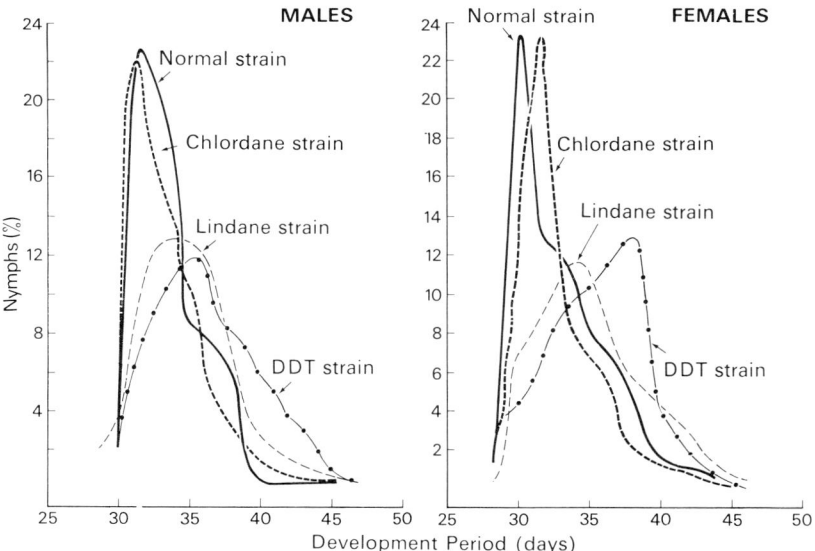

Fig. 181. Distribution of nymphal developmental periods for males and females of resistant and normal strains of German cockroaches. (From Perkins & Grayson[665]).

The inheritance of resistance to DDT in *Blattella* is consistent with Mendelian principles: the F_2 generation contains three susceptible to one resistant cockroach. Resistance involves only one major locus which is incompletely recessive. There is no evidence of resistance being sex-linked as shown by no important differences in the susceptibilities of the sexes, resulting from matings of resistant males with susceptible females and *vice versa*.[199]

Topical treatment of male German cockroaches with dieldrin, shows 2,000-fold resistance in a population from Aarhus, Jutland where dieldrin lacquer had been used for the previous 5–6 years.[476]

1963 The 'jar test' is published for detecting resistance in cockroaches. It is recommended to pest control operators in perfecting treatments—to establish whether failure is due to resistance or improper application. It was later adopted as the WHO field test method: seventeen out of 21 populations of *B. germanica* collected in the U.S. were found 'highly resistant' to chlordane. No resistance was found among seven strains of *S. longipalpa*, seven strains of *P. americana*, four of *B. orientalis*, or in one strain of *P. brunnea*.[289]

Selection of *B. germanica* through sixteen generations fails to bring about measurable resistance to diazinon.[361] The only proven case, in a natural population,[360] occurred in Kentucky in 1959.

1964 The first authenticated case of malathion resistance occurs in a field strain of German cockroaches (Camp Leroy Johnson, New Orleans). The insects are also highly resistant to chlordane, dieldrin and lindane but show no cross-resistance to diazinon (Table CXX). A further strain resistant to malathion is taken at Denver, Colorado and is said to be resistant also to pyrethrins.[23]

Resistance in *B. germanica* to DDT and dieldrin confers considerable cross-resistance to telodrin.[200] Singh identifies and measures the amounts of eighteen amino acids in the blood of susceptible and malathion-resistant strains of *B. germanica*, but concludes that they do not have any direct role in the tolerance of the insect towards the insecticide.[750]

Rare cases of resistance to DDT and/or dieldrin have arisen among strains of Oriental cockroaches in Czechoslovakia. The latter insecticide has never been used in that country.[683]

1965 An Hawaiian strain of German cockroach ('Manoa', with 5,360- to 12,500-fold resistance to chlordane—the greatest ever reported) shows no cross-resistance to chlordecone and only a low tolerance among females to propoxur.[459]

In studies of the genetics of resistance to chlorinated insecticides, variation in the susceptibility of progeny from 'within strain matings', made Jarvis, Grayson & Levitan[466] believe that multiple-factor inheritance was involved in transmission of chlordane resistance. By using aldrin as the test insecticide, Cochran[195] now confirms that inheritance within two field

TABLE CXX

SUSCEPTIBILITY (LT_{50} AND LT_{90}) OF MALES OF THE CAMP LEROY JOHNSON STRAIN (CLJ) OF GERMAN COCKROACHES RESISTANT TO MALATHION, AFTER BREEDING FOR ONE AND TWO GENERATIONS IN THE LABORATORY. COMPARISON IS WITH TWO SUSCEPTIBLE STRAINS: FSH = FORT SAM HOUSTON STRAIN; ORLANDO = ORLANDO LABORATORY STRAIN (USDA)

(Data from Johnston et al[469])

Insecticide	Strain	Generation	LT_{50} (hours)	Resistance factor	LT_{90} (hours)	Resistance factor
Malathion	CLJ	F_1	11·0	9·2	28·0	11·2
	FSH	—	1·2		2·5	
	CLJ	F_2	15·0	7·9	56·0	5·1
	Orlando	—	1·9		11·0	
Diazinon	CLJ	F_1	0·6	1·2	0·9	1·3
	FSH	—	0·5		0·7	

strains from the United States and from Germany is a simple Mendelian trait. In the second generation derived from resistant × susceptible parentage, only 1 in 4 of the cockroaches is killed by a discriminating dose of aldrin.

Resistance to chlordane and dieldrin is recorded among German cockroaches in Sydney, Australia. Resistance to chlordane also occurs in the Port Moresby area of Papua, New Guinea.[24]

Resistance to organochlorine insecticides by German cockroaches is now 'widespread in the United States, but curiously enough chlordane is still effectively used in some areas'. Although resistance to DDT occurs in natural populations in Europe, 'the only DDT-resistant strain in the U.S. has been produced by selection in the laboratory'.[362]

Resistance to malathion in *B. germanica* does not confer cross-resistance to seven other organophosphorus insecticides, but resistance to diazinon does confer low level tolerance (2- to 5-fold) to all organophosphates tested. 'This demonstrates at least two types of resistance to OP compounds'.[823]

Fourteen-fold resistance to diazinon is obtained after 23 generations of selection. High level resistance to malathion (20- to 30-fold) is demonstrated in two of four field strains from Texas (Fig. 182), but resistance to diazinon is low (less than 6-fold). The resistance factor at the LC_{90} is invariably higher than at the LC_{50} suggesting 'incipient resistance' rather than vigour tolerance, associated with elimination of the more susceptible individuals.[363]

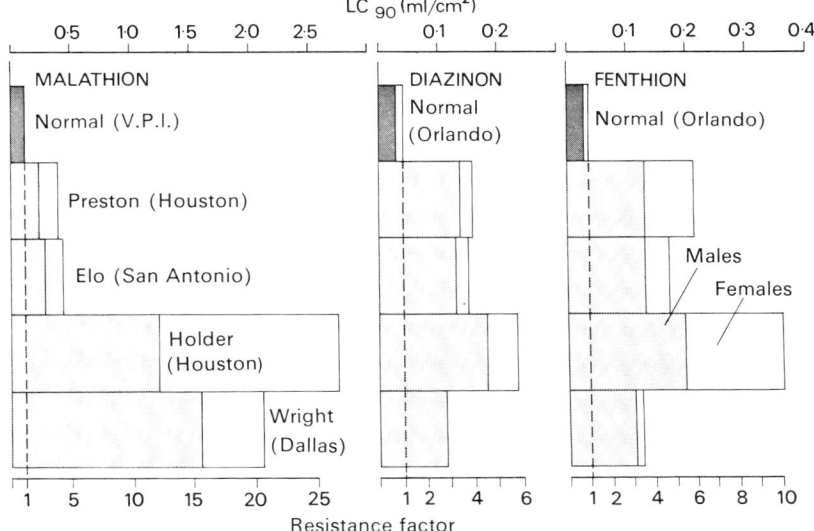

Fig. 182. Resistance factor (based on LC_{90}) of four strains of German cockroach from Texas, to malathion, diazinon and fenthion, compared with laboratory strains from VPI and Orlando. Histograms show the greater susceptibility of males compared with females. (Data from Grayson[363]).

1966 Resistance to chlorinated insecticides extends over a wide area of Japan: all populations show cross-resistance to dieldrin, chlordane and lindane, but not to fenitrothion and diazinon (Table CXXI).

Nineteen field collections of German cockroaches from various locations in Japan, averaged only about 50 per cent mortality after contact for one week with dieldrin ($0.25 g/m^2$ on filter paper): among four strains, 80 per cent of males and 40 per cent of females were able to survive 10 times this application rate.

Two-fold resistance to diazinon and 6-fold to chlordane is detected in a strain of *P. brunnea* from Florida.[519] Evidence is obtained of low cross-resistance between diazinon and some newer carbamate insecticides, U.C. 8454 (Union Carbide) and G.S. 13798 (Geigy), but there is no evidence that cross-resistance extends to propoxur.[364]

There is no cross-resistance between malathion and the carbamates, propoxur and MCA-600; in fact selection with malathion tends to increase susceptibility to these. There is a slight loss in effectiveness of propoxur (about ×2) and MCA-600 (×3) in killing diazinon-resistant German cockroaches.[542]

1967 Sesamex, a pyrethrin synergist, is without synergistic action on dieldrin when applied to susceptible German cockroaches, but it partially or completely removes resistance in various dieldrin-resistant strains.

TABLE CXXI

SUSCEPTIBILITIES (LD$_{50}$ μg/female) OF FIELD-COLLECTED STRAINS OF *B. GERMANICA* TO ORGANOCHLORINE AND ORGANO-PHOSPHORUS INSECTICIDES APPLIED TOPICALLY. KILL ASSESSED AT 1 WEEK

(From Yasutomi et al[876])

Strain	Insecticide				
	Dieldrin	Chlordane	Lindane	Fenitrothion	Diazinon
Susceptible strain 1	0·32	1·55	0·60	0·24	0·50
Susceptible strain 2	0·31	0·83	0·33	0·25	0·39
Antigua (West Indies)	>240	>50	7·49	0·30	0·60
Japanese strains:					
Shirahama A	115	48	6·48	0·24	0·58
Wakayama A	120	50	7·42	0·24	0·59
Nagoya A	120	49	7·25	0·24	0·58
Tokyo	>240	>50	7·47	0·24	0·57
Yokohama A	>240	—	—	—	—
Kawaguchi	>240	—	—	—	—

There is no indication that the effect is related to any biochemical mechanism of defence to dieldrin poisoning.[536]

Penetration of carbaryl through the cuticle is slower and more is excreted by carbaryl-resistant German cockroaches (10-fold) than by susceptible ones (Fig. 183). But these are only contributory factors to carbaryl resistance. More rapid degradation of the insecticide within the cockroach plays an important part in carbaryl resistance.[490]

DDT is regarded as a nerve poison in insects and binds with various components of the nerve cord of the German cockroach (Chapter 14). In cockroaches resistant to DDT, the nerve cord has less binding capacity with the insecticide, than in susceptible insects.[410]

German cockroaches collected from restaurants and bars in 16 localities in Kawasaki City, Japan, during 1966–67 were highly resistant to dieldrin but all were susceptible to diazinon.[779]

1968 From the close similarity in shape of the log time/probit response curve for each insecticide, cross-resistance between dieldrin, lindane and chlordane (the genes being the same in each case) is confirmed in various colonies of German cockroaches (homozygous susceptible (SS), hymozygous resistant (RR), and various heterozygous crosses (SR)). The composition ratios of the three phenotypes (SS, RR and SR) in each colony can be estimated from a plateau which appears on the response curve. The method establishes no cross-resistance whatever between the chlorinated insecticides and diazinon, fenthion (Baytex®) and fenitrothion (Sumithion®).[778]

High levels of resistance to dieldrin and lindane are reported in three strains of German cockroaches in Australia,[439] comparable with those reported by Ishii & Sherman[459] for the highly chlordane-resistant Manoa strain. All three Australian strains are susceptible to diazinon, malathion and fenthion, although organophosphorus insecticides and propoxur have been used in these locations since 1963–64, as well as chlorinated insecticides.

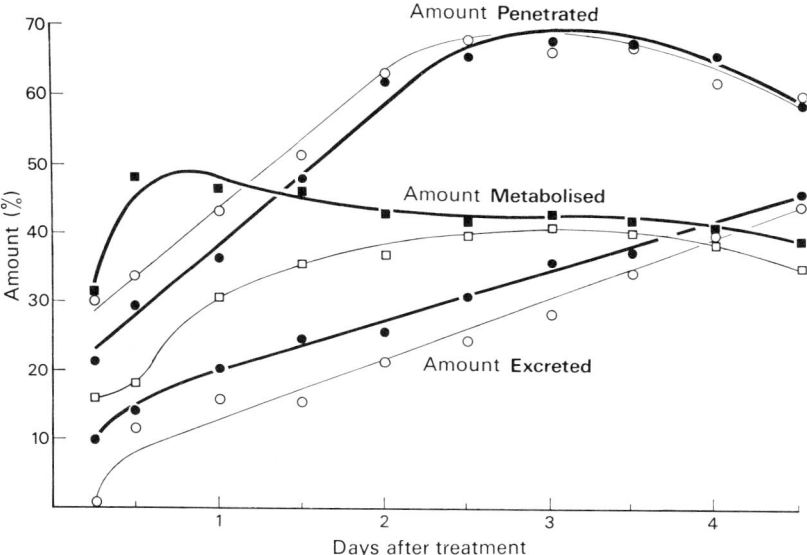

Fig. 183. Rates of penetration, metabolism and excretion of carbaryl in resistant (thick lines) and susceptible German cockroaches (thin lines) at various times after topical application (4 μg carbaryl/insect). The amount metabolised was derived from the proportion of the penetrated dose, recovered as breakdown products in the tissues and excreta. (From Ku & Bishop[490]).

Cockroaches from 7 locations in Louisiana, where problems of control are being encountered, show exceptional resistance to chlordane and marked resistance to malathion (up to 110-fold), considerably higher than previously reported. Resistance to diazinon is 6- to 13-fold and similar to fenthion (8- to 11-fold). Response to propoxur (2- to 15-fold), shows the first definite evidence of resistance to a carbamate in field strains. This may be caused 'wholly or in part by cross-resistance imparted by chlordane, malathion and/or diazinon'.[96]

Carbaryl resistance in B. germanica confers a marked cross-resistance to the structurally similar carbamate, MCA-600 (15- to 22-fold at LD_{90}).

This is apparent by topical application but is not shown when the cockroaches are dipped in insecticide. Resistance to carbaryl causes little reduction in the efficacy of propoxur.[541]

Variations (e.g. in longevity of females) were found in the life histories of chlordane-resistant German cockroaches collected from dwellings in Raleigh, North Carolina, compared with a laboratory, chlordane-susceptible strain. But the first generation bred from field-collected parents showed no significant differences, even though a high level of resistance to chlordane remained. Changes reported from the field 'in the habits and biology of resistant cockroaches' are attributed to the wide range of environmental conditions in infested buildings, rather than to their resistance.[865]

American, German and Oriental cockroaches in Poona, India, are readily killed by fenitrothion and propoxur, but malathion on filter papers (3 g/m^2) fails to kill Oriental and American cockroaches in contact tests for 15 days. This is reported as high level resistance,[825] but may represent simply a marked difference in susceptibility of the insects to these insecticides.

1971 Strains of *B. germanica* from installations of the Third U.S. Army in the Southern United States show resistance to chlordane (in 13 out of 17 strains and to malathion (in 8 of 17 strains), but not to diazinon (highest LT$_{50}$ 1·8 hours).[468]

1972 Resistance in Czechoslovakia occurs widely in Oriental and German cockroaches to organochlorine insecticides, especially to dieldrin, but not to organophosphates.[684]

Difficulty is experienced in the control of American cockroaches in New Orleans, Louisiana, using 30 times the normal concentration of dieldrin or chlordane which failed to give control. Organophosphorus insecticides remain effective. (Grayson,[367] citing personal communication from C.D. Mampe.)

1973 Katz *et al.*[473] report the first study of the inheritance of cross-resistance in German cockroaches resistant to organophosphates. Genetic factors responsible for resistance to diazinon with cross-resistance to propoxur, DDT, pyrethrins and lindane are suggested. A laboratory colony of German cockroaches, selected for resistance to diazinon, develops resistance also to malathion, DDT, propoxur and pyrethrins. Selection was made by applying the insecticide topically. When however the insecticides are injected into the insects, susceptibility to most returns almost to normal, indicating that reduced penetration may be an important resistance mechanism.[209]

Four strains of German cockroach collected from Colorado, Kentucky and Texas show various degrees of resistance to pyrethrins, but not to the extent (75-fold) of a strain selected with pyrethrins for several years in the laboratory.[197]

'The majority of control failures reported have been for reasons other than insect resistance. This is particularly true of indoor pest control where cockroaches represent the primary insect problem'.[46] Referring to the use of organophosphorus and carbamate insecticides, Dr. Grayson says: 'I don't see any problems (in the control of cockroaches) in the immediate future with any of the chemicals we are presently using. There has been no significant increase in resistance to organic phosphates since the problem in Texas in 1963.'

1974 Among groups of German cockroaches taken off four ships and from a Naval hospital, resistance to chlordane occurred in 4; low-level tolerance to malathion in 4; resistance to propoxur in 1 (the hospital); low-level tolerance to diazinon in 1; but no resistance or tolerance to chlorpyrifos.[594]

Resistance to chlordane and dieldrin is confirmed among American cockroaches collected in New Orleans, but they are susceptible to organophosphorus insecticides.[632]

1975 German cockroaches resistant to diazinon and with cross-resistance to propoxur show noticeable differences in susceptibility to these insecticides according to the test method used. Resistance to diazinon is twice as great when the insecticide is applied topically (13-fold) than when injected (6-fold). Conversely, resistance to propoxur is nearly twice as great when injected (14-fold) than when applied to the cuticle (8-fold). Thus if penetration of insecticide into the cockroach is an important resistance mechanism, its contribution varies markedly with the toxicant involved.[210]

Use of a laboratory strain of German cockroaches with multi-resistance to diazinon, propoxur, pyrethrins, lindane and DDT shows that diazinon and propoxur are equally effective as selecting agents for increasing resistance to these insecticides and to the pyrethrins: also in maintaining resistance to lindane and DDT. The implications are that resistance to both the organophosphate, the carbamate and possibly the pyrethrins, should be suspected if resistance to diazinon or propoxur is encountered in field strains. The choice of an alternative to combat resistance in such circumstances 'must be considered carefully' to avoid adding to the problem.[211]

Resistance among cockroaches in the U.K.
The extent of resistance to insecticides among cockroaches in the U.K. is unknown. The earliest reports of difficulties in controlling cockroaches with dieldrin were obtained for infestations on ships in 1956–57. Reports of resistance by the German cockroach to chlorinated hydrocarbons in the U.K. in 1961 indicated that the problem was widespread,[373] although authenticated cases were confined to the U.S.A.

The first confirmed instance of resistance to dieldrin by *B. germanica* in England was reported by Gradidge[355]: one strain was taken from a ship that had been treated extensively with dieldrin lacquer since 1954, and another from an infestation in London. The LT_{50} values exceeded 48 hours.

Tests on cockroaches taken from London showed 5,000-fold resistance to chlordane and 6,000-fold resistance to dieldrin, with some cross-resistance to lindane ($\times 10$) and DDT ($\times 5$).[812] A second infestation of dieldrin-resistant cockroaches in premises was reported in 1961, but this had a normal susceptibility to DDT.[373]

In 1962, tests on dieldrin-resistant German cockroaches infesting two ships visiting British ports showed that some individuals took appreciably longer to become affected by diazinon, compared with three laboratory strains. The conclusion was reached; 'it seems likely that the ships' infestations were of mixed populations containing a small proportion of individuals with some resistance to diazinon.'[813] Two years later, this same author, referring to the satisfactory control commonly achieved of German cockroaches with dieldrin, added 'there have, however, been instances where populations of this insect have developed so high a level of resistance to dieldrin that their control with this chemical has proved impossible.[815]

In 1964 Bills[102] undertook major applications of diazinon against cockroaches resistant to dieldrin, in restaurants and kitchens of multistorey office blocks, but was unable to reduce numbers to tolerable levels. He cites reasons other than resistance as the cause of failure.

In tests with dieldrin, diazinon and propoxur, applied topically to six strains of German cockroaches, taken from infested ships in the Port of London, the most marked difference was their susceptibility to dieldrin.[215] Four strains showed greater than 54-fold resistance in comparison with a laboratory strain. One showed tolerance to diazinon ($\times 3 \cdot 8$). There was no evidence of resistance to propoxur.

The ability to survive

When a resistant cockroach is able to survive an insecticide this indicates that the chemical is no longer causing sufficient biological damage. It could be that the insecticide is unable to reach the site of action in the resistant cockroach because of reduced absorption through the cuticle. The insecticide may be detoxified in the process of getting to the site of action, or get stored in fat droplets away from where the insecticide normally acts. Other possibilities are rapid excretion, or perhaps nerve insensitivity, at least for those toxicants normally acting *via* the insect's central nervous system. All these possibilities have been examined to answer the 'why and how' of resistance in different insects.[589]

Many studies have been made to explain what it is about the resistant cockroach which allows it to survive insecticides of the different chemical groups. Writing about the effects and 'non-effects' of carbamate insecticides, Metcalf & Fukuto[563] conclude that 'nearly all insecticides are subject to rapid detoxication in the insect body: that in general, insecticide-resistant strains arise from the selection of individual variants, containing pre-adaptive genes controlling the level of detoxication enzymes'.

A review of the mechanisms of resistance to chlorinated hydrocarbon insecticides has been made by Perry[666] and Brooks.[123] Because DDT was the first insecticide of the chlorinated hydrocarbons to be used on a world-wide scale—and the first to cause resistance—more studies have been made on resistance to DDT than other compounds. Although DDT-resistance has not

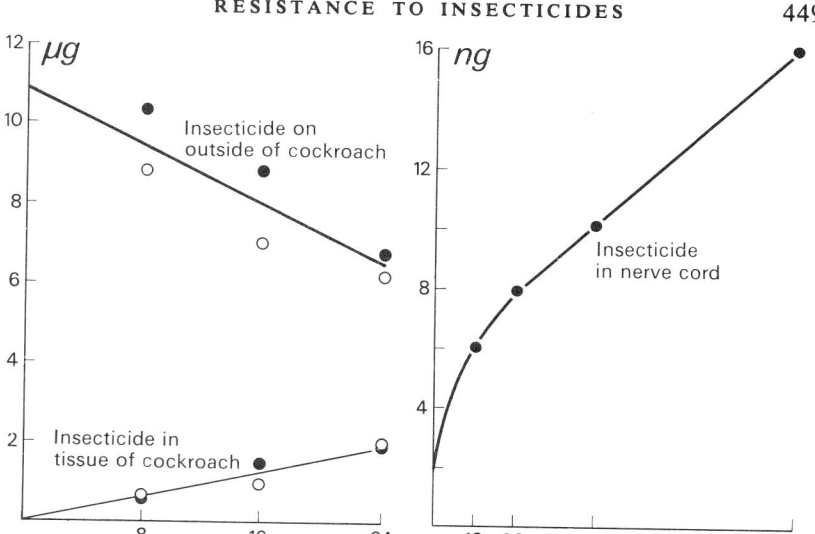

Fig. 184. Uptake of dieldrin by susceptible (open circles) and resistant *B. germanica* (closed circles): (left) relative amounts on the outside and in the tissues after topical application; (right) in the nerve cord of the resistant insect at different applied doses. (After Ray[695]).

become a problem in Oriental and American cockroaches, both have been used as experimental insects to study the problem. With German cockroaches, radioactive DDT was in early studies metabolised at a faster rate by a DDT-resistant than a susceptible strain.[66] Hoskins, Miskus & Eldefrawi[444] found that both susceptible and resistant strains converted DDT to four major metabolites.

Dehydrochlorination of DDT to DDE is the main defence mechanism of insects resistant to this insecticide. But no such breakdown was apparent in an Australian field strain pf *B. germanica*, with 10-fold resistance to DDT, compared with four DDT-susceptible strains. Neither could the resistant strain be identified from speed of penetration of the insecticide through the cuticle.[438]

For a long time the only reaction known to be involved in the breakdown of DDT was caused by a detoxifying dehydrochlorinase enzyme. In 1961, however, German and American cockroaches were both found to contain a microsomal (oxidative) enzyme system, capable of converting DDT to a dicofol-like metabolite. (This is a hydroxyl-type derivative of DDT).[3] 'The relationship between DDT resistance and DDT metabolism in cockroaches still remains largely inconclusive',[667] and because this insecticide is no longer in general use further studies on the subject now seem unlikely.

Males of susceptible and chlordane-resistant German cockroaches contain significantly different quantities of malic dehydrogenase. This enzyme plays a part in the metabolism of carbohydrates, but it is not known how this relates to resistance.[878] No differences occur in the acid and alkaline phosphatase activity of susceptible and chlordane-resistant *B. germanica*.[8]

In the experiments of Ray[695] dieldrin-resistant and susceptible German cockroaches were treated topically with the insecticide: the susceptible insects were prostrate in 6 hours but the resistant ones were unaffected. Unabsorbed insecticide was removed from the outside of the insects with acetone/petroleum ether; nerve cords were also removed, homogenised and subject to dieldrin extraction.

There were no differences in the amounts of unchanged dieldrin recoverable from the tissues of the whole insects, or from the nerve cords of the resistant and susceptible cockroaches (Table CXXII). The amounts of dieldrin in the nerve cords of resistant cockroaches increased with greater amounts applied to the outside of the insect (Fig. 184). These results are not consistent with the presence of a dieldrin-impermeable membrane around the nerve cord of the resistant insect. Resistance is not due to lack of penetration of the insecticide or to metabolism within, but to the ability of the resistant insect to withstand higher concentrations of unchanged dieldrin, within the central nervous system, without showing any signs of poisoning.[695]

How dieldrin poisons insects is not known, but the way the insecticide binds to nerve tissue is believed to play an important role.[532,533] If this is so, nerve components of dieldrin-resistant insects should have a different binding pattern for the insecticide than susceptible ones. German cockroaches topically treated with C^{14} dieldrin, show that dieldrin-resistant cockroaches (Fort Rucker and London (Ontario) strains) have nerve components with less

TABLE CXXII

DIELDRIN (ng) IN NERVE CORDS OF SUSCEPTIBLE AND RESISTANT *B. GERMANICA* AT INTERVALS AFTER TOPICAL APPLICATION
(From Ray[695])

Cockroach	Hours after application			
	8	16	24	Average
Susceptible	4.2	6.2	6.0	5.5
Resistant	5.3	5.1	6.0	5.5

binding capacity for the insecticide (Fig. 185). This supports earlier findings that the ion-transport activities of the nervous system on which nerve conduction depends (see p. 385) are less affected by dieldrin, in dieldrin-resistant cockroaches, compared with susceptible ones.[409] Resistance to lindane is invariably cross-linked to that for dieldrin.

Inhibition of the activity of the enzyme acetylcholinesterase, by organophosphorus compounds, is regarded as the major cause of death in insects, and one might expect to see differences in enzyme depression, between susceptible and resistant German cockroaches. Such a correlation has been demonstrated in a malathion-resistant strain[523]: poisoning causes a faster rate of inhibition of the enzyme in the susceptible strain than the resistant (Fig. 186). In most cases resistance to organophosphates is not associated with a difference in the acetylcholine levels of normal and resistant insects.

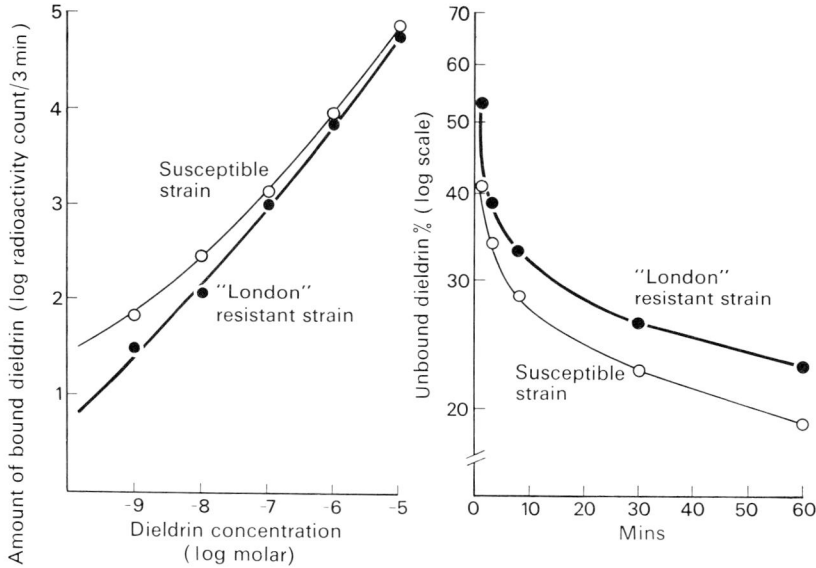

Fig. 185. Binding of C^{14} dieldrin in homogenates of the heads of susceptible and resistant *B. germanica*: (left) amount of bound dieldrin after one hour's incubation with different dieldrin concentrations; (right) effect of time on free (unbound) insecticide after incubation with 1×10^{-6}M dieldrin. (After Matsumura & Hayashi[533]).

In experiments with resistant flies, the fate of insecticides and their breakdown products have been examined using radioactively-labelled insecticides. This method with the American cockroach has shown that it contains at least three types of enzyme (esterases) capable of breaking down organophosphates and a carbamate insecticide.[535] A certain amount of cross-resistance is usually found between these types of compound, probably because both groups are detoxified by the same enzymes.

For a technical appraisal of the biochemical and genetic basis of insecticide resistance the review by Busvine[161] provides a recent summary.

RESISTANCE: THE PROBLEM IN RETROSPECT AND PROSPECT

There are five factors which are important in the development and spread of insecticide resistance in cockroaches:

(1) their rate of reproduction, or the number of generations per year;
(2) frequency of exposure of the insects to the insecticide;
(3) the proportion of the population exposed and the extent of in-breeding;
(4) the inter-relationship of cockroaches with transport;
(5) the ability of the insect to withstand temporary adverse conditions.

Each of these is now examined with the hindsight of experience of the resistance problems which have occurred.

Reproduction and the number of generations per year

Since *B. germanica* has the highest fecundity of the most frequently occurring pest cockroaches, it is not surprising that insecticide resistance has been more pronounced in this than in others. Because of the faster breeding of this species in the tropics, it is again not surprising that resistance was first prevalent in the warm climate of the southern states of America, before being detected in the North. In the U.K. dieldrin resistance in *B. germanica* was first suspected to occur in ships; international traffic not only passes through the tropics, but even in temperate latitudes, the galleys of many ships offer an ideal, almost tropical environment for rapid multiplication of cockroaches. Had we got more detailed information about the existence of resistant strains of cockroaches on land, we might be able to make similar judgements about those environments in buildings which most readily encourage the problem.

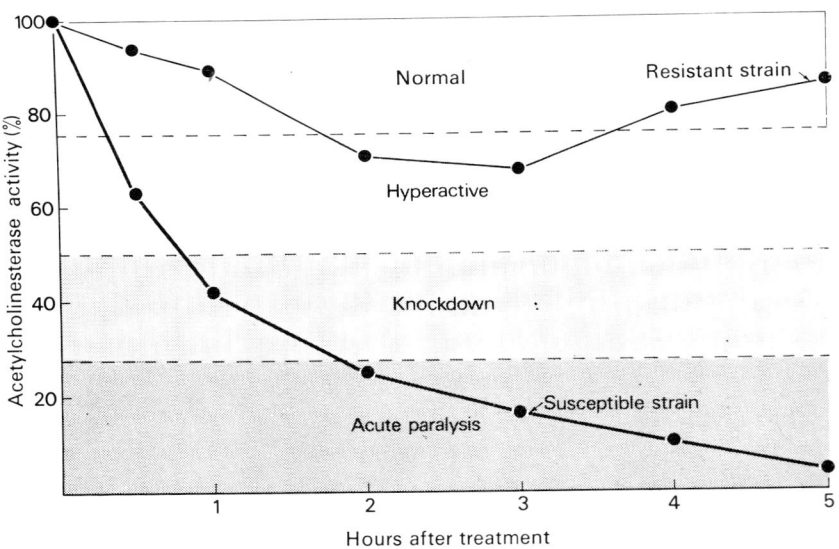

Fig. 186. Inhibition of acetylcholinesterase in *Blattella germanica* by malathion applied topically to a susceptible and resistant strain, in relation to symptom expression with time after treatment. (After Mansingh[523]).

Frequency of exposure to insecticide

A primary requirement for the development of resistance is that an insecticide operates a selection pressure over a number of generations. The longer this pressure is imposed the greater the degree of selection. The pyrethrins, with their extremely short residual life, were used to control cockroaches long before organochlorine insecticides became available, yet resistance to the pyrethrins has, with but few exceptions, reached only tolerance levels. In contrast, resistance to chlordane and dieldrin, insecticides with much longer residual life, was detected in cockroaches within a period of use estimated at about five years. Similarly, malathion and diazinon, now used for periods extending up to 20 years, but with residual lives intermediate between those of organochlorines and the pyrethrins, have resulted in only a few authenticated instances of field resistance. Resistance to propoxur, used for only 10 years seems even less likely to occur.

Clearly, chemical composition of the insecticide and the ability of the insect to detoxify it are of major consequence, but evidence supports the view that persistent compounds afford an extended period of selection, by the possibility of cockroaches being exposed to sub-lethal deposits for many generations. Laboratory evidence shows that Oriental and American cockroaches are more readily killed at lower concentrations, than *B. germanica*, by most of the insecticides commonly used. Resistance, requiring that some insects survive, is therefore more likely to have occurred through failures to control *B. germanica* than other species.

Proportion of the population exposed and extent of inbreeding

The habit of the German cockroach of harbouring within crevices which provide a narrow optimal range of temperature and humidity tends to produce the 'clusters' typical of heavy infestations. An aggregation pheromone (Chapter 4) is known to keep large numbers of cockroaches closely associated and isolates them from adjacent infestations. Indeed as Tyler[815] points out when collecting specimens for insecticide testing, 'since resistance may be localised, cockroaches from different sites, even within one building, should not be mixed but should be tested separately'.

The attempts made to place insecticides as close as possible to, but ideally within the preferred harbourages, ensures that the maximum number of insects in discrete populations, are exposed to treatment. When cockroaches come in contact with sub-lethal deposits of insecticide the two factors, maximum number of insects exposed and 'geographical isolation' become important. They favour a selection pressure being imposed on the greatest number of genes, which are then exchanged in breeding between a closely knit group of individuals, in most instances without dilution from outside sources. The not infrequent possibility of 'back crossing' afforded by progeny mating with parent, further enhances the speed of development of resistance.

Geographical isolation has played a major role in the evolution of new subspecies. Maximum insularity of cockroach infestations probably occurs in ships, where contact with other strains of the same species is infrequent.

Records have been kept of the incidence of German, Oriental, American and Australian cockroaches on cargoes in holds (Chapter 11, Vol. I), but experience in the treatment of galleys and the accommodation of ships fails to support the widely held view that reinfestation of these areas by cockroaches occurs readily when ships are in port. If this were the case, the infestations encountered would comprise many species other than *B. germanica*, but such instances are extremely rare.

Inter-relationship of cockroaches with transport

The close association of cockroaches with man ensures rapid, inadvertent distribution of resistant cockroaches, in ones and twos in all forms of transport, in such things as beverage crates, cardboard cartons and other containers. The speed with which one or two resistant insects may spread genes for resistance among an otherwise susceptible population has not been determined for the cockroach, but transport of all types accelerates these events. In counteraction, cockroaches not subject to insecticidal treatment may, after a number of generations, revert to susceptibility. Nevertheless, with world-wide use of insecticides belonging to the same groups, cross-resistance between chemicals ensures that continued selection for resistance occurs, whether diazinon is used in one country, dichlorvos in a second, or chlorpyrifos or fenitrothion in a third. This was certainly most important—in providing a continuing selection pressure—when cockroach control in the period 1945–65 was carried out almost exclusively with lindane, chlordane and dieldrin.

Ability to withstand temporary adverse conditions

The hazards to which resistant cockroaches are subject in international transport are absence of food and water, low temperature and humidity, and often low pressure. All these factors are examined in Chapter 12, 'Influence of the environment' in Vol. I. From the data of Willis & Lewis[852] it is concluded that cockroaches of many species can survive for relatively long periods, from 5 days to many months, in shipments of material that would not ordinarily be considered food. Although low pressure is suggested as a possible hazard, tests in which cockroaches have been put aboard high speed aircraft have shown that it is without ill effects[775] as long as the temperature does not drop below a certain minimal level, dependent to some extent on the previous temperature experience of the insects.[556] Low temperature appears to be the limiting factor, but resistant insects may often be carried in both the heated and pressurised sections of aircraft.

Low temperatures and pressures do not feature in the accommodation of ships, where conditions are highly favourable to cockroach survival. Marine infestations can provide a direct route for the introduction of resistant cockroaches from one country into ports and adjacent areas of another; baggage from infested accommodation provides a direct link between ship and hotel. It is for this reason, and a number of others, mentioned above, that studies on cockroaches from ships probably give the best advance warning of resistance problems likely to be encountered on land.

REACTIONS OF THE PEST CONTROL INDUSTRY TO RESISTANCE

In 1955 insect resistance became the most important technical problem facing the American pest control industry. Houseflies, bedbugs, cat and dog fleas, certain ticks and several mosquitoes had already become resistant to one or more of the chlorinated hydrocarbon insecticides. The most prevalent insect pest in buildings, the German cockroach, then joined the ranks.

Chlordane as a cheap, effective insecticide—the only synthetic insecticide with which the American service industry had gained much experience—was clearly becoming of little value. The message was that all chlorinated hydrocarbons might eventually become useless against these and other pests. It seemed that the control of resistant German cockroaches would depend on (1) a resort to the pre-war dusts of borax, sodium fluoride and pyrethrins, plus pyrethrin sprays, or (2) employment of the little-used organophosphorus compounds, and a relatively unknown insecticide—chlordecone—in baits. If the answer lay in the use of diazinon and malathion, then the industry recognised that these were going to cost more, and be shorter lived. Also that effective cockroach control was going to require more careful inspections and more frequent and thorough treatments. One of the most important things to be done by the service industry was to explain the problem to its clients, and if necessary to revise prices of contracts.

This drama was never played out in the U.K., where DDT, lindane and dieldrin continued to be used by pest control departments of local authorities into the 1970's. Here, the implications of strong dieldrin resistance among German cockroaches in ships were understood, and for these Rentokil in the U.K. was using diazinon in the early 1960's. Infestations in buildings continued for many years to succumb to a combination of dieldrin and lindane: the major pest cockroach was *B. orientalis*, but infestations of *B. germanica* were recognised as more difficult to control.

The decision taken by Rentokil in 1964 to use organophosphates and discontinue chlorinated hydrocarbons, was not because the chlorinated insecticides had failed, but because questions raised by the publication of 'Silent Spring'[170] clearly indicated that the socially acceptable life of the organochlorines was about to end. The object was to ensure that alternative short-lived insecticides performed adequately in the hands of service staff in the absence of dieldrin and lindane, and to modify cockroach control techniques if necessary.

In the United States, the industry was undoubtedly faced with a more severe problem. Some observers in the mid 1950's believed that the occurrence of resistant German cockroaches in ceilings, door frames and other 'dry areas' was an indication of a different behaviour: the resistant insects survived because they avoided insecticide residues (behavioural resistance). This view was prevalent because it was more difficult for non-technical people to understand the concepts of insects being able to detoxify a chemical and transmit this trait from parent to offspring. With chlordane failing to control infestations, the insects were likely to have been more widespread in buildings.

Recommendations were given to the industry on what action to take if resistance was suspected. To:

1. check that the insecticide used was from fresh stock;
2. check that it had been properly diluted, if a concentrate;
3. ensure that it had been thoroughly applied to all cockroach harbourages;
4. change to another insecticide—to diazinon, malathion or pyrethrins (a wider choice was not available at that time) if live cockroaches still existed after treatment.

If cockroaches then continued to exist, to recheck the thoroughness of the control operation. To:

1. ensure that all harbourages had been found, using a pyrethrins aerosol; the full extent of the infestation might include the premises next door, or above and below if a multistorey building;
2. use dusts; these reach harbourages impossible to treat with sprays;
3. use the full recommended strength of formulations, but not to exceed label recommendations. If resistance exists, doubling of the dose is unlikely to provide eradication. Use generous quantities in all harbourages and potential harbourages;
4. not mix 'insecticidal cocktails';
5. ensure that servicemen have been adequately trained in the biology, habits, inspection techniques and control methods for cockroaches;
6. ensure, wherever possible, that clients have contributed to your obtaining control by improved sanitation within infested buildings;
7. do a 'jar resistance test' with cockroaches from the infested property.

Today, problems in the control of German cockroaches are rarely caused by the chemicals being at fault. Failure, in most cases points to inadequate application methods, although even trained and experienced men may occasionally have problems. Some pest control companies alternate their 'route men' so that each will inspect places the other may have missed. Mampe[902] is unyielding in his view that cockroaches repeatedly found in a treated area means there is a void associated with that location which *must* be treated to get control. Treating the area around will not give control because the cockroaches do not spend much time on treated surfaces.

Resistance to pyrethrins and to diazinon
Because a few cockroaches taken from an infested building, reared to provide sufficient numbers for test, happen to show a measurable level of resistance, there has been a tendency to believe that the insecticide in question has lost, or is about to lose, its value overnight. One suspects that this was the reaction to first reports, in the United States, of resistance by the German cockroach to diazinon and pyrethrins; following as it did resistance to chlordane which had become totally ineffective in some areas.

No criticism is intended here of authors of scientific publications who have reported findings to the pest control industry, but the incidence of resistance, *often as a local problem*, has not been sufficiently stressed. A single instance of measurable resistance should be interpreted with caution. In Labrador[18] and in Florida[509] cockroaches taken from one part of a building were shown to be extremely resistant to chlordane, but those from another part were entirely susceptible. Without tests on large numbers of insects, taken from many geographical areas, it is not possible to give a reliable judgement on the extent

TABLE CXXIII
DOCUMENTED INSTANCES OF FIRST APPEARANCE OF RESISTANCE BY COCKROACHES TO ORGANOCHLORINE AND ORGANOPHOSPHORUS INSECTICIDES
(From Brown & Pal[132])

Species	DDT	Chlordane, dieldrin and lindane	Organophosphorus compounds
B. germanica	1958 Bahamas Cuba Fed. Rep. of Germany France Puerto Rico 1959 Poland Trinidad 1961 England	1951 Texas ⎫ 1955 S.E. ⎬ USA 1956 N.E. ⎭ 1958 Cuba Panama Puerto Rico California 1959 Canada Japan Poland Trinidad 1961 England Fed. Rep. of Germany 1963 Australia Denmark New Guinea Hawaii	1961 Indiana and Kentucky (USA) 1964 Texas (USA) 1966 Louisiana (USA)
B. orientalis	1964 Czechoslovakia	1958 Fed. Rep. of Germany 1964 Czechoslovakia	—
Periplaneta brunnea	—	1965 Florida (USA)	1965 Florida (USA)

and importance of resistance as a problem. Assessments tend to be subjective and need to be based largely on the experience of those actually involved in carrying out control operations.

For those involved directly with practical aspects of pest control, insect resistance is usually an urgent and alarming problem, having commercial implications. 'It is unfortunate that in most cases the first observation under field conditions is the end-point of the resistance problem, the hard fact that the chemical is no longer capable of ensuring the pest's demise'.[849] The choice is a higher concentration (which is inappropriate, and of very limited benefit), or an alternative chemical. There is no doubt that propoxur, introduced at the time diazinon resistance was being detected in cockroaches, had a marketing advantage as an insecticide capable of killing these resistant insects. The U.S. pest control industry anticipated that diazinon would largely disappear from use, as was the threat to chlordane. As it happens, diazinon continues to remain effective.

An up-to-date perspective

The views expressed in 1969 in the United States[630] about resistance in the German cockroach are believed to be pertinent today.

1. *Chlorinated hydrocarbons*: resistance is widespread to these insecticides, being strongly developed to chlordane and dieldrin and moderate to lindane and DDT.

Chlorinated insecticides are now seldom used in the U.S.A., but chlordane is still effective in some locations. For other reasons, insecticides belonging to this group are not now the ones of choice.

2. *Organophosphorus compounds*: there may be locations where the effectiveness of these insecticides is reduced, but in the vast majority of cases, diazinon, malathion, chlorpyrifos and related compounds are adequate for practical purposes.

It was thought in 1969 that significant wide-spread field resistance to diazinon would eventually occur, imparting cross-resistance to malathion and other organophosphates; also perhaps affecting the performance of some carbamates. Since diazinon has in large measure replaced the use of chlordane, the pressure of selection to the organophosphates will most certainly have increased. Currently, however, there is no indication of a practical problem involving resistance by German cockroaches to organophosphorus insecticides. The problem may have been averted by legislative pressures to adopt greater use of the pyrethrins: where diazinon is no longer used, strains of German cockroach lose all their resistance after 6–7 generations.[620]

3. *Carbamates*: resistance to propoxur is possible: in 1969 there was one documented case.

The problem does not appear to have grown, probably because resistance to organophosphates has not materialised. Should resistance to diazinon occur, loss of effectiveness of some of the newer carbamates (e.g. bendiocarb) can be expected.

4. *Other pest cockroaches*

Apart from isolated reports (Table CXXIII) there are no problems of resistance involving *B. orientalis* or species of *Periplaneta*. Additional reports of resistance would have been expected in the last 10 years but none have been made.

5. *In future years*

The levels of tolerance to the insecticides now being used will continue to rise among cockroach populations and may give problems in future years. There is some evidence, however, from laboratory studies, that resistance to diazinon, dursban, propoxur and related compounds, may never become significant in the German cockroach—at least not to create resistance problems of the same magnitude as with the organochlorines. Nevertheless, it is clearly desirable that a variety of insecticides from different chemical groups, and therefore differing mode of action, be permitted for use so that selection pressures are kept low. The alternative: of abandoning insecticides for other methods of cockroach control, does not appear to be within prospect.

16

REARING AND COLLECTING COCKROACHES

Breeding and rearing cockroaches: conditions and equipment; diet; water; setting up cultures; cockroaches of known age; responsibility for cockroach culture; yield of insects; control of mites, psocids and nematodes in cultures; rearing of other cockroach species; handling of cockroaches; CO_2 anaesthesia; immobilisation and insecticide susceptibility—Collecting cockroaches: trap containers; suction methods.

The development of insecticides for the pest control industry involves special tests to demonstrate the usefulness and improved performance of new compounds. In turn, these tests require pest insects in large numbers; it is possible to trap and collect cockroaches from infested premises, but rarely in the numbers required for research. Cockroaches must therefore be reared in the laboratory to satisfy these needs.

In the first part of this chapter we shall examine the methods of breeding cockroaches to provide large numbers of 'standardised' insects for laboratory testing of insecticides. Fortunately all the cockroaches of economic importance can be reared easily, provided an acceptable temperature is maintained, ample food and water are provided, and there is an adequate surface area of harbourage within the culture container.

In the second part, we shall examine methods of collecting cockroaches; some of the old methods of cockroach control depended upon catching the insects. Even today, cockroach traps are marketed for the domestic user who prefers not to use chemicals. Our interest in the use of traps, however, is for collecting cockroaches for test and for assessing levels of infestation. Trapping techniques help test the performance of new insecticides in field trials: by assessing the size of populations before and after treatment we can measure the success or failure of the insecticide used. Trapping is also helpful in establishing whether proven chemicals are performing properly especially where resistance is suspected.

BREEDING AND REARING COCKROACHES

There are many different ways of culturing cockroaches, most of which involve variations in the design of cages or containers, and the materials of construction. They include also different ways of separating developing young from the parental stock. This, however, does not have much effect on the breeding of cockroaches. The essential requirements are a container which can be easily cleaned, food, water, harbourage and warmth.

REARING AND COLLECTING COCKROACHES

The literature on the culturing of cockroaches has been reviewed[111,757] and methods of rearing and handling American and German cockroaches for the evaluation of pesticides are described in two South African Standards.[719,720] The methods of testing sprays and aerosols against cockroaches, laid down by the U.S. Chemical Specialties Manufacturers Association (CSMA), also specify the conditions under which the test insects are to be reared.[25,26]

The production of relatively small numbers of cockroaches for school purposes, for dissection and to teach insect morphology, is relatively easy provided cultures are attended to at least weekly. A similar need can be met for insect physiologists. Because of its size, the most popular species for these purposes is the American cockroach. If the numbers of cockroaches for teaching are small and required infrequently, it is better to obtain them from a biological supplier or research establishment. On the other hand, the culturing of cockroaches by students can stimulate their interest and provide a range of stages to demonstrate moulting and other aspects of insect biology. The production of a hundred adult cockroaches once or twice a year is achieved with inexpensive equipment and presents no real problem except that stock has to be maintained throughout the year, and many more insects may be produced than is really necessary. A small incubator or warm cupboard which can be ventilated is suitable for this purpose.

If the number required is small and seeing their development and behaviour is important, rearing is best done in wide-mouthed glass jars, or all-glass aquaria (Fig. 187). Glass is so easy to clean that there is now no good reason to use containers of wood or metal,[304] or those with wire mesh[221] which are much more difficult to clean and keep in good repair. If it is not important to be able to see the insects, unbreakable plastic containers are best of all.

To supply the insecticide chemist with massive numbers of healthy cockroaches quickly, and with minimum manpower, the insects are best bred in dustbins (Fig. 188). Keeping them in the bins poses a problem, since nymphs of *B. germanica* can climb glass and other smooth surfaces at birth.[853] An 'electric fence' charged by a 22·5v battery has been described to prevent cockroaches escaping from the top of galvanised bins.[830] However, the more modern, light-weight but rigid plastic dustbin is ideal, with the insects confined by PTFE (polytetrafluoroethylene) dispersion applied smoothly as a band below the rim.[690] The room in which the insects are bred should have an air extractor, otherwise it will become heavily fouled. The procedures now described allow German, Oriental and American cockroaches to be reared in the same room using identical equipment, but do not allow the production of cockroaches of known age (see p. 465).

Conditions and equipment

The temperature of the breeding room should be 25–30°C. The relative humidity is of some importance: high values (e.g. about 80 per cent) improve the hatching of oothecae and the survival of young nymphs, but these high humidities may lead to outbreaks of mite infestations in the cultures. For this reason, lower relative humidites (below 60 per cent) are preferred, the minimum

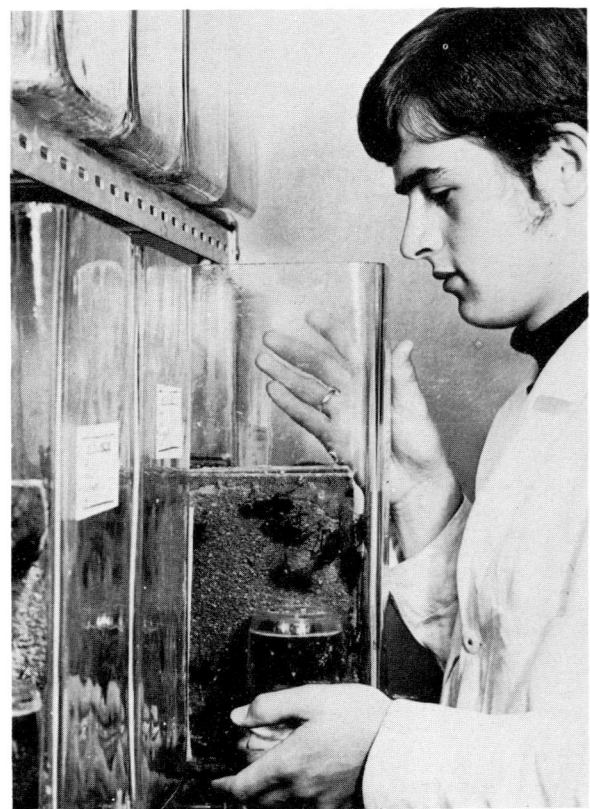

Fig. 187. Small numbers of cockroaches can be reared in glass aquaria which can be readily cleaned, and the insects easily seen.

being of little significance, provided the insects have plenty of water to drink.[402]

Equipping the bins with harbourage, food and water is very simple. Each adult American cockroach needs about 12 cm^2 of surface to produce the maximum number of offspring.[674] About half this is required by *B. germanica* and *S. longipalpa*. A good disposable harbourage is provided by a roll of corrugated cardboard, about 40 cm high and 30 cm across. 'Spacers' of the same card, about 3 cm wide, within the roll (Fig. 189), prevent it from being rolled too tightly, and allow the insects to get between the layers. Use two for the harbourages of German and Oriental cockroaches, and three for *Periplaneta* species. The spacers should be kept at the top of the roll to prevent accumulation of faecal pellets.

The roll of corrugated cardboard is best kept off the bottom of the bin so that the insects can get into the crevices from below: support it on off-cuts of

REARING AND COLLECTING COCKROACHES

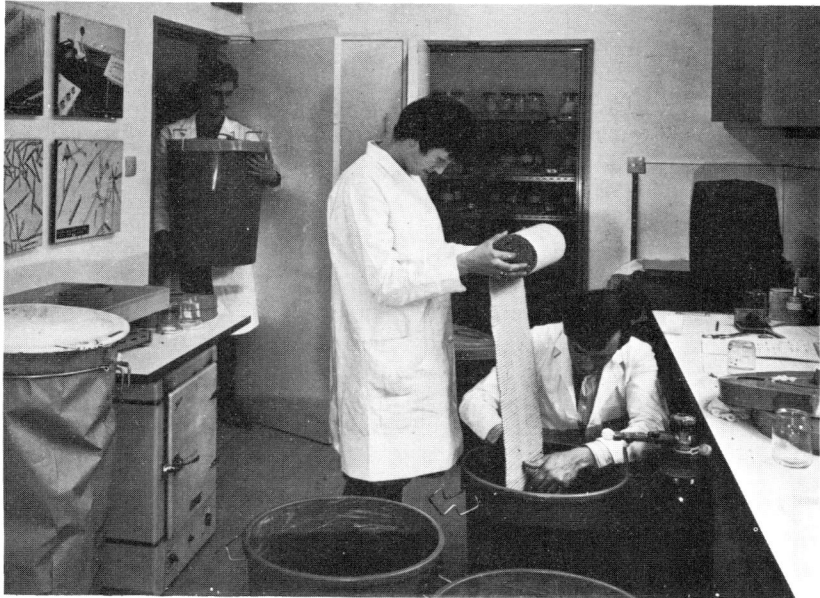

Fig. 188. Setting up cultures of cockroaches in large plastic dustbins. A roll of corrugated cardboard provides the insects with harbourage. The cockroaches are immobilised with carbon dioxide from a pressure cylinder to enable easier handling. The tops of the bins are treated to prevent the insects' escape. (Laboratories of Rentokil, U.K.).

alloy angle which are cheap enough to be thrown away. Sawdust,[332,538] bran,[488] sand or filter paper[879] and other media, are often recommended on the bottom of culture containers to soak up moisture, but this should not be necessary.

Diet

A fortified animal pellet (as given to laboratory rats) or a cereal dog food[115,353] provides an ideal diet. Purina Dog Chow® is mentioned repeatedly in the American literature as being among the best of proprietary products.[331,749] Quite separate from the chemical composition of the diet, it is important when rearing many thousands of cockroaches to provide them with a large surface area from which to feed. Also to keep the food off the bottom of the bin where it will rapidly become mouldy and contaminated with faeces.

Pelleted food, or 'rat nuts' can be offered in a container made from expanded aluminium; a 1 cm mesh stops the pellets from falling out but allows easy entry for very large numbers of cockroaches. A cylindrical container (Fig. 189) is easy to make, maintain and top-up when it becomes less than half full. An alternative for small scale rearing is to prepare a paste from the following and smear a 3 mm layer onto hardboard sheets, again to provide maximum feeding surface area. Allow to dry before use:

>   9 parts rolled oats
>   9 parts wheat feed or middlings
>   1 part fish meal
>   1 part dried yeast powder
>   and water to make a stiff paste.

Water
Cockroaches must have an uninterrupted supply of water: refilling of water containers is vitally important if really large numbers of cockroaches are to be obtained. This is a regular chore and it is therefore best to have the containers accessible, at the top of the bin, where they will also keep reasonably clean. Water can be supplied in 1 lb jam jars, inverted over a cotton wool pad filling a petri dish. The pad should be replaced when moulds appear. Alternatively a roll of filter paper can be used as a wick in a jam jar of water. Two or three jars in each bin are adequate if refilled once a week, but checked twice weekly. The jars can be prevented from falling over if placed in a rack of alloy angle laid on top of the roll of cardboard. The design shown in Fig. 189 has been found most stable; it uses the harbourage and sides of the bin to give support, but should be cut accurately to size or the sides of the bin may be split.

Setting up cultures
The first step is to obtain sufficient numbers to inoculate the bins. This is done with two types of culture: a breeding stock and a rearing stock. The same type of container can be used for both.

With German cockroaches the rearing bins are innoculated with large numbers of first stage nymphs, where they will grow to become 'test' insects. Early in a culturing programme it is best to keep a stock of adults in breeding bins and to separate the young nymphs on a sieve (8 mesh/in.) weekly after anaesthetisation with CO_2. The adults are returned to their container and the nymphs used to establish more rearing bins as required. Additional breeding stocks may be established from time to time, to bring all the rearing bins into use.

With Oriental and American cockroaches the rearing bins are established by inoculating with oothecae. Thus the rolls of corrugated cardboard provided as harbourages, are transferred once a month with egg cases attached from the breeding cultures to new rearing bins. Anaesthetisation with CO_2 will again be found helpful to immobilise adults and nymphs. Faecal pellets in the bottom of the breeding containers are also sieved regularly to separate egg cases and these also transferred. The nymphs which hatch from these can be further subdivided to provide additional sub-cultures.

The procedures described get all the rearing containers into use. Once sufficient insects have been bred, no new breeding cultures are needed: a constant population becomes self-maintained in each bin, dead adults being replaced by maturing nymphs.

Cockroaches of known age

There are many modifications to the method of culturing described. One is to have a culture container consisting of two bins, one fitting into the top of the other (Fig. 190). The base of the top one is of wire mesh, and when this bin contains adult German cockroaches, without harbourage, the young nymphs separate automatically by falling through the mesh and remain in the harbourage provided in the bin below. This helps reduce cannibalism and can provide young cockroaches of a known and narrow age range.

If it is necessary to have large numbers of cockroaches of a particular nymphal stage, the handling of many thousands of insects all at different

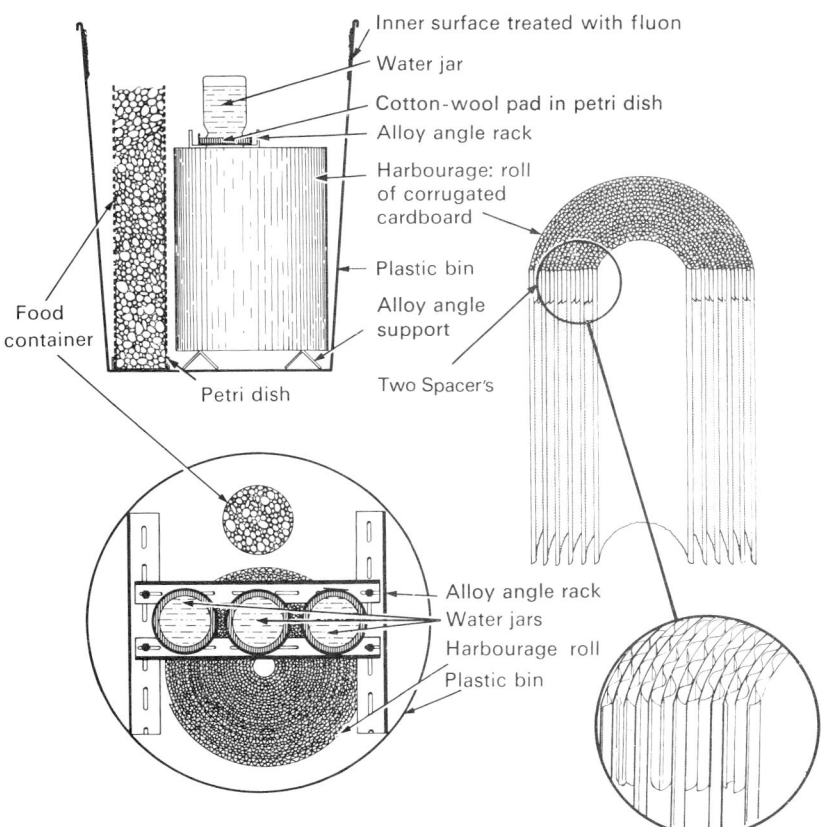

Fig. 189. Container and equipment for culturing cockroaches in large numbers: (top left) section through plastic dustbin; (bottom left) looking down on equipment inside; (right) use of spacers to keep surfaces of corrugated cardboard apart to provide harbourage.

Fig. 190. Rearing containers consisting of two bins: the top one has a base of wire mesh and allows newly hatched nymphs of *B. germanica* to fall into the bottom bin. The offspring can thus be separated from adults automatically and provide test insects of known age. (Communicable Disease Centre, Savannah, U.S.A.).

stages of development cannot be avoided. When adults of a narrow age range (say 7–14 days) are required for test, rearing containers have to be serviced weekly.

Responsibility for cockroach culture

Where cockroaches are reared collectively in large plastic dustbins, many thousands can be reared to maturity each week. Cultures should be cleaned every three months. Where the insects are required for insecticide studies, the person responsible for rearing must be made well aware in advance, of the numbers required so that parental stock can be built up to the appropriate level. This person is usually a laboratory assistant: he must have a keen interest in insect rearing if the programme of work by his scientific colleagues is not to be thwarted by delays.

Very often in a testing programme it is desirable to test the performance of a new insecticide against two or three species of cockroaches at the same time, and against strains which have been reared from supposedly resistant stock. In this type of programme cross-contamination of cultures is fatal to the interpretation of data which may subsequently be obtained. Insect-proof covers on the rearing containers and very strict procedures to prevent mixed cultures occurring are essential.

Yield of insects

Tsuji & Mizuno[804] have recorded the production of oothecae of *P. americana* in stock colonies of increasing population densities (Fig. 191): the numbers vary from 7·5 to 4 egg cases per insect. The most prolific period of ootheca production is during the 100 days between the 150th and 250th day from hatching. This indicates that if new colonies are prepared at intervals of just less than 100 days, oothecae will be constantly available.

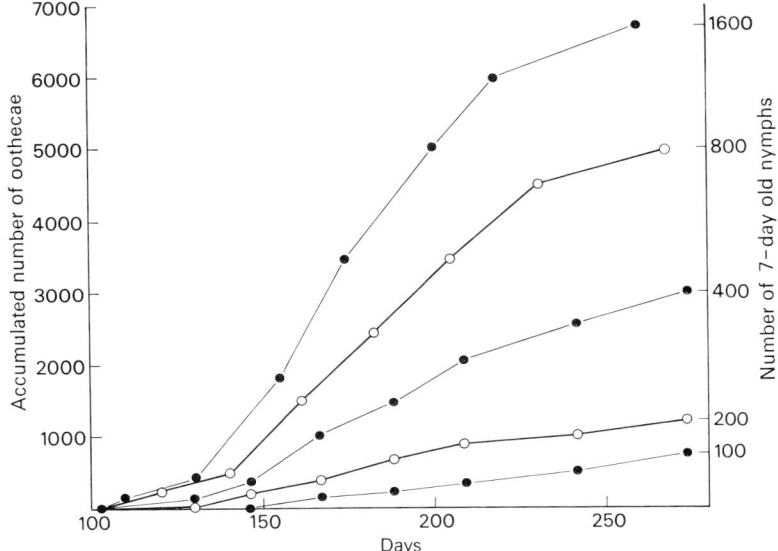

Fig. 191. Accumulated numbers of oothecae of *P. americana* obtained from stock colonies of different numbers of 7-day old nymphs in glass containers (51 × 27 × 35 cm) at 27°C and 75–80 per cent R.H. (From Tsuji & Mizuno[804]).

Mele[555] has studied the growth of populations of *B. germanica* in glass tanks (5 litre capacity) starting with 5 male and 5 female last instar nymphs. Populations stabilised after 4 months at 705 individuals. A study of the population dynamics of mixed cultures[681] has been made by breeding German, Oriental, Brown-banded and American cockroaches together, for 1 year at 25–35°C and 65 per cent RH. The German cockroach was the most productive, the American cockroach less so, and the Oriental and Brown-banded cockroaches were unable to compete under the test conditions.

Control of mites, psocids and nematodes in cultures
If the humidity in the culture room has been kept low, mite and psocid infestation should not arise. Some of the commonest species which attack cockroaches and their oothecae are described under 'natural enemies' in Vol. I. The mites include, *Tyroglyphus* spp. and *Glycyphagus* spp. which thrive on moulds growing on moist cereals, and the predacious *Cheyletus*. A common psocid *Liposcelis divinatorius* also feeds on moulds.

Drastic measures may often be necessary to solve a mite problem, including discarding all the experimental stock. Holding the culture room for a few days at a high temperature, without humidification, will help kill mites in crevices in the walls and shelving. Washing down with ethyl alcohol or formalin should also be carried out. Fumigation can only be contemplated if the building is separate from others.

Should the strain of cockroach being reared have some special qualities (perhaps having been bred for resistance to an insecticide through years of selection in the laboratory) it is possible to wash small numbers of adults and their oothecae without complete loss. Fisk[305] reports controlling mites (of undetermined species) by using a wettable powder of 4-chlorophenyl 4-chlorobenzenesulphate* as a spray and 5 per cent dust: it is reported to have unusual acaricidal properties and limited insecticidal action. One treatment was apparently sufficient.

The nematode, *Leidynema appendiculata*, is an intestinal commensal of *P. americana* reported to cause problems in laboratory cultures.[715] Apparently these worms form a concentration at the junction of the mid- and hind-intestine, blocking movement in the gut and reducing absorption. In tests of different antihelminths in the drinking water, Vanquin® at a dilution of 1 : 100 produced the most effective results with complete elimination of nematode infestation in 5 days.[662]

One or two cockroaches invariably escape from culture containers, or during sub-culturing; it is difficult to prevent this. Treatment of the floor of the culture room with boric acid solution (see p. 195) or the use of chlordecone baits (p. 313) can help prevent infestations becoming established.

Rearing of other cockroach species
Scharrer[732] describes methods of rearing *L. maderae* and Nutting[633] of the giant cockroach *Blaberus*. Dahm[222] gives methods of rearing *L. manderae* and *Blaberus giganteus*. *Supella longipalpa* can be reared by the methods described for the other common pest species.

Handling of cockroaches
Reference has already been made to the use of an electric barrier and PTFE dispersion to confine cockroaches (p. 461). These now replace the previous use of petrolatum, vaseline, liquid paraffin and other far less efficient materials. Teflon 30 FTE (Fluorocarbon Resin Dispersion) is its equivalent in the U.S.A.[262]

Cockroaches are relatively robust insects and can survive gentle sieving. In sub-culturing, or cleaning out culture containers, it is an advantage not to have the cockroaches actively mobile. CO_2 anaesthesia is most commonly used, since the borderline between activity and immobility is more easily controlled than by chilling. Use of CO_2 from a cylinder is also more convenient.

---

* Ovotran® : a 50 per cent wettable powder once marketed by Dow Chem. Co.
Vanquin® : registered trade mark of Parke Davis & Co.

CO_2 anaesthesia

Carbon dioxide when applied for short periods has generally been thought to have no harmful after-effects, since treated insects appear to recover quickly and completely. Unfortunately CO_2 can have detrimental effects on insect growth and Brooks[127] has carried out experiments which should serve as a warning against the over-use of carbon dioxide to immobilise cockroaches.

When nymphs of the German cockroach are exposed to a high concentration of carbon dioxide for 3 minutes each week, until reaching the final moult, nymphal development is retarded by 14–53 per cent and the weight of adults obtained is lower than from non-anaesthetised nymphs (Table CXXIV). Retardation is not influenced by the type of diet, or by rearing nymphs in isolation or in groups. Inexplicably the treatment with CO_2 increases the insects' longevity.

TABLE CXXIV

EFFECT OF CO_2 ANAESTHESIA, BRIEFLY, ONCE A WEEK UNTIL THE FINAL MOULT, ON THE GROWTH, REPRODUCTION AND LONGEVITY OF *B. GERMANICA*

(From Brooks[128])

Measurement	Untreated	Treated
Days to mature (av.)	60	80
Wt of females (mg)	69	61
Wt of males (mg)	48	40
Survival ratio (nymphs : adults)	80 : 63	80 : 63
Reproductive adults	57	63
Egg capsules/female	3·9	4·0
Aborted egg capsules	15·5%	23·3%
Nymphs per ootheca	27	27
Nymphs per female	90	83
No. of weeks to 50% mortality	16	23

In Brooks' experiments her 'control insects' were not anaesthetised and thus not subject to weekly disturbance. This criticism however can be discounted since nymphs anaesthetised with nitrogen (95 per cent) plus carbon dioxide (5 per cent) are little affected by treatment and one group, anaesthetised with 'pure' nitrogen, developed as rapidly as non-anaesthetised cockroaches.

Carbon dioxide applied at intervals throughout the life of *B. germanica* is more deleterious to reproduction than if stopped at maturity.[128] The longer it is used, the greater the number of abortive oothecae; the weight of capsules is reduced, but the number of eggs per capsule is normal (Table CXXIV). Air, chilled to the temperature of expanding carbon dioxide, has no effect on growth rate. The frequency of moulting of anaesthetised cockroaches is unchanged.

These findings indicate that the more often cockroaches are handled during rearing, involving the use of CO_2, the smaller the adults will be, the longer they will take to grow and the fewer young will be produced. This emphasises the value of culture methods (as described) which require the insects to be immobilised least often. Other gases (ether, nitrous oxide, nitrogen and cyclopropane) also have detrimental effects. Nitrogen, ether and chloroform are much inferior to carbon dioxide as anaesthetics for *B. germanica*.[617]

Immobilisation and insecticide susceptibility
German cockroaches exposed to CO_2 for 2·5 hr take several days to die. But the most important question about the use of CO_2 appears not to have been answered: does treatment with CO_2 affect the susceptibility of cockroaches some weeks later when tested with insecticides? No studies appear to have been made. Not surprisingly the response of insects is modified when insecticides are applied *during* CO_2 anaesthesia.[119]

Busvine[162] has reviewed the merits of chilling insects to below their activity threshold as a means of immobilising them. Apart from recovery occurring rather rapidly when the insects are brought into a warm room, he gives two objections to chilling: first its likely effect on the insects' metabolism, especially important if the insects are used in insecticide tests immediately they become mobile again; second, when chilled insects are brought into a warm room, condensation on the cuticle may affect the uptake and action of insecticides. All insects should be 'conditioned' without food or water for 12–24 hours before use, thus avoiding these problems. There seems no objection however to chilling cockroaches to help prevent escape during sub-culturing, or when cleaning out rearing bins, except that the whole container has to be chilled, unless cold air can be piped into the bin and warm air displaced.[395]

COLLECTING COCKROACHES

Methods of catching cockroaches are of interest for a number of reasons:

1. to provide insects for the detection and measurement of insecticide resistance (see p. 48);
2. to assess the practical performance of insecticides, using trap counts before and after treatment;
3. to provide biological information: such as the relative abundance of pest species, the distance of movement of marked cockroaches, and enquiries into disease outbreaks where cockroaches are suspected vectors;
4. for the control of cockroaches: trapping is an antiquated and inefficient method, but is still practised in some countries as an alternative to the use of chemicals.

Methods of trapping are of two types: those in which baited or unbaited containers either attract cockroaches to them or are used as harbourage from which the insects cannot escape; and suction devices which can be used to collect cockroaches in far greater numbers.

In some instances, cockroaches have been collected without using traps: thus, Gould & Deay[352] tried knocking down American cockroaches with pyrethrum powder in a meat-packing factory to establish their sex ratio. The insects could be picked up, but very few survived for susbsequent rearing. Pyrethrins aerosols were used in homes by the City Health Department in Tyler, Texas, to try to locate marked American cockroaches released in nearby sewers.[249] Attempts were also made to determine seasonal changes in cockroach populations of sewers by visible counts, as the manhole covers were lifted.

Trap containers

The simplest trap is a large glass jar or other container with a wide mouth, containing a food lure (Fig. 192). About a tablespoonful of finely divided, highly sorptive clay is shaken in the jar to coat the sides. Any still remaining loose is tipped out. The food—a piece of bread—is placed in the jar and the traps then strategically placed in infested buildings in positions favoured by cockroaches. The dust on the inside of the jar causes the insects to slip back when trying to escape and kills them by desiccation. As many as 1,140

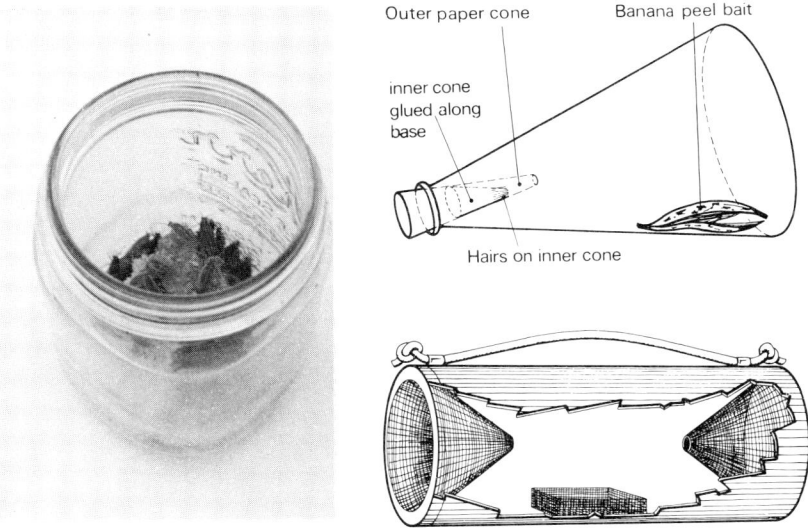

Fig. 192. Simple cockroach traps: (left) wide-mouthed jar baited, and treated internally with dust, vaseline or other material to prevent the insects' escape: (above right) the Graham cockroach trap from which escape is prevented by paper cones; (bottom right) cylindrical metal trap with gauze cones at both ends.

cockroaches have been trapped in a week in one jar.[264] Coca cola syrup, coffee, beer plus yeast and other liquids are more attractive than solids but are not so easy to use: the insects tend to drown and hinder counting. This type of trap has been used by Ebeling and co-workers in many studies of insecticide performance in treated properties in Los Angeles.

Dow[239] used jars to trap cockroaches in a study of dysentery and poliomyelitis in a Latin-American quarter in South Texas, attracting them with bread smeared with lard. Jung & Shaffer[470] used jars coated inside with vaseline and baited with molasses to collect *P. americana* for laboratory transmission studies of ingested Salmonellae.

A very simple trap, which subsequently became known in the literature as 'Graham's trap'—after the maker—consists of a flat-bottomed flask with a paper cone tapered to 1 cm, held in the mouth of the flask by vaseline (Fig. 192). Inside this is a similar cone with one side glued to the larger cone. The smaller one has human hairs glued to its inner end, but these are said to be unnecessary. Banana peel in the trap gave far the best results: 'we have personally tried various contrivances on the market and others of our own devising but find Mr. Graham's trap far better than anything we have met with'.[837]

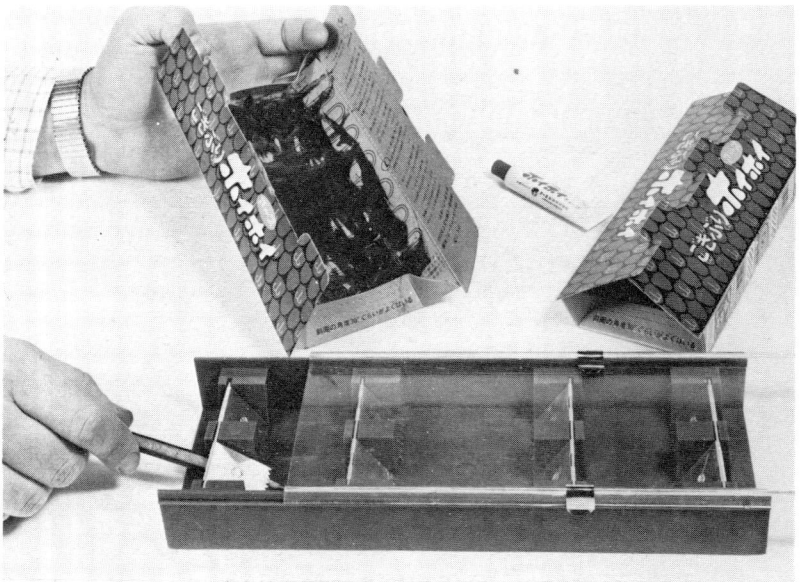

Fig. 193. Examples of traps marketed for cockroach control: (above) a prefabricated toy house of cardboard into which an adhesive paste, incorporating attractants, is applied to the floor from the tube provided; (below) a plastic box with perspex lid into which cockroaches are attracted by bait. Escape is prevented by the hinged flaps, as shown.

Fig. 194. Suction equipment used to collect American cockroaches from Los Angeles sewer manholes. The collecting can contains rolls of corrugated cardboard as resting surfaces. (Courtesy: Ebeling, U.C.L.A.).

Jars with plastic cones held in the mouth by a cover ring were used by Jackson & Maier[460,461] with banana as bait, to collect and study the dispersion of *P. americana* in sewers in Phoenix, Arizona.

A trap consisting of a metal cylinder (45 cm long × 15 cm diameter) with a cone of wire mesh at both ends, and baited with CSMA fly-rearing medium, proved five times more effective than gallon jars baited with dog pellets and beer; it was also ten times better than quart jars containing dog pellets and malt syrup. The baits were contained in wire baskets soldered into the base of the trap (Fig. 192). These were used in sewer manholes and some 25,000 cockroaches were caught in various locations over a period of 3–4 months.

Dried meat used as a bait for dermestid beetles attracted *P. brunnea* in Texas.[267] Specially constructed traps baited with dry commercial fox food

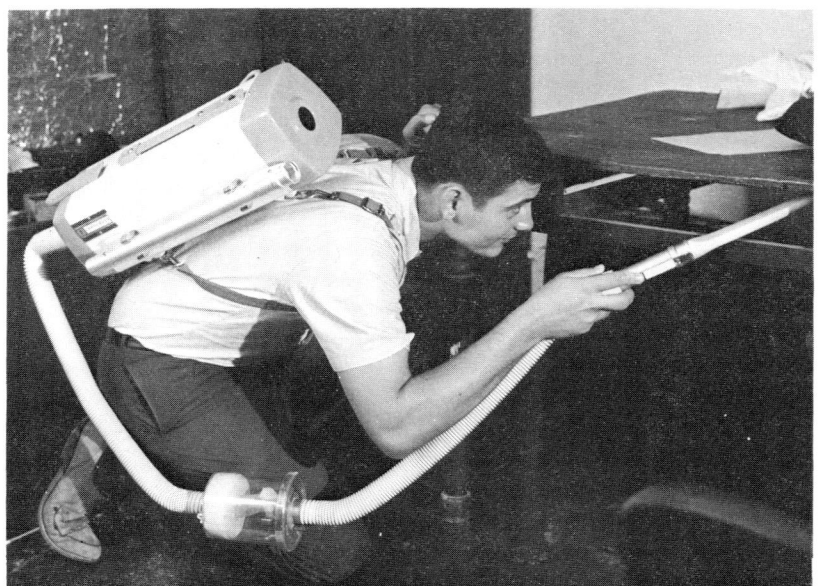
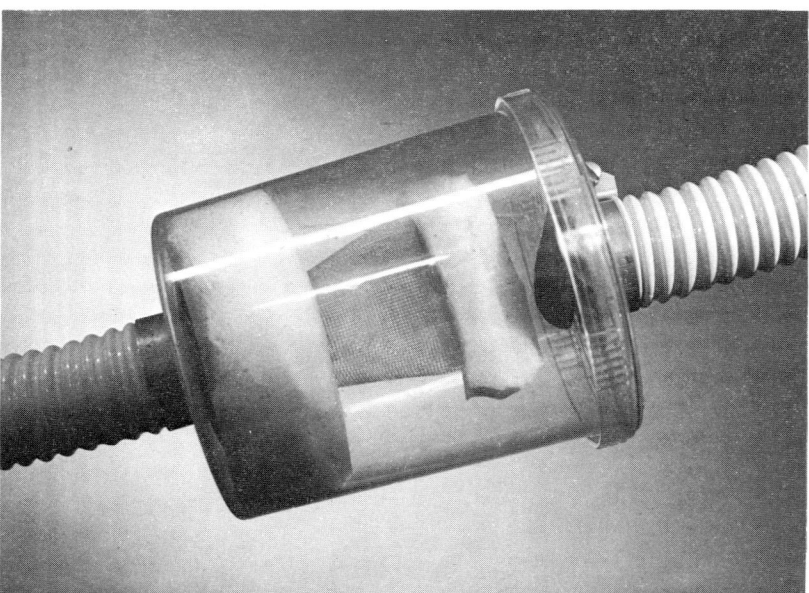

Fig. 195. Portable vacuum cleaner, modified for collecting cockroaches: (top) complete equipment in use; (bottom) detail of collecting container with foam rubber to reduce impact of cockroaches when sucked in. The screen prevents the insects from being drawn beyond the jar. An inlet valve opens when the cleaner is operating. CO_2 is used to anaesthetise the insects before removal. (Courtesy: Wright, North Carolina State Univ., Raleigh, U.S.A.).

were used by Haines & Palmer[392] to study the cockroaches present in homes, privies and sewers in S. W. Georgia.

Traps have also been marketed for cockroach control. 'Trapping is an old recommendation which probably originated in England where roaches were attracted to fermenting beer into which they fell and drowned. Many traps have been devised in this country (U.S.A.), but to date none have effectively eradicated roaches from a heavily infested premise'.[349] Traps provide harbourages from which the insects are unable to escape, either by the design or use of an adhesive bait in which the insects become entangled (Fig. 193). Electrical devices, have also been used: one such trap in which a low voltage shock prevented the escape of the insects, removed 12,000 German cockroaches from a hospital canteen in a year.[152]

Suction methods

A vacuum system has proved useful as a quick method of obtaining cockroaches from sewers.[830] The insects are sucked directly into rearing cans and 'with experience it is possible to collect them at about 20 per minute with very little mortality.' (Fig. 194).

Portable vacuum equipment has been used successfully for collecting large numbers of 'wild' cockroaches, *B. germanica* and *S. longipalpa*, in low income housing.[864] The purpose was to obtain sufficient numbers for testing for resistance, without having to rear through many generations in the laboratory. The vacuum pack is strapped on the back (Fig. 195) and a plastic, screw-capped jar is inserted in the suction line into which the cockroaches are collected (Fig. 195 bottom).

In the next chapter we shall examine the methods developed to test the performance of insecticides and to measure the susceptibility of the different pest cockroaches. These make use of insects reared in the laboratory and collected from infested premises. In both cases the insects have to be handled with care to ensure that they are healthy and representative of pest populations.

17

TESTING INSECTICIDES

Test procedures; principles of testing—Tests of insecticide applied directly to cockroaches: immersion; direct spray methods; CSMA Cockroach Spray Method; CSMA Aerosol Test Method; topical application—Tests of insecticide picked up from treated surfaces; continuous exposure to a single dose; WHO resistance test; continuous exposure to a range of doses; varied exposure and/or multiple doses—Tests of insecticide repellency. Testing compounds for use as repellents.

The professional user of insecticides has little opportunity to evaluate his materials, except by applying them in infested premises, through conventional spraying and dusting equipment. He judges a new insecticide by one criterion: does it work? Inevitably his judgement is influenced by other practical considerations: no odour, no staining and low cost; maximum control for minimum time spent carrying out treatment, speed of action of the insecticide and the client's satisfaction with his service, without 'call-back'.

There are many factors in industrial and domestic properties which affect the performance of an insecticide—not least the man applying it. The aim when testing insecticides in the laboratory is to eliminate as many of these as possible, especially when comparing materials of closely similar properties. Nonetheless, insects in the laboratory are still variable in their response. They are influenced by two sets of factors; some which are determined *before* the test, i.e. season (if the cockroaches have been caught), their condition (whether well-fed if reared in the laboratory), stage of development, age, and sex. Secondly, factors which may have an effect *during* the test, including temperature, disturbance (perhaps light intensity), and how easy it is for the cockroach to get insecticide onto its body (an aspect of formulation).

This chapter is concerned with insecticide test methods. Without these we would not be able to judge the performance of new insecticides or compare them with chemicals already in use. Laboratory methods of test allow us to discover how insecticidal formulations are *likely* to perform in buildings before they are applied for cockroach control. Nevertheless, field trials remain an important part of an insecticide development programme.

Test procedures
Laboratory methods of testing insecticides against crawling insects[658, 860, 861] were examined intensively in the late 1930's, almost in anticipation of the early synthetic insecticides which were to come. These required new techniques of evaluation on a scale much larger than had ever been considered previously, both for effectiveness of the compounds and the uses to which they were being put.[686]

The questions most often put to the technician who carries out insecticide tests are: 'is one insecticide better than another, or is this formulation better than that'? He invariably has a standard against which to make a comparison. His procedures frequently involve testing groups of cockroaches, using two or more insecticides at the same time and each at a range of concentrations. He may also vary the exposure period. Quite often two materials may be very different in their effects at a low dose, but equally efficient at a high one. A comparison at just one concentration can thus give quite misleading information.

The test procedures now commonly used (Fig. 196) can be divided into two types: (1) those in which the *insecticide is applied to the insects*, collectively or individually, the insects having no option but to receive it; and (2) tests in which the *cockroaches contaminate themselves*, their activity influencing to some extent how much they pick up.

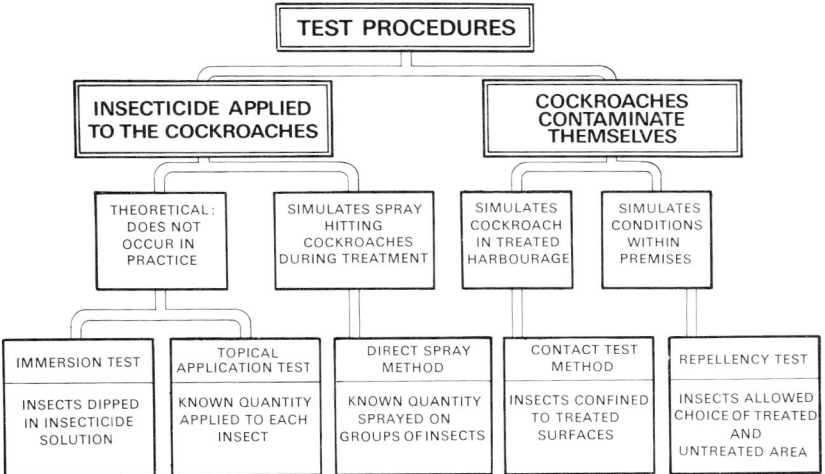

Fig. 196. Methods of testing insecticides and their relevance to practical cockroach control.

Because the reader is unlikely to have the opportunity to carry out tests himself, the various methods used will be described only briefly. They will, however, allow him to see how the data in Tables and Figures in other chapters of this book have been obtained.

Principles of testing

For all the methods described, the end purpose is to determine 'effectiveness'. This is obtained by measuring the dose, concentration, or time for knockdown or kill of half the insects tested (Fig. 197). Not less than ten, but preferably twenty or more cockroaches should make up each batch. In tests in which different amounts of insecticide are used, groups of insects should be exposed to 5 to 8 concentrations (the more the better), killing from 5 per cent to 95 per cent. There is some advantage in separating the values by a logarithmic interval, rather like the aperture settings ('stops') on a camera (2·8, 3·5, 4·5, 5·6, 8, 11, 16, 32). One group must remain untreated as a 'control', to ensure that mortality is not caused by factors other than the insecticide.

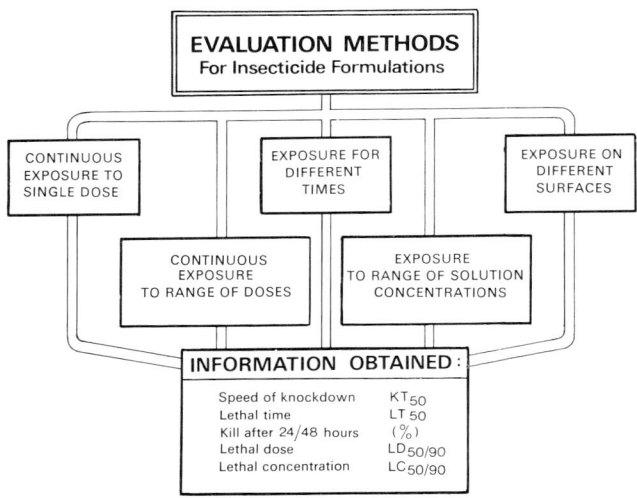

Fig. 197. Methods of evaluating insecticidal formulations and the information obtained.

When the results are plotted graphically (of say dose in mg active ingredient against percentage kill), an S-shaped line is invariably obtained. The use of graph paper in which the base axis is in logarithms (for the dose) and vertical axis in probits (for the per cent response) provides a straight line relationship, which for practical purposes can be drawn by eye, and the dose for 50 per cent kill (LD_{50}) determined by inspection (Fig. 198). Because an accurate calculation of LD_{50} and its confidence limits is a tedious task, many research departments use a computer which is programmed for this calculation. This is especially valuable for those engaged in screening new insecticidal compounds for which a rapid method of data processing is essential.

TESTS OF INSECTICIDE APPLIED DIRECTLY TO COCKROACHES

These tests provide information about the effects of insecticides, without the requirement of pick-up from a treated surface. They cannot therefore give any information about residual life or repellency, and thus very little about the performance of the material when used to treat a building. There are three types of test of increasing complexity:

1. Immersion
2. Direct Spray Methods (a) CSMA Cockroach Spray Method
                                     (b) CSMA Aerosol Test Method
3. Topical application.

Immersion

This is a rapid test method, requiring no complicated apparatus and very little skill. Nevertheless, reproducible results are achieved[309] and those with insects of stored foods compare well in accuracy with results from topical application (Everett, unpublished). Immersion involves dipping groups of insects in different concentrations of insecticide. The LC_{50} is expressed in mg of insecticide per ml of solution (or wt/vol per cent). On immersion, variable amounts of solution are retained by the insects, depending on their size and repellency of the cuticle. However, in addition to the greater speed and simplicity of the immersion test, the relationship of response to concentration is often a much steeper line, (giving narrower confidence limits around the LC_{50}) than is obtained by topical application.[728]

Putting the technique into practice involves first an initial test to determine an appropriate immersion time (between say 30 seconds and 5 minutes) for the concentration range of insecticide, and for the cockroach species being tested. It is best to choose an immersion time for which it appears that a few seconds 'either way' makes little difference to kill. Appropriate concentrations for *B. germanica* immersed in acetone-water solutions, combining a trace of wetting agent are: 5–50 μg/ml for diazinon, 50–1,000 μg/ml for malathion and 100–2,000 μg/ml for chlordane. The last figure assumes some chlordane resistance.[309]

Batches of insects are totally immersed, drained and dried (Fig. 199). The method needs to be practiced before undertaking tests, so that the procedure

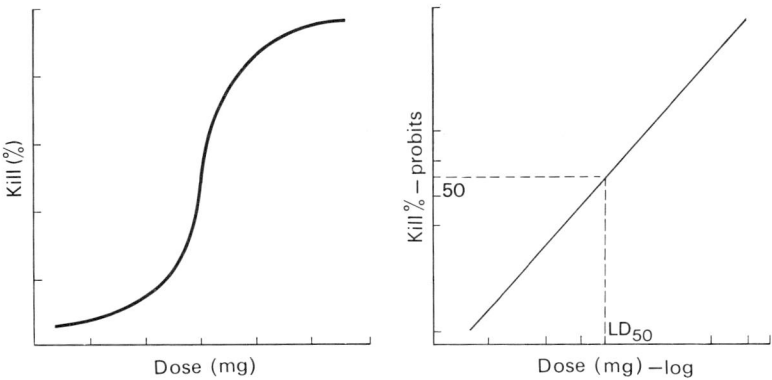

Fig. 198. Typical graphs of kill (per cent) at various doses: (left) when plotted on arithmetic scales; (right) same data when plotted on log/probit scales.

at each step is standardised. Kill is recorded after 24 hours, or sooner, depending on the concentrations and immersion times used.

Direct spray methods

There are many different ways of testing liquid sprays against cockroaches. Miller, Mallis & Easterlin[572] refer to the methods described between 1938 and

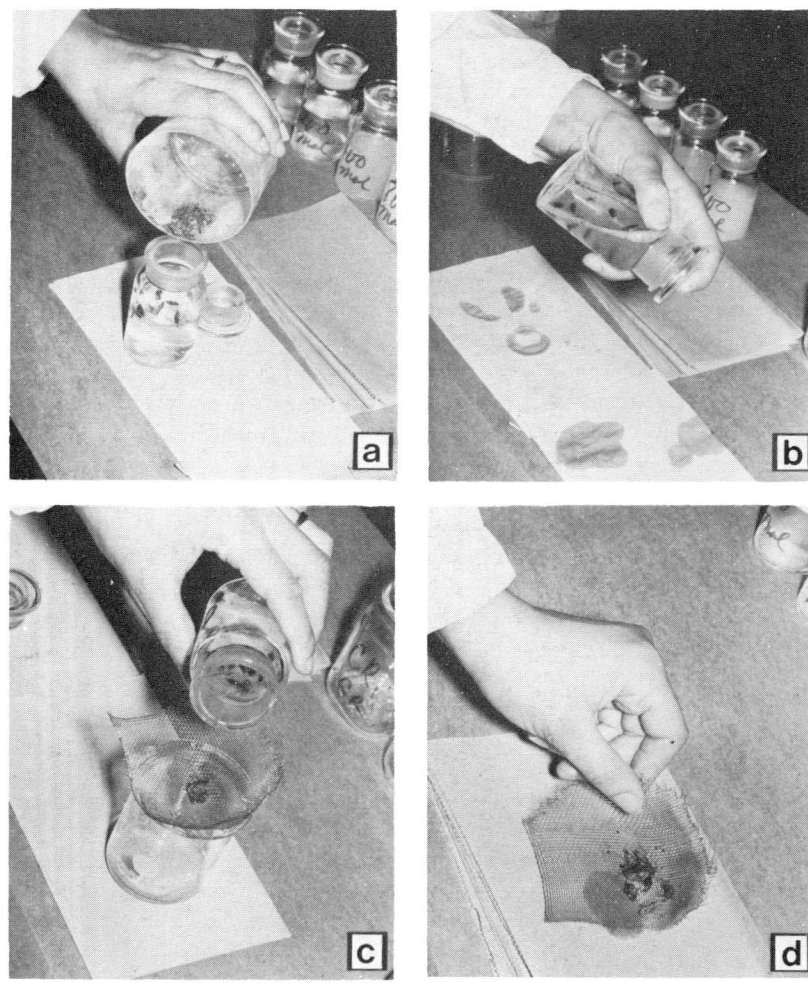

Fig. 199. Stages in the immersion technique for measuring the susceptibility of cockroaches to insecticides: (a) anaesthetised cockroaches are tipped into test solution, (b) shaken to ensure complete wetting, (c) separated from insecticide by straining and (d) blotted to remove excess test solution. (Courtesy: Communicable Disease Centre, Savannah, U.S.A.).

1946. Their own method—the 'racetrack' test—is so called because affected cockroaches have a tendency to run around the base of a hoop, a stainless steel barrier used during the test, to confine the insects on absorbent paper. The spray atomiser is held 50 cm above and 'the gun moved in a circular fashion so that the entire area within the hoop is sprayed'. The cockroaches are exposed for 10 minutes.

(a) CSMA Cockroach Spray Method

This is a well-known test method developed with the co-operation of laboratories of the U.S. Chemical Specialties Manufacturers Association (CSMA), formerly the National Association of Insecticide and Disinfectant Manufacturers Inc. (NAIDM). The preparatory work was done as a sponsored project at Ohio State University from 1937 to 1942, 'on methods suitable for evaluating liquid household insecticides against crawling insects'. The test has subsequently been improved.[25] It determines the relative contact activity of oil based insecticides as sprays, and uses the Official Test Insecticide (OTI) as a basis of comparison.

In summary, adult male German cockroaches, at least three days old, are treated in a specially designed spray chamber at 25·5–28°C and 30–50 per cent relative humidity. The sides are closed, but the bottom is covered with 13 mm mesh. At the top of the chamber is a spray atomiser (De Vilbiss Special No. 5004, as used in the Peet-Grady fly test) with the nozzle 70 cm above the metal containers in which the cockroaches are held. These are 9 cm in diameter and 7·6 cm high, greased to prevent the insects' escape and with 16 mesh wire screen at the base. Twenty cockroaches are treated in each container.

Air is passed continuously through the atomiser at a prescribed pressure. The test insects are sprayed by bringing an accurately measured amount of test spray in a vial in contact with the atomiser intake. At least 10 groups, each of 20 cockroaches, are sprayed at the same dosage. Between 0·5 and 0·9 ml of the OTI gives 70–90 per cent kill of German cockroaches in 48 hours. If a manufacturer claims his product is three times as effective as the standard (OTI), the spray has to be diluted with odourless kerosene to ensure that the average kill falls within this mortality range. The cockroaches remain in the spray chamber for 30 seconds and are then tipped out into mesh-bottomed 'recovery dishes' for observation.

(b) CSMA Aerosol Test Method

An early description of this test[294] involved the use of a Peet-Grady chamber as used for testing flies. The cockroaches were allowed to run in a frame, 76 cm square, lined with glass, and exposed to an aerosol 'delivered with a constant moving motion'. Counts of insects knocked down were said to be 'unreliable for cockroach testing'. The numbers dead were recorded 1, 3 and 5 days after treatment.

A year later, a similar method for testing cockroaches was described[573] quoted as the 'Tentative NAIDM (CSMA) Aerosol Test Method for Flying Insects'. It used the 'Tentative Official Test Aerosol' (TOTA) as a standard.

Subsequently the Association decided that a direct spray (from an aerosol pack), rather than a space treatment, was more appropriate for cockroaches. Also that large nymphs of *B. germanica*, at least three days after moulting, should be used as test insects. Sensibly the test procedure was designed to use the same spray chamber as specified for the CSMA Cockroach Spray Method.

The CSMA Aerosol Test Method has been described in detail[26]: 'aerosol' in this case applies to pressurised formulations which contain 20 per cent by weight or less of volatile ingredients (insecticide, solvent, etc.) and 80 per cent or more of liquified propellant. The aerosol is applied as a direct spray onto the test cockroaches, so there can be no measurement of residual action.

To determine the effectiveness of different insecticides in aerosol formulations, the test is run in comparison with the Official Test Aerosol (OTA) as a standard. The procedure is the same as for the Cockroach Spray Method except that the top of the spray chamber is modified to hold the aerosol containers. The spray rate of the aerosols (g/sec) is determined before use and the contents are then released over a timed interval. The OTA should give 50–75 per cent kill, achieved by releasing 2 to 4g of the contents. The aerosol containers are weighed before and after use to determine the actual amounts of formulations applied in each test.

Topical application

This is one of the most widely used techniques for testing insecticides. Except for micro-injection, topical application is the only way of ensuring that an identical amount of toxicant is applied to each test insect. Nevertheless published results for insecticides tested by this method are extremely variable, because of differences in experimental conditions, and the strain, sex and age of the cockroaches used. When procedures are standardised the technique can give consistent results in successive tests.

Topical application, as the name implies, is the placement of insecticide directly onto the insect's cuticle. The method was first used by applying compounds with a platinum needle or loop.[640]

By more modern techniques, individual cockroaches are picked up on a suction tube connected to a vacuum pump and held against the tip of a syringe in a micro-drop applicator.* A droplet of insecticide, usually dissolved in acetone and always of the same size (often 1 μl) is then applied to each insect (Fig. 200). Cockroaches can be treated in this way without them being anaesthetised.

The first micro-drop applicator for applying measured amounts of liquid insecticide onto the insect integument was described in 1940 by McGovran, Phillips & Mayer.[550] A much simpler piece of equipment for applying small measured doses is described by MacCuaig & Watts[511] but this cannot be used to treat the large numbers of insects that is possible with automatic equipment.

---

* The Arnold Micro-applicator is supplied by Burkard Manufacturing Co. and is fitted with a fully automatic, low voltage, foot-operated micrometer syringe.[58]

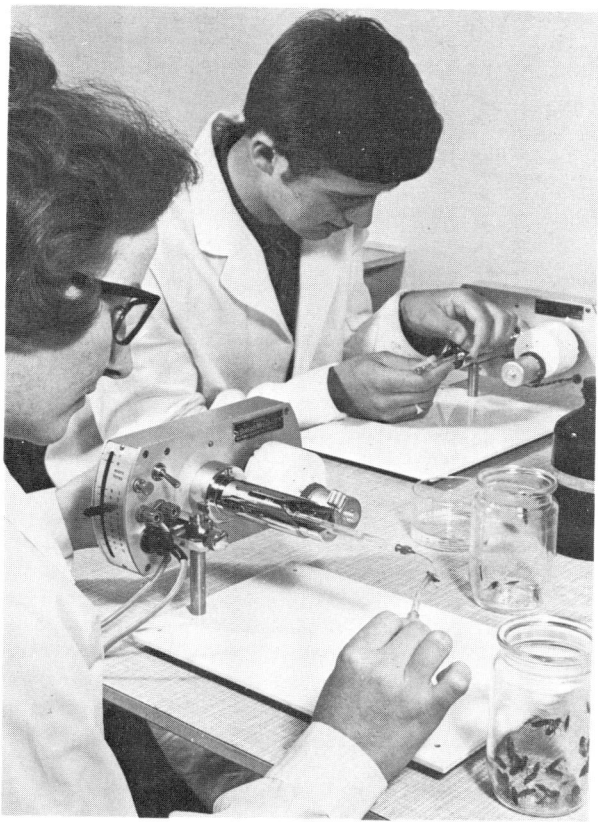

Fig. 200. Micro-drop applicator for the topical placement of insecticide droplets of measured volume onto the cuticle of individual insects held on a suction tube. (Laboratories of Rentokil, U.K.).

The method, in brief, involves treating groups of insects, each preferably not less than 20, at a number of doses, separated by logarithmically increasing intervals. The acetone dries sufficiently rapidly for the cockroaches to be put down immediately after treatment. Five to ten may be placed together in plastic cups without: (1) loss of insecticide, or (2) the insects contaminating each other. Some insecticides at low doses require at least 72 hours to take effect. The number killed is then recorded.

There are some important details of which the user of the technique should be aware. First it is recommended that the test solutions be stored in tightly closed containers over the solvent in a desiccator. This prevents loss of solvent if the solutions are to be used over a period of more than a few days.

Second, he should ensure that the micro-drop applicator is correctly calibrated : that the size of the droplet and thus the amount of insecticide applied is accurate. Risella 17 oil (specific gravity 0·864) can be used to check this. The size of the droplet applied to each insect may occasionally have to be larger than 1 μl if the test compound is relatively insoluble or has a very low activity. Tests with fenitrothion applied in 1 and 3 μl droplets of acetone, but containing the same amount of insecticide, produced exactly the same effects on male *B. orientalis* (Fig. 201).

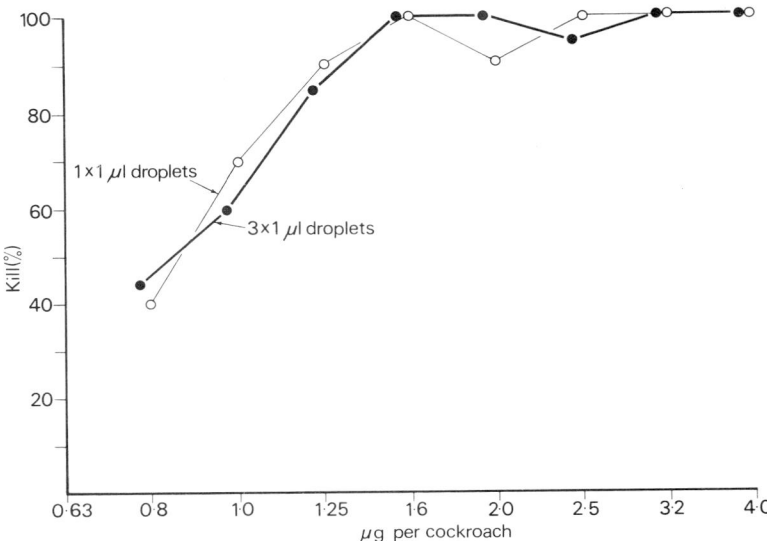

Fig. 20.1. Kill (per cent) of male *B. orientalis* by fenitrothion applied topically as a single 1 μl droplet and as three 1 μl droplets. The total amount of insecticide was the same in both cases. (Fenton, Williams & Bennett, unpublished).

Third, he should select an appropriate solvent. To German cockroaches, fenitrothion in kerosene is three times more toxic, and in xylene twice as toxic, as this insecticide in acetone (Fig. 202). Kerosene and xylene as carriers also make fenitrothion more toxic to female *B. orientalis* than when the insecticide is applied in acetone. The effects of solvent on the toxicity of diazinon applied topically to *B. germanica* is reported by Collins.[210] Solvents may differ in their rate of spread over the cuticle and have different solubilities for cuticular wax. Both these factors may affect rate of penetration.[4]

In the author's laboratory, the use of xylene and kerosene as replacements for acetone when treating *Supella longipalpa* has been found impracticable. Both cause high mortality in controls. Xylene causes immediate knockdown of German and Brown-banded cockroaches; the vapour acts as an anaesthetic, recovery taking about 30 minutes.

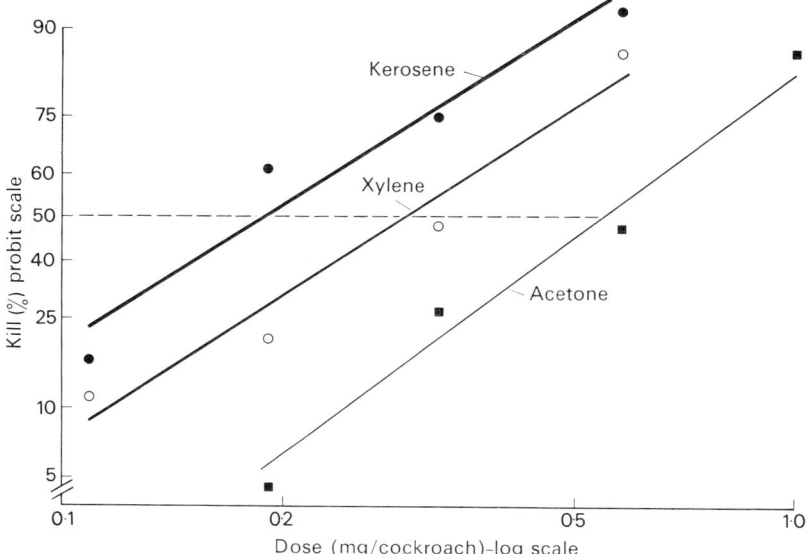

Fig. 202. Kill (per cent) by fenitrothion applied topically in 1 μl droplets of acetone, xylene and kerosene between the hind coxae of German cockroaches. (Fenton, unpublished).

Fourth, a decision has to be made on which part of the cockroach the droplet of insecticide is to be applied: then to treat all the insects in the same way. Usually the insect is picked up by the dorsum, the amount of suction being modified to suit the species. The insecticide can then be applied without hindrance to the underside, between the hind coxae. Application to other parts of the cockroach may influence kill.

The toxicity of DDT to *Musca domestica*, for example,[303] and of malathion to *Schistocerca gregaria*[5] increases as the locus of application approaches the head. Fenitrothion dissolved in acetone applied to both sexes of *B. orientalis* is most rapidly toxic when placed on the membranes of the neck. After 24 hours, however, the effect is the same, regardless of where the droplet is placed (Woolner, unpublished). O'Kane *et al*,[640] fitted cockroaches with a circular disc behind the head so that insecticide applied to different parts of the body was not removed by grooming (Fig. 108). Pyrethrins produced convulsions twice as rapidly when applied to the dorsal surface of the neck than below. The insecticide produced 'no effects of consequence' when applied to the tips of the antennae; whereas application to antennal joints 15–20 produced convulsions in 1 hour, to the first and second joints in 30 minutes and to the mouthparts in 9 minutes. Sensitivity to pyrethrins decreases the nearer application is made to the tip of the abdomen.

It is usual to carry out topical application tests in a room with conditions similar to those for cockroach breeding: 25°C and 60 per cent RH. There must be no insecticide contamination and it is sensible when testing a series of doses to apply the lowest first and to wash out the syringe with acetone before starting the next.

Results are usually expressed as the dose µg/insect, or sometimes mg/g, for 50 per cent kill, the latter taking account of the considerable variation in size of the sexes and the species of pest cockroaches. Typical weights (g) of adults are:

Species	Male	Female
B. germanica	0·047	0·085
B. orientalis	0·451	0·945
S. longipalpa	0·051	0·076
P. americana	1·104	1·518
P. australasiae	0·557	0·909

The application of compounds by micro-injection is not described here because the technique is most often used to study the fate of insecticides within the body, rather than to measure insecticide activity. Neither is the method generally used to screen new insecticidal compounds. Smaller doses normally produce symptoms of poisoning when injected, than when fed to the insect or applied to the cuticle. Nevertheless, it is of interest that the difference in response of male and female *P. americana* to insecticide injected into the haemolymph is less than when fed, or applied topically.[558] Blood stream injection, as a technique in early studies of the action of insecticides has been reviewed.[421]

TESTS OF INSECTICIDE PICKED UP FROM TREATED SURFACES

How often is an infestation of cockroaches controlled by directly contaminating the insects with spray? This happens very rarely. Most cockroaches in infested buildings die through contact with treated harbourages. The majority of laboratory tests, which evaluate the performance of insecticides on treated surfaces, *confine* insects where they cannot escape: this ignores their natural reactions to try to move away from treated surfaces should they be repellent.

The method of test which best resembles a practical situation is to allow cockroaches the choice of walking on treated and untreated surfaces. Better still, to provide them with treated and untreated harbourage. If the insecticide is repellent, the cockroach can then avoid it, and may survive.

We can divide tests which involve the pick-up of insecticide into four types, with the simplest first:

1. continuous exposure to a single dose (e.g. WHO Cockroach Resistance Test);
2. continuous exposure to a range of doses;
3. varied exposure and/or multiple doses;
4. tests of insecticide repellency.

Continuous exposure to a single dose: WHO resistance test

The benefits of detecting resistance in insects early and unequivocally, include:[160]

1. a warning of the need for alternative control measures;
2. an opportunity to offset the problems which resistance might bring if allowed to go unchecked, and
3. elimination of resistance, in some cases, as the reason for failure in control; thus pointing to other causes.

The WHO test method (the 'jar test') for detecting resistance in cockroaches is simple and can be carried out easily with a little practice. The method was originally described by Keller, Clark, Lofgren & Wilson,[478] and adopted by the U.S. Armed Forces Pest Control Board[16] before becoming a test method of WHO. In 1963, Fales & Bodenstein drew attention to its value as a field test by publishing results for the susceptibility of 14 species of cockroach at different stages of development to residues of chlordane.[289]

The object of the test[844] is to compare, under standard conditions, the speed of knockdown of cockroaches taken from an infestation thought to be resistant with those of a normal laboratory strain. Published values exist for laboratory cockroaches so that this part of the test need not be done.

When collecting cockroaches for this test, insects from different parts of the building should be treated separately. It is preferable to use only adult males although this may not always be possible. The following is a summary of the procedure.

The day before the test, obtain or make up 50 ml stock solutions of dieldrin (0·5 per cent), diazinon (0·5 per cent) or other insecticides which it is proposed to evaluate. Add 1 ml of solution to 9 ml of acetone and place 2·5 ml of the mixture in each of 4 jars (1 pint, or about 500 ml). Rotate them so that the solution covers all internal surfaces evenly until the acetone has evaporated (Fig. 203). This gives a residue of 5 mg of insecticide per ft^2 (6 $\mu g/cm^2$). Smear the top of the jars with grease so that cockroaches are unable to escape. Alternatively use fine gauze or muslin.

The following day, in a room free of insecticide, place 10 cockroaches in each of the treated jars. The temperature should be between 20 and 30°C and the relative humidity above 25 per cent. Record knockdown at half-hourly intervals up to 4 hours, then hourly to 7 hours and at 24, 48 and 72 hours. A cockroach is considered knocked down when it is no longer capable of maintaining its normal upright position, normal locomotion and shows evidence of paralysis. Cockroaches which survive beyond 24 hours should be given raw potato.

It is good practice to have some cockroaches in a jar, treated just with acetone (as control), to ensure that the cockroaches are not adversely affected, except by the insecticide. For carbamate insecticides, the test should continue for 5 days; cockroaches resistant to these insecticides may be knocked down but recover a few days later. If this happens, the numbers which recover should be subtracted from the original knockdown figures.

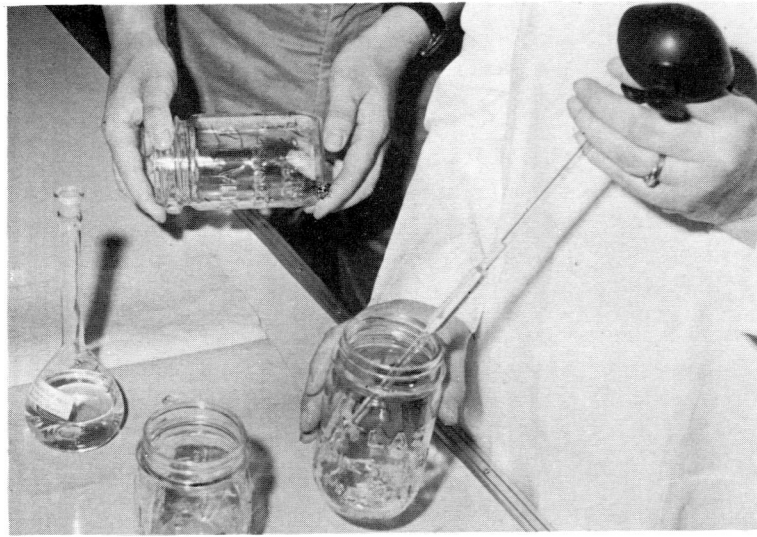

Fig. 203. Treatment of jars with insecticide in acetone, in preparation for the WHO cockroach resistance test. Measured amounts are applied by pipette: the jar is then rotated until the acetone has evaporated. (Courtesy: Fales; Entomology Research Div., U.S. Dept. of Agriculture).

Plot the values (per cent knockdown against time) on log-probit paper and establish the straight line relationship by eye. Compare the times (hours) for 50 per cent and 90 per cent kill with published values for normal strains. The resistance factor (e.g. × 10) is usually the ratio of the LT_{50} of a normal strain to a field strain, although the LT_{90} or LT_{95} may occasionally be specified. Ratios of 3 or less are not normally regarded as an indication of resistance, but of 'low level tolerance'.

The reader should appreciate the limitations of the WHO test: its purpose is primarily to detect resistance, not to measure it. The latter is better done by topical application (see p. 482).

Continuous exposure to a range of doses

Tsuji & Mizuno[804] have described a quick screening test for insecticides using first stage nymphs of *P. americana*. There are advantages in using this stage of the cockroach : large numbers can be obtained easily from oothecae (successively laid by long-living adults) and the nymphs can be handled more easily since they are unable to climb vertical glass surfaces. Not having to rear the insects to adult stage economises in time and labour.

Tests are carried out by pipetting insecticide in acetone solution on to the base of small tubes (5 cm high × 2·5 cm diameter) and allowed to dry. The nymphs are introduced and the tube capped. The method thus measures contact *and* vapour activity. Kill is recorded at 24 hours (Table CXXV). About 0·1–1 μg of insecticide per tube provides mortalities spanning the LD_{50}. To test vapour alone, a strip of treated filter paper, out of reach of the insects, is fixed in the tube between the top edge and the cap: diazinon, lindane, propoxur and dichlorvos all show marked vapour action.

TABLE CXXV

LD_{50} (AT 24 HOURS) OF FIRST STAGE NYMPHS OF *P. AMERICANA* (μg/10 insects) IN CLOSED TREATED TUBES
(Tsuji & Mizuno[804])

Insecticide	LD_{50}
Fenitrothion	0·11
Carbaryl	0·14
Dieldrin	0·27
Malathion	0·69
Lindane	0·90
Fenthion	0·91
DDT	1·80

Varied exposure and/or multiple doses
The method most widely used to test insecticides against cockroaches is to place them on treated surfaces. Rarely would this be used to screen, or select, potentially interesting compounds as new insecticides, but it does provide a test of the merits of different commercially-available formulations. The surfaces used may be of many different types and treated with a range of concentrations. The exposure period of the cockroaches on the surfaces may also be varied.

This type of test gives useful *practical* information. First, the likely performance of the actual product being marketed, which may be quite different from the properties of the active ingredient dissolved in acetone. Second, the interaction of the formulation with the surface to which it is applied: if the cockroach cannot pick-up the insecticide, kill is greatly reduced. Third, the likely time that cockroaches will have to spend on a treated surface to pick up a lethal dose. Other properties may also become obvious whilst spraying the test surfaces; objectionable odour, poor suspensibility (if a wettable powder), or nozzle blockage.

By far the greatest advantage is the opportunity to test the performance of an insecticide after it has aged on a treated surface: continued good kill of cockroaches in treated harbourages, some weeks after insecticide application is important for the control of newly-hatched nymphs. Sufficient numbers of test surfaces can be treated to show the extent of degradation. The technique does, however, have two disadvantages. First, results depend on how the cockroaches are presented to the treated surface: if they are stimulated into activity immediately upon contact, quite different results will be obtained from a method that allows contact at leisure. Second, the insects are confined on the treated surface and cannot avoid the insecticide even though it may be repellent (see p. 177).

Treatment of surfaces
Surfaces in a building sprayed for cockroach control are treated with more liquid than the surface can possibly hold. Credit to the serviceman who knows, before it has happened, when to stop spraying to prevent 'run-off'. How then does one prepare surfaces for test?

An obvious method of treating surfaces for insecticide testing is to do what happens in practice: to spray them at a raised angle of about 60–70° with as much as they can hold. Substances like glass will, of course, retain less than painted hardboard and this less than unpainted board. Moreover, less insecticide will be held at the top of the treated surface and much more at the bottom. Using this method the technician has no control over the amounts applied and he may have some difficulty in interpreting his results when comparing one insecticide formulation with another. It is far better to apply a known amount of spray to all the surfaces to be tested. This can be done, simply, by employing a sufficiently large test surface (say 30 × 60 cm) to ensure that the amount of spray applied can be accurately weighed. Small test surfaces can be placed edge to edge to make up a continuous surface. This may be placed horizontally, on the top of a sensitive pan balance and sprayed finely until the required weight has been achieved. Alternatively, it may be sufficient to apply a number of sweeps of a spray in a standard manner and just check on a balance that the amount applied is within 10 per cent of what is intended. There is some advantage in doing this with a sprayer of the type used by pest control personnel, since it gives the droplet configuration on the test surface as experienced in field application.

Some laboratories have specially designed equipment, in which a spray jet applies insecticide to standard panels moving horizontally on a conveyor beneath. The mechanism is timed to deliver as near as possible a known amount to the test surface (Fig. 204). A Potter Tower can be used to apply a measured amount of insecticide to small test surfaces.

Dusts for cockroach control are normally applied to cavities in buildings which have rough surfaces. Tests with dusts are thus best done on similar substrates. It would be meaningless for example to expose cockroaches to dust applied to glass. The reverse side of hardboard with its 'patterned' texture holds dust well and allows the cockroach to obtain a grip. Dust is easily applied using a pepper-pot dispenser, and made uniform by drawing the edge of a ruler across the surface. The amount applied can again be judged by weighing.

Ageing of treated surfaces
Surfaces which have been sprayed and are dry can be aged in racks. It is im-

Fig. 204. Spray machine, consisting of atomiser head and conveyor, used to treat test panels for insecticide evaluation at the Communicable Disease Centre, Savannah, U.S.A.

portant to decide the temperature and humidity of storage and whether the room is to be ventilated. A treated surface should not be used twice in serial tests, unless it can be marked to show areas which have previously been used. Surfaces treated with dusts, and perhaps wettable powders, should be stored horizontally, using spacers to keep the surfaces apart. With particulate formulations it is important that surfaces should not be allowed to contaminate each other (Fig. 205).

Exposing the insects
At the author's laboratory a simple procedure has been used for many years to compare different insecticides and their formulations. The technique reveals small differences in performance, and results are reproducible. The sensitivity of the test derives from examining different insecticide concentrations (application rates) and exposure times, simultaneously, with the latter kept extremely short.

Fig. 205. Cubicles at 27°C and under negative air pressure for the storage of treated panels between tests at the Communicable Disease Centre, Savannah, U.S.A.

Groups of cockroaches are placed under inverted funnels (8 cm diameter); 10 insects of the smaller species and 5 of the large, with the sexes kept separate. The insides of the funnels are treated with PTFE dispersion (polytetrafluoroethylene) so that the insects cannot climb and are therefore confined to the test surface. The hole allows ventilation (Fig. 206).

Surfaces for test are normally of two types: porous (hardboard) and non-porous (glass) and treated at two rates; 1 per cent and 2 per cent sprays applied at 45 ml/m². These give deposits of 60 and 120 μg of active ingredient per cm². Cockroaches are usually exposed for four different periods, often for only 1 and 2 minutes, and rarely exceeding half an hour. Preferably the time of exposure should be just a few seconds. (If a cockroach can survive after being confined on a treated surface for longer than one hour, the results are of academic interest; the insecticide has little practical merit.) Thus information can be obtained for 16 different treatments with one insecticide.

Exposure of cockroaches to treated surfaces is made by moving the inverted funnel with the insects beneath, slowly and carefully from a 'resting surface' of like material immediately alongside. This must be done without dragging the funnel across the surface and taking insecticide with it. After the appropriate period the funnel and insects are moved back again. Mortality on the 'resting surface' is recorded after 24 and 48 hours: the latter is necessary because of the very short exposures used. Untreated controls are always included and it is an advantage when making initial tests on new insecticides to incorporate surfaces treated with a toxicant for which performance is known (as a standard).

The same method of test, with slight variations, has been used by Flynn & Schoof[307] to examine the performance of 42 compounds applied to four surfaces treated at three application rates (Fig. 207). Aged surfaces were tested over many weeks and on each occasion, chlordane resistant German cockroaches (females) were exposed for three hours. Their results are discussed in Chapter 4 (p. 77) as an example of the interaction of substrate and formulation on insecticide performance.

The same method is used at the Orlando Laboratory of the Entomology Research Division, U.S.D.A., except that known amounts of insecticide as residues, are applied in acetone to plywood panels which dry rapidly and leave a crystalline deposit on the surface. Male German cockroaches are exposed for 30 minutes. Formulations in oils or emulsions would give totally different

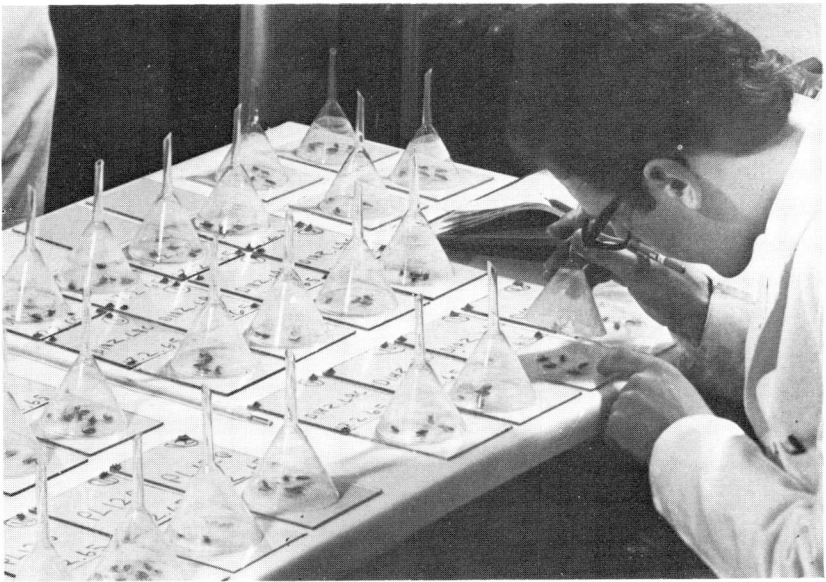

Fig. 206. Contact testing of cockroaches under inverted funnels. Checking the knockdown and kill after exposure. (Rentokil, U.K.).

Fig. 207. Exposure of cockroaches on test panels at the Communicable Disease Centre, Savannah, U.S.A.

responses, because the cockroaches are presented with insecticide in different physical forms, with the insecticide often beneath, rather than on the test surface.

Dr. Grayson at Virginia Polytechnic Institute has standardised on the use of tempered 'Masonite' panels which are dipped in insecticides (180 ml/m^2) and hung to dry. These are then placed in battery jars with female German cockroaches and mortality recorded after continuous exposure for 1 and 3 days.[465] Typical results by this method, for deposits aged for 30 days, and tested against strains resistant to chlordane, diazinon and malathion are given in Table CXXVI.

Dusts are far more difficult to evaluate meaningfully. There is no merit in releasing cockroaches, highly excited by handling, onto a dust-treated surface, as the insects become completely covered in the dust in a few seconds. Experience suggests that if an insecticide performs well as a wettable powder and has good residual life, then the same insecticide will perform at least equally as a dust. Tests involving forced contamination of the burrowing cockroach, *Pycnoscelus surinamensis* by various dusts are described by Kartman, Tanada, Holdaway & Alicata.[471]

A simple way of testing a dust, without exciting the cockroaches, is to apply it directly from a 'pepper pot type' container, with the insects held in a plastic ring (e.g. a section of drain pipe). The ring is removed after a set time and the cockroaches allowed to walk away from the dust.

TABLE CXXVI

KILL (%) OF NORMAL AND RESISTANT STRAINS OF FEMALE *B. GERMANICA* EXPOSED FOR 24 HOURS TO MASONITE PANELS TREATED WITH OIL-BASED INSECTICIDES (250 mg/ft^2) AGED FOR 30 DAYS

(Data from Grayson,[364] except Bendiocarb, Grayson[365])

Insecticide	Normal	Chlordane & diazinon resistant	Chlordane & malathion resistant
Chlordane (3%)	56	16	6
Diazinon (1%)	97	0	100
Malathion (3%)	94	28	22
Propoxur (1%)	100	100	100
Dioxacarb (1%)	100	100	100
Bendiocarb (1%)	100	90	100
Dursban (1%)	100	10	100
Lindane (0·5%)	23	0	12

Another method which overcomes some of the criticisms, and approximates more closely to practical field conditions, is to hold cockroaches beneath an inverted dish surrounded by a ring of dust just a few centimetres wide. When the insects are acclimatised and quiet, to lift the container slowly and allow them to walk from the centre across the dust (Fig. 208). A method similar to this is described by McGovran & Piquett.[549]

TESTS FOR INSECTICIDE REPELLENCY

The way in which the repellency of insecticides affects cockroach control is examined in detail in Chapter 7 together with the various test methods developed (pages 172 to 186). These aim to simulate conditions in infested buildings where insects have a variety of harbourages, not all of which may be contaminated with lethal amounts of insecticide. The principle of the tests is to allow cockroaches to discriminate, in their movements, between contact with treated and untreated surfaces presented to them as simulated harbourages.

The details of the procedures vary between laboratories, but in all cases, the methods test the reactions of cockroaches without them being excited or otherwise disturbed. The mortality rate of cockroaches in choice boxes is greater as population density increases. It appears that more densely crowded insects may, (1) stimulate each other, (2) have less choice of insecticide-free niches in choice boxes and (3) be less able to modify their behaviour so as to avoid repeated contact with the insecticide.[256]

Fig. 208. In tests of insecticidal dusts the cockroaches must not be stimulated into activity as in this photograph. They must be allowed to contaminate themselves in a manner similar to that of cockroaches entering treated harbourages.

In addition to giving cockroaches the opportunity of occupying either treated or untreated harbourages, some tests have compared the kill in choice boxes when the harbourage is either completely or only partially treated with insecticide.[265] Flynn & Schoof[308] have developed a test box, involving plywood panels, in which a variety of test conditions can be examined. They too have shown that where cockroaches can exercise a choice 'the comparative efficacy of candidate compounds may show an order of priority different to that achieved with a technique in which exposure is continuous for a specific time period'. Batth[83] describes a simple test method allowing choice of harbourage, 'for verifying claims of effective residual life' of products registered for cockroach control under the Pest Control Products Act in Canada.

Testing compounds for use as repellents
One of the first methods used to find useful cockroach repellents was the simple expedient of treating the insides of ½ pint ice cream cartons with 5 ml of a 2 per cent acetone solution of the test compounds.[146,345] When dry, a hole was cut in the side of the containers which were inverted to provide dark harbourages with food and water inside.

The test was carried out over a period of days and at each examination the insects were shaken out and the cartons reversed in position so that the insects had to make a new choice. If the treated cartons were inverted on glass, the insects could be counted from beneath without disturbing them. Fenchloric acid was tested concurrently as a standard and acetone-treated cartons included as controls. The effectiveness of a compound as a repellent was judged from the time required for more than 50 per cent of cockroaches to consistently occur in treated cartons. Schwarz, Bodenstein & Fales[736] have used a method similar to this to locate some new repellents.

Goodhue[343] has also used two other methods by which he screened five materials from over 1,000 chemicals tested. By the 'slanting card method', pieces of cardboard (8 × 13 cm) are treated with the test compounds in acetone to give a surface deposit of 0.2 mg/cm^2 and allowed to dry for 24 hours. Treated and untreated cards are placed in containers with cockroaches. The method exploits the tendency of the insects to climb a slanting surface. The numbers of insects on them are counted, but the repellency of a chemical determined in this way is affected to some extent by other chemicals being tested at the same time; the method thus measures comparative repellency.

His other test, 'the glass cylinder method', involves intercommunicating glass cylinders which confine the cockroaches but allow them a choice of contact with treated and untreated filter papers. The reader interested in further modifications of these procedures should consult the studies of Ikeda[452] and Ikeda & Kondo[453] on a feeding comparison method, and a method of Hayashi & Hatsukade,[408] which examines the tendency of cockroaches to enter tubes containing treated filter papers. Reddy[697] describes a choice chamber for separating the liquid and vapour phases of insect repellents.

Progress of the pest control industry requires the evaluation of new insecticides, thus ensuring that those with distinct advantages become available for commercial use. Details are given in this chapter of many of the procedures of the entomologist and development chemist, in their work to test new compounds and formulations for activity against cockroaches. The methods have been developed to answer particular questions about performance and other properties of insecticides.

CONVERSION TABLE

Application rates of insecticides given in the text are in most cases quoted in metric units, after conversion from those given in the published papers. Metric units will be unfamiliar to some users of this book: the following conversion factors may therefore help to give the information in more usual terms. Thus:

To convert	Multiply by
g/m^2 to mg/ft^2	93
g/m^2 to $oz/1{,}000\ ft^2$	3·3
ml/m^2 to ml/ft^2	0·09
m^2 to ft^2	10·8
kg/ha to lb/acre	0·9
mg/m^3 to mg/ft^3	0·03
g/m^3 to $oz/1{,}000\ ft^3$	1·0
g/m^3 to $g/1{,}000\ ft^3$	28
cm^2/m^3 to $in^2/1{,}000\ ft^3$	4·4
m^3 to ft^3	35
$\mu g/$ to mg/ft^3	0·03

1 micron (μ) = one thousandth of 1 mm.
1 nanometre (nm) = one thousandth of 1μ.

BIBLIOGRAPHY AND AUTHOR INDEX

In this bibliography the numbers [in square brackets] at the end of each reference are the pages on which the author is quoted.

1 ABBOTT, D. C., HOLMES, D. C. & TATTON, J. O'G. (1969). Pesticide residues in the total diet in England and Wales, 1966–1967. II. Organochlorine pesticide residues in the total diet. *J. Sci. Fd Agric.*, **20**, 245–249. [142]
2 ADKINS Jr., T. R., KISSAM, J. B. & KREMMS, W. F. (1971). Field evaluation of natural and synthetic pyrethroid water-based pressurized formulations against the House fly. *J. econ. Ent.*, **64** (2), 459–461. [267]
3 AGOSIN, M., MICHAELI, D., MISKUS, R., NAGASAWA, S. & HOSKINS, W. M. (1961). A new DDT-metabolising enzyme in the German cockroach. *J. econ. Ent.*, **54** (2), 340–342. [449]
4 AHMED, H. & GARDINER, B. G. (1967). Effect of mineral oil solvent on the toxicity and speed of action of malathion. *Nature, Lond.*, **214** (5095), 1338–1339. [484]
5 AHMED, H. & GARDINER, B. G. (1968). Variation in toxicity of malathion when applied to certain body regions of *Schistocerca gregaria* (Forsk.). *Bull. ent. Res.*, **57** (4), 651–658. [485]
6 AHMED, H. & GARDINER, B. G. (1970). Penetration of malathion into locusts. *Pestic. Sci.*, **1**, 217–219. [416]
7 ALDRIDGE, W. N. (1971). The nature of the reaction of organophosphorus compounds and carbamates with esterases. *Bull. Wld Hlth Org.*, **44**, 25–30. [414]
8 ALEXANDER, B. H., BARKER, R. J. & BABERS, F. H. (1958). The phosphatase activity of susceptible and resistant House flies and German cockroaches. *J. econ. Ent.*, **51** (2), 211–213. [450]
9 ANNAND, P. N. (1944). Tests conducted by the Bureau of Entomology and Plant Quarantine to appraise the usefulness of DDT as an insecticide. *J. econ. Ent.*, **37** (1), 125–126. [283]
10 ANON. (1943). The insecticide outlook. *Soap, N.Y.* **19** (11), 107, 109, 117. [221, 282]
11 ANON. (1944). Synthetic roach powders. *Soap, N.Y.*, **20** (5), 102–105. [216, 217]
12 ANON. (1953). Techniques and materials for the disinsectization of aircraft. *Bull. Wld Hlth Org.*, **8**, 527–533. [71]
13 ANON. (1957). Tabutrex—a new repellent for roaches, flies and other insects. *Pest Control*, **25** (1), 22, 24. [160]
14 ANON. (1958). Up-date on roach control for the PCO. *Pest Control*, **26** (6), 9, 11, 12–14, 16, 19. [200, 212]
15 ANON. (1958). What composition and combination for roach powders? *Pest Control*, **26** (6), 24, 26, 28, 30, 32. [204, 205]
16 ANON. (1959). Methods for determining the susceptibility of resistance of insects to insecticides. *Armed Forces Pest Control Bd. Tech. Inf. Memo.* No. 3, 13–19. [487]
17 ANON. (1960). American conference of governmental industrial hygienists. *Am. med. Ass. Archs Environ. Hlth*, **1** (2), 140–144. [335]
18 ANON. (1961). Resistance of Canadian roaches to chlordane is finally proved. *Pest Control*, **29** (6), 62. [435, 457]
19 ANON. (1962). Pyrethrum marc. *Pyrethrum Post*, **6** (4), 6. [226]

20 ANON. (1963). *Sumithion Technical Manual.* Sumitomo Chem. Co., Osaka, Japan. 52pp. [352]
21 ANON. (1964). Vapona insecticide. Agricultural News, No. 13, March 1964, Shell Chem. Co. [335]
22 ANON. (1966). Public health pesticides. *Pest Control,* 34 (3), 10–34. [104]
23 ANON. (1967). National communicable disease centre report on public health pesticides. *Pest Control,* 35 (3), 13–40, 65. [441]
24 ANON. (1967). Report of the first session of the F.A.O. working party of experts on resistance of pests to pesticides. (4–9th Oct. 1965). Mimeographed Meeting Report No. PL/1965/18. Rome 1967. [442]
25 ANON. (1967). Cockroach spray method: Official method of the chemical specialities manufacturers association for evaluating liquid household insecticides against crawling insect pests. Latest Revision. *Soap, N.Y.,* 43 (4A), Blue Book Issue, 211–212. [461, 481]
26 ANON. (1967). Cockroach aerosol test method: tentative official method of the CSMA for evaluating aerosols against cockroaches. *Soap, N.Y.,* 43 (4A), Blue Book Issue, 209–210. [461, 482]
27 ANON. (1968). Public health pesticides. *Pest Control,* 36 (3), 9–58. [80]
28 ANON. (1968). Occupational disease in California attributed to pesticides and other agricultural chemicals—1968. *Rep. Dept. Publ. Hlth, Calif.,* 36 pp. [140]
29 ANON. (1968). Licenses for all agricultural pesticides planned, under new British Legislation. *Int. Pest Control,* 10 (5), 21–22. [146]
30 ANON. (1969). Editorial. Year of decision for DDT. *Pyrethrum Post,* 10 (2), 21. [245]
31 ANON. (1969). Occupational disease of California attributed to pesticides and other agricultural chemicals—1969. *Rep. Dept. Publ. Hlth, Calif.,* 33 pp. [140]
32 ANON. (1969). Curbs on panic and pesticides. *Nature, Lond.,* 224 (5226), 1249. [145]
33 ANON. (1969). US committee reports on pesticides. *Int. Pest Control,* 11 (4), 31. [149]
34 ANON. (1970). Vermin control demonstration programme final report. How to control them. *Rep. Dept. Hlth, New Haven, Connecticut,* 93 pp. [58]
35 ANON. (1970). Roach control in a restaurant. Part I. *Pest Control,* 38 (5), 15–18. [70]
36 ANON. (1970). Roach control in a restaurant. Part II. *Pest Control,* 38 (6), 35–42. [70]
37 ANON. (1970). Roach control in a restaurant. Part III. *Pest Control,* 38 (7), 29–34. [70]
38 ANON. (1970). How to ban chemicals without scaring people. *Nature, Lond.,* 225 (5227), 3–4. [145]
39 ANON. (1971). The changing business. *Pest Control,* 39 (6), 13–20. [59]
40 ANON. (1971). Annual report 1970. *Arsberetning Statens Skadedyrlaboratorium,* 86 pp. [91]
41 ANON. (1971). Guidelines for providing data with respect to pesticides in the environment. *Pyrethrum Post,* 11 (1), 34–35. [150]
42 ANON. (1971). Nogos-Nuvan: Ciba-Geigy Handbook. Agrochemicals Division, Basle, Switz. 227 pp. [338]
43 ANON. (1972). Producers are learning to get by on tight budgets. *Chem. Wkly,* 26th July 1972, 18, 42–43. [13]
44 ANON. (1972). Towards cleaner food. Report of the working party on food hygiene. *Ass. Publ. Hlth Inspectors,* 33 pp. [56]
45 ANON. (1972). Report of the aldrin/dieldrin advisory committee (under provisions of F.I.F.R.A.) to the administrator of E.P.A. March 28th. [312]
46 ANON. (1973). Chemical resistance fact and fallacy. *Pest Control,* 41 (3), 19–20, 22. [447]
47 ANON. (1973). The New Law: more responsibility for managers. *Pest Control,* 41 (10), 52. [149]
48 ANON. (1974). Microencapsulated pesticide reaches market. *Chem. Eng. News,* 52 (30), 15–17. [93]
49 ANON. (1974). Interim label granted for diazinon. *Pest Control,* 42 (6), 39. [327]
50 ANON. (1974). Slow-release tape may revolutionize cockroach control. *Pest Control,* 42 (12), 12, 14, 38. [93]
51 ANON. (1975). Controlled release insecticides. *Soap, N.Y.,* 51 (3), 44, 46, 48, 96. [93]

52 ANON. (1975). Is EPA stifling development of new pesticides? *Chem. Wkly,* **117** (18), 25–26. [145]
53 ANON. (1975). Chlordane: the big challenge. *Pest Control,* **43** (9), 11–12. [145]
54 ANON. (1975). Pesticides: U.K. system better than EEC drafts. *Chem. Druggist,* 31st May 1975, 735. [147]
55 ANON. (1975). EPA on trial: is Agency's punitive mentality the will of Congress? *Pest Control,* **43** (8), 10–11, 27. [150]
56 ANON. (1975). Viewpoint. *Pest Control,* **43** (10), 7. [150]
57 APPAIAH, K. M., RAJANNA, A. & RAO, B. Y. V. (1973). Effect of protein and carbohydrate nutrition on the resistance of American cockroaches (*Periplaneta americana* L.) to malathion. *Curr. Res.,* **2** (11), 93. [340]
58 ARNOLD, A. J. (1965). A high speed automatic micrometer syringe. *J. scient. Instrum.,* **42**, 350–351. [482]
59 ARNOLD, B. R. (1975). Safety in the pesticide industry—Part I. *4th Br. Pest Control Conf., Jersey,* Paper No. 4, 3 pp. [131, 333]
60 ARNOLD, T. S. (1975). The control of cockroaches in aircraft. *Environ. Hlth,* **83** (6), 242–244. [71]
61 ARTYUKHINA, I. N., SMIRNOVA, A. S., RYK-BOGDANIKO, M. G., GORBATKOVA, I. E. & BAÏBAK, N. I. (1973). Baits based on mixtures of chlorofos and ammonium carbonate for control of cockroaches. *Medskaya Parazit.,* **42** (3), 320–325. [357]
62 ASHWOOD-SMITH, M. J., TREVINO, J. & RING, R. (1972). Mutagenicity of dichlorvos. *Nature, Lond.,* **240**, 418. [337]
63 AUBIN, F. St. (1974). The label and you. *Pest Control,* **42** (4), 15–16, 40–43. [147]
64 BABERS, F. H. (1949). Development of insect resistance to insecticides. *U.S. Bur. Ent. Pl. Quar.,* E-776. [423]
65 BABERS, F. H. & PRATT, Jr., J. J. (1951). Development of insect resistance to insecticides. II. *U.S. Bur. Ent. Pl. Quar.,* E-818. [423]
66 BABERS, F. H. & ROAN C. C. (1953). The dehydrochlorination of DDT by resistant cockroaches. *J. econ. Ent.,* **46** (6), 1105. [431, 449]
67 BACHMANN, F. & LEGGE, J. B. (1968). Insecticidal properties of a new group of carbamates. *J. Sci. Fd Agric.* (Supplementary Issue: Symposium on pesticidal carbamates), 39–43. [381]
68 BACK, E. A. (1937). Cockroaches and their control. *U.S. Dept. Agric., Wash.,* Leaflet No. 144, 6 pp. [33, 52, 54, 212]
69 BACK, R. C. (1965). Significant developments in eight years with sevin insecticide. *J. agric. Fd Chem.,* **13**, 198–199. [366]
70 BAIG, M. M. H. & MASUD, S. Z. (1971). Some suitable dust diluents of Pakistan. II. Gypsum. *Agriculture, Pakistan,* **22** (2), 219–223. [95]
71 BAILEY, J. (1971). Pest control in air transport. *Proc. 3rd Br. Pest Control Ass. Conf., Jersey,* Paper No. 17, 8 pp. [71]
72 BAKER, G. J. (1963). The 'Dual Synergist System' of piperonyl butoxide and MGK 264. *Pyrethrum Post,* **7** (1), 16–18. [239, 240]
73 BAKER, G. J. (1970). Insecticidal concentrates with improved allethrin. *Soap, N.Y.,* **46** (5), 72, 74, 76, 80. [255, 260, 261]
74 BAKER, G. J. & PREISS, F. J. (1973). A third generation pyrethroid—S-Bioallethrin. *Soap, N.Y.,* **49** (8), 36, 38–40, 44. Conclusion in *Soap, N.Y.,* **49** (9), 50, 52, 62. [265]
75 BARE, O. S. (1945). Boric acid as a stomach poison for the German cockroach. *J. econ. Ent.,* **38** (3), 407. [100, 195]
76 BARLOW, F. & HADAWAY, A. B. (1970). Chemical structure and physical properties of candidate insecticides in relation to residual toxicity to adult mosquitoes. *Pestic. Sci.,* **1**, 117–119. [367]
77 BARNES, J. M. (1966). Human health and pest control. Symposium on Scientific Aspects of Pest Control, 1966. *Nat. Acad. Sci., Wash., Publ.* 1402, 435–452 [284].
78 BARNES, J. M., & VERSCHOYLE, R. D. (1974). Toxicity of a new pyrethroid insecticide. *Nature, Lond.,* **248** (5450), 711. [258]
79 BARNHART, C. D. (1943). Aqueous solutions of boric acid for safe control of German

cockroaches. *Pests*, **11** (1), 8–9. [195]
80 BARNHART, C. D. (1963). Dry ice fumigation. *Pest Control*, **31** (2), 30. [213, 214]
81 BARTHEL, W. F. (1973). Toxicity of pyrethrum and its constituents to mammals. In: Casida, J. E. (Ed.). *Pyrethrum—the natural insecticide*. Academic Press, Chapt. 6. [251]
82 BATES, J. A. R. (1968). Reflections on regulations—certain aspects in the official control of pesticides in various countries. *Chemy Ind.*, (5th Oct.), 1324–1332. [146]
83 BATTH, S. S. (1974). A method recommended for evaluating residual pesticides for cockroach control. *Can. Ent.*, **106** (10), 1081–1085. [496]
84 BEAMENT, J. W. L. (1945). The cuticular lipoids of insects. *J. exp. Biol.*, **21**, 115–131. [208]
85 BEAMENT, J. W. L. (1958). A paralysing agent in the blood of cockroaches. *J. Insect Physiol.*, **2**, 199–214. [405]
86 BEATSON, S. H. (1968). Eradication of pharaoh's ants and crickets using chlordecone baits. *Int. Pest Control*, **10** (2), 8–10. [313]
87 BEATSON, S. H. (1975). Pests associated with hospital catering. *Hlth Social Service J.*, May 25th, *Catering Suppl.*, 17–19. [71]
88 BEATSON, S. H. (1975). Environmental health and hygiene: problems of hospital pest control. *Proc. 4th Br. Pest Control Ass. Conf., Jersey*, Paper No. 7, 3 pp. [71]
89 BEATSON, S. H. & DRIPPS, J. S. (1972). Long-term survival of cockroaches out of doors. *Environ. Hlth*, **80** (10), 340–341. [34]
90 BEDINGFIELD, W. D. (1952). Insecticide resistant roaches? *Pest Control*, **20** (4), 6. [430]
91 BEDINGFIELD, W. D. (1955). Malrin, chlorthion, diperex hold promise of solving the resistant roach problem. *Pest Control*, **23** (5), 24, 38. [432]
92 BEHRENZ, W. & BÖCKER, W. (1965). Baygon, a new, promising public health insecticide of the organic carbamate group. *Pflanzenschutz Nachr.*, **18** (2), 53–81. [374, 380]
93 BEN-DYKE, R., SANDERSON, D. M. & NOAKES, D. N. (1970). Acute toxicity data for pesticides. *Wld Rev. Pest Control*, **9** (3), 119–127. [134]
94 BENNETT, G. W. & ANTONS, I. K. (1975). Controlling German cockroaches with pyrethrin ULV applications. *Pest Control*, **43** (1), 24–28. [123]
95 BENNETT, G. W. & MCNEAL, Jr., C. D. (1974). Low volume, higher concentration: ULV in pest control operations. *Pest Control*, **42** (6), 16, 18, 20 [122].
96 BENNETT, G. W. & SPINK, W. T. (1968). Insecticide resistance of German cockroaches from various areas of Louisiana. *J. econ. Ent.*, **61** (2), 426–431. [445]
97 BERKOVITCH, I. (1974). A new synthetic pyrethroid. *Int. Pest Control*, **16** (1), 20. [277]
98 BERNS, R. E. (1975). Staff training in the United States of America. *Proc. 4th Br. Pest Control Ass. Conf., Jersey*, Paper No. 12, 6 pp. [152]
99 BERNTON, H. S. & BROWN, H. (1967). Cockroach allergy: II. The relation of infestation to sensitization. *Southern Med. J.*, **60** (8), 852–855. [29]
100 BERTHOLD, R. & WILSON, B. R. (1967). Resting behaviour of the German cockroach, *Blattella germanica*. *Ann. ent. Soc. Am.*, **60** (2), 347–351. [172]
101 BHATIA, A. S. (1969). An integrated technique to study the effects of fumigants on respiration of insects. *J. stored Prod. Res.*, **5**, 57–67. [330]
102 BILLS, G. T. (1964). Field observations on resistant cockroach control. *Publ. Hlth Inspector*, **73** (1), 3–6. [448]
103 BILLS, G. T. (1965). Kepone and dichlorvos for controlling cockroaches and vinegar fly. *Int. Pest Control*, **7** (5), 8–11. [99, 332]
104 BILLS, G. T. (1967). Cockroach control at an international airport. *Int. Pest Control*, **9** (6), 17–19. [70, 380]
105 BILLS, G. T. (1969). Successful cockroach control. *Environ. Hlth*, **77** (4), 131–137. [67]
106 BISHOPP, F. (1950). B.E.P.Q. Assistant Chief reports on preliminary results with allethrin. *Agric. Chem.*, **5** (8), 22–24, 76. [260]
107 BLAQUIERE, C. (1972). Legal regulations pertaining to trade and use of lindane. In: Blaquiere, C. *et al. Lindane*, Chap. H., pp. 263–335, Verlag K. Schillinger. [291]
108 BLOCK, E. F. & MCCHESNEY, J. D. (1974). Two new tryptophane metabolites of the American cockroach. *J. Insect Physiol.*, **20**, 1683–1686. [172]

109 BLUM, M. S. & KEARNS, C. W. (1956). Temperature and the action of pyrethrum in the American cockroach, *J. econ. Ent.*, **49** (6), 862–865. [233, 390]
110 BODENSTEIN, O. F. & FALES, J. H. (1962). Residual tests on face flies. *Soap, N.Y.*, **38** (5), 125–128. [269]
111 BODENSTEIN, O. F. & FALES, J. H. (1969). A list of references on the rearing of cockroaches for experimental purposes. *Pest Control*, **37** (7), 30–34. [461]
112 BOND, E. J., ROBINSON, J. R. & BUCKLAND, C. T. (1969). The toxic action of phosphine: absorption and symptoms of poisoning in insects. *J. stored Prod. Res.*, **5**, 289–298. [214, 215]
113 BOOTH, G. M. & METCALF, R. L. (1972). The histochemical fate of paraoxon in the cockroach (*Periplaneta americana*) and honey bee (*Apis mellifera*) brain. *Israel J. Ent.*, **7**, 143–156. [415]
114 BOT, J. (1952). The action of DDT, hexachlorocyclohexane, chlordane and toxaphene. *Documenta Med. Georgraph. Trop.*, **4**, 57–70. [410]
115 BOTTIMER, L. J. (1945). Roach rearing and testing. *Soap, N.Y.*, **21** (12), 151–157. [463]
116 BRACEY, P. (1954). Urea-formaldehyde resin as a vehicle for semi-permanent insecticidal residues to control flies and mosquitoes. *Suppl. to Al-Rendiconti Ist. Superiore Sanita,* 344–393. [89]
117 BRADWELL, L. (1971). Problems of transport: marine-passenger. *Proc. 3rd Br. Pest Control Ass. Conf., Jersey,* Paper No. 19, 3 pp. [71]
118 BRADY, U. E. & ARTHUR, B. W. (1962). Absorption and metabolism of ruelene by Arthropods. *J. econ. Ent.*, **55** (6), 833–836. [414]
119 BRADY, U. E. & STERNBURG, J. (1964). Influence of anaesthesia on the toxicity of TEPP and SD-3562. *J. econ. Ent.*, **57** (1), 173–174. [470]
120 BRANDES, C. H., GÄNGEL, G. & KOWALSKY, H. (1968). The effects of cockroach control on the animal stock of an aquarium and terrarium. *Angew. Zool.*, **7**, 71–98. [72]
121 BREHM, W. L. (1968). Care and maintenance of the one-gallon stainless steel sprayer. *Pest Control*, **36** (5), 16, 18, 20. [124]
122 BROMBERG, A. I. (1974). Insecticidal and insecticidal-rodenticidal preparations obtained by fixation of toxicants to sorbents. *Zh. Mikrobiol. Epidemiol. Immunobiol.*, No. 8, 50–53. [95]
123 BROOKS, G. T. (1968). Mechanisms of resistance to chlorohydrocarbon insecticides. *Wld Rev. Pest Control*, **7** (3), 127–133. [448]
124 BROOKS, G. T. (1971). The fate of chlorinated hydrocarbons in living organisms. In: Tahori, A. S. (Ed.), *Int. Symp. Pesticide Terminal Residues,* Tel Aviv, Israel, 111–136. [281]
125 BROOKS, I. C., HAUS, J., BLUMENTHAL, R. R. & DAVIS Jr., B. S. (1969). SBP-1382—A new synthetic pyrethroid. Part I. *Soap, N.Y.*, **45** (3), 62, 64, 66, 72, 74. [270, 271, 272]
126 BROOKS, I. C., HAUS, J., BLUMENTHAL, R. R. & DAVIS Jr., B. S. (1969). SBP-1382—A new synthetic pyrethroid. Part II. *Soap, N.Y.*, **45** (4), 49–50, 79. [270, 272]
127 BROOKS, M. A. (1957). Growth retarding effect of carbon dioxide anaesthesia on the German cockroach. *J. Insect Physiol.*, **1** (1), 76–84. [469]
128 BROOKS, M. A. (1965). The effects of repeated anaesthesia on the biology of *Blattella germanica* (Linnaeus). *Entomologia exp. appl.*, **8**, 39–48. [469]
129 BROWN, A. W. A. (1951). *Insect control by chemicals.* Wiley, New York, pp. 759–763. [423, 425]
130 BROWN, A. W. A. (1959). Insecticide resistance as a world problem. *Can. J. Biochem. Physiol.*, **37**, 1091–1097. [424, 437]
131 BROWN, A. W. A. (1971). Pest resistance to pesticides. In: White-Stevens, R. (Ed.). *Pesticides in the environment,* Vol. 1, part 2, Dekker, N.Y. [286]
132 BROWN, A. W. A. & Pal, R. (1971). *Insecticide resistance in arthropods.* World Health Organisation, 2nd Edition. 491 pp. [424, 425, 457]
133 BROWN, A. W. A., WENNER, B. J. & PARK, F. E. (1948). Toxicity of selected organic compounds to insects. II. Tests for contact toxicity on nymphs of *Blattella* and *Oncopeltis*, and adults of *Tribolium. Can. J. Res.*, Sec. D, **26** (3), 188–196. [215, 296]
134 BROWN, N. C. (1970). A review of the toxicology of piperonyl butoxide. Report A28/52

(Nov. 1970). Cooper Technical Bureau, Wellcome Foundation Limited. 48 pp. [238]
135 BROWN, N. C., CHADWICK, P. R. & WICKHAM, J. C. (1967). The role of synergists in the formulation of insecticides. *Int. Pest Control,* **9** (6), 10–13. [237]
136 BROWN, V. K. (1968). Solubility and solvent effects as rate-determining factors in the acute percutaneous toxicities of pesticides. S. C. I. Monograph No. 29: *Physicochemical and biophysical factors affecting the activity of pesticides.* Soc. Chem. Ind., Lond., 93–105. [132]
137 BROWN, V. K. & MUIR, C. M. C. (1971). Some factors affecting the acute toxicity of pesticides to mammals when absorbed through skin and eyes. *Int. Pest Control,* **13** (4), 16–21. [132]
138 BRY, R. E., BOATRIGHT, R. E., LAND, J. H. & CAIL, R. S. (1973). Protecting woollen fabric against insect damage with resmethrin. *Soap, N.Y.,* **49** (3), 40, 42, 44. [271]
139 BUEI, K., SHIRO, A., MASAYOSHI, K., AKEO, H. & MINEO, O. (1965). Evaluation of pyrethroids in kerosene and deobase against adults of the Common house fly, *Musca domestica vicina* Macq. by settling mist method. Studies on the biological assay of pyrethroids. 2. *Botyu-Kagaku,* **30**, 37–44. [267]
140 BULL, J. O. (1968). Controlling pests in the bakery. *Biscuit Maker & Plant Baker,* **19** (5), 316–319. [54]
141 BURDEN, G. S. (1967). Cockroach control ... Past, present, future ... *Pest Control,* **35** (9), 20, 22, 24, 26. [22]
142 BURDEN, G. S. (1972). Gas-propelled aerosols and micronized dusts for the control of insects in enclosed areas including aircraft and vans. Part 6. Insects of medical importance. *J. econ. Ent.,* **65** (5), 1458–1462. [246]
143 BURDEN, G. S. (1974). German cockroaches: method of testing for resistance to chlorpyrifos and propoxur. *Pest Control,* **42** (7), 18. [344, 428]
144 BURDEN, G. S., BANKS, W. A. & MADDEN, E. E. (1972). Chlorpyrifos (Dursban) in field tests against German Cockroaches. *Pest Control,* **40** (3), 13–14. [345, 379]
145 BURDEN, G. S. & EASTIN, J. L. (1960). Field tests of dusts and sprays against German cockroaches. *Florida Ent.,* **43** (1), 15–18. [173, 324]
146 BURDEN, G. S. & EASTIN, J. L. (1960) Laboratory evaluation of cockroach repellents. *Pest Control,* **28** (6), 14. [159, 160, 162, 496]
147 BURDEN, G. S., LOFGREN, C. S. & EASTIN, J. L. (1959). Malathion resistance in a laboratory strain of the German cockroach. *Pest Control,* **27**, 38. [437]
148 BURDEN, G. S., LOFGREN, C. S. & GAHAN J. B. (1964). Effect of residual and contact sprays on the resistance of the German cockroach to chlordane. *Florida Ent.,* **47** (2), 109–111. [304]
149 BURDEN, G. S., LOFGREN, C. S. & SMITH, C. N. (1960). Development of chlordane and malathion resistance in the German cockroach. *J. econ. Ent.,* **53** (6), 1138–1139. [438, 439]
150 BURDEN, G. S. & MADDEN, E. E. (1975). *Periplaneta americana*: comparative susceptibility to residuals. *Pest Control,* **43** (1), 20. [304]
151 BURDEN, G. S. & SMITTLE, B. J. (1969). Baygon in field tests against German cockroaches. *J. econ. Ent.,* **62** (1), 262–263. [378]
152 BURGESS, N. R. H., McDERMOTT, S. N. & BLANCH, A. P. (1974). An electrical trap for the control of cockroaches and other domestic pests. *J. R. Army med. Cps.,* **120**, 173–175. [475]
153 BURT, P. E. & GOODCHILD, R. E. (1967). Action of pyrethrum and synergised pyrethrum on the nervous system of *Periplaneta americana* L. *Rothamsted Exp. Sta. Rep.,* 1967, 167–168. [236, 398]
154 BURT, P. E. & GOODCHILD, R. E. (1971). The site of action of pyrethrin I in the nervous system of the cockroach, *Periplaneta americana. Entomologia exp. appl.,* **14** (2), 179–189. [258, 396, 397]
155 BURT, P. E. & GOODCHILD, R. E. (1971). Mode of action of pyrethroids. *Rothamsted Exp. Sta. Rep.,* 1971, 184–187. [392, 393, 394, 398]
156 BURT, P. E., GREGORY, G. E. & MOLLOY, F. M. (1966). A histochemical and electrophysical study of the action of diazoxon on cholinesterase activity and nerve condu-

tion in ganglia of the cockroach *Periplaneta americana* L. *Ann. appl. Biol.*, **58**, 341–354. [417, 418]
157 BURT, P. E., GREGORY, G. E. & MOLLOY, F. M. (1967). The activation of diazinon by ganglia of the cockroach *Periplaneta americana* L. and its action on nerve conduction and cholinesterase activity. *Ann. appl. Biol.*, **59**, 1–11. [417]
158 BURT, P. E., LORD, R. A., FORREST, J. M. & GOODCHILD, R. E. (1971). The spread of topically-applied pyrethrin I from the cuticle to the central nervous system of the cockroach *Periplaneta americana*. *Entomologia exp. appl.*, **14**, 255–259. [232, 387, 389, 390, 396]
159 BUSVINE, J. R. (1953). Forms of insecticide resistance in houseflies and lice. *Nature, Lond.*, **171** (4342), 118–119. [241]
160 BUSVINE, J. R. (1968). Detection and measurement of insecticide resistance in arthropods of agricultural or veterinary importance. *Wld Rev. Pest Control*, **7** (1), 27–41. [487]
161 BUSVINE, J. R. (1971). The biochemical and genetic bases of insecticide resistance. *PANS*, **17** (2), 135–146. [451]
162 BUSVINE, J. R. (1971). *A critical review of the techniques for testing insecticides*. Commonwealth Agric. Bureaux, 333 pp. [470]
163 BUTLER, P. A. (1971). Influence of pesticides on marine ecosystems. *Proc. R. Soc.*, (B) **177**, 321–329. [141]
164 BUTTS, W. L. & DAVIDSON, R. H. (1955). The toxicity of five organic insecticides to resistant and non-resistant strains of *B. germanica* (L.). *J. econ. Ent.*, **48** (5), 572–574. [296, 309, 433]
165 CALSETTA, D. R. & GRASSL, E. F. (1974). Residual activity of new pyrethroid formulation against cockroaches under field conditions. *Pest Control*, **42** (6), 32, 35–36. [272]
166 CALSETTA, D. R. & GRASSL, E. F. (1975). A residual 'SBP-1382' pressurized spray. *Soap, N.Y.*, **51** (4), 41–42, 44. [272]
167 CAMPBELL, F. L. (1942). Pyrethrum vs. Roaches. *Soap, N.Y.*, **18** (5), 90–93, 103. [230, 232, 234]
168 CAMPBELL, W. A., PATEL, K., BECKER, R. A. & HARTMANN, J. F. (1968). Resistance of insect nerve ultrastructure to alteration by pyrethrins. *Pyrethrum Post*, **9** (4), 13–17. [396]
169 CANTWELL, G. E., TOMPKINS, G. J. & WATSON, P. N. (1973). Control of the German cockroach with carbon dioxide. *Pest Control*, **41** (3), 40, 42, 48. [214]
170 CARSON, R. (1962). *Silent Spring*. Hamish Hamilton, London. 304 pp. [223, 286, 455]
171 CASIDA, J. E. (1963). Mode of action of carbamates. *A. Rev. Ent.*, **8**, 39–58. [418]
172 CASIDA, J. E. (1970). Mixed-function oxidase involvement in the biochemistry of insecticide synergists. *J. agric. Fd Chem.*, **18**, 753–772. [236]
173 CASIDA, J. E. (Ed.). (1973). *Pyrethrum—the natural insecticide*. Academic Press, 329 pp. [218]
174 CASIDA, J. E., KIMMEL, E. C., ELLIOTT, M. & JANES, N. F. (1971). Oxidative metabolism of pyrethrins in mammals. *Nature, Lond.*, **230** (5292), 326–327. [251]
175 CASIDA, J. E., MCBRIDE, L. & NIEDERMEIER, R. P. (1962). Metabolism of 2,2-dichlorovinyl dimethyl phosphate in relation to residues in milk and mammalian tissues. *J. agric. Fd Chem.*, **10** (5), 370–377. [335]
176 CATESBY, M. (1747). *Natural history of Carolina*, Appendix, p. 10, London. [14]
177 CHADWICK, P. R. (1961). A comparison of safroxan and piperonyl butoxide as pyrethrum synergists. *Pyrethrum Post*, **6** (2), 30–37. [238, 240, 241]
178 CHADWICK, P. R. (1963). A comparison of MGK 264 and piperonyl butoxide as pyrethrum synergists. *Pyrethrum Post*, **7** (1), 11–15, 48. [238, 240]
179 CHADWICK, P. R. (1971). Activity of some new pyrethroids against *Blattella germanica* L. *Pestic. Sci.*, **2** (1), 16–19. [237, 238, 262, 263, 266, 268, 269, 274, 395]
180 CHADWICK, P. R. (1972). Knockdown times for susceptible German cockroaches in the WHO test. *Int. Pest Control*, **14** (4), 6–9. [287, 294, 295, 344, 381]
181 CHADWICK, P. R. & EVANS, M. (1973). Laboratory and field tests with some pyrethroids against cockroaches. *Int. Pest Control*, **15** (1), 11–16. [262, 265, 274, 275, 276, 278]
182 CHADWICK, P. R. & SHAW, R. D. (1974). Cockroach control in sewers in Singapore using

bioresmethrin and piperonyl butoxide as a thermal fog. *Pestic. Sci.*, **5**, 691–701. [275]
183 CHAMBERLAIN, R. W. (1950). An investigation on the action of piperonyl butoxide with pyrethrum. *Am. J. Hyg.*, **52**, 153–183. [391]
184 CHANDLER, S. E. (1951). Botanical aspects of pyrethrum. *Pyrethrum Post*, 2 (3), 1–9. [225]
185 CHANG, S. C. & CROWELL, H. H. (1953). Effect of successive treatments of DDT on individual susceptibility in the American cockroach. *J. econ. Ent.*, **46** (3), 467–472. [289, 290]
186 CHENG, T. H. & CAMPBELL, F. L. (1940). Toxicity of phosphorus to cockroaches. *J. econ. Ent.*, **33** (1), 193–199. [212]
187 CHITTENDEN, R. H. & GIES, W. J. (1898). The influence of borax and boric acid upon nutrition with special reference to proteid metabolism. *Am. J. Physiol.*, **1** (1), 1–39. [194]
188 CLARK, H. B. & BUTZ, A. (1961). The effects of some insecticides on the metabolites of *Blattella germanica*. *J. econ. Ent.*, **54** (5), 1022–1024. [402]
189 CLARKE, E. G. C. (1975). *Poisoning in veterinary practice*. Ass. Br. Pharm. Ind., London, 34 pp. [138]
190 CLARKE, E. G. C. (1975). Pets and poisons. *J. small Anim. Pract*, **16**, 375–380. [138]
191 CLARKE, T. H. & COCHRAN, D. G. (1959). Cross-resistance in insecticide-resistant strains of the German cockroach, *Blattella germanica* (L.). *Bull. Wld Hlth Org.*, **20**, 823–833. [437]
192 COCHRAN, D. G. (1955). Differential susceptibility of the sexes and developmental stages of the American roach to several insecticides. *J. econ. Ent.*, **48** (2), 131–133. [288, 296]
193 COCHRAN, D. G. (1956). The distribution and metabolism of DDT injected into the American cockroach. *J. econ. Ent.*, **49** (1), 43–49. [288, 399]
194 COCHRAN, D. G. (1961). Further studies on cross-resistance in the German cockroach. *Bull. Wld Hlth Org.*, **24**, 557–561. [366, 439]
195 COCHRAN, D. G. (1964). Insecticide resistance factors and genetic linkage in *Blattella germanica* (Dictyoptera). *Proc. XIIth Int. Cong. Ent.*, London, p. 240. [441]
196 COCHRAN, D. G. (1973). Inheritance of malathion resistance in the German cockroach. *Entomologia exp. appl.*, **16**, 83–90. [341]
197 COCHRAN, D. G. (1973). Inheritance and linkage of pyrethrins resistance in the German cockroach. *J. econ. Ent.*, **66** (1), 27–30. [446]
198 COCHRAN, D. G., GRAYSON J. M. & LEVITAN, M. (952). Chromosomal and cytoplasmic factors in transmission of DDT resistance in the German cockroach. *J. econ. Ent.*, **45** (6), 997–1001. [430]
199 COCHRAN, D. G. & ROSS, M. H. (1962). Inheritance of DDT-resistance in European strain of *Blattella germanica* (L.). *Bull. Wld Hlth Org.*, **27**, 257–261. [430, 441]
200 COCHRAN, D. G. & ROSS, M. H. (1964). Resistance to telodrin in the German cockroach, *Blattella germanica*. *J. econ. Ent.*, **57** (4), 485. [441]
201 COCKS, J. A. (1974). The metabolism of l-naphthyl methylcarbamate by *Periplaneta americana*. *Pestic. Sci.*, **5** (4), 505–510. [419]
202 COHEN, S. H., SOUSA, J. A. & ROACH, F. (1973). Effects of UV irradiation on nymphs of five species of cockroaches. *J. econ. Ent.*, **66** (4), 859–862. [169]
203 COHEN, S. H., SOUSA, J. A., ROACH, J. F. & GINGRICH, J. B. (1975). Effects of UV irradiation on nymphs of *Blattella germanica* and *Periplaneta americana*. *J. econ. Ent.*, **68** (5), 687–693. [170]
204 COLE, A. C. (1932). The olfactory responses of the cockroach (*B. orientalis*) to the important essential oils and a control measure formulated from the results. *J. econ. Ent.*, **25**, 902–905. [99]
205 COLHOUN, E. H. (1958). Acetylcholine in *Periplaneta americana*. I. Acetylcholine levels in nervous tissue. *J. Insect Physiol.*, **2**, 108–116. [414, 415, 416]
206 COLHOUN, E. H. (1958). Physical release of acetylcholine from the thoracic nerve cord of *Periplaneta americana* L. *Nature, Lond.*, **182** (4646), 1378. [415]
207 COLHOUN, E. H. (1958). Acetylcholine in *Periplaneta americana* L. II. Acetylcholine and nervous activity. *J. Insect Physiol.*, **2**, 117–127. [415]

208 COLHOUN, E. H. (1960). Approaches to mechanisms of insecticidal action. *J. agric. Fd Chem.*, **8** (4), 252–257. [410]
209 COLLINS, W. J. (1973). German cockroach resistance. I. Resistance to diazinon includes cross-resistance to DDT, pyrethrins and propoxur in a laboratory colony. *J. econ. Ent.*, **66** (1), 44–47. [446]
210 COLLINS, W. J. (1975). A comparative study of insecticide resistance assays with the German cockroach. *Pestic. Sci.*, **6**, 83–95. [427, 447, 484]
211 COLLINS, W. J. (1975). Resistance in *Blattella germanica* (L.) (Orthoptera, Blattidae): the effect of propoxur selection and non-selection on the resistance spectrum developed by diazinon selection. *Bull. ent. Res.*, **65**, 399–403. [447]
212 COON, B. F. (1944). Effects of paralytic insecticides on heart pulsations and blood circulation in the American cockroach as determined with a fluorescein indicator. *J. econ. Ent.*, **37**, 785–789. [216, 392]
213 CORBETT, J. R. (1974). Neuroactive insecticides excluding inhibitors of acetylcholinesterase. In: *The biochemical mode of action of pesticides*. Academic Press, pp. 165–186. [386, 387, 398]
214 CORNWELL, P. B. (1966). Arprocarb for control of cockroaches and ants. *Int. Pest Control*, **8** (1), 18–21. [375, 380]
215 CORNWELL, P. B. (1968). Cockroaches and their control—with special reference to resistance. *Proc. 2nd Br. Pest Control Ass. Conf., Jersey*, p. 33–38. [448]
216 CORNWELL, P. B. (1970). The incidence of pests dealt with by Local Authorities. *Environ. Hlth*, **78** (7), 267–272, 282. [13, 15]
217 CORNWELL, P. B. (1971). Insecticides for cockroach control used by Local Authorities. *Environ. Hlth*, **79** (9). 279–283. [22, 428]
218 CORRIGAN, J. T. & KEARNS, C. W. (1963). Amino acid metabolism in DDT-poisoned American cockroaches. *J. Insect Physiol.*, **9**, 1–12. [404]
219 CREMLYN, R. J. W. (1974). Organophosphorus insecticides. *Int. Pest Control*, **16** (6), 4–9. [319]
220 CROSBY, D. G, LEITIS, E. & WINTERLIN, W. L. (1965). Photodecomposition of carbamate insecticides. *J. agric. Fd Chem.*, **13** (2), 204–207. [373]
221 CUMMINGS, E. C. & MENN, J. J. (1959). An American cockroach rearing cage. *J. econ. Ent.*, **52** (6), 1227–1228. [461]
222 DAHM, P. A. (1955). A convenient method for rearing large cockroaches. *J. econ. Ent.*, **48** (4), 480–482. [468]
223 DARRELL, R., MADDOCK, M. S., VINCENT, A., SEDLACK, B. S. & SCHOOF, H. F. (1961). Preliminary tests with DDVP vapour for aircraft disinsection. *Publ. Hlth Rep., Publ. Hlth Service, U.S. Dept. Hlth, Education & Welfare*, **76** (9), 777–780. [71]
224 DAVID, J. (1971). The British Pest Control Association. *Int. Biodetn. Bull.*, **7** (1), 3. [145]
225 DAVIES, M. (1971). An account of the development of bioallethrin and bioresmethrin synergised by piperonyl butoxide for the control of *Musca domestica* L. *Proc. 3rd Br. Pest Control Ass. Conf., Jersey*, pp. 35–41. [257, 259, 270]
226 DAVIS, J. J. (1946). DDT to control household and stored grain insects. *J. econ. Ent.*, **39** (1), 59–61. [287]
227 DELHAYE, R. J. (1956). Note Préliminaire sur la Biologie Florale et sur la Fécondation Disigée de Pyrèthre, *Chrysanthemum cinerariaefolium* (Trev.). *Bull. agric. Congo Belge*, **17** (5). [225]
228 DELONG, D. M. (1948). The supermarket's roach problem. *Soap, N.Y.*, **24** (8), 143, 145, 147, 149. [55]
229 DELONG, D. M. (1962). Beer cases and soft drink cartons as insect distributors. *Pest Control*, **30** (7), 14, 16, 18. [160, 167]
230 DEMOZAY, D. & MARECHAL, G. (1972). Biological properties. In: Ulmann, E. (Ed.). *Lindane: Monograph of an insecticide*, Schillinger, Germany, pp. 137–161. [296]
231 DEUTSCH, F. K. (1975). Safety in the pesticide industry—Part II. *Proc. 4th Br. Pest Control Ass. Conf., Jersey*, Paper No. 5, 5 pp. [131]
232 DEWEY, J. E. (1942). The relative effectiveness of dust mixtures against the German cockroach. *J. econ. Ent.*, **35** (2), 256–261. [234]

233 DEWS, S. C. & MORRILL Jr., A. W. (1946). DDT for insect control at army installations in the Fourth Service Command. *J. econ. Ent.*, **39** (3), 347–355. [287]
234 DISNEY, R. W. (1966). A comparison of two methods for the measurement of cholinesterase inhibition in human blood. *Biochem. Pharmac.*, **15**, 361–366. [135]
235 DOBZHANSKY, T. (1941). *Genetics and the origin of species*, 2nd Edition. Columbia Univ. Press, N.Y. [425]
236 DÖHRING, E. (1972). Occurrence and distribution of cockroaches in the Federal Republic of Germany. *Prakt. Schädlingsbekämpfer*, **24** (3), 29–35. [56, 60]
237 DÖHRING, E. (1973). Survey on the presence of cockroaches in the Federal Republic of Germany. (Final Report). *Prakt. Schädlingsbekämpfer*, **25** (4), 47–59. [60, 70, 296]
238 DOMINICK, D. D. (1973). Insecticides in food handling establishments. *Federal Register*, **38** (154), 21685. [151]
239 DOW, R. P. (1955). A note on domestic cockroaches in south Texas. *J. econ. Ent.*, **48** (1), 106–107. [472]
240 DRESDEN, D. (1948). Site of action of DDT and cause of death after acute DDT poisoning. *Nature, Lond.*, **162** (4130), 1000–1001. [408]
241 DRESDEN, D. & KRIJGSMAN, B. J. (1948). Experiments on the physiological action of contact insecticides. *Bull. ent. Res.*, **38** (4), 575–578. [295]
242 DU CHANOIS, F. R. (1956). A preliminary report on resistant cockroach control at Naval installations. *Pest Control*, **24**, 9–10, 12, 36. [430, 433]
243 DUGGAN, R. E., BARRY, H. C. & JOHNSON, L. Y. (1966). Pesticide residues in total-diet samples. *Science, N.Y.*, **151**, 101–104. [308]
244 DYER, K F. & HANNA, P. V. (1974). Has the time come to ban organophosphate insecticides? *Ecologist*, **4** (6), 234–236. [337]
245 DYTE, C. E. (1958). Use of insecticidal lacquers in flour mills. *Milling*, **131** (26), 742–743. [90]
246 DYTE, C. E. (1960). Preliminary tests of an insecticidal lacquer containing malathion. *Pest Technology*, **2** (5), 98–99. [91]
247 DYTE, C. E. (1974). Problems arising from insecticide resistance in storage pests. *E.P.P.O. Bull.*, **4** (3), 275–289. [424]
248 DYTE, C. E. & TYLER, P. S. (1960). The contamination of flour by insecticidal lacquers containing endrin and dieldrin. *J. Sci. Fd Agric.*, **11** (12), 745–750. [90]
249 EADS, R. B. VONZUBEN, F. J., BENNETT, S. E. & WALKER, O. L. (1954). Studies on cockroaches in a municipal sewerage system. *Am. J. trop. Med. Hyg.*, **3** (6), 1092–1098. [471]
250 EAGLESON, C. (1942). Sesame in insecticides. *Soap, N.Y.*, **18** (12), 125–127. [240]
251 EASTIN, J. L. & BURDEN, G. S. (1960). Tests with five silica dusts against German cockroaches. *Florida Ent.*, **43** (3), 99–102. [207, 209, 211]
252 EATON J. L. & STERNBURG, J. G. (1967). Temperature effects on nerve activity in DDT-treated American cockroaches. *J. econ. Ent.*, **60** (5), 1358–1364. [402, 409]
253 EATON J. L. & STERNBURG, J. G. (1967). Uptake of DDT by the American cockroach central nervous system. *J. econ. Ent.*, **60** (6), 1699–1703. [402]
254 EBELING, W. (1964). Tests with Vapona insecticide resin strips. *P.C.O. News*, **24** (4), 23. [331]
255 EBELING, W. & REIERSON, D. A. (1969). The cockroach learns to avoid insecticides. *Calif. Agric.*, **23** (2), 12–15. [199]
256 EBELING, W. & REIERSON, D. A. (1970). Effect of population density on exploratory activity and mortality rate of German cockroaches in choice boxes. *J. econ. Ent.*, **63** (2), 350–355. [495]
257 EBELING, W. & REIERSON, D. A. (1973). Should flushing agents be added to blatticides? *Pest Control*, **41** (6), 24, 46, 48, 50–51. [187, 188, 249]
258 EBELING, W. & REIERSON, D. A. (1974). Bait trapping silverfish, cockroaches and earwigs. *Pest Control*, **42** (4), 24, 36–39. [99]
259 EBELING, W., REIERSON, D. A. & WAGNER, R. E. (1967). Influence of repellency on the efficacy of blatticides. II. Laboratory experiments with German cockroaches. *J. econ. Ent.*, **60** (3), 1375–1390. [173, 179, 190, 193, 195, 196]

260 EBELING, W., REIERSON, D. A. & WAGNER, R. E. (1968). The influence of repellency on the efficacy of blatticides. III. Field experiments with German cockroaches with notes on three other species. *J. econ. Ent.*, **61** (3), 751–761. [185, 187, 197]
261 EBELING, W., REIERSON, D. A. & WAGNER, R. E. (1968). Influence of repellency on the efficacy of blatticides. IV. Comparison of four cockroach species. *J. econ. Ent.*, **61** (5), 1213–1219. [178, 196, 211]
262 EBELING, W. & WAGNER, R. E. (1963). Teflon as a barrier to insects. *J. econ. Ent.*, **56** (5), 715–716. [468]
263 EBELING, W. & WAGNER, R. E. (1964). The treatment of voids under cabinets. *P.C.O. News*, **24** (4), 8–11. [178]
264 EBELING, W., WAGNER, R. E. & REIERSON, D. A. (1965). Cockroach control with Dri-Die and Drione. *P.C.O. News*, **25** (10), 16–22. [207, 209, 472]
265 EBELING, W., WAGNER, R. E. & REIERSON, D. A. (1966). Influence of repellency on the efficacy of blatticides. I. Learned modification of behaviour of the German cockroach. *J. econ. Ent.*, **59** (6), 1374–1388. [173, 185, 188, 189, 496]
266 EBELING, W., WAGNER, R. E. & REIERSON, D. A. (1969). Insect-proofing during building construction. *Calif. Agric.*, **23** (5), 4–7. [54]
267 EDDLEMAN, D. & SIMON, D. (1969). Note on the Brown cockroach, *Periplaneta brunnea* in Texas. *Ann. ent. Soc. Am.*, **62** (3), 678–679. [473]
268 EDDY, G. W. (1961). Laboratory tests of residues of organophosphorus compounds against houseflies. *J. econ. Ent.*, **54** (2), 386–388. [329]
269 EDELSTEIN, A. & TAYLOR, R. B. (1961). Automation and pyrethrum control flies around the clock. *Pyrethrum Post*, **6** (2), 43–48. [223]
270 EDWARDS, C. A. (1970). Persistent pesticides in the environment. *Critical Rev. Environ. Control*, **1** (1), 7–67. [301]
271 EHRHARDT, D. A. & DICKENS, T. H. (1975). Efficacy of acephate against German cockroaches aboard Naval vessels. *J. econ. Ent.*, **68** (1), 41–42. [358]
272 EISA, E. A. (1951). The behaviour of cockroaches (*Periplaneta americana*) towards the different food materials. *Euclides*, **11** (121), 130–131. [99]
273 EISA, E. A. & SOLIMAN, A. A. (1953). The chemoattraction of food constituents to insects. *Bull. Soc. Fouad 1er Ent.*, **37**, 167–172. [100]
274 EL-AZIZ, S. A., METCALF, R. L. & FUKUTO, T. R. (1969). Physiological factors influencing the toxicity of carbamate insecticides to insects. *J. econ. Ent.*, **62** (2), 318–324. [373]
275 ELDEFRAWI, M. E. & HOSKINS, W. M. (1961). Relation of the rate of penetration and metabolism to the toxicity of sevin to three insect species. *J. econ. Ent.*, **54** (3), 401–405. [364, 419]
276 ELLIOTT, M., FARNHAM, A. W., JANES, N. F., NEEDHAM, P. H. & PEARSON, B. C. (1967). 5-benzyl-3-furfuryl chrysanthemate: a new potent insecticide. *Nature, Lond.*, **213** (5075), 493–494. [270]
277 ELLIOTT, M., FARNHAM, A. W., JANES, N. F., NEEDHAM, P. H. & PULMAN, D. A. (1974). Synthetic insecticide with a new order of activity. *Nature, Lond.*, **248** (5450), 710–711. [258, 276]
278 ELLIOTT, M., FARNHAM, A. W., JANES, N. F., NEEDHAM, P. H., PULMAN, D. A. & STEVENSON, J. H. (1973). A photostable pyrethroid. *Nature, Lond.*, **246**, 169–170. [277]
279 ELLIOTT, M., FORD, M. G. & JANES, N. F. (1970). Insecticidal activity of the pyrethrins and related compounds. III. Penetration of pyrethroid insecticides into Mustard beetles (*Phaedon cochleariae*). *Pestic. Sci.*, **1**, 220–223. [390]
280 ELLIOTT, M., JANES, N. F., JEFFS, K. A., NEEDHAM, P. H. & SAWICKI, R. M. (1965). New pyrethrin-like esters with high insecticidal activity. *Nature, Lond.*, **207**, 938–940. [255]
281 ELLIOTT, M., JANES, N. F., KIMMEL, E. C. & CASIDA, J. E. (1972). Metabolic fate of pyrethrin I, pyrethrin II and allethrin administered orally to rats. *J. agric. Fd Chem.*, **20**, 300–313. [251]
282 EL SEBAE, A. H., METCALF, R. L. & FUKUTO, T. R. (1964). Carbamate insecticides: syn-

ergism by organothiocyanates. *J. econ. Ent.,* **57** (4), 478–482. [104, 419]
283 ENAN, O. & GORDON, H. T. (1965). Temperature effects on toxicity of synergised carbamate insecticides on houseflies. *J. econ. Ent.,* **58** (3), 513–516. [419]
284 ENESCU, A. & BALAZS, D. (1974). The influence of temperature on the effectiveness of certain insecticides used to control *Blattella germanica* L. *Archs Roum. Path. Exp. Microbiol.* **33** (1), 87–90. [400]
285 EVANS, M. (1966). Automatic aerosol dispensers for the control of stored food-product moths. *Pyrethrum Post,* **8** (3), 23–25. [223]
286 EVERSOLE, J. W. (1971). Feeding of American and Oriental cockroaches on baits embedded in paraffin. *J. econ. Ent.,* **64** (5), 1316–1317. [315]
287 FABIAN, R., GRIFFEN, T. B. & COULSTON, F. (1971). Occurrence of insecticidal chlorinated hydrocarbons and their breakdown products in man and the resulting toxicological consequences. In: Tahori, A. S. (Ed.), *Int. Symp. Pesticide Terminal Residues, Tel Aviv, Israel.* Butterworths, London, pp. 145–160. [281]
288 FAHMY, M. A. & GORDON, H. T. (1965). Selective synergism of carbamate insecticides on houseflies by aryloxyalkyl-amines. *J. econ. Ent.,* **58** (3), 451–455. [373]
289 FALES, J. H. & BODENSTEIN, O. F. (1963). How to field test for cockroach susceptibility to chlordane. *Pest Control,* **31** (6), 18, 20, 22, 62. [306, 441, 487]
290 FALES, J. H. & BODENSTEIN, O. F. (1966). Evaluation of neopynamin, a promising new insecticide. (Part I). *Soap, N.Y.,* **42** (6), 80–81, 84, 86, 88. [267, 268]
291 FALES, J. H. & BODENSTEIN, O. F. (1966). Evaluation of neopynamin, a promising new insecticide. (Part II). *Soap, N.Y.,* **42** (7), 66–68, 104–106. [267, 268]
292 FALES, J. H., BODENSTEIN, O. F., MILLS, Jr. G. D. & FIELDS, E. S. (1968). Evaluation of aerosols, sprays and other formulations of SBP-1382. *Proc. 55th. annual meeting, Chemical Specialties Manufacturers Ass.,* Washington, D. C., pp. 152–163. [270, 273]
293 FALES, J. H., BODENSTEIN, O. F., MILLS, G. D., YEOMANS, A. H. & FIELDS, E. S. (1966). Tests with a dichlorvos aerosol for control of cockroaches on buses. *Pest Control,* **34** (10), 28–30. [333]
294 FALES, J. H., BODENSTEIN, O. F. & PIQUETT, P. G. (1951). A method for testing aerosols against cockroaches. *U.S. Dept. Agric., Bur. Ent. Plant Quarantine* No. ET-297, 6 pp. [268, 272, 481]
295 FALES, J. H., BODENSTEIN, O. F., WATERS, R. M. & FIELDS, E. S. (1972). Insecticidal evaluation of prothrin, a synthetic pyrethroid. *Soap, N.Y.,* **48** (8), 48–49, 51, 87. [277]
296 FALES, J. H., BODENSTEIN, O. F., WATERS, R. M., FIELDS, E. S. & HALL, R. P. (1971). Insecticidal evaluation of d-*trans* tetramethrin. *Soap, N.Y.,* **47** (5), 58, 60, 62, 64, 92. [268, 269]
297 FALES, J. H., BODENSTEIN, O. F., WATERS, R. M., FIELDS, E. S. & HALL, R. P. (1971). Insecticidal evaluation of SBP-1390. *Soap, N.Y.,* **47** (9), 54, 56, 58, 60, 62, 73. [272, 273]
298 FALES, J. H., BODENSTEIN, O. F., WATERS, R. M., FIELDS, E. S., HALL, R. P. & DURBIN Jr., C. G. (1971). USDA studies insecticide effectiveness—development of aerosol formulations containing resmethrin alone and in combination with tetramethrin or d-*trans* allethrin for use against flies and mosquitoes. Part I. *Aerosol Age,* **16** (12), 52, 55–57, 61–63, 65. [272]
299 FAN, H. Y., CHEN, T. R. & RICHARDS, A. G. (1948). The temperature coefficients of DDT action in insects. *Physiol. Zool.,* **21**, 48–59. [401]
300 FARNHAM, A. W. (1971). Changes in cross-resistance patterns of houseflies selected with natural pyrethrins or resmethrin (5-benzyl-3-furylmethyl ($\pm$)-*cis-trans*-chrysanthemate). *Pestic. Sci.,* **2**, 138–143. [241]
301 FINE, B. C. (1963). The present status of resistance to pyrethroid insecticides. *Pyrethrum Post,* **7** (2), 18–21, 27. [241]
302 FINLEY, E. L., MCDERMOTT, F. G. & GROSS, H. R. (1968). Degradation of fabric by American cockroach, House cricket and Striped earwig. *J. econ. Ent.,* **61** (6), 1552–1557. [48]
303 FISHER, R. W. (1952). The importance of the locus of application on the effectiveness of

DDT to the housefly, *Musca domestica* (Diptera: Muscidae). *Can. J. Zool.,* **30**, 254–266. [485]
304 FISHER, R. W. & JURSIC, F. (1958). Rearing houseflies and roaches for physiological research. *Can. Ent.,* **90** (1), 1–7. [461]
305 FISK, F. W. (1951). Use of a specific mite control in roach and mouse cultures. *J. econ. Ent.,* **44** (6), 1016. [468]
306 FISK, F. W. & ISERT, J. A. (1953). Comparative toxicities of certain organic insecticides to resistant and non-resistant strains of the German cockroach, *Blattella germanica* (L.). *J. econ. Ent.,* **46** (6), 1059–1062. [309, 432]
307 FLYNN, A. D. & SCHOOF, H. F. (1966). Evaluation of toxicants as residues against *Blattella germanica* (L.). *J. econ. Ent.,* **59** (5), 1270–1274. [77, 493]
308 FLYNN, A. D. & SCHOOF, H. F. (1966). A simulated-field method of testing residual insecticide deposits against cockroaches. *J. econ. Ent.,* **59** (1), 110–113. [496]
309 FLYNN, A. D. & SCHOOF, H. F. (1970). Immersion technique for measuring susceptibility of house flies and cockroaches to insecticides. *J. econ. Ent.,* **63** (3), 883–886. [479]
310 FLYNN, A. D. & SCHOOF, H. F. (1971). Control of German cockroaches aboard U.S. naval surface ships on the East Coast. *J. econ. Ent.,* **64** (5), 1176–1179. [324, 379]
311 FRISHMAN, A. M. (1973). The certification exam—37 ways to help you pass. *Pest Control,* **41** (4), 52–54. [155]
312 FRISHMAN, A. M. (1973). *Questions and answers for pesticide applicators.* Frishman, Farmingdale, New York, 33 pp. [145]
313 FROELICHTER, V. (1944). The story of DDT. *Soap, N.Y.,* **20** (7), 115, 117, 119, 145. [288]
314 FUJIMOTO, K., KADOTA, T., FUJITA, Y., OKUNO, Y. & KODA, H. (1970). Evaluation of some synthetic pyrethroidal compounds as an active ingredient of pressurized insecticidal spray. *Jap. aerosol Congr.,* Tokyo, Japan. [259, 267, 268]
315 FUJIMOTO, K. & OKUNO, Y. (1972). Insecticidal activity of cynock (O,O-dimethyl O-4-cyanophenyl phosphorothioate). *Jap. J. Sanit. Zool.,* **23** (1), 35–40. [348]
316 FUKAMI, J-I. & SHISHIDO, T. (1972). Selective toxicity of diazinon and other non-systemic insecticides. *Proc. IInd Int. IUPAC Congr. Pestic. Chem.* **I**, 29–49. [326]
317 FUKUTO, T. R., METCALF, R. L. & WINTON, M. (1962). The synergism of substituted phenyl N-methylcarbamates by piperonyl butoxide. *J. econ. Ent.,* **55** (5), 341–345. [363]
318 FULTON, R. A., YEOMANS, A. H. & SULLIVAN, W. N. (1963). Ethylene oxide as a fumigant against insects. *J. econ. Ent.,* **56** (6), 906. [213, 214]
319 GAHAN, J. B. & KNIPLING, E. F. (1944). Efficacy of DDT as a roach powder. *J. econ. Ent.,* **37** (1), 138–139. [287, 288]·
320 GAINES, T. B. (1960). The acute toxicity of pesticides to rats. *Toxicol. appl. Pharmac.,* **2** (1), 88–99. [134]
321 GALLEY, R. A. E. (1967). Review of *Organic pesticides in the environment.* (Advances in Chemistry Series No. 60), edited by Gould, R. F.: 309 pp. *Nature, Lond.,* **214** (5083), 69. [283]
322 GANELIN, R. S., CUETO, C. & MAIL, G. A. (1964). Exposure to parathion. *J. Am. med. Ass.,* **188**, 807–810. [135]
323 GEORGACAKIS, E. & KAHN, M. A. Q. (1971). Toxicity of the photoisomers of cyclodiene insecticides to freshwater animals. *Nature, Lond.,* **233** (5315), 120–121. [142]
324 GEORGHIOU, G. P. & ATKINS, E. L. (1964). Temperature coefficient of toxicity of certain N-methylcarbamates against honeybees and the effect of the synergist, piperonyl butoxide. *J. agric. Res.,* **3** (1), 31–35. [419]
325 GEORGHIOU, G. P. & METCALF, R. L. (1961). The absorption and metabolism of 3-Isopropylphenyl *N*-Methylcarbamate by susceptible and carbamate-selected strains of house flies. *J. econ. Ent.,* **54** (2), 231–233. [364]
326 GEORGHIOU, G. P. & METCALF, R. L. (1962). Carbamate insecticides: comparative insect toxicity of sevin, zectran and other new materials. *J. econ. Ent.,* **55** (1), 125–127. [364, 373]
327 GEROLT, P. (1969). Mode of entry of contact insecticides. *J. Insect Physiol.,* **15** (4), 563–580. [106]

328 GERSDOFF, W. A. (1949). Toxicity to houseflies of synthetic compounds of the pyrethrin type in relation to chemical structure. *J. econ. Ent.*, **42** (3), 532–536. [259]
329 GIANNOTTI, O. & ARRUDA, H. V. (1973). American cockroaches: joint action of DDT and ouabain on adults. *J. econ. Ent.*, **66** (5), 1228–1229. [409]
330 GIANNOTTI, O., METCALF, R. L. & MARCH, R. B. (1956). The mode of action of aldrin and dieldrin in *Periplaneta americana* (L.). *Ann. ent. Soc. Am.*, **49**, 588–592. [309, 312, 410]
331 GIER, H. T. (1947). Growth rate in the cockroach *Periplaneta americana* (Linn.). *Ann. ent. Soc. Am.*, **40**, 303–317. [463]
332 GIBLERT, I. H. (1964). Laboratory rearing of cockroaches, bedbugs, human lice and fleas. *Bull. Wld Hlth Org.*, **31**, 561–563. [463]
333 GILLENWATER, H. B. & BURDEN, G. S. (1973). In: Casida, J. E. (Ed.). *Pyrethrum—the natural insecticide*. Academic Press, Chapter 13. [218, 246]
334 GINGRICH, J. B. (1973). Behaviour and survival of American cockroaches exposed to different ultraviolet and white light regimens. *J. econ. Ent.*, **66** (5), 1143–1145. [169, 170]
335 GINGRICH, J. B. (1975). Ultraviolet-induced histological and histochemical changes in the integument of newly moulted American cockroaches, *Periplaneta americana* (Dictyoptera: Blattaria: Blattidae). *Can. J. Zool.*, **53** (2), 154–159. [169]
336 GINSBURG, J. M. (1930). Test to determine toxicity of pyrethrum vapours to honeybees. *J. agric. Res.*, **40** (11), 1053–1057. [230]
337 GINSBURG, J. M. (1944). Toxicity of DDT to *Blattella germanica* as compared with sodium fluoride, derris and pyrethrum. *J. econ. Ent.*, **37** (1), 122. [201, 287]
338 GITHINJI, P. M. (1973). The effects of drying air temperature and drying time on pyrethrins content of pyrethrum flowers. *Pyrethrum Post*, **12** (2), 77–82. [226]
339 GLYNNE JONES, G. D. (1973). Pyrethrum production. In: Casida, J. E. (Ed.). *Pyrethrum—the natural insecticide*. Academic Press, Chapter 2. [225]
340 GODIN, P. J., SLEEMAN, R. J., SNAREY, M. & THAIN, E. M. (1966). The jasmolins, new insecticidally active constituents of *Chrysanthemum cinerariaefolium* Vis. *J. Chem. Soc.*, **100**, 332–334. [228]
341 GODIN, P. J., STEVENSON, J. H. & SAWICKI, R. M. (1965). The insecticidal activity of jasmolin II and its isolation from pyrethrum (*Chrysanthemum cinerariaefolium* Vis.). *J. econ. Ent.*, **58** (4), 548–551. [228]
342 GOLZ, H. H. & SHAFFER, C. B. (1956). *Malathion: summary of pharmacology and toxicology*. Central Med. Dept. of Amer. Cyanamid Co., N.Y., 14 pp. [343]
343 GOODHUE, L. D. (1960). New techniques for screening cockroach repellents. *J. econ. Ent.*, **53** (5), 805–810. [159, 161, 497]
344 GOODHUE, L. D. & HOWELL, D. E. (1960). Repellents and attractants in pest control operations. *Pest Control*, **28** (8), 44, 46, 48, 50. [160]
345 GOODHUE, L. D. & TISSOL, G. L. (1952). Determining the repellent action of chemicals to the American cockroach. *J. econ. Ent.*, **45** (1), 133–134. [159, 496]
346 GORDON, H. T. & ELDEFRAWI, M. E. (1960). Analog-synergism of several carbamate insecticides. *J. econ. Ent.*, **53** (6), 1004–1009. [365, 381]
347 GORHAM, J. R. (1962). Insecticide resistance-susceptibility tests with German cockroaches (*Blattella germanica* Linnaeus) in Puerto Rico. *J. agric. Univ. P. Rico*, **46**, 219–225. [439]
348 GOTO, M. (1971). Organochlorine compounds in the environment in Japan. In: Tahori, A. S. (Ed.)., *Int. Symp. Pesticide Terminal Residues, Tel Aviv, Israel*, Butterworths, London, pp. 105–110. [291]
349 GOULD, G. E. (1943). Recent developments in roach control. *Pests*, **11** (12), 12–13, 22–24. [95, 195, 475]
350 GOULD, G. E. (1945). Roach control tests. *Soap, N.Y.*, **21** (2), 113–115, 121. [196]
351 GOULD, G. E. (1948). The newer insecticides against roaches. *Soap, N.Y.*, **24** (3), 147, 149, 177, 179. [200, 201]
352 GOULD, G. E. & DEAY, H. O. (1938). The biology of the American cockroach. *Ann. ent. Soc. Am.*, **31**, 489–498. [471]

353 GOULD, G. E. & DEAY, H. O. (1940). The biology of six species of cockroaches which inhabit buildings. *Bull. No. 451, Agric. Exp. Sta., Purdue Univ.* [463]
354 GOULDING, R. (1975). Pesticide safety and fail-safe precautions. *Proc. 4th Br. Pest Control Ass. Conf., Jersey*, Paper No. 3, 3 pp. [139]
355 GRADIDGE, J. M. G. (1960). Resistance of *Blattella germanica* to dieldrin. *Pest Technol.*, **2**, 229. [447]
356 GRAYSON, J. M. (1951). Response of the German cockroach to sublethal concentrations of DDT and benzene hexachloride. *J. econ. Ent.*, **44** (3), 315–317. [288, 430]
357 GRAYSON, J. M. (1953). Effects on the German cockroach of twelve generations of selection for survival to treatments with DDT and benzene hexachloride. *J. econ. Ent.*, **46** (1), 124–127. [431]
358 GRAYSON, J. M. (1954). Differences between a resistant and a non-resistant strain of the German cockroach. *J. econ. Ent.*, **47** (2), 253–256. [295, 296, 432]
359 GRAYSON, J. M. (1960). Insecticidal resistance and control in cockroaches. *Misc. Publs, ent. Soc. Am.*, **2** (1), 55–58. [438, 439]
360 GRAYSON, J. M. (1961). Resistance to diazinon in the German Cockroach. *Bull. Wld Hlth Org.*, **24**, 563–565. [439, 440, 441]
361 GRAYSON, J. M. (1963). Further selection of normal and chlordane-resistant German cockroaches for resistance to malathion and diazinon. *J. econ. Ent.*, **56** (4), 447–449. [441]
362 GRAYSON, J. M. (1965). Resistance to insecticides in cockroaches. *Proc. XIIIth. Int. Congr. Ent., Lond.*, 501. [442]
363 GRAYSON, J. M. (1965). Resistance to three organophosphorus insecticides in strains of the German cockroach in Texas. *J. econ. Ent.*, **58** (5), 956–958. [442, 443]
364 GRAYSON, J. M. (1966). Results of 1965 NPCA-sponsored research at VPI on cockroach control. *Pest Control*, **34** (6), 12–15. [382, 443, 495]
365 GRAYSON, J. M. (1970). V.P.I. research on cockroach control. *Pest Control*, **38** (2), 31–35. [367, 370, 495]
366 GRAYSON, J. M. (1972). Co-operative VPI-NPCA Project—1971 roach control research. *Pest Control*, **40** (2), 30–33. [357]
367 GRAYSON, J. M. (1974). '73 Cockroach control research: co-operation VPI-NPCA project. *Pest Control*, **42** (2), 32, 34, 37. [446]
368 GRAYSON, J. M. & COCHRAN, D. G. (1955). On the nature of insect resistance to insecticides. *Virg. J. Sci.*, **6** (N.S.) (3), 134–145. [431]
369 GRAYSON, J. M. & COCHRAN, D. G. (1968). The phenomenon of cross resistance in insects: empirical, theoretical and genetical considerations. *Wld Rev. Pest Control*, **7** (4), 172–174. [427]
370 GRAYSON, J. M. & MESSERSMITH, D. H. (1959). Latest on resistant roach control research at VPI. *Pest Control*, **27** (2), 26–27. [365, 437]
371 GRAYSON, J. M. & PERKINS, B. D. (1960). Results of 1959 cockroach control tests at VPI. *Pest Control*, **28** (6), 9, 11, 58. [366]
372 GRAYSON, J. M. & TOWNSEND, H. G. (1962). Results of recent cockroach control tests at VPI. *Pest Control*, **30** (6), 14, 16, 18. [337]
373 GREEN, A. A., KANE, J. & TYLER, P. S. (1961). Field experiments on the control of dieldrin-resistant cockroaches. *Sanitarian*, **70** (1), 3–7. [447, 448]
374 GREEN, A. A., TYLER, P. S. & ROBBINS, B. (1969). Insecticides. *Pest Infestation Research* 1968, 47–48. [381]
375 GREEN, L. R. & DOROUGH, H. W. (1968). House fly age as a factor in their response to certain carbamates. *J. econ. Ent.*, **61** (1), 88–90. [363]
376 GREEN, M. J. (1973). Outdoor infestation of cockroaches. *Environ. Hlth*, **81** (1), 16–17. [34]
377 GRIFFIN, C. S. (1973). Mammalian toxicology of pyrethrum. *Pyrethrum Post*, **12** (3), 50–58. [251]
378 GRIFFITHS, J. T. & TAUBER, O. E. (1943). Evaluation of sodium fluoride as a stomach poison and as a contact insecticide against the roach, *Periplaneta americana* L. *J. econ. Ent.*, **36** (4), 536–540. [202, 203, 204]

379 GROTHAUS, R. H., SULLIVAN, W. N., SCHECHTER, M. S. & COX, E. L. (1972). Resmethrin odor, performance improved. *Soap, N.Y.*, **48** (9), 54, 56, 58. [272]
380 GUNTER, F. A., BLINN, R. C., CARMAN, G. E. & METCALF, R. L. (1954). Mechanisms of insecticidal action. The structural topography theory and DDT-type compounds. *Archs. Biochem.*, **50**, 504–505. [398]
381 GUPTA, A. P. (1972). German cockroach and non-lethal dose of DDT. *Pest Control*, **40** (6), 22, 24. [289]
382 GUPTA, A. P. & DAS, Y. T. (1974). Orthene against German and American cockroaches. *Pest Control*, **42** (1), 15–16. [323]
383 GUPTA, A. P., DAS, Y. T., GUSCIORA, W. R., ADAM, D. S. & JARGOWSKY, L. (1975). Effectiveness of 3 spray-dust combinations and the significance of 'correction treatment' and community education in the control of German cockroaches in an inner-city area. *Pest Control*, **43** (7), 28, 30–33. [55]
384 GUPTA, A. P., DAS, Y. T., TROUT, J. R., GUSCIORA, W. R., ADAM, D. S. & BORDASH, G. J. (1973). Effectiveness of spray-dust-bait combination and the importance of sanitation in the control of German cockroaches in an inner-city area. *Pest Control*, **41** (9), 20–26, 58–62. [55]
385 GUPTA, M. R. RADHAKRISHNAMURTY, R. & MAJUMDER, S. K. (1972). Digestion and distribution of tricalcium phosphate in the cockroach, *Periplaneta americana* Linnaeus. *Indian J. Ent.*, **34** (1), 46–49. [195]
386 GUTHRIE, F. E. (1950). Effect of temperature on toxicity of certain organic insecticides. *J. econ. Ent.*, **43** (4), 559–560. [290, 390, 401, 410]
387 GYSIN, H. (1954). Uber einige neue insektizide. *Chimia*, **8**, 205–220. [363]
388 HAAS, G. (1965). Thirty months' experience with Baygon at the zoological garden, Wuppertal. *Pflanzenschutz Nachr.*, **18** (2), 82–92. [381]
389 HABER, V. R. (1919). Cockroach pests in Minnesota with special reference to the German Cockroach. *Minnesota agric. Exp. Sta. Bull.*, **186**, 3–16. [18]
390 HADAWAY, A. B. & BARLOW, F. (1951). Studies on aqueous suspensions of insecticides. *Bull. ent. Res.*, **41**, 603–622. [77]
391 HADAWAY, A. B., BARLOW, F. & TURNER, C. R. (1970). The effect of particle size on the contact toxicity of insecticides to adult mosquitoes. *Bull. ent. Res.*, **60**, 17–21. [77]
392 HAINES, T. W. & PALMER, E. C. (1955). Studies on distribution and habitat of cockroaches in South western Georgia. *Am. J. Trop. Med. Hyg.*, **4** (6), 1131–1134. [475]
393 HALLER, H. L., LAFORGE, F. B. & SULLIVAN, W. N. (1942). Effect of sesamin and related compounds on the insecticidal action of pyrethrum on houseflies. *J. econ. Ent.*, **35** (2), 247–248. [241]
394 HARDY, J. L. (1970). Laboratory tests on dursban 2E insecticide in combination with synergised pyrethrum for the control of German cockroaches. *Down to Earth*, **26** (2), 27–30. [343]
395 HARRIS, R. L. & FRAZAR, E. D. (1968). A device for immobilizing insects with cooled air. *J. econ. Ent.*, **61** (6), 1755–1756. [470]
396 HARTLEY, J. B. & BROWN, A. W. A. (1955). The effects of certain insecticides on the cholinesterase of the American cockroach. *J. ecøn. Ent.*, **48** (3), 265–269. [410]
397 HARTLEY, G. S. & WEST, T. F. (1969). *Chemicals for pest control*. Pergamon Press, 316 pp. [96]
398 HARTZELL, A. (1945). Histological effects of certain sprays and activators on the nerves and muscles of the housefly. *Contr. Boyce Thompson Inst. Pl. Res.*, **13**, 443. [394]
399 HARTZELL, A. & SCUDDER, H. I. (1942). Histological effects of pyrethrum and an activator on the central nervous system of the housefly. *J. econ. Ent.*, **35** (3), 428–433. [394]
400 HARTZELL, A. & WEXLER, E. (1946). Histological effects of sesamin on the brain and muscles of the housefly. *Contr. Boyce Thompson Inst. Pl. Res.*, **14**, 123. [394]
401 HARVEY, G. T. & BROWN, A. W. A. (1951). The effect of insecticides on the rate of oxygen consumption in *Blattella*. *Can. J. Zool.*, **29** (1), 42–53. [304, 404, 410]
402 HASKINS, K. P. F. (1962). A new system for rearing the American cockroach.

Entomologist, 95 (1184), 27–29. [462]
403 HAWKES, C. (1974). Experiments with chlordecone in the formulation of baits for cockroach control. Int. Pest Control, 16 (3), 12–17. [103, 313, 314, 315]
404 HAWKINS, W. B. & STERNBURG, J. (1964). Some chemical characteristics of a DDT-induced neuroactive substance from cockroaches and crayfish. J. econ. Ent., 57 (2), 241–247. [407]
405 HAYASHI, A. (1968). Studies on the increment of efficacy of insecticides. (V). Effect of synergists on the respiration of American cockroach, Periplaneta americana L. Jap. J. Sanit. Zool., 19 (4), 263–264. [391]
406 HAYASHI, A. (1972). Pouvoir insecticide de pyréthroïdes synthétiques. Parasitica, 28 (4), 111–120. [277]
407 HAYASHI, A. (1973). Studies on the increment of efficacy of insecticides. (Part XII). On the effects of combining two pyrethroids. Botyu-Kagaku, 39 (1), 10–12. [277]
408 HAYASHI, A. & HATSUKADE, M. (1966). A method of testing cockroach repellents. Jap. J. Sanit. Zool., 17 (1), 68–70. [497]
409 HAYASHI, M. & MATSUMURA, F. (1967). Insecticide mode of action. Effect of dieldrin on ion movement in the nervous system of Periplaneta americana and Blattella germanica cockroaches. J. agric. Fd Chem., 15 (4), 622–627. [309, 411, 450]
410 HAYASHI, M. & MATSUMURA, F. (1967). Interactions of DDT with the nervous system of resistant and susceptible German cockroaches. Nature, Lond., 215, 1510–1512. [444]
411 HAYASHI, A. & TANAKA, T. (1973). A study of the insecticidal activity of d-trans-allethrin. Botyu-Kagaku, 38 (1), 29–32. [260]
412 HAYES, W. J. (1960). Pesticides in relation to public health. A. Rev. Ent., 5, 379–404. [144]
413 HAYES, W. J. (1964). Occurrence of poisoning by pesticides. Archs Environ. Hlth, 9, 621–625. [140]
414 HAYES, W. J. (1967). Toxicity of pesticides to man: risks from present levels. Proc. R. Soc. (B), 167, 101–127. [140]
415 HAYES, W. J. & PIRKLE, C. I. (1966). Mortality from pesticides in 1961. Archs Environ. Hlth, 12, 43–55. [140]
416 HAYES, W. J., QUINBY, G. E., WALKER, K. C., ELLIOTT, J. W. & UPHOLT, W. M. (1958). Storage of DDT and DDE in people with different degrees of exposure to DDT. Archs ind. Hlth, 18, 398–406. [142]
417 HAYES, W. P. & LIU, Y-S. (1947). Tarsal chemoreceptors of the housefly and their possible relation to DDT toxicity. Ann. ent. Soc. Am., 40 (3), 401–416. [76]
418 HAZLETON, L. W. & HOLLAND, E. G. (1953). Toxicity of malathion: summary of mammalian investigations. Archs ind. Hyg., 8, 399–405. [342]
419 HEAL, R. E. (1942). Bloodstream of the American cockroach as an indication of the relative toxicity of insecticides. Doctorate Thesis, Rutgers Univ. [288]
420 HEAL, R. E. (1971). The American pattern of legislation. Proc. 3rd Br. Pest Control Ass. Conf., Jersey, Paper No. 2, 2 pp. [150]
421 HEAL, R. E. & MENUSAN, H. (1948). A technique for the bloodstream injection of insects and its application in tests of certain insecticides. J. econ. Ent., 41 (4), 535–543. [202, 204, 486]
422 HEAL, R. E., NASH, K. B. & WILLIAMS, M. (1953). An insecticide-resistant strain of the German cockroach from Corpus Christi, Texas. J. econ. Ent., 46 (2), 385–387. [423, 427, 430]
423 HESLOP, J. P. & RAY, J. W. (1959). The reaction of the cockroach Periplaneta americana to bodily stress and DDT. J. Insect Physiol., 3, 395–401. [405]
424 HEWLETT, P. S. (1952). Piperonyl butoxide as a constituent of heavy-oil sprays for the control of stored product insects. I. Piperonyl butoxide as a synergist for pyrethrum and its effect on the persistence of pyrethrum films. Bull. ent. Res., 42, 293–310. [236]
425 HEWLETT, P. S. (1968). Synergism and potentiation in insecticides. Chemy Ind., Issue 22, 701–706. [235, 236]
426 HIGHLAND, H. A. & MERRIT, P. H. (1973). Synthetic pyrethroids as package treatments to prevent insect penetration. J. econ. Ent., 66 (2), 540–541. [157]

427 HILL, E. G., FISHWICK, F. B. & THOMPSON, R. H. (1973). Pesticide residues in foodstuffs in Great Britain: organochlorine residues in imported cereals, nuts, pulses and animal foodstuffs. *Pestic. Sci.*, **4**, 33–39. [142]
428 HIMEL, C. M. (1974). Analytical methodology in ULV. *Br. Crop Prot. Counc. Monogr.*, No. 11, 8 pp. [120]
429 HINE, C. H., HALL, F. B. & TURKEL, H. W. (1968). Forensic toxicology and the practicing physician. *Clin. Toxicol.*, **1**, 71–80. [299]
430 HIRAKOSO, S. (1962). A record of colony of German cockroaches resistant to lindane and dieldrin in Japan. *Jap. J. exp. Med.*, **32** (2), 207–210. [438]
431 HOCKENYOS, G. L. (1933). The mechanism of absorption of sodium fluoride by roaches. *J. econ. Ent.*, **26** (6), 1162–1169. [202, 203]
432 HOCKENYOS, G. L. (1933). Effect of dusts on the Oriental cockroach. *J. econ. Ent.*, **26** (4), 792–794. [205]
433 HOCKENYOS, G. L. (1936). Mechanism of absorption of pyrethrum powder by roaches. *J. econ. Ent.*, **29** (2), 433–437. [203, 231, 232]
434 HOCKENYOS G. L. (1939). Factors influencing the absorption of sodium fluoride by the American roach. *J. econ. Ent.*, **32** (6), 843–848. [203]
435 HOLAN, G. (1969). New halocyclopropane insecticides and the mode of action. *Nature, Lond.*, **221**, 1025–1029. [409]
436 HOLT, J. J. H. (1916). The cockroach: its destruction and dispersal. A comparison of insecticides and methods. *Lancet*, **190**, 1136–1137. [192, 196]
437 HOLZHACKER, E. L. & GIANNOTTI, O. (1967). Involvement of suboesophageal ganglion on the symptoms caused by DDT in the cockroach *Periplaneta americana* L. *Arq. Inst. Biol. S. Paulo*, **34** (3), 213–222. [407, 408]
438 HOOPER, G. H. S. (1969). Toxicology and physiology of DDT resistance in the German cockroach. *J. econ. Ent.*, **62** (4), 846–849. [449]
439 HOOPER, G. H. S. & GOWARD, J. L. (1968). Resistance to insecticides in some Australian populations of *Blattella germanica* (L.). *Univ. Queensland Papers, St. Lucia*, **2** (5), 85–100. [445]
440 HOPF, H. S. (1952). Studies in the mode of action of insecticides. I. Injection experiments on the role of cholinesterase inhibition. *Ann. appl. Biol.*, **39**, 193–204. [415]
441 HOPKINS, D. P. (1971). Pesticides. *Manuf. Chem. Aerosol News*, **42** (7), 62–63. [145]
442 HOPKINS, L. O. & MACIVER, D. R. (1965). Tropital—a new synergist for pyrethrins. *Pyrethrum Post*, **8** (2), 3–5. [239]
443 HOPKINS, T. L., RAO, N. R. & AMEEL, J. T. (1970). Physiological effects of parathion on the cockroach gut in vivo and correlation with external symptoms of poisoning. *J. econ. Ent.*, **63** (4), 1086–1091. [418]
444 HOSKINS, W. M., MISKUS, R. & ELDEFRAWI, M. E. (1958). In: Pan American Sanitary Organisation and seminar on the susceptibility of insects to insecticides. Panama, Washington D.C. p. 239. [449]
445 HOYLE, G. (1953). Potassium ions and insect nerve muscle. *J. exp. Biol.*, **30**, 121–135. [415]
446 HUNT, E. G. (1966). Biological magnification of pesticides. *Symp. Sci. Aspects Pest Control, Nat. Acad. Sci., Wash., Publs* 1402, 251–262. [286]
447 HUSAIN, S. & FISK, F. W. (1955). Comparison of certain organic insecticides as sprays or baits against *Blattella germanica* (L.). *J. econ. Ent.*, **48** (5), 576–578. [309]
448 HUTZEL, J. M. (1942). The activating effect of pyrethrum upon the German cockroach. *J. econ. Ent.*, **35** (6), 929–933. [388]
449 HUTZEL, J. M. (1942). Action of pyrethrum upon the German cockroach. *J. econ. Ent.*, **35** (6), 933–937. [389]
451 IHNDRIS, R. W. & SULLIVAN, W. N. (1958). Laboratory fumigation tests of organic compounds. *J. econ. Ent.*, **51** (5), 638–639. [329]
452 IKEDA, Y. (1959). Insect control chemistry. *Botyu-Kagaku*, **24**, 83–86. [497]
453 IKEDA, Y. & KONDO, M. (1961). A method of determining the effectiveness of roach repellent and the efficiency of certain repellents to female German cockroaches, *Blattella germanica* L. *Botyu-Kagaku*, **26**, 112–116. [497]

454 INCHO, H. H. (1970). New insecticide for aerosols. *Soap, N.Y.,* **46** (2), 37–40, 68–69, 72. [267]
455 INCHO, H. H. & ODENEAL, J. F. (1963). A study of two new synergists for pyrethrins, allethrin. *Pyrethrum Post,* **7** (2), 37–43. [240]
456 INGLE, L. (1965). *A monograph on chlordane: toxicological and pharmacological properties.* U.S.A., 88 pp. [308]
457 ISHII, S. (1970). An aggregation pheromone of the German cockroach, *Blattella germanica* (L.). *Appl. Ent. Zool.,* **5** (1), 33–41. [172, 280]
458 ISHII, S. & KUWAHARA, Y. (1967). An aggregation pheromone of the German cockroach *Blattella germanica* L. (Orthoptera: Blattellidae). *Appl. Ent. Zool.,* **2** (4), 203–217. [172]
459 ISHII, T. & SHERMAN, M. (1965). Resistance of a Hawaiian strain of the German cockroach to several insecticides. *J. econ. Ent.,* **58** (1), 46–50. [441, 445]
460 JACKSON, W. B. & MAIER, P. P. (1955). Dispersion of marked American cockroaches from sewer manholes in Phoenix, Arizona. *Am. J. trop. Med. Hyg.,* **4** (1), 141–146. [473]
461 JACKSON, W. B. & MAIER, P. P. (1961). Additional studies of dispersion patterns of American cockroaches from sewer manholes in Phoenix, Arizona. *Ohio J. Sci.,* **61** (4), 220–226. [473]
462 JACOBSON, M., BEROZA, M. & JONES, W. A. (1960). Isolation, identification and synthesis of the sex attractant of Gypsy moth. *Science, N.Y.,* **132**, 1011–1012. [102]
463 JACOBSON, M. & CROSBY, D. G. (1971). *Naturally occurring insecticides.* Dekker, N. Y., 585 pp. [253]
464 JAGER, K. W. (1970). *Aldrin, dieldrin and telodrin: an epidemiological and toxicological study of long-term occupational exposure.* Elsevier: Amst., Lond., N.Y., 233 pp. [311, 312]
465 JARVIS, F. E. & GRAYSON, J. M. (1957). Residual effectiveness of insecticide formulations in killing resistant and non-resistant German cockroaches. *J. econ. Ent.,* **50** (5), 604–605. [494]
466 JARVIS, F. E., GRAYSON, J. M. & LEVITAN, M. (1957). Further evidence for autosomal, multiple-factor inheritance of chlordane resistance in the German cockroach. *J. econ. Ent.,* **50** (2), 185–187. [441]
467 JENKINS, D. L., TAYLOR, J. M. & BLOW, D. P. (1975). Permanence and repellency action of insecticides in relation to pest control operations. *Proc. 4th Br. Pest Control Ass., Conf., Jersey,* Paper 15. [179, 181]
468 JOHNSON, C. W. & YOUNG, W. W. (1971). Insecticide resistance in natural populations of German cockroaches from the Third United States Army area. *J. econ. Ent.,* **64** (2), 450–451. [446]
469 JOHNSTON, L., PARSONS, R. E. & BURDEN, G. S. (1964). Malathion resistance in a field strain of German cockroaches. *Pest Control,* **32** (6), 34. [442]
470 JUNG, R. C. & SHAFFER, M. F. (1952). Survival of ingested *Salmonella* in the cockroach *Periplaneta americana. Am. J. trop. Med. Hyg.,* **1**, 990–998. [472]
471 KARTMAN, L., TANADA, Y., HOLDAWAY, F. G. & ALICATA, J. E. (1950). Laboratory tests to determine the efficiency of certain insecticides in the control of arthropods inhabiting poultry manure. *Poult. Sci.,* **29** (3), 336–346. [494]
472 KASA, P. (1968). Acetylcholinesterase transport in the central and peripheral nervous tissue: the role of tubules in the enzyme transport. *Nature, Lond.,* **218** (5148), 1265–1267. [412]
473 KATZ, A. J., COLLINS, W. J. & SKAVARIL, R. V. (1973). Resistance in the German cockroach (Orthoptera: Blattellidae): the inheritance of diazinon resistance and cross-resistance. *J. med. Ent.,* **10** (6), 599–604. [446]
474 KEARNS, C. W., INGLE, L. & METCALF, R. L. (1945). A new chlorinated hydrocarbon insecticide. *J. econ. Ent.,* **38**, 661–668. [301]
475 KEARNS, C. W., WEINMAN, C. J. & DECKER, G. C. (1949). Insecticidal properties of some new chlorinated organic compounds. *J. econ. Ent.,* **42** (1), 127–134. [309]
476 KEIDING, J. (1964). Resistance to dieldrin in cockroaches. *A. Rep. Govt. Pest Infestation*

Lab., Springforbi, Denmark, 1963, 44. [441]
477 KELLER, J. C., CLARK, P. H. & LOFGREN, C. S. (1956) Susceptibility of insecticide-resistant cockroaches to pyrethrins I. *Pest Control*, **24** (11), 14–15, 30. [241]
478 KELLER, J. C., CLARK, P. H., LOFGREN, C. S. & WILSON, H. G. (1956) Cockroach control. Results of USDA-sponsored research tests on cockroach control. *Pest Control.*, **24** (9), 12, 14, 17, 19–20. [269, 429, 433, 434, 487]
479 KELLER, J. C. & LIANG, T. T. (1962). The acute oral toxicities of some insecticides to American cockroaches. *J. econ. Ent.*, **55** (1), 144–145. [288, 289]
480 KENAGA, E. E., DOTY, A. E. & HARDY, J. L. (1962). Laboratory insecticidal tests with dimethylamino-3,5-xylyl methylcarbamate. *J. econ. Ent.*, **55** (4), 466–469. [381]
481 KENAGA, E. E., WHITNEY, W. K., HARDY, J. L. & DOTY, A. E. (1965). Laboratory tests with dursban insecticide. *J. econ. Ent.*, **58** (6), 1043–1050. [344]
482 KENT, N. L. & McCANCE, R. A. (1941). The absorption and excretion of 'minor' elements by man. I. Silver, gold, lithium, boron and vanadium. *Biochem J.*, **35**, 837–844. [194]
483 KITAGAKI, T., NAKAYAMA, I., SUGIYAMA, S. & SAKAMOTO, A. (1973). Effectiveness of Dowco-214 on some insects of public health importance. I. Laboratory evaluation tests for cockroaches. *Jap. J. Sanit. Zool.*, **24** (1), 9–15. [345, 346]
484 KLINGER, H. (1936). Die insektizide Wirkung von Pyrethrum-und Derrisgiften und ihre Abhängigkeit vom Insektenkörper. *Arb. Physiol. angew. Ent. Berlin-Dahlem*, **3** (1), 49–69; (2), 115–151. [230]
485 KLOSTERMEYER, E. C. (1943). Roach powders. *Soap, N.Y.*, **19** (2), 98–99, 109. [196]
486 KOLBEZEN, M., METCALF, R. L. & FUKUTO, T. R. (1954). Insecticidal activity of carbamate cholinesterase inhibitors. *J. agric. Fd Chem.*, **2** (17), 864–870. [363]
487 KOOISHA, G. (1950). Contribution to the knowledge of the action of acetylcholine in the intestine of *Periplaneta americana* L. *Physiologia comp. Oecol.*, **2**, 75–80. [418]
488 KOSHY, T. & MALLIK, D. (1968). An improved method for rearing and maintaining large colonies of American cockroaches in the laboratory. *J. econ. Ent.*, **61** (6), 1748–1750. [463]
489 KRUEGER, H. R., O'BRIEN, R. D. & DAUTERMAN, W. C. (1960). Relationship between metabolism and differential toxicity in insects and mice to diazinon, dimethoate, parathion and acethion. *J. econ. Ent.*, **53** (1), 25–31. [326]
490 KU, T-Y. & Bishop, J. L. (1967). Penetration, excretion and metabolism of carbaryl in susceptible and resistant German cockroaches. *J. econ. Ent.*, **60** (5), 1328–1332. [444, 445]
491 KURIHARA, N., NAKAJIMA, E. & Shindo, H. (1970). Whole body autoradiographic studies on the distribution of BHC and nicotine in the American cockroach. In: O'Brien & Yamamoto (Eds.), *Biochemical toxicology of insecticides.* Academic Press, pp. 41–50. [410]
492 KURIHARA, N., UCHIDA, M., FUJITA, T. & NAKAJIMA, M. (1974). Studies on BHC isomers and related compounds. VI. Penetration and translocation of BHC isomers in the cockroach and their correlation with physicochemical properties. *Pestic. Biochem. Physiol.*, **4**, 12–18. [293]
493 LAAKE, E. W. & WILLIAMSON, B. (1955). German roach resistance in Texas. *Pest Control*, **23** (5), 26. [433]
494 LAING, F. (1946). The cockroach, it's life history and how to deal with it. *Br. Mus. (Nat. Hist.) Econ. Series* No. 12, 28 pp. [20]
495 LALONDE, D. I. V. & BROWN, A. W. A. (1954). The effect of insecticides on the action potentials of insect nerve. *Can. J. Zool.*, **32**, 74–81. [304, 412]
496 LEE, J. (1969). Aerosol insecticide formulations—review of recent developments. *Pyrethrum Post*, **10** (2), 9–13. [239]
497 LEHMAN, A. J. (1952). Chemicals in foods: A report to the Association of Food & Drug Officials on current developments. *Q. Bull. Ass. Fd Drug Off., U.S.*, **16**, 85–91. [297]
498 LEMON, R. W. (1971). 2,2-dimethyl-1,3-benzodioxol-4-yl N-methylcarbamate: a new broad spectrum experimental insecticide. *Proc. 6th Br. insectic. fungic. Conf.*, pp. 570–576. [367]

499 LE PELLEY, R. H. (1973). The start of pyrethrum growing in Kenya. *Pyrethrum Post,* **12** (1), 32. [220]
500 LEVER, R. J. A. W. (1943). Entomological notes: cockroaches and their control in households. *Agric. J. Fiji,* **14** (2), 40–41. [198]
501 LHOSTE, J., LAMBERT, J. & RAUCH, F. (1967). Etude de l'action insecticide du d-*trans*-chrysanthemate de dl-allethrolone sur *Musca domestica. C.r. hebd. Séanc. Acad. Agric. Fr.,* 31 mai, 686–691. [265]
502 LHOSTE, J., MARTEL, J. & RAUCH, F. (1970). A new insecticide 5-benzyl 3-furylmethyl d-*trans* ethanochrysanthemate. *Proc. 5th Br. insectic. fungic. Conf.,* **2**, 554–557. [276]
503 LHOSTE, J. & RAUCH, F. (1969). Remarques sur quelques chrysanthémates insecticides de synthèse. *Revue Zool. agric. path. veget.,* **68** (4–6), 53–66. [276, 279]
504 LHOSTE, J., RAUCH, F. & LAMBERT, J. (1968). Action du d-*trans* chrysanthemate de dl-allethrolone sur quelques insectes. *Phytiatrie-Phytopharmacie,* **2**, 143–150. [260, 263, 264, 266]
505 LINDQUIST, D. A. & DAHM, P. A. (1956). Metabolism of radioactive DDT by the Madeira roach and European corn borer. *J. econ. Ent.,* **49** (5), 579–584. [399, 400]
506 LINTNER, J. A. (1882). First annual report on the injurious and other insects of the State of New York, Albany. [191]
507 LIVADES, G. A. & GEORGOPOULOS, M. D. (1953). Development of resistance to DDT by *Anopheles sacharovi* in Greece. *Bull. Wld Hlth Org.,* **8**, 497–511. [423]
508 LOFGREN, C. S. & BURDEN, G. S. (1958). Tests with poison baits against cockroaches. *Florida Ent.,* **41** (3), 103–110. [104, 357, 359]
509 LOFGREN, C. S., BURDEN, G. S. & CLARK, P. H. (1957). Experiments with insecticides for the control of German roaches. *Pest Control,* **25** (7), 9, 10, 12, 47. [304, 305, 306, 307, 435, 457]
510 LOWENSTEIN, O. (1942). A method of physiological assay of pyrethrum extract. *Nature, Lond.,* **150** (3817), 760–762. [396, 397]
511 MACCUAIG, R. D. & WATTS, W. S. (1968). A simple technique for applying small measured quantities of insecticides to insects. *Bull. ent. Res.,* **57** (4), 549–551. [482]
512 MACDONALD, B. C. & HUVAR, A. J. (1961). Kepone—the pelleted ant and roach bait. *Pest Control,* **29** (10), 62, 64. [103, 313]
513 MACIVER, D. R. (1966). The development of tropital, a polyalkoxy acetal of piperonaldehyde as a potent synergist for pyrethrins. *Pyrethrum Post,* **8** (3), 3–6, 18. [239]
514 MACIVER, D. R. (1971). Synthetic pyrethrins. *Nature, Lond.,* **234** (5324), 113. [279]
515 MACQUILLAN, M. J. (1975). Influence of crystal size and size of insect on the toxicity to ants of insecticidal residual deposits. *J. econ. Ent.,* **68** (2), 143–144. [95]
516 MAGEE, P. N. (1970). Toxicology and certainty. *New Scientist,* **46** (696), 61–62. [133]
517 MAHAN, J. G. & GRAYSON, J. M. (1956). Morphological comparisons of resistant and non-resistant strains of the German cockroach, *Blattella germanica* (L.). *Virg. J. Sci.,* **7** (NS), (3), 166–169. [435]
518 MALLIS, A. (1972). Household insecticides: past, present and future. *Soap, N.Y.,* **48** (3), 44, 46, 120. [150]
519 MALLIS, A., ESTERLIN, W. C. & ASTOR, R. J. (1966). Resistance in a large cockroach, *Periplaneta brunnea* Burmeister in Florida. *Pest Control,* **34** (6), 22. [443]
520 MALLIS, A., ESTERLIN, W. C. & MILLER, A. C. (1961). Keeping German cockroaches out of beer cases. *Pest Control,* **29** (6), 32–35. [160, 168]
521 MAMPE, C. D. (1972). The relative importance of household insects in the continental United States. *Pest Control,* **40** (12), 24–27, 38. [13, 58]
522 MANSINGH, A. (1965). Water loss in malathion-intoxicated German cockroaches. *J. econ. Ent.,* **58** (1), 162–163. [341, 342]
523 MANSINGH, A. (1965). Cholinesterase activity of susceptible and resistant strains of malathion-poisoned German cockroaches. *J. econ. Ent.,* **58** (3), 580–581. [451, 452]
524 MARCOVITCH, S. & STANLEY, W. W. (1942). Fluorine compounds useful in the control of insects. *Univ. Tennessee agric. Sta. Tech. Bull.,* 182. [198, 200, 201, 203]
525 MARKKULA, M. (1969). Pesticide regulations in Finland. *Span,* **12** (2), 100–102. [147]

526 MARKKULA, M. & TIITTANEN, K. (1970). Prevalence of bed bugs, cockroaches and human fleas in Finland. *Ann. ent. Finn.*, **36** (2), 99–107. [60]
527 MARLATT, C. L. (1896). Cockroaches and ants. *U.S. Dept. agric. Div. Ent. Circ.*, **4** (NS), 84–99. [211]
528 MARLATT, C. L. (1908). Cockroaches. *U.S. Dept. agric. Div. Ent. Circ.*, No. 51. [14, 18, 20]
529 MARTIN, H. (1946). Insecticides: chemical constitution and toxicity. *J. Soc. chem. Ind., Lond.*, **65**, 402–405. [399]
530 MATSUMURA, F. (1963). The permeability of the cuticle of *Periplaneta americana* L. to malathion. *J. Insect Physiol.*, **9**, 207–221. [341]
531 MATSUMURA, F. & BROWN, A. W. A. (1963). Studies on carboxyesterase in malathion-resistant *Culex tarsalis*. *J. econ. Ent.*, **56** (3), 381–388. [427]
532 MATSUMURA, F. & HAYASHI, M. (1966). Dieldrin: interaction with nerve components of cockroaches. *Science, N.Y.*, **153**, 757–759. [450]
533 MATSUMURA, F. & HAYASHI, M. (1969). Dieldrin resistance: biochemical mechanisms in the German cockroach. *J. agric. Fd Chem.*, **17** (2), 231–235. [450, 451]
534 MATSUMURA, F. & O'BRIEN, R. D. (1966). Interactions of DDT with components of American cockroach nerve. *J. agric. Fd Chem.*, **14** (1), 39–43. [402]
535 MATSUMURA, F. & SAKAI, K. (1968). Degradation of insecticides by esterases of the American cockroach. *J. econ. Ent.*, **61** (3), 598–605. [451]
536 MATSUMURA, F., TELFORD, J. N. & HAYASHI, M. (1967). Effect of sesamex upon dieldrin resistance in the German cockroach. *J. econ. Ent.*, **60** (4), 942–944. [444]
537 MATTHEWS, G. A. (1975). Developments in ultra-low volume equipment. *Proc. 4th Br. Pest Control Ass. Conf.*, Jersey, Paper 18. [118]
538 MCCAY, C. M. & MELAMPY, R. M. (1937). Care and rearing of *Blattella germanica*. In: Lutz, F. E., Welch, P. L., Galtsoff, P. S. & Needham, J. G. *Culture methods for invertebrate animals*. Dover, pp. 283–284. [463]
539 MCCLUSKEY, R., WRIGHT, C. G. & YAMAMOTO, R. T. (1969). Effect of starvation on the responses of male American cockroaches to sex and food stimuli. *J. econ. Ent.*, **62** (6), 1465–1468. [102]
540 MCDONALD, L. L. (1968). Relative effectiveness of tropital and piperonyl butoxide as synergists for pyrethrins against stored product insects. *J. econ. Ent.*, **61** (6), 1645–1646. [230, 239]
541 MCDONALD, I. C. & COCHRAN, D. G. (1968). Carbamate cross-resistance in a carbaryl-resistant strain of the German cockroach. *J. econ. Ent.*, **61** (3), 670–673. [366, 374, 378, 446]
542 MCDONALD, I. C. & GRAYSON, J. M. (1966). Toxicity of two carbamate insecticides to resistant and normal strains of the German cockroach. *J. econ. Ent.*, **59** (6), 1407–1409. [377, 382, 443]
543 MCDUFFIE, W. C., GAHAN, J. B., KELLER, J. C. & EDDY, G. W. (1953). Insecticide-resistant insects. *Pest Control*, **21** (8), 9–10, 12, 14, 16, 18. [430]
544 MCGOVERN, T. P., BODENSTEIN, O. F., FALES, J. H. & BEROZA, M. (1974). Amides of heterocyclic amines: highly effective as repellents against four species of cockroach. *J. econ. Ent.*, **67** (5), 639–640. [159]
545 MCGOVERN, T. P., BODENSTEIN, O. F., FALES, J. H. & BEROZA, M. (1975). *N,N*-disubstituted *n*-aliphatic amides as repellents for four cockroach species. *J. med. Ent.*, **12** (2), 259–260. [159]
546 MCGOVERN, T. P., GOUCK, H. K., BURDEN, G. S., SARMIENTO, R., BEROZA, M. & SCHMIDT, C. H. (1974). *N,N*-substituted *n*-alkanesulfonamides as repellents for the yellow fever mosquito and the German cockroach. *J. econ. Ent.*, **67** (1), 71–73. [159]
547 MCGOVRAN, E. R. & FALES, J. H. (1942). Roach sprays. A preliminary report of a new laboratory method for testing. *Soap, N.Y.*, **18** (3), 101–103, 105, 107, 117. [233]
548 MCGOVRAN, E. R., FALES, J. H. & PIQUETT, P. G. (1943). The relative resistance of *Periplaneta americana* and *Blattella germanica* to pyrethrum spray. *J. econ. Ent.*, **36** (5), 732–733. [234]
549 MCGOVRAN, E. R. & PIQUETT, P. G. (1946). Roach powder tests. A comparison of the

toxicity to roaches of four common ingredients of roach powders: sodium fluoride, pyrethrum, DDT and the gamma isomer of benzene hexachloride. *Soap, N.Y.*, **22** (8), 157, 159, 181. [202, 295, 495]
550 McGovran, E. R., Phillips, G. L. & Mayer, E. L. (1940). A measured drop method of applying liquid insecticides. *U.S. Dept. agric. Bur. Ent.*, ET-165, 5 pp. [482]
551 McGovran, E. R., Richardson, H. H. & Piquett, P. G. (1944). Toxicity of DDT to bedbugs, cockroaches, the Mexican bean beetle and housefly larvae. *J. econ. Ent.*, **37** (1), 139–140. [287]
552 McLaughlin, G. A. (1973). History of Pyrethrum. In: Casida, J. E. (Ed.). *Pyrethrum—the natural insecticide*. Academic Press, Chapter 1. [219]
553 Meichsner, J., Meyer, R., Muller, P. & Reinhardt, R. (1974). Fekama-dichlorvos 50 used by self-vapourising procedure against the German cockroach. *Angew. Parasitol.*, **15** (2), 84–101. [330]
554 Melander, A. L. (1914). Can insects become resistant to sprays? *J. econ. Ent.*, **7**, 167–172. [422]
555 Mele, M. R. (1972). Factors influencing the population dynamics of the German cockroach, *Blattella germanica* (L.). *Masters Thesis, Fairleigh Dickinson Univ., Madison, N.J.* 69 pp. [467]
556 Mellanby, K. (1939). Low temperature and insect activity. *Proc. R. Soc.*, (B) **127**, 473–487. [454]
557 Mello, E. J. R., Mello, D. & Arruda, H. V. (1970). Sensibilidade de *Periplaneta americana* L. ao inseticida clorofosforado dichlorvos, nas condições de laboratôrio. *Arq. Inst. Biol., S. Paulo*, **37** (2), 85–87. [335]
558 Menusan, H. (1948). Comparative toxicity of insecticides administered in various ways to several species of insects. *J. econ. Ent.*, **41** (2), 302–313. [202, 216, 230, 233, 486]
559 Merrill, R. S., Savit, J. & Tobias, J. M. (1946). Certain biochemical changes in the DDT poisoned cockroach and their prevention by prolonged anaesthesia. *J. cell. comp. Physiol.*, **28** (3), 465–476. [403]
560 Metcalf, R. L. (1955). *Organic insecticides, their chemistry and mode of action*. Interscience, 392 pp. [283, 293]
561 Metcalf, R. L. (1955). Physiological basis for insect resistance to insecticides. *Physiol. Rev.*, **35**, 197. [437]
562 Metcalf, R. L. (1962). Meet the carbamates. *Pest Control*, **30** (5), 20, 26, 28. [362]
563 Metcalf, R. L. & Fukuto, T. R. (1965). Carbamate insecticides: effects of chemical structure on intoxication and detoxication of phenyl N-methylcarbamates in insects. *J. agric. Fd Chem.*, **13**, 220–231. [420, 448]
564 Metcalf, R. L., Winton, M. Y. & Fukuto, T. R. (1964). The effects of cholinergic substances upon the isolated heart of *Periplaneta americana*. *J. Insect Physiol.*, **10**, 353–361. [419]
565 Metzger, V. R. & Trier, K-H. (1975). Zur bedeutung der aggregations-pheromone von *Blattella germanica* und *Blatta orientalis*. *Angew. Parasitol.*, **16** (1), 16–27. [172]
566 Micks, D. W. (1960). Insecticide resistance: a review of developments in 1958 and 1959. *Bull. Wld Hlth Org.*, **22**, 519–529. [435]
567 Mielke, U. von & Schuschke, G. (1972). Erfolgreiche Schabenbekämfung in einem Großkrankenhaus durch ein fortpflanzungsbiologishes orientiertes vertragsgebundenes Bekämpfungsregime. *Hygiene Grenzgebiete*, **18**, 325–327. [71]
568 Miesch, M. D. (1964). Ecological and physiological mechanisms influencing food finding in Blattaria. *Ph.D. Thesis, Oklahoma State Univ., Stillwater, Oklahoma.* [100]
569 Miesch, M. D. & Howell, D. E. (1967). An evaluation of baits for cockroaches. *Pest Control*, **35** (6), 16, 18, 20. [99]
570 Mikalonis, S. F. & Brown, R. H. (1941). Acetylcholine and cholinesterase in the insect central nervous system. *J. cell. comp. Physiol.*, **18**, 401–403. [414]
571 Miles, J. W., Fetzer, L. E. & Pearce, G. W. (1970). Collection and determination of trace quantities of pesticides in air. *Environ. Sci. Tech.*, **4**, 420–425. [143]
572 Miller, A. C., Mallis, A. & Esterlin, W. C. (1954). A testing procedure for evaluating liquid sprays against cockroaches. *J. econ. Ent.*, **47** (1), 23–26. [480]

573 MILLER, A. C., MALLIS, A. & SHARPLESS, R. V. (1952). Aerosol insecticides: their evaluation against houseflies and cockroaches. *Soap, N.Y.*, **28** (2), 143, 145, 147, 149, 151, 153, 181. [481]
574 MILLER, D. (1973). Editorial. *Pest Control*, **41** (5), 6. [22]
575 MILWARD, A. F., RUDGE, A. J. B. & TAYLOR, J. K. (1973). The use of pesticides in bakeries. *Baking Industries J.*, **6** (2), 8–10. [23]
576 MISKUS, R. P. & ANDREWS, T. L. (1972). Stabilization of thin films of pyrethrins and allethrin. *Pyrethrum Post*, **11** (4), 135–151 [228].
577 MISSIROLI, A. (1950). The control of domestic insects in Italy. *Am. J. trop. Med.*, **30** (5), 773–783. [423]
578 MISSIROLI, A. (1951). Resistenza agli insecticide di alcune razze di *Musca domestica*. *Riv. Parasit.*, **12** (1), 5–25. [423]
579 MITLIN, N. & BABERS, F. H. (1955). Relative toxicity of topically applied allethrin and pyrethrins to houseflies and cockroaches. *J. econ. Ent.*, **48** (6), 747–748. [260]
580 MIYATA, T. & SAITO, T. (1968). Toxic properties of NS 2662 against the American cockroach and the mouse. *Botyu-Kagaku*, **33** (1), 13–21. [413]
581 MIZUNO, T. & TSUJI, H. (1974). Harbouring behaviour of three species of cockroaches, *Periplaneta americana*, *P. japonica* and *Blattella germanica*. *Jap. J. Sanit. Zool.*, **24** (3), 237–240. [172]
582 MOORE, J. B. (1950). Relative toxicity to insects of natural pyrethrins and synthetic allyl analog of cinerin I. *J. econ. Ent.*, **43** (2), 207–213. [260]
583 MOORE, J. B. (1973). In: Casida, J. E. (Ed.). *Pyrethrum—the natural insecticide*. Academic Press, pp. 293–306. [252]
584 MOORE, N. W. (1969). Reduction of pesticide hazards to wild life: an appraisal of experience gained in Britain 1960–67. *Int. Pest Control*, **11** (1), 27–31. [142]
585 MOORE, R. C. (1971). Chemical control of German cockroaches in urban apartments. *Bull. Connecticut agric. Exp. Sta.*, No. 717, 11 pp. [331]
586 MOORE, R. C. (1972). Boric acid—silica dusts for control of German cockroaches. *J. econ. Ent.*, **65** (2), 458–461. [197, 198, 208]
587 MOORE, R. C. (1973). Cockroach proofing: preventive treatments for control of cockroaches in urban housing and food service carts. *Bull. Connecticut agric. Exp. Sta.*, No. 740, 13 pp. [48, 58, 195]
588 MOOREFIELD, H. H. (1958). Synergism of the carbamate insecticides. *Contr. Boyce Thompson Inst. Pl. Res.*, **19**, 501–507. [363, 365, 414, 418]
589 MOOREFIELD, H. H. (1959). Mechanisms of resistance to chlorinated hydrocarbons. *Can. J. Biochem. Physiol.*, **37**, 1099–1103. [383, 448]
590 MORRILL, A. W. (1944). DDT as a roach poison. *J. econ. Ent.*, **37**, (1), 138. [287]
591 MORSE, A. P. (1920). Manual of the Orthoptera of New England, including the locusts, grasshoppers, crickets and their allies. *Proc. Boston Soc. nat. Hist.*, **35** (6), 197–556. [14, 58]
592 MOSNA, E. (1947). Su una carratteristica biologica del *Culex pipiens autogenicus* di Latina. *Riv. Parasit.*, **8** (23), 125–126. [423]
593 MULLINS, D. E. & COCHRAN, D. G. (1973). Tryptophan metabolite excretion by the American cockroach. *Comp. Biochem. Physiol.*, **44** (B), 549–555. [29]
594 MULRENNAN, J. A. & BURDEN, G. S. (1974). German cockroaches: evaluations for insecticide resistance in field strains. *Pest Control*, **42** (3), 21–22. [447]
595 MULRENNAN, J. A., GROTHAUS, R. H., HAMMOND, C. L. & LAMDIN, J. M. (1971). A new method of cockroach control on submarines. *J. econ. Ent.*, **64** (5), 1196–1198. [335]
596 MUNGLER, F. & SIEGLER, E. H. (1937). Insecticide tests on roaches—the poison pill and rubber collar methods for testing insecticides against the American cockroach. *Soap, N.Y.*, **13** (10), 94–97. [202, 203]
597 MUNSON, S. C. (1953). Some effects of storage at different temperatures on the resistance of the American roach to DDT. *J. econ. Ent.*, **46** (5), 754–760. [402]
598 MUNSON, S. C. & GOTTLIEB, M. I. (1953). The differences between male and female American roaches in total lipid content and in susceptibility to DDT. *J. econ. Ent.*, **46** (5), 798–802. [288, 400]

599 MUTTRIE, M. P., PAPWORTH, D. S. & TAYLOR, J. K. (1976). The use of pesticides by Local Authorities in Great Britain: April 1973 to March 1974. *R. Soc. Hlth J.* (In press). [23]
600 NAGASAWA, S. & SHIBA, M. (1964). Differential susceptibility of the sexes of the German cockroach, *Blattella germanica* L., to the lethal effect of carbaryl, with special reference to the estimation of dosage-mortality curve from individual records. *Jap. J. Sanit. Zool.*, 15 (4), 258–262. [365]
601 NAIDU, M. B. (1955). Physiological action of drugs and insecticides on insects. *Bull. ent. Res.*, 46, 205–220. [392]
602 NAKATSUGAWA, T. & DAHM, P. A. (1965). Parathion activation enzymes in the fat body microsomes of the American cockroach. *J. econ. Ent.*, 58 (3), 500–509. [418]
603 NANDA, D. K. (1974). Impact of insecticides on the brain neuroglandular elements of *Periplaneta americana*. *Naturwissenschaften*, 61 (10), 451–452. [416]
604 NARAHASHI, T. (1962). Effect of the insecticide allethrin on membrane potentials of cockroach giant axons. *J. cell. comp. Physiol.*, 59, 61–65. [258, 398]
605 NARAHASHI, T. (1962). Nature of the negative after-potential increased by the insecticide allethrin in cockroach giant axons. *J. cell. comp. Physiol.*, 59, 67–76. [258, 398]
606 NARAHASHI, T. (1963). The properties of insect axons. *Adv. Insect Physiol.*, 1, 175–256. [386]
607 NARAHASHI, T. (1971). Mode of action of pyrethroids. *Bull. Wld Hlth Org.*, 44, 337–345. [391]
608 NARAHASHI, T. (1971). Effects of insecticides on excitable tissues. *Adv. Insect Physiol.*, 8, 1–93. [402, 410]
609 NARAHASHI, T. & YAMASAKI, T. (1960). Mechanism of increase in negative after-potential by dicophanum (DDT) in the giant axons of the cockroach. *J. Physiol, Lond.*, 152, 122–140. [407]
610 NARAHASHI, T. & YAMASAKI, T. (1960). Behaviour of membrane potential in the cockroach giant axons poisoned by DDT. *J. cell. comp. Physiol.*, 55, 131–142. [407]
611 NEELY, J. M. & MATTINGLY, C. L. (1966). Control of American cockroaches, (*Periplaneta americana*) with kepone ant and cockroach paste. *Pest Control*, 34 (6), 16–17. [99]
612 NEGHERBON, W. O. (1959). *Handbook of toxicology*, Vol. III. Saunders, Philadelphia. [251, 396]
613 NELSON, J. O. & MATSUMURA, F. (1973). Dieldrin (HEOD) metabolism in cockroaches and houseflies. *Archs Environ. Contamination Toxicity*, 1 (3), 224–244. [410]
614 NEUBECKER, F. P. J. (1960). Beitrag zur Biologie von *Blaberus craniifer* Burm. (Orthoptera, Blattidae) und vergleichende Untersuchungen zum Wirkungsmechanismus der chlorierten Kohlenwasserstoffe Chlordan und Heptachlor. *Z. angew. Ent.*, 47 (3), 302–333. [412]
615 NISWANDER, R. E. & DAVIDSON, R. H. (1948). A comparison of the toxicity of some new insecticides to the German roach. *J. econ. Ent.*, 41 (4), 652–653. [201, 202, 295]
616 NOBEL-NESBITT, J. (1970). Structural aspects of penetration through insect cuticles. *Pestic. Sci.*, 1 (5), 204–208. [106]
617 NOLAND, J. L., LILLY, J. H. & BAUMANN, C. A. (1949). Vitamin requirements of the cockroach, *Blattella germanica* (L.). *Ann. ent. Soc Am.*, 42 (1), 154–164. [470]
618 N.P.C.A. (1956). Diazinon registered for PCO use against resistant roaches. *Tech. Release*, No. 1–56. [321]
619 N.P.C.A. (1961). Kepone bait registered. *Tech. Release*, No. 17–61. [98]
620 N.P.C.A. (1961). German roach resistance and control. *Tech. Release*, No. 8–61. [458]
621 N.P.C.A. (1962). Carbamate insecticides. *Tech. Release*, No. 4–62. [362]
622 N.P.C.A. (1963). Safe use of diazinon. *Tech. Release*, No. 6–63. [321]
623 N.P.C.A. (1964). Baygon (Formerly Bayer 39007). *Tech. Release*, No. 16–64. [377].
624 N.P.C.A. (1965). Insects and insecticides most important to PCO's. *Tech. Release*, No. 22–65. [13, 14]
625 N.P.C.A. (1965). Safe disposal of empty pesticide containers. *Tech. Release*, No. 23–65. [142]

626 N.P.C.A. (1966). DDVP. *Tech. Release*, No. 23–66. [329]
627 N.P.C.A. (1968). Dursban. *Tech. Release*, No. 19–68. [344]
628 N.P.C.A. (1968). Dipterex. *Tech. Release*, No. 20–68. [357]
629 N.P.C.A. (1969). 1969 Research report: new insecticides for control of resistant German cockroaches—Virginia Polytechnic Institute. *Tech. Release*, No. 21–69. [429]
630 N.P.C.A. (1969). Cockroach control as it relates to resistance. *Tech. Release*, No. 15–69. [176, 458]
631 N.P.C.A. (1970). Control of cockroaches in food carts. *Tech. Release*, No. 2–70. [71]
632 N.P.C.A. (1974) Insecticide resistance in cockroaches. *Tech. Release*, No. 4–74. [447]
633 NUTTING, W. L. (1953). Giant cockroaches of the genus *Blaberus* as laboratory animals. *Turtox News*, **31** (8), 134–137. [468]
634 O'BRIEN, R. D. (1957). Esterases in the semi-intact cockroach. *Ann. ent. Soc. Am.*, **50**, 223–229. [415]
635 O'BRIEN, R. D. (1959). Comparative toxicity of some organophosphorus compounds in insects and mammals. *Can. J. Biochem. Physiol.*, **37**, 1113–1122. [130, 141, 318, 388, 417]
636 O'BRIEN, R. D. (1961). Esterase inhibition in organophosphorus poisoning of House flies. *J. econ. Ent.*, **54** (6), 1161–1164. [414]
637 O'BRIEN, R. D. (1967). *Insecticides—action and metabolism*. Academic Press, 332 pp. [135, 309, 312, 319, 320, 386, 387, 410]
638 OGAMI, H., YOSHIDA, Y., KATSUDA, Y., MIYAMOTO, J. & KADOTA, T. (1970). Insecticidal activity of a new synthetic chrysanthemic ester, 5-propargylfurfuryl chrysanthemate (Prothrin). *Botyu-Kagaku*, **35** (2), 45–55. [277]
639 O'HANLON, S. R. (1967). Pesticides and persistence. *PANS* (C) **13** (4), 278–281. [146]
640 O'KANE, W. C., WALKER, G. L., GUY, H. G. & SMITH, O. J. (1933). Studies of contact insecticides. VI. *Tech. Bull. New Hampshire agric. Exp. Stn.*, No. 54, 23 pp. [232, 482, 485]
641 OKUNO, Y., FUJIMOTO, K., KADOTA, T., MIYAMOTO, J. & HAMURO, K. (1969). Insecticidal activity of a synthetic pyrethroidal compound, 5-benzyl-3-furylmethyl-dl-cis, trans-chrysanthemate (NRDC-104, Chryson). *Botyu-Kagaku*, **34**, 157–165. (English summary). [270, 271]
642 OKWELOGU, T. N. (1968). The toxicity of malathion applied to washed concrete. *J. stored Prod. Res.*, **4**, 259–260. [338]
643 OLSON, W. P. (1973). Dieldrin transport in the insect: an examination of Gerolt's hypothesis. *Pestic. Biochem. Physiol.*, **3** (4), 384–392. [410]
644 OLTON, G. S. (1975). Slow-release formulation shows promise. *Pest Control*, **43** (10), 20, 53. [91]
645 OMARDEEN, T. A. (1959). Entomological report and report of the Curepe field station. *Ann. Rep. Malaria Division, Hlth Dept., Trinidad & Tobago*, pp. 21–45. [437]
646 ONO, S. & TSUJI, H. (1974). Influence of temperature on the harbouring behaviour of four species of cockroaches. *Periplaneta fuliginosa, P. americana, P. japonica* and *Blattella germanica. Jap. J. Sanit. Zool.*, **25** (1), 95–98. [172]
647 ORSER, W. B. & BROWN, A. W. A. (1951). The effect of insecticides on the heartbeat of *Periplaneta. Can. J. Zool.*, **29**, 54. [216, 410]
648 OSMANI, Z. & NAIDU, M. B. (1970). Mechanism involved in negative temperature coefficient of toxicity of pyrethrum. *Indian J. Ent.*, **32** (2), 152–158. [392]
649 OZKAZANC, A. N. (1968). The effect of a new poison bait prepared with boric acid sulfathiazole and powdered confectioners sugar on cockroaches (*Blattella germanica* L.). *Ankera Univ. Vet. Fak. Derg.*, **15** (2), 196–205. [195]
650 PAGE, A. B. P. & BLACKITH, R. E. (1949). Bioassay system for the pyrethrins. II. The mode of action of pyrethrum synergists. *Ann. appl. Biol.*, **36** (2), 244–249. [394]
651 PAGE, A. B. P., STRINGER, A. & BLACKITH, R. E. (1949). Bioassay systems for the pyrethrins. I. Water-base sprays against *Aedes aegypti* L. and other flying insects. *Ann. appl. Biol.*, **36** (2), 225–243. [394]
652 PAINTER, R. H. (1930). The biological strains of hessian fly. *J. econ. Ent.*, **23**, 322–326. [424]

653 PAPWORTH, D. S. (1963). Implications of the notification and clearance scheme. *Proc. 1st Br. Pest Control Ass. Conf., Oxford,* 12–15. [146]
654 PAPWORTH, D. S. (1965). Legislation and control of pesticides. *J. Forensic Sci. Soc.,* **5** (2), 66–72. [146]
655 PAPWORTH, D. S. (1971). The United Kingdom pattern of legislation. *Proc. 3rd Br. Pest Control Ass. Conf., Jersey,* Paper No. 14, 8 pp. [146]
656 PAPWORTH, D. S. (1975). Registration procedures and fail-safe procedures. *Proc. 4th Br. Pest Control Ass. Conf., Jersey,* Paper No. 2, 7 pp. [151]
657 PAPWORTH, D. S., TAYLOR, J. K., CUTLER, J. R. & MUTTRIE, M. P. (1972). Quantities of pesticide used by U.K. Local Authorities. *R. Soc. Hlth J.,* **92** (1), 35–38. [23]
658 PARKER, B. M. & CAMPBELL, F. L. (1940). Relative susceptibility of the ootheca and adult female of the German cockroach to liquid household insecticides. *J. econ. Ent.,* **33** (4), 610–614. [250, 476]
659 PARKIN, E. A. (1965). Sesame oil—synergist for pyrethrins in the Second World War. *Pyrethrum Post,* **8** (2), 21–25. [240]
660 PATEL, N. G. & CUTKOMP, L. K. (1968). Biochemical response of the American cockroach to immobilisation and insecticides. *J. econ. Ent.,* **61** (4), 931–937. [407]
661 PATTON, R. L., GARDNER, J. & ANDERSON, A. D. (1959). The excretory efficiency of the American cockroach *Periplaneta americana* L. *J. Insect Physiol.,* **3**, 256–261. [400]
662 PAWLIK, J. (1966). Control of the nematode *Leidynema appendiculata* (Leidy) in laboratory cultures of the American cockroach. *J. econ. Ent.,* **59** (2), 468–469. [468]
663 PEARCE, G. W., SCHOOF, H. F. & QUARTERMAN, K. D. (1961). Insecticidal vapours for aircraft disinsection. *Bull. Wld Hlth Org.,* **24**, 611–616. [71]
664 PENCE, R. J. (1961). *Tribolium* and cockroach control with kepone bait in fabric insect culture cabinets. *J. econ. Ent.,* **54** (4), 821–822. [98]
665 PERKINS, B. D. & GRAYSON, J. M. (1961). Some biological comparisons of resistant and non-resistant strains of the German cockroach, *Blattella germanica. J. econ. Ent.,* **54** (4), 747–750. [439, 440]
666 PERRY, A. S. (1·50). Biochemical aspects of insect resistance to the chlorinated hydrocarbon insecticides. *Misc. Publs ent. Soc. Am.,* **2** (1), 95–113. [383, 448]
667 PERRY, A. S. (1964). The physiology of insecticide resistance by insects. In: Rockstein, M., (Ed.). *Physiology of insects.* Academic Press, N.Y., Vol. 3, Chapter 6, pp. 285–378. [449]
668 PERTI, S. L., MENON, P. B. & O'LEARY, F. D. (1970). Cockroach control in naval ships. *Labdev J. Sci. Tech.,* **8** (B) (3), 175–176. [99]
669 PILLMORE, P. R. (1973) In: Casida, J. E. (Ed.). *Pyrethrum—the natural insecticide.* Academic Press, Chapter 7. [252]
670 PIMENTAL, D. (1958). Ecological and physiological requirements of cockroaches. *Pest Control,* **26** (6), 20–22, 52. [99]
671 PIMENTAL, D. & KLOCK, J. W. (1954). Disinsectization of aircraft by residual deposits of insecticides. *Am. J. trop. Med. Hyg.,* **3** (1), 191–194. [71]
672 PIQUETT, P. G. (1948). Benzene hexachloride and cornstarch as a roach-control combination. *J. econ. Ent.,* **41** (2), 326–327. [99]
673 PIQUETT, P. G. & BOWEN, C. V. (1951). Effect of abrasive diluents on the toxicity of lindane to the American cockroach. *J. econ. Ent.,* **44** (1), 118–119. [95]
674 PIQUETT, P. G. & FALES, J. H. (1952). Rearing cockroaches for experimental purposes. *U.S.D.A. Report,* ET-301. [462]
675 PLAPP, F. W. & BIGLEY, W. S. (1961). Carbamate insecticides and ali-esterase activity in insects. *J. econ. Ent.,* **54** (4), 793–796. [414]
676 PLAPP, F. W. & VALEGA, T. M. (1967). Synergism of carbamate and organophosphate insecticides by noninsecticidal carbamates. *J. econ. Ent.,* **60** (4), 1094–1102. [419]
677 POONAWALLA, N. H. & KORTE, F. (1964). Metabolism of insecticides. VIII (1): excretion, distribution and metabolism of α-chlordane-^{14}C by rats. *Life Sci.,* **3**, 1497–1500. [307]
678 PRADHAM, S. (1949). Studies on the toxicity of insecticide films. Part II. Effect of temperature on the toxicity of DDT films. *Bull. ent. Res.,* **40**, 239–265. [401]

679 PRICE, M. D. (1961). Progress with insecticidal resins. *Pest Technology*, 3 (8), 187–189. [91]
680 PRICE, R. G. (1963). The evaluation of repellents with four species of roaches. Unpublished Ph.D. Thesis, Oklahoma State, Univ., Stillwater, Oklahoma. [160]
681 PRICE, R. G. & HOWELL, D. E. (1969). Population changes in four species of cockroaches maintained together in small containers. *J. econ. Ent.*, 62 (5), 1164–1165. [467]
682 PRICE-JONES, D. (1974). The changing pattern of pesticides research and development. *Biologist*, 21 (4), 179–181. [13, 25]
683 PŘÍVORA, M. (1965). Development and present status of insecticide resistance in insects in Czechoslovakia. *Proc. XIIth Int. Congr. Ent, London*, 1964, p. 835. [441]
684 PŘÍVORA, M. (1972). Susceptibility of *Blattella germanica* (L.) and *Blatta orientalis* L. to insecticides in Czechoslovakia. *Čslká Epidem. Mikrobiol. Imunol.*, 21 (3), 113–118. [446]
685 PUL'VER, K. Yu. (1973). Tests on the control of synanthropic cockroaches *Blatta orientalis* L. and *Blattella germanica* L. in some districts of a town. *Medskaya Parazit.*, 42 (5), 606–612. [104]
686 QUARTERMAN, K. D. (1960). Test methods for establishing levels of susceptibility and detecting the development of resistance in insects of public health importance. *Misc. Publs ent. Soc. Am.*, 2 (1), 95–101. [476]
687 QUARTERMAN, K. D. & SULLIVAN, W. N. (1953). Disinsectization of aircraft by lindane vapours from filters in the ventilating system. *J. econ. Ent.*, 46 (4), 715–716. [71]
688 QUATTROCHI, L. P. (1965). Let's talk about the advantages of bait. *Pest Control*, 36 (6), 8–10, 12, 14. [104]
689 RACHESKY, S. (1969). Cockroach control in Chicago's Lincoln Park Zoo. *Pest Control*, 37 (6), 10, 14, 20. [72]
690 RADINOVSKY, S. & KRANTZ, G. W. (1962). The use of fluon to prevent the escape of stored-product insects from glass containers. *J. econ. Ent.*, 55 (5), 815–816. [461]
691 RAMSEY, J. A. (1935). The evaporation of water from the cockroach. *J. exp. Biol.*, 12, 373–383. [208]
692 RASMUSSEN, W. A., JANSEN, J. A., STEIN, W. J. & HAYES, W. J. (1963) Toxicological studies of DDVP for disinsection of aircraft. *Aerospace Medicine*, 34 (7), 593–600. [71]
693 RATHBURN, C. B. & BOIKE, A. H. (1975). ULV ground tests of adult mosquito control insecticides. *Pest Control*, 43 (7), 16–18. [120]
694 RAUCH, F., LHOSTE, J. & BIRG, M. L. (1972). Propriétés insecticides du d-*trans* chrysanthémate de *d*-alléthrolone. *Meded. Fakult. Landbouw-Wetenschappen*, 37, 755–759. [265]
695 RAY, J. W. (1963). Insecticide absorbed by the central nervous system of susceptible and resistant cockroaches exposed to dieldrin. *Nature, Lond.*, 197 (4873), 1226–1227. [310, 449, 450]
696 RAY, J. W. (1964). The free amino acid pool of the cockroach (*Periplaneta americana*) central nervous system and the effect of insecticides. *J. Insect Physiol.*, 10, 587–597. [404, 405]
697 REDDY, M. J. (1972). The mode of action of insect repellents. I. Choice chamber experiments with the German cockroach, *Blattella germanica* (L.). *Quaestiones Entomolgicae*, 6 (4), 339–352. [497]
698 REIERSON, D. A. (1973). Field tests to control German cockroaches with ULV aerosol generators. *Pest Control*, 41 (1), 26, 28, 31, 32. [187]
699 REIERSON, D. A. (1975) Acephate control of German roaches. *Pest Control*, 43 (12), 16–20. [125, 357]
700 RICCI, M. (1948). DDT action on *Blatta orientalis*. *Riv. Parasitol.*, 9, 143–167. [288, 423]
701 RICHARDS, A. G. & CUTKOMP, L. K. (1945). Neuropathology in insects. *Jl N.Y. ent. Soc.*, 53, 313–349. [216, 395]
702 RICKETT, F. E. & TYSZKIEWICZ, K. (1973). Pyrethrum dermatitis. II. The allergenicity of pyrethrum oleoresin and its cross-reactions with the saline extract of pyrethrum

flowers. *Pestic. Sci.*, **4**, 801–810. [252]
703 RICKETT, F. E., TYSZKIEWICZ, K. & BROWN, N. C. (1972). Pyrethrum dermatitis. I. The allergenic properties of various extracts of pyrethrum flowers. *Pestic. Sci.*, **3**, 57–66. [252]
704 ROAN, C. C. (1959). Roach resistance: what is it? Where will it end? *Pest Control*, **27** (6), 34. [425]
705 ROBBINS, W. E. & DAHM, P. A. (1955). Absorption and excretion, distribution and metabolism of Carbon-14-labelled DDT by the American cockroach. *J. agric. Fd Chem.*, **3**, 500–508. [399, 400]
706 ROBINSON, J. & ROBERTS, M. (1968). Accumulation, distribution and elimination of organochlorine insecticides by vertebrates. In: S.C.I. Monograph No. 29, Physico-chemical and biophysical factors affecting the activity of pesticides. *Soc. chem. Ind., Lond.*, 106–119. [312]
707 RODGERS, J. W. (1975). Staff training in the United Kingdom. *Proc. 4th Br. Pest Control Ass. Conf., Jersey.*, Paper No. 11, 8 pp. [152]
708 ROEDER, K. D. (1948). The effect of anticholinesterases and related substances on nervous activity in the cockroach. *Johns Hopkins Hosp. Bull.*, **83**, 587–599. [414]
709 ROEDER, K. D. & WEIANT, E. A. (1946). The site of action of DDT in the cockroach. *Science, N.Y.*, **103**, 304–306. [408, 409]
710 ROEDER, K. D. & WEIANT, E. A. (1948). The effect of DDT on sensory and motor structures in the cockroach leg. *J. cell. comp. Physiol.*, **30**, 147–172. [408]
711 ROEDER, K. D. & WEIANT, E. A. (1951). The effect of concentration, temperature and washing on the time of appearance of DDT-induced trains in sensory fibres of the cockroach. *Ann. ent. Soc. Am.*, **44** (3), 372–380. [408]
712 ROGERS, R., Roth, L.O. & PRICE, R. G. (1973). Spray patterns and drift from PCO hand sprayers. *Pest Control*, **41** (3), 24, 26, 28. [115]
713 ROMER, J. D. (1962). Report on pest control in Hong Kong for the financial year, 1961–62. In: Annual report of the Urban Council of Hong Kong for 1961–62, pp. 4–5. [439]
714 ROTH, L. M. & COHEN, S. H. (1973). Aggregation in Blattaria. *Ann. ent. Soc. Am.*, **66** (6), 1315–1323. [172]
715 ROTH, L. M. & WILLIS, E. R. (1960). *The biotic association of cockroaches*. Smithson. misc. Collns., **141** (4422), 470 pp. [468]
716 ROTH, L. O. & PRICE, R. G. (1973). How much spray is the right amount? *Pest Control*, **41** (5), 19–20. [115]
717 ROY, D. N., GHOSH, S. M. & CHOPRA, R. N. (1943). The mode of action of pyrethrum on the cockroach *Periplaneta americana* L. *Ann. appl. Biol.*, **30** (1), 42–47. [394]
718 RUSSELL M. P. & FRISHMAN, A. M. (1965). Effectiveness of dichlorvos in resin strips for the control of the German cockroach, *Blattella germanica. J. econ. Ent.*, **58** (3), 570–572. [330, 331, 332]
719 SABS 457 (1970). Rearing and handling the American cockroach (*Periplaneta americana* L.) for the evaluation of pesticides (metric units). Council of the S.A. Bureau of Standards. 3 pp. [461]
720 SABS 458 (1970). Rearing and handling the German cockroach (*Blattella germanica* L.) for the evaluation of pesticides (metric units). Council of the S.A. Bureau of Standards. 3 pp. [461]
721 SACCA, G. (1947). Sull'esistenza di mosche domestiche resistenti al DDT. *Riv. Parasit.*, **8** (23), 127–128. [423]
722 SALING, T. (1928). Über das wirksame Prinzip von Pyrethrum-Insekten-pulvern und eine neue biologische Methodik ihrer Wertbestimmung. *Z. Desinf. Gesund.*, **20** (3), 33–42. [233]
723 SAVIT, J., KOLLROSS, J. & TOBIAS, J. M. (1946). Measured dose of gamma hexachlorocyclohexane and a comparison with DDT. *Proc. Soc. exp. Biol. Med.*, **62**, 44. [295]
724 SAWICKI, R. M. (1961). The effect of safroxan on the knockdown and the 24 hour toxicity of commercial pyrethrum extract against houseflies (*Musca domestica* L.). *Pyrethrum*

Post, **6** (2), 38–42. [241]
725 SAWICKI, R. M. (1962). Insecticidal activity of pyrethrum extract and its four insecticidal constituents against house flies. II. Synergistic activity of piperonyl butoxide with the four constituents. *J. Sci. Fd Agric.*, **13**, 260–264. [237]
726 SAWICKI, R. M. (1962). Insecticidal activity of pyrethrum extract and its four insecticidal constituents against house flies. III. Knockdown and recovery of flies treated with pyrethrum extract with and without piperonyl butoxide. *J. Sci. Fd Agric.*, **13**, 283–292. [237]
727 SAWICKI, R. M. (1962). Insecticidal activity of pyrethrum extract and its four insecticidal constituents against house flies. V. Knockdown activity of the four constituents with piperonyl butoxide. *J. Sci. Fd Agric.*, **13**, 591–598. [237]
728 SAWICKI, R. M. & FARNHAM, A. W. (1964). A dipping technique for selecting houseflies for resistance to insecticides. *Bull. ent. Res.*, **55** (3), 541–546. [479]
729 SAWICKI, R. M. & LORD, R. A. (1970). Some properties of a mechansim delaying penetration of insecticides into houseflies. *Pestic. Sci.*, **1** (5), 213–217. [106]
730 SAXENA, S. C. & SRIVASTAVA, J. P. (1968). On histopathology and histochemistry of insecticide-treated insects. I. Non-specific phosphatases in the midgut and caeca of pyrethrins-treated *Periplaneta americana* L. *Pyrethrum Post*, **9** (3), 9–13. [393]
731 SAXENA, S. C. & SRIVASTAVA, J. P. (1969). The histopathology and histochemistry of insecticide-treated insects. II. Glycogen in the mid-gut of *Periplaneta americana* L. treated with pyrethrum (Blattaria: Blattidae). *Pyrethrum Post*, **10** (1), 12–13, 23. [393]
732 SCHARRER, B. (1951). The Woodroach. *Scient. Am.*, **185** (6), 58–62. [468]
733 SCHECHTER, M. S., GREEN, N. & LAFORGE, F. B. (1949). The synthesis of cyclopentenolones of the type of cinerolone. *J. Am. chem. Soc.*, **71**, 1517. [254, 259]
734 SCHOOF, H. F. (1970). Physiological resistance and development of resistance in field populations. *Misc. Publs ent. Soc. Am.*, **7** (1), 45–55. [424]
735 SCHOOF, H. F., JENSEN, J. A., PORTER, J. E. & MADDOCK, D. R. (1961). Disinsection of aircraft with a mechanical dispenser of DDVP vapour. *Bull. Wld Hlth Org.*, **24**, 623–628. [71]
736 SCHWARTZ, M., BODENSTEIN, O. F. & FALES, J. H. (1970). Compounds related to cyanoacetic acid as repellents for cockroaches. *J. econ. Ent.*, **63** (2), 429–432. [159, 497]
737 SCHWARTZ, M., BODENSTEIN, O. F. & FALES, J. H. (1971). Compounds related to cyanoacetic acid as repellents for cockroaches. II. *J. econ. Ent.*, **64** (3), 576–578. [159]
738 SCORER, R. (1975). The danger of environmental jitters. *New Scientist*, **66** (955), 702–703. [145]
739 SEDLAK, V. A. (1965). Solubility of benzene hexachloride isomers in rat fat. *Toxicol. appl. Pharmacol.*, **7**, 79–83. [297]
740 SHAFER, G. D. (1911). How contact insecticides kill. Pts. I & II. *Michigan agric. Col. Expt. Stn. Tech. Bull.*, **11**, 65 pp. [230]
741 SHAFER, G. D. (1915). How contact insecticides kill. Pt. III. *Michigan agric. Col. Expt. Stn. Tech. Bull.* **21**, 67 pp. [192, 202, 203, 230]
742 SHANKLAND, D. L. & KEARNS, C. W. (1959). Characteristics of blood toxins in DDT-poisoned cockroaches. *Ann. ent. Soc. Am.*, **52** (4), 386–394. [406]
743 SHANKLAND, D. L. & SCHROEDER, M. E. (1973). Pharmacological evidence for a discrete neurotoxic action of dieldrin (HEOD) in the American cockroach, *Periplaneta americana* (L.). *Pestic. Biochem. Physiol.*, **3** (1), 77–86. [410]
744 SHEPARD, H. H. (1939). *The chemistry and toxicology of insecticides*. Burgess, Minn. [200]
745 SHEPARD, H. H. (1942). The early use of sodium fluoride as an insecticide. *Pests and their control*, **10**, 28. [200]
746 SHEPARD, H. H. (1951). *The chemistry and action of insecticides,* Chapter 8, Pyrethrins and Rotenone. McGraw-Hill, 504 pp. [211, 219]
747 SHIPLEY, A. E. (1916). *More Minor Horrors*. Smith Elder, London, 163 pp. [20]
748 SHOTWELL, T. K. (1975). Patterns in federal regulation of pesticides. *Pest Control*, **43** (1), 16, 18, 19, 22. [145]

749 SIEBURTH, J. F., BONSALL, M. G. & MCLAREN, B. A. (1951). A simplified biological assay method using the cockroach, *Periplaneta americana* Linn. for protein utilisation. *Ann. ent. Soc. Am.*, **44** (3), 463–468. [463]
750 SINGH, A. M. (1964). The free amino acids of the haemolymph of malathion-resistant *Blattella germanica* L. *Indian J. Ent.*, **26**, 247–250. [441]
751 SLADE, R. (1945). The gamma-isomer of hexachlorocyclohexane (Gammexane). *Chemy Ind.*, **40**, 314–319. Hurter Lecture, summarised in *Chem. Trade J. Chem. Eng.*, **116**, 279–281. [295]
752 SLOMINSKI, J. W., GOJMERAC, W. L. & BURKHOLDER, W. E. (1969). Oils: their effect on black carpet beetle larvae when applied to different types of surfaces. *J. econ. Ent.*, **62** (2), 507–508. [82]
753 SMALLMAN, B. N. & FISHER, R. W. (1958). Effect of anticholinesterases on acetylcholine levels in insects. *Can. J. Biochem. Physiol.*, **36**, 575–586. [414]
754 SMIRNOVA, A. S., RYK-BOGDANIKO, M. G., ZAGROBA, V. I., LEUTSKAYA, V. F., LAUTSIN, A. M., KUZNETSOVA, R. M. & BUDYLINA, A. A. (1974). Effectiveness of chlorofos baits with ammonium carbonate for control of cockroaches (*Blatta orientalis* L. and *Blattella germanica* L.). *Medskaya Parazit.*, **43** (1), 53–57. [357]
755 SMITH, D. S. & TREHERNE, J. E. (1963). Functional aspects of the organisation of the insect nervous system. *Adv. Insect Physiol.*, **1**, 401–484. [386]
756 SMITH, E. H. & WAGENKNECHT, A. C. (1959). The ovicidal action of organophosphate insecticides. *Can. J. Biochem. Physiol.*, **37**, 1135–1144. [412]
757 SMITTLE, B. J. (1966). Cockroaches. In: Smith, C. N. (Ed.). *Insect colonization and mass production*. Academic Press, pp. 227–240. [461]
758 SMITTLE, B. J. & BURDEN, G. S. (1965). Dichlorvos as a vapour toxicant for control of roaches, bedbugs, fleas. *Pest Control*, **33** (10), 26–32. [331, 333]
759 SMITTLE B. J. & BURDEN, G. S. (1968). Lacquers containing dieldrin, malathion or diazinon as controls for the German cockroach. *J. econ. Ent.*, **61** (3), 702–705. [92]
760 SMITTLE, B. J., BURDEN, G. S. & BANKS W. A. (1968). Cockroach insecticides: how repellent are they? *Pest Control*, **36** (11), 9–10. [187]
761 SNETSINGER, R. & CARROLL, D. (1972). Evaluation of dursban and dowco 214. *Pest Control*, **40** (5), 24, 26, 28, 30, 32. [343, 344]
762 SPEAR, P. J. (1967). Insecticide needs of pest control operators. *Soap, N.Y.*, **43** (3), 94 and (4), 84–86. [13, 21, 22]
763 STAPP, R. R. (1964). Susceptibility to chlordane, diazinon, naled and malathion of natural populations of *Blattella germanica* from the Fifth U.S. Army area. *J. econ. Ent.*, **57** (3), 327–328. [437, 438]
764 STAUDINGER, H. & RUZICKA, L. (1924). Insektentotende stoffe. I-VI and VIII-X. *Helv. chim. Acta.*, **7**, 177–201, 201–211, 212–235, 236–244, 245–259, 377–390, 406–441, 442–448, 448–458. [230]
765 STEDMAN, E. (1926). Position isomerism in relation to miotic activity of some synthetic urethanes. *Biochem. J.*, **20**, 719–734. [363]
766 STERLING, P. D. (1966). The biological evaluation of spray additives and solvents with *Blattella germanica* (Linn.) and *Periplaneta americana* (Linn.). Unpublished Ph.D. Thesis, Oklahoma State Univ., Stillwater, Oklahoma. [176]
767 STERNBURG, J. G., CHANG, S. C. & KEARNS, C. W. (1957). DDT-induced toxins in insect blood. *Fedn. Proc.*, **16**, 124–125. [406, 407]
768 STERNBURG, J. G. & KEARNS, C. W. (1952). The presence of toxins other than DDT in the blood of DDT-poisoned roaches. *Science, N.Y.*, **116**, 114–117. [406]
769 STEVENSON, D. E. & CARTER, B. I. (1975). Pesticides and domestic animals. *Vet. Rec.*, **97** (9), 164–169. [138]
770 STORY, K. O. (1972). Control of cockroaches and other domestic pests with a new carbamate insecticide. *Int. Pest Control*, **14** (6), 6–10. [368, 369]
771 STORY, K. O. (1975). The international potential of bendiocarb insecticide in relation to pest control operations. *Proc. 4th Br. Pest Control Ass. Conf.*, Jersey, Paper 17. [367, 370]
772 STRONG, V. E. (1972). It's ominous, It's titanic . . . It's the Law. *Pest Control*, **40** (6), 15,

16, 18, 22, 24. [153]
773 STYCZYNSKA, B. & KRZEMINSKA, A. (1973). The action of carbamate insecticides on larvae of the cockroach *Blattella germanica* L. *Roczn. Panstwowego Zakladu Hygieny*, **24** (3), 377–381. [381]
774 SUDERSHAN, P. & NAIDU, M. B. (1967). Effect of insecticides and insecticide treated cockroach blood on the heart beat of *Periplaneta americana* L. *Indian J. exp. Biol.*, **5** (4), 215–218. [392]
775 SULLIVAN, W. N., Du CHANOIS, F. R. & HAYDACK, D. L. (1958). Insect survival in jet aircraft. *J. econ. Ent.*, **51** (2), 239–241. [454]
776 SULLIVAN, W. N., PAL, R., Wright, J. W., AZURIN, J. C., OKAMOTO, R., McGUIRE, J. U. & WATERS, R. M. (1972). World-wide studies on aircraft disinsection at 'blocks away'. *Bull. Wld Hlth Org.*, **46**, 485–491. [71]
777 SULLIVAN, W. N., SCHECHTER, M. S., CAWLEY, M. & KENNEDY, J. (1975). Promising pyrethroid and organophosphate insecticides with low mammalian toxicity. *Soap, N.Y.*, **51** (10), 44–46. [272]
778 SUZUKI, T. & MATSUNAGA, H. (1968). Cross-resistance in dieldrin-resistant colonies of *Blattella germanica* (L.). *Jap. J. Sanit. Zool.*, **19** (1), 72–76. [445]
779 SUZUKI, T., MATSUNAGA, H. & SHIMAMURA, M. (1968). A survey of resistance to dieldrin-group in the German cockroach, *Blattella germanica* collected from Kawasaki, Japan. *Jap. J. Sanit. Zool.*, **19** (3), 207–209. [444]
780 SWEETMAN, H. L. & LAUDANI, H. (1942). Sodium fluoride, a study of its toxic action on roaches indicates that it is of little value as a stomach poison in practical control. *Soap, N.Y.*, **18** (4), 90–93. [202]
781 TABARU, Y. & KOBAYASHI, A. (1971). Outdoor hibernation of *Periplaneta japonica* (Blattaria: Blattidae) in a snowy area. *Jap. J. Sanit. Zool.*, **22** (2), 76–77. [39]
782 TABARU, Y., ONO, S. & TSUJI, H. (1974). Laboratory evaluation of several insecticides as feeding inhibitors against the German cockroach, *Blattella germanica* (L.). *Jap. J. Sanit. Zool.*, **25** (2), 147–152. [103]
783 TARRANT, K. R. & TATTON J. O'G. (1968). Organochlorine pesticides in rain water in the British Isles. *Nature, Lond.*, **219** (5155), 725–727. [142]
784 TARSHIS, I. B. (1959). UCLA tests with desiccant dusts for roach control. *Pest Control*, **27** (6), 14, 16, 17, 18, 20, 22, 24, 26–28. [205, 208]
785 TARSHIS I. B. (1959). How to apply sorptive dusts for roach control. *Pest Control*, **27** (6), 30–32. [208]
786 TARSHIS, I. B. (1964). The use of silica aerogel insecticides, Dri-Die 67 and Drione, in new and existing structures for the prevention and control of cockroaches. *Lab. Anim. Care*, **14** (3), 167–184. [195]
787 TARSHIS, I. B. (1967). Silica aerogel insecticides for the prevention and control of arthropods of medical and veterinary importance. *Angew. Parasit.*, **8** (4), 210–237. [206, 208, 209]
788 TELFORD, J. N. & MATSUMURA, F. (1970). Dieldrin-binding in subcellular nerve components of cockroaches. An electron microscope and autoradiographic study. *J. econ. Ent.*, **63** (3), 795–800. [412]
789 TELFORD, J. N. & MATSUMURA, F. (1971). Electron microscopic and autoradiographic studies on distribution of dieldrin in the intact nerve tissues of German cockroaches. *J. econ. Ent.*, **64** (1), 230–238. [412]
790 TELLE, H. J. (1970). Difficulties in controlling *B. germanica* and *B. orientalis* in hospitals in Niedersachsen, Germany. *Z. angew. Ent.*, **66**, 291–294. [71]
791 THOMSON, I. F. (1970). Tackling a cockroach problem in an English hospital. *Environ. Hlth*, **78** (9), 332–334. [71]
792 THORPE, W. H. (1931). Biological races in insects and their significance in evolution. *Ann. appl. Biol.*, **18**, 406–414. [424]
793 TOBIAS, J. M. & KOLLROSS, J. J. (1946). Loci of action of DDT in the cockroach, *Periplaneta americana*. *Biol. Bull.*, **91** (3), 247–255. [286, 408]
794 TOBIAS, J. M., KOLLROSS, J. J. & SAVIT, J. (1946). Acetylcholine and related substances in the cockroach, fly and crayfish, (*Periplaneta americana* L., *Musca domestica* L.,

and *Cambarus*) and the effect of DDT. *J. cell. comp. Physiol.*, **28** (2), 159–182. [410]
795 TOMPKINS, G. J. & CANTWELL, G. E. (1973). The use of dry ice to control German cockroaches in hospital food service carts. *Pest Control*, **41** (11), 24, 26. [214]
796 TOWNSEND H. G. (1963). Insecta-Lac: new roach killer brushes on like paint. *Pest Control*, **31** (2), 40, 42, 64. [89]
797 TREON, J. F. & CLEVELAND, F. P. (1955). Toxicity of certain chlorinated hydrocarbon insecticides for laboratory animals, with special reference to aldrin and dieldrin. *J. agric. Fd Chem.*, **3**, 402–408. [311]
798 TRUMAN, L. C. (1961). Lesson No. 6, Cockroaches. *Pest Control*, **29**, (6), 21–28. [48]
799 TRUMAN, L. C. & BUTTS, W. L. (1967). *Scientific guide to pest control operations*. 2nd Ed. Pest Control Magazine. 187 pp. [202]
800 TSAO, C-H., SULLIVAN, W. N. & HORNSTEIN, I. (1953). A comparison of evaporation rates and toxicity to house flies of lindane and lindane-chlorinated polyphenol deposits. *J. econ. Ent.*, **46** (5), 882–884. [295]
801 TSUDA, K., ABE, Y. & FUJITA, Y. (1972). Comparative activity of pyrethrins I, pyrethrins II and other synthetic pyrethroidal compounds. *Botyu-Kagaku*, **37** (11), 48–56. [226]
802 TSUJI, H. (1965). Studies on the behaviour pattern of feeding of three species of cockroaches, *Blattella germanica* (L.), *Periplaneta americana* L., and *P. fuliginosa* S., with special reference to their responses to some constituents of rice bran and some carbohydrates. *Jap. J. Sanit. Zool.*, **16** (4), 255–262. [101]
803 TSUJI, H. (1966). Attractive and feeding stimulative effect of some fatty acids and related compounds on three species of cockroaches. *Jap. J. Sanit. Zool.*, **17** (2), 89–97. [101]
804 TSUJI, H. & MIZUNO, T. (1971). Laboratory use of first instar nymphs of the American cockroach, *Periplaneta americana*. *Jap. J. Sanit. Zool.*, **22** (1), 1–7. [466, 467, 488, 489]
805 TSUJI, H. & MIZUNO, T. (1973). Behavioural interaction between two harbouring individuals of the Smoky brown cockroach, *Periplaneta fuliginosa* S. *Jap. J. Sanit. Zool.*, **24** (1), 65–72. [172]
806 TSUJI, H. & ONO, S. (1969). Laboratory evaluation of several bait factors against the German cockroach, *Blattella germanica* (L.). *Jap. J. Sanit. Zool.*, **20** (4), 240–247. [101, 104, 105]
807 TSUJI, H. & ONO, S. (1970). Glycerol and related compounds as feeding stimulants for cockroaches. *Jap. J. Sanit. Zool*, **21** (3), 149–156. [101]
808 TSUJI, H. & ONO, S. (1970). Wide application of baits against field populations of the German cockroach, *Blattella germanica* (L.). *Jap. J. Sanit. Zool.*, **21** (1), 36–39. [105]
809 TURTLE, E. E. (1966). Assessing likely risks to wildlife from new uses of pesticides: the position under the Pesticides Safety Precautions Scheme in the United Kingdom. *J. appl. Ecol.*, **3** (Suppl.), 283–285. [146]
810 TWAROG, B. M. & ROEDER, K. D. (1956). Properties of the connective tissue sheath of the cockroach abdominal nerve cord. *Biol. Bull.*, **111**, 278–286. [415]
811 TWAROG, B. M. & ROEDER, K. D. (1957). Pharmacological observations on the desheathed last abdominal ganglion of the cockroach. *Ann. ent. Soc. Am.*, **50**, 231–237. [415]
812 TYLER, P. S. (1961). Dieldrin-resistant German cockroaches. *Pest Infestation Research*, 1961, A.R.C., H.M.S.O., p. 36. [447]
813 TYLER, P. S. (1962). Resistant German cockroaches. *Pest Infestation Research*, 1962, A.R.C., H.M.S.O., p. 42. [448]
814 Tyler, P. S. (1964). Kepone bait for the control of resistant German cockroaches. *Int. Pest Control*, **6** (5), 10–11, 13. [99, 313, 315]
815 TYLER, P. S. (1964). A test for indicating resistance to dieldrin in the German cockroach. *Sanitarian*, **72** (5), 251–252. [448, 453]
816 TYLER, P. S. (1974). The biology and control of insect hygiene pests in food manufacturing premises. Paper presented at British Food Manufacturers Assoc., Leatherhead, July 1974. [56]
818 ULEWICZ, K. & BAROWSKI, S. (1974). Methyl bromide for disinsection of Polish ships. *Angew. Parasitol.*, **15** (1), 36–42. [215]

819 ULMANN, E. (Ed.), (1972). *Lindane*. Verlag K. Schillinger, 384 pp. [299]
820 VALDES-DAPENA, M. A. & AREY, J. B. (1962). Boric acid poisonings. Three fatal cases with pancreatic inclusions and a review of the literature. *J. Pediat.*, **61**, 531–546. [194]
821 VAN ASPEREN, K. (1955). Toxicity and interaction of stereo-isomers of benzene hexachloride in cockroaches. *Bull. ent. Res.*, **46**, 837–843. [296, 297]
822 VAN DEN HEUVEL, M. J. (1971). Pesticide safety: safe packaging and labelling. *Proc. 3rd Br. Pest Control Ass. Conf., Jersey*, 4 pp. [144]
823 VAN DEN HEUVEL, M. J. & COCHRAN, D. G. (1965). Cross resistance to organophosphorus compounds in malathion and diazinon-resistant strains of *Blattella germanica*. *J. econ. Ent.*, **58** (5), 872–874. [442]
824 VAN DEN HEUVEL, M. J. & SHENKER, A. M. (1965). Cockroach control using non-persistent insecticides. *Pest Technology*, **7** (6), 10–11. [250, 275]
825 VARMA, R. N., DIXIT, R. S. & SOMAYA, C. I. (1969). High malathion resistance in Poona cockroaches. *Labdev J. Sci. Tech.*, **7** (B) (1), 76. [446]
826 VEVAI, E. J. (1974). Malathion. Know your pesticides: its salient points and uses in pest control. *Pesticides*, **8** (7), 16–28. [338]
827 VINSON, E. B. & KEARNS, C. W. (1952). Temperature and the toxic action of DDT on the American roach. *J. econ. Ent.*, **45** (3), 484–496. [289, 401]
828 VOLKOV, Y. P., POLESHCHUK, V. D., ZHAROV, V. G., & VASHKOV, V. I. (1967). An investigation of the sexual attracting substance of the female German cockroach, *Blattella germanica*. *Medskaya Parazit.*, **36** (1), 45–48. (In Russian). [102]
829 WACHS, H. (1947). Synergistic insecticides. *Science, N.Y.*, **105**, 530–531. [236]
830 WAGNER, R. E., EBELING, W. & CLARK, W. R. (1964). An electric barrier for confining cockroaches in large rearing or field-collecting cans. *J. econ. Ent.* **57** (6), 1007–1009. [461, 475]
831 WALLER, J. B. & LEWIS, S. E. (1961). The effect of gamma-BHC and other insecticides on the ACh levels in the cockroach. *J. Insect Physiol.*, **7**, 315–323. [410]
832 WALTER, E. V. (1918). Experiments on cockroach control. *J. econ. Ent.*, **11** (5), 424–429. [193, 195]
833 WALTER, V. (1968). A roach by any other name. *Pest Control*, **36** (2), 32. [67]
834 WAMBERA, E., WINMILL, A. E. & BROWN, A. W. A. (1965). Survey of insecticide resistance in the German cockroach. Envir. Prot. Report No. 9. Directorate of Biosciences Research, Defence Res. Board, Ottawa, Canada. Sept. 1965, 4 pp. [438]
835 WANG, C. M. & MATSUMURA, F. (1970). Relationship between the neurotoxicity and in vivo toxicity of certain cyclodiene insecticides in the German cockroach. *J. econ. Ent.*, **63** (6), 1731–1734. [411]
836 WANG, C. M., NARAHASHI, T. & YAMANDA, M. (1971). The neurotoxic action of dieldrin and its derivatives in the cockroach. *Pestic. Biochem. Physiol.*, **1**, 84–91. [411]
837 WASHBURN, F. L. (1913). A successful trap for cockroaches. *J. econ. Ent.*, **6**, 327–329. [472]
838 WEBB, J. E. (1961). Resistance of some species of cockroaches to organic insecticides in Germany and France. 1956–59. *J. econ. Ent.*, **54** (4), 805–806. [436]
839 WELSH, J. H. & Gordon, H. T. (1947). The mode of action of certain insecticides on the arthropod nerve axon. *J. cell. comp. Physiol.*, **30** (2), 147–171. [396]
840 WEST, T. F. & CAMPBELL, G. A. (1950). *DDT and newer persistent insecticides*. Chapman & Hall, London. (Chapter X: DDT against household pests, pp. 250–282). [287]
841 WHARTON, D. R. A. (1971). Ultraviolet repellent and lethal action on the American cockroach. *J. econ. Ent.*, **64** (1), 252–255. [169]
842 WHITNEY, W. K., HARRISON, R. P. & HOWE, R. G. (1967). Cockroach control with dursban insecticide. *Pest Control*, **35** (6), 25–28. [343]
843 W.H.O. (1960). Insecticide resistance and vector control. Xth Report of Expert Committee on Insecticides. *WHO Tech. Rep. Series*, No. 191. [438]
844 W.H.O. (1970). Insecticide resistance and vector control. *WHO Tech. Rep. Series*, No. 443, pp. 130–133. [428, 487]
845 WICKHAM, J. C. (1971). The laboratory evaluation of synthetic pyrethroids as insecticides. *Proc. 3rd Br. Pest Control Ass. Conf., Jersey*, pp. 30–34. [270, 276, 279]

846 WICKHAM, J. C. & CHADWICK, P. R. (1975). Synthetic pyrethroid development. *Proc. 4th Br. Pest Control Ass. Conf., Jersey*, Paper 16. [258, 270, 273, 274, 275, 277]
847 WIGGLESWORTH, V. B. (1945). Transpiration through the cuticle of insects. *J. exp. Biol.*, **21**, 97–114. [208]
848 WILEY, H. W. (1907). The excretion of boric acid from the human body. *J. biol. Chem.*, **3**, 11–19. [194]
849 WILKINSON, C. F. (1968). The role of insecticide synergists in resistance problems. *Wld Rev. Pest Control*, **7** (3), 155–168. [25, 458]
850 WILKINSON, C. F. (1968). Detoxification of pesticides and the mechanism of synergism. In: Hodgson, E. (Ed.). *Enzymatic oxidations of toxicants*. North Carolina State Univ. Press, Raleigh, pp. 113–149. [236]
851 WILKINSON, C. F. (1971). Insecticide synergists and their mode of action. *Proc. 2nd Int. Congr. Chem.*, **2**, 117–159. [236]
852 WILLIS, E. R. & LEWIS, N. (1957). The longevity of starved cockroaches. *J. econ. Ent.*, **50** (4), 438–440. [454]
853 WILLIS, E. R., RISER, G. R. & ROTH, L. M. (1958). Observations on reproduction and development in cockroaches. *Ann. ent. Soc. Am.*, **51**, 53–69. [461]
854 WILSON, I. B. (1967). In: Burger, A. (Ed.). *Drugs affecting the peripheral nervous system*. Dekker, N.Y., pp. 381–397. [414]
855 WINNEY, R. (1974). Pyrethrins, pyrethroids and mixtures. *Soap, N.Y.*, **50** (5), 56, 58, 60, 61. [257]
856 WINTERINGHAM, M. G. (1973). Pharaoh's ants—the modern plague. *Environ. Hlth*, **81** (7), 131–132. [367]
857 WINTHROP, G. J. & FELICE, J. R. (1959). A field study of workers during spray operations with a chlorinated hydrocarbon insecticide. *Am. Med. Ass. Archs Ind. Hlth*, **19**, 68. [312]
858 WINTON, M. Y., METCALF, R. L. & FUKUTO, T. R. (1958). The use of acetyl thiocholine in the histochemical study of the action of organophosphorus insecticides. *Ann. ent. Soc Am.*, **51**, 436–441. [419]
859 WOKE, P. A. (1939). Inactivation of pyrethrum after ingestion by the southern army worm and during incubation with its tissues. *J. agric. Res.*, **58**, 283–295. [232]
860 WOODBURY, E. N. (1938). Test methods on roaches. *Soap, N.Y.*, **14**, 86–90, 107, 109. [233, 250, 275, 476]
861 WOODBURY, E. N. & BARNHART, C. S. (1939). Tests on crawling insects. *Soap, N.Y.*, **15** (9), 93–107, 113. [476]
862 WRIGHT, A. (1974). U.S. environmental ban for two Shell pesticides. *Chem. Age*, **109** (2882), 8. [313]
863 WRIGHT, C. G. (1965). Identification and occurrence of cockroaches in dwellings and business establishments in N. Carolina. *J. econ. Ent.*, **58** (5), 1032–1033. [59]
864 WRIGHT, C. G. (1966). Modification of a vacuum cleaner for capturing German and Brown-banded cockroaches. *J. econ. Ent.*, **59** (3), 759–760. [475]
865 WRIGHT, C. G. (1968). Comparative life histories of chlordane-resistant and non-resistant German cockroaches. *J. econ. Ent.*, **61** (5), 1317–1321. [446]
866 WRIGHT, C. G. (1971). Efficacy of dichlorvos mini-strips for German cockroach control in enclosed kitchen cabinets. *J. econ. Ent.*, **64** (1), 278–280. [332]
867 WRIGHT, C. G. & HILLMAN, R. C. (1973). German cockroaches: efficacy of chlorpyrifos spray and dust, and boric acid powder. *J. econ. Ent.*, **66** (5), 1075–1076. [59, 196]
868 WRIGHT, C. G. & JACKSON, M. D. (1971). Propoxur, chlordane and diazinon on porcelain china saucers after kitchen cabinet spraying. *J. econ. Ent.*, **64** (2), 457–459. [151]
869 WRIGHT, C. G. & MCDANIEL, H. C. (1969). Abundance and habitat of five species of cockroaches on a permanent military base. *J. econ. Ent.*, **62** (1), 277–278. [59]
870 WRIGHT, C. G. & MCDANIEL H. C. (1973). Further evaluation of the abundance and habitat of five species of cockroaches on a permanent military base. *Florida Ent.*, **56** (3), 251–254. [59]
871 WRIGHT, C. G., MCDANIEL, H. C., JOHNSON, H. E. & SMITH, C. E. (1973). American

cockroach feeding in sewer access shafts on paraffin baits containing propoxur or kepone plus a mold inhibitor. *J. econ. Ent.*, **66** (6), 1277–1278. [104, 315]
872 WÜNSCHER, K. & ACKER, L. (1969). Über das Vorkommen von chlorierten Insektiziden im Fettgewebe des Menschen. *Medizin Ernahr.*, **10**, 75–80. [298]
873 YAMAMOTO, I. (1970). Problems in mode of action of pyrethroids. In: O'Brien, R. D. & Yamamoto, I. (Eds.). *Biochemical toxicity of insecticides*. Academic Press, N.Y., pp. 193–200. [235]
874 YAMASAKI, T. & ISHII, T. (1954). (In Japanese) *Botyu-Kagaku*, **19**, 39–46. English translation (1957) in: *Japanese contributions to the study of the insecticide-resistance problem*. Kyoto Univ., for WHO, pp. 155–162. [391]
875 YAMASAKI, T. & NARAHASHI, T. (1958). Resistance of house flies to insecticides and the susceptibility of nerve to insecticides. Studies on the mechanism of action of insecticides. XVII. *Botyu-Kagaku*, **23**, 146–157. [410]
876 YASUTOMI, K., INOUE, Y., OHTAKI, T. & ASAHINA, S. (1966). A comparative study of insecticide resistance of the German cockroach in Japan. *Jap. J. Sanit. Zool.*, **17**, 214–217. [444]
877 YEAGER, J. K. & MUNSON, S. C. (1945). Physiological evidence of a site of action of DDT in an insect. *Science, N.Y.*, **102** (2647), 305–307. [408]
878 YOUNG, R. G. (1958). Dehydrogenase systems from fat body of susceptible and chlordane-resistant *Blattella germanica* (L.). *J. econ. Ent.*, **51** (6), 867–869. [450]
879 ZABINSKI, J. (1928). The growth of black beetles and of cockroaches on artificial and on incomplete diets. Part I. *Br. J. exp. Biol.*, **6** (2), 360–385. [463]
880 ZEID, M. M. I., DAHM, P. A., HEIN, R. E. & MCFARLAND, R. H. (1953). Tissue distribution, excretion of $^{14}CO_2$ and degradation of radioactive pyrethrins administered to the American cockroach. *J. econ. Ent.*, **46** (2), 324–336. [389, 391]
881 ZEIDLER, O. (1874). Verbindungen von Chloral mit Brom- und Chlorbenzol. *Dt. chem. Ges. Ber.*, **7**, 1180–1181. [283]
882 ZONG, M. S., KIM, S. J., KOO, S. H. & HAN, Y. I. (1972). Effectiveness of boric acid as a stomach poison for the German cockroach (*Blattella germanica* L.) control. *Korean J. Parasit.*, **10** (2), 95–99. [195]
883 ZWICK, R. W. (1959). German cockroach resistance tests in the Panama Canal Zone. *J. econ. Ent.*, **52** (6), 544–545. [435]

References Added In Proofing

884 ANON. (1976). Kepone manufacture draws news coverage. *Pest Control*, **44** (1), 30. [317]
885 ANON. (1976). Draft common names for pesticides. *BSI News*, 1976/02, 23. [259]
886 ANON. (1976). Actellic—a broad spectrum pesticide for agriculture and public health. *Int. Pest Control*, **18** (1), 4–6, 18. [359]
887 BOYER, A. C. (1975). Sorption of tetrachlorvinphos insecticide (Gardona) to the haemolymph of *Periplaneta americana*. *Pestic. Biochem. Physiol.*, **5** (2), 135–141. [417]
888 BURDEN, G. S. (1975). Repellency of selected insecticides. *Pest Control*, **43** (6), 16, 18. [176]
889 BURK, T. & BELL, W. J. (1973). Cockroach aggregation pheromone: inhibition of locomotion (Orthoptera: Blattidae). *J. Kans. ent. Soc.*, **46**, 36–41. [102]
890 CHADWICK, P. R. (1976). Application of different pyrethroids against cockroaches. *Int. Pest Control*, **18** (1), 15–18. [84]
891 EBELING, W., REIERSON, D. A., PENCE, R. J. & VIRAY, M. S. (1975). Silica aerogel and boric acid against cockroaches: external and internal action. *Pestic. Biochem. Physiol.*, **5** (1), 81–89. [195]
892 ENESCU, A. & CHADLI, A. (1974). Evaluation of the action of orthoisopropoxyphenyl-carbamate on *Blattella germanica* L. *Archs Inst. Pasteur, Tunis*, **51** (4), 311–320. [378]
893 GADIAN, T. (1976). Toxicology—the basic science of poisons. *Chemy Ind.*, March 6th, 206–207. [133]

894 GIANNOTTI, O. & HOLZHACKER, E. L. (1972). Changes in the electrical activity of the central nervous system of the thorax of the cockroach (*Periplaneta americana*) brought about by the direct application of p,p' DDT to the thoracic and suboesophageal ganglia. *Seção de Praguicidas do Instituto Biológico, São Paulo, Brazil*, **15** (2), 337–342. [408]

895 GRAYSON, J. M. (1976). Cockroach control research in 1975: comparative effectiveness of various insecticides against cockroaches. *Pest Control*, **44** (2), 30–32, 39. [176]

896 HACH, V. & MCDONALD, E. C. (1973). Terpenes and terpenoids. IV. Some esters and amides of thujic acid. *Can. J. Chem.*, **51** (19), 3230–3235. [159]

897 HAYES, W. J. (1957). Dieldrin poisoning in man. *Public Health Reports*, **72** (12), 1087–1091. [312]

898 HAYES, W. J. (1959). The toxicity of dieldrin to man. Report on a survey. *Bull. Wld Hlth Org.*, **20**, 891–912. [312]

899 HAYES, W. J., FERGUSON, F. F. & CASS, J. S. (1951). The toxicology of dieldrin and its bearing on field use of the compound. *J. trop. Med.*, **31** (4), 519–522. [311]

900 HERREWEGE, C. van. (1974). Regulation of food consumption by males of the German cockroach under various alimentary conditions after a period of fasting. *Entomologia exp. appl.*, **17** (2), 234–244 [99]

901 KRAYBILL, H. F. (1975). Pesticide toxicity and potential for cancer: a proper perspective. *Pest Control*, **43** (12), 10–16. [133]

902 MAMPE, C. D. (1976). Answers. *Pest Control*, **44** (2), 16. [370, 456]

903 MANKOWSKA, H. & STYCZNSKA, B. (1973). Insecticidal action of a new carbamate insecticide Ficam 80W. *Roczniki Panstwowego Zakladu Higieny*, **24** (4), 515–520. [368]

904 MULRENNAN, J. A., LAMDIN, J. M., BOLTON, H. T. & HAMMOND, C. L. (1975). Atmospheric levels of propoxur aboard submarines after residual spraying. *J. econ. Ent.*, **68** (6), 755–756. [381]

905 N.P.C.A. (1976). Train suspends all PCO uses of chlordane/heptachlor except subterranean termite control. *Governmental Affairs*, ESPC 023003–6. [145]

906 N.P.C.A. (1976). Misuse actions by E.P.A. against PCO's. *Governmental Affairs*, ESPC 023007–8. [150]

907 N.P.C.A. (1976). Results of OSHA inspections of PCO's. *Governmental Affairs*, ESPC 023011–14. [153]

908 N.P.C.A. (1976). OSHA confirms that employers of ten or fewer employees need not record or report occupational injuries or illnesses. *Governmental Affairs*, ESPC 023021. [140]

909 PENCE, R. J., VIRAY, M. S., EBELING, W. & REIERSON, D. A. (1975). Honey-bee abdomen assays of haemolymph from stressed and externally poisoned American cockroaches. *Pestic. Biochem. Physiol.*, **5** (1), 90–100. [405]

910 RIDDIFORD, L. M., AJAMI, A. M. & BOAKE, C. (1975). Effectiveness of insect growth regulators in the control of populations of the German cockroach. *J. econ. Ent.*, **68** (1), 46–48. [26]

911 RUST, M. K., BURK, T. & BELL, W. J. (1976). Pheromone-stimulated locomotory and orientation responses in the American cockroach. *Anim. Behav.*, **24**, 52–67. [102]

912 SAWICKI, R. M. (1974). Resistance of insects to insecticides. *Chemy Ind.* (24), 980–981. [278]

913 SCHULZE, T. L. & HANSENS, E. J. (1975). Synergism of resmethrin in the house fly. *J. econ. Ent.*, **68** (6), 807–809. [271]

914 SENGUPTA, R., BASAK, S., SARKAR, D. & GHOSH, J. J. (1975). Effects of acute and multiple dose administration of Sumithion (*0,0*-dimethyl *0*-(3-methyl-4-nitrophenyl) phosphorothionate) on some enzymes of *Periplaneta americana* (Linn.). *Pestic. Biochem. Physiol.*, **5** (1), 52–56. [418]

915 SKALSKY, H. L. & GUTHRIE, F. E. (1975). Binding of insecticides to macromolecules in the blood of the rat and American cockroach. *Pestic. Biochem. Physiol.*, **5** (1), 28–34. [399]

916 SUGAWARA, R., KURIHARA, S. & MUTO, T. (1975). Attraction of the German cockroach to cyclohexyl alkanoates and *n*-alkyl cyclohexanacetates. *J. Insect Physiol.*, **21** (5),

957–964. [100]
917 SUMERFORD, W. T., HAYES, W. J., JOHNSTON, J. M., WALKER, K. & SPILLANE, J. (1953). Cholinesterase response and symptomatology from exposure to organic phosphorus insecticides. *A.M.A. Arch. Ind. Hyg. Occup. Med.*, **7**, 383–398. [319]
918 WINNEY, R. (1976). Performance of pyrethroids as domestic insecticides. *Int. Pest Control*, **18** (1), 11–14. [257]
919 WINTER, C. E., GIANNOTTI, O. & HOLZHACKER, E. L. (1975). DDT-lipoprotein complex in the American cockroach haemolymph: a possible way of insecticide transport. *Pestic. Biochem. Physiol.*, **5** (2), 155–162. [399]
920 WRIGHT, A. (1976). World pesticides worth $14 billion by 1990. *Chem. Age*, Feb. 20th, 10. [24]
921 WRIGHT, C. G. & HILLMANN, R. C. (1975). Efficacy of Dowco 214 and Orthene in control of German cockroaches. *J. Georgia ent. Soc.*, **10** (1), 42–49. [357, 360]

SUBJECT INDEX

Acaricides, carbamates as, 364
Acceptable Daily Intake (ADI)
  chlordane, 307
  dieldrin, 307
  malathion, 342
acephate, 177, 357–358
acetone, 484
acetylcholine, 386, 410, 412, 414–415
  accumulation at nerve endings, 414
  cats and dogs, in, 135
  injection of, 415
  measurement in cockroaches, 414
  temperature and, 414
acetylcholinesterase, 320, 386, 412, 414–415
  carbamates and, 363, 412, 414
  levels in man, 327
  measurement in cockroaches, 414
  organochlorines and, 418
  organophosphates and, 412, 416
  plasma and blood cell, 351
  poisoning and, 135, 384
  resistance and, 450–451
  tests for, 141
Actellic, see pirimiphos-methyl
action potential, 385, 398, 412
additives, 78–79, 81
adverse publicity and food contamination, 29
advice to client, 67, 69
aerosol generator, see Micro-gen
aerosols
  diazinon in, 323
  dichlorvos in, 105, 109, 332–333
  disadvantages for cockroach control, 121
  inspection with, 69, 108
  intermittent type, 223
  malathion in, 339
  packs, 107, 120, 121
  propellants, fluorocarbons, 145
  pyrethrins in, 69, 71, 108, 242, 272
  pyrethroids in, 254, 268, 272
  use in aircraft, 71
aggregation pheromone, 18, 26, 102, 170, 186
air-conditioning units, 41
aircraft
  insecticides used in, 70–71
  resistant insects and, 424, 454
  treatment of, 333
air currents, cockroach response to, 102
airports, introduction via, 70
aldrin, 308, 309, 310, 312, 433
aldrin-epoxide, see dieldrin
aliesterase, 414
alkane sulphonamides, 159

allergen, carried by cockroaches, 29
allergy, caused by pyrethrum, 252
allethrin, 259–260
  discovery of, 254
  insecticidal activity of, 255, 259, 260
  compared with
    bioallethrin, 255, 260–262
    biotetramethrin, 269–270
    pyrethrins, 258, 260–261
  MGK 264 and, 240
  physiological action of, 258, 391, 396, 398
  properties of, 259
  safroxan and, 240
  tolerance to, 438
aluminium phosphide, 71, 211, 214
American cockroach, see *Periplaneta americana*
amino acids, 403–404
ammonium carbonate, 357
anaesthesia, 464, 469
analytical techniques, 143
Anarsia lineatella, 423
animal laboratories, use of baits in, 98
animals
  cockroaches introduced with, 70
  diagnosing poisoning in, 137–138
  risk to, in zoos, 72, 98
anti-caking agents, 79, 195
antidote(s), 128, 141, 200
anti-helminths, 468
anti-oxidants, 79
ants and
  bendiocarb, 367
  chlordane, 300
  chlordecone, 313
  DDT, 95
  dieldrin, 309
  malathion, 339
  propoxur, 373
apartments, see homes
apple oil, attractant properties of, 99
approval schemes
  insecticides and, 25, 75, 141–142, 146–150
  policing of, 147, 150
  undesirable effects of, 145
aquaria, control in, 72
aquarium tanks, 461
arolium, 76
arprocarb, see propoxur
arsenic, 198, 288
artificial respiration, 140
atropine, 128, 135
Attagenus megatoma, 81, 271

537

attics, 41, 123, 208
attractants, 99–102, 472–473
Australia, resistance in, 442, 445
Australian cockroach, see *Periplaneta australasiae*
avoidance of insecticides, 173
axonic transmission, 385

Bacteria, 29, 56
bait(s)
  adhesive type, 475
  ageing of, 104
  application of, 71, 316, 379
  attractants and, 99–102
  boric acid/borax in, 195
  chlordecone in, 313–316, 357
  colour of, 100
  composition of, 97–98
  containers, 103
  dichlorvos in, 328
  dieldrin in, 309
  early use of, 18
  equipment for applying, 123
  factors affecting acceptance of, 101
  feeding stimulants and, 99
  fly, 339
  food bases for, 100
  gel formulation of, 99, 105
  malathion in, 339
  mental homes, use in, 71
  mould inhibitor in, 104, 315
  pellets, use of, 103
  performance of, 103–105
  phosphorus in, 211
  practical use of, 105
  propoxur in, 372, 379
  repellency of, 103
  sodium fluoride in, 198, 200, 202
  sodium fluorosilicate in, 198
  speed of kill with, 104
  thallium sulphate in, 213
  trichlorphon in, 356–357
  unpopularity of, 98
bakers shops and bakeries, 22, 60
bananas
  as bait attractant, 18, 472–473
  attractant properties of oil, 99
  cockroaches carried with, 161–162
barrier cream, 128, 136
bars, 43, 46, 50, 57
basements, *P. americana* in, 39
Basudin, see diazinon
bathrooms, 46, 58, 59
bats, 41
Baygon, see propoxur
Baytex, see fenthion
bed bugs, see *Cimex lectularius*
bedrooms, 59
beef broth, as bait base, 99
beer
  association with, 50, 57
  bait attractant, 18, 100, 472, 473
  crates, 159, 160, 165

behaviour, insecticides and, 173, 179, 181
bellows duster, 109
bendiocarb, 366
  crack and crevice treatment (USA), 152
  properties (general) of, 367–370
  repellency of, 177, 179
  use experience in USA, 370
  wettable powder of, 84
benzene hexachloride (see also, lindane), 292–293
  beta isomer of, 298
  imported foods in, 142
  movement of isomers in cockroaches, 293
  resistance, 430
  use of, 293
BHC, see benzene hexachloride
bioallethrin, 259–262
  discovery of, 255
  physiological action of, 395
  properties (general) of, 259, 260–262
biological control, 20
biology, importance in control, 67
bioresmethrin, 270
  flushing action of, 264, 274
  insecticidal activity of, 258, 270, 272–273, 275
    compared with
      NRDC *106*, 275–276
      RU *11679*, 276
  oothecae, effect on hatching of, 274–275
  physiological action of, 395
  properties of, 270
  use against flies, 270, 272
biotetramethrin, 267
  aerosol, performance of, 268
  flushing action of, 264
  properties (general) of, 267, 268–270
"Birkenhead experiment", 370
Blaberus spp.
  effect of Dri-Die on, 208
  transport of chlordane in, 412
black carpet beetle (*Attagenus megatoma*), 81, 271
Blatta orientalis
  insecticide resistance, first instance of, 423
  pest status, 13, 27
  weight of, 486
Blattella germanica
  insecticide resistance, first instance of, 423
  military bases (USA), in, 59
  pest status, 13, 27
  population growth of, 467
  transport of, 58
  weight of, 486
Blattenex, see propoxur
body fat, dieldrin levels in, 312
boiler rooms, 60
boiler suits, 126
book bindings, 48
booklice (*Liposcelis divinatorius*), 467
Boophilus decoloratus, resistance in, 241
borax, 191–196
  bait, 195

INDEX 539

borax—*cont.*
 crack and crevice treatment (USA), 152
 insecticidal activity, 181, 196
 properties of, 193, 194
 pyrethrum and, 226
 repellency of, 178
 sodium fluoride and, 200
 use
  against cockroaches, 195
  influence of resistance on, 455
boric acid, 191–197
 application equipment for, 111
 bait, 99, 101, 103, 104, 195
 crack and crevice treatment (USA), 152
 dust, 95, 123
 insecticidal activity of, 181, 195
  compared with malathion, 340
 proofing with, 54, 195, 217
 properties of, 193, 194
 pyrethrins and, 185, 226
 repellency of, 100, 178, 185, 195
 use in
  culture rooms, 468
  homes, 195, 217
 wall void tests and, 181–182
Boston (USA), cockroaches in, 58–59
brain (cockroach)
 acetylcholinesterase inhibition in, 416
 ultra-structure, pyrethrins poisoning and, 396
breeding
 denying conditions for, 54
 laboratory cultures, 460–470
breweries, 168
brickwork
 lacquer and, 90
 wettable powders on, 85
bromophos, 352, 353
Brown-banded cockroach, see *Supella longipalpa*
Brown cockroach, see *Periplaneta brunnea*
buildings, types infested, 62–63
bulb duster, 109
buses, treatment of, 105–106, 333
business
 establishments, use of repellents in, 159
 loss of by infestation, 29
butadiene-furfuryl copolymer, see MGK R-*11*
N-isobutylundecyleneamide, 236
butyric acid as bait attractant, 100

Cab-o-sil, 195, 205
cafeterias, 46, 61, 66
campaniform organs, DDT and, 408
Canada, resistance to dieldrin in, 435, 438
cancer-producing agents, see carcinogens
cannibalism in cockroach rearing, 465
canteens, 46
carbamate insecticides, 362
 cross-resistance, 427, 443
 early use of, 362

 physiological action of, 412, 418–419, 421, 451
 recovery from, 362
 resistance to, 363, 426, 427, 445, 458
 synergism of, 363–364, 419
 temperature, effect on bees, 418
 toxicity of, 133, 135
 use against cockroaches, 20
 WHO resistance test and, 487
carbaryl, 364
 crack and crevice treatment (USA), 152
 cross-resistance, 366, 437, 439
 Hercon roach tape, 92
 insecticidal activity of, 364–366
 physiological action of, 414
 properties of, 364
 resistance to, 445–446
  cuticle penetration and, 444
  influence on use of, 319
 synergism of, 365, 419
 toxicity of, 366
carbon bisulphide, early use of, 15
carbon dioxide
 cockroach handling and, 464, 469, 470
 fumigation with, 213
carborundum, dust containing, 95
carcinogens (alleged), 29, 133
 chlordane, 145
 dieldrin, 313
 heptachlor, 145
carpet beetles, 81, 271, 339, 367
carrier in dusts, 94–95
Carson, Rachel, 223, 286
cartons
 as carriers of cockroaches, 157, 159, 161, 162
 treatment with repellents, 160
casein glue, 48
cat(s)
 acetylcholine in, 135
 bendiocarb, toxicity of, 370
 dieldrin, toxicity of, 310
 Dri-Die, toxicity of, 207
 parasite control, 339
 poisoning of, 138
catering facilities, 50
cattle tick, resistance in, 241
cellars, use of smoke generators in, 96
central heating, 46
certification procedures, 144, 150, 152, 155
cesspools, 39
Cheyletus species, 467
children, poisoning risks to, 137, 139, 154
chilling
 cockroach growth rate and, 469, 470
 immobilisation by, 468
china clay, 78, 94
chlordane, 299
 crack and crevice treatment (USA), 152, 300
 cross-resistance, 426–427, 430, 431, 433, 437, 441, 443, 444, 445, 447
 early use of, 193

chlordane—*cont.*
  environment, in, 291
  Hercon roach tape, 92
  immersion tests, 479
  insecticidal activity of, 179, 181, 201, 287, 288, 301
    compared with
      carbaryl, 365
      propoxur, 378–379
    malathion, admixture with, 338
  physiological action of, 304, 412
  preference for, in USA, 21
  properties of, 301
  repellency of, 179
  residual life of, 306, 453
  residues on kitchen utensils, 151
  resistance, 204, 224, 300, 304, 321, 433, 435, 439, 442, 443, 445, 446, 447, 453, 455
    B. germanica (first instance of), 423, 430
    control failures, 435
    malic dehydrogenase, 449
    residual life, 453
  suspension of use in USA, 145
  toxicity of, 307
  use in homes, 201, 291
chlordecone, 313
  baits, 99, 101, 103, 104, 313–316
  cross-resistance to, 441
  environment, in, 291
  insecticidal activity compared with trichlorphon, 357
  physiological action of, 412
  safety in use of, 316
  toxicity of, 316
  use
    against ants, 313
    in culture rooms, 468
    in kitchens, 316
    influence of resistance on, 455
    on ships, 314
chlorinated hydrocarbons, see organochlorine insecticides
chlorpyrifos, 343
  application methods, 123
  crack and crevice treatment (USA), 152
  insecticidal activity of, 84, 344–345, 347, 360
    compared with
      chlordane, 301
      fenitrothion, 347
      propoxur, 378, 379
  lacquer, 91
  repellency of, 177
  toxicity of, 347
  use
    in homes, 196
    on ships, 324
    in USA, 429
chlorpyrifos methyl, 343, 345, 347, 360
choice boxes for repellency tests, 178–179, 495

choline acetylase, 418
cholinesterase, see acetylcholinesterase
Chrysanthemum species, 218–219
cigarette beetle (*Lasioderma serricorne*), 329
Cimex
  hemipterus, resistance in, 241
  lectularius
    bendiocarb and, 367
    DDT resistance in, 423
    fumigation of, 213
    malathion and, 339
cinemas, 50, 61, 167
circadian rhythm, 172
cismethrin, 276
  flushing action of, 264
classification of pesticides, 150–151
claws, pick up of insecticide and, 76
clays, sorptive, 205, 471
clearance of pesticides, see approval schemes
client, co-operation by and advice to, 67–70
cloakrooms, infestation in, 163
Clostridium welchii, food poisoning and, 56
clothing
  cockroaches carried on, 162–163
  protective, 67, 69, 108, 126–127, 132, 136, 153
clubs, 46, 61
Coca-cola, as attractant, 472
cockroach eradication, 67–73
  failure of, 81
  key factors in, 75
cockroaches
  casual intruders, as, 73
  collecting, 460, 470–475, 487
  congregation of, 51
  control, early methods, 14
  control, modern methods, 67–72
  damage by, 30
  disease carrying by, 27
  Finland, in 60
  food finding by, 100
  food poisoning and, 56
  geographical distribution of, 58–66
  habitat of, 27
  immigrant, 44
  military bases, in, 59
  moisture requirements of, 46
  odour of, 29
  pest species of, 27
  pigeons and, 37
  piggeries and, 34
  public attitude toward, 33
  rearing, 460–470
  resistance
    first detection of, 423
    history of, 428–447
  response to odours, 100
  seasonal changes of, in USA, 59
  Singapore, in, 58
  starvation and, 402
  transport of, 14, 39, 43, 70, 73, 161–168, 454

cockroaches—*cont.*
   U.K., in, 60–66
   U.S.A., in, 58–59
   West Germany, in, 56–58, 60
coconut palms, 39
coffee, as attractant, 472
collecting cockroaches, 460, 470–475, 487
commodities
   cockroaches on, 43
   entry into buildings in, 73
Common cockroach, see *Blatta orientalis*
complaints of food contamination, 29
computer rooms, use of baits in, 99
concentrates, 78
   accurate dilution of, 69
   dermal risk from, 132
   spillage and, 154
concrete, insecticide absorption into, 84
condensation, 46
Confused flour beetle, see *Tribolium confusum*
congregation, of cockroaches, 51
conservationists, organochlorines and, 281
contact action of sodium fluoride, 202–203
contact dust (rodenticidal), 110
containers (pesticide)
   dispensing from, 137, 144
   disposal of, 137
   first aid advice, 140
   misuse of, 139
containers for cockroach rearing, 461, 465
contamination
   eating utensils, of, 137
   insecticides, by, 74
   protection from, 154
   washing and, 136
controlled release by
   lacquers, 89
   microencapsulation, 93
conveyors, harbourage in, 168
Coopermatic aerosol, 223
coral, 39
cordials, 46
Corpus Christi, 430, 431, 432
correspondence courses, 145
corrugated cardboard
   cockroach harbourage in, 164
   cockroach rearing and, 462
co-solvents, 80
cotton
   pests of, 198
   ULV treatment of, 120
cows, carbaryl and, 366
crack and crevice treatment (USA), 22, 67, 151–152, 154, 300, 309, 327
cracks, sealing of, 20, 54
crawl spaces, 39
crayons, sodium fluoride in, 200
crickets, 107, 373
   control of, 198
cross-resistance
   carbamates, 427, 443
      carbaryl, 366, 437, 439

      propoxur, 446
   insecticide use and, 454
   organochlorines, 317, 427
      aldrin, 433
      chlordane, 426–427, 430, 431, 433, 437, 441, 443, 444, 445, 447
      DDT, 366, 427, 430, 437, 439, 441, 446, 447
      dieldrin, 309, 427, 431, 433, 437, 441, 443, 444, 447
      heptachlor, 433
      lindane, 427, 430, 431, 433, 443, 444, 446, 447
      methoxychlor, 437
      telodrin, 441
   organophosphates, 335, 427, 442, 446
      diazinon, 443, 445, 446, 447
      fenitrothion, 445
      fenthion, 445
      malathion, 427, 437, 441, 445, 446
   pyrethrins, 241, 427, 441, 446
cross-tolerance (vigour), 426
cryolite, 198
crystal formation
   lacquers and, 89
   suspension concentrates and, 87
crystallisation
   of insecticides, 77
   of propoxur, 81
crystals, DDT, insecticidal activity of, 95
CSMA aerosol test method, 481–482
CSMA cockroach spray method, 481–482
Culicidae, see mosquitoes
culverts, 39
cuticle
   abrasion of, 95
   cleaning of, 230
   effects of UV light on, 169
   penetration by
      carbaryl, 364
      dieldrin, 310
      malathion, 340
      pyrethrins, 230, 387, 390
   thickness of, 76
   water-proof properties of, 208
cyanoacetic acid, 159
cyclamates, 141
Cydia pomonella, resistance and, 423
Cythion, see malathion
Czechoslovakia
   DDT resistance in, 441
   dieldrin resistance in, 446

Dairies, 46
damage by cockroaches, 30
date sugar, bait containing, 100
dead spaces
   application of dust to, 95
   elimination of, 54
deaths from pesticides, 140
decor
   cockroach harbourage and, 52
   wettable powders and, 83

DDE, 284, 399
DDT, 282
  baits, 287
  cross-resistance, 366, 427, 430, 437, 439, 441, 446, 447
  discovery of, 283
  early use of, 200, 220, 283, 284, 287
  environment, in, 223, 245, 284, 286, 291
  insecticidal activity of, 287–289
    compared with
      chlordane, 301
      lindane, 295
      sodium fluoride, 201, 287, 288
  litigation (in USA), 141
  malathion, admixture with, 338
  physiological action of, 398–409, 420
    degradation, 399–400, 449
    electric shocks and, 407
    excretion, 400
    fats, solubility in, 398
    induced toxin, 406–407
    nerve function, 398, 407–409, 444
    penetration and distribution, 399
    poisoning symptoms, 286–287, 289, 398, 400
    speed of, 287
  properties of, 283–284
  residual life of, 283
  residues
    in diet (USA), 142
    in imported foods (UK), 142
    medical significance of, 286
  resistance, 286, 426, 427, 428, 430, 431, 434, 435, 437, 439, 441, 444, 447, 448, 449
    biological characteristics and, 439
    cockroaches (USA), in, 428
    insects, in, 423
    mechanism for, 448
    nerve cord, binding to, 444
  topical application tests, in, 485
  use
    in agriculture (USA), 141
    military requirements, 283
    replacement by lindane, 291
    in UK, 22–23, 455
  wildlife and, 286
  world production of, 283
DDVP, see dichlorvos
delivery areas and *P. americana*, 39
deodorants, repellency of, 176
deodorised insecticide, 78
depallethrine, see bioallethrin
dermal absorption, 132
  diazinon and, 326
  first aid for, 140
dermatitis, pyrethrum and, 252
derris, 221, 282, 283
desiccant dusts, 205–209
desiccation, 95
developmental stages
  effects of U.V. light on, 169
  susceptibility to pyrethrins, 233

dextrin, bait formulations and, 357
diatomaceous earths, 205
diazinon, 320
  advantages of, 320–321
  crack and crevice treatment (USA), 152
  cross-resistance, 443, 445, 446, 447
  early use of, 181, 319
  formulations of, 84, 89, 91, 92, 323
  insecticidal activity of, 84, 91, 295, 323–325, 360
    compared with
      carbaryl, 365
      chlorpyrifos, 344, 345
      dichlorvos, 329
      fenitrothion, 347, 349
      propoxur, 377, 380
  lacquer, 89, 91, 92, 323
  oothecae, effects on, 250
  physiological action of, 326, 414, 417
  repellency of, 179
  residual life of, 204, 306, 323, 324, 325, 453
  residues on kitchen utensils, 151
  resistance, 325, 374, 429, 438, 439, 441, 442, 443, 445, 446, 447, 448, 453, 456, 458
  tests
    immersion, 479
    topical, effect of solvent on, 484
    wall void, 182
    WHO resistance, 487
  tolerance to, 92, 447, 448
  toxicity of, 325
  use
    in homes, 196, 201, 209, 323–324
    on ships, 324
    in USA, 21, 224, 321, 429, 455, 458
  vapour action of, 105, 489
diazoxon, 326, 417
Dibrom, see naled
dibutyl succinate, see Tabutrex
dichlorvos, 327
  aerosols, 105, 106, 109, 328, 332–333
  baits, 99, 328
  chlorpyrifos, admixture with, 343
  crack and crevice treatment (USA), 152
  development of, 319
  formulations of, 327–328
  flushing action, 328, 332
  insecticidal activity of, 288, 329–335
  maximum allowable concentration of, 335
  mechanical dispensers and, 71
  misting and fogging of, 246, 330
  physiological action of, 320
  properties of, 327
  resin strips, 105, 327, 328, 331–332
  toxicity, 335
  vapour action of, 105–106, 215, 330, 331, 489
dieldrin, 308
  cross-resistance, 309, 427, 431, 433, 437, 441, 443, 444, 447
  environment, in, 286, 291

INDEX 543

dieldrin—cont.
  insecticidal activity of, 91, 92, 287, 295, 309
    compared with bendiocarb, 367
  lacquer, 89, 90, 91, 92, 309
  physiological action of, 310, 400, 402, 410–412, 450
  properties of, 308–309
  residual life of, 309
  resistance, 92, 99, 426, 433, 435, 437, 438, 441, 442, 443, 444, 445, 446, 447, 448, 450, 453
    B. germanica (first instance of) UK, 447
    cuticle penetration and, 450
    mechanism for, 309–310
    mosquitoes, in, 423
    penetration of nerve cord and, 450
  toxicity of, 310–313
  use in bakeries (UK), 23
  WHO resistance tests, 487
diet for cockroach rearing, 463–464
diethyl nonamide, 159
diethyl toluamide, 157
diluent, 78
  in dust formulations, 94
  functions of, 78
  in wettable powders, 84
dilution rate of insecticides, 79
dimethyl phthalate, 157
dimetilan, 363, 365, 381
dining rooms, cockroaches in (USA), 59
dioxacarb, 381
Dipterex, see trichlorphon
direct spray test method, 480–482
diseases carried by cockroaches, 27
dispersing agents in wettable powders, 84
distress caused by cockroaches, 29
distribution of cockroaches in UK, 64
dobbin duster, see dust blower
dogs
  acetylcholine in, 135
  diagnosis of poisoning in, 137, 138
  parasite control, 339
  toxicity of
    chlordecone, 316
    dieldrin, 310
    Dri-Die, 207
    sodium fluoride, 200
    trichlorphon, 357
dose, importance in human poisoning, 139
Dowco-*214*, see chlorpyrifos methyl
drains, 39, 56, 69
  baits in, 104
  cockroaches in, 163
Dri-Die *67*, 205–209
  anti-caking agents, 195
  application, equipment for, 111
  crack and crevice treatment (USA), 152
  insecticidal activity of, 206–207, 208
  oothecae and, 208
  proofing with, 54, 217
  toxicity of, 207
  wall void tests with, 182

driers in lacquers, 88
drilling holes and use of dust, 71, 110, 123, 209
Drione
  composition of, 207
  dust, use of, 197, 209
  insecticidal activity of, 209
  sewers, treatment with, 209
drug stores, 50
dry cleaners, cockroach entry into, 163
ducts, 51
  in hospitals, 71, 85
  in ships, 71
  use of smoke generators, 96
Dursban, see chlorpyrifos
dusts, 94–95
  application of, 95
  colouring of, 200
  desiccant, 205–209
  first-aid and, 141
  flushing agents in, 187
  insecticide tests with, 490, 494
  physiological action of, 202–203
  properties of, 77, 94
  propoxur, 374
  pyrethrum/sodium fluoride, 95
  repellency of, 94, 172–173, 179
  toxicity of, 131, 132
  use of, 22, 84, 95, 109–111, 123, 208–209
  wall void tests and, 181–182
dust bins for cockroach rearing, 461
dust blowers, 109–111
dust coat, 126
dust mask (Martindale), 127, 128
dyes, 79
dysentery, 472

Effluent, 39, 46
egg case, see ootheca
electrical switch gear, treatment of, 99
electric devices for confining cockroaches, 461, 475
electronic equipment, treatment of, 214
elevator shafts, 48
embarrassment caused by cockroaches, 29
emetic, 131
emulsifiers, 78, 82
  repellency tests on, 176
emulsions
  advantages of, 83
  comparison with suspension concentrates, 86
  convenience of, 84
  disadvantages of, 83
  poor performance of, 84, 377
  popularity of, 88
  properties of, 82, 84
  spray nozzle for, 113
endrin, 312
  excretory efficiency and, 400
  toxicity, 282
entomophobia, 29

entry into buildings, 43–44, 54, 70, 71, 73
environment, 161–168
  concern for, 223
  contamination of, 74
  DDT and, 141, 223, 245
  E.P.A. and, 149–150
  levels of pesticides in, 142
  monitoring of pesticides in, 141
  protection of, 137, 141–142
  pyrethrins and, 245
  risks to, 133
Environmental Protection Agency (USA), 149–150
  crack and crevice treatment, 151–152
  pesticide registration and, 150
enzymes
  insecticidal action and, 384, 393
  insecticide detoxication and, 451
Ephestia elutella (tobacco moth), 329
equipment
  care of, 123–124, 154
  choice of, 108
  clean use of, 108
  for inspection, 108–109
  motorised, 117–122
  proper use of, 154
  (safety) legislation and, 153
  sophistication of, 108
  for self-protection, 125–128
eserine, 415
essential oils as bait attractants, 99
ethyl alcohol for mite control in cultures, 467–468
ethylene oxide, 213
Europe, cockroach resistance in, 429, 435, 442
European Economic Community
  approval scheme for pesticides, 146–147
  movement of goods in, 161
excretion (cockroach), insecticidal poisoning and, 400
eyes
  contamination of, 132, 140
  irritation of, by pyrethrins, 252
  protection of, 128
  sensitivity tests for, 133

Faecal pellets, aggregation pheromone and, 102
false ceilings, 51
Famid, see dioxacarb
fat body
  DDT susceptibility and (cockroaches), 399–400
  dieldrin levels in (man), 312
  insecticide activation by (cockroaches), 418
fat loss, DDT poisoning and, 403
fear
  of cockroaches, 29
  of pesticide effects, 145
Federal Environmental Pesticide Control Act (1972), 150

Federal Insecticide, Fungicide and Rodenticide Act (1947), 148, 150
Federal Occupational Safety and Health Act (1971), 153
feeding stimulants in baits, 99, 101
fenchlorphos, 357
  crack and crevice treatment (USA), 152
fencholic acid, 159, 497
fenitrothion, 347
  baits, 104
  cross-resistance, 445
  development of, 319
  formulations of, 84
  insecticidal activity of, 186, 295, 347–350
    compared with
      bendiocarb, 368
      chlorpyrifos, 345
      malathion, 340
      propoxur, 377, 379
      resmethrin, 271
  oxo-sumithion, activation to, 351
  physiological action of, 414, 416, 418
  properties of, 347
  repellency of, 179
  residual life of, 324
  stored food pests and, 353
  topical application tests, in, 484, 485
  toxicity of, 350–351
  use by Dept. Public Health (UK), 23
fenthion, 357
  crack and crevice treatment (USA), 152
  cross-resistance, 445
  resistance to, 445
Ficam 80W, see bendiocarb
filter flies (*Psychoda* spp.), 329
filters for masks, 128
Finland,
  cockroaches in, 60
  pesticide regulations in, 147
first-aid, 128, 136, 140
fish, toxicity to
  bendiocarb, 370
  DDT, 307, 337
  dichlorvos, 337
  dieldrin, 307
  iodofenphos, 356
  lindane, 307–308
  malathion, 337
  pyrethrins, 252
flammable liquids, safety with, 136
flats
  cockroaches in, 61
  proofing of, with chemicals, 54
  in Singapore, 58
  in USA, 58–59
fleas
  bendiocarb and, 367
  carbaryl and, 366
  DDT resistance in, 423
flies
  iodofenphos and, 352, 353
  malathion and, 339
  repellents against, 159

flit-gun, see sprayers
flushing
  agents, repellency tests on, 176, 187
  by dichlorvos, 328
  by propoxur, 157, 374
  by pyrethrins, 157, 187, 247–249, 272
  synthetic pyrethroids and, 264, 272
  by ULV, 122–123
fog(s)
  application equipment, 117, 120
  bioresmethrin in, 275
  disadvantages for cockroach control, 121, 330
  inhalation risks and, 131
  pyrethrins in, 242
  use in homes, 246
food
  carts, 48, 71, 214
  contamination, with insecticides, 131, 137, 159
  contaminants, cockroaches as, 29
  crack and crevice treatment (USA), 151–152
  dichlorvos in, 338
  dieldrin in, 312
  finding by cockroaches, 100
  laws regulating wholesomeness of, 29
  movement of cockroaches in, 164
  pesticide levels in UK imports, 142
  poisoning, cockroaches and, 56
  requirements of cockroaches, 48, 50
  taint, by cockroaches, 29
food manufacturing premises, 60
  aerosols in, 120, 223
  cockroach entry into, 44, 163
  hygiene, importance in, 54, 163
  lacquers in, 89
  meat and poultry, 152
  P. americana in, 60
  protective clothing in, 126
  supplies to, 164
  treatment problems in, 184, 252
formalin for mite control in cultures, 467–468
formulations
  availability of, 21
  contact action and, 75
  correct choice of, 75
  properties and performance of, 74–106
  toxicity and, 133
free-flowing agents, dusts containing, 95
fruit flies, 329
fumigants, 213–215, 294, 330, 333
fumigation
  aircraft, of, 70–71
  early methods of, 15–18
  food carts, of, 71
  masks and, 127–128
  "misting", misnomer for, 244
  mite control in cultures and, 467–468
  poisoning risks and, 131
fungicides, carbamates as, 364

Gamma BHC, see lindane
ganglia
  diazinon, effects on, 417
  neurone damage by pyrethrins in, 397
  ultra-structure, pyrethrins poisoning and, 396
garages, 43
garbage cans, see refuse containers
gel, bait formulations of, 99, 101, 103, 105
genetic variability, resistance and, 425
geographical
  distribution in UK, 64–66
  spread of cockroaches, 58
German cockroach, see *Blattella germanica*
Gesarol, see DDT
Getz powder blower, 109
giant fibres, electrical activity in, 396
gloves, protective, 126–127, 154
glucose and DDT poisoning, 402
glutamine and insecticide poisoning, 404
glycerides as feeding stimulants, 101
glycerol, 103
glycogen and insecticide poisoning, 393, 402
glycols, feeding response to, 101
Glycyphagus spp. 467
goggles, protective, 128
Graham's trap, 472
grasshoppers, control of, 198
groundnut oil as bait attractant, 99
gunpowder, cockroach control by, 18
gut, action of pyrethrins in, 393
Gyplure, 102

Hands, contamination of, 131
harbourages
  cockroach rearing and, 462
  detection of, 247
  dichlorvos, penetration of, 331
  indoors, 50–52
  insecticide absorption into, 84
  outdoors, 39–43
  partial treatment of, 179
  repellency of insecticides and, 175–189
  requirements for, 172
  response of cockroaches to, 178
  treatment of, 69, 173, 175, 176, 208–209, 247, 253
hard hat, see helmet
hazards, classification of pesticides and, 150–151
Health and Safety at Work Act (1975), 153
health and safety, attitudes to, 154
health risks
  ill-maintained equipment, from, 124
  insecticide use and, 67
  protection against, 126
  training in, 153
haemolymph
  DDT binding in, 399
  organophosphorus insecticides and, 417
  toxic components in, 390
  volume, pyrethrins and, 392

heart rate
  acetylcholine and, 419
  chlordane poisoning and, 304
  lindane poisoning and, 410
  pyrethrins poisoning and, 392
Heathrow airport, 380
hedgehogs, biological control and, 20
helmet, 126
Henschoutedenia spp., 161
heptachlor
  chlordane, impurity in, 301, 307
  cross-resistance, 433
  speed of action of, 287
  suspension of use (in USA), 145
Hercon roach tape, 92
heterocyclic amines, 159
hexyl hexanoate, attractant properties of, 100
hexyl pentenoate, attractant properties of, 100
Hi-Fog, 121
home(s) and apartments, 44, 46, 51
  attitudes towards pest control in, 163
  baits (paste) in, 104, 212, 357
  boric acid in, 196
  chlordane in, 201, 305, 435
  chlorpyrifos in, 196, 345
  diazinon in, 201, 305, 323–324
  dichlorvos in, 331
  Dri-Die in, 209
  Drione in, 209
  dust application in, 109
  emulsion and oil sprays in, 85
  entry of cockroaches into, 44, 54, 161, 163
  hygiene in, 55, 163
  low income, *B. germanica* in, 59
  malathion in, 201, 305, 323–324
  mist treatment in, 243, 246
  poisoning in the, 138
  proofing with chemicals, 54, 195
  propoxur in, 378
  repellents in, 159
  resmethrin in, 272
  retail products, use of in, 163
  service contracts and, 85
  Singapore, in, 58
  sodium fluoride in, 201, 305
  sodium fluorosilicate in, 198
  U.K., in, 61, 62
  U.S.A., in, 58, 59
  West Germany, in, 60
Hong Kong, control failures with dieldrin in, 439
hose (sprayer), 124
hospitals, 48, 60, 71
  cockroach control in, 71
  disease transmission in, 56
  Dri-Die in, 209
  Drione in, 209
  lacquers in, 89
  propoxur in, resistance to, 447
hotels, 43, 46, 51
  cockroach entry into, 161, 167
house(s), see homes

houseflies, see *Musca domestica*
householder
  insecticide performance and, 204
  protection of, 137
humidity
  cockroach rearing and, 461
  cockroach requirements for, 172
hydrogen cyanide, 15, 213
hygiene
  effects on cockroaches, 55
  in homes, 163
  improvements in, 69
  in kitchens (Germany), 70
  standards of, 39, 44, 52
hyperactivity and DDT poisoning, 403

Identification of pest cockroaches, 67
immersion tests, 479
immobilisation of cockroaches, 468–470
India, malathion resistance in, 446
indoor infestations, 46–55
infestation
  assessing levels of, 460
  effluent and, 39
  factors encouraging, 46
  lack of concern for, 46, 52
  refuse tips and, 37
  sanitation and, 39
  temperate climates, in, 33–39
  tropical climates, in, 39, 41, 44, 46
ingestion
  poisoning by, 131
    first aid for, 140
inhalation
  poisoning by, 131–132, 252, 326
    first aid for, 141
injuries (occupational), recording of, 140
inorganic insecticides, 191
insect growth regulators, 26
insecticides
  approval for use of, 25, 69
  benefits from, 13
  development of, 13, 384
  early types of, 191
  efficiency of use and, 75
  formulations of, 74–106
  future outlook for, 24
  maximising the effect of, 69
  mode of action of, 383
  mutagenic properties of, 425
  nervous system of insects and, 384–386
  performance of
    claims for, 69
    on ships, 71
  physiological action of, 383
  pick up by insects, importance of, 348
  preferences for, 21–23
  principal users for cockroach control, 13
  properties, importance of, 67
  repellency of, 172–187
  resistance to, 422–459
  restrictions in use of, 252
  screening of, 384

INDEX

insecticides—*cont.*
  side effects of, 20
  specificity of, 318, 384
  storage of, 136
  susceptibility of sexes to, 176
  test methods for, 476–497
insorbicides, 95
inspection, 69–70
insulation as cockroach harbourage, 163
iodofenphos, 352
  baits, 105, 355
  development of, 319
  formulations of, 353
  insecticidal activity of, 353–355, 360
    compared with
      bendiocarb, 368
      fenitrothion, 353, 354
  properties of, 352
  suspension concentrate, 353
  toxicity of, 325, 355–356
ironing board cupboards, 52
isolan, 363, 365, 381

Japan
  pesticide production in, 24, 255
  resistance to chlorinated insecticides in, 443, 444
Japanese cockroach, see *Periplaneta japonica*
jars for
  cockroach rearing, 461
  cockroach trapping, 471, 472
juke boxes, cockroaches in, 159
jute sacking, 90
Jutland, dieldrin resistance in, 441

Keatings powder, 219
Kenya Pyrethrum Growers Association, 220
Kepone, see chlordecone
kerosene in
  oil sprays, 78
  topical application tests, 484
kitchens, 46
  cockroaches in, 57, 60
  environment of, 61
  in Germany, 57, 60
  grease in, 78
  in homes (USA), 58
  hospitals and, 71
  insecticide repellency tests in, 178
  lacquers in, 89
  slow release (dichlorvos) in, 331, 337
knapsack equipment, 110
kraft paper sacks, 90

Label(s)
  information on, 147, 150
  instructions for use and, 136, 137, 143, 147–150
  pesticide containers and, 79, 147
  precautions for safe use and, 148
  toxicity classification and, 151

lacquers
  diazinon, 323, 379–380
  dieldrin, resistance to, 441, 447
  fenitrothion, unsuitability in, 347
  Heathrow airport, use at, 379–380
  properties and use of, 88–92, 123
  propoxur, 372, 379–380
Lasioderma serricorne (cigarette beetle), 329
laundries, 46, 71, 163
lead arsenate, resistance and, 423
LC_{50}, 427, 479
LD_{50}, 133, 427, 478
Leidynema appendiculata, 468
legislation
  functions of, 130
  insecticide development retarded by, 361
  pesticide use and, 141–155
  policing of, 147
  pyrethrins and, 253
  training in, 152–155
  violations of (USA), 153
lethane, 215–216, 282
Leucophaea maderae
  allethrin and, 261
  chlordane and, 305
  Dri-Die and, 208
  parathion and, 418
  pest status, 27
  propoxur and, 374
lice
  DDT and, 283, 284
  DDT resistance in, 423
  lindane and, 299
  pyrethrum and, 220
light fume mask, 128
lindane, 290
  baits, 99, 104
  cross-resistance, 427, 430, 431, 433, 443, 444, 446, 447
  dust, 95
  environment, in, 291
  formulations of, 294
  insecticidal activity of, 201, 262, 287, 295
    compared with
      chlordane, 301
      malathion, 340
  legislation and, 291
  maximum allowable concentration, 298
  physiological action of, 289, 295, 410
  properties of, 292–295
  repellency of, 186
  resistance to, 296, 426, 433, 434, 435, 437, 438, 439, 445, 447
  smoke generators, 95–96
  stored food pests and, 353
  toxicity of, 297–299
  use
    in bakeries (UK), 22
    in Dept. Public Health (UK), 23, 455
  vapour action of, 105, 489
  vaporisers, 71, 299
lipoproteins
  DDT, binding and, 399

Liposcelis divinatorius (booklice), 467
living quarters, see homes
liver microsomes, 297, 307, 311
locker rooms, 46, 163
Local authorities, see public health departments
logarithmic interval in insecticide tests, 478, 483
LT_{50}, 427
lungs, inhalation risk and, 127

Madeira cockroach, see *Leucophaea maderae*
maintenance of equipment, 123–125
malaoxon, 320, 343, 416, 417
malaria
  DDT and, 284
  eradication, setbacks in, 423
  insecticide resistance and, 423
malathion, 338
  crack and crevice treatment (USA), 152
  cross-resistance, 427, 437, 441, 445, 446
  development of, 319
  fog, 246
  immersion tests, in, 479
  insecticidal activity of, 91, 92, 246, 340–341, 360
    compared with
      chlorpyrifos, 345
      dichlorvos, 329
      fenitrothion, 350
  lacquer, 89, 91, 92
  malaoxon, activation to, 320, 343, 416, 417
  odour of, 78
  physiological action of, 320, 341, 343, 414, 416–417, 427
  properties of, 338–339
  repellency of, 186
  residual life of, 269, 273, 306
  resistance, 341, 437, 438, 442, 445, 446
    acetylcholinesterase depression and, 450–451
    amino acids and, 441
    B. germanica (first instance of), 441
    residual life and, 453
  stored food pests and, 353
  tolerance to, 447
  topical application tests, in, 485
  toxicity, 290, 342
  use
    in homes, 201, 323–324
    influence of resistance on, 455
    on ships, 324
malt extract, as bait attractant, 100, 473
maltose, as bait attractant, 100, 101
Malrin, 432
mannitol, feeding stimulation by, 101
markets, 43
masks, 127–128, 136, 154
Maximum Allowable Concentration (MAC), 298, 335
MCA *600*, 382, 443, 445

meat, as cockroach bait, 473
mercuric chloride, as bait toxicant, 99
meter points, 39
methyl bromide, 215
methyl myristate, as bait attractant, 101, 105
methylene chloride, 81
methoxychlor, 284
  cross-resistance, 437
  malathion, admixture with, 338
  physiological action of, 401
  toxicity, 282
mexacarbate, 364, 381
MGK
  R-*11*, 160
  R-*55*, 160
  R-*874*, 160
  264, 240
    allethrin, synergist for, 240
    bioallethrin, synergist for, 260
    crack and crevice treatment (USA), 152
    pyrethrins, synergist for, 160, 236
    repellency of, 176
    tolerance in food, 253
micro-drop applicator, 482
microencapsulation, pyrethrins and, 93
Micro-gen, 109, 121–123
military bases, cockroaches in, 59, 433, 435, 437, 446
milk products, 46
mist
  blowers, 117, 120
  disadvantages for cockroach control, 121, 175, 242, 246, 330
  inhalation risks and, 131
  treatment of homes by, 243–244
mites
  cockroach rearing and, 461, 467
  iodofenphos and, 353
moisture, cockroach need for, 46
molasses, as bait attractant, 472
molluscicides, carbamates as, 364
mortality/dose response curve, 478, 488
mosquitoes (Culicidae)
  bendiocarb and, 367
  control by ULV, 118
  DDT and, 284
  dichlorvos and, 329
  malathion and, 339
  particle size and, 77
  poisoning incidents in control of, 299
  propoxur and, 373
  pyrethrins and, 220
  repellents against, 159
  resistance in, 423, 424, 425
  synthetic pyrethroids and, 254
moth control
  malathion and, 339
  sodium fluorosilicate and, 198
motors, cockroach harbourage in, 163, 167
Musca domestica
  allethrin and, 259, 267
  bioresmethrin and, 270, 272
  biotetramethrin and, 269

carbamates and, 363
carbaryl and, 364
DDT and, 431, 485
diazinon and, 321, 326
dichlorvos and, 329
MGK *264* and, 240
propoxur and, 373
prothrin and, 277
resistance in, 241, 423, 425, 427
resmethrin and, 267, 270
safroxan and, 240, 241
sesame oil and, 240
synergised carbamates and, 363, 419
synergised pyrethrins and, 237, 239
synthetic pyrethroids and, 254, 279
tetramethrin and, 267
mustard beetles, 390
mutagenic compounds, 29

Naled, 357
National Poisons Information Centres, 139
naval installations, chlordane resistant cockroaches in, 433
NC *6897*, see bendiocarb
negative after-potential, 386, 407
nematodes, cockroach rearing and, 467, 468
Neocid, see DDT
nerve function
   acetylcholine and, 386, 414
   acetylcholinesterase and, 386, 414
   DDT and, 407–409
   lindane and, 410
   pyrethrins and, 393–398
nervous system
   DDT binding and, 408, 444
   dieldrin binding, 411, 450
   insecticide action and, 384–387
   insecticide sensitivity and temperature, 391
   pyrethrins and, 393–398
neurones, 385
night inspection, 55, 70
nitrogen
   anaesthetisation of cockroaches by, 469, 470
   cockroach exposure to, 214
Notification of Pesticides Scheme, see Pesticides Safety Precautions Scheme
NRDC
   106, 255, 275–276
   108, 255
   119, see cismethrin
   143, see permethrin
   161, 258
nucleating agent in suspension concentrates, 87
Nuvan, see dichlorvos
Nuvanol-N, see iodofenphos

Odour
   of cockroaches, 29
   response of cockroaches to, 100
Official Test Aerosol (OTA), 482

Official Test Insecticide (OTI), 481
oil rigs, 164
oil spray
   absorption of, 81
   disadvantages of, 80
   nozzle for, 113
   properties of, 80
oothecae
   bioresmethrin, hatching and, 274–275
   delayed hatching of, 173
   diazinon effects on, 250
   dichlorvos effects on, 331
   Dri-Die effects on, 208
   introduction into buildings, 163
   production in culture of, 467
   pyrethrins effects on, 249–250
orange (oil) as attractant, 99
ordeal bean, 363
organic thiocyanates, 215
   carbaryl synergism by, 419
   cockroaches, effects on, 216
organochlorine insecticides, 281
   cross-resistance, 317, 427
   dermal poisoning by, 132
   in diet (UK), 142
   environmental risks and, 141, 281
   health risk from, 281
   legislation and, 282, 429
   non-recovery from, 181
   physiological action of, 398–412
   preference for, 20
   public alarm and, 281
   pyrethrins in combination with, 316
   resistance to, 21, 426, 427, 447, 448, 458
   use in (USA), 281
   wildlife and, 142
organophosphorus insecticides, 318
   cross-resistance, 335, 427, 442, 446
   development of, 319
   environmental risks and, 318
   physiological action of, 320, 412–418, 451
   preference for, 20, 318, 320, 429
   resistance, 426, 427, 458
      first instance of, 424
      influence on use of, 319
      progress (since 1963), 447
      types of, 442
   safety record of, 144
   tolerance to, 442
   toxicity of, 133, 135, 251, 253, 319
Oriental cockroach, see *Blatta orientalis*
Orthene, see acephate
Oryzaephilus surinamensis, 353
outdoor infestations, 33–44
ovens, 46, 48
oxo-sumithion, 351

Packaging, see cartons
paint(s)
   emulsions and, 84
   insecticides incorporated in, 93
   interaction with insecticides, 71
   oil sprays and, 80

P.A.M., see pralidoxime chloride
Panama Canal Zone, resistance to chlordane in, 435
Panchlora viridis, 161
pantries, 46
Papua, chlordane resistance in, 442
paraffin wax blocks, 104, 314
paranitrophenol, 104, 315
parasites (ecto-)
   diazinon and, 321
   malathion and, 339
parathion, 290, 319, 325, 347, 415, 418
Parcoblatta spp., 27
particles, health risks and, 127
passenger baggage (air), cockroaches in, 70
paste, chlordecone in, 103, 314
pea aphid, strains of, 425
Pediculus humanus, resistance in, 241
people, as carriers of cockroaches, 162–163
pepsin, as bait component, 100
peripheral nerves, insecticide action and, 393, 407
Periplaneta
   americana
      pest status, 27
      weight of, 486
   australasiae
      pest status, 27
      weight of, 486
   brunnea
      chlordane/diazinon, resistance to, 443
      pest status, 27
      resistance tests on, 441
      synergised pyrethrins and, 241
   fuliginosa
      insecticide tests on, 345, 348
      pest status, 27
      in USA, 59
   japonica
      pest status, 27
peristaltic contractions, insecticide poisoning and, 418
permethrin, 277, 279, 280
persimmon, as bait component, 100
perthane, 432
pest control contractor, 55
pest status of cockroaches, 29–33
Pesticide Residue Analysis Information Service, 142
Pesticides Safety Precautions Scheme (UK), 146
petroleum distillates
   oil sprays and, 78
   price and availability of, 25
pets, 44, 69
   pesticide use and, 146
   poisoning risks to, 137, 138
   repellent sprays for, 160
pet shops, treatment of, 72, 98
pharmaceutical works
   protective clothing in, 126
   use of UV light in, 170

pheromones, response to, 102
phosphatase
   chlordane and, 450
   fenitrothion and, 418
   pyrethrins and, 393
phosphine (Phostoxin), see aluminium phosphide
phospholipids, insecticidal poisoning and, 393
phosphorus
   baits (paste) containing, 99, 212
   early use of, 18, 211
   properties (general) of, 211–212
photodecomposition
   pyrethrins and, 228, 252
   synthetic pyrethroids and, 259, 267
Physostigma venosum, 363
physostigmine, 363, 384, 413
pictures, harbourages behind, 51
pineapple oil, as attractant, 99
piperonyl butoxide, 236
   allethrin and, 259, 260–261
   bioallethrin and, 260–261
   bioresmethrin and, 274
   biotetramethrin and, 270
   carbamates and, 373, 418–419
   carbaryl and, 363, 364, 418–419
   crack and crevice treatment (USA), 152
   first use of, 220
   metabolism of, 236
   mexacarbate and, 363
   propoxur and, 363
   pyrethrins and, 236, 398
   resmethrin and, 270–271
   synthetic pyrethroids and, 257, 279
   tetramethrin and, 267, 268
   tolerance in food, 253
   toxicity of, 238
pirimiphos-methyl, 359
plants, damage by sodium fluoride, 198
plaster, use of lacquer on, 90
plaster of paris, baits containing, 18
poisoning of man, 130–135
   antidotal treatment and, 128, 135
   incidents, 139–140, 143–144, 299
   protection from, 136–137
poliomyelitis, 472
pollution, 141
   E.P.A. and, 150
polytetrafluroethylene (PTFE)
   confining cockroaches by, 461, 468
   insecticide tests and, 492
potassium ions
   DDT poisoning and, 398, 407, 409
   dieldrin poisoning and, 411
   nerve impulse and, 385, 398
potato, as bait base, 100
potentiation, 235, 323, 335, 357
poultry, toxicity of chlorpyrifos to, 347
poultry mite
   carbaryl and, 366
   malathion and, 339

pralidoxime chloride, 128, 135
precautions, insecticide application and, 136, 143
premium grade (insecticide), 78
pressure spraying equipment, 111–117
pressurized canisters, dust application by, 111
preventive pest control, 52–55
privies, cockroaches in, 475
proline, DDT poisoning and, 404
proparthrin, 277
propoxur, 371
  baits, 99, 103, 104, 372, 379
  bioallethrin and, 260
  crack and crevice treatment (USA), 152
  cross-resistance, 446
  dust, 94
  emulsion of, 84
  flushing action of, 157, 374
  formulations of, 372
  insecticidal activity of, 186, 360, 374–380
    compared with
      bendiocarb, 367–368
      chlordane, 301
      chlorpyrifos, 344, 345
      fenitrothion, 347–348, 349
      resmethrin, 271
  lacquer, 89, 91, 92
  oil spray of, 81
  properties of, 372–373
  recovery from 181
  repellency of, 177, 179
  residual life of, 324, 372, 374
  residues on kitchen utensils, 151
  resistance, 447, 453
    B. germanica (first instance of), 445
  tolerance to, 92, 441
  toxicity of, 380–381
  use
    in homes, 196
    on ships, 324, 379
    in UK, 23, 195–196
    in USA, 21, 224, 362, 372, 458
  vapour action of, 489
  wall void tests and, 181–182
prosecution for food contamination, 29
prostigmine, 363
protam chloride, see pralidoxime chloride
protective clothing, 67, 69, 125–128, 132, 136
  client and, 108
  laundering of, 126
  legislation and, 153
  problems of wearing in tropics, 126
protective treatment, 73
  boric acid, with, 195
  Dri-Die, with 209
prothrin, 277
psocids, cockroach rearing and, 467
Psychoda spp. (filter flies), 329
psychological harm caused by cockroaches, 29
PTFE, see polytetrafluoroethylene

public
  attitude to cockroaches, 33, 163
  concern about organochlorines, 281
  insecticide restrictions and, 143
  responsibility to, 154
public halls, 61
public health departments, insecticides used by, 22, 23
public houses, cockroach entry into, 66, 167
publicity, pesticides and, 145
Puerto Rico, chlordane and dieldrin resistance in, 439
puffer packs, 107
Pybuthrin, 186, 236
pyrethrins, 218, 225
  admixture with
    chlorpyrifos, 343
    DDT, 221
    diazinon, 323
    Dri-Die, 207
    malathion, 339
    residual insecticides, 187, 247
    sodium fluoride, 203, 204, 216
    synthetic pyrethroids, 280
  aerosols
    cockroach collecting and, 471
    inspection with, 69, 108–109, 247
    intermittent type of, 223
    patent for, 220
    incorporation in, 71, 242, 279
  boric acid, and, 193
  composition of, 226
  crack and crevice treatment (USA), 152
  cross-resistance, 241, 427, 441, 446
  degradation
    in insects, 235
    by light, 228, 252
    in man, 251
  dusts, 95
  environment and, 245
  extraction of, 219–220
  flushing by, 122, 157, 187, 247–249, 272, 279
  fog, 246, 330
  insecticidal activity of, 201, 229–230, 232–233, 246, 257, 278, 287
    compared with
      bioresmethrin, 272
      dichlorvos, 329
      lindane, 295
      resmethrin, 271–272
  manufactured products (USA) containing, 236
  microencapsulation of, 93
  oothecae, effects on, 249–250
  photodecomposition of, 228, 252
  physiological action of, 230–232, 289, 387–398, 420
  properties of, 228
  recovery from, 235, 261
  repellency and, 157, 160, 176, 177, 185, 248
  residual insecticides and, 187, 247

pyrethrins—cont.
  resistance, 241, 258, 434, 447, 456
    Fort Rucker strain, 433
    selection pressure and, 453
    stored product pests and, 220, 252
  synergism of, 220, 235–236, 391
  tolerance in food, 253
  tolerance to, 438
  topical application tests, 230, 387, 485
  toxicity of, 251–252
  ULV application of, 121–122, 225
  use
    in bakeries (UK), 22–23
    in insect control, 242–249, 279–280, 429
    in USA, 22, 218, 224, 455
  World War II and, 282
pyrethrins I and II
  composition of, 226
  insecticidal activity of, 230
pyrethrum, 218
  allergic reactions to, 223, 252
  Chrysanthemum species, 218–219
  cultivation of, 220, 221–223, 225
  dermatitis and, 252
  dust, 226, 231–232
  early history of, 219
  early use of, 14
  flowers, 225
  Keatings powder, 219
  military use of, 215
  physiological action of, 235
  sodium fluoride and, 200
  synthetic pyrethroids, influence on, 224
  thanite, synergism by, 215
Pyrethrum Board of Kenya, 220
pyrethrum extract, 218, 221, 226
  constituents, synergism of, 236
  pale extract, 226
pyrethrum marc, 200, 226
pyrolan, 363, 381

Quartz, dust containing, 95

Radiators, 46
rain water, organochlorines in, 142
rats for toxicity and carcinogenicity tests, 133
raw materials
  inspection of, 54
  reinfestation of, 44
recovery
  insecticide avoidance and, 181
  propoxur, from, 181, 377
  pyrethrins, from, 235
  sub-lethal doses, from, 173
refrigerated display units, 52
refrigerators, 46, 99, 109
refuse, 37
  collection of, 39
  containers, 39, 57
  disposal of, 54
  dusting of, 110
  treatment of, 107, 242
registration of pesticides, see approval schemes
regulations, by government, see approval schemes
reinfestation, 69, 70, 73, 99, 173
repellency
  insecticides, of, 157, 172–189
  insecticide testing and, 176–187, 486, 490
  reinfestation and, 173
  treatment of harbourages and, 173–176
repellents, 157, 159–160
  applications for, 161–170
  beverage crates and, 165, 168
  early use of, 13, 15
  soft drinks and, 165
  tests for, 495–497
residual insecticides
  crack and crevice treatment (USA), 151–152
  flushing agents and, 187
residual life
  emulsions and, 83
  resistance and, 453, 455
  wettable powders and, 86
resistance
  Camp Leroy Johnson strain, 441
  carbamates, 363, 426, 427, 445, 458
    carbaryl, 445–446
    propoxur, 445, 447, 453
  characteristics of, 424–425
  cockroach behaviour and, 455
  cockroach rearing and, 466, 468
  cockroaches, morphological features and, 430, 432
  Corpus Christi, 430
  definition of, 422
  detection of, 427, 487
  development, factors influencing, 451–452
  early history of, 422–424
  factor, 427
  field tests for, 427, 487
  Fort Rucker strain, 433
  genetic factors and, 441, 442, 446, 451
  geographical isolation and, 453
  in-breeding and, 453
  influence on insecticide use, 319
  inheritance and, 425, 441, 442, 446
  insecticide detoxication and, 448–449
  insecticide development and, 25
  $LC_{50}/LD_{50}/LT_{50}$ and, 427
  local incidence of, 457
  Manoa strain, 441
  Mendelian principles and, 441, 442
  organochlorines, 21, 426, 427, 447, 448, 458
    benzenehexachloride, 430
    chlordane, 204, 224, 300, 304, 321, 423, 430, 433, 435, 439, 442, 443, 445, 446, 447, 453, 455
    DDT, 286, 423, 426, 427, 428, 430, 431, 434, 435, 437, 439, 441, 444, 447, 448, 449

INDEX 553

resistance—cont.
  dieldrin, 92, 99, 309–310, 426, 433, 435, 437, 438, 441, 442, 443, 444, 445, 446,, 447, 448, 450, 453
  lindane, 296, 426, 433, 434, 435, 437, 438, 439, 445, 447
  organophosphates, 319, 424, 426, 427, 442, 447, 458
    diazinon, 325, 374, 429, 438, 439, 441, 442, 443, 445, 446, 447, 448, 453, 456, 458
    fenthion, 445
    malathion, 341, 437, 438, 441, 442, 445, 446, 450–451, 453
  pest control industry and, 455–459
  pyrethrins, 241, 258, 433, 434, 447, 453, 456
  residual life and, 453, 455
  reversion to susceptibility, 431, 433, 437, 458
  selection for, 425, 426, 438, 453, 459
  sex-linkage and, 441
  ships and, 71, 99, 447, 448, 452, 454
  speed of development of, 425
  status of, 69
  synthetic pyrethroids, 258, 278
  trapping techniques and, 460
  treatment inadequacy confused with, 456
resmethrin, 270
  aerosol, 272
  fly control and, 270
  flushing action by, 272
  insecticidal activity of, 271–272
  photodecomposition of, 259, 270, 272
  residual life of, 272
  toxicity of, 270
respiration
  poisoning in cockroaches via
    allethrin, 391
    chlordane, 304
    DDT, 405
    lindane, 410
    pyrethrins, 391
  poisoning in man via, 131–132
respirators, see masks
restaurants, 43, 46, 51, 61, 66, 70
  cockroach entry into, 44, 161, 164, 167
  disease transmission in, 56
  treatment arrangements in, 69
rest homes, cockroach control in, 71
retail products of pesticides used in homes, 163
Rhizopertha dominica, diazinon and, 321
rice bran as attractant and feeding stimulant, 101
risk symbols, on labels, 147, 151
Ronnel, see fenchlorphos
roof spaces, see attics
rotary dust blower, 110
rotenone, see derris
RU
  11679, 276, 280
  12061, see NRDC *106*
  12063, see cismethrin
  15525, 276, 280
run-off of insecticides, 117
Rust-red flour beetle, see *Tribolium castaneum*

Sachet packs, 144, 367
safety, 130
  code of, 135–137
  factors influencing, 130
  features of spraying equipment, 114
safroxan, 240, 241
Salmonellae
  carried by cockroaches, 29
  food poisoning and, 56
  transmission studies of, 472
sanitation, see hygiene
San Jose scale, resistance and, 422
S-bioallethrin, 264
Schistocerca gregaria, malathion and, 485
schools
  breeding cockroaches for, 461
  disease transmission in, 56
  Dri-Die in, 209
  Drione in, 209
schradan, 319
screening agents, 79
seasonal changes of cockroaches
  in UK, 61–62
  in USA, 59
sebaceous glands, dermal poisoning and, 132
secondary poisoning, 72
seed dressing, dieldrin and, 308
selection
  resistance and, 425, 426
  varying insecticide use and, 459
sensory nerves
  DDT and, 402, 408
  pyrethrins and, 394
services, cost of, 70, 84
serving counters, 48
sesame oil, 220, 236, 240
sesamex, 236, 258, 279, 363, 364, 419, 443
sesamin, 236, 241
sesamolin, 236, 241
sesoxane, 363
setae, insecticide pick-up on, 120
Sevin, see carbaryl
sewers,
  baits in, 104
  bioresmethrin fogs in, 275
  chlordecone blocks in, 314–315
  cockroach trapping in, 473, 475
  dichlorvos (USA) in, 331
  drione treatment in, 209
  inspection plates and, 39
  mists/aerosols in, 129
  P. americana and, 39, 473
  smoke generators, use in, 96
sex attractant, 26, 102
sexes
  insecticide susceptibility and, 176
  propoxur and, 378

sexes—*cont.*
　　pyrethrins and, 233–234
　　sodium fluoride and, 201
sex pheromone, see sex attractant
shame of disclosing infestation, 52
sheep blow fly, diazinon and, 321
shipping containers, repellent treatment of, 162
ships, cockroaches on
　　acephate for, 358
　　baits for, 99
　　chlorpyrifos for, 379
　　control of, 71, 324
　　diazinon susceptibility in, 448
　　dichlorvos for, 333, 358
　　harbourages of, 51
　　in-breeding of, 453
　　lacquers for, 89, 92, 99
　　malathion, tolerance to, 447
　　propoxur for, 379
　　resistance in
　　　chlordane, 447
　　　dieldrin, 99, 447, 448, 452
　　　spread of, 71, 452, 454
　　water supplies and, 39
shops, 50, 52, 57
　　hygiene, importance in, 54
　　packaging materials in, 164
shower rooms, 46
silica aerogel, see Dri-Die 67
silica dust(s), 205, 208
silverfish
　　bendiocarb and, 367
　　malathion and, 339
　　propoxur and, 373
simulated packages, tests with, 106
Singapore
　　cockroaches in, 58
　　treatment of sewers in, 275
sinks, 46, 99
Sitophilus species, 321, 353
skin, see dermal absorption
skirting boards, 51
slanting card test, 160, 497
slow-release products, 331, 337
smoke
　　inhalation risks and, 131
　　properties of, 99
smoke generator (smoke bomb), 95–97
　　poisoning and, 299
　　propoxur in, 372
smoke ovens, 52
Smokey-brown cockroach, see *Periplaneta fuliginosa*
smoking, contamination from, 131
sodium chlorate in smoke generators, 95
sodium fluoride
　　bait, repellency of, 100
　　borax, admixture with, 200
　　borax, replacement by, 191
　　contact action of, 203
　　developmental stages and, 201
　　dust, 95, 197–205

insecticidal activity of, 191–192, 200–204, 288
　　compared with
　　　DDT, 287
　　　lindane, 295
　　manufacture of, 198–199
　　physiological action of, 203–204
　　plants, damage to, 198
　　properties of, 198–199
　　pyrethrins, alleged synergism with, 203
　　pyrethrum, admixture with, 95, 200, 204, 226
　　toxicity of, 199–200
　　use, 197–198
　　　influence of resistance on, 455
　　wall void tests and, 181–182
sodium fluorosilicate
　　properties of, 199
　　toxicity of, 200
　　uses of, 197–198
sodium ions
　　DDT poisoning and, 398, 407, 409
　　dieldrin poisoning and, 411
　　nerve impulses and, 385, 398
soft drinks, 46, 50
　　cartons of, 159, 163, 165
　　dispensers, 57
　　manufacturing plants of, 165
solvents, 78, 80, 82, 87
　　dermal poisoning and, 132
　　repellency tests on, 176
　　topical application tests and, 484
sorbitol, feeding stimulation by, 101
space treatment, see mist; fog; ULV
specificity, insecticidal action and, 318, 384
spillage, 154
　　dermal poisoning and, 140
　　removal of, 69, 123, 137
spiracles, water loss, insecticides and, 341
spot treatment (USA), 152
　　with bendiocarb, 367
　　with diazinon, 321
　　with dichlorvos, 335
spray(s)
　　application rates of, 117
　　cockroach avoidance of, 173
　　flushing agents in, 187
spray drift, 117
spray droplets
　　first aid and, 141
　　size and number of, 76, 115
　　ULV and, 120
sprayers, 88, 107–108, 111–120
spray jet, care of, 124
spray nozzles, 113
stability, additives in formulations for, 78
stadia, 43
staining, risk of, 80
starch flour as bait base, 101
starvation, cockroaches and, 99, 102
Staphylococci, food poisoning and, 56
steam pipes, cockroach harbourage and, 163
stock rotation, 54

storage
  insecticides, of, 136
  security of, 136
  treatment with cockroach repellents, 160
stores of hospitals, 71
stress, physical, DDT poisoning and, 404, 407
sub-lethal doses, recovery from, 173
submarines, 333
suboesophageal ganglion, DDT poisoning and, 407
sucrose, as bait component, 101
sugar in bait formulations, 357
sugar alcohol, feeding response to, 101
sulfoxide, 357
sulphur dioxide, early use of, 15, 18
sulphur lime, resistance and, 422
Sumithion, see fenitrothion
Supella longipalpa
  apartments (W. Germany), in, 60
  chlordane susceptibility, 304
  homes (USA), in, 59
  pest status, 27
  resistance, tests on, 441
  Singapore, in, 58
  weight of, 486
supermarkets, 55
  entry of cockroaches into, 161, 167
  packaging materials in, 164
supplier, infested raw materials and, 164
surfaces
  absorptive and non-absorptive, 77, 80–82
  insecticide tests and, 490–495
  pick up of insecticide from, 76
  suspension concentrate and, 87
  treatment without visible wetting, 120
  wettable powders on, 84–86
surfactants, see wetting agents
surveys of cockroaches in
  Germany, 56–57, 60
  UK, 60–66
  USA, 58
survival outdoors, 33–41
suspended floors, 51
suspension concentrates
  iodofenphos in, 353
  properties of, 87
sweat glands, dermal poisoning and, 132
sweet orange (oil) as attractant, 99
swimming pools, 43
synaptic transmission, 386
  carbamates and, 412, 418
  DDT poisoning and, 409
  dieldrin poisoning and, 411
  organophosphorus insecticides and, 412
Synchro-Mist, 223
synergism, 235–236
  carbamates, of, 363, 364–365, 373, 414, 419
  cockroaches, action in, 237–238
  definition of, 235
  factor, 237
  houseflies, action in, 237, 239–241
  pyrethrins, of, 203, 220, 236, 239
  ratios, 237
  stored food pests, action in, 237
  synthetic pyrethroids, of, 236, 257, 260, 262, 264, 267, 268, 270, 271, 277, 279
  temperature effect on, 419
synergists, 78
  MGK 264, 236, 240, 253, 260
  mode of action of, 235–236, 398
  piperonyl butoxide, 220, 236–238, 253, 257, 259, 262, 267, 268, 270, 271, 274, 279, 363, 364, 373, 419
  repellency tests on, 176
  safroxan, 240, 241
  sesame oil, 220, 236, 240
  sesamex, 236, 258, 363, 364, 419
  sulfoxide, 363
  temperature and, 391
  Thanite, 215
  tolerances in food, 253
  Tropital, 236, 238–239, 261
synthetic pyrethroids, 254
  aerosol for use in aircraft, 71
  cockroach control, combinations for, 279–280
  development, history of, 255
  dichlorvos, comparison with, 329
  flushing action of, 247, 279
  knockdown by, 279
  physiological action of, 258
  properties (biological) of, 257, 278
  pyrethrum production, influence on, 224
  recovery from, 261
  repellency and, 157, 177
  resistance to, 241, 258, 278
  safety in use of, 258, 259
  synergism of, 236, 257, 260, 262, 264, 267, 268, 270, 271, 277, 279
  toxicity of, 251, 259
Systox, 319

Taint, 352–353
talc, 78, 94
tarsi, pick up of insecticide on, 76
Tabutrex, 159
TDE, 284
tea urns, 46
technical material (insecticide), 77
Teflon, 468
telephones, harbourage in, 52
television cabinets, harbourage in, 52
telodrin, cross-resistance to, 441
temperature
  cockroach rearing and, 461
  insecticidal activity and, 73, 390, 400
  mite control and, 467
  requirements of cockroaches, 46, 48, 172
termites (soil poisoning)
  chlordane and, 300
  dieldrin and, 308
tests (procedures)
  ageing of surfaces for, 490–491

tests (procedures)—*cont.*
  cockroaches, for, 476–497
  contact tests, with treated surfaces, 486–495
  CSMA aerosol test method, 481–482
  CSMA cockroach spray method, 481, 482
  direct spray method, 480–482
  dusts, for, 490, 494–495
  exposing insects in, 491–495
  glass cylinder (repellency) method, 497
  immersion, 479
  insecticides for, 476–495
  insecticide repellency, for, 176–186, 495–496
  micro-injection, 486
  Official Test Insecticide (OTI), 481
  repellents, for, 496–497
  resistance, for, 425, 487
  slanting card (repellency), 497
  topical application, 479, 482, 484, 485–486
  treatment of surfaces for, 490
  USDA, 493
  Virginia Polytechnic Institute (VPI), 429, 494
  wall void, 181–182
  WHO (jar test), 441, 487
tetraethylpyrophosphate (TEPP), 319, 431
tetramethrin, 267
  insorbicide containing, 95
  introduction of, 255
  photodecomposition of, 259
  properties (general) of, 267–270
  synergism of, 277
thalidomide, 141
thallium sulphate, 213
Thanite, 215, 216
theatres, 50, 61, 167
thujic acid, 159
ticks, carbaryl and, 366
tiles, harbourage under, 51
timber preservatives, 198, 308
Tineola bisselliella, resmethrin and, 271
tobacco moth (*Ephestia elutella*), 329
toilets, 46, 60
Tokyo, resistant cockroaches in, 438
tolerance of cockroaches to insecticides
  allethrin, 438
  diazinon, 92, 447
  malathion, 447
  organophosphates, 442
  propoxur, 92, 441
  pyrethrins, 438
  WHO test and, 488
tolerance(s) of insecticides in food, 145, 147, 149, 152
  chlordane and, 307
  Federal Food and Drug Administration (USA) and, 149
  malathion and, 343
  MGK *264* and, 253
  piperonyl butoxide and, 253
  pyrethrins and, 253

tool kit, 123
topical application tests, 230, 479, 482–486
torch, 69, 108
towns, cockroaches in, 60, 61
toxicity
  classification, label and, 147
  insecticides, of, 131–135
  measurement of, 133
toxic waste, disposal of, 137
trade associations, 145
training of personnel, 106, 144, 150, 152–155
trains, treatment of, 333
transmission of nerve impulses, 384–386
transport
  of cockroaches, 58, 60, 63, 159
  of pesticides, 151
  spread of resistance and, 454
traps
  attractants in, 102
  cockroach control by, 460, 475
  jar, 18, 99, 471, 472
  suction type, 471, 475
trapping techniques
  baits and, 97, 472–475
  early use of, 18, 20
  insecticide use and, 460
trees, cockroach entry *via,* 41
tree frogs, biological control and, 20
Tribolium species
  diazinon and, 321
  fenitrothion and, 353
  lacquers, effects on, 90, 91
tricalcium phosphate, 195
trichlorphon, 356
  baits, 99, 104, 357
  crack and crevice treatment (USA), 152
  insorbicide containing, 95
  properties (general) of, 356–358, 360
Trinidad, resistance to dieldrin in, 437
Triton, repellency of, 176
Tropital, 236, 238–239, 261
typhus, 220, 284
Tyrophagus species, 467

Ultraviolet light
  absorbers, 79
  cuticle, effects on, 169
  lethal effect of, 169
  repellent action of, 169–170
ULV application, 78, 117–123, 225, 246
United Kingdom
  cockroaches in, 60–66
  pesticide sales in, 24
  resistance in, 447–448
United States of America
  cockroaches in, 58–59
  lacquers in, 92
  legislation on pesticides in, 147–152
  pesticide sales in, 24
utensils, insecticide residues on, 151

Valves, shut-off, 124

INDEX 557

Vapona, see dichlorvos
vapour, poisoning by and first aid for, 131–132, 141
vehicles
  infestation in, 168
  movement of cockroaches in, 161, 164
  pesticides in, 137, 139
  pyrethrins, use in, 246
  security of, 69
  treatment of, 246, 333
vending machines, 159, 167
ventilation
  cockroach rearing and, 461
  ducting, 51
  inhalation risks and, 131–132, 136
ventral nerve cord, 385
vinyl tiles, damage to, 80
Virginia Polytechnic Institute (VPI), 429
vomiting, first aid and, 140

Walls, 51
wallpaper paste, 48
warehouses, 54, 60, 161
washers, equipment maintenance and, 124
washing of equipment, 124
washrooms, 48, 60
waste traps, 56
water, cockroach rearing and, 464
water dispersible powder, see wettable powder

water-proofing agents, dusts containing, 79
weed killers, carbamates as, 364
West Germany
  cockroach survey in, 60
  hospitals, cockroaches in, 71
  resistance and cockroaches, 296
wetness, affecting treatment, 70
wettable powder, 83, 84–87, 113
wetting agents, 78, 84, 176
Whitmire prescription aerosol, 121
WHO resistance test, 441, 487–488
wildlife, pesticides and, 142, 146
wood-boring beetles, 425
woodwork, lacquer and, 90
world market, pesticides in, 24

Xylene in topical application tests, 484

Yeast, as bait attractant, 472

Zectran, see mexacarbate
zoos
  baits, use in, 98
  B. germanica in, 63
  cockroach control in, 72
  P. americana in, 60
  propoxur and, 381